CW01082666

# ARABIAN Sinai

## NABONIDUS AND THE EXODUS

# ARABIAN Sinai

## NABONIDUS AND THE EXODUS

JANET TYSON

Pirištu Books
Norwich
2024

Covers: Sleeve Front: Image licensed through Adobe Stock. Back: Arabian Peninsula and the Red Sea (Google Earth 2024). Case cover (Author's own design,. Front: Nabonidus' triad of Sin, Shamash, and Ishtar, plus the serpent; Back: Re on his barque, protected by the *mehen* serpent (Image: Budge, *From Fetish to God*, 166).

British Library Cataloguing in Production Data. A catalogue record for this book is available from the British Library.

ISBN 978-1-7393154-6-7

# CONTENTS

ABBREVIATIONS   i

LIST OF FIGURES   v

PREFACE   vii

1. PEOPLE   1
*Defining identities and relationships that cross the boundaries of Genesis and Exodus*

In Genesis: Terah  (2) | Abraham (6) | Sarah (9) | Nahor (14) | Iscah (14) | Milcah (16) | Hagar (16)  | Ishmael (18)

In Exodus: Moses and his Foster Mother (19): *Thermuthis and Renenutet (20); Merris (23)* | Aaron (24) | Zipporah (27) | Miriam (30) | Elisheba and Reumah (33): *The Four Sons (35)* | Joshua and Lot (36)

2. MIRRORING   41
*The journeys of Abraham and Moses reveal specific mirrored details that serve as clues to the historical situation*

Nabonidus and Cyrus (43) | Ur Layout as a Mirror to Exod 14:2 (47): *The Harbours (48); Nabonidus and Hiram of Tyre (52); Ziggurat Complex (56); Harbour Palace and Temple (56); Defensive Tower (57); Migdol (57); Canal (58); Enki's Temple*

(58); *Sea (59); Pi-Hahiroth (62)* | Stolen (63) | Hiram's Deal (70) | The Escape in Legend (72)

## 3. OLD BOYS' CLUB    74
*Nabonidus builds working relationships with former allies and legitimates his presence in the region*
Hittite Burial Site (75)

## 4. EGYPT    82
*Finding significant meaning in three Egyptian toponyms*
Pithom (83): *Pithom and Osiris (84); A Note on Nomes (85)* | Rameses (88): *Corvée (88)* | Goshen (92)

## 5. PLAGUES    98
*Osirian influences reveal Nabonidus' interest in conflating solar and lunar worship*
Snake Eats Snakes (101) | Hardened Heart (102) | Osiris' Nile (105) | Darkness (107) | Death (109) | "Today, in the month of Abib" (110): *Ten Months in Egypt? (113)* | Auspicious Days (114) | Judgement of ~~Osiris~~ Nabonidus (116)

## 6. CROSSING THE "SEA"    123
*Route from Egypt to Arabia; from the Great Wall to Solomon's port*
Wilderness of Shur (123): *Another Shur (129)* | Ezion-geber (130): *A Note on Aqaba (130)* | Eloth (136): *Elusive Heir and Ezion-geber (138)* | Bitter Water (142)

## 7. COVENANT OF SALT    146
*Affirming relations with the peoples of Tayma via a local custom*
Elim (146) | Manna (148)

## 8. WHY "CUSHITE" IS A PROBLEM    155

## 9. WATER AND BLOOD    161
*Nabonidus' growing megalomania and short temper ends in the death of a much-loved character*
"… shall we bring water?" (161) | Strike (163) | Blood Curse (168) | Kadesh-barnea (170)

## 10. OLD HABITS    176
*Nabonidus is tested; his previous lifestyle proves unsavoury to the early Jews so he must prove he has relinquished old habits*

Blood-Lickers (176) | Massah, Meribah (181): *Pillars of Melqart (182)* | Eldad and Medad (183) | Gerar (184); *Gerrha in Strabo (187)*

## 11. FURNACE AND FIRE  **189**
*Metallurgical influences on Nabonidus' new religion*

Qenites (189) | Volcanoes (195) | Fire (197): *Burning Bush (197); Sparks (198)* | Strange Fire (201) | Sheshbazzar (203)

## 12. SINAI  **205**
*Following etymological clues in toponyms and using old maps and travelogues, Sinai is discovered in an unexpected location in Northwestern Arabia*

Horeb (205) | Deuteronomy Names (206): *Suph (207); A Note on the Red Sea (207); Paran (209); Tophal (209); Laban (209); Hazeroth (210); A Link to Numbers (210); Di-zahab (213)* | Locating Sinai (214) | Mountain of God (217): *Getting High Up-High? (222); A Note on the Physiological Effects of Arsenic-Copper (223)*

## 13. JOSEPH'S BONES  **225**
*The acquisition of Egyptian royal bones to serve as a solar relic in the proposed amalgamation of solar and lunar deities*

The "Double" (229): *Zaphenath-paneah (232)* | A Woman's Secret (233) | Sanctuary (236) | Osirian Aspects (240) | Cosmological Context (244) | Jochebed and the Divine Birth (246) | Black Box (251) | "Back" of the Sun (253) | Sinai's 12, 40, and 73 (257): *12 (257); 40 (259); 73 (259)* | Sapphire (260) | Image (261) | Darkness Within (262) | Ra-meses (264)

## 14. CHERUBIM  **267**
*Serpentine guardians of the ark's contents; bovine guardians of the ark*

"… there I will meet with you" (267) | Solomon's Cherubim (271)

## 15. SERPENT KING  **275**
*Serpentine myth and iconography related to Moses/Nabonidus*

Mother Serpent (277) | Petra-glyphs (278) | Sloughing at Sinai (280) | Hobab the Snake (281): *Levite (283)* | Nehushtan (284)

## 16. MOSES IN TAYMA  **286**
*Evidence of local recollections of Nabonidus in Tayma and how they reflect "Moses" and "Solomon"*

Deification (286) | Tayma Stone (296): *Salm (297); Salmshezib the Priest (301); Salm of Hagam (302)* | Rock Inscriptions (302) | Jewish Tayma (306): *Nabonidus' Local Names (307)*

## 17. SCRIBAL CRAFT   310

*Types of tablets and their significance to Nabonidus*

Tablets (310): *Clay Tablets (310); Stone Tablets (313); Fate Tablets (314); Women and Tablets (316)* | Nabonidus and Tablets (317): *Reading and Writing (317); Usurper of the Fates (321); Blessings/Curses (324); The "Book" (324); Tantrum (328)*

## 18. IDOLS   330

*Attempted aniconism, familiar deities for the masses, Daniel's warning, and Nabonidus' penchant for statues*

"I AM" (330) | *A Note on 1 Chr 3:20-3 (335)* | "… out came this calf!" (335) | Daniel's Statues (340): *Four Metals and Clay (341); Golden Statue (345); A Note on "666" (348)* | Nabonidus' Statues (351)

## 19. END DAYS   353

*The deaths of the leading characters put an end to the original triad*

Revelry and Massacre (353) | Aaron's Demise (360): *Hor (362); Seir (363); Ithamar (367); Heber and the Harraat (367)* | Death of Moses (368) |

## APPENDICES   373

1. The Song and its 'Mad' King (373)
2. Primary Commission Names (376)
3. Abraham, Isaac, and Solomon (378)
4. 400 or 430 Years in Captivity? (382)
5. Numbers 33 and the 40 Camps (383)

## BIBLIOGRAPHY   391

Primary Sources (391)
Secondary Sources (393)

## INDEX   413

# ABBREVIATIONS

| | |
|---|---|
| *AAE* | *Arabian Archaeology and Epigraphy* |
| *Abarim* | *Abarim Publications* |
| *AD* | *Archaeological Discovery* |
| *AE* | *American Ethnologist* |
| *Ag. Ap.* | *Against Apion* |
| *A.J.* | *Antiquities of the Jews* |
| *A.JA* | *American Journal of Archaeology* |
| *AJSL* | *American Journal of Semitic Languages and Literatures* |
| *ÄL* | *Ägypten Und Levante* |
| *AMN* | *Acta Musei Napocensis* |
| ANET | Pritchard, James B., ed. *Ancient Near Eastern Texts Relating to the Old Testament.* 3rd ed. Princeton: Princeton University Press, 1969 |
| *AO* | *Antiguo Oriente: Cuadernos del Centro de Estudios de Historia del Antiguo Oriente* |
| *AOr* | *Aula Orientalis* |
| *AS* | *Anatolian Studies* |
| *ATLAL* | *Journal of Saudi Arabian Archaeology* |
| *BA* | *Biblical Archaeologist* |
| *BAR* | *Biblical Archaeology Review* |
| *BASOR* | *Bulletin of the American Schools of Oriental Research* |

| | |
|---|---|
| BASORSup | Bulletin of the American Schools of Oriental Research, Supplementary Studies |
| *BChr* | *Babylonian Chronicle* |
| BDB | Brown–Driver–Briggs Lexicon |
| *BJIM* | *British Journal of Industrial Medicine* |
| *BV* | *Bulletin of Volcanology* |
| *BW* | *The Biblical World* |
| *CBQ* | *Catholic Biblical Quarterly* |
| *ClQ* | *Classical Quarterly* |
| *CP* | *Classical Philology* |
| *CRB* | *Comptes Rendus Biologies* |
| *CS* | *Cristianesimo nella Storia* |
| DSS | Dead Sea Scrolls |
| *DWO* | *Die Welt des Orients* |
| *EA* | *Egyptian Archaeology. The Bulletin of the Egypt Exploration Society* |
| *EAO* | *Egypte, Afrique, & Orient* |
| *EB* | *Encyclopedia of the Bible* |
| *EIr* | *Encyclopedia Iranica.* Edited by Eshan Yarshater. London: Routledge & Kegan Paul, 1982-. |
| ENiM | Ecole Nationale d'Ingénieurs de Monastir |
| *ER* | *Entangled Religions* |
| ETCSL | Black, J.A., et al., The Electronic Text Corpus of Sumerian Literature (http://etcsl.orinst.ox.ac.uk/), Oxford 1998-2006. |
| HB | Hebrew Bible |
| *HEQ* | *History of Education Quarterly* |
| *Hist.* | Herodotus, *Histories* |
| *Hist. Nat.* | *Natural History* |
| *Historia* | *: Zeitschrift Für Alte Geschichte* |
| *HR* | *History of Religions* |
| *HS* | *Hebrew Studies* |
| *HUCA* | *Hebrew Union College Annual* |
| *IEJ* | *Israel Exploration Journal* |
| *IGJ* | *Iraqi Geological Journal* |
| *JAEI* | *Journal of Ancient Egyptian Interconnections* |
| *JAF* | *Journal of American Folklore* |
| *JALS* | *Journal of Arid Land Studies* |
| *JANES* | *Journal of the Ancient Near Eastern Society* |

| | |
|---|---|
| *JAOS* | *Journal of the American Oriental Society* |
| *JAS* | *Journal of Archaeological Science* |
| *JBAA* | *Journal of the British Astronomical Association* |
| *JBL* | *Journal of Biblical Literature* |
| *JCEA* | *Journal of Civil Engineering and Architecture* |
| *JCS* | *Journal of Cuneiform Studies* |
| *JCSMS* | *Journal of the Canadian Society for Mesopotamian Studies* |
| *JE* | Singer, Isidore; et al., eds. *The Jewish Encyclopedia.* New York: Funk & Wagnalls, 1901-1906. |
| *JEA* | *Journal of Egyptian Archaeology* |
| *JESHO* | *Journal of the Economic and Social History of the Orient* |
| *JHA* | *Journal for the History of Astronomy* |
| *JJLP* | *Journal of Jewish Lore and Philosophy* |
| *JM* | *Journal of Maps* |
| *JMC* | *Le Journal des Medecines Cuneiformes* |
| *JNES* | *Journal of Near Eastern Studies* |
| *JQR* | *The Jewish Quarterly Review* |
| *JQS* | *Journal of Qur'anic Studies* |
| *JSAA* | *Journal of Saudi Arabian Archaeology* |
| *JSJ* | *Journal for the Study of Judaism in the Persian, Hellenistic, and Roman Period* |
| *JSOT* | *Journal for the Study of the Old Testament* |
| JSOTSup | Journal for the Study of the Old Testament Supplemental Series |
| *JSQ* | *Jewish Studies Quarterly* |
| *JSS* | *Journal of Semitic Studies* |
| *JTS* | *The Journal of Theological Studies* |
| JVL | Jewish Virtual Library |
| *LO* | *Liminology and Oceanography* |
| LXX | Septuagint |
| *Minerva* | *Minerva: The International Review of Ancient Art & Archaeology* |
| *MJ* | *Museum Journal* |
| *MLN* | *Modern Language Notes* |
| *MR* | *Massachusetts Review* |
| *MW* | *Muslim World* |
| *Nab* | *Nabonidus* (see W&N inscriptions) |
| *Nab Chr* | *Nabonidus Chronicle* |
| *NEA* | *Near Eastern Archaeology* |

| NOBSE | The New Open Bible Study Edition |
| NRSV | New Revised Standard Version |
| OREA | Oriental and European Archaeology |
| *PDE* | *Plant Diversity and Evolution* |
| PERSGA | Regional Organization for the Conservation of the Environment of the Red Sea and Gulf of Aden |
| *PSAS* | *Proceedings of the Seminar for Arabian Studies* |
| PT | Pyramid Texts |
| *RB* | *Revue Biblique* |
| *RChr* | *Royal Chronicle* |
| *RQ* | *Revue de Qumrân* |
| *RSE* | *Rassegna Di Studi Etiopici* |
| SAA | State Archives of Assyria |
| *SAA* | *Studia Antiqua et Archaeologica* |
| *SAK* | *Studien Zur Altägyptischen Kultur* |
| *SEL* | *Studi Epigrafici e Linguistici* |
| *SLR* | *Stanford Law Review* |
| *SMEA* | *Studi Micenei ed Egeo-Anatolici* |
| *SS* | *Sound Studies* |
| *Strong's* | *Strong's Exhaustive Concordance of the Bible*, Biblehub.com |
| *TDOT* | *Theological Dictionary of the Old Testament, Vol. 9.* Edited by G. J. Botterweck, H. Ringgren, H. L. Fabry. Translate by D. Green. Grand Rapids: Eerdmans, 1974. |
| *Tradition* | *Tradition: A Journal of Orthodox Jewish Thought* |
| *UF* | *Ugarit-Forschumgen* |
| VA | Verse Account of Nabonidus |
| *VEcc* | *Verbum et Ecclesia* |
| *Vita Apoll.* | *Vita Apollonii* |
| *VT* | *Vetus Testamentum* |
| W&N | Frauke Weiershäuser and J. Novotny. *The Royal Inscriptions of Amēl-Marduk (561-560 BC), Neriglissar (559-556 BC), and Nabonidus (555-539 BC), Kings of Babylon.* The Royal Inscriptions of the Neo-Babylonian Empire, Vol. 2. University Park: Eisenbrauns, 2020 |
| *WZKM* | *Wiener Zeitschrift Für Die Kunde Des Morgenlandes* |
| *ZDP* | *Zeitschrift Des Deutschen Palästina-Vereins* |
| *ZOA* | *Zeitschrift für Orient-Archäologie* |

# LIST OF FIGURES

1. Detail of the Harran Stele showing the three icons of Sîn, Shamash, and Ishtar (4)

2. An Arabian Ghirbal, or "timbrel" (#20) that looks like a garden sieve (31)

3. Mirrored elements in the Genesis and Exodus narratives (44)

4. A simplified schematic of Ur in Nabonidus' day (48)

5. Artist's rendition of the harbour at Tyre with its statue (53)

6. Nomes 8 and 20 on the route to Tahpanhes from the south (87)

7. Lunar eclipse 03574 for Ipip, 522 BCE (113)

8. The Wall of eastern Egypt, as defined by Trumbull (126)

9. The Wall as Diodorus defines it (127)

10. Doughty's map showing routes through and around the Harraat and along the coast of the Red Sea (137)

11. Suggested itinerary of Nabonidus (Moses) from Egypt to Sinai (138)

12. Split Rock in the desert of al-Ula about 50 km from Tayma (163)

13. Potential site of Kadesh-barnea and the mirrored Wildernesses (175)

14. Keyhole (pendant) graves near Khaybar (212)

15. Qurayyah mesa (220)

16. Caves area (to right) and extensive rockfall (221)

17. Amun-Re on his barque with serpent-staff, surrounded by *mehen* serpent (253)

18. The ark as an olfactory stimulus for divination (269)

v

19. Lamassu (273)

20. A modern Aurochs (273)

21. Snake in a boat from rock with Nabonidus inscription near Tayma (279)

22. Wadjet (285)

23. Author's rendition of Nabonidus as he appears in relief (303)

24. Author's rendition of a press-release photo showing Nabonidus and a serpent motif (304)

25. Ringed staff of Nabonidus (305)

26. Marduk with multiple tablets adorning his robe (315)

27. Hair-like lava in the Harraat (365)

28. The stark reality of the Harraat (366)

# PREFACE

The aim of this eclectic analysis is to prove that

* Abraham and Moses are characters based on the same historical person: Nabonidus, King of Babylon (556-539 BCE).

* Sinai is to be found in Northwestern Arabia, relatively near the eastern shore of the Red Sea.

* The "exodus" involved a handful of people (probably fewer than one hundred); it was from Babylonia, not from Egypt, and began in 538 BCE.

* Much of what the character Moses does, in the context of religion, is coloured by Nabonidus' fascination with Osirian/solar funerary rites and rituals.

* Much of what he does, in the context of his private life, is coloured by the relationships Nabonidus made in Tayma, and his inability to harness his hubris or his temper.

The current predicament with our conventional understanding of "the exodus" is summed up by a few scholars:

Biblical literature provides a useful source alongside archaeology and other historical materials for much of the periods of the separate kingdoms of Israel and Judah, as well as the conquest of Babylon by Cyrus which led to the liberation of the Jewish elite from exile, and the post-exilic period. Here modern knowledge is augmented by much of the biblical story. It is the earlier periods – patriarchal, Egyptian period, Exodus, conquest and the united kingdom of David and Solomon – where history and archaeology diverge from the biblical narrative.[1]

After a century of exhaustive investigation, all respectable archaeologists have given up hope of recovering any context that would make Abraham, Isaac, or Jacob credible "historical figures" [...] archaeological investigation of Moses and the Exodus has similarly been discarded as a fruitless pursuit.[2]

The biblical account of the early history of Israel is mainly a literary-theological construction, directed by the ideological and religious objectives of the late scribes who wrote the history.[3]

This is precisely the situation for which a much-needed paradigm shift is required. Many maintain convention, determined to prove the veracity of the traditionally understood Hebrew Bible (henceforth HB).[4] I feel, however, not enough credit is given to the original authors, who were masters of their scribal craft; they knew how to play with their language to create entirely hidden landscapes beneath a seemingly simplistic narrative.

The following investigation is not another commentary on the book of Exodus, nor a biography of "Moses." It is a fresh new perspective on the exodus narratives, which are, for the purposes of this discussion, Genesis, Exodus, Numbers, and Deuteronomy. With an open mind, a little leeway for historical conjecture, and a determination to get to the bottom of anything marked as "meaning unknown," it is hoped that the overwhelming evidence for a 6th Century BCE exodus can be, if not proven, certainly advanced as a serious premise for further discussion.

---

[1] Robbin Derricourt, *Antiquity Imagined: The Remarkable Legacy of Egypt and the Ancient Near East* (London: I. B. Taurus, 2015), 188.

[2] William G. Dever, *What Did the Biblical Writers Know, and When Did They Know It?: What Archaeology can Tell Us about the Reality of Ancient Israel* (Grand Rapids: Eerdmans, 2002), 98-9.

[3] Nadav Na'aman, "From Conscription of Forced Labor to a Symbol of Bondage: Mas in the Biblical Literature," in *"An Experienced Scribe who Neglects Nothing": Ancient Near Eastern Studies in Honor of Jacob Klein*, (Bethesda: 2005), 746-58, here 747.

[4] I use the NRSV Bible for quotations, unless otherwise stated.

This is an extensive exploration of such things as the etymology of names and toponyms within the alternative paradigm; the filial connections between the major characters; cosmological symbolism; geographical boundaries, routes, etc.; historical inscriptions; and Egyptian, Osirian myths/beliefs.

The Song of Solomon is the first episode, if you will, of the Nabonidus story in the HB, i.e., my previous book *She Brought the Art of Women*[5] revealed that the Song is an account of the tumultuous marriage between Nabonidus and his Egyptian princess-bride, Nitocris II, during his seven-year residence at Tayma, Arabia. That is, Nabonidus *is* "Solomon." It's a lot to take in, I know, but I would advise you look at this argument before diving into the current study, for the exodus narratives continue the tale, chronologically (i.e., after the Persian invasion and the Edict of Cyrus). There is a short precis of *She Brought* in Appendix 1, and the entire book is free to download online.

The exodus was, initially, rather a diminutive event, with a handful of people including Nabonidus' family and a preliminary contingent of Jews; it was not from Egypt but from Babylonia; and the original chronicle of the migration to Canaan was probably very short, lacking in miracles, and written by two groups of people. Both groups travelled with Moses but one had a positive experience, the other a more negative one. Thus, we see Exodus and Numbers recounting the more sinister, violent, and questionable aspects of the experience, and Genesis and Deuteronomy being more lenient. The man who inspired these biblical diaries, travelogues, and/or memoirs is not a very nice human being; he is an impressive, dominant, intriguing character but he is not the Sunday-school (or Hollywood) Moses we grew up with.

The exodus narratives, together with the cuneiform inscriptions we have to date, depict Nabonidus as a strange but captivating character. Think of him as a cross between Pharaoh Akhenaten and England's King Henry VIII; on the one hand a man with a singular vision, with a desire to create a new religion by amalgamating the familiar pantheon into one deity, while on the other, a megalomaniac who demands to have his own way, leaving death (often that of women) in his wake. He has his supporters but he has more dissenters. The HB contains diametrically opposed depictions of him, from curses in the Song of Solomon and accusations of murder in Exodus, to the gushing praise of Psalm 72. Each must decide which is the version of the man they can see in the evidence presented here.

---

[5] Janet Tyson, *She Brought the Art of Women: A Song of Solomon, Nabonidus, and the Goddess* (Norwich: Pirištu Books, 2023).

It is self-evident that as historians we rely on what others have recorded about their experiences, be they of battles, journeys, or other people. It has long perplexed me why many scholars, even today, refuse to read the Bible as a collection of historical documents. In certain cases, these texts may be the *only* historical record of key events, yet they are all too often ignored or rejected as too religiously imbued to be of any concrete use. I respectfully suggest that it is we who have made it thus; we have turned chronicles into dogma. Due to the paucity of contemporaneous alternative sources for most of these events, the accuracy (or legitimacy) of the texts has been doubted or explained away by reference to divine authorship, etc. What I suggest is that the Bible is *all* historical (even the more arcane, esoteric texts); we just lack enough parallels in contexts we are familiar with.

The original impetus that made the early HB authors invest so much effort into each and every word of their histories would have diminished over the generations, and other motivations would naturally supersede the old ones, but the desire to encode vital information within the etymology of names, for instance, proved so strong, it was retained even by authors of the New Testament. Such chroniclers were privy to a world of related information that would have made their references far clearer, perhaps, but we don't have that luxury (at least not until the last century or two, with the discovery of cuneiform tablets, etc.). We have the biblical accounts, and if accepted as History, they can help fill in the gaps in our understanding.

I do not claim that any of the assertions herein are definitive; they are intended as examples of what might be discovered if boundaries are removed. Nothing is deemed too sacred, nothing taboo; everything is up for debate. Is that not the point of academia? I hope, however, they provide a few new insights and/or avenues of investigation hitherto not considered. There are so many hidden gems in the old familiar narratives that are just begging to be investigated.

One cannot present a new paradigm in one book, or even three, perhaps not in a single lifetime … but it's a start.

"If you wish to strive for peace of soul and pleasure, then believe;
if you wish to be a devotee of truth, then inquire."

— FRIEDRICH NIETZSCHE, TWILIGHT OF THE IDOLS

# 1

## PEOPLE

T he brilliance of the early Hebrew scribes is reflected in their ability to make every name *mean* something within the immediate context. Some are blatant, i.e., where an interpretation is provided in parentheses, but most are obscure and require investigation. In my work with the Gospel of John, I called these context-specific designations "commission names." For instance, I suggest both Mary and Lazarus have several commission names that echo each stage of their respective rise in status. On a simplistic level, it allows the narrator to tell independent stories/accounts without having to provide linking material to explain how that person got into the current situation. On a more profound level, it permits a multitude of symbolic allusions to be made simultaneously by playing with the etymology. This is how the characters in the exodus narratives must be approached. To this end, I provide below a synopsis of each important person in the subsequent discussion; *some details will require further attention at the right moment.* I ask that you suspend your criticism or disbelief until you see how this information permeates the rest of the analysis. Because this paradigm is quite new, and because I argue that *all* biblical nomenclature is precise and relevant (I never agree with "meaning unknown" definitions), these synopses are basically a breakdown of the etymology, and how the resulting meaning plays with or reflects the historical 6th Century BCE/Nabonidus context.

1

First, a note about the three main *historical* characters that you have been, or will be, introduced to from the Song of Solomon: Nabonidus, Nitocris, and Jehudijah (please also read the precis in Appendix 1).

Nabonidus was the last King of Babylon, who lost his empire to Cyrus the Great in 539 BCE. He is best known today for being a rather eccentric character who, like Akhenaten, went into the desert to worship his own deity, the way he wished to; some argue he attempted to impose his views on everyone else, some suggest he didn't. His personal favourite god was Sîn, the Moon-god, whose temples were at Harran in the north, and Ur in the south of Babylonia. He created a second capital at Tayma, in Northwestern Arabia, where he (evidently) married Nitocris II, high priestess and daughter of Pharaoh Ahmose III. She is "Solomon's" Egyptian bride, i.e., "Pharaoh's daughter."

The marriage was stormy and complex but was recorded by someone who was in attendance at court and witnessed everything, i.e., Jehudijah, the author of the Song of Solomon. Jehudijah was one of Nabonidus' harem women, who became his second-wife. She is mentioned in 1 Chr 4:18 as "the Judean wife"; some (like me) consider this a disguised name. In fact, it is but one of several pseudonyms for this woman, who figures strongly in the exodus narratives.

Without recognizing the importance of these three central 6th Century BCE historical figures to the exodus narratives, the story of Moses (and Abraham) will never reveal its original nature and meaning. Brace yourself for a journey into an ancient, secret world that has been hidden between the lines all along.

# In Genesis

# Terah

Abraham's father Terah is the one who suddenly gets the urge to up sticks and leave for Canaan (Gen 11:31), but why? There is no initial hint in Genesis that Abraham's family knows anyone from Canaan, nor any suggestion this move is instigated by some divine prophecy of a promised land, etc. It is only after Terah dies that Abram receives a divine calling to go to Canaan in the context of inheriting the land (Gen 12:1). Something must have instigated the sudden desire to move, but I think searching for a rationale on the basis of "Terah" being an actual person, is misguided; there are too many clues to suggest this is a fabricated character, i.e., a literary necessity. There are a few of these, intermingled with real people.[1]

The name "Terah" is defined by *Strong's* as "*Terach*: Abraham's father, also a place in the desert" and "of uncertain derivation." Not too helpful. The BDB suggests "delay," which could very well marry with Nabonidus' delayed return to Babylon due to his enforced penance[2] and the time-consuming problems with the seemingly volatile Nitocris. It might also pertain to the delay in getting to Canaan (e.g., either the stopover at Harran, or the "forty years" in the desert). Or it can suggest a link to the "delay" in Exod 32:1, where Moses remains up Mount Sinai for longer than expected.

In the Book of Jubilees (12:1-6), Terah is said to be a *maker* of idols, and Abraham supposedly sees the light and destroys them.[3] Written centuries after Nabonidus' reign (possibly 100 BCE but perhaps earlier), we can see here the unmistakable hand of someone attempting to negate the forefather Abraham's possible link to the Babylonian king, which is already becoming evident in the early stages of this analysis. Nabonidus openly hails his own father, Nabû-balṭsu-iqbi, as a "reverer of the gods and goddesses";[4] to a Babylonian, of course, there is no higher praise but to the Israelites/Jews, this would be an abomination.

NOBSE translates "Terah" as "wanderer." This connotation is strikingly clear: Nabonidus refers to himself as a "wanderer" in the desert, on a public stele;[5] but it also suggests the Moon, i.e., as the celestial wanderer. In Tayma, the lunar deity worshipped in Nabonidus' day is called "Ter/Teri," or "Ilteri."[6] It is not too far a stretch to consider the name of the "father" of Abraham is an intentional allusion to the Moon god.

If Terah represents the Moon (in Hebrew, *yareah*), he must represent Nanna/Sîn who, himself, represents the cosmic "Father," father of the gods, etc., A "Hymn to the Moon-God" demonstrates this affectionate title:

---

[1] For "Terah" as the literary pivot in the mirroring technique I discuss in the next chapter, see my paper, "Nabonidus and the Arabian Genealogies (Genesis 10 and 11)" (2024), www.academia.edu. I discovered this too late to include here.

[2] Tyson, 6-7.

[3] Cf. *teraphim* in 1 Sam 19:13. Rabbinic literature takes it a step further by calling Terah "wicked" (Numbers Rabbah 19:1; 19:33), and an "idolatrous priest" (Midrash HaGadol on Genesis 11:28).

[4] Raymond. P. Dougherty, *Nabonidus and Belshazzar: A Study of the Closing Events of the Neo-Babylonian Empire* (Eugene: Wipf & Stock, 1929, repr. 2008), 17-18.

[5] C. J. Gadd, "The Harran Inscriptions of Nabonidus," *AS* 8 (1958): 35-92, here i 26; ii 9-10 (57-9); Paul-Alain Beaulieu, *The Reign of Nabonidus King of Babylon 556-539 B.C.* (New Haven: Yale University Press, 1989), 169; W&N, 6, n. 45.

[6] Beaulieu, *Reign of Nabonidus*,184; VA 5.3. See also Julius Lewy, "The Late Assyro-Babylonian Cult of the Moon and its Culmination at the Time of Nabonidus," *HUCA* 19 (1945): 405-89, here 427-33.

Father Nanna, lord Sîn, hero of the gods,
Father Nanna, lord of Ur, hero of the gods.[7]

The link to Nanna/Sîn is also a link to Ur and Harran, the two cities in Abraham's Mesopotamian-based narrative, and the two centres of Sîn-worship made famous by Nabonidus.

*Figure 1: Detail of the Harran Stele showing the three icons of Sîn, Shamash, and Ishtar. (Image: BM 90837)*

In most myths, Sîn has three children (four, if one includes Ishkur/Adad, but this is a limited reference), i.e., Utu/Shamash (the Sun), Inanna/Ishtar (the Evening Star/Venus), and her twin sister, Ereshkigal (goddess of the Underworld). The *sacred* (Neo-Babylonian) triad is commonly Sîn, Shamash, and Ishtar: Moon, Sun, Star(s). Sîn's wife is Ningal "Great Lady/Queen," daughter to Ninhursag and Enki, and goddess of the reeds. Ningal is associated with visions and dream interpretation; her daughter, Ishtar, is the predominant avatar for Nitocris in the Song of Solomon; Nitocris is also "Queen" and is trained in remote viewing (visions).[8] So, we have, tentatively (with further explanation to follow), the triad of :

Abraham (Moon) | Nahor (Sun) | Sarah (Star[s])

In the forthcoming analysis of the Moses section of the exodus story, this will equate to:

Moses (Moon) | Aaron (Sun) | Miriam (Star[s])[9]

The cosmic aspect of "Terah" or Sîn, is replaced in the narrative with that of "Yahweh."

The purpose of mentioning "Terah" is twofold: 1) To introduce the notion of a triad, i.e., Abraham, Nahor, and Sarah. Just as Sîn/"Father" is the first born, so Abraham/"Father" is the eldest of the triad; in Gen 20:12, Abraham informs Abimelech that Sarah is the daughter of Terah by another

---

[7] "Hymn to the Moon-God," ANET, 386.

[8] Tyson, 79-80; 96.

[9] Which is why we see Micah suggest God's three leaders were Moses, Aaron, and Miriam (Mic 6:4). It also explains why Deut 4:19 prohibits the worship of sun, moon, and stars, i.e., not because there is anything inherently wrong with praising the heavens, but because they represent the Babylonian influence from which the later generations wish to disassociate.

mother, making her Abraham's half-sister, emulating the incestuous "sister-bride" motif of the Song, but also making her the third child of the Moon/"Terah" and third in the sacred triad. 2) It establishes this triad as a signature within the narrative, i.e., of Nabonidus' preference for the very same deities, whose icons appear on every inscription: Sîn (Moon), Shamash (Sun), and Ishtar (Star). Early audiences who knew anything of the ex-king probably knew that much, so they would be aware from the start who "Abraham" represents.

Dougherty writes:

> Arabian interest in the moon god was a distinct phase in the development of religion among the Semites. …the moon god was worshipped with much veneration … [and] different names were ascribed to the lunar deity (e.g., Wadd, Haubas, Amm, Ilmuqah, and Sîn) …. The sun god was also granted a prominent place … but the persistence of nomadic forms of life kept homage of the moon god to the fore.[10]

In my assessment of the Song of Solomon, I highlight the prevalence of lunar names associated with the relevant characters, e.g., Ahmose III is "The Moon is Born"; "Bithiah" means "Daughter of the Moon"; Ennigaldi-Nanna is "High Priestess of the Moon God," etc.[11] I also suggest throughout that the lunar deity Iah, also spelled Yah, may suggest a lunar affiliation in many, if not all, the biblical names ending in –*yah*. Thus, as we will see later, the desert tribes Moses associates with in Arabia are highly likely to be lunar worshippers, with a form of Iah/Yah as their deity, something familiar to Nabonidus, of course, but also to Jehudijah,[12] which will prove more significant later.

So, "Terah" "dies" in Harran, which is fitting, for this is the ultimate Sîn city; he dies at two hundred and five years old. This is not the age of a human; in gematria, 205 is the number of Adar/Atar, the solar deity,[13] who is synchronised with Nusku the fire-god, a reference that will crop up again. The symbolic "death" of Terah, the Moon, occurs when Nabonidus' ambitions turn more decisively "solar," as we shall soon see. Also, there is a sixty-year difference between Abraham's age of seventy-five, and Terah's age at his death. The number 60 may represent (in gematria) an allusion to *genebah*, "a theft, or something stolen" (from *ganab*, "to steal"), which is not as random as it might seem, for this is a *significant* motif in the exodus narratives; the entire tale begins and ends with 'stolen things'!

---

[10] Dougherty, *Nabonidus and Belshazzar*, 155.
[11] Tyson, 229-30.
[12] Tyson 198-9.
[13] Bill Heidrick, "205," Hebrew Gematria, https://www.billheidrick.com.

# ABRAHAM

Abraham's original name, Abram, means "exalted father," from *ab*, "father," and *rum*, "to be elevated," or from the verb *abar*, "to be strong or to protect," and *am*, "their." The root *br*, means "to be strong" or "to protect."

We see this notion of protection as part of Nabonidus' initial depiction in the Song of Solomon, where his strength and protective nature (i.e., toward Nitocris, at least in the beginning), is related in terms of a lofty tree casting its shade (Song 2:3), etc., i.e., the epitome of a Babylonian king. Most interestingly, however, the derived nouns *ebrah/eber* suggest the pinion(s) that make up a bird's wings. The motif of protective wings is central to Mesopotamian iconography, with its multiplicity of winged creatures and deities.

Another curious connection between Abraham and Nabonidus is the camel. Abraham is often thought of as a nomad (and yet not *the* ancestral nomad) and this suggests a *lifestyle*, not merely traversing a great distance to get where you have been sent. Heb 11: 9 says of Abraham: "… he stayed for a time in the land he had been promised, as in a foreign land, living in tents, as did Isaac and Jacob …."[14] He didn't have to; it was a choice.

The noun *gamal*, meaning "camel," comes from the identical verb *gamal*, which means "to trade or invest."[15] Thus we should, perhaps, be seeing Abraham's journey more in terms of assessing the territory of Canaan from a trader's perspective. The name "Canaan" is thought to mean "Land of the Purple," from the term *kinahnu*, "purple dye" (which, of course, relates to the Phoenician trade in royal purple dye), but it has also adopted the connotation of "trade, merchant," etc., from biblical contexts.[16] We must also recognise that Harran, Abraham's residence for the period between leaving Ur and heading out to Canaan, is also a significant trading post, being in a strategic location near both the Euphrates and the Tigris, and at the junction of at least two major caravan routes. It was set up as a trading outpost by Ur, specializing in luxury goods (cf. Ezek 27:23).[17]

This is just the view of Nabonidus many scholars adhere to, i.e., that he goes to Arabia to secure trading rights. Why would he not do so on his

---

[14] Note how many times the imagery of tents, herds of cattle, etc., is used, e.g., Gen 12: 8; 13: 3, 5, 18, etc.

[15] Cf. Gen 12:16; 24:5-8, 10.

[16] Michael C. Astour, "The Origin of the Terms 'Canaan,' 'Phoenician,' and 'Purple'," *JNES* 24. 4 (1965): 346-50, here 347.

[17] Tamara M. Green, *The City of the Moon God: Religious Traditions of Harran* (Leiden: Brill, 1992), 19.

way through Canaan?

When you see how many times the narrative of Genesis mentions Abraham's belongings, the goods and chattels, etc. (e.g., Gen 12:5, 20; 13:2, 6, etc., and in 14:16, Abraham focuses on securing the "goods" before he returns Lot!), it becomes evident that this motif is not just coincidental, it is showing us what Abraham is doing there. He is surveying the land, trading as he goes, building a new empire on the backs of his camels (in 13:6 the combined possessions of Abraham and Lot are "so great that they could not live together"—this only makes sense if they are beginning to tread on each other's toes in a trading context, i.e., "this trade route isn't big enough for both of us!"). This is not a slur; it is part of the process Nabonidus must go through to fulfil his dream (plan?), to create a new place of worship, a new temple, ostensibly in Jerusalem, i.e., the city *needs* "goods." (But will they end up in Jerusalem?)

In connection with this idea of Abraham's potential trading caravan, Dougherty notes that camels are scarcely mentioned as commodities in cuneiform literature but that there is a sudden increase in examples when Nabonidus moves to Tayma, as his food (i.e., probably favourite luxuries he cannot procure in Tayma) is delivered by camel from Erech and other cities. The camel-drivers are, apparently, issued with receipts in case of loss of or injury to the beast, as they must have been worth a great deal of money.[18] So one might suggest Nabonidus is the original inventor of "home delivery" and instrumental in the sudden increase of camels at Tayma:

> Preliminary analysis of the animal bones shows a very limited occurrence of camel bones in occupation period 4, whereas in the subsequent period (Iron Age) there is an increasing number of camel bones (nearly 20%).[19]

It is not too far a leap to then suggest that due to his status and the relative novelty of seeing a caravan of camels wander through the suburbs of Israelite towns, Nabonidus (as Abraham) is also responsible, at least in part, for the influx of camels in Canaan and Phoenicia around the time of the fall of his kingdom. This effect alone is enough to reconsider the sudden disappearance and/or anonymity of Nabonidus post-539 BCE.

---

[18] Dougherty, *Nabonidus and Belshazzar*, 114-17. Interestingly, Dougherty mentions that camels were called "Beasts of the Sea" (115); he presumes this meant they were imported via the Persian Gulf (!) but it must surely mean "Beast/ship of the Desert," i.e., on the sea of sand.

[19] "Archaeological research at the oasis of Tayma, Saudi Arabia," General Commission for Tourism and Antiquities, Riyadh, and the German Archaeological Institute, Berlin, https://studylib.net/doc/7406744.

That modern archaeologists can trigger a media storm by insinuating that the tale of Abraham and his camels might prove an anachronism in the biblical tale, due to the lack of evidence for domesticated camels in the Levant before the 9th Century BCE, does hint at a genuine concern for clarifying why the story of Abraham, set hundreds of years earlier, can suggest this character owned many.[20] And yet, camels *are* familiar beasts of burden to Egyptians, Arabians, and Babylonians;[21] according to Judg 7:12, the Midianites' camels are "without number, countless as the sand on the seashore" (cf. Isa 60:6). Midian is Nabonidus-Moses territory, as the king of Babylon he has links to both Egypt (via his wife) and Mesopotamia, so the transference of this commodity to anywhere we can trace him should not seem so surprising; it's just a case of deferring to *historical* events and evidence (and the HB is part of that historical evidence, if you can accept it as such).

Another interesting correlation is that in the commission name of "Abraham" (with the shift from Abram) is a direct link to one of Nabonidus' pseudonyms in the Song of Solomon. In Gen 17:5, Abraham is told: "I have made you the ancestor (father) of a multitude of nations," but in the Hebrew this reads "*ab hamon goyim.*" The word *hamon* means "tumult, uproar, commotion," etc., as that coming from a large crowd, a multitude. It is used in Song 8:11 in the name "Baal-hamon," a pun employed to signify Nabonidus as the ruler/leader of the noisy Babylon (which itself is considered the centre of the world), in an allusion to the *Atrahasis* myth, i.e., the "Flood Myth."[22] Abraham becomes the "father of many nations" right after the flood narrative of Genesis 10. Such continuity in applied etymology is surely worthy of more extensive analysis by scholars.

Note also that Abraham is called "the friend of God" in 2 Chr 20:7, Isa 41:8, and James 2:23 (on the basis that he met and interacted with the deity via angels, voices, dreams, etc.). In Exod 33:11, Moses is called the "friend of God."[23] Similarly, in Genesis 22 Abraham's loyalty is tested by God (i.e., the sacrifice of Isaac); in Exodus 19 Moses is tested (the battle with Amalek). These are just the beginnings of a long list of parallels.

---

[20] Christopher Eames, "Camels: Proof That the Bible Is False?" Armstrong Institute of Biblical Archaeology (March 28, 2019), https://armstronginstitute .org.

[21] Renato Sala, "The Domestication of Camel in the Literary, Archaeological and Petroglyph Records," *JALS* 26.4 (2017): 205-11.

[22] Tyson 205-6.

[23] Reuel (Exod 2:18) is a name that actually *means* "friend of God," from *ra'a*, "to be a friend," and *el*, God."

# SARAH

"Sarah" means "princess," feminine of the noun *sar*, i.e., "chieftain, ruler, official, prince." The noun *shiryon* means "body armour" and *shirya* denotes a weapon like an arrow or spear.[24]

This proves intriguing, as I previously noted that in the etymology of the "rose of Sharon" in Song 2:1, this same etymology is alluded to, and that it accurately defines the princess, Nitocris, in terms of her avatar Ishtar, i.e., the mistress of the bow and arrow.[25] In the narrative of the Song Nitocris is the *dominant* one, the (royal) *leader*, so again the etymology is apt.

I posit, therefore, that Sarah is a literary construct based on the character of Nabonidus' first wife, Nitocris. The authors of the exodus texts *know* Nabonidus; they lived under his rule in Babylon, or Tayma, perhaps ride with him through the desert. There is no Nitocris, now (I have suggested she dies when Cyrus takes Babylon) but she had such a hold over Nabonidus, and was so divisive, she is considered necessary to the tale of the exodus. *Why?*, you are thinking. Why not just forget about her, if she was such a negative influence and is dead anyway? I argue it is because of Jehudijah, Nabonidus' second-wife, who is still alive and with him on this journey. The castigation of Nitocris does not end with the Song of Solomon's hidden curses; it is continued in the tale of Sarah and her allegedly miraculous pregnancy.

Sarah is barren (Gen 11:30); Nitocris is *considered* barren in the Song, as she refuses to get pregnant after aborting her first pregnancy; Jehudijah curses Nitocris' womb, stating it is a veritable "wilderness."[26] We learn that Jehudijah is the one who gives birth to Nabonidus' children, not Nitocris.[27] The refusal to conceive is linked to Nitocris' sacerdotal position and her sacred blood; she *chooses* not to give this up.

Sarah is considered beautiful; Abraham makes a conscious decision *before* anything happens, to allow her to be considered available by instructing her to say she is his "sister," not his "wife" (Gen 12:11-13). This is a purely selfish plan, as the passage makes clear, i.e., by, effectively, pimping out his wife to the pharaoh, Abraham's profits are greatly increased; trade goes well (12:16). We see this happen to an even greater degree in the Song, where the "beautiful" Nitocris is forced to provide her sacred blood Elixir to all and sundry on a whim, when Nabonidus invites his "friends" to

---

[24] P. J. Williams, "Shirya," Semantics of Ancient Hebrew Database, www.sahd.div.ed.ac.uk/media/lexeme:pdf:njx-shirya-williams_p-cam-1998p.pdf.

[25] Tyson, 64-5.

[26] Tyson, 111-19; 97, respectively.

[27] Tyson, 213-14.

partake (Song 5:1).[28] This is followed up with an allusion to his bringing the practice to Babylon after the family's departure from Tayma, i.e., Nabonidus creates a new form of temple prostitution based on the popularity of the Elixir; it, too, is very profitable.[29]

In fact, a strong allusion to this is made in Gen 20:2-16. Abraham has seen that his lovely wife is an asset. She can bring in the money. Having acquired a great deal of "goods" from Pharaoh, he tries his luck a second time, with King Abimelech of Gerar. When the king is told in a dream that Abraham is duping him, Abimelech sends Sarah away. Abraham thus leaves without making a trade deal with the king. Then there is a strange episode where Abimelech tells Sarah that he has given Abraham a "thousand pieces of silver" anyway. Firstly, why would the king bother to explain this to a woman (who is, by the way, over ninety years old, according to Gen 17:17; would she still be so irresistible, one wonders, or is there another explanation)? Secondly, and more importantly, this amount is exactly the same as the money charged to men procuring the blood-giving virgins in the temple at Babylon (Song 8:11).[30] This is too coincidental for my liking and thus I consider it to be an intentional correlation; Abraham is Nabonidus, up to his old tricks.

The Islamic version of this scenario, of Abraham allowing his wife to pretend she is not married so that he can profit from the arrangement, includes a very interesting echo of the Song of Solomon. In Song 7, Nitocris is visited by a group of men, whom I suggest are Egyptians, i.e., from her home town. They are, at first, flattering, but their flattery soon turns to lechery, making the queen feel uncomfortable and threatened. Their praise of her lists every part of her body, from her feet, up to her head.[31] In the Quran version of the praise of Sarah by three visiting "princes of Egypt," *her* body is systematically praised, from head to toe:

> (col. 20)
> [… line 1 and first half of line 2 missing ….] … how excellent and beautiful is the expression on her face! And how pleasing [and how] delicate is the hair of her head! How beautiful are her eyes, and how pleasing is her nose and all the bloom of her face … how lovely is her breast, and how beautiful is all her fairness! Her arms, how beautiful! And her hands, how perfect! Any glimpse of her hands is to be desired! How lovely are her palms, and how long and slender are all the fingers of her hands! Her feet, how beautiful! And how perfect are

---

[28] Tyson , 123.
[29] Tyson, 206-9.
[30] Tyson, 206-9.
[31] Tyson, 162-89.

her thighs! No maidens or brides who enter the bridal chamber are more beautiful than she is! The beautifulness of her beauty is superior to (that) of all (other) women, and her beauty is high above all of them! And with all this beauty she possesses much wisdom, and the work of her hands is beautiful.[32]

In the midst of all this unsettling ogling is the mention of "wisdom," which seems rather odd, as the HB Sarah is not known for her intellect. However, Nitocris is. She is the high priestess, the embodiment of Egyptian esoterica and ancient wisdom. She is Nabonidus' teacher, feeding him with little gems of insight to keep him satiated in his quest for hidden knowledge. In accordance with this perception of Nabonidus, the Quran's Abraham says:

> three men who were princes of Egypt [came ... ...] of Pharaoh Zoa[n] about my affairs and about my wife,[33] and they presented [me numerous gifts and aske]d m[e to teach them] values, wisdom, and truth. So I read in their presence the [book of] the words of [En]och ... with much eating and [much] drinking [... ... ] wine ....[34]

Nabonidus loves a party; we see this in the Song, especially when he starts sharing the Elixir (Song 5:1), and we see it in Daniel 5, when he gets all his yes-men drinking from the Jewish temple vessels the night before the fall of Babylon. But, as Solomon, he is renowned for "wisdom"; the Queen of Sheba is enthralled with his knowledge and wit (1 Kgs 10); the King of Tyre supposedly enjoys his riddles (Josephus, *A.J.* 8.5). In Eccl 1:1-17, the aging Solomon allegedly reminisces that he had acquired great wisdom (at a cost); and Nabonidus himself, at least according to the Verse Account (5.3), claims to have learned more about "hidden things" than the best of the

---

[32] John C. Reeves, "Translation Of 1Q Genesis Apocryphon II-XXII," https://pages.charlotte.edu/john-reeves/course-materials/rels-2104-hebrew-scripturesold-testament/translation-of-1q-genesis-apocryphon/. The potentially incestuous marriage between Abraham and Sarah is a reflection of the "sister-bride" motif in the Song but also another dig at Nitocris, who was erroneously seen as lascivious and incestuous because of her misunderstood cultic rituals and her negative depiction in the Song (e.g., Tyson, 54-6; 107). In contrast, most "Muslim sources ... identify Sarah as the daughter of Abraham's paternal or maternal uncle, or daughter of the king of Haran, and therefore unrelated to Abraham," which sidesteps the issue altogether (Suzanne Pinckney Stetkevych, "Sarah and the Hyena: Laughter, Menstruation, and the Genesis of a Double Entendre," *HR* 36.1 [1996]: 13-41, here 39, n. 62).

[33] In *She Brought* (Tyson, 165), I conjecture that the Egyptian visitors are possibly sent, initially, from Ahmose to spy on the couple, as he supposedly had misgivings about how she might have been kept by the Babylonian king (i.e., as a concubine, rather than as a queen). I had not read the Quran version at that time.

[34] Reeves, "Translation" (as above).

Babylonian sages.[35] This is a profoundly significant aspect of both the legends of Solomon and the actual evidence for Nabonidus. The Quran thus seems to conflate legend with reality, in combining elements from the Song, the legends of Solomon, and the known history of Nabonidus, to create its own version of "Abraham."

One other aspect of Sarah demands explanation, i.e., the fact that she "laughs" when she is told she will conceive even though she has become old (Gen 17:17) and has not menstruated for *many* years (Gen 18:11).[36] I should make it clear that I do not consider miraculous intervention a suitable or helpful resolution to such issues. This must be seen in terms of pragmatic, realistic, everyday life, or it cannot help us understand what is really behind the narrative. I think this is further evidence of a vendetta against the memory of Nitocris.

In the Song of Solomon, Nitocris is vilified for being an Egyptian, for being black, for being the king's favourite, and for being loyal to her own faith. She never stands a chance in Nabonidus' court; her ill-fated pregnancy is seen as her own callousness, her beating by the guards payback for her alleged scheming and manipulation. In her reprise as "Sarah" she is supposedly given the blessing of pregnancy, despite the impossibilities inherent in the set-up, and the first thing she does is "laugh." This is not, I argue, a joyful laugh but one of symbolic significance.

*Strong's* defines *tsachaq* as "mock, play, make sport ... to laugh outright (in merriment *or scorn*)." Nitocris' character, as seen through the pen of another woman scorned (Jehudijah), is one of selfishness, amorality, and impertinence. If, as herself, she had been told many years later that *she* would bear her husband's offspring, I *can* see her laughing, as if to say "you *must* be ***** joking!" She suffered greatly at the hands of Nabonidus; she tried very hard to change his ways and show him a different path, but he persisted with what brought him instant gratification and wealth. If the Song echoes anything of her true nature, it reveals that Nitocris had not a single moment's desire to become the mother of Nabonidus' children.

Jewish exegetes notice immediately the not-so-pure intent of the passage, for Sarah is caught out in a lie immediately (Gen 18:15), by claiming she had not laughed, and that her laughter "remained hidden in her heart. That laughter—bitter and maybe even angry—came from hidden knowledge and foreboding ...."[37]

---

[35] Tyson, 123-4.

[36] For an interesting discussion on the theme of menstruation in the "Sarah" narrative see Stetkevych, "Sarah and the Hyena."

[37] Esther M. Shkop, "And Sarah Laughed ..." *Tradition* 31.3 (1997): 42-51, here 42-3. Shkop argues that this trepidation is more to do with Sarah's age and the impracticalities of motherhood, but also the potential for reprisals concerning *the*

By effectively *forcing* this pregnancy upon Sarah, Nitocris must posthumously succumb to the very fate she dreaded and fought against. The authors of Genesis have maintained Jehudijah's version of events and make Nitocris "mother" (to Nabonidus' offspring) for eternity. It is almost as if Jehudijah is there, standing over the scribes, laughing smugly as they write, making sure this curse gets into the final copy.

Isaac (whose name means "he will laugh," from the verb *sahaq*, "to laugh or make fun") is devised to *represent* the one thing Nitocris could not, or would not, deliver, i.e., Nabonidus' child. The "laugh" is on Nitocris, for she will not only be linked to motherhood, thereby negating all her wishes and her sacerdotal beliefs and practices, but also to the multitude of Nabonidus-Abraham's descendants, personified by "Isaac," who is destined to laugh at her down the ages. When we discuss Isaac again, later, we find that he is, indeed, Nabonidus' biological son, making him utterly disassociated, genealogically, from the Israelites; Genesis is a pro-Nabonidus text, however, and preserves this manufactured connection proudly.

Sarah's original name, "Sarai" means "*my* princess," which suggests that the moment the prospect of pregnancy is mentioned (Gen 17:15-16), she transforms from Nabonidus' personal, specific "princess" (Nitocris), into a generic, universal, symbolic representation of what happens when you resist conformity. She loses her individuality and identity, which is what the HB authors (including Jehudijah) seem to think she deserves.

In the similar name "Sara" is a subtle allusion to Nitocris as the embodiment of Ishtar, played against the Tammuz character of Nabonidus in the Song (to appeal to audiences already familiar with this mythology; discussed throughout *She Brought*). "Sara" is an Akkadian/Babylonian name for Inanna-Ishtar, as used in the opening lines of Enheduanna's hymn to the goddess, "*Nin me šara*," i.e., "Mistress of the innumerable *me*," more commonly known as "The Exaltation of Inanna."[38] As a sacerdotal poetess, Jehudijah wrote the Song of Solomon with Nitocris in the role of the "whore of Babylon," Ishtar; Jehudijah is now amongst the caravan Moses leads; she may well inspire the authors of Genesis' "Abraham" story to name this version of Nitocris along the same lines, for continuity.

There is one other aspect of the depiction of Sarah that comes into play very subtly, but this can *only* be seen when we know the real-life story of the Song of Solomon, for "Sarah" is also an potential avatar of Ennigaldi-Nanna, Nabonidus' daughter. This won't make sense until later, so I shall come back to this in due course.

---

*legitimacy* of Isaac, i.e., he may not have been her son after all?), 48.

[38] ETCSL, 4.07.2, 1-12 (opening words).

# NAHOR

Nahor, brother of Abraham, is the Genesis version of Aaron, brother of Moses. "Nahor" means "snort, scorched" (a strange combination) from the verb *nhr*, "to snort" which is related to *harar*, i.e., "to be hot, burned, charred." The root *hwr* in cognate languages means "to bend or turn"; as a noun, it means "hollow or depressed ground"; the noun *hor*, means "hollow."

Such etymology suggests a metallurgical foundation, with the "heat" of the furnaces, which are often simple basins dug into the soil/sand, and the bending/turning/"twisting" (which is repeated elsewhere) of the metals.

As for the "snorting" aspect, I have my own interpretation. In Gen 2:7, Yahweh breathes into his creation, into Adam, to bring him to life. The verb used to describe this "blowing" is *naphach*, ("to inflate, blow hard, scatter, kindle," etc.). Dougherty writes that Yahweh blows into the nostrils of Adam to give life, much as a smith would use a blowpipe to stir the fire in the furnace – the root of the word *naphach* "is the exact equivalent of the Babylonian root *napâḫu* which refers primarily to the activities of a smith in kindling fire by means of blowing."[39] Thus, the "snorting" idea is just a variation on the puffing or blowing of the smith, and the ultimate inspiration (in the literal sense) of the deity.

The "*hor*" element brings to mind Mount Hor; the "scorched" element of "Nahor" comes into play in this capacity, but the discussion must await the section on Seir, later. This aspect is key to linking Aaron and Nahor.

# ISCAH

Abarim translates this name from the root *sakak*, "to weave a protection"; *sakak* suggests an interwoven hedge i.e., of "prickly branches"; *Strong's* says: "From an unused root meaning 'to watch; observant'."

Several Hebrew sources identify Iscah with Sarah (Sanhedrin 58b:6, 69b:13; Sifrei Bamidbar 99, etc.).[40] From my perspective, too, this is correct and leads to the identification of Iscah with Nitocris but there are issues, e.g., there are two dominant theories; one is weak and one is forced. Firstly, there is the theory that the two women are identical because both are deemed beautiful and

---

[39] Raymond P. Dougherty, *The Sealand of Ancient Arabia*, Yale Oriental Series 29 (New Haven: Yale University Press, 1932), 180.

[40] See also Eliezer Segal, "Sarah and Iscah: Method and Message in Midrashic Tradition," *JQR* 82.3/4 (1992): 417-29.

men "look" upon them. Secondly, which is more interesting, focus is placed on the "seeing/looking" aspect in terms of being a "seer," for instance:

> And Rabbi Yitzḥak says: Iscah is in fact Sarah. And why was she called Iscah? Because she envisioned [*shesokha*] hidden matters by means of divine inspiration .... Alternatively, Sarah was also called Iscah, because all gazed [*sokhim*] upon her beauty.
>
> Sanhedrin 69b:13

> [Sarah] was a helpmate worthy of Abraham. Indeed, in prophetical powers she ranked higher than her husband. She was sometimes called Iscah, "the seer," on that account.
>
> *Legends of the Jews* 1.5

Nitocris is the "seer"; she knows of "hidden" things; she can induce dreams whilst awake, i.e., she views remotely (Song 3:1; 5:2); she is an Egyptian high priestess, trained in *heka* and the esoteric rites of the God's Hand and of Neith.

I offer two other pieces of evidence to support the identification not only of Sarah with Iscah, but of both these characters with Nitocris.

1. The etymology of "Iscah" includes a strong reference to a protective hedge, yet this is not dealt with by the rabbis. In the Song of Solomon, there are two distinct "protective hedges," i.e., a) Nabonidus is likened to a hedge of prickly henna shrubs that protects his "vineyards" (where "vineyards" equate to nubile females) in Song 1:14;[41] and b) Nitocris is described as having a "protective fence" upon her belly, as a symbol that she is (supposedly) pregnant (where the hedge is made of lilies to signify a female child), in Song 7:2.[42]

2. In Sifrei Bamidbar 99, Iscah and Sarah are equated in the context of a debate concerning whether Iscah or Zipporah is the "Cushite" woman (mentioned by Miriam and Aaron in Exodus 12), or the Midianite woman (from Exodus 2;18). This is so intriguing, as Nitocris *is* the "Cushite" wife and Jehudijah *is* the Midianite wife, but the debate more or less reduces to the comparison of beauty again. They missed the clues.

Nothing else is said of "Iscah" because, as an avatar of Nitocris, she is defunct in the forthcoming narrative, i.e., Nitocris is dead.

---

[41] Tyson, 60-1.

[42] Tyson, 170-1. The irony is that Nitocris is *not* pregnant in Song 7:2, Jehudijah is; and the same etymology is given for Jehudijah's son Soco (1 Chr 4:18), suggesting continuity. As the two women are more or less superimposed onto one another in the Song, this potential dual identification as Iscah is intentional, too.

# MILCAH

Milcah is Miriam. Although this name is commonly understood to mean "Queen" (*malka*) it can also mean "chief, ruler, court-lady," etc. (just as *melek* can mean king, chief, leader), e.g., a high priestess or even a judge, like Deborah, perhaps. This is further supported by the other translation of "counsel" or wise-woman. Milcah is married to Nahor, i.e., Abraham's "brother," i.e., she is married to Aaron, Moses' "brother." Ennigaldi-Nanna would be the ruling *entu* by now, so she is fits the notion of "wise-woman/counsel," and a large part of her training would be as a dream interpreter, visionary. As the wife of Aaron, the "prophet" (*nabi*, "a spokesman, speaker, prophet" in Exod 7:1), she fits the etymology of "prophetess" (see "Miriam").[43]

The motif of the two-wives/sisters is consistent through the Song of Solomon, with Nitocris and Jehudijah; Genesis, with Sarah and Hagar; and Exodus, with Zipporah and "the Cushite" woman (Nitocris). In the case of Milcah and Iscah, things are slightly different, for Iscah is Nitocris, and Milcah is Ennigaldi, i.e., the "little sister" of Song 8.

Milcah has eight sons with Nahor (Aaron), according to Gen 22:19-24; remember, the group has sojourned for many years after leaving Ur, so it is plausible. One of these children is Hur, the man who helps Aaron support Moses' arms in Exod 17:12, and who is left in charge of the crowd at Sinai, again with Aaron, in Exod 24:14. Father and son work as a team.

# HAGAR

"Gerar," the region where Abraham settles for a while in Gen 20:1, and where he attempts to bribe Abimelech with Sarah's charms, means "dragging, sojourning," from the verb *garar*, "to drag or drag away." As will be discussed shortly, Jehudijah is practically dragged away from her position at the temple by Nabonidus. Although "Gerar" appears in the context of Sarah (Nitocris), the etymological synchronicity with "Hagar," i.e., "flight," "to be dragged off" or "to be pressed into service" (Abarim), must be intentional. I suggest this is a subtle reminder to the audience that Jehudijah, Nabonidus' living wife, is the one who is accompanying him on this trip, even though Nitocris' ghost is haunting the narrative. It also echoes the insinuation, discovered in the Song, that Jehudijah feels she had lived under the shadow of Nitocris at Tayma; by using Nitocris-Sarah as the main wife in

---

[43] Tyson, 200-4 (the *entu* was allowed to marry, if not expected to).

Genesis, Jehudijah is once again subjugated to her old nemesis. It isn't until the Moses part of the narrative that she becomes a character in her own right.

Jehudijah fits the description of Hagar to a tee. She is the second-wife, the one who is fertile and who bears (Nabonidus') children, while Sarah (Nitocris) is initially "barren." She is treated badly by the first wife (in the Song, it is Nitocris who devises the plan to steal Jehudijah's child) and the two women are at odds with each other, e.g., the one reference to exemplify Solomon's wisdom is in 1 Kgs 3:16-28, where the two women vie for the right to keep a child—this is an account of Nitocris and Jehudijah battling over Ennigaldi.[44] The phrase concerning Hagar in Gen 16:4, "... she looked with contempt on her mistress," hits the nail on the head; the Song of Solomon is steeped in anger, resentment, and vengeful allusions.

When Sarah, in Genesis 16, tells Abraham that she is unhappy with Hagar, he shrugs his shoulders and defers authority to Sarah (echoing Nabonidus' attitude both in the Song and, it would seem, in his role as King), telling her to do as she pleases. The verb used by Sarah in 16:5 for "judge" ("May the Lord judge between you and me"), i.e., *shapat*, is echoed by the noun *mishpat* ("judgement") used to signify Solomon's decision in 1 Kings 3. Solomon-Nabonidus replaces God as "judge," but the inference is that these two scenes are connected by the two same women portrayed in each.

Because Nitocris dies before Nabonidus leaves Babylonia for good, and because it was clearly deemed important to acknowledge the underlying events of Nabonidus' reign, such allusions to the ex-king are woven into Genesis without mention of Nitocris, but via her ghostly avatar, Sarah. If the author had made Sarah an Egyptian, so much more would have to be explained, e.g., why would Abraham marry an Egyptian?; he doesn't end up in Egypt until much later. The Egyptian element is vital to the tale of Nitocris, however, so it is included but applied to Hagar, the slave, the bondwoman. That would make more sense to the average audience of the time. Those in the know, however (e.g., those who knew the women, those on the exodus, etc.), are fully cognisant of the fact that the two wives of Nabonidus are being referred to in the Genesis narrative. In *She Brought*, I suggested that Jehudijah *might* be an Egyptian Jew from Tayma's elite, as she would have had to understand Egyptian mythology and rituals, which she writes about in the Song.[45] However, since researching for *this* book, I realise there is more to her depiction and this identification has to be revised as we go along (e.g., I was unaware of the "Hagar" connection at that point).

Hagar is the epitome of the long-suffering "afflicted" second-wife (Gen 16:11). Nikaido suggests she is "...surrounded with attributes that

---

[44] Tyson, 220.
[45] Tyson, 217.

make her Abraham's true companion in tribulation and fitting counterpart with regard to his patriarchal role."[46] In the Song, Jehudijah is the voice behind the once loyal and gushing exuberance over "Solomon," but in the exodus stories she fares little better than poor Nitocris.

# ISHMAEL

This is, I think, the most difficult character to comprehend (perhaps intentionally so). The tale of Ishmael is, I posit, invented to explain the already extant social/religious/familial connections between Nabonidus and Arabia.

Hagar flees into the desert with her child, Ishmael ("God Hears," from the verb *shama*, "to hear," and the word *el*, "God"). The rationale for her action is that Sarah has issues with Hagar and her son and wishes them gone. Abraham leaves the responsibly firmly in Sarah's hands, who then sends Hagar from the home.

Two very interesting aspects need further attention by exegetes: the fact that Ishmael grows up to be an "archer" and the fact that he supposedly marries an Egyptian. Both these statements lead us back to Nitocris, who is the embodiment of Ishtar in the Song, i.e., the Mistress of the Bow, and also the archetypal "Egyptian" in the HB, "Pharaoh's daughter." Why would such connections be made? Is it possible that the Arabian mind-set proved more lenient to the legendary Nitocris than their Mesopotamian and Jewish counterparts?

In *She Brought*, I show the parallels between the narrative of Nabonidus and Nitocris in the Song of Solomon and the Arabic legend of "Layla and Majnun," in which the female character is just as celebrated (if that is the right term), as the male.[47] This legend seems to have its roots in the historical/geographical site of Tayma. Thus, it is worth considering that "Ishmael" is the representation of the Arabian contingent who supported Nitocris, or who, at least, did not denounce her, and this is why Ishmael must, in effect, be banished from Jewish Canaan. He is said to go to live in Paran (Gen 21:21), near Sinai ... not far from Tayma, in Arabia. "Tema" is said to be one of Ishmael's twelve sons (Gen 25:15), and some scholars take this literally, suggesting the population in/around Tayma were Ishmaelites, i.e., "their place is called after their name."[48] In Genesis, however, Joseph is

---

[46] S. Nikaido, "Hagar and Ishmael as Literary Figures: An Intertextual Study," *VT* 51.2 (2001): 219-42, here 228-9.

[47] Tyson, 247-50.

[48] Hatoon Ajwad Al-Fassi, "The Taymanite Tombs of Madā'in Ṣāliḥ (Ḥegra),"

sold to a caravan of "Ishmaelites" who are also called "Midianites" (Gen 37:25–28, 36; 39:1; also Judg 8:22-24); would there have been enough time between the generations for a society of "Ishmaelites" to have developed?

I don't think Ishmael is based on a single historical person; rather, he is a representation (not progenitor, as convention holds) of the northern Arabian tribes Nabonidus has dealings with, i.e., those who are possibly renowned for their war-faring skills and, as such, are favoured by him, thereby earning *their* continued support. According to Isa 21:17, the Qedarites, whose territory spans much of northern Arabia, are known as skilful archers. Later, Nabonidus' potential association with the Qedarites is discussed, in terms of them perceiving him as a leader. However, from the perspective of the Genesis author(s), what we see in Ishmael, a warrior living in Arabia, with an Egyptian wife, is a mirror-image of Nabonidus and Nitocris at Tayma, a generation later. This is the supposedly doomed inheritance of those who do not return to Canaan, to Jerusalem, to Yahweh. The character Ishmael is said to live to one hundred and thirty-seven years old (Gen 25:17); the gematria of 137 suggests a meaning of "inheritance."[49] This age is also given for "Levi" and "Amram" (Exod 6:16, 20; a genealogical addendum); both these names are linked to "Ishmael" in that both pertain to the same group of people, i.e., the Arabs of the northwest.[50]

# In Exodus

## Moses and his Foster Mother

Moses being pulled out of the water to inherit a profound destiny is an echo of the legend of King Sargon of Akkad (ca. 3800 BCE):

> My mother, the princess, conceived me, in a secret place
> she gave me birth.
> She placed me in a basket of reeds and closed the lid with pitch.
> She cast me into the river which overwhelmed me not.
> The river bore me along. To Akki, the irrigator, it brought me.
> Akki, the irrigator, reared me to boyhood as his own son.[51]

---

*PSAS* 27 (1997): 49-57, here 51.

[49] "Numbers 1-40 and their meanings," Hebrew Linguistics and the Bible, www.gods-abcs.com.

[50] For the Levitical connection, see pp. 283-5; for "Amram" see discussion on Aaron, below.

[51] Original Sources, www.originalsources.com.

The obvious parallels to Moses' story need not be laboured upon but what is germane to this discussion is "Akki," i.e., the person who draws Sargon out of the water has a name that pertains to the drawing/using of water ("the irrigator"). Pharaoh's daughter is said to call the child she finds "Moses" because she had "drawn him from the water" (Exod 2:10), from the verb *mashah* ("to draw, pull out"). Early audiences could easily identify Moses with Sargon, whose legend loomed large in Babylonian lore (and education).

## *Thermuthis and Renenutet*

These initial potential links between Moses and Nabonidus require another look at the discussion on Mered and Bithiah from 1 Chronicles 4, which proved a vital key to unravelling the Song.[52]

In Midrashic literature (BT Megillah 13a) it is said that "Bithiah" of 1 Chronicles 4 was none other than the daughter of Pharaoh who adopted Moses (she is *not* named in the HB); apparently, she chose to convert to Judaism and was given the name, traditionally translated as "daughter of God," in honour of her bravery and her service to the Israelite nation:

> God told her: "Moses was not your son, yet you called him your son; you are not My daughter, but I call you My daughter."
>
> Lev. Rabbah 1:3

The name "Bithiah," however, was adopted *from* the notoriously difficult passage in 1 Chr 4:18 which mentions Mered and Bithiah in the genealogies. The Midrash reveals that the early rabbis felt the need to explain why a son of Judah had married an Egyptian princess:

> God said: "Let Caleb, who rebelled against the counsel of the spies, marry the daughter of Pharaoh, who rebelled against the idols of her father's house."
>
> Megillah 13a

They had linked Mered to Caleb in a bid to hide his true identity perhaps, but because Caleb simply means "dog," with connotations of loyalty and faithfulness (Num 14:24), there was a need to explain why he was renamed so negatively, so the rabbis explained that he was given the name "Mered" because he rebelled *(marad)* against the counsel of the spies (Num 13-14). The name has more negative connotations, however,

---

[52] Tyson, 22-4.

20

suggesting not mere disagreement but a deeply concerning rebellion against the divine, against God. So, by suggesting Caleb marry the daughter of Pharaoh, God is equating him with the undesirable Egyptian. This, I have claimed, is precisely how Nabonidus was seen by his dissenters.

Josephus (*A.J.* 2.9.5) and the Book of Jubilees (47:5), on the other hand, declare "Thermuthis" was the king's daughter, Moses' Egyptian foster-mother.[53] What proves intriguing for the current investigation is that "Thermuthis" is the Hellenized version of the Egyptian protector goddess, Renenutet. Renenutet was said to be a fertility goddess, a nurse to children, the protector of the harvest but also *of the pharaoh*. I have previously explained how the Song of Solomon depicts Nitocris, on one level, as a fertility idol/goddess.[54] In the afterlife Renenutet would become a fiery cobra who could defeat any foe with her gaze; cf. "Turn away your eyes from me, for they overwhelm me" (Song 6:5). Moses' adoptive mother is, effectively, a serpent goddess.

Renenutet was also said to be the one who gave children their true name; the Egyptian word '*rn*' (*ren*) means "name" (and refers to an aspect of the soul).[55] Apt for the royal woman who would name Moses and protect him. In the Song, Nitocris gives Nabonidus a special name and she does attempt to protect him (from himself, really) by nursing his soul. Eventually, the goddess became amalgamated with Isis, the Great Sorceress. Nitocris, of course, uses magic in the Song to manipulate the king.

> The Jews thought that the Egyptians saw this pagan goddess as the Mother of the young Pharaoh-Moses. We can conclude that the *interpretatio Judaica* of Pharaoh's daughter was articulated in Egypt by Egyptian Jews in the third century BCE, or at the latest, in the first half of the second century BCE.[56]

So, the glorification of Genesis' "Pharaoh's daughter" took root, potentially, about three hundred years after the fall of Babylon. One might wonder why it took so long for her to be recognised as an important figure if she had lived a thousand years prior, as tradition maintains (as Moses' step-mother). Perhaps the reason why the rabbis felt so compelled to make Bithiah a convert was because they could not challenge the increasingly robust worship of Thermuthis *and* Moses who, Artapanus suggests, was

---

[53] David Flusser and Shua Amorai-Stark, "The Goddess Thermuthis, Moses, and Artapanus," *JSQ* 1.3 (1993): 218-19.

[54] Tyson, 162-71.

[55] Shesh Kemet Egyptian Scribe, https://seshkemet.weebly.com/the-egyptian-soul.html.

[56] Flusser and Amorai-Stark, 220.

revered by the Hellenistic Jews as Thoth-Hermes, the founder of Egyptian culture![57] Diodorus writes:

> Thus, for these reasons Moses was loved by the masses, and being deemed worthy of divine honour by the priest, he was called Hermes because of his ability to interpret [*hermeneia*] the sacred writing.
>
> (*Praep. Ev.* 9.27.6)[58]

Flusser and Amorai-Stark suggest the early Jews jumped on the bandwagon, so to speak, in a demonstration of Jewish-Hellenistic apologetics, in order to survive in an ever-increasingly anti-Semitic world.[59]

However, Chronicles is considered a postexilic text; the question is then *why* did the rabbis draw attention to the difficulty of Mered and Bithiah appearing in the genealogies? Clearly, the couple's presence in the Jewish record did not sit well with someone; this someone, it seems, could be Ezra, the supposed author of Ezra-Nehemiah (see Bava Batra 15a:2). This proves interesting because I previously discussed Ezra as the one who had the most acerbic attitude toward the high-ranking females within the sojourning group. He really has a problem with strong women, especially foreign strong women (cf. Ezra 10:10-15).[60]

As discussed in *She Brought*, the biblical pattern of dealing with issues concerning powerful or awkward females is to ridicule them, bump them off, or convert them.[61] I suggest the rabbis knew full well who Mered and Bithiah were but were unable to remove their names from the record; a radical interpretation was needed to allay any misunderstandings that Nabonidus and Nitocris were honoured with a direct mention within the genealogies, so hey-presto, the Egyptian princess is given a new identity and made a convert.

The overall effect of this is that Moses is brought up by a 'serpent goddess', under the influence of the Egyptian royal court. He is compared to Thoth-Hermes because of his search for wisdom and his ability to read/write (sacred) texts, and because of his association with serpents and magic. This is precisely the Moses we shall discover in this analysis.

---

[57] Flusser and Amorai-Stark, 226.

[58] Caterina Moro, "Hero and Villain: An Outline of the Exodus' Pharaoh in Artapanus,") in *Israel's Exodus in Transdisciplinary Perspective: Text, Archaeology, Culture, and Geoscience*, T. E. Levy, T. Schneider, W. H. C. Propp, B. C. Sparks, eds. (Heidelberg: Springer 2015), 365-76, here, 368.

[59] Flusser and Amorai-Stark, 225.

[60] See Tyson, 34-8 and 214-16. The most powerful women who are not overtly Israelite/Jewish are mentioned out of a duty to chronicle the events in question but they are commonly given derogatory and humiliating names, somehow ridiculed and demeaned within the narrative, or have their identity deeply obscured.

[61] Tyson, Chapter 3, 30-42.

# *Merris*

Artapanus called Bithiah "Merris," a name Christianity would later adopt for the foster-mother of Moses. She, the historian argued, was the wife of Chenephres, a supposed king of the "lands beyond Memphis"[62] (i.e., Sais) for whom there is no record. However, could the fickle hand of fate have led to a misinterpretation of an ancient manuscript, a misreading? Could it have once read, or implied "Khenemibre"? This, of course, is Ahmose III's true name. In addition, Caterina Moro makes the comment: "Chenephres becomes king only because he married the daughter of the previous king"[63] and it is commonly thought today that Ahmose, who seized the throne, probably married the daughter of his predecessor, Apries, to legitimise his position.

However, what is even more pertinent is the associated legend that this Merris (a feminised version of "Mered" perhaps?) was barren, and that she *feigned pregnancy*, taking another woman's child as her own.[64] In discussing Nitocris' situation, as it appears within the narrative of the Song of Solomon, I state that *she feigns her pregnancy*, in an effort to appease the king (Nabonidus) whilst maintaining her sacred duty as a priestess of Amun. This I then link to the fleeting mention of "Genubath," whose name means "stolen" (1 Kgs 11:20); he, too, was brought up in the palace by an Egyptian Queen—a queen and a place that have potential links to Nabonidus.

Finally, there has been published a comparison between a pre-Hellenistic Egyptian hymn to Thermuthis (Renenutet) and the Bible's Psalm 107.[65] Both declare that the route to salvation must come from within the heart of the one pleading for it, i.e., the person must "call out" for help. In the Egyptian song it is Thermuthis who must be actively sought out and appealed to; in the Psalm, it is God, of course. In my assessment of the Song, the final stanzas reveal *precisely the same sentiment*: Anyone searching for spiritual redemption, for insights into the divine, etc., must "call out," must use their voices and ask directly (in the first instance this teacher was Nitocris, but after her death, Jehudijah took over, I claim).

So, consider this: *If* the "daughter of Pharaoh" of the Exodus tradition,

---

[62] George Archer, "A Short History of a 'Perfect Woman': The Translations of the 'Wife of Pharaoh' Before, Through, and Beyond the Qur'ānic Milieu," 4-5, https://pubs.lib.uiowa.edu/mathal/article/2738/galley/111540/view/.

[63] Caterina Moro, "Hero and Villain: An Outline of the Exodus' Pharaoh in Artapanus,") in *Israel's Exodus in Transdisciplinary Perspective: Text, Archaeology, Culture, and Geoscience,* T. E. Levy, T. Schneider, W. H. C. Propp, BC. Sparks, eds. (Heidelberg: Springer 2015), 365-376, here 368.

[64] Joseph Jacobs, et al., "Moses" §"In Hellenistic Literature," *JE* www.jewishencyclopedia.com.

[65] Flusser and Amorai-Stark, 232-2.

Thermuthis, Bithiah, or Merris, *is* Nitocris II, daughter of Ahmose III, and if we accept that in the Song Nitocris treats Nabonidus as a child, a novice/student (especially note the invective at the end of the Song), then we can suggest that Moshe/Moses *can* be equated with Nabonidus, and Thermuthis/Renenutet to Nitocris.

If the pharaoh who was ruling at the time Thermuthis and Moshe met was, indeed, Ahmose III, the issue of chronology comes into play, as it is claimed in Exod 2:23 that this particular pharaoh dies ("after a long time"; duration unspecified), allowing Moses to return to Egypt. We know that Ahmose III died in 526 BCE, which was over a decade *after* Cyrus' original edict, and that his son Psamtik III took over only for a matter of months. Psamtik proved inconsequential and would not have earned the right to be mentioned as the lead figure in such a significant tale (it was Ahmose who left an indelible mark on Egypt as the last great pharaoh).[66] We also know that the migration from Babylonia occurred in waves, spanning at least *several* decades.[67] So perhaps there is no conflict here; Ahmose III, I posit, is the pharaoh whose death is marked by Exod 2:23. There is more to be said on this in due course.

# AARON

Aaron is Nahor in Genesis. The character begins with such high expectations. "Amram" (Exod 6:20), whose name means "people bound together," or "an exalted people" (from the verb *aram*, "to bind or grip"; and/or from the noun *am*, "people," and the verb *rum*, "to be high"), is said to be "father" to Moses and Aaron, and in 1 Chr 6:3, also Miriam. The chronicler clearly understood the symbolism of Genesis, for this means Amram is the avatar of Terah, the lunar, figurative "father" that sires the triad.

"Aaron" means "light, or shining" or "mountain/hill" (from *or*, "to be or become light, to shine" and/or from the noun *har*, "mountain, hill." From the root *rn*, is the verb *ranan* ("to produce a ringing cry"); the BDB suggests it might be onomatopoeic, and means (in Arabic) "to cry aloud." The plural noun *renanim*, denotes the "piercing cries" of birds. Aaron is said to be three years older than Moses, i.e., 83 (Exod 7:7) but while Moses' age may well have root in reality, given Nabonidus' advanced years (it is thought he is in his sixties when he becomes King), I suggest most, if not all ages in the HB

---

[66] Tyson, 21.

[67] Arguments abound concerning the dating of Joshua and Zerubbabel's leadership, for instance, which some contend occurred as late as the mid-5th century BCE, under Darius II (e.g., Henry Englander, "Problems of Chronology in the Persian Period of Jewish History," *JJLP* 1.1 (1919): 83-103, here 89-90.

are symbolic, *not* literal, and must be deconstructed to find their meaning in the immediate context. I am drawn to investigate the possible reason for announcing Aaron's age, as it seems superfluous at first glance.

As we shall see, the HB uses numbers in a very specific way; not one, I will wager, is as simple as it seems. I posit that the difference, 3, is intended as symbolic gematria, in that the number 3 denotes something relevant to the entire Sinai narrative to come. The meaning of the number 3 is "the blending of disparate elements into a harmonious whole," or "the ability to combine two contrasting forces—to bring about integration."[68] Aaron initially represents the "Sun" in Nabonidus' new triad; he is the opposing force, the opposite of Moses' identity as Moon. These forces will be symbolically melded at Sinai. As this investigation gathers evidence, there can be no doubting Aaron is Nahor, and as biblical genealogies usually list the offspring in descending order, we can safely assume Nahor is younger than Abraham, so "Aaron" must be understood as being *younger* than "Moses."

In Exod 4:14, Aaron is called "the Levite" but his genealogy, provided later in 6:14-25, is most certainly an addendum. "Levite," apart from being a term associated with a group of Israelites who are *later* linked with Aaron and the priesthood/temple, originally meant "one who joins" (i.e., "Levi" means "joined, joiner" from the verb *lawa*, "to join or connect"; the assumed root *lwh* exists in Arabic with the meaning of "to turn, twist or wind"). Traditionally, the Levites are given no land as a result of their behaviour after the rape of Dinah (Gen 49:5-7); they are thus considered, for all intents and purposes "nomads." As Levites are seen as attendants to Aaron, the high priest, the use of "Levite" for Aaron himself before the priesthood is created must insinuate either editorial manipulation or an alternative understanding. I think the nomadic element is alluded to here but also, a specific association with Moses which is necessary for them to be considered "brothers" and thus serve as the basis of the mythological triad (with Miriam).

Who or what does Aaron "join" and where? On one level he joins Moses in the "wilderness"; he is brought to Moses (ostensibly by God) in Exod 4:14 to serve as his "mouth" (*peh*), or mouthpiece/spokesperson because Moses declares himself not "eloquent" enough for the job. God says Aaron is "fluent" in speech but then he tells Moses to *put the words into Aaron's mouth*; God will "be with" *both* "mouths" and will teach them *both* what to do (i.e., "teach you" here is plural). When we understand what occurs later in the narrative, this simple scene takes on deeper meaning, for the "speech" being alluded to here includes magical "utterances," not just everyday talk. Nabonidus is showing his trademark lack of expertise; he likes to think he is a master of everything but in this instance, with so much

---

[68] Raskin, "Gimmel," www.chabad.org.

apparently at stake, he accepts that Aaron is more suited to the task.

Nabonidus would have learned rudimentary Egyptian (Demotic) whilst living with Nitocris; she would have taught him certain prayers, spells, invocations, etc. (i.e., as "Solomon"); he would have conversed with Ahmose on several occasions, but perhaps through an interpreter. To be "fluent" in such matters as will be expected, e.g., in the famous plagues scenes, is a priest's job, a magician's job, an "enchanter's" job.[69] Confronting an Egyptian pharaoh in the context of divine signs would *necessitate* a skilful and precise speaker. Words, especially magical words, are highly important and profoundly powerful, so for Nabonidus to charge in without some sort of professional by his side would be catastrophic.[70]

Much more comes to light about Aaron's identity and role as this investigation continues but we must proceed with one major element of identification, i.e., the allusion to "joining, twisting," etc., anticipates his association with snakes *and* his training as a metallurgist, a smithy/artisan (i.e., the ringing or piercing sound [*ranan*] alluded to in his name is reminiscent of the high-pitched ringing after metal strikes metal on a forge). Aaron is Miriam's Midianite husband, who is originally *not* associated with Sinai; he is called to be with Moses from somewhere else (Exod 4:27).

"Amram" is thus a pseudonym for Jethro, who is the Midianite priest and who knows Aaron via this connection to a central cult; he is Moses' father-in-law and Aaron's sacerdotal (not biological) "father." The age/gematria of 137 (i.e., the age given for "Amram") therefore links the "levites" (discussed in due course), the high priest, and the eventual tribal/racial group of the Northwestern Arabian "Ishmaelites." Amram also becomes the Exodus equivalent of "Terah" in Genesis, i.e., the symbolic "father" of the two main characters, and who, we will see, probably worships a lunar deity.

---

[69] Although Egyptian kings were considered on a par with the high priest, if not higher, in terms of knowing the liturgy, etc., Mesopotamian rulers were not always au fiat with anything other than the traditional rites and ceremonies. For a fascinating discussion on magic in terms of speech/words see Robert Kriech Ritner, *The Mechanics of Ancient Egyptian Magical Practice* (Chicago: Oriental Institute of University of Chicago, 1993), 35-57. The Coptic word for "enchanter" means "a man who speaks" (49).

[70] The modern perception of Moses having a "speech impediment" is unfounded. With all the ridicule that was thrown at Nabonidus after the fall of Babylon, it seems likely a stammer, or lisp, etc., would have been mentioned (as a perceived weakness, perhaps). The dominant depiction of Aaron as the one who speaks is a subtle reminder of the VA's accusations, i.e., that Nabonidus wouldn't listen to the authority of those better informed. Moses soon speaks for himself quite efficiently.

# ZIPPORAH

"Zipporah" is usually translated as "bird," i.e., from *tsipor (sippor)*, "bird." This noun stems from the verb *sapar*, which can mean to "make a noise" i.e., (singing?) like bird, presumably.

Zipporah is mentioned three times in the exodus narrative, i.e., Exod 2:21; 4:25-6; and 18:2. In the first account, Moses has just fled Egypt and arrived in Midian. He stops at a well, the most blatantly symbolic of all motifs in the Bible, I think, i.e., symbolising marriage and/or sexual attraction (cf. Gen 24:10-14 29:1-12); the waters of the well being a long-standing euphemism for female fertility. The very next sentence states that the "priest of Midian had *seven* daughters," so we instantly know that Moses will marry one of them. However, there is far more to this short scenario:

☆ The "well" is linked to a priest's "seven" daughters; I suggest this is the Arabian "Beersheba," which means "Well of Seven" or "Well of the Oath" (i.e., that made between Abraham and Abimelech in Gen 21:32, where "seven" lambs are given to Abimelech in exchange for the rights to the well).[71]

☆ This is the same well Hagar comes across as she wanders in the wilderness with Ishmael (Gen 21:14-19), thus linking her with Zipporah.

☆ Both Hagar and Zipporah are avatars of (or commission names for) Jehudijah, Moses' Midian second-wife. In *She Brought*, I postulate that Jehudijah is the daughter of an elite family of Tayma, or thereabouts, taken into Nabonidus' harem; now I see she is Jethro's daughter, i.e., daughter of the high priest. Nabonidus has known her for years; she was already one of the love-struck ladies at court when Nitocris was introduced to Tayma in ca. 549 BCE. Though legally she has the rights of a second-wife, the pro-Moses Genesis narrative reveals its misgivings and depicts her as a concubine for the following reason:

The second scene in Exodus 4 is intriguing. Why on earth would God wish to "kill" Moses after setting up his entire life, it seems, for the sole purpose of freeing the Israelites? What a waste! This is highly indicative of a Mesopotamian influence, where the gods are always annoyed with, angry

---

[71] For the "blood covenant" allusion in the Beersheba pericopes see H. Clay Trumbull, *The Blood Covenant: A Primitive Rite and its Bearings on Scripture* (Kirkwood, Mo.: Impact Books, 1975), 263-71.

with, or perturbed by humans and decide, on a whim, to destroy them (e.g., *Atrahasis*). Here, it is a construct to illicit Zipporah's actions and words. When she throws down (*naga*, "to reach, strike, touch, throw," etc.) the bloody flesh from her son's circumcision, the blood splattering onto Moses' foot, she says: "Truly you are a bridegroom of blood to me!" (Exod 4:25). She doesn't tell Moses to get himself circumcised, note. On a superficial reading, this might seem to be a precursor to the first "Passover" blood, long before the Israelites are told to paint blood on their doors; it is an arcane ritual, possibly, reminiscent of Jehudijah and Nitocris' mutual hanging-up of the children's umbilical cords over their doors when Ennigaldi is born (Song 7:13).[72] It would serve as a protection against the wrath of God.

However, the term used for "blood" here is actually in the plural, and this almost always pertains to something more sinister, i.e., "blood-guilt," or spilt blood,[73] i.e., Zipporah is accusing Moses of being a "murderer." He is, of course, for he has killed an Egyptian (Exod 2:11-15). Propp suggests that Zipporah only realises Moses' fugitive status at this moment and that she acts quickly; by "shedding the blood of their son Zipporah has improvised a blood expiation rite," thereby clearing Moses of his blood-guilt.[74]

I would argue, however, that Jehudijah, here given the commission name "Zipporah" (she is a poet and probably a singer of songs, therefore the "bird" epithet fits) is *fully* aware of Moses' blood-crime and that she is not doing anything in this scene to help her husband; she is, in fact, cursing him (again). In the Song, in the very first few words, we discover that Jehudijah is a woman scorned; she once adored Nabonidus (from afar) but when Nitocris came to court, everything went just a bit crazy (literally). Nabonidus lost his mind thanks to a mixture of the hallucinogenic Elixir and Nitocris' sympathetic magic. Even when the feigned pregnancy and the stolen child were discovered by Ahmose's emissaries, Nabonidus remained oblivious. Jehudijah watched from a distance as Nitocris was abused and other women were exploited. In those few short words opening the Song, she hexes the king for eternity by stating that his name means nothing, it is "empty,"[75] i.e., one of the worst things you could say to a Babylonian king.

Jehudijah has no concern for Nabonidus' wellbeing at this point. She has no concern for the memory of Nitocris. In fact, on one level, you could say she seizes this opportunity to symbolically *negate* Nitocris' long-held

---

[72] Tyson, 187-9. One has to wonder why, if Moses was supposed to have been raised an Egyptian he was not already circumcised (he is, supposedly, at the age of 99, in Exod 17:24), as Egyptians employed the practice, too, whilst Babylonians did not.

[73] William H. Propp, "That Bloody Bridegroom (Exodus IV 24-6)," *VT* 43.4 (1993): 495-518, here 502.

[74] Propp, 505.

[75] Tyson, 49-51.

association with blood in Nabonidus' life. Jehudijah is the one who has borne his children, she is the one who made all the sacrifices, but she never got the attention Nitocris did for *her* blood. Surely, the symbolic sacrifice of the pure blood of a child to save his life surpasses anything Nitocris' foreign blood gave him? Her defiant tone, however, is not one of a loving wife but a long-embittered, jealous, and vengeful woman who makes a sudden decision to humiliate Moses by taking the matter into her own hands (like Jael). It may be due to this prolonged resentment that she wipes Moses' "feet" with the blood (feet and marriage are linked also in Ruth and the Gospel of John), i.e., she is marking Moses as *a* "husband"; but she does not claim him as *her* husband.

Aware of this dramatic and liberated female intervention, the Genesis authors choose to reduce the impact of this woman on their version of Nabonidus' tale, so they diminish her to the rather pathetic concubine who runs away at the first sign of trouble.

Spoiler alert! The third episode in Exodus 18 involves Jethro bringing Zipporah "back" to Moses. When Miriam, her daughter, suffers under Moses' hand (in Exodus 17), Jehudijah also flees, but because she has had enough of Nabonidus' treatment of the women in his life, perhaps even fearing for her own safety. The forlorn woman and her child (as Hagar and Ishmael) head to Beersheba, i.e., to the "Well of Seven," to her father, Jethro's home.[76] This is why we suddenly see Zipporah being returned to Moses by Jethro in Exodus 18, when there had been no explanation for why she had been away in the first place. I think Exod 4:24-6 is a misplaced recollection (or an intentionally anachronistic one) of a publically-performed curse, i.e., a hex, placed by Jehudijah on the man she now hates; she is claiming the right of blood-revenge in the only way she can. This will have to await further discussion once the scene with Miriam is explained. However, it becomes increasingly evident that the author of Exodus, while being anti-Nabonidus, is pro-Jehudijah, and I think this is primarily because she has already written the Song of Solomon and her followers (on the journey) know how she feels about the ex-king.

I think there is a far more apt etymology for this woman, whose claim to fame is circumcision. The verb *sapar* has an unusual connection to, of all things, the cutting of hair. Apparently, the verb *sapar* that is used to denote "haircut" doesn't appear in the HB but becomes standardised "in the Jewish lexicon from the Mishna and the Targumim."[77] There is a Neo-Babylonian

---

[76] I discuss "Beer-lahai-roi" (Gen 16:14) in my forthcoming book on the Queen of Sheba. The two names are compatible.

[77] The information in this paragraph thanks to Rabbi Reuven Chaim Klein, "Haircut Time" (April 2022), The Anatomy of a Mitzvah, https://ohr.edu/this_week/the_anatomy_of_a_mitzvah/9811.

word, *sirpu/sirapu*, which means "scissors" (or "shears") but the term was used specifically for the shearing of animals; the Hebrew/Aramaic *sapar* was used to denote the cutting of human hair. It has been suggested that *sapar* stems from a collection of *spr* words that have a core meaning of "circle" or "round" (and that a barber is called a *sapar* because he cuts hair in a circular motion around the head).

So, applying this to "Zipporah," you can see how this woman, with a sharp, flint object in her hand, *cuts* her son's foreskin, which leaves a *circle* of flesh. Because this particular version of *sapar* is not in the HB, I suggest the term for "haircut/barber" was adopted from this very scene by later rabbis.

What makes this even more plausible is the fact that the idea of a sharp instrument (like scissors, or a flint knife) does figure again, in relation to Jehudijah, much later in the analysis, linking her again to Zipporah.

# MIRIAM

The etymology for "Miriam" is described as "rebellion" and/or "bitter," potentially from the verb *mara*, "to be rebellious," or the verb *marar,* "to be strong or bitter," which can apply to tastes and smells, but also feelings, situations, etc. There is also "myrrh" from the word *mor*, and "beloved," from the Egyptian.

Miriam has many of the characteristics of Jehudijah, e.g., her name implies "bitterness" (Jehudijah is bitter about her relationship with Nabonidus, as evidenced in the Song); she sings a song of praise (Exod 15:20-1), which links her to Jehudijah's etymology (e.g., "songs of praise"); and she has a connection to wells/water (Numbers 20), just as Hagar does.

The fact that she is seen to be playing a musical instrument, i.e., a timbrel (*toph*, "timbrel, tambourine" from *taphaph*, "to sound the timbrel, beat"), proves not only fascinating but highly significant. Most commentators simply suggest this must demonstrate some sort of sacerdotal office, e.g., she is a temple priestess. I want to take this further: Miriam is Ennigaldi-Nanna, Nabonidus' *entu* daughter, from the temple at Ur. Part of her training would have been as a temple singer, a "songstress."

Teeter and Johnson describe the life of an Egyptian songstress called Meresamun (8th Century BCE); the Mesopotamian cognate is less articulated in the records but other very close parallels between the two cultures and their temple procedures, etc., suggests the Babylonian temple-singers can be loosely described by this outline:[78]

---

[78] Emily Teeter and Janet H. Johnson, eds. *The Life Of Meresamun: A Temple Singer In Ancient Egypt*, The Oriental Institute Museum Publications 29 (Chicago:

✶ Young girls learned their role from their mothers, in incremental stages.

✶ The job was hereditary.

✶ Mother-daughter pairs could simultaneously bear "the prestigious title Singer in the Interior of the Temple of Amun."

✶ When performing outside the temple they often accompanied dancers by beating out the rhythm on a drum.

✶ Many holders of the title chose to retain it, "in preference to other titles," even when they no longer served in that capacity.

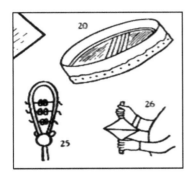

*Figure 2: An Arabian Ghirbal, or "timbrel" (#20) that looks like a garden sieve (Image: Galpin, 71)*

Ennigaldi's biological mother, Jehudijah, who weaned her in Tayma and stayed as her nurse through the Ur days (with Nitocris as the acting *entu* and cultic mother), is a poetess, a psalmist, like the famous Enheduanna (the world's first known author and the *entu* daughter of Sargon I who reigned ca. 2334-2279 BCE). Nitocris' own mother, Ankhnesneferibre[79] was originally a temple "songstress" at Karnak.[80] Music runs in the 'family'.

In Mesopotamia there are two types of timbrel used by temple musicians/singer, i.e., 1) a copper instrument that shakes, like a tambourine or a sistrum, making a "ringing" sound (in Assyrian *timbu*) that is deemed soothing to the gods,[81] and 2) a non-jingling tambourine with just a skin, called a *mezu* or *manzu* (ME-ZE), which is approximately 50 cm

---

University of Chicago, 2009), 27-8. For parallels, see Lloyd D. Graham, "King's Daughter, God's Wife: The Princess as High Priestess in Mesopotamia (Ur, ca. 2300-1100 BCE) and Egypt (Thebes, ca. 1550-525 BCE)," www.academia.edu/34248896.

[79] For my discussion on the relationship between Ankhnesneferibre and Nitocris, see "Ankhnesneferibre and Nitocris II: A Question of Filiation," 2023, www.academia .edu.

[80] On the Ankhnesneferibre Stele, Ankhnesneferibre's original titles are listed as: "Great songstress of the residence of Amun, the one who carries the flowers in the chapel, chief of the enclosure of Amun, first prophet of Amun, king's daughter ...." (Anthony Leahy, "The Adoption of Ankhnesneferibre at Karnak," *JEA* 82 (1996): 145-65, here 148).

[81] Francis W. Galpin, *The Music of the Sumerians and their Immediate Successors, the Babylonians and Assyrians*, (Librairie Heitz: Strasbourg University Press, 1955), 9. The creation of this form of timbrel was attributed to Tubel, the archetypal coppersmith (Gen 4:19-22). The "ringing" sound thus links to the etymology of Aaron, the smith.

in diameter and played with the fingers/palm.

The latter style was excavated from a royal tomb at Ur by Woolley, and is akin to "the large Arab *Ghirbal* ...which had no jingles and is described by early writers as "like a sieve.""[82] According to "ceremonial glosses on some of the temple hymns which were intended to indicate ... the proper form of accompaniment ... the *mezu/menzu* ... seems to have been especially linked with joyful outbursts ...."[83]

So, in Miriam's first scene we see her beating out the rhythm of the song, encouraging the singers and dancers, with this drum-like instrument that looks like a "sieve." This links *directly* to the notion of "Miriam's Well" (which will make sense when Exodus 17 is discussed):

> Rabbi Ḥiyya said: One who wants to see Miriam's well, should do the following: He should climb to the top of Mount Carmel and look out, and <u>he will see **a rock** that looks like a sieve in the sea</u>, and that is Miriam's well. Rav said: A spring that is portable, i.e., that moves from place to place, is ritually pure and is regarded as an actual spring and not as drawn water. And what is a movable spring? It is Miriam's well.
>
> Shabbat 35a:6

In Exodus, Miriam is called a "prophetess" and the "sister of Aaron."[84] The word for "prophetess" is *nebiah*; *Strong's* defines this as, "Feminine of *nabiy*; a prophetess or (generally) inspired woman; by implication, a poetess; by association a prophet's wife."

The word for "sister" is *achoth*, which commonly means a biological sister, half-sister, etc., but as with "son," there is scope for a broader non-biological meaning (e.g., intimately connected, by religion, marriage, etc.). *Strong's* has: "another, sister, together; Irregular feminine of *'ach*; a sister ... literally and figuratively—(an-)other, sister, together." This means she need not be a true sister at all but the insinuation, by emphasising her relationship with Aaron, and not to both him *and* Moses, is that she is closely linked to *Aaron* in a sense that would make them of the same generation (as siblings would be), perhaps. I therefore suggest that Miriam and Aaron are either lovers or are married, and that her relationship with Moses must be as a daughter.

This suggests Aaron is Moses and Jehudijah's son-in-law.[85] This is how the two men know each other and why they are called "brothers" (in a non-biological sense).

---

[82] Galpin, 10.

[83] Galpin, 9-10.

[84] In Num 26:59 and 1 Chr 6:3, "Miriam" is the "sister" of Moses and Aaron. This is, I suggest, a remnant of the triad structure mentioned above (in "Terah").

[85] See Chapter 14, "Hobab the Snake."

Shemot Rabbah 1.13 suggests that "Miriam" was also called "Puah," for her *insolence to her father*, i.e., her rebelliousness, which is an echo of the scene in Num 12:14, where Miriam's punishment is sanctioned by reference to her father's (hypothetical) anger.

What really confirms it, however, is that in 1 Chr 4:17, "Miriam" *is* the daughter, the "firstborn," of Mered (Nabonidus-Moses) and Bithiah (Nitocris); in the Song this is the child Nitocris pretends is hers, but is really Jehudijah's, i.e., Ennigaldi-Nanna.[86]

With this, we can now see that both Jehudijah and her daughter, Ennigaldi (Miriam's historical, sacerdotal name) are most certainly on the journey with Nabonidus.

# ELISHEBA AND REUMAH

I see Exod 6:14-25 as a later addendum. It sticks out like a sore thumb from the rest of the narrative and I really don't think the original story of Moses suits, or contained, lengthy genealogies. This suits more the era of Ezra-Nehemiah. However, we must address the mention of Aaron's wife, Elisheba. The name means "God of oaths, or God of seven," from the word *el*, "god," and *shaba*, "seven" or "to swear." These are distinctive elements of the story behind the naming of Beersheba in Gen 21:25-34, as discussed under "Zipporah." Zipporah is Jehudijah, one of the seven daughters of Jethro (aka "Amminadab": "my kinsman is noble/generous," from the noun *am*, "kinsman or people," and the verb *nadab*, "to willingly give"),[87] so I think "Elisheba" is the commission name given to Jehudijah as Aaron's concubine (second-wife), i.e., the same position Jehudijah has in relation to Nabonidus. Elisheba bears Aaron *four* sons, who prove to be more significant to the story than she is (i.e., Nadab, Abihu, Eleazar, and Ithamar; the first two are infamous for offering "strange fire" in Lev 10:1-2 and for being punished with death, and the latter two become relevant figures in the ensuing narrative).

In Gen 22:24, the *concubine* of Nahor (Aaron) is called Reumah ("exalted, or wild ox," from the verb *ra'am*, "to rise," or the noun *re'em*, "wild ox"); she bears Nahor *four* sons (together, symbolically, Nahor/Aaron has twelve children, the other eight with Milcah, i.e., Miriam [Gen 22:20-

---

[86] Tyson, 160-61, et al.

[87] Jethro fits the definition for "Amminadab" in that he is of high rank ("noble") and is willing to "give" or share his religious wisdom. The name is also in Song 6:12 as two words (translated as "my noble people"; Tyson, 159-60); now we can see that Jehudijah is the voice behind the Song, this suggests she is speaking of her own people, the Qenites (I could not make this connection until now).

3],). The Reu- prefix reminds us of Reuel (Jethro), thereby suggesting a filial connection perhaps, but "Reumah" has a very subtle and interesting etymology which may confirm her identity as Jehudijah.

There are four potential roots for this name: *rwm*, *rmm*, *r'm*, and *'rm*. From these are derived several terms but the most germane are: *re'em*, "wild ox" i.e., a sign of strength or a challenging behaviour; the verb *ramam* "to be exalted"; the verb *rama* (1 and 2), meaning (1) "to throw or shoot" and (2) "to beguile, deceive, or mislead"; and the noun *romam*, "praise."

There are also more negative connotations, such as the root *rmm*, which exists in Arabic as "to grow rotten or decay." It is used in Exod 16:20, 24 in the context of the "worms" in the manna. Linked to this is the noun *rimmon*, "pomegranate"; Abarim offers a lengthy discussion on the symbolism of the pomegranate and associates it with the more negative concept of rotting/decay by suggesting a "state of over-ripeness," i.e., when the fruit is passed its best and is decaying.[88]

The following is my take on these ideas as they relate to Jehudijah:

* She is one of the strongest, "bull-headed" women in the Bible.

* She challenges Nabonidus in both her Song of Solomon and during the exodus, especially in Exod 4:24-6, where she casts the bloody flesh from Ishmael's circumcision to Moses' feet (i.e., in anger).

* Later in the exodus narrative she is in a situation where she is deemed to be a liar, i.e., to be deceitful.

* Jehudijah's name means "praise."

* One of Jehudijah's signature themes in the Song is "weaning," i.e., she incorporates it into the secret code that identifies her as the author of the Song.[89] The weaning refers to her position as wet-nurse for Ennigaldi. In the scene where Nabonidus and Nitocris first go to collect Ennigaldi from her nurse, there is a play on the concept of ripeness insinuating that the child is ready to be taken and that timing is of the essence (Song 6:12-13): The pomegranates must be in bloom and the "mandrakes" must "give forth fragrance" (Song 7:13). The latter do so only for a very brief period, after which they decay and are foul-smelling.[90]

---

[88] Cf. Tyson, 66, et al.
[89] Tyson, 216-17.
[90] Tyson, 186-7.

> ✶ In *She Brought* I used the analogy of the fruit/wine in my discussion concerning the womb-blood of both Nitocris and Jehudijah, i.e., one womb is for sacerdotal, symbolic "wine," the other is for getting pregnant.

Thus, I have no doubt Jehudijah is Genesis' Reumah, in the context of Aaron's (Nahor's) concubine. This is how she will be understood later in the Exodus story, but already we see that she has relations with both Nabonidus and Aaron, with sons resulting from both encounters. My own guess is that all of this was a relatively long time ago, as the sons are adults and Jehudijah has been in Babylonia for the last four or five years. Aaron is now married to Jehudijah's daughter, Miriam (Ennigaldi), which makes the whole thing a little confusing but no more so than many relationships today!

The point to all of this is to demonstrate just how much more there is inherent in the personal names and toponyms, if you just delve a little more and apply some imagination, as the original authors did in creating them. The connections are there, waiting to be rediscovered, layer after layer, like a fractal. Until you understand the Song of Solomon, many inferences are lost. Because it was such an early work, and because Jehudijah's reputation as a great temple poetess was appreciated from the start, many insights come from this one, great example of her work (but there is more, I suspect, in the HB, and more, I hope, yet to be discovered in the ruins of Babylonia).

## *The Four Sons*

"Nadab" means "willing, volunteer," from the verb *nadab*, meaning "to willingly give, incite, or impel" as in volunteering for war (Judg 5:2, etc.); from the noun *nedaba*, meaning "freewill offering." It seems he is named after his grandfather, Elisheba's father Amminadab, aka "Jethro." The most obvious echo of this trait or character is in the scene of the slaying of Cozbi and Zimri in Num 25:6-15 by Phinehas, who is described as having "such zeal" for taking it upon himself to do the job (i.e., he volunteers, inciting the situation that follows his action). This has more significance, also, and must be dealt with at the proper juncture. Nadab seems to be Aaron's "son," a Midianite, by virtue of the link to Jethro.

On the other hand … Abihu has a questionable genealogy, for this name means, according to Abarim, "he is father," or "whose father is he?" Etymology is from the noun *ab*, "father," and *hu'*, "he." The concept of "father" in the HB, however, is complex, like that of "son" or "daughter" in that all can pertain to filial and non-filial relationships, especially in the context of sacerdotal hierarchies.

This is just the sort of riddle Solomon would be proud to have devised! The identity of the biological father is obscured by the priority of the social interpretation, yet once you understand the connections between all these names, via their etymology, you know that he is most probably Moses (Nabonidus), the "father" (i.e., Abraham), the one person at the centre of the community, the leader. Making this even more pronounced is the fact that the name "Abihu" is related to "Baal-hamon" (i.e., *hemma* means "they"; *hama* means "to be noisy"; *hamon* denotes "a noisy multitude"). "Baal-hamon" is the Song's pseudonym for "Nabonidus, King of Babylon" (Song 8:11)[91] and means something like "lord of the noisy multitude." Thus, "whose Father is he?" suddenly suggests, "who is his father?"

Abihu, therefore, is probably Moses' "son." So far, Elisheba seems to have at least one child with each man, which is significant in the analysis of the event that ensues in Numbers (yet to be discussed). Whether we accept "sons" as pertaining to immediate offspring, descendants, or members of a group, what is also evident is a schism, a division between Aaron and Moses supporters. This will become more evident in the Sinai scenes.

"Eleazar" means "God has helped," from *el*, "God," and the verb *azar*, "to help, support." He is the father of Phinehas (Exod 6:23, i.e., the one who performs the deed in Numbers). Eleazar is strongly linked to commanding roles/situations, e.g., in Num 20:28, he becomes (high) priest; in Num 26:3-4 he is put in charge of the census, which is taken prior to the entry into Canaan; he is also depicted in leader mode in Numbers 31, where Moses' (symbolically charged) battle with the Midianites leaves much booty to be inventoried and distributed, and Eleazar, as (high) priest, gets quite a substantial cut (as offerings to God). This demonstrates how he can be described as being "helped by God"; he is charmed, favoured. Eleazar is certainly Aaron's "son," i.e., successor.

# JOSHUA AND LOT

"Joshua" means "Yah Saves, Yah will Save, Yah is Salvation," from *yah*, "God," and the verb *yasha'*, "to save." Num 11:28 suggests he has served under Moses from his youth (*bechurim* or *bechuroth*).

Joshua is a military man through and through, which, if he succeeds

---

[91] Tyson, 205-6. In my book on the Gospel of John (*The Testament of Lazarus: The Pre-Christian Gospel of John* [Norwich: Pirištu Books, 2023]), I argue that this linguistic subterfuge is precisely how the gospel presents both Lazarus and Jesus, i.e., as potential fathers of the same child, thereby hiding the truth behind a literary ambiguity, and thus protecting the child in question. Perhaps this name "Abihu" is where the author of John's gospel gets the idea.

to Moses' role, must mean Moses is a military man, too, something not very often suggested, even though much of Exodus pertains to battles or preparations for invasion, etc. Nabonidus, of course, is a military leader. Joshua is the one commissioned to lead the battle with Amalek at Rephidim (Exod 17:8-16) because Moses is getting old and weak. Joshua appears as if from nowhere.

Later, Joshua is given his full title: "Joshua, son of Nun." "Nun" means "posterity, or fish," from the verb *nun*, "to propagate or greatly increase." This is hugely exciting (to me), as it suggests something I have been wondering all along, i.e., it suggests the possibility that Joshua is none other than Belshazzar, Nabonidus' firstborn son (his progeny)!

First, the name "Nun" itself needs some explaining. In Mesopotamian mythology, the fish is a prolific symbol for fertility, pregnancy, birth, regeneration, etc.[92] It is linked to the deity Enki (Ea) and the waters of the Apsu. Enki's firstborn son is Marduk, who "emerges as a national and popular god of the second [younger] generation, who exercises influence in every walk of life as the healer and saviour of the Babylonians."[93] The emblems and cultic statues of Marduk went into "captivity" many times, especially under Assyrian rulers who did not favour this deity (e.g., Sennacherib). "The return of the statue of Marduk, which was always connected with Babylonian resurrection, was interpreted as a theological change of destiny and as a punishment inflicted by Marduk on Babylon's enemies."[94] Marduk is called "the fish of Enki/Ea."[95]

According to Beaulieu, there are three archival texts that potentially shed a little light on what happens to Belshazzar in the final years of Nabonidus' reign. In Nabonidus' fourteenth year, i.e., the year 542, BCE, a year (or less) after the royal family leaves Tayma to return to Babylonia, he is listed as receiving "travel provisions."[96] His name is absent from the local records from the year before, i.e., as soon as Nabonidus returns, his son is summarily relieved of his royal duties and seemingly stationed on some distant front. In *She Brought*, I suggest there may be reason to consider a possible alliance between Nitocris and her stepson Belshazzar, which later is misconstrued as having a sexual context (due to Nitocris' reputation).[97]

---

[92] For a brief discussion, see Gavin White, *Queen of the Night: The Role of the Stars in the Creation of the Child* (London: Solaria, 2014), 59-64.

[93] JVL, "Marduk," www.jewishvirtuallibrary.org.

[94] JVL, "Marduk."

[95] W. Muss-Arnolt, "The Names of the Assyro-Babylonian Months and Their Regents" (Part 2) *JBL* 11.2 (1892): 160-176, here 174.

[96] Paul-Alain Beaulieu, *Reign of Nabonidus King of Babylon 556-539 B.C.* (New Haven: Yale, University Press, 1989), 204-5.

[97] Tyson, 245-7.

It is easy to forget that Belshazzar is a field marshal, a leader of men in battle. He is mentioned in the Nabonidus Chronicle (ii 13) as being with his solders at Dūr-karšu, near Sippar, when his grandmother, Adad-guppi dies in 547 BCE. Beaulieu states, however, that the provisions sent to the prince must indicate he is too far from a Babylonian city to procure them locally; he further suggests Belshazzar might well be patrolling the northern and eastern borders of Mesopotamia and Syria,[98] which is relatively close to where all the exodus action is taking place (in northern Arabia). There is also an argument that Belshazzar is sent to live in Tayma, presumably to keep things ticking over for Nabonidus in his absence (i.e., knowing he would return one day?); Beaulieu doesn't put much store in this idea[99] but now, having worked through the research for this book, it *does* make complete sense. Either way, the archival evidence from Babylonia means that a) Belshazzar was *not* at the "feast" in Babylon the night before the fall of the city, as Daniel seems to suggest (Dan 5:30). It may be that Daniel, third in command of Babylon, and friend/ally of Belshazzar, is in on the exodus-ruse and publically declares the prince "dead" on the night of the invasion, in order to leave him free to go under-cover as "Lot" (see below)[100]; and b) it is possible Belshazzar *is* in the right place at the right time to join his father at/near Tayma. It would seem that any possible feud between father and son is history.

Marduk, alluded to in the etymology of "Nun," via Enki symbolism, is thus the son of a deity (recall from the Song of Solomon that Nabonidus is self-deified; see precis in Appendix 1). Marduk is both a valiant soldier and a "saviour" (Joshua defeats Amalek, the embodiment of evil, in battle; as this is just south of Tayma, the theory that this is where the prince might have been sent is further supported). He is seen as being resurrected. It is Joshua who leads the new Israel into Canaan and conquers all the lands north of Sinai (Josh 10:41; 11:16-17), thereby marking the shift away from the

---

[98] Beaulieu, *Reign of Nabonidus*, 203-5.

[99] Beaulieu, *Reign of Nabonidus*, 205.

[100] Daniel makes it clear that he neither likes nor trusts Nabonidus; he probably perceives Belshazzar *as* "King," not merely crown prince. His declaration is a parting affirmation of his loyalty, i.e., he will not tell. The ambiguity, with respect to the naming of the "King" as Belshazzar is intentional, i.e., to comply with the rule of not mentioning Nabonidus' name, perhaps, but then why not just leave it as "the Chaldean king"? There must be another reason for this far too blatant error; I suggest it is because Belshazzar, given his pro-Marduk reputation was probably expected to remain in Babylonia in some lofty role after the Persian takeover but he absconds. As the narrative unfolds, we will learn what (potentially) happens to him. For more on Daniel's opinion of Nabonidus see Tyson, 223-4.

Mosaic world of the Arabian Desert (for the Jews).[101]

So, thanks to a very subtle allusion hidden deep within a very short name, there are potential clues to support Belshazzar being brought back into Nabonidus' fold (resurrected) as his military advisor/assistant. As the final entry into Canaan is ostensibly an invasion, a conquest, Moses needs a good general.[102]

It wasn't until I recognised Belshazzar in Joshua that my long-standing confusion concerning who Lot might represent in Genesis was resolved: Lot is Belshazzar, also.

The name "Lot" comes from the verb *lut*, meaning "to wrap closely or to envelop." It has two derivatives, i.e., the noun *lat/la't*, meaning "secrecy," and the noun *lot*, "covering." A related verb, *malat*, suggests a rescue, a salvific action, which tallies with the allusion to being saved in Joshua's name; the allusion in "Lot" is the same, i.e., the saving of Belshazzar from certain death (i.e., as part of Nabonidus' deal with Cyrus, possibly, but I have another idea; see Appendix 2). The "secrecy" inherent in the etymology of "Lot" speaks for itself: Lot is disguised as Abraham's "nephew" just as Sarah is feigning to be his "sister."

Lot, once the awkward piece of the puzzle that just wouldn't fit, now *does*. Look again at the scenario of him and Abraham parting company in Genesis 13, and notice where he goes:

> Lot looked about him and saw that the plain of the Jordan was well watered everywhere … like Egypt, in the direction of Zoar; this was before the Lord had destroyed Sodom and Gomorrah. … And Lot journeyed eastward [and] settled among the cities of the Plain and moved his tent as far as Sodom.
>
> Gen 13:10-12

Abraham has taken them to Bethel, i.e., the Bethel in the land of Ephraim, the place of the "first" altar (Gen 13:4; not the second one, down south by the Dead Sea).[103] So Lot, standing in the Arabah heads "East," i.e.,

---

[101] By "Arabian Desert" I mean the that of the Arabian Peninsula, not the "Arabian Desert" east of the Nile.

[102] Just as a comment, note that Josh 5:15 is a repetition of Moses removing his sandals in Exod 3:5. This is standard scribal technique for suggesting we "pay attention!" A son reflects the father.

[103] "Bethel" is traditionally translated as "house of God," from the noun *beth*, "house," and *el*, "God." However, a baetyl is an aniconic sacred stone which many consider to be a form of natural idol, i.e., in that it is revered as representing a certain deity. "Such stones have been identified in sites such as Gezer, Megiddo, Hazor, Shechem, Tell el-Hayyat and Tel Kitan, mostly in open-air cult places" (A. Yasur-Landau, "The Baetyl and the Stele: Contact and Tradition in Levantine and Aegean Cult," in *Metaphysics Ritual,*

farther into Arabia, probably moving from oasis to oasis, all the way to Sodom, which is mentioned again in the discussion on Seir later, i.e., Lot makes his way to the same general area where Tayma lies, in the Hijaz.

Thus, the allegedly unfounded theory proposed by a few scholars and rejected by Beaulieu, that Belshazzar was sent to Tayma at the fall of Babylon, may just have firm footing in the historical record within the HB after all.[104]

One other little thing: Beaulieu mentions that Belshazzar, in the extant documents, appears to have become an astute *private* businessman, which was not the norm for members of the royal family in Neo-Babylonian times.[105] This would surely stand him in good stead to take the reins in the trading hub of Tayma and serve as Nabonidus' business partner.

---

*Myth, and Symbolism in the Aegean Bronze Age,* Aegaeum 39 (Leuven: Peeters, 2016) 415-22, here 416. For a helpful synopsis see Robert Wenning, "The Betyls of Petra," *BASOR* 324 (2001): 79-95, here 80 (and note the strong Phoenician/Tyrian connection). They are heavily debated but are probably comparable to the altars Abraham (and Jacob in Gen 28:22) erects (12:7, 8).

[104] I have not forgotten "Keturah"; she is discussed in my book *Nabonidus and the Queen of Sheba: Roots of a Legend* (Norwich: Pirištu Books, 2024), 31-51.

[105] Beaulieu, *Reign of Nabonidus,* 91.

# 2

# MIRRORING

It may seem a strange claim that Nabonidus is the inspiration for both Abraham *and* Moses but they are mirror images of each other, e.g., with respect to the itineraries and evidence of specific Nabonidus traits and behaviours; ultimately, one tale is not complete without the other. As my focus is predominantly on Moses and the exodus, I shall provide only enough information on Abraham to illustrate how this profoundly clever scribal technique creates two distinct legends from one (extended) historical event.

The tale of Abraham is quite simplistic, compared to that of Moses. There is not such a significant focus on locations, e.g., he seems to travel from one place to the other without too much incident, and many opportunities to add detail to his sojourn are simply overlooked. Even the very strange and unexpected diversion to Egypt is given next to no explanation or embellishment (other than to say there was a famine, which provides an excuse, but no elucidation).

It might be easy to assume that a simpler text would predate a more sophisticated one perhaps, but I don't think Genesis was necessarily written before Exodus; I suggest it was written either at the same time or even afterwards. The overall pattern of the two texts is such that a single perspective, an overriding familiarity with both itineraries and both characters is necessary to produce the effect I call "mirroring." That is, the story of Abraham's journey from Ur, all the way to Egypt, and back to "Mamre"/"Hebron," mirrors Moses' sojourn to Egypt (from "Midian") and back down to Tayma. *Figure 3* shows how this looks on paper, though the details, especially of Moses' journey, have yet to be discussed.

I am not of the opinion that so many people, together with all their belongings, and all of their animals, were involved in this first wave of repatriation. I think it was a trial run, a reconnaissance trip, in a sense. The fascination with such huge numbers throughout the narrative(s) is either a later addendum (e.g., to illustrate the strength and potential of the new nation of Israel), or is symbolic in some way (e.g., as gematria, which would be a book in its own right, given the extent of the figures). Many thousands of people would never fit into the small villages/towns on the route. The animals would slow them down too much and probably would not survive (e.g., sheep are notorious for not travelling well, losing much of their body fat/milk if trekked too much between grazing lands). One might suggest they need the animals for food but then why are they so hungry they need a chance influx of birds and "manna" to survive (Exod 16:13-26)? You could argue that they needed the animals for sacrificing in the desert, but this stipulation has yet to be put into law at Sinai; the first sacrifice, Passover, is a one-off, yearly event, and as they would eventually come to another settlement, farm, village, etc., other animals would become available when it was time.

The whole idea of half-a-million-plus leaving all at once, and descending on the unsuspecting and ill-prepared villages, wherever one places their journey, is rather preposterous.

Once the Arabian context of the Mosaic narrative (in Exodus, Numbers, Deuteronomy) is recognised, and knowing the geographical layout of the itinerary, it becomes clear that subsequent generations have transposed significant locations onto the Canaanite landscape, as if an Arabic connection is just anathema and must be negated. It is a shame, as it has thwarted our understanding of history, of fascinating people and events that have influenced most of the modern world via Judaism, Christianity, *and* Islam. The exodus was from Babylonia, not Egypt; Moses *did* enter the "Promised Land"; and much of his story *is* rooted in Arabia, the land Nabonidus made his second home.

Note how Abraham's journey and Moses' have identical landmarks within the narrative (*Fig. 3*), i.e., both 1) begin in marshlands; 2) include the abduction of an individual from the marshland areas; 3) use boats to travel some of the way; 4) encounter a wall-like structure (in Genesis this is not explicit but archaelogy provides the evidence, see below); 5) stay for some time at their old homes; 6) arrive at a sacred site; and 7) end in precisely the same place, i.e., Tayma. The first account involves an excursion into Egypt and then back into Arabia; the second begins in Egypt, with a trip down to

Midian and back. (The elements of this map relate to discussions throughout this analysis.)

I suggest this "mirroring effect" is not coincidental but intended to link the two narratives whilst allowing each to retain its own distinct identity and its own significance to the emerging Israel. However, *both itineraries tell of the first exodus from Babylonia after the Edict of Cyrus, led by Nabonidus* (referred to as "Sheshbazzar" in Ezra 1:8, 11; he will be discussed later).

The two marshland starting points are the key, as these tie the stories together symbolically; this is not so simple to see, though, as salient details have to be in one's knowledge-database to begin with, such as the layout of Ur. To early audiences, especially those coming from Babylonia on this first expedition to Canaan, the allusions and references would have been more familiar but today it is quite an arduous task to unravel the intricacies.

# NABONIDUS AND CYRUS

The reason why there are two stories to explain the exodus from Babylonia is because there are two distinct missions. Nabonidus, as we know, loses his kingdom to Cyrus the Great (558-529 BCE) in 539 BCE. Next to nothing is known about what happens to him from that point on. There is one rumour, from the 3rd Century BCE Babylonian, Berossus, who suggests Cyrus sends the ex-king to Carmania (in what is now the province of Kerman, Iran), as a vassal king, and that Darius I (522-486 BCE) quickly confiscates certain lands from Nabonidus.[1] Three centuries is quite a long time for memories to remain accurate, without some form of contemporaneous record of the events to draw upon, yet there is nothing before this. We see in Herodotus' accounts that even the lifespan of a person is enough to blur the facts, and rumours are often unfounded or utterly confused.

The Dynastic Prophecy, ca. 330 CE (after the Persian king Darius III and the Achaemenid Empire are replaced by Alexander and his Macedonian Empire), i.e., *eight hundred* years after the events in question, is the only other document we know of to mention the fate of Nabonidus after Cyrus' invasion; it states:

---

[1] "Berossus," *EIr*, www.iranicaonline.org; Eusebius: "Chronicle" (41), www.attalus.org; Josephus, *Ag. Ap.* 1.20.

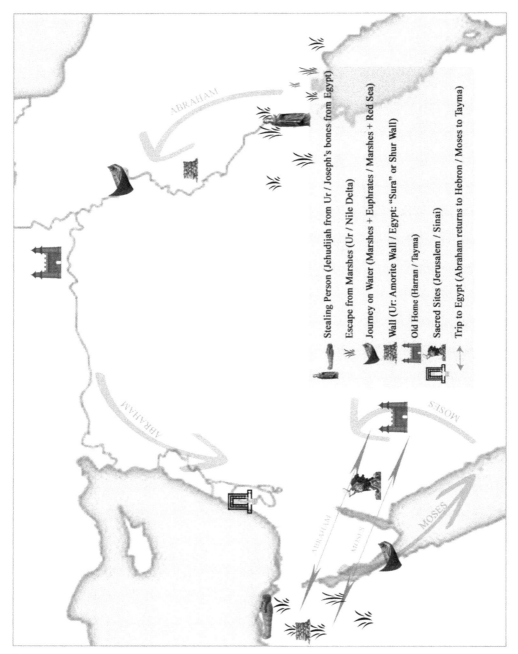

*Figure 3: Mirrored elements in the Genesis and Exodus narratives (Image: Author's schematic)*

A king of Elam will set out. The royal sceptre he will [take from him]. From his throne he will remove him and he will seize the throne and the king whom he made rise from the throne the king of Elam will change his place. In another land he will settle him.[2]

The VA demeans and humiliates the deposed king in a way no other Persian-conquered rulers seem to have experienced. In fact, Cyrus is normally (at least superficially) relatively magnanimous, allowing incumbent rulers to remain on their thrones, and to maintain their own businesses, laws, etc., so long as they behave and don't cause trouble.[3] Tyre is a case in point, as Hiram is allowed not only to keep his throne but also his trading ships and contracts with other countries, including Egypt. Tyre is considered not so much a vassal as an ally, it seems (though this is challenged under Cambyses, when he expects Tyre to take his side against the Carthaginians and they refuse, as they are related by blood [*Hist.* 3.13-19]).

My suggestion is that in 539 BCE, Nabonidus knows that Cyrus is on the offensive; he slips away from Babylon and meets the Persian king on the outskirts of Opis, where battle is about to begin. His aim is to make a deal.

Nabonidus seems to have begun his political career as a peacemaker, an arbitrator during the so-called "Eclipse Battle" between the Lydians and the Medes, in 585 BCE, under the auspices of Nebuchadnezzar.[4] He certainly made a treaty with Ahmose and the other countries, when the coalition against Cyrus' earlier advancement was formed, in 549 BCE. Why would he *not* attempt to negotiate terms with Cyrus? Some historians believe he might well have negotiated directly with Cyrus sometime around 556 BCE (when the Medes challenged the security of Harran), so there might be another precedent.[5]

The last Babylonian king has been underestimated, considered a laughing-stock, a failure perhaps but, despite his eccentricities, it is clear he is a very resourceful and indomitable man. He is not going to just lay down and accept the consequences; neither is he in any sense prepared for a major confrontation (as his rather lacklustre, perhaps misguided relocation of the

---

[2] "Dynastic Prophecy" (ii 17-21) § "Cyrus," www.livius.org. For perspectives on Nabonidus' capture, see W&N 13, n. 103.

[3] H. Jacob Katzenstein, "Tyre in the Early Persian Period (539-486 BCE)," The *BA* 42.1 (1979): 23-34, here 26.

[4] H. M. T. Cobbe, "Alyattes' Median War," *Hermathena* 105 (1967): 21-33, here 26. Also, Dougherty, *Nabonidus and Belshazzar*, 33-7 (citing Herodotus, *Hist.* 1.74).

[5] Sidney Smith, *Isaiah XL-LX: Literary Criticism and History* (London: Oxford University Press, 1944), 33. Cf. Beaulieu, *Reign of Nabonidus*, 109; Dougherty, *Nabonidus and Belshazzar*, 144.

cultic statues suggests, i.e., his only preparation for the looming onslaught).[6] The one option available to him is to come to a mutually-beneficial agreement with the conqueror, Cyrus.

The attack on Opis, one short, sharp show of intent is granted, which is enough to frighten the other cities into surrender; with no strong king to say otherwise, they have little choice. We can look at this two ways: Either Nabonidus effectively throws his people under the bus, not caring what will happen to them, knowing he will be gone soon; or, he sacrifices his kingdom for the sake of his people, knowing Cyrus has the power to decimate the nation if he so chooses. I think the former is more probable. Nabonidus cannot wait to leave everything behind him.

As there *is* a rumour about Cyrus granting Nabonidus governorship of a vassal state, yet there is no record of him (to date) being active in that capacity in Carmania, it may just be possible that the deal is to allow Nabonidus a governorship of somewhere else, where he can live out his days without too much interference (so long as he behaves himself). If he is considered such a terrible king, with so many negative attributes, as the Persians seem to claim (publicly), why would Cyrus consider granting him a governorship at all? This does suggest something else is going on behind the scenes.

I propose that Nabonidus offers himself as the governor of this 'new' Jerusalem he has heard the Jews (probably Daniel) talk about. Cyrus would be sending someone there anyway, and Nabonidus is being offered "another land" to settle in, so why not kill two birds, so to speak? He will take a pioneering group to set things up, i.e., to organize the political infrastructure. It must be remembered that anything in Jerusalem before the exile would have been small, rudimentary, and provincial. The task of building a temple requires a lot of preparation, let alone construction, and this is substantiated by how long it actually takes and all the troubles the project has to overcome.

In the Song of Solomon, "Jerusalem" is used where "Tayma" is meant, in order to maintain the idea of a belittled Nabonidus, but there *has* to be some historical basis for Nabonidus (as Solomon) being reckoned the "King of Israel" by later authors; I think this is it. That is, Nabonidus does,

---

[6] Nab Chr iii 9-12. Beaulieu cites three instances of this occurring before Nabonidus' day and suggests the king was, indeed, preparing for war by attempting to preserve the cultic statues, which might be taken as booty by the Persians (*Reign of Nabonidus* 223). However, one has to wonder why some cities failed to send their statues to Babylon for protection (220-4), i.e., perhaps it was *not* considered the normal thing to do and Nabonidus had his own reason for accumulating as many cultic statues as he could. Perhaps he believed many gods surrounding him would work to his benefit, just as the selfish motivation of forcing his wife into veritable prostitution was to serve *his* best interests).

indeed, enter the Promised Land, but he does so under the guise of Genesis' "Abraham."[7] The biblical account may be the *only* written record of Nabonidus taking a small group of exiles (and others) to the land of Canaan, perhaps as the new governor, or perhaps just as a scout. As such, he has the seal, the authority of the new King of Babylon, Cyrus, and this gives him access and rights few can boast. Though he is no longer King, as we will see, he maintains the authority of a king—in Tayma.

However, this is Nabonidus the rule-breaker, the impatient and self-obsessed man who insists on doing things *his* way. Knowing what happened in Tayma, with his passion for esoteric rituals, secret knowledge, etc., and remembering that he actually deified himself there,[8] Nabonidus already has a plan in place, I am certain. He has no interest, really, in Jerusalem at this stage (hence the scene in Dan 5:23, where he makes a mockery of the "vessels" allegedly stolen from the original Jewish temple; this echoes his making a mockery of Nitocris' Elixir in Song 5:1); he just wants to go home, to Tayma, but he must follow through, until Cyrus is convinced the job is done and the Jews in his charge have been settled.

So, with this potential foundation in place, the interpretation of the exodus narratives must begin with an explanation of Abraham's part of the mission. Because the two stories, i.e., Abraham's and Moses', are two sides of the same coin, we must understand how the two accounts connect with each other. To this end, the following discussion is provided on the symbolic starting point of Nabonidus' final sojourn from Babylonia, i.e., from Ur. Before he sets out, he has something he needs to do, and this instigates the first escape from the marshlands.

# UR LAYOUT AS A MIRROR TO EXOD 14:2

In Exod 14:2, Moses is told to halt the Israelites in their tracks and to turn them around to face the oncoming Egyptians, just before they cross the Red Sea:

… camp in front of <u>Pi-hahiroth</u>, between <u>Migdol</u> and the <u>sea</u>, in front of <u>Baal-zephon</u>, you shall camp opposite it, by the sea.

---

[7] And this allows for a superficial disassociation from the historical Nabonidus who, as Moses, is not allowed to enter the Promised Land. This is a concrete rejection of the Babylonian king; later, of course, we see many names that should really be recognised as Arabian sites, being commandeered as Canaanite landmarks, presumably to disassociate the new nation from its unsavoury past connection with Nabonidus.

[8] Tyson, 103-7.

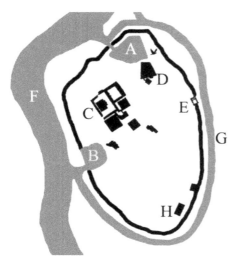

A. North Harbour
B. West Harbour
C. Ziggurat Complex
D. Harbour Palace and
   Temple
E. Defensive Tower
F. Euphrates River
G. Canal
H. Enki's Temple

*Figure 4: A simplified schematic of Ur in Nabonidus'
day (Image: Author's adaptation of Woolley's [Ur of the
Chaldees, 182])*

Hoffmeier has argued that all four sites, i.e., Pi-hahiroth, Migdol, the sea, and Baal-zephon, have contiguous parallels "in the very same area of the ancient eastern Delta, (i.e.,) present-day North Sinai."[9] This is both expected and necessary, if my idea of the "mirroring effect" can have any substance. The Hebrew authors of Exodus knew precisely this correlation; they exploited it! They had *been* there, with Nabonidus-Moses and when the time came to write of their experiences, they purposefully transposed one region (eastern Nile Delta) upon the other (Ur) for symbolic significance and to link the two stages of the exodus to each other.[10] Whereas the subsequent narratives bring Arabian names into Canaan, this time, we see Egyptian sites mirrored in Babylonia. It is a consistent scribal technique.

To comprehend how this works, and what occurs during Nabonidus' departure from Ur, we need to look at the various sites within Ur itself and the significance of each to the overall narrative.

## A & B. The Harbours

One of the two harbours (as yet unresolved but potentially the North Harbour, as this accommodates boats coming down the Euphrates) was

---

[9] James K. Hoffmeier, Ancient Israel in Sinai: The Evidence for the Authenticity of the Wilderness Tradition (Oxford: Oxford University Press, 2005), 108.

[10] I had first called the "mirroring effect" the "ouroboros effect" as it initially seemed a simple circular representation, but as we see, it's a bit more complicated than that, e.g., a coiled snake, perhaps (which really would be fitting, symbolically).

probably the "pure quay of Nanna" mentioned in Ur III texts, at the point of which stood a statue, so Jacobsen describes.[11] Harbour statues depicting deities affiliated with ships and sailors would be familiar to and expected by trading vessels, such as those of the Phoenicians, who perform "rituals of departure," to appease land gods who might refuse to release their ships, as well as rituals associated with "landings and entering harbours" (i.e., in respect of local deities).[12] I suggest Ur's "Baal-zephon" is such a statue, i.e., if not physically, at least implied for the symbolism of the narrative.

Nabonidus is known to have made a unique statue/idol of Sîn, to suit his own perception of the deity;[13] with the refurbishments at Ur, in preparation for the inauguration of the new *entu* priesthood, he reclaims land from the exposed harbour bank (after the Euphrates starts to change its flow), in order to build the palace there.[14] It would be a good time to erect a new harbour statue, too, i.e., one that means something to *him*.

The name "Baal-zephon" is almost invariably translated as "lord of the North," (from the verb *ba'al*, "to be lord," and the noun *sapon*, "north or darkness." Tahpanhes, on the outer regions of the eastern Nile Delta, is deemed a centre of worship for Baal-zephon, according to a 6th Century BCE Egyptian papyrus, which reads: "Baal-zephon and all the gods of Tahpanhes."[15]

A certain *Ba'ali-Tsapuna* (Mount Baal-zephon)[16] is named in inscriptions of Tiglath-Pileser III (745-727 BCE) and his son Sargon II (745-727 BCE), and referred to as the "great copper mountain" in northern

---

[11] Thorkild Jacobsen, "The Waters of Ur," *Iraq* 22 (1960): 174-85, here, 183. Called "Amar-dEnzunak"; I attempted to find another reference to this statue , even approaching several scholars in the Ur III field of study, but to no avail. The Sumerian word *amar means* "calf; young animal"; *amaru* means "destructive flood (water + to go + to send)"; the Akkadian Dictionary has *amaru* defined as "to see, behold, inspect, meet, to be checked, verified, etc."; *enzu* means "goat" (female), but it is also defined as "the constellation Lyra … also (a kind of bird)."

[12] Mark A. Christian, "Phoenician Maritime Religion: Sailors, Goddess Worship, and the Grotta Regina," *DWO* 43.2 (2013): 179-205, here 198.

[13] Tyson, 154-7.

[14] Leonard Woolley, *Ur Excavations, Vol 9, The Neo-Babylonian and Persian Periods*, Publications of the Joint Expedition of the British Museum and of the University Museum, University of Pennsylvania, to Mesopotamia (London, 1962), xi.

[15] W. F. Albright, "Baal-Zephon," in *Festschrift, Alfred Bertholet zum 80* (Geburtstag: J. C. B. Mohr Tübingen, 1950), 1-14, here 9. (Baal-zephon was also worshipped at Memphis.)

[16] A "mountain called Mons Casius (Jebel Aqra on the Syrian coast) was known in earlier times as Baal-zephon); there are several other proposed locations (JVL, "Baal-Zephon," www.jewishvirtuallibrary.org).

Syria.[17] It would seem there are several potential Baal-zephon centres, sites, sanctuaries, etc., which is unsurprising. We need to find the one that fits the clues and the narrative.[18]

The verb *sapa* can mean "to look out or watch"; derivatives are the nouns *sippiya*, meaning "lookout post" and *mispeh*, "watchtower" or "lookout point." This seems fitting for a statue overlooking a harbour. The verb *sup* relates to the flow of liquid, e.g., honey, water, etc., "to flow or overflow" (the verb *sapa* means "outflow"); again, a fitting allusion to a harbour where "sea," river, canal, and harbour converge.

The verb *sapan* means "to hide or store up"; it suggests hiding someone or something as an act of protection; this verb is used in Exod 2:2, where Moses is "hidden" for three months by his mother. Abarim suggests the most literal translation is "lord of hidden things" and this I find most satisfactory, as much of the Song of Solomon centres on "hidden things," i.e., hidden wisdom Nabonidus seeks[19] but also, later in the analysis, we find that something is *actually* "hidden" at Baal-zephon. This could be why the authors of Exodus insist on *naming* this particular deity; they wish us to see that there are hidden layers to their story, and that the exodus itself perhaps only happens because Nabonidus is on another quest to find arcane wisdom.

There is also a mythological connection that needs to be understood. The earliest mention of Baal-zephon as a deity comes from a 14th Century BCE Ugaritic poem:

> O mountain Baal-zephon, O holy Phoenix
> O barque, Glorious Phoenix
> Phoenix of wide wings.[20]

---

[17] Lewis B. Paton, "The Civilization of Canaan in the Fifteenth Century BC," *BW* 20.1: 25-30, here 30. Paton adds: "Copper was found ... in early times in Mount Lebanon and Mount Hermon. Remains of ancient mines have been discovered in these regions, and later historians bear testimony to their productiveness."

[18] "Baal-zephon" is also mentioned in Papyrus Sallier 4 (ca. 1270-50 BCE): "...to Baaltis, to Qudshu, to the Barque of Baal-zephon ... to Sopdu"; these are all shrines thought by Albright to be along the coastline, from the eastern Nile Delta up to Byblos and Tyre ("Baal-Zephon," 6-8). Nome 20 is ruled by the deity Sopdu, which might suggest it is not on the coastline, but Nome 14, wherein sits Tahpanhes, this would hint at a potential coastline location for the "barque of Baal-zephon" (i.e., the outer limits of the deity's realm, signified by a boat on the waters?) if not the primary sanctuary (which is in apparently Tahpanhes).

[19] Tyson, Chapter 5.

[20] Albright, "Baal-Zephon," 3. Phoenix (the son of Agenor) is thought to be the eponym of the Phoenicians.

Albright suggests the Greeks probably adopted the legend of the phoenix from the Phoenicians; Herodotus attributes the bird's significance to the priests of Heliopolis (*Hist.* 2.73; i.e., the HB's "On"): "Since the phoenix was *par excellence* the symbol of resurrection, it is quite likely that Baal-zephon and his *ḥôl* (associated mythical bird) were connected with immortality and the afterlife of kings ...."[21] This is an amazing clue to much that transpires later in the exodus narratives.

In the *Legends of the Jews* (3.1, 11-12), God refrains from harming the deity Baal-zephon during his plague-campaign against the Egyptian pantheon for the sole purpose of using him to thwart the Jews' immediate escape and thus prove his own greatness. He lets the Egyptians keep this idol, to allow them to believe they still retain a powerful deity and will thus fight on (again, such a manipulative deity, with very human motivations, is very Mesopotamian in nature).

The legend goes on to say that the Israelites go to Pi-hahiroth "where two rectangular rocks form an opening, within which the great sanctuary of Baal-zephon [is] situated." What is more, *Legends* says that Joseph himself hides a great treasure in that sanctuary, i.e., under the protection of Baal-zephon, but the Israelites run off with it! The verb *sapan* ("to hide or store up") in "zephon," the potential meaning of "lord of hidden things," and the hiding of something by Joseph at the Baal-zephon sanctuary, I suggest, have *specific* meaning to the exodus narrative, providing the rationale behind Nabonidus' second visit to Tahpanhes (after his stint in Midian).

In Exod 19:4, is a strange phrase, i.e., "I bore you on eagles' wings to me." If truly wandering about for forty years, that's hardly "on eagles' wings"! This must mean that Moses is spirited away *quickly*, is figuratively flown to where God is.[22] In the pragmatic world of canals, rivers, etc., this can only mean leaving in a boat (rather than on foot).

Note in the verse above the reference to the "barque" of Baal-zephon. In the *Odyssey* (xi 125)[23] the "banks of oars" are called "wings of the ship" (i.e., *mknpt*, or "wingspread").[24] If the Greeks took the phoenix legend from the Phoenicians, perhaps this notion was adopted from them, too, which might suggest that the HB's "eagles' wings" reference *is* an allusion to boats, i.e., boats from Phoenicia, from Hiram of Tyre (cf. Isa 60:8-9; ships 'flying').

---

[21] Albright, "Baal-Zephon," 4, n. 2.

[22] The Akkadian *Epic of Etana*, in which a snake, an eagle, and a tree are again at the core of the myth, includes a veritable flight on an eagle's wings, and should be examined more closely for potential symbolic import here. See, e.g., Jonathan Valk "The Eagle and the Snake, or *anzû* and *bašmu*?: Another Mythological Dimension in the Epic of Etana," *JAOS* 140.4 (2020): 889-900.

[23] Homer, *Odyssey*, Samuel Butler, trans. (1900) www.perseus.tufts.edu.

[24] Albright, "Baal-Zephon," 3, n. 4.

## Nabonidus and Hiram of Tyre

An ancient myth telling of Tyre's rocky foundation is told, ostensibly, by Heracles[25] to Dionysus in a 4-5th Century CE tale by Nonnus of Panopolis.[26] Two floating rocks, "which Nature has named the Ambrosial Rocks," drift freely along the coastline. On one rock grows an olive tree; in its upper branches lives an eagle, with a bowl (nest?) perched on the highest branch. At the roots of the tree lives a snake, who wraps his body around the trunk. The eagle and the snake live in harmony. Heracles, however, suggests that the eagle must be sacrificed to Zeus if the rocks are to be secured and a city and quays built. He instructs the locals on how to build a sea-faring boat and orders them to catch the eagle. Remarkably, the bird sacrifices himself to this cause and the two rocks become one, i.e., the city of Tyre.

Although this Hellenized version of the tale is the most well-known, it is thought to be based on a much older account of the deity Melqart, son of Baal, who becomes Tyre's patron god.[27] As the protector of Tyrian ships/traders, each Phoenician colony builds a temple in his honour[28] but no statue of Melqart is placed in the temple until the 1st Century CE; instead, there are apparently two "pillars."[29] Herodotus mentions them (*Hist.* 2.44) but employs the word *stelae*,[30] which has the connotation of being inscribed. However, a Melqart temple in modern Cadiz, Spain (then called Gades), contains actual *pillars* of either bronze (Strabo, 3.5.5) or gold and silver (Philostratus, *Vita Apoll.* 5.5); Philostratus also says the pillars are inscribed.

In the description of Solomon's temple in 1 Kgs 7:21, there are two bronze pillars, which are named "Jachin" and "Boaz." These are of huge interest to scholars, and yet no consensus on their true meaning is forthcoming. In 7:41, however, these two pillars are said to be topped with, of all things ,

---

[25] Tyrians called Melqart "Heracles" or "Hercules" but this predates the Greek Heracles/Hercules.

[26] Nonnus, *Dionysiaca*, (Cambridge, MA: Harvard University Press, 1940) § 40.448-510, https://topostext.org/work/529.

[27] María Eugenia Aubet provides a concise summary of the various foundation myths and their earliest known sources, suggesting that "the one of Philo of Byblos and the one of Nonnus, contain early features that are clearly oriental and probably emerged from the same original tradition" ("Tyre before Tyre: The Early Bronze Age Foundation," in *Nomads of the Mediterranean: Trade and Contact in the Bronze and Iron Ages, Studies in Honour of Michal Artzy*, Ayelet Gilboa and Assaf Yasur-Landau, eds. [Leiden: Brill, 2020], 14-30, here 27).

[28] Gabriela Ingrid Bijovsky, "The Ambrosial Rocks and the Sacred Precinct of Melqart in Tyre," XIII Congreso Internacional de Numismatica, Madrid – 2003. Actas – Proceedings – Actes I. Madrid (2005): 829-34, here 831.

[29] Bijovsky, 831.

[30] Bijovsky, 830.

"bowls" (*gullot*). Nothing similar appears anywhere else, as far as I am aware.

It is blatantly obvious that Hiram of Tyre and his artisans have a very strong influence on the design and construction of the temple "Solomon" builds, so it would seem this is where we find the inspiration for the pillars, i.e., from the Tyrian worship of Melqart. The pillars might then represent the mythical tree, with its lofty bowl/nest, the "wreath-work" the winding serpent body, etc.[31] While it is to Nabonidus-Solomon that this iconography relates, it also has a significant bearing on Nabonidus-Moses, in that serpent imagery is essential to the exodus narratives (and it is a factor pertaining to Nabonidus' inscriptions, as will be seen).

*Figure 5: Artist's rendition of the harbour at Tyre with its statue (Image: Public Domain).*

In the 7th Century BCE, the Assyrian king, Assurbanipal, seizes Tyre but his grip on the city soon weakens and life goes on very much as normal for the Phoenicians, including a lucrative arrangement with Egypt, i.e., in exchange for exclusive rights to the cedars of Lebanon, Tyre is given a trading quarter in Memphis.[32] When Nebuchadnezzar, in the 6th Century BCE, then lays siege to Tyre, an action

---

[31] Two interesting alternative interpretations include: R. B. Y. Scott, "The Pillars Jachin and Boaz," *JBL* 58.2 (1939): 143–49 (who considers the pillars to be connected with coronation and covenant ceremonies); and Carol Meyers, "Jachin and Boaz in Religious and Political Perspective," *CBQ* 45.2 (1983): 167-78, (who argues the pillars represent a symbolic gateway to the hidden abode of God but also a legitimisation of the dynastic power behind the temple itself).

[32] Kristin Kleber and C. van der Brugge, "The Empire of Trade and the Empires of Force: Tyre in the Neo-Assyrian and Neo-Babylonian Periods," in *Dynamics of Production in the Ancient Near East 1300-500 BC*, J. C. Moreno García, ed. (Oxford: Oxbow Books, 2016), 187-222, here 197.

Josephus claims lasted thirteen years (*A.J.* 11.10.1), the city becomes a vassal to Babylonia. Then a new Egyptian Pharaoh, Apries, comes to the throne and decides he wants the Phoenician ports for Egypt, so another battle ensues, this time by land *and* sea (the Babylonians have no navy), and Tyre hedges its bets by acquiescing to the greater power, i.e., Egypt, thus alienating Babylonia. "Eventually Tyre capitulate[s] and negotiate[s] the turnover of the city into Nebuchadnezzar's hands, perhaps against the right to remain a (vassal) state with its own king."[33] The kingdom phase lasts only a short while, then there is a period of "judges," or *shoftim,* that rule the city under Babylonian control:

> Tyre's kingship was reintroduced in 558/7. No source informs us about the reasons for this decision. … The royal house of Tyre was in Babylonian captivity: Josephus relates that when king Balatorus died, his successor Merbalos (Mahar-ba'al) was brought from Babylon. When he died four years later, his brother Hiram III was fetched again from Babylon.[34]

It is *this* Hiram III (551-32 BCE) Nabonidus-Solomon knows, *not* Hiram I (978-44 BCE), whom most biblical scholars ascribe to the conventional dating of the Solomon stories.

Because Babylonia gains control over Phoenicia, it has, potentially, exclusive rights to its resources. Although historians generally agree that the city of Tyre becomes a shadow of its once illustrious self, in terms of international commerce, from the Babylonian perspective this means a greater share of the "goods and chattels." So while the period after Hiram I's heyday in the 10th Century BCE, with the various machinations of Egypt, Assyria, and Babylonia taking their toll, might not be considered a suitably affluent time for the kind of business relationship we see in 1 Kings, with Nabonidus-Solomon, there is ample scope for the newly restored kingdom of Tyre, under Hiram III, to form such an alliance. After all, the natural resources are still in the ground, or growing on the mountains; the ships are still sailable, the craftsmen are still working; the only real difference is that now Babylon (whether ruled by Nabonidus or the Persians) gets first dibs and everyone else, probably, gets what is left.

Thus, although the descriptions of the riches made available to Solomon are potentially exaggerated for effect, I do not agree with some who claim that such grandeur must be totally invented.[35] When Nabonidus-

---

[33] Kleber and van der Brugge, 199.

[34] Kleber and van der Brugge, 201.

[35] Nadav Na'aman, "Hiram of Tyre in the Book of Kings and in the Tyrian Records," *JNES* 78 (2019): 75-85, here 85.

Solomon builds his temple in Tayma, he replicates the (Southern) Palace in Babylon, so the VA claims (ii 8); we now know that Tyrians were involved in the building of *that* palace also:

> In the *Hofkalender*, an inscription that mentions Nebuchadnezzar's 7th year (598/7 BC), Tyre is listed next to Gaza, Sidon, Arwad, and Ashdod as having contributed to the building of the South Palace in Babylon.[36]

So, the goods procured by Nabonidus-Solomon for his "temple" (i.e., in 1 Kgs 7) are not, I think, destined for the temple at Jerusalem but are a *memory* of the temple/palace at Babylon and/or Tayma. The Jews have witnessed this construction; some of them might have worked on these buildings, perhaps under corvée labour (cf. VA ii 9; 1 Kgs 5:13).

> [He] made the city resplendent (and) buil[t a palace]. He built it (just) like the palace of Babylon, ... [... He constantly placed] the treasures of the city and l[and inside it]. He surrounded it with a garris[on ...]."
> VA ii 28-31[37]

When the time comes for Nabonidus to take steps toward building the temple at Jerusalem, it is reasonable to suppose that the expectations of the Jews are high for a similarly opulent place of worship, hence the lavish and lengthy descriptions of, basically, what they *want*, rather than what actually transpires.[38]

As Abraham, however, Nabonidus builds his business platform in Canaan (discussed shortly). He must already know Hiram III from Babylon, where the Tyrian king has been retained.[39] I suggest this is where and when Nabonidus and Hiram might agree to take on Jerusalem, and the wider Canaan territory, as a joint business venture, probably unbeknownst to Cyrus. Hiram would naturally go into this relationship with Nabonidus-Solomon thinking he would make a fortune.

---

[36] Kleber and van der Brugge, 197.

[37] Translation from W&N 11 and n. 89.

[38] According to Josephus (*A.J.* 11.4.7), the temple wasn't completed until the ninth regnal year of Darius, ca. 513-512 BCE but others suggest a much later date.

[39] Nabonidus, when he was King, had numerous troops stationed at Gaza (Nab 28 i 33-4); he likely went there on his military excursions and so he has already been to (through) Canaan long before the exodus. Dealings with Tyre/Sidon would have been unavoidable. Hiram III is first noted as king in 551 BCE, i.e., he is returned to Tyre by Nabonidus' orders. It is the later phase of their friendship I suggest relates to "King Solomon of Israel" and the 'temple'.

## C. *Ziggurat Complex*

The Ziggurat of Ur Nammu, the original ziggurat on this site, was dedicated to the Moon god Nanna (Sîn) and dates back to the reigns of the Third Dynastic kings, Ur-Nammu (2112-2095 BCE) and Shulgi (2095-47 BCE). Woolley discovered three of the stages/platforms of this early ziggurat but was confident Nabonidus, who renovated the site in the 6th Century BCE had constructed seven,[40] a well-attested design and probably astronomically symbolic.[41] This new ziggurat, *Ekišnugal* ("House of the seed of the throne"), is where the young *entu*, Ennigaldi-Nanna, Nabonidus' daughter is officially High Priestess, even though she is only about three when dedicated. As I explain in *She Brought*, Nitocris, the girl's official mother and a high priestess herself, serves as regent (in Egypt she was First Prophet of Amun; at Ur she is the acting-*entu*).[42]

## D. *Harbour Palace and Temple*

The structure here is extensive, with eighty rooms, courtyards, and chambers. It, too, was comparable to the Southern Palace in Babylon,[43] which may provide substantiation for the description of the Tayma palace and the expectations of the Jews for an opulent temple under Nabonidus' aegis. Attached by a passageway is a small temple of ten rooms specifically geared for religious rites and services. I have previously suggested that the site at Ur was effectively handed over to Nitocris to run as she pleased;[44] she and Nabonidus (as the Song of Solomon attests) did not get on and there seems to have been a very serious issue concerning purity rites.[45] As an acting-*entu*, or even as Queen, Nitocris would be entitled to her own palace

---

[40] Leonard Woolley, *Ur of the Chaldees* (London: Book Club Associates, 1982; rev. ed. 1929), 235.

[41] Peter James and Marinus Anthony van der Sluijs present multiple examples of seven-tiered ziggurats (63-4) and conclude that this was possibly to represent a sevenfold understanding of the cosmos, which was then conflated with the seven planets (the five known planets plus the Sun and Moon) (73-4). In "Ziggurats, Colors, and Planets: Rawlinson Revisited," *JCS* 60 (2008): 57-79.

[42] Tyson, 200.

[43] Woolley, *Ur of the Chaldees*, 249.

[44] Woolley suggests the *entu* could even be active in the design/construction of her temple, citing a 20th Century BCE *entu* who left her name on the bricks of her Great Court (*Ur of the Chaldees*, 150). This sort of authority, of course, is just what Herodotus attributes to Nitocris (*Hist.* 1.185-7).

[45] Tyson, 126-7; 201.

and her own ritually pure place of worship.

After her demise, the next in line, i.e., the deputy *entu*, if you will, is Jehudijah, Ennigaldi-Nanna's biological mother, who, as we see at the end of the Song of Solomon, has inherited and perhaps superseded Nitocris' position and significance. This palace becomes (briefly) *Jehudijah's* home.

## E. Defensive Tower

A substantial, fortified watch tower, at the foot of which were discovered the foundations of a number of residential houses dated to the Isin-Larsa period (20-18th Century BCE) and a fortified watchtower/fort from the Kassite period (15-12th Century BCE). "Of its interior walls nothing remained, but an elaborate gateway approach of Kuri-Galzu and heavy mud-brick foundations of a Neo-Babylonian fortress showed that whatever had stood here was an important element in the city's defences."[46]

Migdol

"Migdol" is a Hebrew word meaning "bound together; strength; force; greatness; magnitude; elevation; great height; tower; watchtower, elevated stage." Woolley describes the Temenos (the walled enclosure, i.e., the black line in *Fig. 4*) that protects the sacred area as having been planned as a …

> work of military defence. … in the east corner of the Temenos there was an immensely solid square structure which cannot be regarded as anything other than a fortress tower; it could hardly have served a religious purpose. In girdling Nanna's Sacred Area with a work of defence such as might be built round the palace of an earthly king the Babylonian monarch was certainly reviving a very ancient conception of the god as Ruler of the city and its leader in war whose house would be the final rallying-point for resistance against an enemy….[47]

We can thus ascribe the tower on the map (D) the name "Migdol," and have immediately introduced the concept of an impending standoff, if not a battle. The area is, indeed, a "rallying-point," as shall be seen.

---

[46] Leonard Woolley, "Excavations at Ur, 1929-30," *MJ* 21. 2 (June, 1930): 81-105, here 83.

[47] Woolley, *Ur of the Chaldees*, 241.

## G. Canal

Woolley found that "Ur was ringed with a moat and only by the south could be approached by land."[48] We know that several canals served Ur, allowing water flow from/to several directions.[49] It is one of the few cities to which "everlasting waters of abundance" are "secured by the digging of a great canal called 'Hammurabi is the abundance of the people'."[50]

The canals were constantly in use, if not for travel/trade (i.e., with access to the Euphrates via the two harbours), for ceremonial purposes, such as the ritual visitation of deities (i.e., their cultic statues):

> [Nin-khursag] would emerge in procession from her dwelling, borne on her priests' shoulders, with attendant gods to right and left and behind her, a sacred emblem going before, and a courier leading to clear the way. At the canal she was taken aboard a boat, and thus floated down, where the track of the stream can still be seen, past the south-west front of the ziggurat at Ur.[51]

Nabonidus himself is responsible for creating a wide gate in the wall of the Temenos, so that such statues could be brought close to the south-west side of the ziggurat by boat (reminiscent of a Venetian church with its steps lapped by the canal waters).[52]

Woolley suggests that the "northeast wall of the city was washed by the waters of a broad canal whose bed is today clearly marked by a deep depression which separates the mounds of the walled town from those of its north-east suburbs"; two Persian-period burials were discovered there, suggesting that not long after the reign of Nabonidus, the water supply to Ur becomes increasingly precarious.[53]

## H. Enki's Temple

The small temple in the southern part of the site was named for Enki, the Sumerian god of freshwater, wisdom, and magic.

Eridu, rather than Ur, was Enki's official home; the marshland

---

[48] Woolley, *Ur of the Chaldees*, 138.

[49] Thorkild Jacobsen, "The Waters of Ur," *Iraq* 22 (1960): 174-85, here, 182-4.

[50] C. J. Gadd, *History and Monuments Of Ur* (London: Chatto & Windus, 1929), 186.

[51] Gadd, *History and Monuments*, 64.

[52] Gadd, *History and Monuments*, 240.

[53] Woolley, "Excavations," 2.

surrounding this, the oldest of the Mesopotamian sites, was called the *abzu (Apsu)*, i.e., Enki's watery domain that came to represent the Cosmic Ocean. His Eridu temple was seen as "an artfully built mountain which floats on the water" (ETCSL 1.1.4, 71-82). The *abzu*, or marshland/sea, was praised for its bounty; it was profoundly productive and the people made use of everything it provided, most especially the reeds, which stood some eight feet tall and were used to make boats and, in the marshes themselves, floating rafts with (reed) huts on top (these are still evident in the area to this day).

The iconography of Enki is usually water with fish in it but the marshland was just as much a haven for birds:

> He shaped lagoons in the sea. He let fish and birds together come into existence by the sea. He surrounded all the reed beds with mature reeds....
>
> ETCSL 5.3.3, 26-32

Modern ornithologists claim that these marshes, "situated on the routes of the migratory birds ... are chiefly significant for [they] set up a main wintering and staging area for waterfowl travelling between breeding grounds"; the African "Sacred Ibis" is one of the now endangered species that migrated to the marshes in their droves many centuries ago.[54] Moses has a mythical connection to the ibis, discussed later, and it is my thought that the statue of Baal-zephon (if it existed) took the form of a bird (e.g., eagle or phoenix).

## Sea

The "sea," if we superimpose the instruction of Exod 14:2 onto the map, lies beyond the canal, in almost every direction. This may seem an odd thing to say, making Ur seem as though it were an island city; in fact, it *was* in ancient times, for the land surrounding Ur, Eridu, and even Babylon farther north, was marshland. Ur was once situated at the mouth of the Euphrates and Tigris River system, their flow somewhat thwarted by the *heavily*-reeded marshes which simply transitioned into the Arabian Gulf. The actual coastline of the Arabian/Persian Gulf receded from Ur over the centuries but marshland is still prevalent and is affected by the tides of the Arabian Gulf, which can raise water-levels to ten-feet or more.

The marshes today consist of three main marshlands, i.e., the Al-

---

[54] Laith Jawad, et al, "The Southern Marshes of Iraq," § The Birds of the Iraq Marshes; Ornithological Society of the Middle East the Caucasus and Central Asia, 7th August, 2021, https://osme.org.

Hammar, Central, and Al-Hawizeh; Ur is located in the Al-Hawizeh Marshes region, which is described thus:

> The water is slightly brackish owing to its location near the Gulf, eutrophic and shallow. It reaches a maximum depth of 1.8 m and about 3 m at a high watermark. The Euphrates River is the main supplier of water to this marsh. A substantial amount of water from the Tigris River, spilling over from the Central Marshes, also sustains the Al-Hammar Marshes. ... The enormous reed beds offer an ideal environment for breeding birds, while the mudflats support many waders.[55]

The *Ekišnugal* temple at Ur is described in Sumerian literature as the temple "whose shadow extends out into the midst of the sea" (ETCSL 4.13.07, B 10-17), i.e., the marshes, or Sealand, as it was named. A. M. Bagg writes:

> We know that the Sealand was located in the southernmost part of Babylonia, roughly in the marshy region east of Ur, but the information about its extent is scarce. It is clear from the sources that the Sealand extended to the Arabian Gulf. In the inscription on Shalmaneser's throne base concerning his Babylonian campaign on behalf of Marduk-zākir-šumi, when his brother rebelled against him, we read: "I received tribute from the kings of Chaldea as far as the sea (and) imposed my powerful might upon the Sealand."[56]

Although alluvial sedimentation gradually forced the shoreline south, the extent of this is not really understood, and it is still just a guess where the original shore lay and how long ago the changes to the shoreline, in terms of the area having access to the Arabian Gulf, took effect. In its heyday, however, merchant ships did access Ur's harbours; large ships were detained in deeper waters (both on the Euphrates and in the Gulf) while the registry formalities were completed at Ur, then the ships were allowed into the harbour(s). Four clay cones were discovered at a site just north of Ur (called Diqdiqah), where the Euphrates effectively "stops," and where was once (probably) a large lake or lagoon. The cones read: "In the registry place the ships of Megan of Nanna by the might (?) of Nanna my master I verily detained in Ur. I verily cleared them."[57] Presumably, the cones were handed

---

[55] Jawad, § "Geological Perspectives." The eutrophication (an excess of nutrients that can limit oxygen in water) is a modern phenomenon, e.g., runoff phosphorous and nitrogen from industry/farming.

[56] A. M. Bagg, "The Unconquerable Country: The Babylonian Marshes in the Neo-Assyrian Sources," *Water History* 12, 57-73 (2020): 59.

[57] Thorkild Jacobsen, "The Waters of Ur," *Iraq* 22 (1960): 174-85, here, 184-5.

to the ships' captains as a sort of passport and they were returned when the ships left again.

Jacobsen suggests that the Diqdiqah lagoon, the extensive marshes, and the Arabian Gulf were considered one, rather sprawled out and varied, "sea."[58] Similarly, "[t]he body of water [at Borsippa] was so impressive that in the sixth century the morass … began to be called *tâmtu*, the 'Sea'."[59]

These marshes were also referred to (in Shalmaneser III's inscriptions) by the

> … term *marratu*, which denotes a body of salty water, refers usually—especially in the Neo-Assyrian royal inscriptions—to the Arabian Gulf. In Shalmaneser III's inscriptions, it is explicitly explained that the "Sea of Chaldea," namely the Arabian Gulf, was also called *marratu* the "Bitter Sea." However, … *marratu* was also used to denote a lagoon in the Sealand. It is striking that in Sargon's inscriptions, Bīt-Jakīn is referred to as the land "at the shore of the Bitter Sea (*marratu*)." *Marratu* can denote here the Arabian Gulf or a lagoon or both.[60]

Thus, we see a heavily-reeded marshland, with a salt-water lagoon, colloquially known as "the Sea" or the "Bitter Sea"; compare this to the Hebrew *marah*, i.e., "bitter," applied to the "bitter waters" of Exod 15:23. The sea, in keeping with Jacobsen's statement (above), also includes the Ur canal and the harbours, for these are inextricably linked to the waters beyond.

Birds and fish are not the only things hunted in the marshes, i.e., people are, too. Bagg suggests:

> This particular landscape with its marshes, swamps, canebrakes, lagoons and intertidal flats was much more than a rich natural environment, it was the perfect refuge to hide from pursuers and an excellent base to launch military operations against the Assyrian enemy and its confederates.[61]

Sargon, Sennacherib, and Ashurbanipal each had cause to pursue adversaries into the marshes, only to lose their quarries amidst "the sea":

> "He fed alone and escaped to the land Guzummānu, where he entered the swamp and marshes and (thereby) saved his life …"

---

[58] Jacobsen, 185.
[59] Bagg, 62.
[60] Bagg, 62-3.
[61] Bagg, 64.

... he "flew away like a bird to ... the midst of the sea .... But the King of Babylon could not be found";

... "For five days they sought him out, but his (hiding) place could not be found."[62]

This provides a vital clue to Nabonidus' *original* departure from Babylonia; although it is Abraham who "leaves Ur," seemingly without incident, it is the first stage of the migration to Canaan, and it provides the Exodus account of the "escape" a plausible rationale within the bounds of recorded history. A subtle allusion to a "rallying point," a defensive tower, and a known history of rebels hiding amongst the reeds creates a certain tension in the narrative, in anticipation of what might occur.

## Pi-Hahiroth

Pi-hahiroth means something along the lines of "house of [....]" or "mouth of [....]." Etymologically, the prefix seems to stem from the Egyptian noun *pr* ("house"), as used in Pi-Ramesses, etc., or from "the Hebrew noun *pi*, ("mouth"); the suffix might come from *hur*, "cavern, hollow." The Akkadian word *harāru* means "to dig or hollow out,"; a canal/harbour is made by digging/hollowing out the ground.[63] or from *hara*, "to burn or ignite," figuratively, "to get angry."

The *Jewish Encyclopedia* says:

The Mekilta (Beshalla, Wayehi, 1) identifies the place with Pithom, which was called Pi-hahiroth (= "the mouth of freedom") after the Israelites had been freed from bondage, the place itself being specified as a valley between two high rocks.[64]

"Mouth of the marshes," suits the geographical context (marshes being depressions filled with water) but there are two other "geographical depressions," in a sense, i.e., the canal, and the harbour(s), so "mouth of the canal"[65] or "mouth of the harbour" are both potential interpretations.

---

[62] Bagg, 65-6. For illustrations of marsh-battles from Sennacherib's Palace at Nineveh, see 69.

[63] Hoffmeier suggests a "canal" reference is most suitable in the Egyptian context of the site (107).

[64] Emil G. Hirsch and M. Seligsohn, "Pi-hahiroth," www.jewish encyclopedia.com/articles. Note the "two rocks" reference.

[65] James K. Hoffmeier, *Ancient Israel in Sinai: The Evidence for the Authenticity*

The other possibilities are actually connected. In 1922, an Egyptologist suggested the name Pi-hahiroth may mean "House of Hathor."[66] This has not been given much, if any attention by scholars today but I think there is a very strong basis for accepting this interpretation, but only with the hindsight of understanding the Song of Solomon as the story of Nabonidus and Nitocris.

The harbour palace is the residence of the *entu*, i.e., Ennigaldi, but also Nitocris, as regent. In the Song, Nitocris is represented as an avatar of Hathor during her feigned pregnancy scenes; it is a very precise and powerful depiction, filled with episodes of anger from several sides, and one that highlights her Egyptian heritage and her power.[67] It is possible that the harbour palace at Ur might have received the colloquial "House of Hathor" attribution (perhaps sarcastically, as she was not much liked) but I don't think the "anger" element of Pi-hahiroth fits; it is not strong enough (with respect to Nitocris' character in the Song)[68] to warrant this focus in the etymology. I think the anger comes from elsewhere and it turns out to be a very strong factor in not only this toponym but in the continuing tale of the exodus.

The anger potentially alluded to in Pi-hahiroth is that of Jehudijah, who now dwells in the palace, after Nitocris' demise. Her wrath, her scorn, has made this site the "House of Anger," for she is the one who *had* harboured a great love for Nabonidus (in Tayma) and yet was overlooked and exploited. She has come to realise the man's true colours and in her most famous song of praise, the Song of Solomon, she turns the tables and curses him for eternity. She is *not* a happy woman.

# STOLEN

Why then, if Nabonidus has made a deal with Cyrus to take his expedition to Jerusalem, is there any need for an escape from Ur?

---

*of the Wilderness Tradition* (Oxford: Oxford University Press, 2005), 105-6.

[66] A. H. Gardiner, "House of Hathor," *Recueil D'études Égyptologiques Dédiées à la Mémoire de Jean-François Champollion* (Paris: 1922), 213.

[67] Tyson, 65-6; 162, et al.

[68] Note should be made, however, of the term *chor*, which means "hole", this is deemed to be a potential root for the latter part of Pi-hahiroth; it appears in Song 5:4 in reference to the aperture Solomon thrusts his hand into. As this is a highly erotic and violent scenario (where the king is, essentially an addict forcing himself on Nitocris for her part of the Elixir, and where "hand" may be a euphemism for penis; see Tyson, 125-9), it may be that the author(s) of Exodus is, for the umpteenth time, insulting the memory of Nitocris, hailing her a veritable "whore" but, in the process, reiterating her connection to the harbour palace.

If Nabonidus and Cyrus have made an agreement in secret, nothing would be recorded. The sarcastic and vicious diatribe against Nabonidus in the VA might well be a cover, i.e., a diversion. Show the people that they were right to want their king gone, that he was a useless ruler, that he really didn't care about his kingdom, and then send him to a far off, relatively measly little town, which needs someone to sort things out anyway, and nobody need see or hear from him again. It could suit all parties.

The only thing is, Nabonidus has included in this deal (I suggest), that he takes Jehudijah and his children (specifically Ennigaldi) with him, and that the ultimate destination is Tayma. He has invested much there and sees it is his home.

The plan for the escape, it seems, is encoded in Exod 14:2's very specific instructions, i.e., a (small) group is to assemble in the place where all four sites are located, i.e., in the Temenos of Ur, i.e., in front of Pi-hahiroth (D, the Palace); between Migdol (E, the Tower) and the sea (A, the Harbour); in front of Baal-zephon (near the statue). This is, I suggest, in order to facilitate a hasty retreat, for Nabonidus intends to seize Jehudijah and her children (Ennigaldi is about seven or eight, if this takes place ca. 538 BCE) against their will. Why should he wish to do this? We can only speculate, of course, but it seems to me that Nabonidus, having once known the benefits of an Egyptian princess as wife, e.g., the riches and contacts that go with such a conciliatory marriage, hopes that he can rely on his father-in-law to help him regain his fortunes in this new, post-King world. I think he is planning to offer the return of Pharaoh's grandchild in exchange for a healthy pay-out that will fill the coffers for his new adventure.

The narrative of Exodus/Numbers demonstrates, without a shadow of a doubt (I am confident I can convince you) that Jehudijah and her children *are*, indeed, on the journey with Nabonidus. The plan, however, is not as straightforward as he thinks it will be, as we shall see.

In the Song of Solomon, there is a very subtle inference that Nitocris was also taken against *her* will, from Egypt, when she had been made Nabonidus' conciliatory bride (i.e., in Song 1:4 the verb *mashak* is employed to describe her leaving; this means "to draw [away], to drag, to seize"). In 1 Chr 4:17, and 1 Kgs 3:1, both alluding to the marriage between Nabonidus and Nitocris, this same perception is clear; she was forced.[69] Now, Nabonidus is about to force Jehudijah away; as "Hagar," recall, the etymology of her name speaks of "flight," and being "dragged off" or "pressed into service."

Nitocris (in Song 7) is visited by members of the priestly fraternity who knew her in her role as God's Hand (potentially) and First Prophet

---

[69] Tyson, 51.

(certainly) at Karnak; they are the "brothers" who are said to be "angry" with her.[70] They are angered because she is deemed the purest source of the Elixir and, Ahmose's treaty notwithstanding, they want her back. Once I realised Jehudijah is Moses' second-wife, it became even more apparent that her account of Nitocris is coloured by her *own* experiences and feelings more than I had previously suspected. The scene in Song 7 with these men might well have been inspired by what is about to transpire at Ur, i.e., the confrontation at this location is potentially between Nabonidus (and his crew) and the priests of Ur, who are attempting to protect Jehudijah and Ennigaldi.

I can quite easily see Cyrus not being concerned with this squabble in far-off Ur, between a man and his concubine. Turning a blind eye would be prudent perhaps, so long as the coup is successful and quick and Nabonidus gets out of Babylonia for good.

It is, as we have seen, fairly simple for people to purposefully conceal themselves in the marshes; if Nabonidus has procured a number of small river boats, they could well have slipped into the reeds and disappeared. A "wilderness" does not need to be an arid desert ... it can just as likely be a mountain range, or an endless swamp/sea (e.g., Isa 21:1 "the wilderness of the sea").

Not only would the brackish water be unwise to drink, it would also be sufficiently deep for people to drown in, even at a normal level. Also, by leaving the area in boats, there is a practical and pragmatic explanation for the miraculous escape, i.e., they do, indeed, "go into the sea" on "dry ground" (*chareb*) but instead of sand or soil beneath their feet, they have rushes, or wood (i.e., whatever the boats are made of). Poetic license.

Exod 14:21-2 suggests the waters "divide" and form walls on either side of those escaping their pursuers; the Hebrew verb for "divide" is *baqa*, which means, according to *Strong's*, "to cleave; to rend, make a breach," What do boats do in the water? They breach the surface, forcing bow waves on either side, like little walls of water, i.e., the faster they travel, the greater the size of the waves. The noun *chomah* here suggests a surrounding wall like that of a city or fortress, i.e., a protective, encompassing wall; this suits the context, for bow-waves do seem to hug the boat moving in the water, providing that notion of an embracing protection. In Ps 78:13 God is said to make the waters "stand like a heap," suggesting a low wall, not a towering edifice, making the wave suggestion a stronger possibility.

These boats are likely to be river boats, not sailing boats, as the group heads straight into the marshes, to hide (sails would not function well and would be seen above the reeds). This is why Moses says "you only have to

---

[70] Tyson, 54-6.

keep still" (Exod 14:14); they only have to sit still and keep quiet, so they won't be discovered.

The "eagles' wings" of Exod 19:4 might come into play here, i.e., the eagle signifying a Tyrian connection. It is quite possible that Nabonidus (aka Solomon) has arranged with his friend Hiram to have boats conveniently at the ready farther up the Euphrates (having been sent down the river on a trading trip, they may already be on their way back home).[71] The statue of Baal-zephon (whether actual or symbolic) is thus also a sign to those assisting Nabonidus that the escape from Ur will be a speedy one, assisted by allies.

They wait until just before dawn, at the quietest, darkest time (Exod 14:21 suggests nothing is done "all night"), and then they make their move, grabbing the *entu* and her children from their beds, slipping into the depths of the low-tide marshes, untraceable. From Sennacherib's report we learn about the effect of the tide in this southernmost part of the Sealand: "The high tide of the sea rose mightily, and (then) entered my tent and completely surrounded my entire camp. For five days and nights, on the account of the strong water, all of my soldiers had to sit curled up as though they were in cages."[72] At "dawn" (14:27), Moses symbolically raises his arm again and the water returns to its normal flow, trapping in the mire those who had ventured farther than they should in the half-light. Nabonidus, being keen to know everything, is bound to be aware of the tidal calendar in the Gulf and when the marshes will rise again to their most dangerous level. He has timed things perfectly.

In *She Brought*, I mention a possible connection between the tale of Hadad fleeing to Egypt, i.e., to Tahpanhes (although the toponym is weakly disguised as the name of the queen, "Tapenes"), and Nabonidus.[73] I suggest that the "sister" to the queen is an allusion to Jehudijah; she gives birth to a child, here a son (which is to be expected, given the prevalent disinterest in females), whom she *weans* "in Pharaoh's house" (1 Kgs 11:20). "Weaning," recall, is Jehudijah's catchphrase, helping to identify her as the author of the Song.[74] The child in 1 Kings is named "Genubath," which means "stolen."

Nabonidus effectively steals his wife and children, most significantly Ennigaldi-Nanna, from under the noses of their guardian priests. Previously, I hinted at the possibility that the mysterious sarcophagus of Tashentihet, discovered in the tomb of Ahmose's chief wife, Queen Nekhtbastetru, and

---

[71] Travelling up the Euphrates means travelling against the wind, so rowing would be slower than sailing, but with a decent crew, certainly faster than paddling or walking.

[72] Bagg, 67. Today, the Karun River.

[73] Tyson, 231-7.

[74] Tyson, 216-17.

their son, Ahmose (at Giza), might well be Ennigaldi,[75] returned to what Nabonidus saw as her family (being unaware of the feigned pregnancy). On further investigation, here, I realise this cannot be the case, for she is identified with Miriam in the Exodus narrative and she does not leave the group until much later.

However, I maintain that the return of Ennigaldi could well be the motivation for the trip into Egypt (the "famine" in Gen 12:10 acts as a narrative device to shift location with minimal explanation). Nabonidus has the intention, it does seem, to return what he sees as Nitocris' child to "Pharaoh's house" by taking her to Tahpanhes, in some feigned remorseful gesture in order to get back into Ahmose's good books (Nitocris' death might have been avoided if Nabonidus had bothered to intervene, and he must be aware her father would be resentful at the very least).[76] If you read *She Brought*, Chapter 7, you will see that the visitors who come to Tayma from Egypt (in Song 7) taunt Nitocris when she does not give them what they desire; they have discovered that she has lied about the pregnancy and that Nabonidus (then King) is blissfully unaware. They blackmail her, threatening to tell the king and probably her father. I suggest this *is* what happens, i.e., the emissaries from Ahmose, during the final year or so in Tayma (i.e., the royal family leaves in 543 BCE), inform the pharaoh that Ennigaldi is not really his own flesh and blood. This assessment is based on many snippets of historical information and textual (HB) nuances; as this analysis continues, I hope the proposed scenario won't seem so fanciful as you may think it at present.

Making the connection to Tahpanhes is highly significant, as it provides a concrete location for Abraham's excursion and Moses' return trip to Egypt. It also links the tales of Abraham, Moses, and Solomon (all avatars of Nabonidus).

Relatively recent excavations at the site of Tahpanhes, or as it is now called, Tell Defenneh, Tell Dafana, or simply Daphnae,[77] have demonstrated that the town was built not as a military fortress but as a "temple-town."

---

[75] Tyson, 234.

[76] I think the tale of Ahmose III and Polycrates in *Hist.* 3.40-3 is another misattributed rumour by Herodotus. The story of the discarded signet ring (note this is also applicable to Solomon in the Ashmedai legend), the precariousness of unbounded wealth, the fortuitous second chance, etc., all fit Nabonidus, and seems to echo the final attitude of Ahmose after this scene with the girl he discovered was not his daughter's child.

[77] Most of the information on Daphnae (unless otherwise noted) thanks to François Leclère and Jeffery Spencer, *Tell Dafana Reconsidered: The Archaeology of an Egyptian Frontier Town* (London: British Museum, 2014). For a full explanation of the variation in names, ancient sources, etc., see especially 2-4.

Built during the Saite Period (Dynasty 26),[78] its secluded position on the eastern-most "diffluent of the Pelusiac branch of the Nile" meant that it remained relatively isolated, with "limited cross-cultural connections." The surrounding terrain was swampy and in the Late Period, the river nearby becoming more and more difficult to navigate, a canal was dug a few kilometres away.

Thus, the site might serve well for a clandestine meeting between Ahmose and Nabonidus, especially with the sacerdotal nature of the town, i.e., considering Ennigaldi, the *entu*, is being (potentially) brought there in the context of her priestly significance. The swampy, difficult terrain makes access tricky, and while it is thought that most visitors arrive along the desert road from Pelusium, if one is trying to remain discreet, as Moses and his group are (also avoiding the busy "Way to Shur" and Edom), arriving from an alternative direction may be more risky but certainly less noticeable. Boats travelling from Tyre along the coast, then clandestinely upstream a short way into the Nile marshes, would be the perfect route.

A Demotic text mentions that Pharaoh Psamtik (it is presumed to be Psamtik I) stayed at Daphnae before heading into Syria; he died and was embalmed in the vicinity. Another text suggests he was imprisoned here and "received his daily pittance from the nearby royal palace." This not only supports the biblical understanding that Tahpanhes was a royal residence, but also substantiates my own claim that the entire story of "Tahpenes" and "Hadad" in the story of Solomon *must* be rooted in Dynasty 26.[79] While I was considering this part of Nabonidus' mission, I did wonder if a pharaoh would actually deign to visit such an outpost but now I see that I had no reason to doubt it.

Soon after the death of his daughter in 539 BCE, Ahmose III makes a change to the laws concerning women's rights in marriage (allowing them *more* rights),[80] suggesting he is not merely mourning but furious, i.e., furious with Nabonidus. The irony is that Nabonidus himself never comprehended what Nitocris was up to, so he spent years believing Ennigaldi was Nitocris' daughter and that Jehudijah was hired as her nurse. Even though the latter had been a woman of the harem, with so many, as we learn from the Song, he probably couldn't recall each one, especially once they got pregnant. This

---

[78] Attributed to Psamtik I. A stele discovered in the area refers to Pharaoh Apries using Daphnae as a base from which he planned an expedition deeper into the Sinai region (Leclère and Spencer, 135-6).

[79] Tyson, 233-7.

[80] Annalisa Azzoni, "Women and Property in Persian Egypt and Mesopotamia" (paper presented at the Women and Property Conference, Centre for Hellenic Studies, Harvard University, n.d.), 1-28, here 4.

lies at the root of Jehudijah's bitterness after all (i.e., that she was always in the shadows).

So, when Nabonidus and his *little group* turn up near Tahpanhes, with every intention to hand the young girl over, the situation takes a turn for the worse and Nabonidus finds himself being set upon by Ahmose's henchmen. He is not welcome, and neither is the poor, probably bewildered, girl. They are summarily sent on their way, with an unfriendly escort.

This scenario is represented, I think, in Gen 12:11-20, where Abraham and Sarah are effectively booted out of Egypt, with an escort, because Abraham has allegedly allowed his "sister/wife" to be admitted into Pharaoh's house (12:15). The tale is adjusted to suit the overall context and focus of Genesis' Nabonidus, which is far more positive in nature than his representation in Exodus; if "daughter" were employed here, too much of the unsavoury history would need to be aired. So, one interpretation might be that Ennigaldi is taken to Pharaoh, he keeps her in his house for a while, probably telling her everything he discovered about Nitocris and her feigned pregnancy, etc., then returns her to Nabonidus, sending them both on their way, perhaps with a warning not to come back (which is then echoed in Exod 10:28-9).

An ancient tradition holds that there is an "old watercourse called *Ḳanâet Bint el-Ḳafir*, i.e., the Conduit of the Infidel's Daughter, running west of the mound in the direction of Ramleh," not far from Gezer.[81] This would be on Abraham's route through Canaan. When Petrie discovered Tahpanhes (Daphnae), he found a great fortress/tower, the local name of which, so his Arabian guides informed him, was "*el Kasr el Bint el Yahudi*," "Castle of the Jew's Daughter."[82] So we now learn of this mysterious "daughter" at the very site I suggest is Nabonidus-Abraham's destination in Egypt.[83] This fortification on the Nile Delta is remembered as the place where this "daughter" visited Pharaoh, and for the kafuffle her presence

---

[81] R. A. Macalister, *The Excavation of Gezer*, Vol. 1 (London: John Murray, 1911), 20-1. Also, Tyson 17-18. In *She Brought* (18), I considered this a derogatory recollection, but now my assessment is reversed; I think it was a term of endearment for *her* (as "Miriam"), but not for Nabonidus.

[82] "The Antiquary's Note-Book (Ancient Egypt: Remarkable Discovery)" in *The Antiquary: A Magazine Devoted to the Study of the Past*, Vol 14 (London: Eliot Stock, 1886), 82. Also, Tyson, 234.

[83] Many have presumed this to be a reference to Jer 43:5-7 and the daughters of Zedekiah ("princesses"). Like the Conduit, however, the singular is explicit, i.e., only one "daughter." As Nabonidus is attending/leading the "Jews" (as Abraham at this point in the narrative), he would be considered one of them (which is the entire basis of the Moses-as-a-child myth). In Exod 2:19, Moses is called "an Egyptian" by the Midianites; this ambiguity also appears in the Gospel of John, where Jesus is called a Samaritan in Judea, and a Jew in Samaria.

made (Nabonidus being seen by later generations probably as a crazy leader of the Jews who tried to swindle Ahmose).

This then allows for the potential explanation of "Sarah" being, in part, another avatar of Ennigaldi, as mentioned earlier (i.e., the daughter reflects the mother, just as the son reflects the father) for it is probably Nabonidus' *daughter* that he tries to pimp out (to Abimelech), not his aged wife (and it might be *she* who gets pregnant, in reality, for Sarah/Nitocris is dead).[84] If the young girl is only about eight when she leaves Ur, with the time supposedly spent in Harran (Gen 12:4), for which there seems to be no other rationale, she might still only have been about twelve (on the cusp of becoming a woman) when she is taken to Pharaoh. If Nabonidus has delayed in order that she might begin menses, he may have in mind to offer her back to the Egyptian temple as a replacement for Nitocris (once First Prophet and, as I have suggested, keeper of the Elixir Rubeus), still thinking she is of royal/priestly blood. Perhaps they would pay well for her.

When things don't go to plan, Ennigaldi leaves Egypt with Nabonidus, but in Genesis this backtrack is dealt with as Abraham returning to Mamre, or "Hebron" (i.e., stipulated in the addendum as the one "in Canaan") where his story ends. This simply means Nabonidus leaves Tahpanhes (in disgrace) and returns to Tayma (see below); this will become the basis for Moses' flight to Midian after angering "Pharaoh."

# HIRAM'S DEAL

Hiram of Tyre potentially aids Nabonidus by securing travel arrangements from Ur up the Euphrates, but also from the Phoenician coast into the marshes of the Nile Delta. Herodotus tells us that the "Tyrians had a quarter in the city of

---

[84] There are many rabbinic sources that claim the legal age for sexual penetration of a girl is three years and one day (based on the ages of Sarah, Isaac, and Rebecca (!): Isaac "waited for her (Rebecca) until she would be fit for marital relations-three years-and then married her" (Gen. Rabbah 57:1). Might this not just mean she was too young to have her first period? See also Jacob Neusner, *The Comparative Hermeneutics of Rabbinic Judaism: Seder Tohorot. Tohorot through Uqsin, Vol. 6* (United States: Academic Studies in the History of Judaism, 2000), 52; Isaac Klein, *A Guide to Jewish Religious Practice* New York: Jewish Theological Seminary of America, 1979, 1992), 396. Marriage (intercourse) with an underage girl was permitted upon an agreed payment from the man to the father. This might explain why Abraham (Nabonidus) can leave with both the money *and* the girl, i.e., suggesting an even more unsavoury ruse, perhaps, where Nabonidus offers his daughter as a (virgin) *bride* to Pharaoh, not suggesting she was Nitocris' child at all. The ruse backfires when Ennigaldi reveals who she really is, having learned the story of Nitocris from her mother, Jehudijah. Just a thought.

Memphis assigned to them, probably from an early date,"[85] which means he can probably get the fugitive and his daughter *into* the region surreptitiously, and out again *swiftly* (again, by boat, through the marshes).[86]

1 Kgs 9:10-14 tells of Solomon (Nabonidus) giving Hiram twenty cities in "the land of Galilee." However, Hiram is displeased because the lands are "*cabul.*" The NRSV translates this as "in the land of Cabul" and adds a note explaining this means "a land good for nothing." However, the BDB suggests: "√ of following = 'bind'; Late Hebrew 'bind', 'fetter'; Aramaic id.; Arabic 'bind', 'fetter'." *Strong's* says possibly "from *kebel,*" which means "fetter." The lands are thus given as a pledge, a binding agreement, an oath.

From the Song of Solomon, we learn that "fetters" are something significant in the dealings between Nabonidus and Nitocris; they symbolise the bond between teacher and student, between the initiate and the master, and between a besotted king and the object of his desire.[87] Such fetters originate in innocence but soon, in Nabonidus' world, they become millstones and remembrances of things gone wrong. They are a portent of concern.

The numerical difference between the *twenty* pieces of land and the "*one hundred and twenty* talents of silver*" (1 Kgs 9:14) is important. In *She Brought*, I discuss the gematria of "twenty" as it relates to Nabonidus (as

---

[85] *Hist.* 2.112; see also H. Jacob Katzenstein, "Tyre in the Early Persian Period (539-486 BCE)," *BA* 42.1 (1979): 23-34, here, 30. Also, Tyson, 226.

[86] It is easy to imagine the eastern Nile Delta marshlands as abandoned, empty territory but archaeologists have uncovered many settlements and defence structures, showing this was an active and protected area. It would have taken someone with great navigational skills and travel permission from the Egyptians to get through, especially as the Egyptians were on their guard against marauders they "called Shasu and 'Sand Crossers', i.e., Arabians, coming up from the desert (Eliezer D. Oren, "Migdol: A New Fortress on the Edge of the Eastern Nile Delta," *BASOR*, 256 [1984]: 7-44, here 8-10). Nabonidus knows this, so enters (this time) via the marshes under the aegis of Hiram's trading access. In 2000, the ancient Egyptian port of Thonis-Heracleion was discovered just 35 km from Alexandria; this was the central hub of trade from the Mediterranean and would probably have been where Hiram normally conducted his trade with Egypt. However, excavations revealed that almost all of the boats in the harbour were local river-boats, i.e., many traders had to transfer their goods to the smaller vessels that could transport them upstream along the Nile ("Thonis-Heracleion: Finding a Legendary Port Under the Sea," https://the-past.com). As Tyre also had an enclave at Memphis, Hiram's river-boats would be a constant sight on the Nile and would not be considered suspicious (even if the motley crew had to feign being sailors). See my paper "Nabonidus, Tarshish, and Ophir," www.academia.edu.

[87] Tyson, e.g., 195-6; 249.

Solomon, in 1 Kgs 9:10) and the plots of land;[88] the resulting impression is one of a scoundrel who will con even his best ally for his own gain.

A similarly negative interpretation arises for the value of *one hundred*, which is represented by the Hebrew letter *kuf*. This is the nineteenth letter of the alphabet and has the meaning of "monkey." It represents "one who ventures below the acceptable, an individual who violates the circumscribed boundaries of the Torah"; it is considered an "unholy" letter that symbolises "falsehood and impurity" and "ultimate death."[89] That does not bode well for a deal/oath with Nabonidus! At the very end of the Song (8:6-7), Nabonidus' dismal fate is symbolically sealed, for he chooses the wrong path, spiritually; he chooses lust over love, gratification over wisdom, and prosperity over honesty; his fate is *sheol*.[90]

So, Nabonidus (Solomon) palms off twenty plots of scrap land for a comparatively large cash payment (probably hoping Hiram would never bother to investigate);[91] we then learn that he ends up with the lands anyway, and that he places "the people of Israel" in them (2 Chr 8:1-2). This may suggest that during his first sojourn through Canaan (as Abraham), Nabonidus drops off those of the exiles who wish to remain there instead of following him all the way to Tayma. This could be the point at which the foundation of Genesis' exodus narrative is created by those who see themselves as having been returned home; they don't wish to know what happens to the others and end their account on a motivationally positive note with Abraham returning to them and coming to a peaceful end there. That the lands are not of the best quality does bolster the idea that Nabonidus is not truly interested in his charges' wellbeing; he just wants to get the job done (he dumps them on otherwise useless land) and move on.

Hiram, who goes out of his way to assist Nabonidus on more than one occasion, is left out of pocket.

# THE ESCAPE IN LEGEND

In the *Legends of the Jews* is a section called "The Sons of Moses" which has a very odd but potentially illuminating account of a group of Jews who

---

[88] Tyson, 241-3.

[89] Raskin, "Kuf," www.chabad.org.

[90] Tyson, 196.

[91] Josephus (*Ag. Ap.*, 1.17; *A.J.*, 8.5.3) suggests the money from Hiram was a payment of a debt incurred whilst betting on the outcome of riddles; the two friends supposedly exchanged riddles and whoever failed to decipher the meaning had to pay a forfeit.

"escape" the exile (under "Nebuchadnezzar")[92] by being miraculously hidden from their pursuers by a pillar of fire and cloud:

> At the fall of night a cloud descended and enveloped the Sons of Moses and all who belonged to them. They were hidden from their enemies, while their own way was illuminated by a pillar of fire. The cloud and the pillar vanished at break of day, and before the Sons of Moses lay a tract of land bordered by the sea on three sides. For their complete protection God made the river Sambation to flow on the fourth side. This river is full of sand and stones ....[93]

Three sides water, the fourth desert and rocks. This sounds very much like Arabia, from the perspective of Ur, i.e., the Arabian Gulf, the Arabian Sea, and the Red Sea, with everything else "sand and stones." The Sambation "river" is metaphorical, of course, suggesting the harshness of the desert roads that would thwart any but the most determined and best prepared; the desert is its own protection. In subsequent Jewish lore, the name "Sambation" was used to denote an "unruly" child, i.e., one who is rebellious.[94] This begs the question of whether the first group to leave the immediate control of a Persian-ruled Babylonia *was* considered rebellious. It is very clear from the account of Moses killing an Egyptian, challenging the Pharaoh, having to turn and face the enemy pursuing them, etc., that a battle/escape scenario is being portrayed; we cannot ignore that, but if this *is* an account of the departure from Babylon of the exiles after the Persian conquest, we must consider that Nabonidus and his "mixed" crew are truly on the run. They are not simply walking out of Babylonia in some joyous departure with Cyrus' blessing, gifts of silver and gold, etc. Moses' story begins with confrontation, violence, and battle imagery. Nabonidus may have the seal of Cyrus to show the guards along the route, but there are possibly those who want him, dead or alive (hence the disguises of "Abraham," "Sarah," and "Lot").

---

[92] *The Legends* state that "This Babylonian king was a son of King Solomon and the Queen of Sheba," § "Nebuchadnezzar," https://sacred-texts.com.

[93] Book X: "The Exile," https://sacred-texts.com.

[94] Britannica Encyclopedia, "Sambation," www.britannica.com.

# 3        OLD BOYS' CLUB

M ost modern scholars suggest the reference, "A wandering Aramaean is my father" (Deut 26:5), refers to Jacob but in the 12th Century CE there was a hint that "Abraham" was meant and that the "wandering" referred to *his* journeys between Harran (i.e. Aram) and Egypt.[1] It is quite evident that the narrative of Jacob echoes that of Abraham in terms of the erecting of sacred stones/altars, the nomadic existence, and even the repeated pimping out of a wife to the same king! The designation of Jacob as the Aramean, and as the ancestor of Israel, stands however, despite *Abraham* being the one who wanders even farther (i.e., from Ur), who travels up and down Canaan (rescuing Lot, etc.), and who first goes into Egypt and back again. Abraham is the one divinely designated as "father/ancestor" (Gen 17:5), so why is he disregarded? To me, there can be no doubt the "Aramean" in question is Abraham, especially when the identification with Nabonidus is accepted, and I think this is precisely why the Jewish lineage runs from Jacob, and not Abraham, i.e., because Abraham *is* Nabonidus, a connection that simply cannot be admitted. As we see later, in the discussions concerning Belshazzar, Nabonidus' own son has links to tribal 'descendants', while Nabonidus does not.

---

[1] Daniel Machiela, "Who is the Aramean in Deut 26:5 and What is He Doing?: Evidence of a Minority View from Qumran Cave 1 (1QapGen 19.8)," *RQ* 23.3 (91) (2008): 395–403, here 397.

Millard proposes that the phrase "wandering Aramaean" in Hebrew (*arammi obed*) was taken to mean "fugitive," based in part on a similar phrase in the annals of Sennacherib, who called the Aramaeans "the runaway(s)," concluding that the figure must have been a "political refugee and a social misfit."[2] So far, this sounds like Nabonidus.

Historically, Nabonidus was, and still is to some extent, considered an Aramaean by descent. Adad-guppi, his mother, an influential devotee of Sîn at Harran, is considered to have been Aramean, and Tayma, his chosen second-capital, was strongly Aramaean before his arrival.[3] He is also a self-proclaimed wanderer.[4] On these wanderings, I posit, the ex-king rekindles his relationship with Hiram of Tyre (for his own benefit), but also finds that someone else he once knew has made a new life in this land of plenty.

# HITTITE BURIAL SITE

In Genesis 23 we are provided a rather detailed and somewhat emphatic rendition of the purchase of a burial site for Abraham's wife, Sarah. There are two angles of approach I wish to discuss: 1) the symbolic nuances imposed by its author, and 2) the historical veracity of an arrangement between a "Hittite" and Nabonidus.

Sarah is said to die at Kiriath-arba, which means "City of Four" from the noun *qiryah*, "city," from the root *qarar*, "to compact (forcibly, i.e., pound down)," and the cardinal *raba*, "four," although the verb *raba* means "to stretch or lie down" (often sexual).

In the Song of Solomon, Nitocris, through the hidden voice of Jehudijah, refers to herself as a "Wall." It is a metaphor for a strong woman, based on a mythological perception of the goddess Ishtar as a "broad wall" that protects the city (ETCSL 2.1.4, 12-24). In Song 8, Ennigaldi-Nanna is the "little sister" whose fate is debated by the priestesses at the temple in Ur, i.e., will she be like her mother and be a "wall" or will she be weak, like a "door"?[5] It may just be another strange coincidence but the verb *qarar* is used in only one place in the HB, in Isa 22:5, where walls are being torn down. Together with the connotation of laying down in a sexual manner, which echoes the accusations of prostitution hurled at Nitocris in the Song,

---

[2] Alan R. Millard, "A Wandering Aramean," *JNES* 39.2 (1980): 153-55, here 153.
[3] Raymond P. Dougherty, *Nabonidus and Belshazzar: A Study of the Closing Events of the Neo-Babylonian Empire* (Eugene: Wipf & Stock, 2008), 18-27, here 24. See also W&N, 4.
[4] W&N, 6, n.45.
[5] Tyson, 201-4.

one begins to see a familiar pattern emerging. Nitocris is *once again* being vilified and humiliated. Not only is she forcefully beaten down from her lofty position as the "Wall," she is again targeted as a loose woman; together, these two images play on the actions of Song 5:6-7, where Nitocris runs through the streets after Nabonidus in her night attire and is beaten/knocked down by the sentinels. With the previous suggestion that Nitocris-Sarah is forced to be remembered as the mother of Nabonidus' child against her wishes, the book of Genesis' depiction of Sarah is far from a remembrance of a much loved, iconic female; it is a carefully thought out and sustained vilification of the woman the early Jews *hated*, i.e., "Pharaoh's daughter," Nitocris.

Not only that, the gematria of Sarah's supposed lifespan of 127 years (the only such record for a woman in the HB) is *very* much a matter of debate, as the convoluted and highly symbolic Kabbalistic interpretations attest.[6] I prefer to keep things on a more simple footing, one that a basic understanding of the gematria of the Hebrew alphabet can explain.[7] In this case, 127 is broken down into its constituent parts: 100 + 20 + 7 (I have used the most germane definitions):

100 = *kuf*, "monkey" – symbolising a thing that is unholy, base, negative

20 = *kaf*, "bend, crown," desire/pleasure – to submit to the Crown

7 = *zayin*, "sword, crown" – suggesting the might of the Crown

These potential understandings of the age of Sarah suggest that she has succumbed to the strength of the Crown, perhaps by the use of a weapon. In *She Brought*, I posit a theory that Nitocris is killed a few days after the Persians seize Babylon, i.e., possibly thrown from the Ishtar Gate by men who would have been armed.[8] Taking this a little less specifically, it just means she succumbs to the will of a higher, forceful authority.

The final insult is that the Cave of Machpelah is said to be to the "east

---

[6] For example: "The Strength of Sarah," www.chabad.org; Jeffrey Meiliken, "Sarah Lives Continued: There's Much More than Meets the Eye" (Nov 25, 2008), https://kabbalah secrets.com.

[7] While secret knowledge is stored within names, numbers, etc., to protect it from getting into the wrong hands, as every sophisticated civilization has demonstrated, there is no point in making it so obscure it becomes indecipherable over time. The pre-Kabbalistic gematria would have been taught to many; if they are learning this, they have access to the hidden wisdom of the narratives.

[8] Tyson, 225-7; it is quite possible that Nabonidus himself is "the crown," for her father, Ahmose III, seems to blame Nabonidus for her death.

of Mamre," with an addendum to certify this is "Hebron" *in Canaan*, i.e., hinting that the location might be misconstrued, which then implies there may be two such sites. This is easily done, when so many names are mirrored between Arabia and Canaan. If we ignore the obvious instruction to ignore the Arabian version of events, this means that the "double" of Mamre in Canaan is the Mamre we will find near Tayma (discussed in "Gerar," 182-6). "Hebron" means "place of joining/alliance," from *habar*, "to join."

In 585 BCE, Media and Lydia establish a peace-treaty after the famous "Eclipse Battle"; the two arbitrators are Syennesis of Cilicia and "Labynetus" of Babylonia (*Hist.* 1.74). Although some early scholars argued against Labynetus being Nabonidus, most now accept the suggestion (and with the added insights from the Song of Solomon suggesting a conciliatory marriage between the king and Nitocris, Herodotus' claim that Labynetus was married to "Nitocris, Queen of Babylon" [*Hist.* 1.188] is corroborated). So, Nabonidus has an intimate working knowledge of Lydia.

The parties involved in this treaty are the Median king, Cyaxares, and Alyattes, king of Lydia. One of the terms of the agreement is a conciliatory marriage between Alyattes' daughter Aryenis and Astyages, the son of the Median king. Alyattes is also Croesus' sister, i.e., Croesus the famous, almost mythical King of Lydia, renowned for his wealth. Nabonidus thus also has experience in negotiating conciliatory marriages (which probably proved useful to him when bargaining with Ahmose for Nitocris' hand). More importantly, Nabonidus very probably *meets* Croesus at this earlier time. As we have seen regarding Nabonidus' ally Hiram of Tyre, the ex-Babylonian king has a practice of garnering allies in the most strategic and/or productive regions.

Later, in ca. 549 BCE, the coalition between Pharaoh Ahmose III, Polycrates of Samos (Sparta), Croesus, and Nabonidus is formed to protect the member states against the marauding Persians (Cyrus).[9] Nabonidus has been in Arabia for a few years and has settled at Tayma; this is the ideal place for an international summit, as it is extremely difficult for strangers to navigate through its hostile and dangerous land. The oasis boasts everything stately visitors should want, however, and is situated in neutral territory. This, I suggest, is the meaning of "Kiriath-arba," i.e., the "City of Four" is the location of the famous coalition of four major powers, at Tayma, in 549 BCE. As "Hebron" also alludes to a location where an alliance is formed, we can deduce it also pertains to Tayma; it is no wonder, then, that Abraham (Nabonidus) ends his days at Hebron (Gen 25:9-10). The author of the

---

[9] A. T. Olmstead, *History of the Persian Empire* (Chicago: University of Chicago Press, 1948), 39. Also, "Anatolia from the end of the Hittite Empire to the Achaemenian Period," www.britannica.com.

clarification, in parentheses, makes a concerted effort to redirect us to Canaan.

Thus, Sarah is said to be buried "facing" Tayma, the city she hated, where everyone hated her; she was miserable there. She cannot leave the Book of Genesis narrative; she is stuck there forever, symbolically, with everything she denounced, railed against, and tried to overcome. The early Jewish authors have made her an example of what happens to women, especially foreign women, who stray from the path set for them, or who refuse to be subjugated. If Jehudijah has any influence (even posthumously) in the writing of these "Sarah" passages, we can see that the venom once channelled through the Song of Solomon has not abated.

Sarah does not live a long and happy life by her husband's side, merrily getting pregnant in her (very) old age, and finally dying and being buried in a special place bought by Abraham to keep her corpse safe for eternity. Sarah is the avatar of the doomed and maligned Nitocris, who dies in Babylon (also east of Mamre) alone, unloved, and far from the tombs of her ancestors.

In the Song, a simple passage in 3:11 points to a memorable historical event that allows us to date the composition quite easily: It records the visit of Nabonidus' mother, Adad-guppi, for the wedding celebrations in 547 BCE. She dies on the way there, or the way back, and her death is widely publicised and mourned.[10] This, I think, is a recurring scribal technique and is here found in the story of Sarah's burial, which seems otherwise a little out of place; it is, in part, a calendrical marker, a clue to the historical context of the narrative that will outlive any immediate reference to dates which can vary from society to society (i.e., the 549 BCE coalition date is the starting point, certainly recorded in the respective nations' annals).

What of the "Hittite" association? Croesus, one of the delegates at the Tayma summit, is the last Anatolian king. He inherits a cultural, if not blood lineage that is rooted in the ancient Hittite civilization. Although the Hittites were conquered and dispersed, their shadows can be traced in the resulting city-states (e.g., Ionia to the south, and Aeolis to the north), including neo-Hittite states such as Carchemish and Syria. At its zenith in the late 8th Century BCE, however, the Phrygian kingdom "made up so large a part of Anatolia that geographically it can in a sense be characterized as the political heir to the Hittite empire" (the other legendary "rich" king, King Midas, was a Phrygian); the Lydians themselves were relative newcomers to Anatolia, but their "language is classified in the Anatolian branch of Indo-European and resembled Hittite ...."[11] The Phrygians and the Lydians were fairly

---

[10] Tyson, 89-90.

[11] "Anatolia from the end of the Hittite Empire to the Achaemenian Period," www.britannica.com.

friendly neighbours and both succumbed to Cyrus in 547 BCE. For all intents and purposes, in the context of the Genesis narrative, the general depiction as a "Hittite" fits Croesus.

To make certain we get the hint: The man who originally owns the land Abraham is seeking to purchase is called "Ephron," which means "place of dust, ore, malleability," from the verb *aphar*, "to be malleable or dust-like." Croesus is famous for being one of the richest men in history. He got rich from gold, which is abundant in his neck of the woods. He is also famous for being the first to mint gold (as well as silver, and also electrum) coins,[12] i.e., he makes the metal "malleable" enough to strike coinage.

After his defeat by Cyrus, Croesus is said, just like Nabonidus it seems, to be publically humiliated and punished (i.e., he is prepared for burning on a pyre but is miraculously reprieved) and sent off somewhere undisclosed to remain a high-status consultant to the Persian king.[13] Herodotus suggests Croesus was, like Nabonidus, a man in search of wisdom (*Hist.* 1.29 ff.), inviting the Greek sage Solon to visit, to discuss philosophy (Solon also visited Ahmose III).

Consider the possibility that Cyrus acts astutely by publically denouncing the defeated Croesus, only to quietly allow him safe passage elsewhere, to live out his life, so long as he doesn't revolt (as with Nabonidus). What if Canaan is the original "Klondike"? It is clearly advertised as the "land of milk and honey"; why wouldn't displaced rulers with a penchant for the good life make it their next abode, to see what fortunes lay there?

Croesus leaves Anatolia eight years before Nabonidus leaves Babylonia, which gives him plenty of time to become settled in Canaan. The cavalier manner in which "Ephron" brushes off any idea of payment for the burial plot, e.g., "…four hundred shekels of silver—what is that between you and me?" (Gen 23:15) demonstrates his wealth but it suggests something else, too. It hints at an elite "old boys club"; Nabonidus, Hiram, Croesus, all rich and powerful leaders, now commune in the land of Canaan, away from prying eyes ("…you are a mighty prince among us" [Gen 23:6]). They are all international traders/merchants (cf. Gen 23:16) but Hiram is the only one still in power and still using his own name. Croesus and Nabonidus are incognito (to the masses); they are just wealthy men, and now Nabonidus

---

[12] Ata Akcil, "Mining History in Anatolia - Part 1" CIM Magazine 1.1 (2006): 90-92, here 92, www.researchgate.net.

[13] "As a pensioner at the Persian court the ex-king could be imagined exerting a quietly civilizing influence on the new regime; it was in no one's interest to discourage this notion. The circulation of such tales no doubt convinced Herodotus that Croesus must have survived the sack of Sardis" (Stephanie West, "Croesus' Second Reprieve and Other Tales of the Persian Court," *ClQ* 53.2 (2003): 416-37, here 421).

wants to get his foot on the property ladder.

The land being purchased has the value of 400 shekels of silver, which is the equivalent of just under a thousand US dollars today; I suspect that this measly price is symbolic but because an explanation requires information not yet provided, I shall return to this in due course.

The scene represents a legally binding covenant between the two men, in the context of land purchase, which is why it is fleshed out so meticulously, e.g., there is a preamble, telling of Sarah's demise, the need for a gravesite, the fact that Abraham is a "stranger," etc.; there is specific mention of witnesses and a public setting by the gates of the city (where judges, priests, etc., hear legal cases); and there is an agreed price very carefully noted, despite Ephron's initial reticence to take Abraham's money.[14]

The legal covenant may be inserted here to bolster the Hittite context, for it brings to mind the first real international "treaty" (a form of covenant) we know of, i.e., that between Egypt and the original Hittites in 1253 BCE, signed by Hattušili III and Pharaoh Ramses II at Kadesh (not the Arabian Kadesh but the one in northern Canaan/Syria).

On the other hand, the scene *may* be influenced, in some oblique way, by Croesus and his fascination with Greek wisdom (did the two ex-kings discuss Greek and Egyptian philosophy over a goblet of wine/Elixir, perhaps?). Herodotus (*Hist.* 1.67-8) tells the tale ("in the time of Croesus") of the supposed finding of the bones of Orestes, the son of Agamemnon, located under a blacksmith's forge in Tegea. The Oracle at Delphi had apparently stated that the missing bones of this hero had to be repatriated before a Spartan victory over the Tegeans could be granted, but the tale has similarities to the one in Genesis:

⋆ Both stories centre on finding a burial site

⋆ In *Hist.* 1.68, we learn that the man who finds the grave is a "stranger" in the land

⋆ He tries to offer money as rent for the site but the smith refuses; eventually they come to an agreement

⋆ Croesus allies himself with the Spartans and when he hears they have ordered gold for a statue from Sardis (Croesus' capital), the Anatolian king waves the cost and gives it to them, gratis

⋆ They form an alliance

---

[14] According to Midrash (Bereishit Rabbah, 5), there are three *truly* Israelite sites, i.e., the Cave of Machpelah, purchased by Abraham; the Temple Mount, bought by David; and the portion of Joseph in Shechem, paid for by Jacob.

I posit this is what we see happening in Genesis 23; Nabonidus and Croesus are becoming allies via a transference of land-ownership, set in the semi-mythical context of the "power of bones."[15] In *The Oresteia*, the concepts of morality and legal process are at the fore, and the "transferal of Orestes' bones from Tegea to Sparta [leads] to the *appropriation of an identity* (emphasis mine)."[16] Nabonidus is seeking legitimisation in this new land[17] (and as Abraham honouring Melchizedek, for instance, in Gen 14:18-20, he demonstrates a sobriety and a revived skill at deal-making and etiquette that seem to be lacking in his personal life); the scene with Jethro (Exodus 18) and the creation of the "judges" seems to fit into this perception. Did Croesus himself relate this story to Nabonidus and his followers?

At any rate, the scene of Abraham securing a place to bury the "dead" and the relocation of a hero's bones turns out to be a precursor, or perhaps a well-disguised parallel, to a theme found in the book of Exodus, with Moses and the ark of the covenant. There is a *possible* historical link to be made between the actual escape from Egypt and the creation of the ark. This will be discussed in due course.

This excerpt from a Nabonidus inscription supports the notion that he had material support from the Hittites even in the remotest parts of his kingdom (the "obstructed roads" and the "ten years" are direct allusions to his time in Arabia and specifically Tayma, known for its arduous approaches):

> The god Šamaš, the lord of command(s) ... made the people of the lands of Akkad and Ḫatti, whom he had placed in my hands, have common cause with and a loyal heart towards me so that they can fulfil (their) duties to m[e] (and) fully carry out (all of) my commands in the remote mountains region(s and on) the obstructed road(s) that I marched on for ten years.
>
> Nab 47 ii 3-11

---

[15] For a fascinating discussion on the mythical significance of bones and burials see Chandra Giroux, "The Power of Bones: An Intertextual and Intermaterial Reading of the Retrieval of Theseus' Bones in Plutarch's *Life of Cimon*," *The Dynamics of Intertextuality in Plutarch* (Leiden: Brill, 2020), 539-550.

[16] Mary Fragkaki, "Spartan Identity and Orestes' 'Repatriation'," in *Ancient History: Interdisciplinary Approaches*, Carmen Soares, José Luís Brandão (2018), 287-298, here 287. doi:10.14195/978-989-26-1564-6.

[17] I suggest Mamre/Hebron is Tayma, so east of here is the corridor of land, culminating at the Mediterranean, that the reigning "King of the Arabs" had control over (mentioned again later). It is possible Croesus had purchased some of this territory when he first arrived in Canaan, to give him access to Arabia.

# 4

# EGYPT

There is a current debate concerning whether or not the Israelites were ever in Egypt at all, let alone as slaves. Hopefully, by the end of this analysis, there will be a little more clarity on the issue, but my aim here is to reveal what lies beneath the veneer of simplicity, and what Nabonidus was really up to. To this end, it is necessary to be somewhat ruthless, to separate wheat from chaff, history from religious dogma. I therefore make one statement to begin with: The Israelites who accompany "Moses" (Nabonidus) never *lived* (long-term) in Egypt. Once you can accept that Abraham's and Moses' stories are connected, the respective interludes in Egypt become just one aspect of the extended exodus/sojourn, but because Nabonidus' *personal* mission changes at this point (i.e., the second visit to Tahpanhes), the narrative begins in Egyptian territory.

The introduction to Exodus, telling of Moses' birth, is, as discussed earlier, to be seen as purely symbolic, placing both Moses and his mission firmly in the realms of familiar mythological and royal precedents. However, the first historical/geographical allusions are embedded into the narrative at Exod 1:11, i.e., "forced labour," "supply cities," and "Pithom and Rameses," in order to provide a social context, a reference point for the physical location, and an indication of what Nabonidus has planned. As with most clues in the HB, they really become apparent once the overall story is understood, so that when you look back, you (the intended audience) get the impression of divine prophecy, omens, etc. i.e., "it is written." If the clues are missed, the words of the god(s), the truth, cannot be known. This has been the way the Bible has worked for so long as a profound source of "power and glory" for those who would obscure the hidden aspects for their own ends.

# PITHOM

It has been surmised that the geography of Exodus

> corresponds with the sixth century BCE. …This also agrees closely with the perceived threat on the northeastern border, expressed in Exodus 1, because from the time of the late Assyrian and the Babylonian periods onward invasions from this direction were a constant threat. As a consequence, it is precisely in the Saite period that narratives expressive of xenophobia make their appearance in Egypt and become a staple of the Egyptian self-consciousness.[1]

In Exodus, Numbers, and Deuteronomy fiction is punctuated by moments of history and fact, i.e., little details that speak of first-hand experience, things witnessed, places visited. These are what we need to find and see how they relate to the 6th Century world of Nabonidus. Pithom is a real place, in Egypt, and in just the right position to be a significant element in the story of Nabonidus' second visit to Tahpanhes, both physically and symbolically.

The following discussion should be read bearing in mind the early assessment of the Ur escape; the details there also apply here, of course, as they are part of the Moses story, not Abraham's. The alluded to abduction of Jehudijah from the temple, the hiding in the marshes, being pursued by an angry mob, etc., all happen at the very *beginning* of Nabonidus' departure from Babylon. Because Genesis' Abraham is a positive perspective on the ex-king, in terms of how he got the first wave of exiles back to Jerusalem (Canaan), any hint of collaboration (e.g., a deal with Cyrus), or scandal (kidnapping) is avoided and left to those who don't see Nabonidus as a hero, but a tyrant and a murderer, i.e., "Moses" (in Exodus, especially). For narrative effect these events are exploited to build the Egyptian expedition up into a profoundly symbolic and ultimately damning appraisal of Moses' strange mission.

From the very beginning of Exodus we learn that "Moses" has an

[1] John Van Seters, "The Geography of the Exodus," in *The Land that I Will Show You: Essays on the History and Archaeology of the Ancient Near East in Honour of J. Maxwell Miller*, J. Andrew Dearman and M. Patrick Graham, eds. JSOTSup 343 (Sheffield: Sheffield Academic Press, 2001), 255-76, here 275.

interest in Osiris. This is not random, but central to the entire mission that constitutes the bulk of the exodus narratives. It's just very subtle.

## Pithom and Osiris

Uphill states that "Archaeologists and biblical scholars are both agreed that ("Pithom" is) derived from Pi Tum, i.e. Pi Atum or Per Atum,"[2] i.e., "House of Atum" (the ancient Egyptian solar deity).

Pi Tum is otherwise known as Heroopolis. Naville, perhaps the most frequently cited authority on Pithom, argues that in LXX Gen 46:28, which deals with the meeting of Jacob and Joseph, replaces "Goshen" with "Heroopolis" in the *land of* Ramesses; the Coptic translation then reverts to the ancient name for Heroopolis, i.e., "Pithom."[3] He then cites several ancient references to "Pithom," including an inscription from the city itself, describing a Ptolemaic priest as "'the keeper of the storehouse' .... the storehouse was one of the principal parts of Pithom, which had been constructed as a store-city."[4]

Then there is the statue of Osiris discovered at Pithom, which mentions a man who is called an "inspector of the palace," i.e., "the good recorder of Tum" (Pithom).[5]

In addition, there is a tablet known as the "Stone of Pithom" which bears an inscription by the king, Ptolemy Philadelphos (284-246 BCE), who is depicted offering *maat* to the gods, the first of whom is Tum, "the great god of Succoth," followed closely by Osiris, "the lord of Ro Ab (the Arabian city), who resides at Pikehereth."[6] Ro Ab represents "Arabia," i.e., the nome of Arabia (see below); Osiris is thus the "lord of Arabia."[7] Part of the inscription reads: "They arrived in the Eastern Nome of the Harpoon; it was the city of their father Atum."[8]

From two inscriptions at Denderah is found: "Thou art in Pithom of Arabia," and "Thou art living in Pithom of Arabia, living like the living God."[9]

---

[2] E. P. Uphill, "Pithom and Raamses: Their Location and Significance." *JNES* 27.4 (1968): 291-316, here 291.

[3] Edouard Naville, *The Store-City of Pithom and the Route of the Exodus* (London: Trübner, 1885), 7.

[4] Naville, 7

[5] Naville, 13.

[6] Naville, 16.

[7] Naville, 8.

[8] "Translations of Hellenistic Inscriptions: 258," c. 264 BCE (Pithom Stele), Cairo CG 22183 [TM 58344], Eduard Naville, transl., www.attalus.org.

[9] Naville, 8.

So, Pikehereth (or Pikerehet) is the *city of Osiris* in Succoth, which is in the Arabian Nome 20. Naville argues that the capital region of Succoth had two cultic centres, one dedicated to Atum (Pi Tum), the other to Osiris (Pikehereth) that were near each other[10] (as would, I suggest, be represented by the order and proximity of the deities in the inscription). Although no Ramesside temple to Osiris has been found here, to date, the Latin name for Pikehereth is "Serapin"; a sanctuary of Osiris is called a Serapeum. Naville claims it to be the only such sanctuary known to have existed in the region.[11]

PT utterance 247, "possibly the earliest extant hymn to Osiris, calls Osiris 'the Complete', *tem*, associating him thereby with Atum, his great-grandfather."[12]

The deity Tum is associated with Nome 8, also called "Harpoon" (East).[13]

## A Note on Nomes

The nomes, or administrative districts, of Egypt have their roots in the tale of the dismembering of Osiris:

> The nome lists which we have for study are mostly of a late period; but the lists of cities where ceremonies took place, or where the fourteen or sixteen parts of Osiris were deposited, shew us what were the principal centres at a very early date.[14]

As political influences changed over the years, more and more subdivisions were added to the list until there became forty-two nomes but, as Petrie states, the original Osiris-based nomes were perpetuated for religious/ritual purposes right to the end of the kingdom.[15] Petrie argues that the Arabian nome was (Lower) Nome 20 and was a much later addition to the list as it claimed no "relic" of Osiris (i.e., the body parts had all been

---

[10] Naville, 20.

[11] Naville, 20. Osiris-Apis is named in Greek, "Serapis," or "Serapin." Not to be confused with "Serapeum," the name given to the area (farther south-east) separating Lake Timsah from the Bitter Lakes.

[12] Edward P. Butler, "Osiris," Henadology: Philosophy and Theology, https://henadology.wordpress.com.

[13] Naville, 8; Diane Leeman, "The Nomes of Ancient Egypt" (2019), 1-40, here 22, www.academia.edu.

[14] W. M. Flanders Petrie, "The Nomes of Egypt," in *Historical Studies,* British School of Archaeology in Egypt: Studies Vol. 2 (London: 1911), 22-9, here 22.

[15] Petrie, 25.

applied to other nomes[16]) but was identified as a "turquoise amulet" instead.[17] The Pelusiac branch of the Nile, upon (or near) which stand Tahpanhes and Heroopolis, was worshipped "as one of the legs of Osiris."[18]

The Nile Delta region had been occupied by a series of chieftains for a long time before the invading Assyrians effectively dissolved the nomes, leaving Psamtik I (Dynasty 26) "to establish himself as the sole king of a reunified country. Many of the ancient nomes were reinstated during this period,"[19] i.e., as part of the archaistic movement that would culminate with the reign of Ahmose III. So, in Ahmose's/Nabonidus' world, the districts would be indicative of the contemporaneous Osirian revival.

***

The mention of Pithom in Exodus has remained such an enigma, many historians have given up on it claiming, for instance, that its inclusion in Exodus "has nothing to do with the old history of Israel" but is simply part of the "their own fictitious picture of the sojourn of the Israelites."[20] I think there is a significance to "Pithom" that *means* something not only to the pericope in which it is found, but to the entire exodus narrative. It relates to the history of the Israelites who leave Babylon, yes, but not to a "fictitious," enslaved nation residing in Egypt.

Years after Moses kills the Egyptian and flees to Midian (Tayma), i.e., when the original pharaoh has died, he returns to Egypt. This means the route to Tahpanhes is not via Pelusium, as is the norm, but from the south, i.e., from Tayma in Northwestern Arabia. It is likely the group passes through Nomes 8 and 20 to reach their destination on the Nile (the HB text does not provide any information on this particular journey but the route suggested in *Fig. 6* is discussed shortly).

Therefore, it is possible that Pithom (Pi Tum) is recounted as a first-hand experience, i.e., again, the most obvious site to mention would be Pikehereth, or its Serapeum but as with every other Nabonidus-linked name, it must not be mentioned (as it vindicates the man's memory, which the early Jews do not want). The two sites of worship laying directly in his path to Tahpanhes, Pi Tum and Pikehereth, represent the Sun and Moon together,

---

[16] "The relic of Heroopolis was called *Tem*, and was probably *tem*, the skin" (Petrie, 28).

[17] Petrie, 24.

[18] Trumbull, *Kedesh-Barnea*, 348.

[19] Leeman, 13.

[20] Niels Peter Lemche, "Is it Still Possible to Write a History of Ancient Israel?," in *Israel's Past in Present Research: Essays on Ancient Israelite Historiography*, Vol. 7, V. Philips Long, ed. (USA: Eisenbrauns, 1999), 391-414, here 399.

foreshadowing Nabonidus' Sinai plan.

These "store-cities" (from the noun *miskenoth*, i.e., "supply, storage") appear in the HB as the fortified cities (or storage magazines) in five contexts: 1) Exod 1:11 (Pithom and Rameses); 2) 1 Kgs 9:19; 2 Chr 8:4,6 (Solomon's building projects); 3) 2 Chr 16: (Ben-hadad's raid against the store-cities of Naphtali); 4) 2 Chr 17:12 (Jehoshaphat's building projects); and 5) 2 Chr 32:28 (Hezekiah's "storehouses"). Neither Numbers nor Deuteronomy mention any such structures. Is this because the reference to them in Exodus is a later addendum, or because the authors of the latter two texts knew that the Israelites were never resident in Egypt (to that extent; some might have been living there by choice, of course) and didn't quite know what to make of the reference, so chose to omit it?[21]

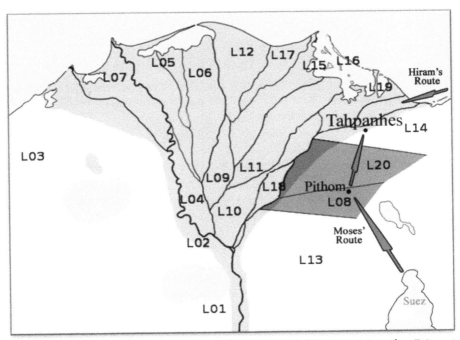

*Figure 6: Nomes 8 (containing Pithom/Sun-god) and 20 (containing the "city of Osiris,"/Moon-god, Pikehereth) on the route to Tahpanhes from the south (Image: Author's adaptation of Wikimedia map).*

---

[21] Num 33:3, 5 mention Rameses but not Pithom.

# RAMESES

Pithom's storehouses were, as far as Naville's archaeological investigations revealed, built by Ramesses II.[22] Uphill notes how the city of Bubastis, also on the Pelusiac branch of the Nile, contained more statues of Ramesses II than any other city;[23] it would seem this eastern side of the Nile, from Pelusium to Heliopolis, was very obviously Ramesside, wherever Pi-Ramesses might have been located. Thus, the reference to "Rameses" in relation to Pithom, *may* be as the LXX Gen 46:28 suggests, i.e., "the *land* of Ramesses," rather than a city. This, however, begs the question of why the author of Exod 1:11 uses the plural for "cities" and not the singular.

Because my own idea about the use of "Rameses" in Exod 1:11 involves details yet to be discussed, I shall return to this at a more appropriate juncture.

## *Corvée*

The Israelites never lived in slavery in Egypt. The oppression the HB speaks of relates to what they know of Assyrian and Babylonian corvée practices, from the 8th to the 6th Centuries, BCE.

Nebuchadnezzar, for instance, is said to have forbidden the captured Israelites to pray (Midrash Eicha Rabbah 5.5) and forced them, unnecessarily, to march with speed to Babylon, as if they were being chased by lions (Ginzei Shechter 1:273).

Just as in Dan 5:23, and the (symbolic) profane employment of the Israelites' "vessels," the Babylonian kings are held responsible for ridiculing the Israelites' faith; Nebuchadnezzar is depicted as performing a similar gesture toward Torah:

> The king noticed that the princes of Judah, though they were in chains, bore no load upon their shoulders, and he called to his servants: "Have you no load for these?" They took the parchment scrolls of the law, tore them in pieces, made sacks of them, and filled them with sand; these they loaded upon the backs of the Jewish princes. At sight of this disgrace, all Israel broke out into loud weeping.
>
> *Legends of the Jews*[24]

---

[22] Naville, 11.

[23] E. P. Uphill, "Pithom and Raamses: Their Location and Significance," *JNES* 28.1 (1969): 15-39, here 25.

[24] In 4.10, The Exile, §"Transportation of the Exiles," https://sacred-texts.com.

In Exodus, the sacks of sand are replaced by bricks, mortar, and field work; in Exod 5:15-19, Pharaoh makes their work even harder by not allowing them enough straw to make their bricks, turning the Israelites, really for the first time, against Moses, for they blame him for making their lot worse, not better. This is the beginning of the "complaining" that will run right through the exodus narratives, and will set the tone for the relationship between Nabonidus and the exiles.

Evidence from a cylinder attributed to the Babylonian King Nabopolassar (626-605 BCE) reveals that he proudly used corvée labour: "I mustered the workmen of the gods Enlil, Šamaš, and Marduk and (then) I made (them) carry hoe(s and) imposed (on them the carrying of) basket(s)."[25] However, as Ouysook notes, these labourers were taken from the general population of Nippar, Sippar, and Babylon, i.e., not from a distinct race, or as a form of enslavement/punishment.

Also, slavery is an aspect of Mesopotamian life from distant days; at Uruk, for instance (Ur III Period), an inscription tells of "herded people," i.e., captives, who might well have become "coerced and commoditised workers";[26] and many records of slave sales are known. Although conquest might inject a few more slaves into the system, the majority of enforced workers were local residents and most of those were placed in this position due to debt they could not repay.[27]

In Nabonidus' day, we see two sorts of corvée labour, i.e., that imposed as a temporary levy, and that imposed as a permanent subjugation.

In the former case:

I raised up my extensive troops from the land (of the city) Gaza (on) the border of Egypt (and) the Upper Sea ... to (re)build Eḫulḫul, the temple of the god Sîn ... which is inside the city Ḫarrān ....
Nab 28 i 33-40

And in the latter:

To carry basket(s), I gave to the gods Bēl (Marduk), Nabû, and Nergal, the gods who march at my side, 2,850 (people) from an

---

[25] Peerapat Ouysook, "A Study of the Composition of Nebuchadnezzar II's Royal Inscriptions" (PhD diss., Department of Archaeology University of Cambridge, 2021), 165.

[26] John Nicholas Reid, "Slavery in Early Mesopotamia from Late Uruk until the Fall of Babylon in the Longue Durée" (PhD diss., University College, 2014), 56. For a discussion on the notion/definition of "slavery" as it pertains to Near Eastern studies, see 14-29.

[27] Reid, 59-72. Enslavement as punishment was not so common, as financial recompense was the norm, but if the family fell into debt by paying this to the injured party, they might be forced into slavery (84).

(enemy) army, booty from the land Ḥumê, which the lord, the god Marduk, had placed in my hands ....

Nab 3 ix 31-41

When he returns from Tayma (543 BCE) to place Ennigaldi, Nitocris, and Jehudijah in their refurbished temple at Ur, Nabonidus makes a point of excusing the priesthood there from corvée, which means even they were expected to comply with this obligatory service to the nation at some point:

> the lower-ranking priesthood who are named (here) by their title(s), from their corvée labour and established their freedom from service obligations.

Nab 34 ii 26-7

With respect to Nabonidus as "Solomon," there are two main statements about his use of labourers that reflect just this two-tier system. In 1 Kgs 5:13 we read that Solomon "conscripted forced labour out of all Israel .... He sent them to the Lebanon ... in shifts; they would be a month in the Lebanon and two months at home." The Hebrew term for this "forced labour" is *mas* or *mis*, i.e., a "body of conscripted labourers, a taskforce, etc." which *Strong's* defines it as a "levy, a burden, i.e. A tax in the form of forced labour." The fact that they go in "shifts" and spend only a month in the Lebanon (i.e., they are probably sent to Tyre to work for the craftsmen) and then come "home" makes it clear this is not oppression or slavery. The Israelites are simply subject to the same conditions of corvée as everyone else under Babylonian rule.

In 1 Kgs 9:15-23, however, the idea that Israelites might be considered as "slave labourers" is clearly anathema. Those who became slaves are the indigenous peoples, i.e., the *residents* of the land (1 Kgs 9:20-1), just as in the Ur III comment above. The author of 1 Kings then makes it abundantly clear that Solomon employed the Israelites as his army and the "chief officers" (taskmasters, ironically) to oversee the work (9:22-3). The Hebrew terminology here changes from *mas/mis*, to *mas obed*, which has the connotation of forced labour that includes subservience, as in obeying a master, worshipping, being a (permanent) servant, etc. This is why the author takes such pains to delineate between the two contexts.

We need to bear in mind that Solomon, too, is based on Nabonidus, and all of this labour, whether in shifts as citizens bound by the law, or as slave labour taken from the local population or prisoners of war, is performed in Tayma and Nabonidus' outlying projects, *not* Jerusalem (as below).

> This is the account of the forced labour that King Solomon conscripted to build the house of the Lord and his own house, the

Millo and the wall of Jerusalem[28] …as well as Solomon's storage
cities … and whatever Solomon desired to build ….

1 Kgs 9:15-19

In the scathing assessment in the VA, the dethroned Nabonidus
supposedly sets all the people of Tayma to work on his own palace/temple
there (before murdering them, naturally):

The inhabitants became troubled. The brick form and the brick basket
he imposed upon them.

VA ii 9

Today, the concept of slavery enforced upon the Israelites is
becoming harder and harder to accept by those who seek historical evidence,
especially when a centuries-long residence in Egypt is ruled out (which
seems to be the way things are going, at last). Even the notion of an
*oppressive* captivity during the Assyrian/Babylonian exile has to be
seriously questioned. A cache of about a hundred cuneiform tablets made
available to researchers in 2015 were dated to Nebuchadnezzar's reign and
revealed a strong Jewish community doing well, economically: "They were
free to go about their lives, they weren't slaves …. Nebuchadnezzar wasn't
a brutal ruler in that respect. He knew he needed the Judeans to help revive
the struggling Babylonian economy."[29]

Nabonidus is a man of his time, in many respects, even though he is
quite a unique character; his admiration for his predecessors, especially the
Assyrian kings, means he maintains certain inherited traditions and policies,
and corvée is one of them. He doesn't invent it; perhaps he relies on it more
than other kings, but he is a man with a vision and apparently very rich
investors. It is quite possible that the inhabitants of Tayma *are* put to work,
and that some of the Jews who travel with Nabonidus and live there for
several years, also have to earn their keep. It wouldn't be anything out of the
ordinary, but in the anti-Nabonidus VA account (and Exodus) it has to be
shown in a negative light.

In the end, I have to think that the Jewish authors of Exod 1:11, and of 1
Kgs 9:15-23 are speaking of the same experience, i.e., of witnessing the
enforced labour of fellow residents, perhaps even themselves or their families,
at certain times, for particular building projects throughout Babylonia.

---

[28] In *She Brought* I suggest the "Millo" is actually the *majal*, the walled cemetery
of the *entus* at Ur; this probably equates to the "wall of Jerusalem," i.e., where Jerusalem
is a pseudonym for Tayma, recall. Tyson 25-7.

[29] Luke Baker, "Ancient Tablets Reveal Life of Jews in Nebuchadnezzar's
Babylon," Feb 23 2015, www.reuters.com.

# GOSHEN

Goshen is, regardless of semantics, etymology, and the countless variations of interpretation, traditionally situated to the east of the Nile Delta (e.g., Gen 46:28, 29, 34; Exod 13:17; 1 Chr 7:21).

My first thought was that Goshen might be an allusion to the *stratopeda* described by Herodotus (*Hist.* 2.154), i.e., the camps on either side of the Pelusiac branch of the Nile filled with Greek mercenaries by Psamtik I. These camps, one of which is thought to be Daphnae/Tahpanhes, were supposedly decommissioned by the end of Ahmose III's reign, when he wanted the soldiers to guard Memphis, but archaeological evidence suggests a strong Greek contingent remained in the area.[30] It is plausible that whilst visiting the region during the two excursions we know of, Nabonidus' chroniclers learn of this relatively recent history and assume a similar notion for the Israelites, back-dating it to an ancient time (i.e., in Genesis). Herodotus claims that before Psamtik I, "no foreigners had ever taken up their residence in that land," so "Goshen," if truly a land handed over to the Israelites, would have to have been beyond the Wall of Shur, i.e., not *in* Egypt at all. When you consider the topography in this Pelusiac region, the marshes, lagoons, the thick reeds, crocodiles, etc., it is hardly the "best part of the land" ("in the land of Ramesses"; Gen 47:11) and certainly not capable of sustaining hundreds of thousands of people and their livestock. In fact, this description doesn't really work for what lies just beyond either, with the mountains to the east and then the desert beyond. The emphasis is more on the *act* of granting this home, i.e., royal largess, than on the land itself; it is an appropriated concept to bolster a growing narrative of the new nation of Israel.

What I am more interested in is the possibility that "Goshen" extends into Arabia (proper).

The book of Judith is commonly dated to the 2nd-1st Century BCE, and is considered a retrospective, fictional account of the conquest of good over evil, piety over idolatry, etc. It has obvious anachronisms, such as claiming Nebuchadnezzar was the King of Nineveh (1:1).[31] Such a blatant error in the very first verse must be intentional, i.e., to indicate that the entire story is myth, a fable. Many toponyms are rattled off in succession, pointing us to the Genesis/Exodus narratives, including "Tahpanhes" and "Raamses" but suddenly there is another rather glaring error; what the English

---

[30] Alan. B. Lloyd, *Herodotus, Book II Commentary 99-182*, 2nd ed. (Leiden: Brill, 1993), 137.

[31] Assyria is often used to denote Babylonia and, as we have seen, "Nebuchadnezzar" is used to denote Nabonidus, but Nineveh was defeated and destroyed even before Nebuchadnezzar's time (i.e., ca. 612 BCE).

translation insists is "Goshen" is, in fact, "Gesem" (or "Geshem") (Jdt 1:9), and this name appears also in LXX Gen 45:10 and 46:34, raising some interesting questions.

The 1901 *Jewish Encyclopedia* entry for "Goshen" claims that the HB version of the word *must* be considered more authentic than "Gesem" because the name "Goshen" appears in a Dynasty 12 papyrus, and probably only relates to the "Arabian nome," as discussed earlier.[32] I prefer to speculate on *why* the change in name might have occurred.

Looking at "Gesem," for instance, we find the name appears in Neh 2:19; 6:1, 2, 6, as one of the opponents to the rebuilding of the walls of Jerusalem, i.e., he is called "Geshem the Arab." LXX Gen 45:10 states that the sons of Jacob lived in the "land of Gesem of Arabia." Retsö states:

> Since eastern Egypt and some cities in the eastern delta are said already by Hecataeus to be in Arabia, this extent of the Arabian kingdom was probably already established in the sixth century BC, probably in connection with the Persian conquest.[33]

An archaeological find at Pithom (Pathoumos) has revealed a connection between Pithom and Gesem, in the form of an inscribed votive silver bowl that mentions the name "GSM king of QDR"; this is to be identified as "Gesem of Qedar."[34] So, if the name "Gesem" was employed instead of "Goshen" by later Hebrew texts, was this because they knew the former to be more accurate, more pertinent, historically? Were they aware of the fictitious nature of the Egyptian captivity?

For me, if a Hebrew author retains in their work (in the HB texts) an obvious anomaly, it is a signal to the reader that something different is meant, i.e., that something is hidden beneath the text. I think this may be a case in point regarding the book of Judith, a book that openly claims to be fiction from the start, that includes an odd-one-out toponym; it provokes examination without being explicitly contradictory.

"GSM king of QDR" implies two things: 1) GSM is a person's name, not a place, and 2) his territory is that of the Qedarites. It is evident that the Qedarites and the "Arabs" were considered two distinct entities in the Neo-

---

[32] Isidore Singer, ed., "Goshen" *JE* (1901), www.studylight.org.

[33] Retsö, 251. Hecataeus of Miletus is the first known Greek historian (550-476 BCE). He would have had information contemporaneous with Nabonidus' reign and the exodus thereafter.

[34] Retsö, 250-1. This GSM is thought to be the man mentioned in Nehemiah 2, as the bowls date to about the same time, but there might have been a succession of rulers called "GSM," like there were several Hirams of Tyre.

Assyrian Period, but their proximity and similarities are enough to consider them, at least for our current discussion, one group of people.[35] We know that their vast territory included the lands east of the Nile Delta, i.e., the "Wilderness of Shur" (which would include the Sinai peninsula) right down to Tayma and Dadan, and including much of Syria as far as Palmyra (Tadmor).[36] In other words, the Qedarites inhabit every region we find Moses (Nabonidus) in, much of which falls under the aegis of "Edom."[37]

Shuaib notes that

in Genesis 25:13, Qedar was one of the descendants of Ishmael and the indication in Song 1: 5 is that the Qedarites were Bedouin living in black tents. Thus, we may conclude that 'the Arab' of the text of Nehemiah is one of the sons of Ishmael who lived in tents near Palestine.[38]

"Ishmael" is (I claim) an eponymous name given to those in the south, i.e., the Nitocris/Nabonidus sympathisers from whom the early Jews wished to be disassociated. Of course, I am not suggesting the Qedarites owe *their* existence to Nabonidus; they had been around for centuries before his time, but the HB seems to be hinting at a strong connection between them and our gone-native king, and I think there are other snippets of information that might shed further light.

Nabonidus has history with the Qedarites from his early days as King of Babylon, spending the first few years of his Arabian campaign conquering various cities before settling in Tayma. A rock relief at Sela (about fifty kilometres north of Petra) is thought to commemorate his victory over Edom (Nab 55); the Royal Chronicle (v 13-24) describes the difficult terrain he had to overcome around Dadan (i.e., the Harraat[39] lowlands), well within Qedarite territory; and Nab 47 (i 45 - ii 2) also suggests military confrontation with the Arabs.

Dumbrell suggests that the Qedarites' power must have been diminished by the presence of Nabonidus at Tayma, who would not

---

[35] Retsö, 163.

[36] "Qedar," 12 October 2020, www.livius.org.

[37] The zenith of Edom's territorial expansion was in the first half of the 6th Century BCE (Ernst Axel Knauf, Robin M. Brown, "Edom" [2018], Oxford Bibliographies, doi: 10.1093/OBO/9780195393361-0258.

[38] Marwan G. Shuaib, ;'The Arabs of North Arabia in later Pre-Islamic Times: Qedar, Nebaioth, and Others" (PhD diss., University of Manchester, 2014), 60.

[39] The Harraat is the expanse of lava fields in Northwestern Arabia; the singular is "Harra" unless placed before a toponym, in which case it is "Harrat ____." Peter Vincent, *Saudi Arabia: An Environmental Overview* (London: Taylor & Francis, 2008), 22.

otherwise have had such a free rein in the land.[40] But what if Nabonidus made friends of his once-enemies, as he did with Ahmose III? What if he now considers himself one of *them*? He certainly seems to have adopted much of the nomadic, Bedouin lifestyle (as Abraham), and yet seems also to retain much authority and prestige in Tayma, as a quasi-king/priest (as Moses *and* Solomon).

What if the Israelites are told they will live in the land of "Gesem" because they (at least those who experience the Exodus part of the journey, not just the Genesis part) are going to live (for several years) in the land that *is* Gesem's, i.e., Arabia. Technically, this includes the lower regions of Canaan, of course, but the bulk of Qedarite territory is farther south. This might suggest that "Gesem" in the LXX context is to be equated with Nabonidus. He takes his group with him to Tayma, to the far side of Edom, a land he has conquered himself, and into whose hands he now offers himself as a fellow Arab (by partaking of the covenant of salt and amalgamating with their religion [discussed later]). If the GSM dynasty of Qedarites was strong and well known in the region, it would not be too big a leap to imagine the early Jews identifying the two troublemakers; in the Song, Nabonidus (whose name is not to be mentioned, recall) is equated with Baal (Song 8:11),[41] and Rome is later depicted as Babylon (e.g., 2 Esdras 3, Revelations 14), etc. It is a common enough technique.

So, the Israelites (who follow Nabonidus to Tayma, and who write Exodus) live in the land of Nabonidus (Gesem) of Arabia. The idea of Goshen, a land granted to them by royal appointment is based on the idea that at least two pharaohs granted Nile-delta lands to foreigners. If we take Gen 46:34 as a clue, i.e., "all shepherds are *abhorrent* to the Egyptians" (employing the noun *toebah*, "abomination"), it is easy to see the land of the Qedarites, the land of the Ishmaelites, and the land of the Shasu, i.e., the pastoral, nomadic tribes the Egyptians were determined to keep out of their land,[42] as indistinguishable. "Shasu" means "wanderers"; Abraham is a wanderer, and Nabonidus puts this epithet in stone. I often have a chuckle at the profoundly clever scribal machinations in the HB; I hope this one was intentional.

The rejection of the Shasu are mentioned in the Anastasi Papyri (VI) in direct association with Pi Tum; they are allowed to pass through the defences to water their flocks, but only on one specific day. As I mention

---

[40] William J. Dumbrell, "The Tell El-Maskhuta Bowls and the 'Kingdom' of Qedar in the Persian Period." *BASOR* 203 (1971): 33-44, here 40.

[41] Tyson, 205.

[42] James K., Hoffmeier, Thomas W. Davis, and Rexine Hummel, "New Archaeological Evidence for Ancient Bedouin (Shasu) on Egypt's Eastern Frontier at Tell el-Borg," *ÄL* 26 (2016): 285-311, here 286-7.

above, for the HB it is the *act* of granting the Israelites Goshen that carries weight in the narrative, not the land itself, and this appears to echo the Anastasi papyrus: Goedicke suggests this superficial generosity toward people otherwise abhorred, was simply for show, as an appeasement to the god Set. "To grant the Shasu permission to proceed to water their flocks seems a gesture more intended for Set than for the people concerned, in order to win the god's grace on his "birthday.""[43] Although Goedicke goes on to say there can be no comparison to the Israelite's situation,[44] this is only because he maintains the traditional perception of the Genesis story. Shift the context to that of the 6th Century BCE Qedarites and the antagonism between the early Jews and their Arabic neighbours, and it makes more sense. Though I doubt anyone in Nabonidus' caravan had access to the papyri, such a memory of an annual amnesty on Set's birthday might have been easily uncovered in and around Pithom, if it was not still in effect.

This brings to mind another familiar account that I like to consider a *potential* reference to Nabonidus in his later role as king in Tayma.

In Herodotus' brief account of Cambyses' journey through the desert to get to Egypt in 525 BCE (*Hist.* 3.4-7) he states that the Persian king had to ask for "safe conduct" through the territory under the control of the "king of the Arabs." This would have been the "Way to Shur" along the Phoenician coast and the Abarah, under the control of the Qedarites. Let's consider, just for argument's sake, that there was more than one King GSM of QGR, i.e., a father, or grandfather by the same name. That would mean it is *possible* that Cambyses has to ask permission from an Arab king[45] who at least knows Nabonidus, a major player in the region by now. If "Gesem" is yet another pseudonym for Nabonidus, to illustrate his Arabian persona, and "GSM" is historically the name of a king of the Qedarites/Arabs, is it beyond all possibility that the generic "king of the Arabs" Cambyses seeks passage from is none other than Nabonidus?[46]

Still *acting* the king at Tayma, i.e., as the HB's "Solomon," he does seem to have control of lands Cambyses would need to traverse. It might be the case that such permission is provided by proxy and the two never have to

---

[43] Hans Goedicke, "Papyrus Anastasi VI 51-61," *SAK* 14 (1987): 83-98, here 87.

[44] Goedicke, 89.

[45] Dumbrell suggests that "both 'kingdom' and 'king' are convenient, but somewhat inexact terms" as "the probable type of Arab leadership" did not include "conventional kingship" (33, n. 4).

[46] As mentioned earlier, it is possible Nabonidus purchases some of this land from Croesus, who would have bought it from a previous Arab leader; this would certainly give a plausible context for Nabonidus having control over access between the Levant and Egypt, as well as between the Mediterranean and Arabia.

meet, so Cambyses would never be aware that this "Arab" is Nabonidus (and neither would Herodotus, as he knew very little of this Babylonian king).

With this potential allusion to Nabonidus in mind, look at the related etymology, i.e., of the Hebrew "Gesem/Geshem," not the Egyptian "Goshen":

- ★ *Strong's* (1654). Geshem or Gashmu, from the same as *geshem*
- ★ (1653) *geshem*, "rain, shower" (used in Song 2:11)
- ★ (1655) *geshem*, "the body" (used only in Dan 3:27, 28, 4:33; 5:21; 7:11)

Later, I discuss Moses' first action when he reaches the other side of the Red Sea, i.e., *his* territory. Without pre-empting myself, it is sufficient to say this has to do with *rain*. It might also explain the odd usage of the same word as "body" in Daniel 1-5, i.e., the one author beyond the exodus narratives who seems to have an insight into what is going on in Arabia. The location of this rain event has an etymological connection to the notion of a "body," so my suggestion is that Daniel 1-5 uses this term (*geshem*) as code, to refer to Nabonidus. It is a declaration that he knows where he is (perhaps defying Cyrus' orders?).

# 5

# PLAGUES

[May Ha]dad [pour (over it)] every sort of evil (that exists) on earth and in heaven and every sort of trouble; and may he shower upon Arpad [ha]il-[stones]! For seven years may the locust devour (Arpad), and for seven years may the worm eat.

Sefire 1.25-28[1]

The original exodus narrative was a far simpler affair than what has come down to us. The first clue to this being the case is the specific reference to the death of the firstborn in Exod 4:22-3. This is supposedly the pinnacle of all the plagues, the final and strongest statement of God's power, yet the game is given away at this early stage in such a lacklustre way.

From the historical perspective, it seems unlikely a face-to-face confrontation between the new pharaoh and Nabonidus ever takes place. The first trip to Tahpanhes, with Nabonidus as Abraham, does seem to be a personal encounter (which did not end with a great escape but an expulsion), but not this one, as "Moses." We must also remember that the confrontational aspect of the Ur departure is what may be the inspiration for

---

[1] Plagues as a curse. J. A. Fitzmyer, trans., *The Aramaic Inscriptions of Sefire*, 2nd ed. (Rome: Pontifical Biblical Institute, 1995), 45.

the more dramatic scenes mirrored in the context of Egypt. Although, Cambyses remains in Egypt for three years after his victory, he visits many cities and might be anywhere; the proximity of Tahpanhes to Pelusium, the site of the battle that won him Egypt, together with the resentment of the later priestly scribes creates a wholly fictitious but strongly symbolic anti-Egypt, anti-Babylon statement (Cambyses representing both, now).

If the connection to Pithom is historically plausible, then it makes the Osirian symbolism all the more entrenched, and this suggests a predominantly artificial insertion of the lengthy plagues-narrative by a later scribe who knows of Nabonidus' Osirian interests and plans, and who builds the Nile pericopes around them. Having discovered this connection to "Pithom," I am even more convinced of this, and would suggest Nabonidus (as Moses) never makes any grand gesture at the Nile (barring a private supplication to Osiris, perhaps, in light of what follows).

I see the death of the firstborn as the original and *only* punishment ("judgement") threatened by God. There are rabbis who agree with this,[2] so I don't feel I've put myself out on a limb here.

That most of the so-called "plagues" depict wholly natural phenomena experienced by anyone living in Egypt, Mesopotamia, or Arabia[3] lessens the miraculous nature of most of the plagues, perhaps. My first attempt to understand this section was to compare it to the epic of Marduk and Tiamat, with the struggle against the eleven monsters of the water (i.e., the eleven "signs" being the ten so-called plagues, plus the serpent-rod trick).

> *The eleven creatures who were laden with fearfulness,*
> *The throng of devils who went as grooms at her right hand,*
> *He put ropes upon them and bound their arms,*
> *Together with their warfare he trampled them beneath him.*
> Enuma Elish, 4.115-18[4]

While there is reason to assume a Marduk-based theme running through the Abraham/Moses narratives, in terms of the characters proving to be saviours of a sort, and this being a familiar context in which one might

---

[2] For example see Rabbi David Frankel, "The Death of Pharaoh's Firstborn: A One Plague Exodus," www.thetorah.com.

[3] Charles M. Doughty, *Travels In Arabia Deserta* [1888] (New York: Random House, reprint 1921), e.g., gnats 1.431; 2.451; gnats and frogs 2:119; 2.565; flies 1.147; 2.90; locusts 1.500.

[4] Joshua J. Mark, "Enuma Elish: The Babylonian Epic of Creation," 4 May 2018, www.worldhistory.org.

set these tales (for Babylonians), it is not an approach that offers much to this current analysis and was ultimately scrapped when I discovered that the *number* of plagues varies according to the source:

> … why does the number ten never appear in Exodus in relation to the plagues? Biblical scholars have shown that the plague narrative there is composite, comprised of two or three sources that have been melded together. None of these sources had all ten plagues. The redactor, who combined these sources together, is responsible for creating a story with ten plagues, but he was fundamentally conservative, and thus tended not to add to his earlier sources—he would not have inserted the number ten into his narrative. Thus, it was up to later sources to note and emphasise the ten plagues.[5]

To me, the addition of the more pragmatic material still serves a purpose that supports what this analysis is aimed at proving, i.e., that the early Jews desired to detach themselves from anything Nabonidus-related and in doing so, adjusted certain aspects of the received chronicle of the exodus in order to make their point. As will be seen later, this happens with many of the Exodus pericopes, e.g., the water from the rock, the battle with Amalek, etc. Each is apparently based on an experienced event but is written as a parable, often a disguised jibe at Nabonidus.

The later authors turn a potentially simple account (written by a Jewish author who felt an eye for an eye was just, given the situation of the exile) into a familiar epic ordeal for their own propagandistic purposes, i.e., to illustrate the Egyptian influence on Nabonidus' new deity/religion, which must then be countered by, effectively, setting him up as the instigator of his own downfall. This is what happens in the Song of Solomon, where the king's behaviour with Nitocris leads to his temporary madness and forms the foundation of his eventual fall. Nabonidus is his own worst enemy and his fate is apparently sealed by the end of the Song of Solomon, but the Fates are fickle and with the conquest of Babylon comes a new lease of life for the wandering ex-king. With a strong character that does not really change, the exodus narratives reveal a man who deems might is right, who cannot comprehend that his way is not the *only* way, and who needs some serious anger-management therapy. The "plagues" scenarios depict Moses in such a way that on the surface he seems the hero, but just beneath the familiar imagery lies a bitter resentment and an intentional castigation of everything he stands for.

So, the "signs" and "wonders" that provide the most insight into the

---

[5] Marc Zvi Brettler, "Some Biblical Perspectives on the Haggadah," www.thetorah.com.

meaning of the "plagues" are the snake-rods, the bloody Nile, the darkness, and the death of the firstborn. Only the last is to be interpreted as a "divine judgement" as per Exod 4:22-3; the rest are demonstrations of Nabonidus' intent and the Jewish response.

# SNAKE EATS SNAKES

Recall that Moses' adoptive mother is mythologically linked to the Egyptian goddess Renenutet. The traditional iconography of this goddess is that of a woman with the head of a cobra. She is also the mother of a rather more significant deity called Nehebkau, who is a fully-fledged serpent god. In more ancient stories he was an evil entity, untrusted and a threat to Re (cf. Apep) but, the legend goes, Atum touched the snake's spine with his fingernail and it became gentle, benevolent, and a protector/assistant to Re (eventually succeeding him in the hierarchy of the afterlife). A complete turnaround (which may have a bearing on understanding the relationship between Egypt and Babylon during the reign of Nabonidus). One of the most striking legends pertaining to Nehebkau is that *he devoured seven snakes* and from then on was *impervious to danger from magic, fire, and water.*[6] He is depicted as a multi-coiled snake and his likeness was used as an amulet against evil, ill omens, etc.

Aaron is the one who is responsible for this first sign; although Moses is shown how to perform it at Sinai, Aaron is the one who displays his magical prowess and the superiority of the serpentine symbolism. This is a direct foreshadowing of things to come, for Aaron is strongly associated with snake mythology and magical ritual, as we shall see.

Interestingly, the word used for "snake/serpent" in Exod 4:3, i.e., the noun *nachash*, is derived from an unknown word but the verb *nachash* means "to practice divination, observe signs." A play on words is evident here. This is the first sign, conducted as a warning, an *omen* to Pharaoh. However, when the scene shifts to Aaron's snake eating those of the priests (Exod 7:12), the word for the animal also shifts, i.e., to *tannin*, which has been translated as "serpent, dragon, sea-monster, crocodile," etc., depending on the context (e.g., in Gen 1:21 *tannin* is used to denote the first sea creatures; in Deut 32:33, they are venomous snakes). In Ezek 29:3; 32:2, though, *tannin* is employed as a metaphor for Pharaoh which, if translated as "crocodile" (and the description of this beast thrashing about in the Nile, making the waters muddy, etc.,

---

[6] Pharaoh does likewise in PT utterance 318: "The King is a serpent … who swallowed his seven uraei" (Edward P. Butler, "Wadjet," Henadology: Philosophy and Theology, https://henadology.wordpress.com.

sounds like a crocodile, rather than a snake that glides), links him directly with the deity Sobek. So, if the Pharaoh with the hardened heart is equal to Sobek, this suggests he is *also* linked to Renenutet, as in the mythology. See "Hardened Heart," below.

By demonstrating that Aaron can not only turn his rod into a snake but can have that snake devour all the others, is an outright usurpation of the power of Nehebkau, i.e., Aaron and Moses seize the upper hand from the start, ensuring they and the Israelites will not be harmed by anything that is to occur (and this is made explicit in the narrative). *They* now have the magical protection of the snake deity, which, again, is central to the discussion later, concerning the amalgamation with the Qenites of Midian. The snake is, at the very least, a talisman Moses takes seriously, but it becomes the symbol of *everything* Nabonidus will come to represent, quite literally. But there is much to discuss before we get to that.

It is important to remember that Nabonidus has "returned" to Egypt after Ahmose III's death. He is there for a particular reason that is significant to *him*, to his own, personal desire (and not to free Israelite "slaves"); something that becomes a familiar theme in the Song and the VA. It is too early in the analysis to discuss this reason in detail, but what ensues between Pharaoh and Moses in these few episodes is linked directly to Nabonidus' keen interest in the Osirian resurrection myths, which is why the generalised climatic and agricultural "plagues" don't *seem* to fit. They do, however, have a purpose, i.e., they provide evidence of time passing (following the agricultural seasons), and this is important.

# HARDENED HEART

The Israelites brought to Babylonia by Nebuchadnezzar split between those who decided to make a go of it and find work, build families, etc., all as if they *were* Babylonians and those who chose to make new Jewish enclaves, keeping themselves segregated.[7] Already this is hinting at a potential precedent for the alleged schism at Sinai and the rift between Samaria and Judea. When Cyrus announces the edict, as evidenced on the Cyrus Cylinder (ca. 539 BCE), which is a far more concise and vague declaration than generally considered, thanks to Ezra's suspiciously generous rendition,[8] it is

---

[7] Elias J Bickerman ("The Edict of Cyrus in Ezra 1," *JBL* 65.3 (1946): 249-75) tells how many of the Jews in exile in Babylonia chose to isolate themselves as much as they could, living in small enclaves, headed by a chief.

[8] The Cyrus Cylinder states: "I returned the images of the gods, who had resided there, [in Babylon] to their places and I let them dwell in eternal abodes. I gathered all their

probably the distanced, isolated Jews who jump at the chance to leave.

The early migrants, however, are cognisant of the potential for a change of heart by the Persian ruler if they do not respect his rules once they are in Canaan. They are not free, per se, they are still vassals of the King of Babylon—just a *different* king, this time *a pharaoh too*. The timeframe for the application of the edict remains uncertain (but may be hinted at in the extended five-year stay in Harran by Abraham); Cyrus dies in 530 BCE; allowing for time spent in Canaan, Tayma, etc., Nabonidus arrives in Egypt the second time, with Aaron, post-526, *after Ahmose's death*). Cambyses is the figure they must now contend with. That is, Cambyses II, the *alleged* Caligula/Nero of the Persian sphere (but see below).

Notice that Ezra never mentions Cambyses (just as Nabonidus is never mentioned in the HB). The narrative jumps from Cyrus, to "Darius," to Artaxerxes, who reigned 465-425 BCE, which is long time after the Edict of Cyrus and the first wave of emigrants.[9] The scenario of the Jews writing a letter to the King of Persia to request support for the building of the temple after neighbouring factions prove hostile (Ezra 4) is echoed by Josephus, who is certain that it *was* Cambyses who received this letter:

> But when Cambyses, the son of Cyrus, had taken the kingdom, the governors in Syria, and Phoenicia, and in the countries of the Ammonites and Moabites, and Samaria, wrote a letter to Cambyses …

He goes on to explain Cambyses' response:

> … this city (Jerusalem) hath always been an enemy to Kings; and its inhabitants have raised seditions, and wars. We also are sensible that their Kings have been powerful, and tyrannical; and have exacted tribute of Celesyria and Phenicia. Wherefore I give order, that the Jews shall not be permitted to build that city; lest such mischief as they used to bring upon Kings, be greatly augmented.
>
> *A.J.* 11.2.1

Note the opposite sentiment and outcome in Josephus' rendition, in relation to Ezra's exuberant account.

There is certainly a reticence when it comes to the HB authors

---

inhabitants and returned to them their dwellings." Translation of Fragment B: "The people of Babylon blessed my kingship, and I settled all the lands in peaceful abodes." www.livius.org.

[9] Ezra 6:15 implies the royal warrant to build the temple was still being sanctioned in the time of Artaxerxes, yet goes on to say it was completed in Darius' reign. The Jewish Chabad.org suggests the temple wasn't complete until 349 BCE ("The Second Temple is Built," https://www.chabad.org).

discussing contemporaneous Kings of Babylon; Nebuchadnezzar is dead (he is mentioned); Nabonidus receives pseudonyms; Cyrus is dead (he is mentioned); Cambyses is completely omitted. One plausible reason for this omission would be to assuage any repercussions if the texts get into the wrong hands and are considered seditious to the ruling power of the time, be it Cambyses for the early texts, or perhaps Xerxes (485-465 BCE), who was also rather ruthless. The Jews are writing for themselves, for their own descendants; only *they* are required to comprehend the allusions, the symbolism, etc. The *original* significance of their written words, poured out for posterity very soon after the move away from Babylonia, is intentionally obscured from those not within the clique.

Cambyses[10] is thus, I posit, the "pharaoh with the hardened heart" who refuses to let the Israelites worship their own deity in their own sacred space —Jerusalem.

Herodotus' depiction of Cambyses is exemplified by at least three major incidents, namely, the murder of his pregnant wife, the slaying of the sacred Apis bull, and the loss of 50,000 soldiers in the desert. On a closer examination, however, knowing how Herodotus' confusion over the marriage of "Nitetis" ended up revealing an erroneous assumption concerning the identity of the groom,[11] it may well be that the power of the legends of Nabonidus has been greatly underestimated.

The account of Cambyses and his sister-wife is remarkably familiar because it has a potential parallel in the exodus narratives. Herodotus claims the Egyptian side of the story is that Cambyses' wife compared a "stripped lettuce" to the state of Cyrus' empire in the hands of her husband, who had murdered his own brother "Smerdis." It was an insult he reacted to by attacking her, though she was pregnant; she miscarried and died (*Hist.* 3.32). Nabonidus, of course, had a wife who miscarried and (later) died, but in Exodus/Numbers, we see Moses attacking a woman, who dies as a direct consequence of his action (she *may* be pregnant).

Smerdis' "murder was a secret. Whether Cambyses' wife knows for sure, or just suspects, that she speaks openly of murder is clearly an affront; but is it motive for further killing ...."[12] In the scene with Zipporah (Exodus 4) and the blood of the circumcision, we see that this exact scenario is echoed, i.e., the husband is seen as a murderer by the wife, who makes a public show of her knowledge of the "secret"; Moses is also motivated to more killing and Zipporah meets her fate later in the narrative, not by Moses'

---

[10] Whose Egyptian name becomes "Mesuti-Ra [born of Re]" (from the naophorus of Wedjahor-Resne [Vatican Museum, Rome]), www.livius.org.

[11] Tyson, 7-8.

[12] R. Drew Griffith, "Honeymoon Salad: Cambyses' Uxoricide According to the Egyptians (Hdt. 3.32.3-4)," *Historia* 58.2 (2009): 131-40, here 132.

hand but by his command. The fact that Moses had murdered an Egyptian and had kept this a secret, and that he is openly humiliated by a woman who knows this secret is too coincidental, given the proximity of the historical characters (Nabonidus and Cambyses), to be considered unrelated. Again, Herodotus probably hears some salacious gossip but ascribes it to Cambyses, knowing very little about Nabonidus.

Then there is the Apis killing, of which Herodotus says: "Now this Apis, or Epaphus, is the calf of a cow … fire comes down from heaven upon the cow, which thereupon conceives Apis" (*Hist.* 3:28); when Cambyses discovers the Egyptians worshipping it, he kills them all (3.27). Cambyses then kills the calf-bull (3.29). This could be a misconstrued rumour regarding the golden calf scenario at Sinai, which sees Moses destroying the calf-bull (Exod 32:20), Aaron explaining that the idol was miraculously born from the flames (32:24), and the subsequent murder of "three thousand" of the worshippers (32:28). Egyptian sources, meanwhile, show that Cambyses was respectful to the Egyptian deities and "a dutiful adherent of the Apis cult."[13]

These two scenarios are often referred to in discussions on the "madness" attributed to Cambyses but I argue that they are a further remnant of the famed "madness" of Nabonidus.[14]

Herodotus (*Hist.* 3.26) also tells the tale of the missing army of 50,000 men Cambyses takes to a certain "Oasis"; a freak sandstorm rises up and buries them all, never to be found again. This, to me, sounds rather like the many "thousands" said to be on the exodus, traces of whom have never been found (and rumours of such would have been met with incredulity by anyone living and travelling as a nomad in such places, knowing this to be all but impossible in the terrain).[15] Clearly these tales stem from the same period, and both relate to Egypt, deserts and oases, etc. Herodotus might easily have been conflating information (again) and not quite getting things straight.

# OSIRIS' NILE

Osiris has a brother, Set; he also has two sisters, Isis and Nephthys. When Isis and Osiris, united by marriage in the womb, prove to be popular to the

---

[13] John Dillery, "Cambyses and the Egyptian Chaosbeschreibung Tradition," *ClQ* 55.2 (2005): 387-406, here 400.

[14] For a full discussion of Cambyses' "madness," see Rosaria V. Munson, "The Madness of Cambyses (Herodotus 3.16-38)," *Arethusa* 24.1 (1991): 43-65.

[15] In 2009 two brothers claimed to have discovered evidence for the lost army but scientists and archaeologists have urged caution because of their reputation as filmmakers. See "Sands of Time," www.pulpinternational.com.

Egyptians, Set becomes jealous and kills his brother, dismembering his body and casting it over the land of Egypt which itself becomes synonymous with the body of Osiris. There is another myth that proves highly significant, i.e., that Osiris is cast into the Nile, where his decomposing corpse creates an efflux of blood and pus. The inundation of the Nile is said to begin with the death of Osiris and Isis' tears when she heard of it. The blood and pus from Osiris' decaying body cause the river to overflow; this, in turn feeds the Nile valley with fertilizer, making everything grow. Hence, Osiris is depicted with green skin and/or corn growing from his mummified body. This is the time of the "Green Nile," i.e., about May/June. "Osiris of the Green Nile was … the personification of (celestial) malachite" that made vegetation green.[16]

This is also the time when Pharaoh is equated with the crocodile deity, Sobek, and I think this is enough to substantiate the invented context of a face-to-face meeting between Moses and Pharaoh in the narrative, i.e., Moses faces the Nile; he faces Pharaoh Sobek:

> I have come today from out of the waters of the flood; I am Sobek, green of plume, watchful of face, raised of brow … I have come to my waterways which are in the bank of the flood of the Great Inundation, to the place of contentment, green of fields, which is in the horizon.
>
> Pyr. 507-8[17]

The "Red Nile," the famous bloody Nile of Exodus, comes when the waters rise enough to disturb the soil in the surrounding valley and loosen the oxide sediments. The redness of the waters is attributed to the blood and pus of Osiris. What is key here, however, is that this process is believed, by the ancient Egyptians, to "purify the land: The canals are filled, the waterways are flooded by means of the purification[18] which issued from Osiris (Pyr. 848)."[19] The rise of the Red Nile is in Egypt's midsummer (August), when Osiris is reborn, his "bones" being gathered and reconstituted, so that Isis can become pregnant. By October, the third month (when women often realise they are pregnant), the White Nile symbolises a

---

[16] Terje Oestigaard, "Osiris and the Egyptian Civilisation of Inundation: The Pyramids, the Pharaohs and their Water World," in *A History of Water Vol 5: River and Society. From the Birth of Agriculture to Modern Times,* Terje Tvedt and Richard Coopey, eds. (London: I. B. Tauris, 2017), 72-99, here 86.

[17] Oestigaard, 87.

[18] The Egyptian word *hsmn* ("purification") is also the term for menstruation; it presupposes a positive attitude toward female blood as fecund and sacred, not 'a curse', as in the Hebrew tradition.

[19] Oestigaard, 87.

mother's milk.[20]

In the Egyptian month of Choiak, the fourth month of the Flood (Inundation), i.e., November, the annual Festival Of Osiris takes place. On 26 Choiak, the dismembered body of Osiris is symbolically transformed into the solar Osiris, drawn on his barque in a solemn procession.

Nabonidus is exploiting this festival for his own mission (much like Jesus uses festivals to accentuate his teachings), here in the Nile Delta; another Osiris avatar will be drawn away in a mock-barque, to become the solar aspect of the new chimeric deity at Sinai.

> *I made the Ulāya River flow with ... blood;*
> *I dyed its water red like a red-dyed wool.*
> Ashurbanipal 9 (ii 62-4)[21]

# DARKNESS

The penultimate sign is a "darkness that can be felt" (or a "dense darkness") throughout the entire land of Egypt (Exod 10:22); this is the result of Moses "stretch[ing] out his hand toward the heavens" (10:21). Clearly, this is an astronomical sign (with the obligatory exaggeration of its effects to suggest the Israelites remained unaffected, i.e., the Egyptians could just as easily have lit torches, as the Israelites seem to have done).

From the point of view of celestial divination, the most important synodic moments of the moon's cycle were conjunction, i.e., the day of the first lunar crescent or the first day of the month, and opposition, the day of full moon, ideally on the 14th day. "The lunar section of *Enuma Anu Enlil* is itself divided into two parts focused on these times in the lunar synodic cycle ...."[22]

In Exodus 10, the three-day period of darkness is an allusion to the "disappearance of the moon" just before new moon. Modern astronomical calculations reveal that the new moons of Mesopotamia would have been sighted on the 30th or 31st of the (ending) month (i.e., from our perspective today, but designated the first day of the new month to the ancients),[23] but

---

[20] Oestigaard, 88.

[21] Jamie Novotny and Joshua Jeffers, *The Royal Inscriptions of Ashurbanipal (668-631 BC), Aššur-etel-ilāni (630-627 BC) and Sîn-šarra-iškun (626-612 BC), Kings of Assyria, Part 1.* Royal Inscriptions of the Neo-Assyrian Period, Vol. 5. (Winona Lake: Eisenbrauns, 2018), 196.

[22] Francesca Rochberg, *In the Path of the Moon: Babylonian Celestial Divination and Its Legacy* (Leiden: Brill, 2010), 263.

[23] "The prime importance of the day of the New Moon and the Crescent is also

this is not definitive. Accuracy of such sightings was sometimes limited by atmospheric conditions, and in such cases post-dated predictions were used to register the new moon, and thus the new month. In Exodus, of course, there has supposedly just been a great storm that made conditions perfect for locusts, so atmospheric conditions delaying the sighting of a new moon might actually have occurred (if we accept the storm as historical[24]). It is perfectly possible that a new moon crescent might not be seen by the naked eye for three full days.[25] From another Neo-Assyrian astrological report, there is this description:

> The moon disappeared on the 27th; the 28th and the 29th it stayed inside the sky, and was seen on the 30th; when (else) would it have been seen? It should stay inside the sky less than 4 days, it never stayed 4 days.[26]

The oppression of the darkness adds to the general idea of it being darkest before the light, of the necessary transition through the realms of the netherworld (Egypt) in order to be reborn, etc., which will soon become central to this analysis. I have a thought that the pharaoh's words to Moses in Exod 10:28, and Moses' response in 10:29 might be interpreted astronomically; there is another omen which reads:

> If on the 13th day [the m]oon and sun are seen together: ... there will be steps of the enemy; the enemy will plunder in the land. **If the moon ... is not seen with the sun on the 14th or on the 15th day: there will be deaths; a god (i.e. pestilence) will devour.**[27]

---

shown by Semitic words for 'month': they originally mean 'New Moon'" (Marten Stol, "The Moon as seen by the Babylonians," in *Natural Phenomena: Their Meaning, Depiction and Description in the Ancient Near East*, D. J. W. Meijer, ed. [Amsterdam: Royal Netherlands Academy of Arts and Sciences, 1992], 245-77, here 264, n. 11).

[24] An omen from the *Enuma Anu Enlil* combines a storm, locusts, and a darkened moon (though the latter is already in progress): "If on the 13th day of Arahsamna the watch passes and the moon is dark; his features are dark like sulphur fire; attack of locusts [in(?) the la]nd; Adad will thunder and there will be lightning; ... locusts will attack and devour the harvest of Akkad" (Rochberg, 107-8). Logically, these omens are constructed after an event, to provide warnings if the same conditions recur; the combination in the Exodus warning is thus plausible.

[25] For a detailed analysis of the timings of new moons, invisibility, etc., see S. Stern, "The Babylonian Month and the New Moon: Sighting and Prediction," *JHA* 39.1.134 (2008): 19-42.

[26] Rochberg, 264.

[27] Rochberg, 264.

That is, the Sun (Re), personified by Pharaoh (as Horus), and the Moon (Osiris), represented by Moses (Nabonidus) fail to "see" each other again after Exodus 10 (i.e., opposition is not visible/recorded). Plunder, death, and a devouring god follow. It is not that the Babylonian omen is the direct inspiration for the Exodus account but the elite, educated priests and scribes, the ones writing the HB, would certainly be aware of such omens and portents. A general influence of their inherited Babylonian culture is suggested.

Knowing that Nabonidus is an avid lunar-deity worshipper, and is known for his support of the main triad of deities (Shamash, Sîn, and Ishtar, i.e., Sun, Moon, and Stars), it seems fitting that a sign from the divine "above" is included (and not just earthly wind/hail). In the context of his Mesopotamian cultural heritage (as well as the Egyptian mythologies), an all-encompassing, heavy darkness is equated with two things, i.e., the night, and the underworld. In the context of Egyptian lunar/solar mythology these two notions also become conflated, for it is through the dark hours of night that the Sun-god travels to reach the new dawn, i.e., he passes through the underworld (more on this in due course).[28]

It is under the cover of this darkness that the Israelites "plunder" the Egyptians (Exod 12:36), presumably at the behest of Moses, which is why Exod 11:3 is added by someone who seems to think this was going just a bit too far (but given all the other things Moses does in the narratives, this is by far the least objectionable).

# DEATH

The death of the firstborn is hard to justify on any level; it seems cruel and unnecessarily broad in its application. It didn't happen, of course. This is another case of those clever first authors who want to turn the tables on Nabonidus and use him as his own foil in the narrative.[29]

Once you are aware of the association between the Osirian, solar-lunar myths, as applied to the Exodus signs, the "death of the firstborn" of Egypt seems synonymous with the death of Osiris, firstborn of the gods. It also resonates with the unspeakable concept of the death of Horus, firstborn son of Re/Osiris.

---

[28] This can be likened to the journey of Gilgamesh, who traverses the netherworld but survives, essentially reborn (Mehmet-Ali Ataç, "The 'Underworld Vision' of the Ninevite Intellectual Milieu," *Iraq* 66 (2004): 67-76, here 68).

[29] For an overview of various attempts to explain the problem with Exodus 4 and 11 and the threat by God, see Rabbi David Frankel, "The Death of Pharaoh's Firstborn: A One Plague Exodus," www.thetorah.com.

Osiris' identity is mingled with death from start to finish; everything he represents relies on his death, so threatening to kill Osiris is futile. Threatening to kill Horus, i.e., Pharaoh, his earthly avatar, on the other hand, is tantamount to threatening the entire nation. I submit that the final curse, judgement, plague, whatever you wish to call it, is a direct threat aimed at Nabonidus in light of what happens to Cambyses (see below). Elaborated, as each of the signs are, the imposed death expands to its fullest range, targeting the nation as a whole. Killing Horus draws a frighteningly fine line between *maat* and chaos, between immortality and the dreaded "second death" in the afterlife. It is the son's duty to bury and tend the grave of the deceased father, in order that the latter might fulfil his passage to the afterlife safely and be reborn. Without the son Horus, Osiris cannot be replenished in the underworld. The domino-effect of this is that the entire Egyptian theology is *figuratively* brought down, and the repercussion for Moses (Nabonidus) is that everything he is going to do in the ensuing narrative will be for nought, i.e., rendered null and void.

Thus, the "death of the firstborn" is actually a veiled caveat for anyone supporting Nabonidus, who is investing so much in this foreign religion, which is itself denounced and brought low by the whim of the Israelite god before it has even begun. Just as in the Song, Nabonidus is burdened with the ironic distinction of instigating his own downfall. This subtle allusion to the potential "second death" of Ahmose is a thus stark foreshadowing of Moses' activities and intentions at Sinai. This is why the death of the firstborn "plague" is sufficient on its own.

# "TODAY, IN THE MONTH OF ABIB"

In Exod 13:4, Moses tells the people that they are leaving Egypt "in the month of Abib" but this translation blurs the fact that the word for "month" is *chodesh*, i.e., "new moon," which not only confirms that the "darkness" plague signifies the disappearance of the moon as I claim, it also sets up the calendrical context of the journey from Egypt to Sinai.

"Abib," mentioned in Exod 13:4; 23:15; 34:18, and Deut 16:1, is so often shrugged off as merely an ancient name for Nisan, the Hebrew month (March/April) designated as the first of their calendar year, according to Exod 12:2. However, looking a little deeper, we soon discover that "Abib" is an Arabic term for the Egyptian month of Ipip, the 11th month in the Egyptian calendar, which is actually in June/July.[30]

---

[30] See "The Egyptian - Coptic Calendar," www.ucl.ac.uk; "Egyptian Civil Calendar," Sesh Kemet Egyptian Scribe, https://seshkemet.weebly.com. I perused several

In the sacred hymns to Osiris they invoke "Him that is carried within the arms of the Sun," and on the 30th day of the month (Ipip) they celebrate "the Birthday of the Eyes of Horus," when the Sun and the Moon are come into one straight line, inasmuch as they consider not the Moon alone, but the Sun also as the eye and the light of Horus.

Plutarch, *Osiris* 45 (LII)

In the Sokar chapel at Dendera, the rising sun is depicted on the eastern horizon, the setting moon on the western, illustrating the solar and lunar disks in opposition, which only occurs during a full moon; "This situation may explain the unusual ring-like hieroglyph of the moon, normally reserved for the sun, because it is perhaps a deliberate iconographic device to express the equal status of the full moon with the solar disc."[31] We have just seen allusions to the death/rebirth of Osiris, the resurrection of Re, and the birth of Horus. The disappearance of the moon darkens the heavens for three days (cf. Exod 10:22), then the phases of the waxing moon (Osiris) culminate on the fourteenth/fifteenth day, when Osiris officially "enters the moon" and shines as the bright full moon. This celestial opposition marks the starting point for Nabonidus' mission, which will ultimately end with a celestial conjunction, i.e., of Re and Osiris, at Sinai.

The sun has been dominant in the sky for three months but the summer solstice (ca. June 21) marks "the beginning of the retrograde motion of the Sun-god."[32] This is the prerequisite state of affairs, celestially speaking, for the ensuing symbolic actions performed by Nabonidus at Sinai, as we shall see, particularly as the name "Ipip" is linked etymologically to "Apep," the serpent in the nocturnal underworld through which Re journeys; the hieroglyphs for Ipip read, "the spitter."[33]

I went in search of some astronomical information to see what might have been going on in the skies around the time I suggest these events take place, i.e., after the Persian invasion of Egypt (525 BCE). As with Nabonidus' highly significant 13 Ululu lunar eclipses (which I discuss in *She Brought*),[34] I wondered if another lunar eclipse had occurred anywhere near the time of his alleged confrontation with Pharaoh, that might have influenced his

---

sources and it seems there is yet to be a consensus on the exact dates of the Egyptian months, some differing as much as a couple of weeks either way, so an estimate remains the best we can do.

[31] Gyula Priskin, "The Depictions of the Entire Lunar Cycle in Graeco-Roman Temples," *JEA* 102 (2016): 111-44, here 119.

[32] W. Muss-Arnolt, "The Names of the Assyro-Babylonian Months and Their Regents," (Part 1) *JBL* 11.1 (1892): 72-94, here 85.

[33] Shesh Kemet Egyptian Scribe, "Egyptian Civil Calendar," https://seshkemet.weebly.com/calendar.html.

[34] Tyson, 154-7.

decision when to leave Egypt. I discovered, on NASA's Lunar Eclipse site, that a highly visible, substantial, partial eclipse occurred on July 17, 522 BCE.

According to Brown, Ipip "began June 25th, at about the time of the summer solstice .... Moreover, according to Plutarch and others, the moon was fullest on the 17th of the Egyptian lunar month"; this, he argues, may indicate that Horus' "Birthday ... was at one time a new-moon festival, Plutarch's 'one straight line' then being referable to a conjunction of the sun and moon."[35] However, both Nisan as the Jewish new year, and Josephus' claim that Aries was the constellation visible at the time of the departure from Egypt (*A.J.* 3.10.5) are post-biblical; neither is mentioned in the exodus narratives. All we are given is "Abib." If the month Abib/Ipip is the same as their familiar Babylonian Nisan, why do the Israelites need to be *told* this particular day/month is now going to be the start of *their* year?[36]

The answer lies in how the respective new years are defined. For the Babylonians, and subsequently the Jews, the first sighting of the first new moon crescent after the vernal equinox dictates the start of the year (in Nisan, or March/April). The ancient Egyptian new year, on the other hand, is heralded by

> the cosmic rising of Sirius on July 7th. On this day, Sirius rises together with the Sun and it is still invisible. It is not until July 19th that Sirius rises early enough to become observable at dawn: this epoch is called its heliacal rising.[37]

---

[35] Lawrence Parmly Brown, "The Cosmic Eyes," *The Open Court* (n.d.): 685-701, here 609. https://opensiuc.lib.siu.edu.

[36] Emmeline Plunkett (*Calendars and Constellations of the Ancient World* [London: Senate, 1997, 1903] proposes that the fourteenth night of Abib, far from being a fixed date in the calendar and having to do with "waving the corn before the Lord," is actually an ancient reference to the first sighting of Abib, an Arabic-influenced name for Spica, the star depicted as the ear of corn in the "Virgin's" hand (i.e., the constellation Virgo). On this basis, Plunkett suggests an Arabian context for Moses' "forty years" and a much later date for the book of Exodus (170). However, this does imply that Plunkett is also swayed by the traditional Aries/Spring argument of the later Jewish tradition, rather than what is preserved in the text. An astronomy website states: "This association with harvests may arise because the Sun moves into Virgo in the fall. The association with spring is interesting as well, as Virgo first becomes visible in the evenings right around the spring equinox" (Daniel Johnson, "Meet Spica, the Ear of Grain," Sky & Telescope [May 6, 2019], https://skyandtelescope.org). We can't have it both ways; either the corn motif means harvest, then a time later in the year, or we focus on the heliacal rising of the constellation, which emphasises the equinox. Also, another astronomy site (based in Jordan) suggests Virgo is best seen in June ("Virgo Constellation," Arabian Nights, https://arabiannightsrum.com).

[37] Rita Gautschy, "The Star Sirius in Ancient Egypt and Babylonia," § "Sirius and its phenomena in the course of the year," www.gautschy.ch.

The first sighting of Sirius is more complex than the sighting of the first lunar crescent, as it depends on various cosmological and geographical factors, so there is no hard and fast definition for this new year; in fact, there are records of sightings as early as Pharmuthi 23 (IV Peret) and as late as Ipip 9 and 28 (III Shemu).[38] Pharmuthi equates to the Hebrew month Nisan, the month of the rising of Aries. I suggest that without the HB's specific mention of "Abib" (Ipip), there would be no reason to question the tradition of the exodus beginning in March/April. But we *do* have this "Abib" to deal with and it does point to a very Egyptian perception of the new year.

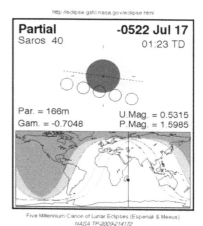

*Figure 7: Lunar eclipse 03574 for Ipip, 522 BCE (Image: Eclipse Predictions by Fred Espenak, NASA/GSFC Emeritus)*

This is why subsequent generations shift the new year to fit the Nisan dating and obscure the meaning of "Abib" (without deleting anything), i.e., they are not lying, just bending the truth a bit (which means they must have access to astronomical or calendrical information for Egypt, to know that this much range in the rising of Sirius is even possible).[39]

What makes lunar eclipse 03574 even more exciting is that it occurs in the very month Cambyses is killed in Syria (i.e., July 522).[40] This adds verisimilitude to the idea that it is Cambyses who is the pharaoh of the hardened heart in Exodus, whether the two men actually meet or not (Cambyses, as Horus, is killed on his journey home from Egypt to Persia). It is just the sort of thing an early scribe might, with hindsight, incorporate into the narrative. So the death of the firstborn seen as a reference to the death of Horus/Pharaoh makes even more sense, in hindsight; the heavens apparently predicted it.

## Ten Months in Egypt?

Whether Nabonidus and his group hang around for the full four months of the flood is impossible to say, but they don't leave until Ipip, meaning they

---

[38] Gautschy, § "Comparison with ancient observations." An example for a new year in each of the three months is provided.

[39] For more on Abib see my paper "Scorpion Rising: Nabonidus and the Ascent of Akrabbim," 8-9, www.academia.edu.

[40] "It is clear from the Bīsotūn inscription and Babylonian legal documents that Cambyses died after 1 July 522 B.C." (*EIr*, "Cambyses," https://www. iranicaonline.org).

do stay in Egypt for a lengthy period. If they symbolically, or in reality, arrive before the Nile becomes red, which seems to make sense, given Moses' action, and we use Moses' epithet of "Thoth" as a clue, we can suggest that the "ten" plagues correspond to ten months in Egypt, with the arrival in the first month of the Inundation, in the month Thoth, and departure in Ipip, giving us ten months. Thus, the "ten" plagues may simply be a means of preserving this timeframe (if original to the narrative).

# AUSPICIOUS DAYS

The Babylonian month of June/July is Araḥ Dumuzu, equivalent to the Hebrew month Tammuz; in Jewish tradition *this* is the month that is said to be when Moses reaches Sinai. The people, having come from Babylonia, would be fully aware of the significance of the timing but to them, this would be attributable to the worship of Tammuz, Ishtar's consort, whose imminent demise and retreat to the underworld are the focus of this month's observances. The yearly event is preserved in Ezek 8:14 where women publically mourn for the dying Tammuz, i.e., the dying of the vegetation under the harsh rays of the summer sun but also the dying of the Sun itself in winter.[41]

This fourth month is ruled by the god Adar, who, apart from being hunter/warrior, is also a judge, known as "the decider," "destroyer of the faithless," and "king of heaven and earth"; Adar is a solar deity.[42] Perhaps more germane, Adar, due to his identification with the sun, is also recognised as Nusku, the protective fire-god whom Nabonidus sees as being the source of his kingly attributes:

> … the god Nusku, the martial one, decorated him with the brilliance
> of kingship, became his *šēdu* in order to give orders, hold counsel,
> and investigate matters, (and) sent the great gods to his aid so that (he)
> could exercise his leadership.
>
> Nab 19 i 12-18

Nusku's sacred number is 10,[43] which *may* be an alternative inspiration for the ten commandments (but see below).

Just for synchronicity, the zodiacal sign for this fourth month is

---

[41] Muss-Arnolt, 1, 85.
[42] Muss-Arnolt, 1, 85.
[43] Muss-Arnolt, 1, 86.

*nangar(u)*, an Assyrian word meaning "workman."[44] This is relevant later, so I will mention it again at the appropriate juncture.

Moses, I claim however, stands at the "bloody" Nile at the time of the Festival of Osiris, in November (Choiak), and the group leaves Egypt in June/July (Ipip), which, by the way, is also the month of the official "birthdays" of both Osiris and Horus.[45] Maintaining the Egyptian dating (as the narrative refers back to "Abib"), the group arrives at Sinai on the third "new moon" after their departure (Exod 19:1), i.e., the month of Phaophi (September/October). The Sept/Oct month in the Hebrew reckoning is the month of Tishrei. This really *is* interesting!

Tishrei, is called the "month of the pure, brilliant Lord," "the month of the sacred mound/dwelling," i.e. "the mountain, or place, of the fates."[46] This must already be seeming quite apt, not only with the reference to a sacred mound but also to the home of the "fates" (taking into consideration what I have suggested concerning Nabonidus' symbolic sin and why he was sent out of Babylon, i.e., the metaphorical stealing of the Tablet of Destinies).[47] The deity presiding over Tishrei is none other than Shamash, the Babylonian Sun-god, otherwise referred to as "the light-bearer," or "Lord of the universe"; he is the "protector of laws (and) avenger of justice."[48]

Tishrei, or rather the Babylonian Tashritu, is special for Nabonidus. It seems to him to be an auspicious month for major plans. In Nab 28 (ii 60-5), he tells of securing the foundations of Shamash's temple Ebbabar (in Sippar) in the month of Tashritu. Far more significantly, however, two of the most iconic moments in Nabonidus' history (to date) occur in this month: In Nab 17 (i 1-11) and Nab 47 (ii 3-11), it is recorded that he chooses to leave Tayma for Babylon on 17 Tashritu after first consulting the omens, etc.; and from Nab Chr (iii 12-16) we learn that the confrontation (or deal?) with Cyrus at Opis takes place in Tashritu, followed by the fall of Babylon and the arrest of its king a couple of days later. One must ask whether such momentous events coincidentally landed in the same propitious month, or if Nabonidus planned things thus. I think the latter, especially as we now see him orchestrating the arrival at Sinai in the very same month (which would have necessitated a stopover at Tayma in the interim, as the journey itself would not have taken much more than two weeks, three at most, but there is a span of three months between the full moon of "Abib" and the "third new moon" of their arrival at Sinai).

---

[44] Muss-Arnolt, 1, 87.

[45] For the birthdays of the five major gods see Anthony Spalinger, "Some Remarks on the Epagomenal Days in Ancient Egypt," *JNES* 54.1 (1995): 33-47.

[46] Muss-Arnolt, 2, 161.

[47] Tyson, 5-6.

[48] Muss-Arnolt, 2, 161.

I suggest the "third day" of 19:15 is the first day of a visible moon crescent (echoing the three days of darkness in Exod 10:22):

> The Moon is in turn a symbol of death and resurrection, the eternal recurrence. The Moon remains the high symbol of the dead and resurrecting god ... three days in the tomb, just as the Moon is three days dark.[49]

The new moon, of course, is when Osiris is resurrected:

> Raise thyself up, Osiris ... Thou purifiest thyself on the first of the month, thou dawnest on the day of the new moon ....
> PT Utterance 483 (1012a; 1012c)[50]

"Abib" therefore leaves in its wake an embarrassing truth, yet it is not stricken from the record, just left to fall into obscurity. I suggest it later becomes incorporated into the festival of Rosh Hashanah, held on 1 and 2 Tishrei, marking the beginning of the *civil* year; in this respect it is also known as the "Month of Beginning."[51] Perhaps it was intentionally displaced from its once strongly religious (and thus ecclesiastical) origins; in Ezek 40:1 the author refers to "the twenty-fifth year of our exile, at *the beginning of the year*," using *rosh* ("head") and *shanah* ("year"), but this predates the festival. Like many references to Nabonidus' influence on the early Jewish religion, the HB authors seem to think that what God must know as fact cannot be obliterated ... but that doesn't stop them obscuring what they don't wish to acknowledge openly.

# JUDGEMENT OF ~~OSIRIS~~ NABONIDUS

The tale of Set and Osiris, two brothers at odds, includes a very formal, legal trial in which the two are pitted against eachother in a court of law, or rather, a court of "Truth."

Set, having murdered Osiris, is jealous of his brother's popularity even after death; Set attempts to convince the gods that Osiris should not be allowed to enter their heavenly realm (and thus become a god). The first ploy is to destroy Osiris' body, which would make it impossible for him to be reborn, of

---

[49] Joseph Campbell, *Myths of Light: Eastern Metaphors of the Eternal* (Novato: New World Library, 2003), 16.

[50] Samuel A. B. Mercer, trans., *The Pyramid Texts* (1952) §22 "A Miscellaneous Group, Utterances 453-486," https://sacred-texts.com.

[51] Muss-Arnolt, 2, 163.

course. When Thoth discovers the lengths Set will go to, he decides the matter must be put to the vote and a formal hearing is declared; this is held on the night of the death of Osiris, in a great Hall of the Aged God (i.e., Re) at Heliopolis (On, in the HB, i.e., where Joseph's wife comes from).[52]

The outcome of the trial is that Set is declared a liar, and Osiris (representing himself) speaks the Truth. This is where the idea of "True of Voice" comes from, i.e., *maa(t) kheru*. His words are judged to be true, so Osiris wins the case and is admitted into the heavens to become a divine king and the eternal judge of the dead. All Egyptians thenceforth pray to be judged as "True of Voice" on their own day of judgement, by appealing to Osiris. In the Song, there is an episode where this *maa(t) kheru* comes into play, i.e., in Song 5:10-16, Nitocris makes a poppet/idol of the king for magical purposes and one of the last things she refers to is his "speech" that is "sweet." In the context of the Song's verses here, this does seem to be an intentional allusion to death and the (Osirian) afterlife.[53]

The scribes who tell the tale of Moses at the Nile are erudite, well-versed in all manner of ancient wisdom, magic, mythology, etc. The Osirian myths are potentially the most common and widespread, even beyond Egypt itself, so there is every chance connections are made between what Nabonidus is doing (i.e., in terms of his fascination with Egyptian religion) and the above legend. It is an example of a fundamental challenge, a setting right of things, under the judgement of a god. For Hebrew audiences, this has to be translated into something more familiar, and in the 6th Century BCE (when I claim the story of the exodus took place and was written about), this means a Babylonian frame of reference.

The authors have lived in Babylonia all their lives and despite being self-segregated, *have* been influenced by the culture. They have their own oral legends, handed down from those originally made captives, and some written accounts, perhaps from the so-called "Prophets" (who, in my opinion, are simply astute observers of bureaucracy and can write in such a manner as to suggest precognition, but in fact, write after the event, just as "omens" are recorded). The rather convenient and highly suspect finding of the "the book" amongst the rubble of old Jerusalem (2 Kgs 22:3-20; 2 Chr 34:8-28) seems to support this claim. The books of Genesis, Exodus, Numbers, Joshua, etc., are the post-Tayma accounts of Nabonidus through the eyes of different witnesses (or recipients of tales, like Herodotus).

Nabonidus' part in the history of Israel is so indelible, yet so undesirable to *most* early Jews, many clever scribal techniques and much

---

[52] E. A. Wallace Budge, *Osiris and the Egyptian Resurrection*, Vol. 1 (London: Warner, 1911), 89-91.
[53] Tyson, 141-2.

imagination are invested to create a legitimate "history" of this reborn nation. It must be truthful, as God is watching. It must chronicle the facts, as this is the legacy for future generations. Nabonidus has both supporters (e.g., the authors of Genesis and Deuteronomy) and dissenters (the authors of Exodus and Numbers), so it must appear to be balanced. By appreciating both positive and negative perspectives of the same (or linked) events, one can come to an acceptable compromise that evens out the biases and preserves the facts.

Each dramatic episode, in Exodus especially, carries a heavy responsibility; it must show the Israelites as overcoming all the odds to reach the Promised Land, because God wills it but at the same time, it must denounce Nabonidus, the man whose name is anathema but whose dynamism and unique drive gets them out of Babylon and (eventually) "home." They have a choice, i.e., they can either invent a history, which would be untruthful and thus not condoned by their God, or they take what *really* happened and give it a spin, as in this case. If Nabonidus can do it, why can't they?

> The decisions at its place of reaching the great judgment
> -- the river of the ordeal –
> let the just live and consign to darkness the hearts that are evil.
> ETCSL 4.80.1, 48-56 (Temple Hymn)

In Exod 7:4 God declares he will deliver the Israelites out of Egypt by "great acts of judgement."[54] The judgement may pertain to Egypt's ruler but primarily, it is a judgement of Nabonidus, within the context of his Osirian fascination but also of his Babylonian heritage; it is one of many such judgements throughout the exodus narratives. Egypt "is" Babylon (especially post-525 BCE), as Tayma "is" Jerusalem in the Song,[55] and such a castigation must be understood by a Hebrew audience, not an Egyptian one, so while the Osirian allusions *are* at the root of the situation, the overall gist of the episode is one of a formal, even *legal*, rejection of Nabonidus' theological plans in terms the Jews from Babylon can comprehend.

From Mesopotamia, right up to the Neo-Babylonian era, there was a *legal process* by which the guilt or innocence of an accused or an accuser could be judged; it was an ordeal by water.[56] Held at a specific river, e.g., in

---

[54] Cf. Exod 12:12: "On all the gods of Egypt I will execute judgements," which is probably the inspiration for commentaries that attempt to identify each plague with a specific deity.

[55] Just as Rome is depicted as Babylon in, e.g., 2 Esdras 3, Revelations 14.

[56] The following description of the ordeal thanks to Wilfred H. van Soldt, "Ordeal A. In Mesopotamia," in *Reallexikon der Assyriologie*, Erich Ebeling and Ernst F. Weidner,

Nebuchadnezzar's day, the Ordeal by Water took place on the banks of the Euphrates just north of Sippar, often with an "ordeal-priest" present, the process could take many forms, depending on the case but the party escaping unscathed would be proven innocent. It could be initiated by an individual or a group, so long as they were subjects of the same ruler. Although the river-god (commonly called "Id" or Idlurugu "divine river"; in some cases, *mu*, "water," as mentioned above, concerning the potential etymology of "Moses") was deemed the head judge for the event, the ultimate judgement came from the Apsu/Abzu (the marsh/swap), i.e., from Enki/Ea, the primary river/water deity. The king was almost always present, as was Marduk (in statue form), in the Neo-Babylonian period.

Accusations judged by this Ordeal were mostly of adultery, sorcery, treason, and sacrilege. If one party refused the Ordeal, they automatically lost, unless an agreement was made between the parties. There was always a warning period before the Ordeal, i.e., a sort of cooling off time when the entire argument could be resolved between the parties before things turned ugly.

This Ordeal sounds like what might be happening here in Exodus, i.e., Moses and Aaron are challenging Pharaoh on the "riverbank" (Exod 7:15); a warning has already been given in the form of the snake eating the snakes; an ordeal is presented involving the waters of the Nile; only the Egyptians are affected, suggesting the Israelites are the innocent party.

What is the accusation in this particular Ordeal of Water? Well, superficially, it is the pharaoh's refusal to let the Israelites go into the wilderness to make sacrifices to their god but this in itself is not a legal issue, in context. When we consider the most pertinent and prolific themes elsewhere in the postexilic texts, we find adultery and sacrilege at the top of the list, with a healthy smattering of sorcery for good measure. When you begin to see the exodus story as a record of the earliest Jews denouncing the Babylonian "whore" and their entire experience in spiritual captivity there, how they represent their attack on their oppressors becomes clearer and clearer. That is, they see their suppression as an imposed state of adultery (not originally of their choosing but some, of course, give in and become Babylonians by nature, if not by name). Thus, the deities thrust upon them and their own sense of having fallen out of favour with *their* god find voice throughout the HB, especially in the Prophets, as a *mea culpa*, a pleading for forgiveness for having been adulterous and having been led by evil forces into sacrilegious behaviour—worshipping other deities.

Now, the Ordeal by Water in Mesopotamia nearly always took place where there was a temple by a river; the most prolific of these proved to be

---

eds., (Berlin: 2019), 124-9. Other textual evidence of the Ordeal to be found in Joanna Töyräänvuori, "Trial by Water through the Ages," *SAA* 27.2 (2021): 301-30.

temples dedicated to Ningal, i.e., Ishtar's mother. This proves insightful, as in my book on the Song of Solomon, I discuss the Jewish perception of Ishtar, the "whore of Babylon," especially in connection with her *blood*.[57] A highly sexual and violent goddess, Ishtar was renowned for enjoying blood and she is depicted in a variety of myths as bathing in it, drinking it, and lusting after it; there is, however, another side to consider. This antipathy toward her and all she represents is transferred from Babylonian females (who worship and embody her) to Jewish females, in the guise of *niddah*, the rabbinic laws pertaining to menstruation. This is a dominant theme in the Song of Solomon, where the drinking of menstrual blood (and semen) in an ancient esoteric ritual now referred to as imbibing the Elixir Rubeus is at the forefront.[58]

According to Lev 15:28, a menstruating woman is considered "unclean" or *niddah*, for a *full seven days*; on the eighth day she must cleanse herself or she can touch no one and no *thing*, lest others who touch objects she has touched become *niddah*, too (of course, the rabbinic laws transform this rudimentary prohibition into one of the most complex and sometimes baffling institutions in early Judaism). Exod 7:25 makes it perfectly clear that the Nile remains in its bloody form for seven days *before* the next sign is given to Pharaoh. It never says that the Nile turns back to its fresh flow again, just that the Egyptians have to dig for drinking water. The insinuation, then, is that the Nile itself, the life of Egypt, the symbol of everything sacred to the Egyptians, is unclean, is *niddah*. It is not cleansed on the eighth day (i.e., the Egyptian priests clearly have the power to reverse the condition of the water but they just repeat the action/curse/plague), so it remains unclean indefinitely, unless Pharaoh acquiesces and allows the Israelites to leave.[59]

Even the wooden and stone vessels are *niddah* (to the Israelites), for they are tainted with the blood also, meaning that even though the Egyptians can find fresh water underground, if they try to carry it home, it becomes just as tainted as if it came straight from the river. It could be said this is a precursor to the blood on the door posts, for it serves as a line in the sand, a defined segregation of Jew from Egyptian, of foreign gods from Israelite (Jewish).

The river of blood must, I submit, be an allusion to Nabonidus' fascination with and addiction to menstruating women and/or the postexilic Jewish obsession with *niddah* rules. It is the only context (I can think of) in which such a scene can retain its original power for a wholly Jewish audience.

As stated above, the Mesopotamian Ordeal of Water procedure most

---

[57] Tyson, 30-40. Examples run throughout the book.

[58] Tyson, 31-4.

[59] To a Babylonian, there was no defined sabbath day (and here in Exodus there is no reason to interpret the "seven days" as an allusion to such, as the seventh day is not mentioned) but the foundations of the Jewish/Christian sabbath do stem from the mythology of Ishtar and the pattern of her menstruation! Tyson, 38-9.

often took place where there was a temple to Ningal, Ishtar's mother. This is also identified with the river where Ishtar would bathe annually (in the month of Ululu), to cleanse herself and reaffirm her "virginity."[60] So, by making the Nile turn to a flow of blood, it not only makes it and everything it touches *niddah*, i.e., by making it, in effect, a menstruating woman, it creates a strong allusion to the most hated of all menstruating women, Ishtar. She is, in essence, the very first target of the Jews' attack. She is the Most Wanted, the top of their hit list, so to speak.

The Egyptian priests repeat the sign themselves, which seems a little odd, even in this miraculous context. Why would they simply repeat the process, supposedly putting their own people under duress for a second time? Why not just negate Aaron's sign by returning the Nile to normal? The fact that this reversion is not forthcoming suggests the Jewish author is intentionally tarring the Egyptian priests with the same brush he uses to castigate Nabonidus/Babylon.[61]

The anti-Nabonidus authors insinuate that no matter what lofty ideas he may have, anything he adopts from Egypt will be tainted, will be *niddah*, and thus profane, not sacred. The "purification" of Osiris' blood is necessarily deemed a fallacy, and is therefore parodied by Moses' action. The seeds for an ultimate rejection of Nabonidus' partly Egyptian "I AM" are sown from the very start of his campaign.

Osiris is judged to be True of Voice and is made King and a god in the heavens; Nabonidus would very much like this to be his fate, perhaps. It may very well be from this Osirian influence on his actions and his new deity that rumours arise (i.e., begun by those who do not grasp his arcane intentions) of Nabonidus attempting to make himself a "god" (more on this later). For instance, if Nitocris had provided him with a copy of the Book of the Dead, he would have known that the deceased would recite such words as:

> I am Osiris, the first-born of the divine womb, the first-born of the gods, I am Horus, the first-born of Ra of the risings.

> ... I have become a divine being, I have come, and I have avenged mine own body. I have taken up my seat by the divine birth-chamber of Osiris, ... I have become mighty, ... I am brought forth with him, I

---

[60] Tyson, 39. This anticipates the Jewish practice of *tevila*, or immersion in a *mikvah* (ritual cleansing river/pool).

[61] Paul John Frandsen ("The Menstrual 'Taboo' in Ancient Egypt," *JNES* 66.2 (2007): 81-106, here 99-100) suggests there was no overriding menstruation taboo in ancient Egypt; if anything, such women were apparently *protected* from metaphysical/ spiritual harm during menses.

renew my youth ....[62]

To a Jewish mind of the time this apparent hubris would be the opposite of being "True of Voice," just as it is presented in Song 5. It becomes a parody of virtue that simply results in the perception of Nabonidus—as Solomon in the Song and here, as Moses—as a heathen (infidel) with delusions of grandeur.

Two little asides might be worth mentioning for future investigations:

1. In the myth, once Set is denounced, he is thrown to the ground and, as Budge puts it, "Thoth led [Osiris] to the place where Set was lying, and made Osiris to take his seat upon him as a sign of his triumph and of the victory of righteousness over evil."[63]

Cf. Jer 43:8-13 and the "clay pavement" at Pharaoh's palace in Tahpanhes, upon which the Babylonian King Nebuchadnezzar is said to sit on his throne over the stones as a sign of victory.

2. Osiris becomes the eternal Judge (of the dead), the Lord of Maat. It is said that the deeds of every person are known to him, that he carefully weighs the evidence and then makes his judgement. Everything is written in books by scribes, and the entire process is treated as if it were a court of law.[64]

Cf. Moses setting himself up as the sole judge (Exodus 18). Jethro apparently feels compelled to intervene so that others might shoulder some of the responsibility (i.e., he can see where this is going and makes sure others have a degree of authority).

---

[62] "Coming Forth by Day" (Papyrus of Mes-em-neter), https://en. wikisource.org.

[63] Budge, *Osiris*, 311.

[64] Budge, *Osiris*, 308-9.

# 6

## CROSSING THE "SEA"

T he escape from Ur at the very start of Nabonidus' new mission should really belong to the tale of Abraham, for it is he who is said to leave Ur (abruptly and without explanation). The experience of this probably made quite an impression on those who were with him, some of whom would continue by his side on his extended journeys to and fro, down to Arabia, and then back into Egypt, etc. I personally think that the second marshland escape, from Egypt, was far less dramatic and impressive, and some of the adventurous tone and details are transferred *to* the Exodus narrative for effect. That is why we get the Ur departure in Moses' depiction, i.e., the Abraham followers do not wish to represent their forefather as being forced from his homeland, or as being a criminal or troublemaker. Exodus is basically anti-Nabonidus, so the memories are better suited to this version of events.

## WILDERNESS OF SHUR

In Exod 13:17, it is written that God leads the Israelites away from the "land of the Philistines" because he fears they will "change their minds" if they have to face "war." Verse 18, however, states that the Israelites are "*prepared* for battle," so why this strange interjection about the route taken?

It has been proposed that the Israelites are attempting to avoid military installations where their identities and purposes of travel can checked by guards at imposing forts on the border of the Nile Delta region.[1] This would imply they are doing something illegal, i.e., stealing the gold and silver, or maybe something much more valuable?

The noun *shur* means a "wall" (Gen 49:22, Job 24:11) and various ideas have been put forward to explain what and where this wall might be found. *McClintock and Strong Biblical Cyclopedia*, for instance, supports the theory that Shur represents a mountain range:

> This can be no other than the high range to the east of Suez, the continuation of the great chain of Jebel et-Tih northward towards the Mediterranean, forming a sharp ridge or a high wall as seen from a distance east and west, and a grand barrier on the east side of Egypt and to the west of the great plain in the interior of the wilderness called Desert et-Tih.[2]

In Gen 25:18, of course, we get the clarification that "Shur" is where Ishmael is laid to rest; it lies "opposite Egypt in the direction of Assyria." This is Arabia, including the Sinai Peninsula, but also Northwestern Arabia.

Trumbull argues for "Shur," i.e., the "Great Wall," being the ancient remains of a defensive wall to the east of Egypt, built centuries before Nabonidus' day, laying between Pelusium and the Gulf of Suez.[3] He suggests the earliest mention of this Wall comes from Dynasty 12, before the Hyksos invasion, in which a traveller encounters the Wall that had been erected to keep out unwelcome peoples from the east.[4] The Wall is also mentioned in Dynasty 19, in one of the Anastasi Papyri.

Named "Abnu" in Egyptian, i.e., meaning "wall, fence, barrier," the Greeks called it "Gerrhon" (rather similar to "Gershon") and the Hebrews, "Shur." In the 13-14th Century CE an Arabian historian/geographer,

---

[1] James K. Hoffmeier, *Ancient Israel in Sinai: The Evidence for the Authenticity of the Wilderness Tradition* (Oxford: Oxford University Press, 2005), 68-9.

[2] *McClintock and Strong Biblical Cyclopedia*, "Shur," www.biblical cyclopedia.com.

[3] Henry Clay Trumbull, *Kadesh-Barnea* (Philadelphia: Wattles, 1895), 44-58. The information in these "Wall"-related paragraphs is thanks to Trumbull, unless otherwise cited. The ancient port is known as "Clysma" but I will refer to it as Suez.

[4] The Dynasty 12 *Prophecy of Neferti* indicates that "Ameny" (or Amenemhet I) will "build the 'Walls of the Ruler' … to prevent the Asiatics from going down to Egypt" (James K. Hoffmeier, Thomas W. Davis, and Rexine Hummel, "New Archaeological Evidence for Ancient Bedouin (Shasu) on Egypt's Eastern Frontier at Tell el-Borg," *ÄL* 26 (2016): 285-311, here 286.

Abufeda, mentioned the Wall as being on the "Arabian side" (of Egypt) and called it "Sura." (Trumbull suggests the Wall is not to be mistaken for the string of fortresses in the region erected by Ahmose I.)

The Egyptian root *m-z-r* means "enclosure, fortress, boundary," so the Egyptian side of the Wall was referred to as "the Land of Mazor," or Mizraim (as in Hebrew).[5] The land beyond the Wall was known as the Wilderness of Shur, taking its name from the Wall itself. (There is no determined extent of this "Wilderness," so it might just be similar to "beyond here be dragons.") An inscription at Karnak, so Trumbull states, calls the ancient Wall "The Border-Barrier of Mazor."

Diodorus states that the pharaoh "Sesoösis," i.e., Ramesses II,

> made the country secure and difficult of access against attacks by enemies …. He also fortified with a wall the side of Egypt which faces east, as a defence against inroads from Syria and Arabia; the wall extended through the desert from Pelusium to Heliopolis, and its length was some fifteen hundred stades.[6]

Although the Wall was actually begun by Seti I, Ramesses would have taken the credit upon its completion, as was the norm. The fact that Ptolemy II (284-246 BCE) claims responsibility for building the eastern defensive wall on the Pithom Stele demonstrates this point.[7] There is no knowing if the wall remains a substantial obstacle in Nabonidus' day (6th Century BCE), or just an ancient, derelict landmark (as the old Amorite Wall in Mesopotamia), but I do have a suspicion that the latter is the case (which would explain why Ptolemy sees the need to repair/rebuild it). I also suggest that there is a subtle allusion to this Wall, or segments of it that might have remained visible, in Exod 14:22 and the 'walls to the left and the right' (as they passed through a gap in the waterlogged structure, perhaps).

A direct route for the Wall from Pelusium (or just east of the city) down to Heliopolis, Trumbull claims, would not have protected Darius' Red Sea canal which (he suggests) was probably originally cut at about the same time, i.e., in Dynasty 5. The earliest evidence for this canal is from four stelae deposited by

---

[5] *Mazor* is singular and refers to Lower Egypt, while *Mizraim* is plural and signifies Upper and Lower Egypt (Trumbull, *Kadesh-Barnea*, 56-7).

[6] Diodorus Siculus, *Library of History* 1.§57, https://penelope.uchicago.edu /Thayer/E/Roman/Texts/Diodorus_Siculus/1C*.html. Ramesses II is called by the Greeks Sesostris (cf. Herodotus, *Hist.* 2.102).

[7] Mustafa Nourel-Din, "The Great Eastern Canal in Egypt," *ÄL* 32 (2022): 199-230, here 203.

Darius (ca. 515 BCE);[8] Herodotus (*Hist.* 2.158) suggests the structure was first conceived of and begun by Necho II (ca. 600 BCE). Of course, Necho might well have been inspired by ruins of an older canal, as Lloyd suggests.[9]

Trumbull offers an alternative route, suggesting the Wall must have run from Pelusium to the Gulf of Suez, *then* onward to Heliopolis (and claims the distance of "fifteen hundred stades" could accommodate this). According to Abulfeda, evidence for this ancient Wall ("Sura,"), in the form of sporadic ruins along a defined path, reached as far as Syene, Ethiopia.

On the other hand, Trumbull does suggest that other scholars support Diodorus' description of a direct route from Pelusium to Heliopolis. So, how does this affect Moses? If you look at *Fig. 8* and *Fig. 9*, Trumbull's longer, funnel-shaped Wall would, indeed, secure *anything* within that triangle but if the canal is not up and running until at least 515 BCE, either the Wall is not as old as Trumbull thinks it is, and it was built in order to protect the canal, or it was an ancient wall built just as Diodorus suggests, close to the Nile. As the land here is predominantly marshes, and seems not to be the preferred route into Tahpanhes (the usual route was from Pelusium, or along the river from the west), there would seem to be little point protecting such a 'wilderness' before the canal.[10]

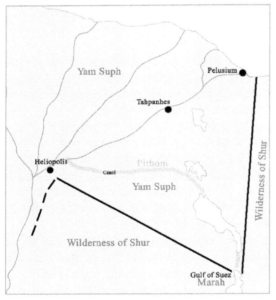

*Figure 8: The Wall of eastern Egypt, as defined by Trumbull (Kadesh-Barnea, 50-2) (Image: Author's construct)*

Diodirus' Wall, set closer to the Nile (perhaps ten to twenty miles from the river?) is my preferred option due to its simplicity, to its relative nearness to the inhabited regions of the Delta, and because of how Exod 15:22 is worded. The group 1) sets out from *Yam Suph*, 2) they go into the Wilderness of Shur, and 3)

---

[8] Nourel-Din, 202-7.

[9] Alan B. Lloyd, "Necho and the Red Sea: Some Considerations," *JEA* 63 (1977): 142-55, here 143.

[10] *Fig. 6* shows Nabonidus' route from Suez to Tahpanhes; he could easily have used the same route the canal *would* take (probably already excavated) as far as Pithom, then northward to Tahpanhes.

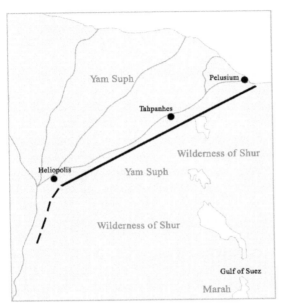

*Figure 9: The Wall as Diodorus defines it (Image: Author's construct)*

they travel for three days before reaching Marah, the waters of which they cannot drink.

A recent study of the potential for "wind setdown" on Lake Tanis (in an effort to provide evidence that the crossing of the Red Sea might have been possible due to this phenomenon)[11] reveals that the topography of the isthmus of Suez is riddled with shallow, ancient lake beds, estuaries, and mud flats, most of which are under water much of the time (the test was modelled on a springtime, low flow of the Nile, but as I have demonstrated, the group leaves in the late summer, during or just after the inundation, which means levels would be higher and probably *inaccessible* to horses and chariots). The same Karnak inscription mentioned above, also describes the Pelusiac branch of the Nile, where Heroopolis and Tahpanhes are situated, as being infested with crocodiles and full of reeds.[12]

It can be no surprise, I think, that infiltrators had found this a dangerous but well-frequented entry point into Egypt, and no wonder anyone pursuing them would either be over-whelmed by the terrain or would simply give up (just like at Ur). Once any pursuers reached the Wall boundary, it would be deemed inefficient or simply not worth the risks to chase miscreants any farther; they would be out of Egyptian territory and in the land (Wilderness) of "Shur."

Strabo (17.1; cf. Herodotus, *Hist.* 2.97), describing the Nile Delta, writes: ... at the time of the rising of the Nile, the whole country is covered,

---

[11] Carl Drews and Weiqing Han, "Dynamics of Wind Setdown at Suez and the Eastern Nile," PLoS ONE 5(8): e12481. doi:10.1371/journal.pone.0012481.

[12] Tell Heboua, just down river from Daphnae (Tahpanhes) is today described likewise, i.e., as having "crocodile infested marshland/lagoons" (Gregory Mumford, "The Sinai Peninsula and its Environs: Our Changing Perceptions of a Pivotal Land Bridge Between Egypt, the Levant, and Arabia," *JAEI* 7.1 (2015): 1-24, here 9).

and resembles a sea, except the inhabited spots, which are situated upon natural hills or mounds ; and considerable cities and villages appear like islands in the distant prospect.

He continues by claiming the ancient Egyptians saw "Egypt" as "that country only which was inhabited and watered by the Nile .... But later writers, to the present time, have included on the eastern side almost all the tract between the Arabian Gulf and the Nile." This supports the theory of an ancient wall that hugs the eastern parameters of the Nile, rather than extending all the way out to the Red Sea.

I suggest, therefore, that *Yam Suph*, an inhospitable, endless sea of reeds is the Nile Delta itself. In Isa 18:2 and 19:5, the Nile is *called* the "sea" (*yam*); Trumbull claims that "it is so known among the Arabs at the present time" and states that the Egyptian word for "sea," *im*, is also used to refer to the Nile.[13]

Beyond the Wall is the Wilderness of Shur, i.e., the land of the Bedouin, the marauders, the strangers.

If Trumbull's configuration is correct, *Yam Suph* would cover everything from Tahpanhes to the Gulf, which means there is no Wilderness of Shur between it and the Red Sea, unless a detour is made to one of the arms of the Wall, which seems pointless. Exod 15:22 states that it takes the group three days to reach "Marah"; the brackish swampland from Tahpanhes to Suez (technically still *yam*, especially during flood season) covers a distance of about 140 kilometres which can be accomplished in that time, in rowboats.

"Marah," I claim, is the Red Sea.

If you take Diodorus' configuration, *Yam Suph* ends at the Wall, then there is a wide expanse of nothingness, *midbar*, or wilderness. The group enter the official Wilderness of Shur beyond the Wall and take three days to travel to Marah, i.e., Suez, where they encounter the "bitter" salt-water of the Gulf.[14] There are no time specifications for the journey on the Red Sea itself, but the distance (about 600 km; see below) suggests they could be rowing/sailing for about another week, with rests, to get to the other side and

---

[13] Trumbull, *Kedesh-Barnea*, 348. Cf. Herodotus, *Hist.* 2.97.

[14] The narrative is obviously condensed to highlight the major episodes but a *specific* number of days should be reckoned as a geographical marker, just as days mentioned in other contexts are calendrical markers. Note that this is precisely the period demanded of Moses in Exod 8:27 ("we must go a three-day journey into the wilderness"); this seems to be a clue to (or rational for) the events later, rather than an original aspect of the chronicle of the event, for it isn't until the plagues begin that this three-day journey is made part of the deal.

landfall.[15] Pragmatically, the group would find water at ports along the shore but the reason for mentioning the lack of fresh water is to highlight the shift in environment, i.e., something the author of Deuteronomy notices (see below); they move from a situation of "water, water, everywhere and not a drop to drink," to hostile, arid desert, where water is even scarcer. When they arrive at their destination, having supposedly gone several days without fresh drinking water, Moses performs a rather strange action that is seldom discussed: He throws a piece of wood into the water, which will prove highly significant.

I submit, therefore, that the hyperbolic (symbolic/propagandistic) account of the miraculous escape and the defeat of the Egyptians did not happen, historically; the trip to Tahpanhes and back was probably discreet, hasty, and relatively uneventful. The reason I say this is because of what Nabonidus *seems* to be doing back at Tahpanhes (for a second time), which doesn't become clear until much later, so bear with me on this one. It just needs to be made clear that a lot rides on this visit and much has to be done in secrecy, so any grand gestures and confrontations are really not apt at this juncture. (Besides, Tahpanhes/Daphnae is one of the most guarded cities in Egypt after the Persian invasion,[16] so to make any threats to the pharaoh, or draw attention to one's self as a troublemaker would not be advisable; Nabonidus would have been dead before he got started.)

## Another Shur

There is another way of deciphering this "wall" mystery. I think there is a riddle here, a play on words, in the manner of "Baal-zephon." The coastal "Way to Shur" (way of the Philistines) leads to Tyre, "The Rock."[17] This potentially safe harbour for the fleeing group would, indeed, be "nearer" (Exod 13:17) but this is not where Nabonidus intends to go. The text is hinting that there is *another* Way to *another* "Rock," only this other rock is south.

The word for "rock" used in Exodus (17:6; 33:21-2) is *tsur* (meaning "rock or cliff"). This is also transliterated as "Zur" ("Rock") the name of the Midianite leader in Num 25:15 (I will come back to this).

---

[15] I checked distances and rowing times for expert rowers, etc., and even modern tourist itineraries, which take only two days to traverse the same route (with stops in between but still going at a relatively slow pace); a week might even be generous.

[16] A. T. Olmstead, *History of the Persian Empire* (Chicago: University of Chicago Press, 1948), 89.

[17] Wallace B. Fleming, *The History of Tyre* (New York: Columbia University Press, 1915), 4.

Another related word is the verb *sur*, which means "to form or fashion," with the noun *sir* meaning "image." This is almost uncanny once we understand what transpires at Sinai, for there Moses a) deals with the "formed/fashioned" golden calf idol; and b) makes it clear that no idol can be made of the deity. The notion of "image" becomes vital to understanding the ritual that takes place at Sinai, and it proves potentially highly significant to the history of Nabonidus in Arabia.

In fact, there are *two* "rocks" in the narrative to follow, i.e., one south of Tayma, which will be another landmark for the sojourners, and the ultimate "Rock," Sinai. Thus, there is a mirrored Wilderness of Shur; one associated with the boundaries of Egypt, and the other with the Arabian Desert (between Sinai and Sela).

# EZION-GEBER

*King Solomon built a fleet of ships at Ezion-geber,*
*which is near Eloth on the shore of the Red Sea, in the land of Edom.*
1 Kgs 9:26

*For the king had a fleet of ships of Tarshish at sea with the fleet of Hiram.*
1 Kgs 10:22

*Ezion-geber and Eloth on the shore of the sea, in the land of Edom.*
2 Chr 8:17

The conventional location of Ezion-geber is said to be at the north-eastern tip of the Gulf of Aqaba. I have never felt comfortable with this, and since researching the influence of Nabonidus on the HB, I am utterly convinced this is wrong. Because Ezion-geber is such a prominent site in the story of Nabonidus-Solomon, and because it is also on the Red Sea, its location needs to be confirmed, for this is where Nabonidus-Moses is headed.

## A Note on Aqaba

The site of Aqaba, archaeologically, shows no evidence of having been a major sea port (i.e., tradition holds it is "Solomon's" grand port) at any time before the Byzantine era from (ca. 300-500 CE) and the later Islamic Period (from 610 CE); the earliest attested name for the site is "Aila" (Byzantine) while the Islamic name is "Ayla," and for most of its history, "the settlement has ... taken its name from the root attested in the Bible, Elath (Eloth) ...."[18] So, here we have, again, the circular reasoning that because someone attributed the site to a place mentioned in the Bible, it is all but universally accepted for millennia, without any material or even further textual evidence to support the claim. A multitude of other places and events are then linked to this site to prove the biblical precedent (and a solely Canaanite heritage). It is very difficult to break free from this but we must, if the understanding of the exodus (and Solomon) narratives is to take a step forward.

Hiram's crews, we know, are used to moving their ships cross-country, disassembled, like flat-packs,[19] so it is feasible that vessels could be transferred from the Nile to the Red Sea by land, even before the canal was functional. Thus, Hiram might maintain a presence there permanently, which would mean he would probably have precedence, if not a monopoly, in both gulfs. The two biblical fleets can sail together for trade purposes (1 Kgs 10:22) with their respective trading harbours far enough away from each other (i.e., like Abraham and Lot) and Hiram can easily send his sailors over to Solomon's ships when needed, from Memphis to Arsinoe, or another port on the western shore of the Sea. It seems most unlikely they would keep two major fleets in the same little harbour and have no presence on the rest of the Red Sea shoreline. That lacks business acumen.

Besides, from a biblical author's perspective, having Solomon's fleet tucked away in this otherwise insignificant place, would not demonstrate his position as the greatest king; he would have to have the prime spot. If, from the historical perspective, the fleet of Solomon was, indeed, right at the tip of a gulf that doesn't even appear on early maps, the location would have been recorded as being in a secluded bay, etc. As it stands, 1 Kgs 9:26 claims Solomon's ships are based "on the shore of the Red Sea," which suggests the Sea *proper*, not the very tip of a narrow gulf.

Some have suggested that Nabonidus' sojourn into Arabia might have been for the purpose of "exerting his authority over the trade-routes in the west and of gaining control of the eastern shore of the Red Sea" because "the old alliance with the Medes had broken down" and he could not make a deal for access; the Persian Gulf had been silting up over a long period, "leaving the king without seaports."[20] If trade is the overwhelming incentive for Nabonidus

---

[18] Donald Whitcomb, "Aqaba," in *Oriental Institute 1994-1995 Annual Report,* William M. Sumner, ed. (Chicago: Oriental Institute, 1995), 14-17, here 15.

[19] Barry J. Beitzel, "Was There a Joint Nautical Venture on the Mediterranean Sea by Tyrian Phoenicians and Early Israelites?" *BASOR* 360 (2010): 37-66, here 47, n. 26; "The city of Opis is where the Assyrian king Sennacherib famously had Syrian-built ships dragged overland on rollers from the Tigris River to the Euphrates River in 694 (BCE)" (W&N, 11 n. 100).

[20] J. M. Wilkie, "Nabonidus and the Later Jewish Exiles," *JTS* 2.1 (1951): 36–44, here 39.

to build a port on the shores of the Red Sea, why not place it in a convenient halfway point, more specifically on the eastern shore, where ships can be unloaded and goods packed off in caravans waiting on the far side of the harbour, ready to set out on the inland trade routes? Why take cargo right to Aqaba, where the immediate trade route is accessed predominantly by the King's Highway, toward the northern regions?[21] This is more convenient for Tyre. During Nabonidus' reign, the goods *he* traded for would be heading for either Tayma or Babylonia. The quickest route would be to Tayma and from there, across the desert to Babylon (via Adummatu).[22] There would be no need to double back or go far north and then down the Euphrates.

Therefore, I suggest it is Hiram, with his Egyptian investors/trade-partners, who dominates ports in both the Gulf of Suez *and* the Gulf of Aqaba, while Solomon (Nabonidus) has his ships somewhere along the shore of the open Red Sea, to service his interests in Arabia. It would make sense for this port to be relatively close to his Tayma kingdom.

***

The evidence for the location of Solomon's port within the biblical texts has remained almost untouched because it was so cleverly hidden— but it *is* there! With a little investigation, the precise location of "Ezion-geber, near Eloth" can be discovered. It is nowhere near Aqaba.

The etymology of "Ezion-geber" is profoundly instructive. The verb *asam* relates to a skeletal structure i.e., a "backbone" that supports the larger structure. The noun *osem* means "might or skeleton," while the noun *osma* means "strength"; the adjective *asum* means "mighty or numerous." The root verb *asam* denotes "strength in numbers," "to be mighty" (Gen 26:16, Dan 8:8), or "to be numerous" (Exod 1:7, Isa 31:1). The BDB suggests, on the other hand, "a land abounding with the trees" (*es* means "tree," *esa* "trees").

The verb *gabar* also means "to be strong or mighty" (Job 21:7, 1 Chr

---

[21] "The road seems to have eased traffic and trade in a north-south direction between the territories of Edom, Moab and Ammon, and probably beyond, but the true path of this route is still unconfirmed" (Fawzi Abudanah, Saad Twaissi, et al., "The Legend of the King's Highway: The Archaeological Evidence," *ZOA*, Band 8 (2015): 156-187, here 157, n. 1; 158).

[22] See Hanspeter Schaudig, "Edom in the Nabonidus Chronicle: A Land Conquered or a Vassal Defended? A Reappraisal of the Annexation of North Arabia by the Late Babylonian Empire," in *About Edom and Idumea in the Persian Period: Recent Research and Approaches from Archaeology, Hebrew Bible Studies, and Ancient Near East Studies,* B. Hensel, E. Ben Zvi, and D. V. Edelman, eds. (Sheffield: Equinox 2022), 251-64, here 252; "Figure 10.1. The main caravan routes in North Arabia in the time of Nabonidus."

5:2), or "to prevail" (Exod 17:11, Gen 7:18). Note that the Exodus example is the scene at Rephidim, with Moses having his hands held up during the battle between Joshua and Amalek. Ezion-geber is, perhaps, a commission name that simply reflects a military site, i.e., a naval base); it is a place of numerous mighty ships (and sailors).

This could be a potential reason for suggesting that Solomon forms an alliance with Hiram, who has similar notions of expanding trade to farther realms perhaps, or in order to strengthen their mutual security, i.e., safety in numbers, as *asam* denotes.

If Nabonidus *is* the inspiration for "Solomon," as I claim, the most logical place to build a port for a "fleet" of large ships is at or near the harbour we know today as al-Wajh. About 600 km down the coastline from the tip of the Gulf of Aqaba, al-Wajh lies at a very strategic point on the Red Sea's eastern shore, i.e., where a well-trodden caravan route leads to the criss-crossing trade trails from the interior, i.e., from Tayma, to Babylon, to the north, and to the south.

In 2013-19 a survey, and then an expedition, was undertaken to examine the potential for ancient caravan access between al-Wajh and al-Ula.[23] The most relevant findings for this discussion were:

⋆ The same routes Doughty took in the 19th Century (*Fig. 10*) turned out to be the more viable ones the expedition tested (though they made no reference to him), i.e., one that took them through the volcanic fields and one that went around

⋆ The most plausible trade route was the one that took the longest time but was much safer and more easily accessible for people and load-bearing beasts

⋆ This route, via the Wadi al-Jizl and Wadi al-Hamd, proved more hospitable, with more frequent access to ground water, forage for camels, and greater easiness underfoot

Num 33:35 says: "They set out from Abronah and camped at Ezion-geber."[24] "Abronah" means "passage, pass" from the verb *abar*, "to pass over,

---

[23] Zbigniew T. Fiema, et al., "The al-'Ulā–al-Wajh Survey Project: 2013 Reconnaissance Season," ATLAL 28.2, 109-31, https://hal.science/hal-03064753 /document. For the 2019 summary see Laïla Nehmé, "Land (and maritime?) routes in and between the Egyptian and Arabian shores of the northern Red Sea in the Roman period," in *Networked Spaces: The Spatiality of Networks in the Red Sea and Western Indian Ocean* (Lyon: MOM Éditions, 2022), doi: https://doi.org /10.4000 /books.momeditions.16486.

[24] In Num 33:34 the group moves to "Jotbathah," which means "Pleasantness, Goodness," from the verb *yatab*, "to be or do good." Compare this to the land Lot chooses

through" (the term "Hebrew" originally implied "nomads" or "travellers").

Similarly, Deut 2:8 reads: "We turned away from the Arabah road ("away from the road of the plain/desert"), which *comes up from* Elath (Eloth) and Ezion-geber, and travelled along the road of the Wilderness of Moab." Doughty mentions an Arabian tribe who frequented a passage from Aqaba to al-Wajh that hugged the shores of the Red Sea; on his map (*Fig. 10*) it is marked by a black line and runs through a region called "Aarab Agaba." "Agaba" in Arabic is the same as Numbers' "Abronah," i.e., "passage/pass"[25]; "Aarab" refers to the nomadic Arabs or Bedouins.[26] Aarab Agaba is thus equivalent to the HB's "Abronah" or "Arabah road."

The port of al-Wajh was known as the "Port of Hegra and Dadan."[27] It is wise to recall that Nabonidus conquers Dadan during his wandering in Arabia (RChr, v 1-24); I am sure he would not overlook its convenient access to a natural port on the Red Sea.

There is a famous handbook from the early 1st Century CE entitled *The Periplus of the Erythraean Sea: Travel and Trade in the Indian Ocean,*[28] which serves as a first-hand guide to merchant sailors traversing the somewhat treacherous but bountiful waters from Arabia to India and beyond. It describes market cities and smaller towns on the coastline, what they trade in, the perils of local sea conditions, winds, peoples, etc. Though dated a few centuries later than the era we are concerned with, it demonstrates the challenges but also the rewards that trade along the coastline of the Red Sea and the Indian Ocean could offer, and this bears uncanny resemblance to what we find in the HB.

*The Periplus* describes a busy trading post that many scholars identify as al-Wajh:

> Now to the left of Berenice, sailing for two or three days from Mussel Harbor eastward across the adjacent gulf, there is another harbor and fortified place, which is called White Village, from which there is a road to Petra,[29] which is subject to Malichas, King of the Nabataeans. It holds the position of a market-town for the small vessels sent there from Arabia; and so a centurion is stationed there as a collector of

---

to move to in Gen 13:10 i.e., "well-watered" and like a garden (see "Joshua and Lot" in Chapter 1).

[25] *Sudan English-Arabic Vocabulary*, Sudan Government, 1925, 211.

[26] Sayyid Abdul Husayn Dastghaib Shirazi, "Greater Sins - Volume 2," § What Does 'Becoming A'arab After Hijrat' Mean? www.al-islam.org.

[27] "Ancient Ports in the Red Sea," 3684, www.ancientportsantiques .com.

[28] *The Periplus of the Erythraean Sea: Travel and Trade in the Indian Ocean by a Merchant of the First Century*, Wilfred Harvey Schoff, trans. (New York: Longmans, 1912).

[29] This could well be the same route mentioned in Num 33:35 and Deut 2:8.

one-fourth of the merchandise imported, with an armed force, as a garrison.[30]

The recent archaeological expedition team states:

...[A]ncient Leuke Kome (White Village) might, in fact, have been located somewhere in a large bay located just south of al-Wajh. Strabo confirms that Leuke Kome was a natural harbour (*hormos*) and so the bay south of al-Wajh would have provided a sufficiently large anchorage to accommodate [a] fleet of 120 large cargo ships. ... al-Wajh is the optimal location for that ancient seaport.[31]

Below this safe harbour, *The Periplus*, continues, "Navigation is dangerous along this whole coast of Arabia, which is without harbour, with bad anchorages, foul, inaccessible because of breakers and rocks, and terrible in every way."[32]

> *Jehoshaphat made ships of the Tarshish type to go to Ophir for gold;*
> *but they did not go, for the ships were wrecked at Ezion-geber.*
> 1 Kgs 22:48

So this really is the farthest south down the (knobbly) "backbone" (recall the etymology of the verb *asam*, above, and also the "body" reference to *geshem*, mentioned earlier) of Arabia one would set anchor before heading out into the open Sea (in this time period, i.e., Jeddah becomes a large port in the 7th Century CE). The site has everything Nabonidus (Solomon) could want for his fleet of ships.

With respect to the tree-related verb *asam* and/or the noun *atseh*, the words also pertain to "wood," e.g., for kindling (Josh 9:23); for building (Gen 6:14, 2 Kgs 12:13); and manufactured goods (Exod 7:19, Deut 19:5), even idols (Deut 4:28). This is why *Hitchcock's Dictionary of Bible Names* and *Easton's Bible Dictionary* both translate "Ezion-geber" as "The Wood of the Man."

What happens when the group first reach the other side of the Red Sea ("Marah")? Moses throws *a piece of wood* into the water (see below). Thus, the name once again denotes the immediate action and thereby preserves the place location (in the context of the journey), a pattern that runs throughout the narrative.

All the indications point to Ezion-geber being al-Wajh.

---

[30] *Periplus*, 19.
[31] Fiema, 112.
[32] *Periplus*, 20.

# ELOTH

"Arabic names often preserve ancient topographic ones, not impacted by town renaming after political changes."[33] "Eloth" is a perfect example of this practice. It means "protrusions, terebinths," etc., from the noun *ayil*, "protruder," stemming from the verb *alal*, "to protrude." There is also a strong allusion in the etymology (i.e., the assumed root *'wl*) to "foolishness" or "worthlessness," especially in connection with idol-worship; this reflects the HB's sentiment toward Nabonidus (predominantly at Tayma).

Eloth, which must be near Ezion-geber, has sea on one side, volcanic rock on the other, so terebinths, or trees, *seem* unlikely. What it does have, in fact, is a large area of mangroves; the entire archipelago that begins at al-Wajh and runs about 100 km south, is rich in ("abounding with") mangrove trees.[34] In Nabonidus' day these would have been much denser, probably, and quite a memorable sight, set against the starkness of the landscape beyond. "Eloth" is, therefore, the area just south of the harbour, i.e., the mangrove forest.

> Along the whole of the coast of the Red Sea, down in the deep, grow trees like the laurel and the olive, which at the ebb tides are wholly visible above the water but at the full tides are sometimes wholly covered; and while this is the case, the land that lies above the sea has no trees, and therefore the peculiarity is all the greater.
>
> Strabo 16.3.6

So, Nabonidus and his fellow migrants make their way in boats from Suez to al-Wajh (Ezion-geber). From there they caravan along the established Wadi al-Jizl and Wadi al-Hamd route, which takes a little longer but is far safer, with access to everything they need for survival. They come from the south, skirting the dangerous lava fields to Dadan and Mada'in Salih (Hegra), before arriving at the oasis of Tayma. Ezek 25:13 states that Edom includes the territory "from Temen to Dedan." Tayma is thus *in* Edom (just), completing the picture. They never need to enter the Sinai Peninsula.

---

[33] Danièle Michaux-Colombot, "Bronze Age Reed Boats of Magan and Magillum Boats of Meluḫḫa in Cuneiform Literature," in *Stories of Globalisation: The Red Sea and the Persian Gulf from Late Prehistory to Early Modernity*, A. Manzo, C., D. J. de Falco, eds. (Leiden: Brill, 2019), 119-53, here 151.

[34] "Status of Mangroves in the Red Sea and Gulf of Aden," PERSGA Technical Series 11 (PERSGA, Jeddah: 2004), 26-7, www.cbd.int.

Figure 10: Doughty's map showing routes through and around the Harraat and along the coast of the Red Sea (Image: C. Doughty, insert)

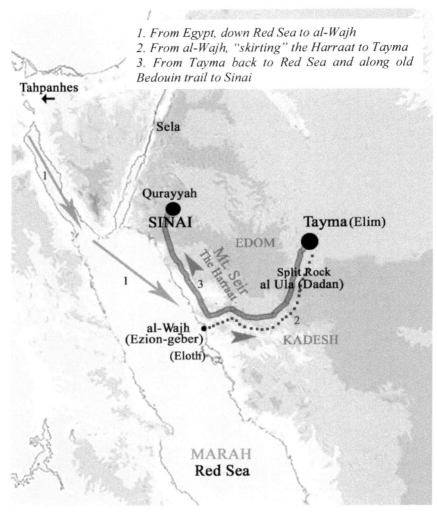

*Figure 11: Suggested itinerary of Nabonidus (Moses) from Egypt to Sinai (Image: Author's construct)*

## Elusive Heir and Ezion-geber

There is another character potentially linked to Nabonidus' son Belshazzar, i.e., Eliezer ("God is Help"), son of Moses, who is also to be understood as "Eliezer of Damascus," the life-long "elder of the household" or "Servant" of Abraham (Gen 15:3; and probably 24:2).

The Kabbalists argue that Eliezer's soul returned as "Caleb" (Chesed

L'Avraham, Maayan 5, Nahar 25), i.e., another link to Nabonidus-Mered of 1 Chronicles 4. Targum Jonathan 14:14 says Eliezer was the son of King Nimrod, described as a "mighty warrior" (Gen 10:9),[35] i.e., making him, symbolically, the son of the King of Babylon, in the current context, Nabonidus, i.e., this son is, therefore, Belshazzar, "Joshua" the soldier.[36]

We are told that Eliezer is the "elder" (*zekan*) of Abraham's home, i.e., his heir (Gen 15:3). What does this word *zekan* imply? According to some, it can be broken into two words, *ziv ikunin*. *Ziv* is Hebrew for "radiance," and *ikun* is Greek for "image," implying that his image was a radiant reflection of his illustrious master. Gen 24:2 then says he "ruled all that he had," i.e., all *Abraham* had. Belshazzar is Nabonidus' firstborn, thus older than any subsequent offspring, so naturally considered the heir. He was the crown prince, put in charge of Babylon while Nabonidus was in Tayma.

As we will see in the discussion concerning the alleged deification of Nabonidus and the associated serpent iconography, the word "image" is significant, and "radiance" is a factor in the worship at Sinai. Nabonidus is deemed "radiant" in the Song (Song 5;10). In his own (later) inscriptions Nabonidus often mentions Belshazzar, in a context of protection, piety, etc., (e.g., Nab 27 i 32-6, ii 23-6, iii 20-4; Nab 28 iii 75-7; 32 ii 23–26; 33 ii 1-5) and the sense I get is that Nabonidus never stopped worrying about his (perhaps headstrong) son, but a son is always understood to be a reflection of his father.

As for "Damascus," this may very well be a reference to where the group first encounter Belshazzar, who, as stated previously, had possibly been sent to Northern Syria just before the fall of Babylon, i.e., perhaps he was in Damascus before he joined his father's caravan. However, there may be a play on the etymology of "Damascus" here, for the name *Dammeseq* means "silence of the sackcloth weaver," which refers to silent mourners. Recall that I suggest Daniel makes his declaration that Belshazzar is dead (Dan 5:30) as a means of severing the crown prince from his life in Babylon, while supporting his 'escape' to a new (incognito) life as "Lot"; he declares his loyalty to Belshazzar by keeping the secret. Might the reference to *Dammeseq* be confirmation of this insider knowledge? That is, the author of Genesis knows this is Nabonidus' son, who is supposed to be dead, but is also 'keeping silent' on the matter because Belshazzar (unlike his father) is deemed a hero (for now).

I am a keen proponent of deciphering gematria, and this is a nice example, for the name "Eliezer" has the numerical value of 318, i.e., the

[35] "Eliezer," www.chabad.org.
[36] In rabbinic literature Nimrod is described as "he who made all the people rebellious against God" (Pes. 94b; Targ. Yer. to Gen. 10:9).

precise number of soldiers sent into battle along with Abraham (Gen 14:14). Early Jewish exegetes interpreted this to mean Abraham took *only* his trusted servant Eliezer.[37]

"Lot," as explained earlier, is the name given to Nabonidus' son as a pseudonym because his identity is intentionally hidden; the etymology speaks of "covering, enveloping, secrecy," etc. Think of a modern super-hero who suddenly changes his/her entire identity with the simplest of tactics (removing glasses, changing an outfit, etc.) to become the mysterious, victorious defender. The early Hebrew authors clearly had imagination; this may well be the earliest example of this super-hero genre, as Lot conveniently disappears from the narrative by virtue of being kidnapped then suddenly, there is Eliezer, fit for battle, charging all over Canaan by Abraham's side, conquering the enemy against all odds. When the battle is over, Eliezer disappears into obscurity again and lo and behold, Lot is brought home.

To me, this entire episode is one of the theft and subsequent rescue of traded goods, *not* of Lot. The action begins in the region of Kadesh, i.e., between Tayma and the Harraat, where Lot (Belshazzar) has been sent; the men make off with a substantial quantity of goods that have probably been sent to Tayma by Nabonidus. Lot is not kidnapped but is in pursuit, meeting up with Abraham (Nabonidus), who then switches to soldier-mode and the two set off to retrieve their goods. When they get beyond Damascus, i.e., not far from the central trading hub of Harran, they catch the men at a place called "Hobah," which means "hiding place," i.e., the men hide the goods before taking to market at Harran. The return of the merchandise is ranked higher in significance than the supposed rescue of Lot because the latter never happened.

If this seems fabricated to you, consider the passage from Xenophon (I, 4.16), who describes a certain "Prince of Assyria" who goes to the borderland between "Assyria and Media" (i.e., "Assyria" is Babylonia in both Herodotus and Xenophon), to "hunt." Ostensibly for his "safety" he brings along a large army; he also acquires many more soldiers from the local area. Suddenly he gets the idea that with such a contingent he can raid the Medes for "booty" and a to-and-fro battle ensues.

Xenophon employs the pseudonym of "King of Assyria" for Nabonidus, so the "Prince" must be his son.[38] Cyrus is hailed the victor, of

---

[37] "Eliezer," www.chabad.org.

[38] Xenophon, like the authors of the HB, uses a fictional tale to recount a historical one. In *Cyropaedia*, a pro-Cyrus text that "results in a cover-up of Cyrus' anti-Median activities," the "King of the Assyrians" is Nabonidus, and the tale of the subjugation of Syria and the Arabs is "most probably … a memory of Nabonidus' actions against Syria and the Northern Higaz during his first years" (Jan Retsö, *The Arabs in Antiquity: Their*

course, resplendent in his shiny armour, but the accompanying notes suggest that this "Prince," though a "fictional" character, does seem to represent Belshazzar.[39] The location is moved to the border of Babylonia and Persia because this book is about Cyrus, but such a perception of a battle over booty involving Nabonidus' son might well have been inspired by the same event (or similar) we see preserved in Genesis.

Another "Eliezer" appears once only, in 2 Chr 20:37, as the son of a man called "Dodavahu of Mareshah." "Dodavahu" means "beloved of Yah," from the verb *dwd*, "to love," and *yahu*, the name of God. In the Song of Solomon *dwd* is highly contentious, as it denotes a particular kind of "love" within the narrative. It also signifies Nabonidus-Solomon, i.e., as *dodi*, the "beloved." "Mareshah" is interesting because it can mean two things that are opposites: "enfranchise, to empower or endow with possessions", or "to disenfranchise," depending on the intended root. The latter would be based on the verb *rush,* which also includes the notion of losing liberty or civil rights (often via conquest). The former would stem from the verb *yarash* ("enfranchise"); the HB uses this verb in only two ways: 1) legal/official transfer of land or goods (Gen 15:3; Jer 32:8), and 2) military conquest/seizure (Gen 15:7, Deut 2:12, Josh 18:13, Amos 9:12).

So which is it? Looking at the context of 2 Chr 20:37, it would seem as though the both meanings are intended. Eliezer is said to be prophesying against Jehoshaphat for going into partnership with King Ahaziah "in building ships to go to Tarshish" from Ezion-geber (20:36). We know that Tarshish is a significant allusion to King Solomon (Nabonidus) who joins with Hiram of Tyre, sending boats out from Ezion-geber (1 Kgs 10:22). Thus, the scenario in 2 Chronicles is set in a context of international trade. This is Nabonidus' specialty.

When re-read with this in mind, the prophecy now sounds more like a threat, i.e., "Dodavahu of Mareshah" represents Nabonidus, and his son "Eliezer," Belshazzar, having moved down to Tayma (as "Lot") to guard his father's interests. Notwithstanding the generations that pass between Solomon and Jehoshaphat, it may very well be the case that the short tale of Jehoshaphat and the ships at Ezion-geber is inspired by a memory of the same incident Genesis 14 is based on, i.e., the theft of Nabonidus' possessions, possibly from his port at al-Wajh. Perhaps Jehoshaphat decided it was time to claim the port for Judah, and descendants of Belshazzar-Eliezer were responsible for destroying the alien ships in 'their' port.[40] This might help explain Edom's

---

*History from the Assyrians to the Umayyads* [London: Routledge, 2003], 186).

[39] Richard Stoneman, "Notes," in *Xenophon: The Education of Cyrus*, H. G. Dakyns, trans. (London: Dent & Sons, 1992 [1914]), n. 4.16, 275.

[40] Again, we don't know if Cyrus grants Nabonidus a relatively free rein as

eventual revolt against Judah (2 Kgs 8:20).

Thus, one party is disenfranchised, the other is enfranchised (via conquest/theft), but then matters are reversed.

# BITTER WATER

The name "Marah" is translated from the Hebrew *marah*, which is the feminine of "bitter," stemming from *marar*, "to be bitter," which can be literal or figurative, i.e., a bitter taste, bitter experience, bitter spirit, etc. The name "Miriam" can also be translated as "bitterness."

The word used to describe what Moses throws ("hurls") into the water on his arrival at al-Wajh (Exod 15:25; i.e., at Ezion-geber, the "Wood of the Man," recall), is the Hebrew noun *ets,* which is from *atsah*; a tree (from its firmness); hence, "wood." This obscure action caused a lot of head-scratching for me, as it incorporates so many possible symbolic meanings. In the end, I think there are two distinct meanings behind this scene; one corresponds to the *act* of throwing a piece of wood into water, and the other to a very serious and sinister turn of events relating to Miriam.

1. The group, having spent three days on the Sea of Reeds (the marshlands) have come to shore of Marah, the Red Sea, still unable to drink the water, for however many days they are afloat, at least metaphorically). The word for "shows" is *yarah* or *yara*, "to throw, or shoot"; it can also mean to teach, or instruct, and it appears in Exod 24:12 in that capacity (where the tablets bearing the commandments are said to be "written for their *instruction*"). The BDB notes in this context: *"Specially of the authoritative direction given by priests on matters of ceremonial observance"*; this proves fascinating because it ties into the idea of Moses and Aaron performing signs and wonders in magical competition with the priests of Egypt but also because it echoes Nabonidus' fascination with the occult and with learning the religious practices of other cultures (especially as "Solomon," who was supposedly "educated in all the wisdom of the Egyptians" [Acts 7:22]).

In this scene, Moses is following an instruction, not from God but from Aaron; he is being taught how to perform sympathetic magic to compel the heavens to open, i.e., Moses is performing a rain spell.

Look at how Josephus describes what Moses does with the piece of wood:

---

governor (wherever he is sent), as seems to be the case with Hiram, but the ex-Babylonian king does seem to be a man who does as he wishes anyway; whether he has permission to use his old fleet or not (i.e., he would simply use Hiram's) is a moot point. I think he returns to Tayma as a local king and acts accordingly. Few would challenge him.

... he took the top of a stick that lay down at his feet, and divided it in the middle, and made the section length ways. He then let it down into the well, and persuaded the Hebrews that God had hearkened to his prayers ... he bid the strongest men among them that stood there, to draw up water; and told them that when the greatest part was drawn up, the remainder would be fit to drink. So they laboured at it till the water was so agitated and purged as to be fit to drink.

*A.J.* 3.1.2

Obviously Josephus was not there to see this, so it must be that he, too, understood the action in the narrative as describing a magical ritual. The spell is to induce rain, which then fills the well (pool) from the bottom to the top via the freshly replenished aquifer. Naturally, the old water (bitter seawater that has seeped into the well) is drawn until the dilution of the remaining water is such that the entire well/pool is relatively fresh to drink.

There is evidence of this magic being performed in ancient Greece (i.e., as recorded in the 2nd Century CE):

Should a drought persist for a long time, and the seeds in the earth and the trees wither, then the priest of Lycaean Zeus, after praying towards the water and making the usual sacrifices, lowers an oak branch to the surface of the spring, not letting it sink deep. When the water has been stirred up there rises a vapour, like mist; after a time the mist becomes cloud, gathers to itself other clouds, and makes rain fall on the land of the Arcadians.[41]

The employment of magic to procure rain is also familiar to the Baal worshippers of Tyre, whose *modus operandi* is to throw sea water into a muddy puddle:

Another testimony of the phenomenon of sympathetic magic was practiced in Tyre in remote periods of history and persisted until the end of the 18th Century. Every year, in October, the water of the Ras el-'Aïn well becomes muddy, to the point where it is no longer possible to make any use of it. It is remedied by throwing five or six jugs of sea water, which clarify the source in less than two hours. The date of the ceremony in October is very characteristic: it is the moment when the sources are impoverished, where the cisterns contain nothing more than mud and where everybody desires and asks (for) the rain.[42]

---

[41] Pausanias, *Description of Greece* (8.38.4), W. H. S. Jones, trans., www.theoi.com.

[42] Ziad Jalbout, "Sacred Water," §3.7. https://phoenicia.org.

The Talmud states that the members of the great Sanhedrin had to be "masters of magic" (Menachot 65a, 2), and that "various rabbis … successfully and legitimately perform magic, including making rain" (b. Berakhot. 20a, 4).[43] It is probable that the rabbis took each of the instances of sorcery in the HB and claimed they had mastered them all (i.e., they knew how it was done). The only magical rite for rain in the HB seems to be here, in Exodus.

That Moses "throws" the wood/branch into the water (i.e., using the Hebrew verb *shalak*, "to throw, hurl, cast"), suggests the same level of insensitivity and uncouthness visible in Nabonidus' depiction in the Song of Solomon. He tries, but he is not subtle; ceremoniously touching the surface of the water is not his style. He just chucks it in. Having come to know Nabonidus over the years, this made me chuckle but the humorous side of things doesn't last long, for there is an ominous potential understanding of this scene.

For historical verisimilitude, Nabonidus himself mentions rains that come to Babylonia (after a debilitating drought) while he is in Tayma (H2 A&B 1.31-7). Gadd finds the comment strange ("confused") because earlier, Nabonidus had claimed the people were impious, etc., but suddenly they receive rains, which are deemed a divine "reward for piety."[44] There is no contradiction, however, if one assumes Nabonidus is referring to his *own* piety, i.e., his penance, which he sees to have been carried out whilst in Tayma.[45] Nebuchadnezzar says about those who respect his memory and are pious: "Rain from the sky, [fl]ood [water] from (the interior of) the earth shall be given to him continually as a present" (ANET, 307).

The magical rite Nabonidus performs in Exodus 15 suggests he believes he can influence the gods again (i.e., a touch of that old hubris coming back).

> *… the heavens are shut up and there is no rain because your people have sinned against you …. Teach them the right way to live, and send rain on the land you gave your people for an inheritance.*
> 1 Kgs 8:35-6

2. The term *atsah* is also a verb, meaning "to shut"; in Arabic it means "to shut the eyes, to wink" (in Hebrew, *asa*):

---

[43] Other forms of magic performed by these men supposedly included "initiating famine, producing money, materializing a witch from a stone, and bringing back the dead." Edwin M. Yamauchi and Marvin R. Wilson, *Dictionary of Daily Life in Biblical and Post-Biblical Antiquity* (Peabody, MA: Hendricksons, 2021), 215-16.

[44] C. J. Gadd, "The Harran Inscriptions of Nabonidus," *AS* 8 (1958): 35-92, here 67, n. 31-7 (c).

[45] Tyson, 5-6 for an explanation of this 'original' sin.

> One who winks the eyes plans perverse things;
> One who compresses the lips brings evil to pass.
>                                         Prov 16:30[46]

There is a play on words here, a typical Hebrew fascination with double meanings, for this first scene with the "water" is a precursor, a foreshadowing of the "rock" episode in Exodus 17. I suggest that Exod 15:25 depicts, in part, the first physical admonition and rejection of Miriam, i.e., the first signs of Nabonidus' "compressed lips" and "winking eye."

In Exod 15:20-1 Miriam sings a verse from Moses' song of praise (a victory song after their successful escape from *Yam Suph*); instead of "I will sing," she *instructs*, "Sing!," her erstwhile temple assistants singing and dancing around her, shaking their timbrels. This directive supports her role as a woman of the temple, a priestess, a leader in her own right but she has made the mistake of taking charge of the situation, stealing some of the glory from Moses; she has upstaged her father, the volatile ex-king. It is a portent of doom for Miriam.

The "bitter water" submits to Moses' action and becomes "sweet." The Hebrew term here is *mathoq* ("sweet or pleasant"), which has a rather disturbing underlying meaning, i.e., "to suck with relish" or "to smack the lips with pleasure" (BDB and *Strong's*). Considering Nabonidus' penchant for drinking female blood, this seems to me an intended allusion, i.e., Moses forces himself on Miriam (he figuratively becomes the "wood" to her "water"). He steals what he wants (sex and/or blood), as payback for her insolence. This finds further substantiation later, but just look at one of the few other examples of this word *mathoq* in the HB: "Stolen water is sweet, and bread eaten in secret is pleasant" (Prov 9:17).

This scenario also hints at the rationale for Moses' exclusion from Canaan, which is related in Exodus 17, again linked to Miriam.

---

[46] Cf. Isa 29:10; 33:15.

# 7

## COVENANT OF SALT

### ELIM

The name "Elim" means "protruders, big trees, terebinths" from the noun *ayil*, "protruder," stemming from the verb *alal*, "to protrude." This links it to "Eloth."

*Strong's* suggests the name means "palms," but also defines *ayil* as meaning "ram," with the explanation that in some instances, this can suggest a "masculine leader, chief," i.e., as a ram leads a flock. It also defines *ayil* as a "terebinth … probably as prominent, lofty tree" and "as marking idol-shrines."

The masculine noun *elil*, means "worthlessness, or a worthless thing." In the HB this noun is used primarily for "vain worship" or "idols" (e.g., Lev 19:4, Isa 2:8, Ezek 30:13). Furthermore, the related word *allon*, meaning "oak," is used as a synonym for a high-place, i.e., of pagan worship (Hos 4:13), or for the wood from which idols are made (Isa 44:14). In the Song of Solomon, one of the very first statements from the mouth of the author, Jehudijah, is the hidden curse to Solomon: "Your name is empty, hollow, cast out," i.e., "worthless," making it anathema.[1] Tayma, by association,

---

[1] Tyson, 50. Even today, there are remnants of this Hebrew practice: In a discussion on the origins of the name "Jew" Rabbi Aaron L. Raskin mentions says, "Hitler—may his

becomes the place of Nabonidus' alleged idolatry, etc., hence the naming of the surrounding area as the Wilderness of Sîn (after the lunar deity).

The related noun *ayyal* means "stag or deer" (Deut 12:15, Isa 35:6); while *ayyala* means doe. In Ps 42:1, the stag "longs for flowing streams," as the man yearns for direction from God; combining this with the rather negative inference of *elil* (above), one gets the impression of a worthless man seeking divine instruction (see Abarim's discussion). In the Song, Nabonidus is depicted as the "stag" and Nitocris the "doe"; the king desperately seeks out hidden gems of wisdom he can glean from his illustrious Egyptian priestess. He constantly makes a fool of himself.

The entire nature of the name "Elim" screams "Tayma!" It also suggests that the author of the original Exodus narrative was already familiar with the Song of Solomon and/or what had occurred in Tayma in earlier years. This is further potential substantiation for a very early writing of the Song, and with the upcoming scenes in Exodus 17, this is made even more clear, with a sense of regret for what happens to Miriam, and a lingering resentment for Nabonidus' attitude and behaviour. It is a sentiment that reaches a peak, perhaps, in Numbers, and the revolt of Korah (Num 16:1-40).

Supporting a Tayma location for Elim is the well at Tayma, built by Nabonidus (called the Haddaj Well, after the Aramean god of water).[2] Today, the base of the well is more or less intact but it has been spruced up for tourists. Nevertheless, its size accommodates about fifty camels drawing water (depending on how much room your camel requires), with fifteen walled divisions. The largest well of its kind in the world, it is very impressive and would have been famous as one of the best watering holes in the desert. It is fed by more than eighty springs, so the allusion to "twelve" in Exodus 16 simply means there was ample for everyone, i.e., all the clans/tribes.

Similarly with the seventy palm trees; there are seventy "elders/judges" (Exod 24:9) who, like Deborah, probably sit under "palm" trees to meet with the people. Tayma is a place also apparently famous for its "wisdom," e.g., "is wisdom no more in Teman? is counsel perished from the prudent? is their wisdom vanished?" (Jer 49:7).[3] There are, symbolically, palm trees for all, too, in this haven.

---

name be erased—forced all Jews to wear a yellow star with the word 'Jude' (i.e., Yehudi) on it" (Rabbi Aaron L. Raskin, "Yod," Letters of Light, www.chabad.org).

[2] Abeer Al-Amoudi, "Haddaj: An enduring well in an ancient oasis" (23 June 2020), www.wafyapp.com.

[3] I think this is a result of Nabonidus' influence (as "Solomon").

# MANNA

In Exod 16:4, not long after Moses' rain spell, God tells Moses "I am going to rain bread (*lechem*) from heaven for you ...." Perhaps not quite what he expected, on a superficial reading, but *lechem* can mean anything from a loaf of bread, to the grain it is made from, to any foodstuff that sustains animal or human; the key element is 'sustain'. One's daily bread is a euphemism for what keeps you alive and functioning; in normal circumstances this *would* probably have been bread of some sort but here, in the dry desert, bread is the last thing a thirsty person would want, so there must be more to this allusion.

Exodus 16 is a test, so some of the narrative is intentionally theological/symbolic but there is, as always, another side to the story, i.e., a pragmatic side. God supposedly provides strict instructions about how and when to collect this *lechem*, with limits on how much each person should take/consume; an "*omer*" (16:36) is about 2.5-3.5 pounds (roughly 7 kg). The advice is perfectly sound, for an overindulgence is life-threatening, for "manna" is salt. An *omer* per person per day? That seems like an excessive ration. This is where the "quail" come in, i.e., the amount of salt is required for the preservation of the meat they have been given (and see below); salting is the best way to conserve meat in the desert but it is also used in both "baking" and "boiling" (Exod 16:23).

The description of the "manna" in Exodus 17[4] is as follows:

1. It appears early in the morning, with the "dew," i.e., *tal*, or "night mist" (hence it appears to come as 'rain' from the sky)

2. It is "fine and flaky ... like frost" (*kphowr*)

3. Stored up, it goes off quickly, exuding a rancid smell and is filled with "worms" (*tola*)

4. Heated by the sun, it "melts" (*masas*)

5. It has the appearance of white "coriander seeds" (*gad* + *zara*)

6. It tastes sweet (like flatbread made with honey)

Each of these descriptions can be explained by reference to salt crystals formed in a sabkha (Arabic terminology but applied internationally)

---

[4] Exod 17:31-6 is clearly an addendum, using not *lechem* but *man*, meaning "What?/Who?" referring back to the question in 16:15; the reference to the "house of Israel" is also a bit of a giveaway.

or salt-flat.[5] There are two types of sabkha, inland and coastal; as the group has left the shores of the Red Sea and has come to Elim, we must be dealing with an inland sabkha, which derives the majority of its moisture from the aquifer and/or runoff from the surrounding area.

1. *It appears early in the morning, with the "dew." i.e., tal, or "night mist" (hence it appears to come as rain from the sky)*: "Some crystals appear on the surface of the solution in the daytime when the temperatures are high. Others arise at the bottom of the pelvis during the night when temperatures are low."[6] Upward seepage of groundwater adds extra moisture.

2. *It is "fine and flaky ... like frost"*: There are different kinds of processes that occur to create different kinds of salt crystals, e.g., needles (that look like shiny quartz crystals); hopper-shaped (that look like clumps of ice/snow); and dendritic (which are tiny crystals with arms, like a snowflake). The form most likely being described in Exodus is the powdery dendritic, as it is compared to frost covering the ground rather than to lumps of rock salt, for instance (16:14).

3. *Stored up, it goes off quickly, exuding a rancid smell and is filled with "worms" (tola)*:

> As the sabkhas dry up, a new salt layer reforms at the surface, thus shielding the residual brine, which can be reached throughout the year beneath the surface crust at depths of only a few centimetres.[7]

Beneath the salty crust is a membrane of brine; within the brine live minute brine-shrimp (Artemia). This is why we see the "quail"/birds flocking in their droves, i.e., they have come to feed on the brine-shrimp and their eggs (cysts). Artemia are generally either red or transparent; the Hebrew noun used for "worms" in Exod 16:20 is the noun *tola*, defined as "worm, scarlet stuff". Uncannily, all species of Artemia are prone to an infection of microscopic tape worms,[8] which heightens their redness but this

---

[5] For a descriptive assessment of sabkhas in general see Yaser B. Mohammad and Salih M. Awadh, "Salt Crystallization and Mineralogy of Sabkhas in Abu Ghraib, Western Baghdad, Abu Graib, Iraq," *IGJ* 56 (2023): 263-272, here 263.

[6] Mohammad and Awadh, 268.

[7] Y. Levy, and J. R. Gat, "Isotope hydrology of inland sabkhas in the Bardawil area, Sinai," *Limnology and Oceanography* 23.5 (Sept 1978): 841-50, here 842.

[8] M. I. Sánchez, B. B. Georgiev, P.N. Nikolov, et al. "Red and transparent brine shrimps (Artemia parthenogenetica): a comparative study of their cestode infections," *Parasitol Res* 100 (2006): 111-14, here, "Abstract" (online), https://link.springer.com.

would not be known to anyone without a microscope. The shrimp themselves can grow to about half an inch in length, with long tails, so they might well be mistaken for wriggling worms. The rotten smell of the salt that is "left until morning," e.g., in a container as in 16:33, occurs when the gasses created by the biological processes of the shrimp are not allowed to escape into the atmosphere (as many who have ever bought sea monkeys will tell you). It could also allude to a fine film of brine adhering to the salt that soon smells fishy.

Looking at Num 11:7, the description of the manna is similar: The salt is likened to "coriander seed" in shape/size and is said to be the *colour* of "gum resin" or *bedolach* (bdellium), which is the same orangey-red colour as the shrimp and their cysts. The crust from a sabkha rich in brine shrimp may well be stained a reddish colour underneath.[9]

Yet, the addendum in Exod 16:31 describes manna as being "white." I am convinced the author of the addendum identified manna with salt, i.e., *white* salt he was familiar with, and that he had, therefore, never been to this site. He was not, perhaps, one of those who had experienced life in the desert.

4. *Heated by the sun, it "melts" (masas)*: The sabkha goes through a cyclical process, whereby moisture either seeps up from the water below ground or it receives runoff from the surrounding land; it continually evaporates; leaving salt crystals on the surface; when these get heavy enough, they slowly sink below the crust.[10] To those unfamiliar with the scientific process, it would, indeed, seem as though the crystals were dissolving or melting.

5. *It has the appearance of white "coriander seeds" (gad + zera)*: This is the later description from Exod 16:31-6. The word *gad* is defined by Strong's as "coriander; a simile for manna" but it is arbitrary, attempting to

---

[9] A "sounding at the northern end of the sabkha showed algae and gastropods attached to the Ordovician bedrock suggesting the existence of a palaeo-lake whose level once was 13 m higher than the present-day surface" ("Archaeological research at the oasis of Tayma, Saudi Arabia," https://studylib.net/doc/7406744). It may not be such a wet environment now, but the biblical evidence does suggest it *was* (at least enough to still harbour Artemia), even in the 6th Century BCE. I have been unable to find any specific reference to red-tinted salt from Tayma in current research papers" but a quick search online provides accounts of many red salt-flats around the world, which can change colour almost on a daily basis, depending on the bacteria, weather, etc. For a broad analysis of sabkha fauna see Peter J. Hogarth and Barbarah J. Tigar, "Ecology of Sabkha Arthropods" in *Sabkha Ecosystems, Vol. 1: The Arabian Peninsula and Adjacent Countries,* H. J. Barth and Benno Böer, eds. (Netherlands: Kluwer Academic, 2001), 1-16.

[10] Mohammad and Awadh, 268-9.

make sense of the imagery by emphasising the scores on the seeds; it could just as easily be any small seed.[11] The key is the second word, *zera*, which means "a sowing, seed, offspring," from *zara*, "to sow or scatter seed." This echoes the tiny dendritic salt crystals covering the ground, i.e., like scattered seeds. Another meaning of *gad* is "a mustering of troops, or together," which could indicate a crust made up of intertwined/bonded crystals.

6. *It tastes sweet (like flatbread made with honey).* Again, this is the addendum version (Exod 16:31), whereas Numbers describes it as having the taste of "cakes baked with oil" (11:8). The latter seems far more pragmatic, with a muted sweetness that olive oil can bring to cooking; the former sounds as though the author is rationalising how the Israelites could possibly have eaten so much of it, for so long, i.e., it had to be "sweet," surely! However, in the real world of deserts and the appreciation for salt, we find sabkha salt really does seem, at least to the locals, to taste *sweeter* than …sea salt."[12] (Coriander is known to bring a sweeter flavour to spiced foods, i.e., in a spice-driven economy, as this region is, it makes sense to describe the manna in terms that would be familiar.)

So, with this information I think we can safely suggest that the scene of the "manna" takes place on a salt-flat. There are sabkhas in the Sinai, in the marshlands of Mesopotamia, and in Arabia, so it is possible that any of these might be the right place, but the location is made clear: "… the wilderness of Sîn,[13] which is between Elim and Sinai." Elim is Tayma.

The events of Exodus 16 are said to take place *between* Elim and Sinai, in the Wilderness of Sîn (16:1), meaning the location is just north of Tayma itself (i.e., Sinai, as will be discussed shortly, is located north of Tayma). The city *is* just south of a 20 km² inland sabkha.[14] Doughty mentions it, suggesting Tayma salt is "the daily sauce of the thousand nomad kettles in all these parts of Arabia":

---

[11] It is also possible to interpret this as the manna having the appearance of semen, i.e., a milky substance, for *zera/sara* often pertains to offspring="seed."

[12] Charles M. Doughty, *Travels In Arabia Deserta* [1888] (New York: Random House, reprint 1921), 340.

[13] I refer to this wilderness as that of Sîn, rather than "Sin" because I think it was so-named originally, due to Tayma being the home of Nabonidus, known for his worship of that lunar deity. It is a name the authors (and audience) would be familiar with.

[14] There is an excellent photograph of the Tayma sabkha illustrating the early stages of the frost-like salt crust (search the following, and click onto the third photograph: Uta Deffke, "The story of a dried-up lake in the North Arabian desert," 24 March, 2022). You can see why the idea of semen/seed might come to mind.

> ... yellow-brown loam may be seen in [the] marl pits. ... The most lower grounds in these deserts are saltish, of the washing down from the land above; after the winter standing-water may be found a salty crust, — such I have seen finger-thick ...[15]

Doughty also mentions a salt-flat within the volcanic landscape of the Khaybar region, describing it as "a rusty fen, white with the salt-warp ... exhaling a sickly odour," echoing the redness (note the "yellow-brown," i.e., orangey colour in the quotation above), the white, and the "stink" elements, of the Exodus narrative. He describes the mirages of "water" in the distance, only to discover these were the salt-flats glistening under the sun. Plus, Doughty even mentions birds: "... we often startled *gatta* fowl ("sand grouse"); they are dry-fleshed birds and not very good to eat" (hence the salting of them not only preserves but also adds flavour).[16]

The general perception of the sabkha in this region, then, seems to be that it has an orangey tint to the underlying ground caused by living organisms, it is white on the surface, it has an unpleasant smell, and it attracts birds. The one in Exodus 16 is just north of Tayma.

That is the scientific version; what about the more esoteric side of things? The allusion to bread and salt is intentional; *this* is the "covenant of salt" mentioned in Lev 2:13,[17] Num 18:19, 2 Chr 13:5, and Ezra 4:14 (and alluded to in 6:8-10; 7:22). Perhaps one of the most Arabic of all the scenes in Exodus, this concept of a bond entered into by two parties, using the most

---

[15] Doughty, 1.340. "Marl" is defined as being a soft sedimentary rock, "formed in marine or freshwater environments, often through the activities of algae."

[16] Doughty, 2.88. For a modern discussion of the sabkha in this area see Arnulf Hausleiter, et al., "Al-Ula, Saudi-Arabia: Archaeology and Environment from the Early Bronze Age (3rd mill. BCE) onwards. Season 2019," from e-Forschungsberichte des Deutschen Archäologischen Instituts, 2021-1, § 1-22. doi: https://doi.org/10.34780/b5t2-t686.

[17] This HB book has the most mentions of the salt of the covenant, as it pertains to sacrificial rites, e.g., burnt offering (Lev 1; 6:8-13; 8:18-21; 16:24); grain offering (Lev 2; 6:14-23); peace offering (Lev 3; 7:11-34); sin offering (Lev 4; 5:1-13; 6:24-30; 8:14-17; 16:3-22); trespass offering (Lev 5:14-19; 6:1-7; 7:1-6). In these rites the salt is sprinkled on the sacrificed meat primarily because it is going to be eaten (by priests and/or donors); it almost seems like a weak homage to some distant memory of a salt covenant, or a compromise, i.e., the salt, once *the* most binding symbol of a contract between Yahweh and his desert people, becomes little more than a sanctified condiment. Ezek 16:4 implies a ritual involving salting a new-born child. Perhaps it is because it is introduced in the context of Nabonidus/Arabia that makes it something later generations feel obliged to maintain for authenticity, but who choose to reduce its significance; in time, the Jews need to be reminded of it.

fundamental of offerings, i.e., the bread and salt of life, is a well-attested, ancient custom in arid lands.[18] The Arabic word for "salt" is *milhat*, a derivative of *malaha*, or "treaty"; there is an old Arabic expression: "There is salt between us"; Ezra "share(s) the salt of the palace" to suggest his loyalty to the Persian king (Ezra 4:14). In his travels through Arabia, Doughty refers to the "sacrament of bread and salt" many times.[19]

The salt covenant is considered by some to be more refined and amiable than the more primitive blood-based contracts.[20] This is a vital aspect to consider, both because the subsequent Israelite religious rites are inexorably blood-rites (sacrifices), with the salt covenant being all but forgotten bar a few vague mentions in the Bible, and (primarily) because we are dealing with Nabonidus; he has a history of blood-contracts, recall, and this entire idea is forced to the fore in the upcoming verses of Exodus 17.

In the context of Exodus, we have seen Nabonidus bringing his "mixed" group of emigrants from Babylonia into the Arabian desert, a hostile, strange place many will feel uncomfortable in, even unsafe, i.e., "… the desert paths leading to Tayma are known as *durûb al-mawt*, roads of death."[21]

The covenant of salt is ostensibly between God and his people, a show of the divine willingness to protect this vulnerable group as they traverse the danger zone of the wilderness. In ordinary situations, the Arabic notion of bonding with salt is to assume a brotherhood, to take on a responsibility, a loyalty; in the theological message of Exod 16, God is seen to be setting his banner of protection over the group, just as Nabonidus had done, in the Song of Solomon, when Nitocris first arrived at Tayma.[22] This is a significant segue, for at the root of this unique scene on the Tayma sabkha is Nabonidus' own knowledge of life in Arabia. He knows the customs; he has become an honorary Arabian, respecting their rituals. For him to bring a motley crew of strangers into the heart of his old kingdom, he must be certain they, too, will act respectfully.[23]

---

[18] For a broad representation of salt in Mesopotamian contexts see Daniel Potts, "On Salt and Salt Gathering in Ancient Mesopotamia," *JESHO* 27.3 (1984): 225-271.

[19] Doughty, 284-5.

[20] Henry Clay Trumbull, *The Covenant of Salt: As Based on the Significance and Symbolism of Salt in Primitive Thought* (New York: Scribners, 1899), 6.

[21] Raymond P. Dougherty, "A Babylonian City in Arabia," *AJA* 34.3 (1930): 296–312, here 312. Also, Nab 47 ii 3-11.

[22] Tyson, 69.

[23] "All Bedouins regard the eating of 'salt' together as a bond of mutual friendship, and there are tribes who—quite in accordance with the Moorish principle, 'the food will repay you'—require to renew this bond every twenty-four hours, or after two nights and the day between them, since otherwise, as they say, 'the salt is not in their stomachs,' and can therefore no longer punish the person who breaks the contract. The 'salt' which gives a claim to protection consists in eating even the smallest portion of food belonging to the protector" (Edward Westermarck, *The Origin And Development Of The Moral Ideas* Vol

So again, there are multiple levels of meaning. There is historical and scientific substantiation for what theologians claim to be a miracle (the "manna"); there is a strong geological and personal link to Nabonidus in Tayma; and then there is the umbrella of divine protection in a potentially hostile environment, a motif that reaches its zenith at Sinai.

I [London: Macmillan, 1924], 589). Thus we see the group gathering and eating the salt on a daily basis, i.e., they were welcome at Tayma for the duration.

# 8 WHY "CUSHITE" IS A PROBLEM

Numbers 12 provides an account of Miriam and Aaron discussing Moses' "Cushite wife"; it appears immediately after the manna/quail episode which I claim happens at Tayma (see entry on "Hazeroth" pg. 208), and which, in Exodus, occurs before the group arrives at Sinai. Numbers, however, places this episode toward the end of the Sinai encampment. For me, Exodus' sequence of events takes precedence, so any extraneous material from other texts needs to be assimilated into Exodus' framework. Thus, I put this scene in the camp at Tayma/Rephidim, not Sinai.

A Cushite is a Nubian, i.e., a person especially noted for their very dark skin (see Jer 13:23). Nitocris is black. She introduces herself in the Song as one who is sunburnt (Song 1:6). The Hebrew term for "black" is *sahar*, which may be a play on Sara/Sarah (Nitocris' avatar in Genesis). The root *yshh* yields the noun *tushiya*, meaning "wisdom, knowledge." Nitocris is the woman with much knowledge.

> *And Miriam and Aaron spoke against Moses because of*
> *the Cushite woman whom he had married;*
> *for he had married a Cushite woman.*
> Num 12:1

The original author(s) of Numbers failed to expand on this, but the rabbis decided it warranted explanation, so they created a detailed Midrash

155

about Moses' missing years that told of his becoming a great soldier (which, of course, Nabonidus was, too) and marrying a Nubian Queen. They chose to translate "Cushite" as "beautiful," however (Sifre 99),[1] which I think is a bit of a cheat; they refused to deal with the tricky fact that Moses might have had a black wife, something that would really give the game away that Moses was, indeed, Nabonidus, and the "Cushite" wife was, indeed, Nitocris. It was a cover-up.

Intriguingly, a 3rd Century BCE dramatist/poet called Ezekiel wrote of Zipporah that she called *herself* a "stranger" in Midian, describing her own ancestral home thus:

> Stranger, this land is called Libya. It is inhabited by tribes of various peoples, Ethiopians, dark men. One man is the ruler of the land: he is both king and general. He rules the state, judges the people, and is priest. This man is my father and theirs. ... My father has given me as spouse to this stranger.[2]

All this makes sense but only if Ezekiel had *not* made the connection to Zipporah (Jehudijah) being Moses' (Nabonidus') *second-wife* ... he is clearly talking about Nitocris, the first wife, the black princess of the Song of Solomon.

Nitocris, I have suggested, is given by her father, Ahmose III, to Nabonidus in a conciliatory marriage during the forming of the alliance against the marauding Cyrus, in 549 BCE. The next passage from Ezekiel's narrative is Moses recounting his dream of being made king atop a great mountain, with all the "stars" at his feet, i.e., exactly what occurs, symbolically, in Song 4:8 (and Nabonidus is known for mentioning dreams on his stelae, etc.).

What interests me, however, is the mention of "Libya," for in *She Brought* I explain how there is a reference in PT Avodah Zarah (1:2, 39c) that identifies the "daughter of Pharaoh" whom Solomon married as being from the dynasty of Necho, and how scholars have chosen to see this as an aberration.[3] I continue to explain that the Necho dynasty hailed from Libya and so they were, very probably, dark-skinned. The "black pharaohs" (Dynasty 25) came from Nubia, so "Cushite" becomes a generalization, *perhaps* derogatory in the HB context, for "black *Egyptian*," not for "black"-skinned people generally.

---

[1] Stanley Schneider, "Moses in Cush: Development of the Legend," Researchgate (2019), www.researchgate.net.

[2] *Ezekiel's Exagoge* (Exodus), Howard Jacobson, trans., 60-7. https://bingweb.binghamton.edu/~jstarks/ezekiel.html.

[3] Tyson, 21-2.

So, it would seem that Ezekiel, the poet/playwright, also knew of, or suspected, this ancestral connection and thus the link between Dynasty 26 and "Solomon," even if he did not know anything about Nabonidus. The description of the "father" certainly fits the bill for him being a pharaoh (Ahmose III).

Then there is the fact that Libya is also called Put (or Phut). Josephus mentions that "Phut also was the founder of Libya," and named the place after himself (*A.J.* 1.6.2). In the Supplemental Notes to *She Brought*, I discuss the various legends that echo my own interpretation of the Song of Solomon. One of these legends is that of Joseph and Asenath. The characters parallel Nabonidus and Nitocris in great detail but for this discussion the following salient points should be noted.

The Jewish Virtual Library's entry for Asenath is:

> ASENATH (… meaning in Egyptian, "she belongs to, or is the **servant of**, [the goddess] **Neith**"), daughter of Poti-Phera, **the high priest** of On (Heliopolis). Asenath, at Pharaoh's instance, married Joseph (Gen. 41:45, et al.). She bore Joseph **two sons**, Manasseh and Ephraim, during the **seven years** of plenty (41:50; 46:20).[4]

✶ Nabonidus and Nitocris dwell in Tayma for seven years; 1 Chr 4:17 suggests she mothers (but may not give birth to) two sons.[5]

✶ Nitocris is the daughter of Ahmose III, Pharaoh and (high) priest of the solar deity (Amun), and "the son of Neith"; as Neith is the tutelary deity of Sais, and Nitocris is High Priest (First Prophet), it is almost certain she would be considered a "servant of the goddess Neith."[6] With the upcoming discussion on Nabonidus and Ahmose as "doubles" and the focus on the solar aspect at Sinai, this entire definition might well have been written for "Nitocris."

✶ Asenath's father is Potiphar in Gen 41:45 but Putiel in the Joseph and Asenath legend. That is, *put* + *iel*. The word *put* is used to denote Libya or Libyans (e.g., Ezek 30:5; 38:5; and Jer 46:9, respectively). Nitocris is from a Libyan Dynasty (Necho's).

Herodotus mentions Ahmose's "Greek" wife Ladice (*Hist.* 2.181), whom he took in a conciliatory marriage but for whom there is no record

---

[4] "Asenath," JVL, www.jewishvirtuallibrary.org. Also be spelled "Aseneth."
[5] Tyson, 213-14.
[6] For a further link between Asenath, Neith, and Nitocris, see Tyson, 120-1.

whatsoever; she is said to come from Cyrene, which is in Libya. The historian considers her the daughter of either "Battus or Arcesilaus, the king" or "Critobulus, one of the chief citizens." In other words, he doesn't know *who* her father was but he knows a few names of important people (compare this to the various suggestions he has for the marriage of Nitetis [*Hist.* 3.1-3], where he has heard a tale but cannot pin down if it involves Cyrus or Cambyses). Herodotus suggests that after the Ahmose's death Ladice is sent home to Cyrene; all evidence of Ankhnesneferibre ends with the Persian invasion of Egypt in 525 BCE. Ahmose is often considered a philhellene because of his magnanimous gestures to Greeks living in Egypt, so Herodotus seems to *assume* this woman to be "Greek" (as opposed to a Libyan by blood).

What is most interesting is that Herodotus tells this tale of Ladice in the context of a woman supposedly "bewitching" her new husband (to make him impotent, i.e., "struck with weakness"), probably so as not to get pregnant. Nitocris, in the Song, uses her magic (and the Elixir Rubeus) to keep Nabonidus from impregnating her. If you have read my paper on Ankhnesneferibre and Nitocris II,"[7] you will know that I lean toward Ankhnesneferibre being Ahmose's wife and Nitocris' biological mother. I suggest there that Ankhnesneferibre might well have resented being Queen and getting pregnant when *she* had been serving as High Priest and God's Wife. It could well be that she assists her daughter (in the Song of Solomon) because she has had a similar experience.[8]

So, even in this seemingly unrelated tale in Herodotus' *Histories*, we find a potential allusion to a Libyan (i.e., dark-skinned) 'sorceress' in a king's court, who uses her womanly wiles to deflate her conciliatory husband, and who disappears just at the time of a foreign invasion (Nitocris, I have claimed, dies when Cyrus invades Babylon[9]). Like mother like

---

[7] Janet Tyson, "Ankhnesneferibre and Nitocris II: A Question of Filiation" (2023), www.academia.edu.

[8] How could anyone possibly know that Ladice had "made a vow internally"? That the account ends with the woman erecting a statue to Aphrodite (Ishtar) is another subtle link to the depiction of Nitocris, who is predominantly depicted as Ishtar in the Song. Why does the statue face away from the city (of Cyrene)? Symbolically, a statue should face those who erect it, to bestow abundance, blessings, etc., on the people. By erecting the statue, effectively with its back to the city, Ladice maintains her defiance against enforced sexuality and impregnation. One might even suggest an allusion to Neith, for this goddess is also represented by a famous statue in Sais that bore an inscription to just this effect, i.e., it purportedly included the phrase "No one has ever laid open the garment by which I am concealed" (*Proclus: The Commentaries of Proclus on the Timaeus of Plato, in Five Books*, Thomas Taylor, trans.[London: A. J. Valpy, 1820], 82).

[9] Tyson, 225-7.

daughter, or another Herodotus mix-up? Her Libyan ancestry is the one thing that identifies the "black and beautiful" Nitocris as an Egyptian princess. Nothing is given to us that might give the game away too easily; Nabonidus and Nitocris have lost their right to be remembered as anything other than lost souls, enemies, etc. Had "Libyan" been used in Numbers 12, this would have provided Nitocris with a posthumous link back to her pharaonic ancestors, something that is painstakingly guarded against through every allusion to her.

What then of Miriam's punishment for discussing the "Cushite wife" with Aaron? We know that in the Mesopotamian belief system of Nabonidus' day, illnesses are associated with sin in some way, and the diviners (exorcists) are the only ones who can discover what sin has been committed and how to rectify this spiritual imbalance. For the Babylonian king, an ulcer is deemed the outward symptom of a spiritual shortfall (i.e., in 4Q242 Prayer of Nabonidus). Thus, Miriam's "leprosy" is not the medical condition we know of today, i.e., it is a ritualised form of punishment known in Judaism as *tzaraat*.[10] The translation of Num 12:11 (i.e., in the NRSV, "do not punish us") is "do not lay sin upon us."

The disease she is struck with (i.e., "leprosy") is seen as a direct result of her perceived sin, i.e., not of being "bitter" but of daring to bring up Nabonidus' past, his ill-fated relationship with Nitocris (Num 12:10-16).[11] Miriam is speaking of her once-mother with her husband; there is no way of discerning whether this was in a positive or negative context; in fact, it doesn't matter. It is the act of mentioning her at all that gets Nabonidus into a rage, and he strikes out at his daughter, banishing her from the camp for seven days. That the crowd insists on waiting for her punishment to end before they all move on indicates, again, a pro-Jehudijah/Ennigaldi sentiment.

In Deut 24:9, there is a reminder of Miriam's skin disease; the people are to guard against it, and to bear in mind her punishment. Clearly, a very serious offense has led to her condition, yet it is so ambiguous, until you know what really happened between father and daughter. Deuteronomy, unlike Exodus, is a pro-Moses text. The insinuation is that Miriam was rebellious toward her father; she humiliated him by stealing his thunder with her victory song, and then by reminding him of his weakest moments, his failure as a husband, etc.; the warning in Deuteronomy is basically, "do as you are told and don't defy your leader/father." (Recall her identification as "Puah" mentioned in Chapter 1's outline of her character.)

---

[10] Rabbi Jill Hammer, "Priestesses, Bibliomancy, and the Anointing of Miriam," 2013, https://rabbijillhammer.com. Sîn was responsible for punishing with "leprosy," according to Esarhaddon's Succession Treaty (SAA 2.6, 419-21); the curse also demanded expulsion.

[11] For the idea of illness being the result of sin, see Tyson, 5-6.

A very interesting detail no one seems to talk about is Aaron's response: "Do not let her be like one stillborn, whose flesh is half consumed when it comes out of its mother's womb" (Num 12:12). This may seem a bizarre thing to say but it is a direct allusion to something in the Song of Solomon. Aaron is married to Miriam, i.e., to Ennigaldi, Jehudijah's biological daughter for whom she has served as a life-long companion/nurse. There is little doubt once the truth is out concerning Miriam's ancestry (mother and daughter talk) secrets are revealed and truths, however painful, revealed.

In the Song, Nitocris aborts her first unwanted pregnancy.[12] When the Egyptian emissaries visit (Song 7), demonstrating that they know what Nitocris has done, they allude to the abortion by referring to her "sandals." In the Talmud, prayers offered up during pregnancy include this one: "Within the first three days a man should pray that the seed should not putrefy; from the third to the fortieth day, he should pray that the child should be a male; from the fortieth day to three months, he should pray that it should not be a sandal ..." (Berakoth 60a). The sandal is "a kind of abortion resembling a flat-shaped fish (*foetus compressus*)."[13] The reference to a "stillborn," misshapen, fleshless foetus cannot be coincidental (no such thing in the HB, in my opinion).[14] Thus, Aaron commits the same sin as Miriam (mentioning the Cushite wife) but he goes further; he pinpoints the exact moment when Nabonidus' marriage to Nitocris began to fail, i.e., the moment she defied him and ended the pregnancy he had waited for.

*It is not the colour of the Cushite woman's skin that is the problem*, it is this blatant reminder of the entire deception that made a fool of Nabonidus that is unforgivable, yet Aaron is not, *at least not immediately*, punished.

The situation is more immediate for Miriam, however, who has become a thorn in Nabonidus' side. This imprudent incident seems to be the final straw for Nabonidus, as far as she is concerned.

---

[12] Tyson, 114-16.

[13] Marten Stol, *Birth in Babylonia and the Bible: Its Mediterranean Setting*, Cuneiform Monographs 14, T. Abusch, et. al., eds. (Groningen: Styx Publications, 2000), 18, n. 95. See also Niddah 31a.

[14] Could this reference be hinting at Miriam's condition? Might Exod 21:22-23 be a direct (Hebrew) response to Nabonidus striking a *pregnant* Miriam? As the potential avatar of Sarah (i.e., as the supposed daughter of Nitocris), I have suggested it is she, not an aged "Sarah," who gets pregnant. Such a situation is accounted for in the Laws of Hammurabi (209-10), where monetary recompense is prescribed, but in Exodus the punishment is basically "an eye for an eye." Miriam is, after all, a much revered woman.

# 9

## WATER AND BLOOD

## "... SHALL WE BRING WATER?"

The story in Exod 17:1-7 of the Israelites complaining in the desert that they have nothing to drink is often considered in terms of the practicalities of nomadic life (i.e., God gives the travelling migrants enough sustenance to survive their journey).[1] In light of this, I went in search of a pragmatic but still biblically sound interpretation of the event from the perspective of Moses physically leading a group of thirsty people through a desert landscape (rather than on some spiritual journey, for instance).

What is there in the territory surrounding Tayma that could account for the strange tale of the water from the rock and the battle with/of Amalek?

Performing a basic search for "rocks near Tayma," thinking I may just find a topographical survey of the land, I was utterly overwhelmed with the plethora of photographs and videos of a rock I had no knowledge of, i.e., the split rock at the al-Naslaa Rock Formations, about fifty kilometres south of Tayma (*Fig. 12*). Split Rock (as I call it) has caused a sensation as more and more tourists are discovering it because of its almost unnatural division; the 7.5m by 3m rock is split completely in two in such a neat and linear way,

---

[1] Nathaniel Helfgot, "'And Moses Struck the Rock': Numbers 20 and the Leadership of Moses," *Tradition* 27.3 (1993): 51-8, here 53-4.

the internet has been brimming with rumours of alien laser technology!

On his travels through Arabia in 1876-8, Doughty witnessed at least two similarly split rocks, i.e., one in Khaybar and one near Mecca; both had Islamic legends attached to them concerning a supernatural (divine) sword wielded in anger.[2] As he found the latter (far less dramatic) rock interesting enough to sketch, as well as several other less impressive rocks, I don't think he ever saw this one (Khaybar is over two hundred kilometres away from the al Naslaa formations), which I'm certain he would have commented on, as it is also inscribed, and he collected inscriptions.

Such unusual and memorable rocks were well known markers to the Bedouin, who would memorise them, allowing them to navigate through an otherwise sparse wasteland. "Strange are the ... forms in this desert of wasted sand-rock spires, needles, pinnacles, and battled mountains, which are good landmarks," Doughty states. He asked a Bedouin if he know them all: "From my childhood, I know as good as every great stone upon all our marches, that may be over three or four thousand square miles."[3] Doughty then claims a Bedouin guide told him the *names* of a few of the rocks, and says another man hinted that such names were secret, to be known only to the Bedouin.[4]

About a day's walk away, to the north, lies Tayma, the oasis, with all the water the group will ever require for both humans and beasts. I suggest the scenario is based, *in part*, on this very distinctive landmark indicating to Nabonidus that the journey is almost over and everyone will find water. Though simplistic, it does sit comfortably in the historical/geographical context.

> *Bring water to the thirsty ...*
> *O inhabitants of the land of Tema.*
> Isa 21:14

Nabonidus knows this land, he has traversed the desert for many years; he knows how close they are to home. He is perturbed by the people's lack of trust in his ability to get them safely to water, i.e., "Why do you quarrel with me? Why do you test the Lord?" (Exod 17:2). These rather forced questions are inserted to anticipate/explain the names that follow in 17:7.

If he has, over the years, gone native to a degree, it is perfectly feasible that he would devise his own names for the landmarks he most relies upon to take him safely back home. We soon see him naming Split Rock.

---

[2] Charles M. Doughty, *Travels In Arabia Deserta,* New York: Random House, 1921. 2.97; 549.

[3] Doughty, 1.284-5.

[4] Doughty, 1.328: "Some murmured, 'Why did Zeyd show him our landmarks?'." The response, in effect, is that the explorer was honoured as a temporary Bedouin.

*Figure 12: Split Rock in the desert of al-Ula, about 50 km from Tayma (Image: Disdero [2021], Wikimedia)*

# STRIKE

The Hebrew word for "strike" in Exod 17:6 is the verb *nakah*. This is not a light tapping of a stick on a rock, nor a firm-handed thwack; this is a powerful, unrestrained, definitive *beating*. It is used throughout the HB in contexts of attacking, slaying, smiting, defeating, killing (e.g., Gen 34:30; 2 Sam 23:10, etc.); *nakah* is used in the descriptions of Moses instigating the plagues, i.e., striking the Nile, the dust, etc. It has the connotation of superiority, power, and dominance. It is the verb used to describe the killing of the Hebrew by the Egyptian in Exod 2:12.

Numbers 20 also uses *nakah*. Moses is told to "command" the rock to release its water but he takes it upon himself to "beat" the rock *twice*. For this single act, ostensibly, Moses is punished by God and he is barred from entering the Promised Land. After all he has done to get God's people out of Egypt, through the desert, and into the land of Canaan, why would something so seemingly trivial turn God against Moses? Clearly, it cannot be that trivial; we have just come too far from the original meaning of the story to recognise what is actually going on here. The sin that allegedly angers God is rooted in the man's very nature; there is much symbolism here.

Edwin M. Good suggests the use of the verb *nakah* in Exod 2:11 "shows that the Egyptian bully was not merely beating the Hebrew but was murdering him,"[5] and yet no one dares to point out that the same verb is used to describe Moses beating the rock in Numbers; but how can you murder a rock?

The answer lies in the rather odd identification provided in rabbinic literature, i.e., the rock's spring (water) is called "Miriam's Well":[6]

## Taanit 9a:9
The well was given to the Jewish people in the merit of Miriam …. When Miriam died the well disappeared, as it is stated: "And Miriam died there" (Num 20:1), and it says thereafter in the next verse: "And there was no water for the congregation" (Num 20:2).

## Shabbat 35a:6
A spring that is portable, i.e., that moves from place to place, is ritually pure and is regarded as an actual spring and not as drawn water. And what is a movable spring? It is Miriam's well.

## Rabbeinu Bahya, Bamidbar 20:2:1
"The congregation had no water." When Miriam died, the well disappeared, because the well was due to the merit of Miriam who merited the water through [watching over] Moses [at the Nile], as it is written, "And his sister was stationed at a distance" (Exod 2:4). And because it disappeared now, with her death, [Israel] realised that it was with them through her merit, and from here [we can infer] that the well was with them for the whole 40 years [of their wandering].

The site of the "bitter waters," Meribah (in Numbers), has the definition of "strife, contention, provocation." "Meribah," however, is also one of the names Moses gives to the area where the water from the rock and the battle with Amalek takes place (Exodus 17), which the rabbis took to mean that Miriam's Well must have followed the Israelites, i.e., from Kadesh to Rephidim at least. However, this is too simplistic and doesn't give the rabbis credit for their astuteness.

This seemingly bizarre interpretation of the rock in Exodus 17 is not as strange as it seems, for buried beneath such archaic and fanciful notions is an element of truth, for the "rock," within the context of the HB as didactic literature, *is* meant to represent Miriam. "Miriam" of course, means "rebellion, bitterness" but the character shows no such temperament, in fact, she is portrayed as quite the opposite, singing and dancing, etc. The only possible

---

[5] Edwin M. Good, "Capital Punishment and Its Alternatives in Ancient near Eastern Law," *SLR* 19.5 (1967): 947-77, here, 952, n. 24.

[6] Compiled by Lisa Batya Feld, on Sefaria, www.sefaria.org.

connection to the idea of rebelliousness might be the moment she is caught gossiping with Aaron about Moses' first "Cushite" wife (Num 12:1-9). I think she is thus named *because* she is Nabonidus' daughter, e.g., in 1 Chronicles 4 "Mered" is the father of "Miriam" and both names mean "rebellious."

In the books of Exodus and Numbers, Nabonidus is being seen to be tested, retrospectively. We have seen the covenant of salt between the Bedouin and the Israelites that will protect them in this strange land, but now Moses (Nabonidus) must prove himself worthy of the leadership he has taken upon himself. Will he be the right leader for the new nation as it finds its way in the Promised Land? If Moses is deemed not worthy after hitting the rock, according to Num 20:12, there *must* be more meaning between the lines.

With the idea of Aaron teaching Moses sympathetic magic back in Exodus 15, it is possible that Moses is getting a little too sure of himself. Like "Solomon" in the Song, he is too hasty, over-zealous, and as a result, things get out of hand. He over-indulges in the sacred Elixir Nitocris revealed to him, he boasts about it, and eventually makes money from it; his antics earn him a reputation in Babylonian history as a madman who thought he knew more than the sages. It seems he has not really changed. By ignoring God's order to speak to the rock (to "command" it) and by *forcibly beating* it instead, whilst saying to the crowd "Shall *we* make water come from this rock?," Nabonidus is basically reverting to form. He is presumptuous and proud, showing himself and Aaron to be the ones with power. Just as he was seen to be usurping the Tablet of Destinies[7] and was admonished for this, having to serve a penance of seven years (according to Dan 4:19-27), so he is once again stealing God's thunder, so to speak. This could be reason enough for divine disapproval; I think, however, there is even more to it.

Back in Song 8, when the young Ennigaldi first enters the temple at Ur, Nitocris and Jehudijah, along with all the other priestesses, swear that no man will harm their "little sister." I wonder if Nabonidus, having learned that the girl is *not* of Egyptian royal blood, i.e., is *not* Nitocris' daughter after all, becomes enraged. Perhaps he now doubts she is really *his* child, which would humiliate him, given how much he publicised her divine election and dedication as *entu*. Ennigaldi would be no more than about seven or eight when Babylon fell, so by my calculations with respect to dating the journey, by the time they get to Kadesh, where she is said to meet her end, she would be about thirty years old, perhaps a little older. She is the *entu*, a high priestess, powerful and sacred in the eyes of her followers and colleagues. She is the wife of Aaron, the mother of his children, yet her father treats her as if she is nothing, now. The first bitter water scene in Exodus 15 serves as the first moment Moses loses his temper with Miriam; he chucks the wood

---

[7] Tyson, 5-6.

into the water in such a way as to show no respect. As suggested earlier, one might even insinuate that this is a euphemism for attempted (sexual) penetration, or perhaps a demand for her (Elixir) blood (considering the ensuing battle with Amalek and its undertones, this is a distinct possibility).

The rationale for Moses being heavy-handed, for beating a woman who dares to make him look diminished or who dares to assert her independence/power, harks back to the scenes in the Song 5:6-7, where Nitocris attempts to seek out the king and is beaten by the guards, seemingly on his command, and to where he attempts to force himself on her in her own rooms.[8] Nabonidus is depicted as a rather uncouth man, a rugged soldier with a propensity to learn things beyond his sphere of capability; he falters, gets mixed up (VA, v 4), and then lashes out in frustration. He uses force because that is what he knows. The story of Moses killing the Egyptian and hiding the body, with his only concern whether or not someone saw him and could tell, is set early in the narrative to give him a *modus operandi*, and to allow us to realise he *is* a violent man.

Nabonidus is recorded to have slain many during his campaigns (e.g., Nab Chr i 11-22; ii 15b-18; iii 12b-16a), but that is the norm for warrior-kings. The Verse Account, being anti-Nabonidus propaganda, makes it appear that he was a slayer of the innocent, too (iii 1); and even today, people still debate whether *he* angrily slaughtered the residents of Opis after the army retreated from Cyrus in 539 BCE (Nab Chr, iii 12b-16a). Throughout the exodus narratives we see him becoming somewhat of a despot, a megalomaniac even, whose answer to everything seems to be "off with their heads!" Exod 32:27-8 is a prime example; he orders the people to kill each other, simply because they worship what is familiar in a frightening place, while Moses is absent. Perhaps it is not Yahweh who is called "Jealous," but Nabonidus. (The extraordinary diatribe in Deut 13:12-18, Deuteronomy being a pro-Moses text, seems to be a consequence of this outburst in Exodus 32.)

It has been argued that the phrase "Moses raised his hand" in Num 20:11 is not like other instances of Moses' lifting the rod before striking the Nile, the dust, etc., and that it should be taken figuratively, i.e., as pertaining to his *state of mind*, in readiness for violent action against a foe.[9] When you raise your hand in anger, it presupposes imminent violence.

The fact that Miriam is equated not just with the rock but also with a well, does have a symbolic resonance, i.e., she is a well of female blood, which is often also referred to as "water" in Babylonian texts.[10] This is why

---

[8] Tyson, 127-8.

[9] Ka Leung Wong, "'And Moses Raised His Hand' in Numbers 20:11," *Biblica* 89.3 (2008): 397-400. Wong concludes that the enemy is God.

[10] Ulrike Steinert, "Fluids, Rivers, and Vessels: Metaphors and Body Concepts in

the "well" scenes in the HB (and even in the Gospel of John) all have to do with forthcoming marriage/procreation. If Nabonidus now doubts he is Miriam's father, and has been humiliated publically, it may be that he seeks a form of revenge he knows will be most abhorrent and demeaning to Ennigaldi, i.e., the Elixir rite, or rather, his version of it.

By standing above her, wooden staff in hand, Nabonidus taunts her, calling out to the crowd, just as he does in the Song 5:1, for them to join the fun and "drink" (i.e., in the Song this is Nitocris' blood he is supposed to keep sacred but he offers it to his friends as if it were alcohol).[11] "Shall we get water (blood) from this stone?" he teases. When Miriam defies Moses, publically, *again*, he loses his temper and thrashes her[12] ... to death. Suddenly the Moses of Exodus 2 re-emerges, violently reacting to something that infuriates him, resulting in the death of another. This time, however, there are many witnesses; he cannot hide from this murder.

Brownsmith suggests that women in ancient Near Eastern texts are often depicted as being objectified as something to consume, be it as food or drink: "objectification is a necessary stage of consumption; to metaphorically eat a woman, one must first dehumanize her into a sexual object."[13] By suggesting to Miriam that he would take her by force, take her blood, Nabonidus not only demeans her, he effectively rapes her (whether he actually sexually assaults her cannot be known); this is what he tries to do to Nitocris in Song 5:4 (which is also left ambiguous with regard to how far he goes). He objectifies her to the point of becoming a "rock" he can beat to procure his favourite tipple, i.e., the blood of a woman. The striking of the

---

Mesopotamian Gynaecological Texts," *JMC* 22 (2013): 1-23, here 4-5. Joann Scurlock, "Medicine and Healing Magic," in *Women in the Ancient Near East: A Sourcebook*, Mark Chavalas, ed. (United Kingdom: Taylor & Francis, 2013), 101-43, here 110. Water is a universal, fundamental symbol of the feminine; it is such in many civilizations over the millennia. In Nabonidus' own culture, the very foundation of the world begins with Tiamat in the creation epic, the Enuma Elish. She represents the saltwater sea, i.e., the bitter water; her husband Abzu (*apsu*; later, this becomes the swamp realm of Enki/Ea), is the fresh (sweet) water. As discussed earlier, Tiamat has another role to play in the exodus saga (in the idea of the plagues) but Exodus 15 and 17 seem a deliberate allusion to the overthrow and slaying of Tiamat by the storm-god Marduk, and thus the imposition of a new world order.

[11] Tyson, 123.

[12] In Egyptian law, beating with a wooden stick is normal practice for corporeal punishment (Müller-Wollermann, 233). Doughty describes witnessing just such a beating in public (of harem women, with a stick, even though their husbands were present), 1.222.

[13] Esther Brownsmith, "To Serve Woman: Jezebel, Anat, and the Metaphor of Women as Food," *Researching Metaphor in the Ancient Near East: An Introduction*, Ludovico Portuese and Marta Pallavidini, eds. (Wiesbaden: Harrassowitz Verlag, 2020), 29-52, here 45.

'bloody' Nile thus becomes a foreshadowing of the death of Miriam.

This is why the water/rock scene of Exodus 17 comes immediately before the battle with Amalek, where the ex-king's peculiar addiction is tackled head on.

> *They angered the Lord at the waters of Meribah,*
> *and it went ill for Moses on their account;*
> *for they made his spirit bitter,*
> *and he spoke words that were rash.*
> Ps 106:32-2

# BLOOD CURSE

> *... anyone who strikes another with a weapon of wood in hand*
> *that could cause death, and death ensues, is a murderer;*
> *the murderer shall be put to death.*
> *The avenger of blood is the one who shall*
> *put the murderer to death ....*
> Num 18-19

Blood is at the centre of the story of Nabonidus, at least during the time of his Tayma residency. Discovering the Elixir Rubeus was a turning point in his life, especially in his search for esoteric wisdom, but it also proved to be instrumental in his downfall. He became addicted and his character changed. The rabbis attempted to explain this away as some sort of possession by an evil demon (Ashmedai),[14] but in reality, it was the physiological and psychological effects of substance abuse that made him a king too weak and obsessed to defend his kingdom. Legend told that he finally regained his senses and returned to his duties as king ... that only lasted a few years. Behind the scenes his penchant for sacred blood rites (and for riches) continued to shape his fate.

Caught in the middle of all this is Jehudijah, the woman Nabonidus had impregnated without even remembering her face, it seems (but that is deemed the way for a Mesopotamian king). Having lived in the shadow of her nemesis, Nitocris, having given up her child to the Egyptian interloper, etc., she finds herself on the exodus with a still-addicted Nabonidus, in the middle of the desert, probably with no other females to support her, save her daughter.

After the death of Miriam is where I propose the circumcision episode in Exod 4:24-6 would better fit. What Jehudijah does with the bloody foreskin of Ishmael, in effect, is to expose Moses as having shed *innocent*

---

[14] E.g., Tyson, 28-9.

blood. The death of the Egyptian he attacked and killed earlier (Exod 2:11-15) is somewhat mitigated by the fact that the man was clearly doing evil himself and had to be stopped (it may be that this is pure fabrication, to explain the trip down to Midian and to provide a *non-magical* rationale for Jehudijah's strange action,[15] which is probably part of the original text, as it is consistent with her character throughout the exodus narratives and the Song). She takes on the role of blood-avenger by physically *touching* Moses with the blood not of the deceased Miriam, but still with the blood of Moses' offspring.

Edward Westermarck, in a lengthy analysis of ancient blood-revenge and related cursing rituals, states that "of all conductors of curses none is considered more efficient than blood."[16] The act of *touching* is key (in Exod 4:25, the verb *naga* is used, i.e., "to touch, reach, strike, throw, etc."):

> ... he grasps with his hands either the person whom he invokes, or that person's child, or the horse which he is riding ; or he touches him with his turban or a fold of his dress. In short, he establishes some kind of contact with the other person, to serve as a conductor of his wishes and of his conditional curses.[17]

Jehudijah holds onto the young Ishmael as she casts the bloody remnant toward Moses' feet, completing her hex.

The traditional "bloody husband" translation is possibly forced, for the word for "bridegroom" is *chathan*, which means "to make oneself a daughter's husband" (*Strong's*). It can also mean "father-in-law," or even "mother-in-law" depending on the context. In effect, the Hebrew verse suggests that Zipporah declares Moses has treated Miriam in such a way as to make her, legally, his bride, i.e., he has either slept with her or has forced her to subject herself to the Elixir ritual, which Jehudijah then takes as tantamount to rape. However, he has also killed his own daughter, an innocent woman.

Westermarck goes on to explain:

> The duty of blood-revenge is, in the first place, regarded as a duty to the dead, not merely because he has been deprived of his highest good, his life, but because his spirit is believed to find no rest after death until the

---

[15] Remember the striking clause in Exod 22:18, "You shall not permit a female sorcerer to live." I think this resonated strongly in the post-Nitocris/Jehudijah Jewish community. Clearly, Moses and Aaron are allowed to perform magic, but Jehudijah's magic is the forbidden "sorcery" of women.

[16] Edward Westermarck, *The Origin and Development of the Moral Ideas*, 2 vols. (London, 1908), 365.

[17] Westermarck, 586.

injury has been avenged. The disembodied soul carries into its new existence an eager longing for revenge, and, till the crime has been duly expiated, hovers about the earth, molesting the manslayer or trying to compel its own relatives to take vengeance on him.[18]

I suggest this is where the original perception of the "Well of Miriam" might be rooted. Those on the journey with Nabonidus, who later put this account into words, reckoned the revenge-seeking soul of Miriam as the entity that seemed to follow them wherever they went. The Well is symbolised by a "rock" that "looks like a sieve" because this is their lasting impression of the joyous, singing and dancing woman, beating the rhythm of the victory song as they had reached the safety of Ezion-geber.

Jehudijah, as Zipporah in Exodus 4, is the one who avenges her daughter's death by cursing Moses with blood, as she had cursed him in the Song, with words.

*This* is why the water-from-the-rock scenario costs Moses the right to enter the Promised Land (though he has already been there, as Abraham).

# KADESH-BARNEA

The verb *qadash* means "to be holy, sacred, purified, etc." The noun *qodesh* refers to the "sacredness" of something, e.g., *qodesh haqodeshim* means "Holy of Holies." The nouns *qadesh* and *qadesha* refer to religious prostitutes (male and female, respectively).

"Meribath-kadesh" in Deut 32:51 is a conflation of the two "water" scenarios of Exodus/Numbers, i.e., the "bitter waters" of Meribah and the striking of the rock at Kadesh, where Miriam dies (both in the Wilderness of Sîn).

Meribath-kadesh is considered the location where Moses and Aaron fail to honour God (Deut 32:51); the first instance involves both Moses and Aaron in a magical invocation (to a storm deity, probably) to bring rain (as well as being the first assault on Miriam), and the second involves Moses boasting about his (and Aaron's) power to procure water from a rock, thereby not giving credit to God (plus the fatal beating of Miriam). Even though the author of Deuteronomy is a pro-Moses writer, unlike the author of Exodus, the reason for God's ultimate rejection of Moses is the same strange incident with/at the rock. Nabonidus' patent inability to stifle his addiction to the Elixir, or his temper, leads to the murder of Miriam and this is the basis of Moses' rejection by God (i.e., by the Israelites). No wonder it is so carefully obscured.

---

[18] Westermarck, 481.

If this first employment of "Kadesh" has such negative connotations, why use it again for "Kadesh-barnea"?

Abarim translates "Kadesh-barnea" as "sacred desert of wandering, holy purifying staggerings" (their explanation is rather lengthy but worth reading in full), derived from the verb *qadash* ("to be holy"), perhaps *bar* ("desert or empty field"), and the verb *nua* ("to stagger or shake"). *Strong's* suggests: "From the same as Qadesh and an otherwise unused word (apparently compounded of a correspondent to *bar* and a derivative of *nuwa* meaning 'desert of a fugitive'); Kadesh of (the) Wilderness of Wandering."[19]

The latter part of the name is potentially from *bar*, the Chaldean, Syriac, and Arabic word for "desert," or from the Hebrew roots *b'r*, *bwr*, or *brr*. The derived nouns of the latter pertain to wells, ditches, pits, etc., as the verbs tend to reflect the act of cutting, digging, breaking (ground). The verb *ba'ar* describes the act of inscribing (tablets); the verb *barar* suggests purifying. The noun *bor* designates a material used in metal purification procedures. The noun *berit* means "covenant," while the verb *berit* denotes divine creativity. Everything about "-barnea" seems utterly Sinaitic. Mount Sinai is in the desert; it is holy, sacred; it is the place where the stone tablets are carved; where the priests are consecrated and made pure; where metal is purified yet to be explained); where a covenant is made; where the new priestly Israel is created.

The verb *nua*, the final element of *barnea* ("to shake, stagger, quiver, tremble, wander, be unstable" etc.) brings to mind Moses at Rephidim, feeling weak and unable to support his own arms at the battle with Amalek, in Exodus 17 (i.e., another confirmation that Aaron is probably younger, as he provides support to the aging Nabonidus). This emphasises the notion of warfare.

So, there seems to be a distinct blend of profaneness *and* sacredness to the name "Kadesh-barnea."

There *is* a location that suits this dual-natured description: Sela. I suggest Sela is the true site of the "crossing of the Jordan" (the Rift Valley, not the river) by Joshua, *et al.*, and the site of the deployment of the spies into Canaan. Sela parallels Sinai on several counts, both structurally and symbolically.

---

[19] A very subtle link can be made to Cain's curse: "You shall be a fugitive and a wanderer on the earth" (Gen 4:12); this is spoken in the context of Abel's blood being in the "mouth" of the ground (i.e., figuratively drinking it). The "fugitive" aspect of Strong's translation stands out here, especially if Nabonidus did, in fact, kidnap Jehudijah, is held responsible for Nitocris' death, and does kill his daughter, Miriam (i.e., Moses is already deemed a fugitive by virtue of killing the Egyptian). The "wandering" reference is germane but the subliminal allusion to drinking blood, together with a reminder that Moses is weak and unsteady, does suggest the site where the two aspects (i.e., blood and instability) converge in Exodus, i.e., Kadesh/Rephidim.

While the significant rocks in the exodus narratives are defined by *tsur*, the name "Sela" is thought to derive from the Arabic root *sl'* meaning "to cleave, split." This echoes the Hebrew roots *b'r*, *bwr*, and *brr* that pertain to the act of "cutting," etc., and this allusion is to the geological structure of the site, i.e., it is a mound that essentially has twin peaks. In a paper online I discuss the "Ascent of Akrabbim" as it relates to Sela, and to Nabonidus' solar-related interests at Sinai; the cleaved, twin-peaked 'mountain' of Sela is key to understanding "Akrabbim."[20] However, this structure also emulates the rock at Kadesh (near Tayma), i.e., Split Rock ("Massah/Meribah"; see below), thereby bringing together Sinai *and* Kadesh references.

Sela is isolated in the landscape; it has caves; it has water; it has a summit sacred space (two actually). The Qenites, who play a huge part in the Sinai story, also seem to be linked to Sela (cf. Num 24:21, where *sela* is used to denote "cliffs"), but then they were nomadic and traversed great swaths of land in the region. On the one hand, Sela is a sanctified 'high-place' that reminds the group of Sinai (and thus the covenant) but on the other, a fortress (on one side of the summit) with a history of combat and conquest. This is why the name "Kadesh-barnea" fits so well, with its sacred/profane dichotomy. It is not to be misidentified as Sinai, however.[21]

In Deut 1:2, we are told it takes "eleven days" to travel from Kadesh-barnea to Horeb (i.e., from Sela to "the *horeb*," or "Rephidim/Kadesh" in the Wilderness of Sîn, see pp. 205-6), via Mount Seir (discussed later). The total distance traversed, between Kadesh (in the *horeb*, south of Tayma) and Kadesh-barnea (Sela) is about 960 km or 600 miles, meaning a pace of approximately 87 km or 54 miles per day (see *Fig. 11*).[22] Camels can walk a hundred miles (not kilometres) in a day without discomfort.[23] I think the addendum was inserted into Deuteronomy 1 because the toponyms mentioned in 1:1 all pertain to the Hijaz/Tayma region (see pp. 206-13) but

---

[20] Janet Tyson, "Scorpion Rising: Nabonidus and the Ascent of Akrabbim" (2024), www.academia.edu.

[21] The sites of Sela and Petra are not identical, either. Petra, as we know it today, is farther south and, as I attempt to convey in a short paper ("Nabataeans, Nabonidus, and the Tribe of Dan," www.academia.edu), is a much later manifestation of the Nabataeans, i.e., the first being here, at Sela. Early archaeologists had a tendancy to name newly discovered locations with reference to biblical toponyms; there was never discovered a sign saying "Welcome to Petra." The carved rocks were a subsequent expression of their society.

[22] Compare the breakdown of walking distances and times in Martin Jacobs, "'A Day's Journey': Spatial Perceptions and Geographic Imagination in Benjamin of Tudela's Book of Travels," *JQR* 109.2 (2019): 203-32, here 217-18. See also Doughty 1.112, who travelled in this region by camel and managed 50 miles in one day.

[23] PBS, "Desert Survival: Transportation," https://www.pbs.org/lawrenceofarabia/revolt/transport.html.

the later scribe wished to emphasise that the story continued northward, to Sela; it is thus included by mentioning the time it took to get there.

I suggest Sela is also to be identified with "Pisgah"; this name means "cleft," from *pasag*, "to pass between." It too is/has a "high place" (Num 23:14). It is allegedly directly opposite Jericho[24] on the Moabite side of the Rift Valley. From it Moses could see a panoramic view of Canaan.

In Num 13:26, the spies return to Moses and Aaron, who have been waiting in "the wilderness of Paran, at Kadesh." The 'original' Wilderness of Paran, as stated earlier, is that which surrounds Sinai; if Sela mirrors Sinai, the Wilderness around *it* must be mirrored, too (see *Fig. 13*). "Kadesh" here is Kadesh-barnea.

From Sela to "Pisgah," to "Mount Nebo," therefore, seems to me to be a straightforward progression, symbolically but also geographically, for the first two are identical and the third is, I suggest, the very clifftop from which Nabonidus' own vast inscription marks his passing (through the wadi), serving as a constant reminder of his role in the exodus but also the symbolic delineation between Canaan and Arabia (in Num 32:38 "Nebo" is mentioned as belonging to the Reubenites who dwelt in the Transjordan). This is Nabû-na'id's 'mountain' if for no other reason than he put his name on it! Thus, Sela once belonged to the Jews but was figuratively kept at arm's length, just as everything else associated with Nabonidus. Ultimately, it is granted to a relatively insignificant tribe that chooses to reside, effectively, in Arabia (i.e., Reuben is granted "Nebo" in Num 33:38).

This makes further sense when we read in Josh 10:41 that Joshua conquers everywhere "from Kadesh-barnea to Gaza," i.e., "from/to" being a common biblical indication of a vast stretch of land, in this case, incorporating everything from their starting point, Sela, all the way up to the Mediterranean coast and Gaza, which recall, is where Nabonidus once held vast troops.[25] Judg 1:36 suggests the boundary of the Amorites' territory, adjacent to that of Israel, also has Sela as the main marker ("from Sela and upward"). Sources have suggested that "the south-eastern frontier of Judah could not have been laid down so far to the south in the time of Moses and

---

[24] *McClintock and Strong Biblical Cyclopedia*, "Pisgah," https://www.biblical cyclopedia.com/P/pisgah.html. See here, "Appendix 6," pp. 387-9.

[25] It is worth noting that Deut 1:4 interjects with a statement concerning Moses' alleged defeat of two kings in the region (the Transjordan), i.e., King Sihon and King Og. Despite rabbinical lore about these brothers being giants, etc. (e.g., Ber. 54b; Shabbat 151b), this *may* pertain to the military campaign for which the vast rock inscription at Sela was created (see pp. 387-8). The territory of these two kings is given to the Jews who remain in the Transjordan, i.e., Reuben, Gad, Manasseh (Num 32:33). Cf. Deut 2:24-35.

Joshua";[26] indeed, but shift the date to the 6th Century BCE, and you find no impediment.

As for "the Jordan," I suggest the name was applied to the river at a later date, in order to further entrench the entire history in Jewish territory. Originally, "Jordan," which means "descending" (from *yarad*, "to descend") simply referred to the Rift Valley that cuts through the entire land, from the Sea of Kinneret to Aqaba.[27] From Sela, the group would indeed be "descending," i.e., into the wadi. That they pass ("cross over") on "dry land" may be an echo of Moses' story[28] but it might also be an echo of a similar play on the logistics, i.e., in Moses' case, the dry land under his feet was actually a boat; here, it is "dry" simply because there is no river in this region of the Arabah. It is another example of burying the truth deep with the symbolic story.

Two thoughts:

The difference between "Sin" (*Ciyn*) and "Zin" (*Tsin*), I think, is that "Sin" originally related to the territory around Tayma, eching Nabonidus' known preference for Sîn, the lunar deity; this was *his* territory. It is referred to *only* as "Sin" in Exodus. Numbers uses both terms; Deuteronomy uses only "Zin." The Wilderness of Zin emulates the Wilderness of Sîn to complete the mirrored effect of the exodus narratives but is slightly altered to allow for it being in Israelite territory, not Nabonidus' (it signifies another rejection of Nabonidus and his beliefs).

The BDB suggests that Sin is Pelusium, on the eastern Nile Delta border, and that the name is akin to the Egyptian *'Imt*, or "clay."[29] In discussions yet to come, we will see that "clay" is one of the defining (symbolic) attributes of Nabonidus, and of the geology of Tayma itself. If the "Egyptian" element is a legitimate aspect of "Sin" it is because of Nabonidus' focus on Egyptian myth and ritual (again, yet to be discussed).

---

[26] *McClintock and Strong Biblical Cyclopedia*, "Akrabbim," https://www. biblicalcyclopedia.com/A/akrabbim.html.

[27] The Wadi Al-'Arabah runs from the Dead Sea to Aqaba; this still marks the geographical division between Israel and Palestine.

[28] E.g., the fact that the group allegedly crosses during the flood season (Josh 3:15) is a direct reflection of Nabonidus at the Nile during its flood season; the waters "heaping" up, etc.

[29] *Strong's* 5512: "Ciyn," https://biblehub.com/hebrew/5512.htm.

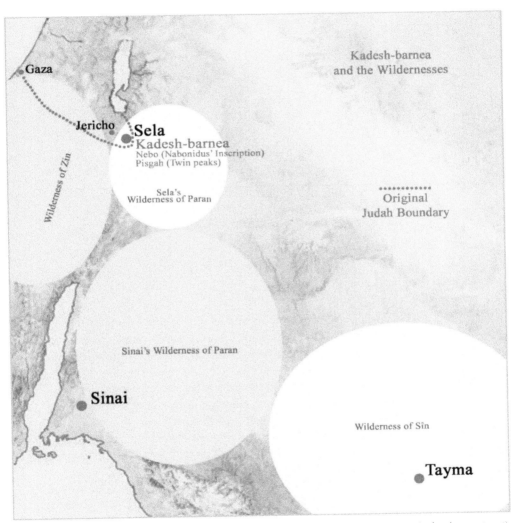

*Figure 13: Potential site of Kadesh-barnea and the mirrored Wildernesses (Image: Author's construct)*

# 10

OLD HABITS

## BLOOD-LICKERS

The Jewish perception of Amalek, even to this day, is one of profound animosity and suspicion. Watching just one video online of a rabbi reading his account of the biblical Amalek, I was stunned by his vocabulary concerning their attack of the Israelites in Exodus 17, i.e., "frenzied; insane; suicidal; inexplicable; cowardly; vicious; hatred; genocidal; obsession; irrational; vicious; destroy; archenemy." This was in the space of about six minutes. His anger and disgust were intense and he seemed to take it all very personally. Yet, so little is known about "Amalek." Perhaps in some Jungian way, the shadowy nature of Amalek's existence makes it/him/them more sinister a threat?

The etymology of Amalek is very interesting, as it allows for a direct symbolic connection to the Song of Solomon and the interpretation I have proposed, i.e., that it tells the story of Nabonidus, Nitocris, and the consequences of their esoteric blood-rite.

"Amalek" is "a composite of *am* and *lak*, i.e., 'the people who came *to lick blood*' (emphasis mine)."[1] In his studies of early Arabian marriage and

---

[1] Rabbi Moshe Weissman, *The Midrash Says: The Narrative of the Torah-portion*

other oaths, Smith writes:

> Now at Mecca within historical times such a life and death covenant
> was formed between the group of clans subsequently known as
> "blood-lickers" (*la'acat al-dam*). The form of the oath was that each
> party dipped their hands in a pan of blood and tasted the contents. But
> the use of blood in sealing a compact was not confined to Mecca. In
> *Agh.* 4₁₅₁, at the conclusion of peace between Bakr and Taghlib, we
> find the phrase "when the blood was brought nigh and they proceeded
> to close the compact."[2]

Bringing things even more into the frame of a Nabonidus scenario is an
inscription found (1999) in an area south-west of Tayma [now] called Ramm
but originally known as Iram; this is very close to Split Rock at Al Naslaa:

> Inscription 1
> 1) I, MRDN the servant of Nabonidus, the king of Babylon,
> 2) came with RBS¹RS¹ [or: army leader] (so?)
> 3) ... *nm* in the attack/invasion [or: 'in the emigration; for
> inspection/supervision'] behind the bare (?) desert.[3]

The etymology of the last word *l'q* is questioned, thought dubious, as
it means "to lick" and the author, H. Hayajneh, believes the word might
mean "bare" (as in "to graze bare") but adds: "It is possible that the word *l'q*
here is the name of the *bdt* 'desert'. But I have to admit that no toponyms
related to *l'q* in North Arabia are known to me."[4] So, we are left with the
interpretation of "lickers."[5]

Note in the above inscription the idea of an emigration, i.e., an exodus.

---

*in the Perspective of our Sages* (Brooklyn, NY: Benei Yakov Publications, 1980), 158.

  [2] William Robertson Smith, *Kinship and Marriage in Early Arabia* (United States: Wipf & Stock, 2023; 1903 reprint), 57.

  [3] Hani Hayajneh, "First Evidence of Nabonidus in the Ancient North Arabian Inscriptions from the Region of Taymā'," in *Proceedings of the Seminar for Arabian Studies, Vol. 31*, Papers from the thirty-fourth meeting of the Seminar for Arabian Studies held in London, 20-22 July 2000 (Archaeopress, 2001), 81-95, here 82.

  [4] Hayajneh, 86.

  [5] For "licking/swallowing" in Egyptian rituals see Robert Kriech Ritner, *The Mechanics of Ancient Egyptian Magical Practice* (Chicago: Oriental Institute of University of Chicago, 1993), 92-110. The act of swallowing (e.g., blood), becomes synonymous with "knowing" in the Book of the Dead; Ankhnesneferibre, Nitocris' mother, pays homage to Sia, the "Great Swallower," deified "Perception," on her sarcophagus (106-7). The Elixir Rubeus ritual, as discussed in *She Brought*, was intended to unite the human with the deity, to allow him to ingest wisdom and thus know the divine (it just went a bit pear-shaped when Nabonidus got hold of this magic).

To "inspect"? Moses sends emissaries to scout ahead (e.g., Num 13:1), to make sure everything is safe, etc. Nabonidus, a seasoned army man would do no less. After the Tayma years, an inscription reveals that the then King was somewhat surprised by how willingly the Arabian people took to him, suggesting either that the VA version of events (i.e., of Nabonidus slaughtering and pillaging his way into Tayma, etc.) really is nothing but propaganda, or, that Nabonidus remained utterly deluded:

> The people of Arabia, who ... [...] weapon(s) [...] of the land of Akkad [...] ... for robbing and taking away the possessions that they had available, but, by the word of the god Sîn, the god Nergal broke their weapons and they bowed down at my feet.
>
> Nab 47 i 45-ii 2

If he is now arriving back in Tayma unannounced, perhaps he is uncertain of his welcome since he lost his kingdom and the city now answers to Cyrus. Sending someone out first is prudent. I mentioned earlier that Belshazzar might have been sent back to Tayma to secure Nabonidus' interests in the city/region.

Num 13:29 locates the Amalek people in the Negeb (desert) which, by convention, is located north(west) of the Gulf of Aqaba (cf. 1 Sam 15:7). Biblical locations we accept today were sometimes quite arbitrary (often by well-meaning but un-travelled theologians or archaeologists intent on proving the veracity of the Bible), based on one or more passages that are, themselves, ambiguous. There is no pinpointing even the Negeb, which is a rather nebulous entity that could well suggest, simply "desert/wilderness." The etymology of *negev* is: "dry, parched" and/or "undulating, rolling hills," from an unused verb *negeb*, "to be dry" and/or from the verb *negeb*, rolling or waving, which in turn comes from the verb *gabab*, "to be concave or convex" (i.e., like sand dunes or low hills). It is also understood to mean, broadly, "The South," especially by early translators of the HB. It may or may not be identical, geographically, to the Negeb we speak of today.

If we assume a little more fluidity in the understanding of *negev*, it could be applied to the general (undefined) expanse of dry, undulating lands anywhere between Egypt and Canaan (Num 13:29; 1 Sam 15:7; 30:10-21) and farther south, into the regions of Sela and even farther into Arabia. Where would one draw the line (literally in the sand)? I suggest the name was originally devised to echo the Nufud, the Arabian Desert, and as such, is simply a continuation of it (the two meld together).

The "bare (?) desert" in the inscription (above) can then be read as: "the *l'q* desert," i.e., the desert of Amalek, the blood-lickers.

> *Then he looked on Amalek and uttered his oracle,*
> *"Amalek was the first of the nations,*
> *But his end shall be destruction."*
> Num 24:20

"Amalek," *if* it is the name of a people (but note Num 24:20 and Deut 25:17, where Amalek is spoken of in the second-person singular, i.e., "he" and "his"), might relate to a band of disparate nomads, opportunistic marauders who travel the broad desert lands without a base, without a defined heritage, like pirates of the sands. Despite the declaration that God will wipe all memory of them from the earth (Exod 17:14; Deut 25:19), they still appear in other books of the HB, e.g., Num 13:29; Judg 7:12-25; 2 Sam 1:1-16, etc., as if they are indestructible. That is the nature of the abstract notion of evil; it persists, from generation to generation.

Exod 17:8 says "Then Amalek came ...," not "Then *the* Amalek(ites) came ...," suggesting something more abstract, i.e., a representation of something more intellectual, more arcane. Amalek comes to represent, I propose, a dangerous and unsavoury aspect of human nature, much as the *yeser*, the demonic force at large in the world, drawing men to their doom (at the hands of women).[6] The rabbinic literature is just as vehemently opposed to the *yeser* as it is to Amalek. It is because of this association with an almost primal malevolence (as its use in Gen 6:5 and 8:21 suggests) that the Ephraimites, the subsequent archenemies of Judea, become equated with Amalek in the "Song of Deborah: "The Ephraimites have their root in Amalek" (Judg 5:14).[7]

The scenario in Exodus 17 is profoundly Nabonidus-based; it is a metaphor of personal choice, the qualities of leadership, and the ability to change. The "blood-lickers," then, can be seen as representing all those

---

[6] Yishai Kiel, "Dynamics of Sexual Desire: Babylonian Rabbinic Culture at the Crossroads of Christian and Zoroastrian Ethics," *Journal for the Study of Judaism in the Persian, Hellenistic, and Roman Period*, 47.3 (2016): 364-410, especially 368-77.

[7] In Judg 7:4-8. Gideon 's vast troops are reduced to a mere 300 by the most unusual method: the troops are taken to a lake to drink – those who kneel down and drink from their hands are eliminated, while those who "lap the water with their tongues, as a dog laps" are chosen to fight (these are the 300). What person would lap like a dog? The Hebrew term here is *laqaq*, "to lap, or lick"; these are Amalekites. The context of the battle here is between Israel and Midian, but the Amalekites are mentioned as being there too. I suggest they are, in keeping with their alleged nature, acting as mercenaries for Gideon. This cannot be 'officially' sanctioned in the HB as Amalek is such an all-encompassing enemy. The number 300 is used to identify these soldiers as the same ones who fought at Kadesh, against Joshua, i.e., 300 in gematria is equated with the letter *shin*, spelled the same as Sin/Sîn, i.e., the Wilderness of Sîn, where the battle takes place in Exodus 17.

"friends" of the king in the Song of Solomon (5:1) who became supporters of Nabonidus in his rather deranged exploitation of the Elixir Rubeus, i.e., those who entered into the covenant of blood under false pretences, making a mockery of the sacred rite Nitocris had introduced to court.[8] They seem to appear at Rephidim as if out of the blue because they are *symbolically* associated with Tayma itself (the king probably invited elite men from all the surrounding lands to partake).[9] As a representation of an intangible force of evil, a tool sent by God to judge Nabonidus himself, Amalek becomes a projection of the dethroned king's conscience. This is a personal battle.

> *By the command of the god Sîn and the goddess Ištar, the kings*
> *of the lands Egypt, Media, (and) Arabia, and all of the hostile kings*
> *sent (their envoys) into my presence for (establishing) goodwill and peace.*
> Nab 47 i 38-45

Nabonidus loved the personal attention being King afforded him, but he didn't seem to enjoy the *office* of King. One can imagine him sitting in his throne room at Tayma, in his opulent palace, meeting and greeting every dignitary, every royal envoy, accepting their gifts, wining and dining, sharing his most special vintage with those who flattered him the most. But he is now an aging, desert-weathered man. He was in his sixties (we think) when he became king, and that was twenty-plus years ago. He has traversed the desert, walked up mountains (*supposedly*), taken on military jaunts (i.e., the "rescue" of Lot), and now he is tired. God sets him a challenge, a test: Confront Amalek, i.e., those he had debauched with, those whom he offered his wife's most sacred and personal attribute. He has to prove himself a convert to the new way of thinking, the new way of behaving. He is no longer the King of Babylon, the one to whom everyone bowed down and flattered, the one who worshipped idols and the blood of women. The author(s) of Exodus are creating a battle that is symbolic; it may well be based on an actual skirmish with a people known as Amalekites but the dreaded enemy is used as a foil, here, to portray Moses nearing the end of his usefulness. Here is what I can see happening in this scene …

Amalek appears suddenly to battle with Israel, in the *horeb*. The first thing Moses does is delegate leadership to Joshua, his much younger assistant. He does not wish to be forced into a situation where he has to openly denounce his past and his once allies. Moses suggests he will go up

---

[8] Interestingly, Hayajneh (82) suggests that the word *ḥlm* in line 1), translated in 1999 by another scholar as "friend," is actually a South Arabian loan word and is thought to have a later provenance (after the rise of Islam); *ḥlm* is therefore replaced with "a variant of *ġlm*," and rendered "servant."

[9] Tyson, 123.

onto a nearby hill ("tomorrow"; why does he procrastinate, unless to show unwillingness?) and watch, with his faithful "staff" in hand, looking the leader but not actually *doing* anything. Notice that the three original leaders i.e., Moses, Aaron, and Miriam, are now Moses, Aaron, and Hur. Miriam is no longer with them.

The old man on the hill raises his hand and this appears to have the effect of bolstering the Israelites' strength; when he lowers his hand, Amalek gains the advantage. When he tires, Aaron and Hur decide to help out; they sit Moses on a rock (this is a natural way of sitting for Arabic nomads in the desert) and take one arm each, holding them up until the battle is over, to even the odds. The glaring question is this: If Moses is supposed to be able to affect the fighting from a distance just by raising his "hand," why do the other men hold up *both* arms? Why not just prop up the one that seems to be getting the job done for Israel, leaving the other hand to hold the mighty staff and thus *not* aid Amalek?

# MASSAH, MERIBAH

The answer is all about the landmark Split Rock, just south of Tayma. Moses' right and left hands raised and supported mirrors the structure of the rocks, side by side, i.e., right- and left-hand rocks. Both boulders are resting on (precariously small) *supports* (that are plugs of the rock that continue under the sand, having been eroded into this dome-shape).

The site is Rephidim; the verb *raphad* means "to spread or support," occurring only three times in the HB, i.e., twice in Job (17:13 and 41:22, where it is used as "spread") and once in, of all places, the Song of Solomon, i.e., where Nitocris, during the *hieros gamos* scene of 2:5 demands to be "sustained" with apples (we later learn that she, too, is "tired," i.e., from Nabonidus' incessant attempts to impregnate her).[10] In Song 3:10, where the king's palanquin is described as having some sort of back-support of gold, the term *rephidah* is employed, i.e., the only such use in the HB. To me, this is intentional intertextuality, with the Song being a known masterpiece by the time Exodus is written. The authors are telling us, quite plainly, that this is Nabonidus, this is Tayma, where the Song is set, and the entire battle that ensues here is one to thrash out, once and for all, Nabonidus' loyalties. (The allusion to Song 2 reminds us of the blood connection; the allusion to Song 3 confirms this is the same route "Solomon" took on his return from Egypt, loaded with goods, i.e., along the same caravan trail.[11]) Will he support his

---

[10] Tyson, 69.
[11] Tyson, 83-4.

old friends, will he make a run for Tayma and leave the Israelites to fend for themselves? Is he over his fascination with the blood rite? Even the mention of the building of an altar and the "banner of the Lord" (Exod 17:16) echo the building of high-places by "Solomon," and the "banner" of Song 2:4 (which is also in the context of a public declaration).[12]

The Hebrew word for "rock" here is *tsur*, which also has the connotation of "cliff"; when you look at the rock in question (*Fig. 12*), one side is uncannily flat, while the other is rugged and rounded. The front of the rock *is* cliff-like, i.e., a sheer vertical (which also allows for the wordplay on *shur*, or "wall," recall).

Moses (or rather the author) names the two sides of the rock—one half is Massah, the other Meribah. "Massah" means "proving, or test," from the noun *massah* ("test, trial, proving"), and/or from verb *nasa* ("to try or test"), from the root *nasas*, which relates to metallurgy. "Meribah" is said to mean "a place of strife," from the noun *meriba*, and/or from the verb *rib*, "to contend." While the explanation in Exod 17:7 is that Israel tests God, the actual testing, we are expected to comprehend, is of Moses *by* God. Notice that the naming comes before the battle in the narrative, just as Miriam's death is announced before the striking of the rock in Num 20:1; it is to foreshadow, prepare the reader for, what is about to occur. It teaches us to pay attention and make the right connections for ourselves. The HB is replete with secrets, codes, allegories, riddles; it does not spoon-feed the intellectually lazy. The vague hint of "metallurgy" in the etymology of "Massah" may seem quite random, but there is meaning even in this, for it alludes to the *region* in which Tayma is located, it has a bearing on the deeds of Nabonidus as "Solomon," and it helps to locate the elusive Mount Sinai.

The Israelites who stood in front of Split Rock must have thought it so rare, so impressive, so touched by God (as people today think it is touched by aliens) that it inspired this symbolism. They created an indelible monument to a profoundly significant moment in their passage from Babylonian exiles to free Israelites; the landmark itself could never be forgotten or demolished. This is a bold testament of their changing perception of Moses and an omen of things to come, i.e., the final rejection of the Babylonian ex-king.

## Pillars of Melqart

In 1 Kgs 7:21 the two bronze pillars said to be at the entrance to Solomon's

---

[12] Tyson, 69; "banners" also appear in Song 6:4, where Nitocris is reaching the pinnacle of her power in Nabonidus' court (146-9).

temple, are *named*, i.e., "Jachin" and "Boaz." I mentioned earlier Meyers' interpretation of these pillars as having to do with the legitimisation of dynastic power.[13] Here is where my take on this comes into play.

Just as in this scene from Exodus, at Rephidim, with Moses naming the two sides of Split Rock, so Solomon in 1 Kings names the two pillars, i.e., a left-hand and a right-hand pillar. If a Tyrian influence is at play in the making of these pillars, they probably pertain to the worship of Melqart, as discussed earlier. The pillars of Melqart have to do with the two rocks of Tyre, seemingly floating. Split Rock now mirrors this notion, with the two sides of the same rock seemingly hovering above the ground, yet rooted to the earth by some divine force. The imagery is thus a direct correlation between Nabonidus' Tayma and Hiram's Tyre.

The name "Boaz" means "in strength," from the prefix *be*, "in," and the verb *azaz*, "to be strong, powerful." "Jachin" means "he establishes," from the verb *kun*, "to be set up, fixed, or established."

Together, Solomon's pillars reflect, the arrogance and audacity of the self-deified Nabonidus (at Tayma), who sees his kingdom as firmly established and strong. This brings to mind the writing-on-the-wall scene of Daniel 5, and the inevitability of hubris leading to a fall. Here, at Split Rock, we are given the first hint that all will not go well for Nabonidus; as Moses, he reveals his true colours, his weaknesses, and his instability. This is then taken up by the authors of 1 Kings and is reconfigured as part of the very fabric of Solomon's temple and the subsequent fall of the united-Israel dream.

It should also be noted that it was also the custom in Egypt for each new pharaoh to erect a pair of pillars at the entrance to a temple;[14] with the allusions to a shared identity between Nabonidus and Ahmose (yet to be fully explained), the erection of Solomon's (Nabonidus') temple pillars may be more Egyptian-influenced, than Tyrian (but one has to wonder if the Tyrians' pillars were inspired by their long-standing Egyptian overlords).

# ELDAD AND MEDAD

In the manner of Moses' testing at Rephidim, with the Amalek representing his rather salacious, sexually liberal past, Numbers preserves another incident (in the same geographical area, near Tayma) that might correlate with this one, i.e., Num 11:26-30, where two men, Eldad and Medad, remain

---

[13] Carol Meyers, "Jachin and Boaz in Religious and Political Perspective," *CBQ* 45.2 (1983): 167-78.

[14] E. P. Uphill, "Pithom and Raamses: Their Location and Significance," *JNES* 28.1 (1969): 15-39, here 25.

in the camp whilst the rest go to the tabernacle. They are accused of "prophesying."

"Eldad" means "beloved of God, God loves," from *el* ("God") and the verb *yadad*, "to love." "Medad" means "beloved, lover," also from the verb *yadad*. The verb *yadad* is predominantly a *sexually*-related expression for "love"; it contains the word *yad*, or "hand" and thus is also used to mean "casting lots" (a physical action that might resemble a sexual act). I think it is becoming clear what this scene is representing, i.e., homosexual relations between two men who skip out of their duty to go to the tent of meeting, in order to have a secret liaison.

The play on "prophesying" is subtle, for the other men who do go to the tent are also said to prophesy (Num 12:25). The verb used is *naba*, which denotes the generally accepted notion of religious ecstasy, divine inspiration, etc., but it also has negative connotations as it is used to denote false prophets (e.g., 1 Kgs 22:10; 2 Chr 18:9; Jer 14:14; Ezek 13:17) and pagan, ritualistic ecstasies (e.g., 1 Kgs 18:29; Jer 23:13). Taken from the latter prospective, especially when the "incident at Peor" is discussed later, we can envision an episode that relates to Nabonidus' own inherited cultural proclivities, i.e., the sexually liberal and uninhibited antics associated with the worship of the goddess Ishtar. Her followers revel in a variety of sexual behaviours in honour of her; they adopt cross-dressing as a symbol of their devotion, and it seems nothing is taboo.

We must remember that whoever wrote the final version of the exodus narratives, especially Exodus itself, had an agendum to depreciate Nabonidus' effect on early Israel. Exodus is a testing of the man, and he falls short of the requirements for Israel's first ruler. Just as he is pitted against his blood-licking friends, the Amalek, to prove a point, here in Numbers he is seen to be sanctioning the two men's behaviour as perfectly normal under the circumstances and merely a sign of their devotion (as it would have been in Babylonia). He sees it as them simply getting carried away with the excitement of being so close to God, etc., but to the Jewish authors this is clearly a demonstration that Nabonidus is unsuitable, still a retrograde in their eyes. Notice that it is Joshua, i.e., Belshazzar, the younger generation, who sees the awkwardness of the situation and urges his father to stop the men. He perhaps realises things are different now and adjustments need to be made, but Nabonidus is too old and set in his ways to see the disparity, let alone address it.

# GERAR

In the first discussion of Sarah, "Gerar" was mentioned as a potentially symbolic name that is linked etymologically to Hagar, e.g., in terms of "fleeing" or being "dragged away," etc. We need to recall that the Abraham and Moses stories are mirror-images of each other to quite a degree; what happens to/with Nabonidus on one leg of his journey may have consequences or echoes in the other. This is either to illustrate the fact that Nabonidus remains true to character in both contexts, or to continue a specific theme or motif across the boundaries of the narratives, in order to draw a thematic connection between the two.

"Gerar" is a case in point. The place is mentioned in Genesis 10; 20; 26, and 2 Chronicles 14, without any other indication of location than a general region or direction in relation to other *known* cities. According to Gen 10:19, Gerar is situated in western Canaan, quite close to Gaza, which is where modern archaeologists have identified a site.[15] The toponym is provided, primarily, in the context of Abraham seemingly pimping out Sarah to Abimelech and, amazingly, his son Isaac doing exactly the same thing with Rebekah. When I discussed Gerar earlier, in the section on Sarah, I said that the context of the action *involves* Sarah but the toponym is linked to Hagar, i.e., because Sarah is the memory, or avatar, of Nitocris but Jehudijah (Hagar) is the one still alive and in the wandering group.

As "Moses," Nabonidus does not miraculously change his nature; he is the same man, with all his proclivities, traits, and motives. Although the name "Gerar" does not appear in the Moses story, its equivalent in Arabia can be located by following the clues in Abraham's itinerary.

The Hebrew Gen 20:1, reads: "Abraham journeyed there to the *negeb* (i.e., the "*south*-country") ... and stayed in Gerar" (i.e., temporarily). Back in Gen 18:1, Abraham is living at the "oaks of Mamre, the Amorite" (note that in 18:16-22 Abraham walks with the three men to show them the way to Sodom and Gomorrah; he does not go there himself). The word for "oak" is *elon*, i.e., "terebinth, or tree"; this is an echo of two places: Eloth and Elim, i.e., al-Wajh and Tayma (as above).

The name "Mamre" caused me a bit of a run-around, but in the end I think I have found the pattern, so bear with me, as I need to include elements yet to be fully discussed.

"Mamre" comes from the noun *memer*, "bitterness"; and/or from the verb *mara*, "to be fat or well fed." Potentially, we see two elements of the Exodus narrative we now comprehend, i.e., the "bitterness" of the water scene in Exod 15:22-5 (which takes place at al-Wajh), and the eating of the "manna" in Exod 16:4-26 (which takes place at Tayma and has the connotation of greed/gluttony in Num 11:33-4).

---

[15] Eliezer D. Oren, Martha A. Morrison, and Itzhak Gilead, "Land of Gerar Expedition: Preliminary Report for the Seasons of 1982 and 1983," BASORSup 24 (1986): 57-87.

Mamre the *man*, is brother to Eshcol and Aner, Abraham's "allies"(Gen 14:13): "Eshcol" is defined as "bunch, cluster; properly the stem or stalk of a cluster";[16] this is precisely how Nitocris is envisioned by the lusty visitors who taunt her in Song 7:8, one threatening to climb the tree and steal her juicy cluster of dates; and exactly how Nabonidus (Solomon) is described in Song 1:4, i.e., as a "cluster of henna" (bushes, for protection)." This suggests Eshcol is Nabonidus. Just to bolster that connection, the noun *esh* means "fire," another aspect of Nabonidus' depiction (and also of Yahweh) at Sinai.

"Aner" means "boy"; Aner is Eshcol's son, i.e., Nabonidus' son, Belshazzar. The "brother" to Nabonidus, in Genesis *and* Exodus is Nahor/Aaron. Thus, the man "Mamre" is, for the exodus narratives, Aaron. When we tie together all the other evidence for Aaron and his home, it seems his territory is somewhere west of Tayma (discussed in the context of his demise, later). So, for Sarah to be buried "east of Mamre," for instance (Gen 23:17), suggests she is (symbolically) interred in or near Tayma.

This might suggest the author of Genesis 14 is playing with his readers, for "Abram" cannot be an ally to himself; it might be an intentional indicator of the parallel nature of the two narratives, i.e., pointing us to idea that Abraham is Nabonidus. The idea of "allies" is actually based on the sealing of a "treaty" between these three characters, Mamre, Eshcol, and Aner (using the term *berith*, or "covenant"; also used for the treaty between Solomon and Hiram, in 1 Kgs 5:12). With the covenant of salt a deliberate indication of an agreement between Nabonidus and his people, and the indigenous peoples around Tayma (including Aaron and his community), this allusion to a "treaty/covenant" echoes the "City of Four" definition I provided earlier, i.e., this is the meaning of "Kiriath-arba," the alleged site of Sarah's Hittite burial site. So we come full circle, arriving again at Mamre, near Tayma.

The Arabian mirror-image of "Gerar," therefore, is to be found somewhere between al-Wajh and Tayma. I propose it is synonymous with the general concept of "Rephidim/Kadesh," *south-west* of Tayma, where Miriam refuses Moses' demands and is killed. Abarim's potential translation of "Gerar" as "to be pressed into service" seems more apt now, perhaps.

This can potentially tell us where "Sodom and Gomorrah" might be located in the Arabian context. As Abraham is in the region of Rephidim in Genesis 18, and the three men continue to walk away from there; and considering what happens at these sites in Genesis 19, I suggest we need to look at the Harraat, i.e., the volcanic ranges that inspire trepidation in any sojourner's heart, as a place of death and danger (discussed again later). The black, charred-looking lava (especially near Khaybar) is the remnant of violent cataclysms over

---

[16] "Eschol," *EB*, www.biblegateway.com.

eons, i.e., volcanic eruptions that would be apt inspiration for the description of the "sulphur and fire" of Gen 19:24. There is even plentiful salt here, in the sabkhas (i.e., for the scene with Lot's wife in 19:26).

If "Sodom and Gomorrah," the two towns known for their supposed sexual depravities (Gen 19:5-12), are south of Tayma, this places them in the same region where Amalek, the symbolic representation of Nabonidus' once-chummy "blood-lickers," does battle with Joshua. The Amalek, recall, are destined for destruction, too (Exod 17:14). The sexual nature of the issues in both Lot's home and the battlefield at Rephidim, and the divine retribution implied in both scenarios, does suggest a common foundation. Whether the actual events occur in Canaan or Arabia, we may never know, but the etymology never lies![17]

## Gerrha in Strabo

Strabo says that on the eastern coastline of Arabia is "Gerrha, a city situated on a deep gulf; it is inhabited by Chaldaeans, exiles from Babylon" (16.3.3).

From the biblical perspective, the Gerrhaeans are said to be the descendants of Hagar: "… a city of the people of Hagar would have become 'han-Hagar', or possibly Hagara', when written in Aramaic. When Hellenized, it would have become 'Gerrha'."[18] This potentially links the place with the legends of Abraham, and also to the region known today as Hegra, i.e., Mada'in Salih, the general area I designate as Kadesh/Rephidim.[19] There may also be an intended play on words with Jehudijah (Zipporah) and Moses' son, "Gershom," ("stranger, exile," from *garash*, "to drive out, cast out").

The fact that the city is identified by its Chaldean population, deemed to be "exiles" from Babylonia, is striking and many have attempted to explain this, e.g., "the historian F. C. Movers suggested in 1856 that it might have been Nebuchadnezzar who exiled the nomadic Gerrhaeans from Mesopotamia as part of a policy to protect his empire from menacing Arab tribes"; on the other hand, "most historians … believe the nomads of Gerrha were expelled during the reign of Achaemenids," possibly when Babylon

---

[17] In terms of the Harraat, the name does not appear in the HB and is Arabic, but notice how many of the *har-* terms in Hebrew fit the notion of a volcanic field, e.g., *hara* (to burn, ignite); *harar* (hot, burned, charred); *harhur* (violent heat), etc.

[18] "The Hagarites/Gerrhaeans," https://nabataea.net.

[19] For a detailed analysis of Paul's use of the Hagar/Arabia/Sinai connection, see Stephen C. Carlson, "For Sinai is a Mountain in Arabia: A Note on the Text of Galatians 4:25," *ZNW* 105.1. (2014):80-101.

fell to the Persians.[20] The Gerrhaeans are Aramaean, not Yemenite or Arabian, ethnically;[21] they are also considered "nomads"[22] Abraham (Nabonidus), of course, is the "wandering Aramaean," and Tayma is strongly Aramaean; his group of exiles/fugitives are domiciled there immediately after Cyrus' amnesty of the exiles.

Gerrha became one of, if not *the*, richest, busiest, most influential and illustrious ports in ancient Arabia, practically monopolising trade with the profoundly wealthy and successful Sabaeans, when the old trade routes through the desert proved insufficient to support the ever-increasing demand for South Arabian incense, spices, etc.[23] Thus there is a link to Abraham the trader, and to the mysterious legend of Solomon and the Queen of Sheba; the trading alliance between the Sabaeans and one of Nabonidus' chief trading ports might easily encourage the notion that "Sheba" is located in southern Arabia. It is possible that early exegetes also recognised this connection and presumed the tales of Solomon reaching the ears of the Queen to be merchants' gossip, i.e., transferred along the incense trail between the two regions.[24]

With this synchronicity, it does seem that the author who devised the tale of Abraham/Isaac at "Gerar" is intentionally alluding to some sort of parallel or connection with the famed trading port of Gerrha. It might be to highlight the trading aspect of Nabonidus/Belshazzar's toing and froing; perhaps the ex-king has solid connections at Gerrha. It is also possible there is an unknown (to us) city near the port of al-Wajh that replicates these features of Gerrha, e.g., somewhat inland from the bay, where Nabonidus would go to make trade deals, etc. It is plausible that as King of Babylon he would have had dealings with this port on the east coast of Arabia. It's certainly worth further investigation, especially if and when any new Nabonidus inscriptions turn up from the eastern regions of the peninsula. The mirroring effect of the entire Nabonidus post-Cyrus era may include far more regions/sites than I have discerned.

---

[20] "The Hagarites/Gerrhaeans," https://nabataea.net.

[21] Shamsaddin Megalommatis, *Meluhha, Gerrha, and the Emirates: Introduction to the Ancient History of the Emirates* (Germany: Dictus Publishing, 2012), 32.

[22] "The Hagarites/Gerrhaeans," Nabataea.net. In the 3rd Century BCE, Nicander of Colophon refers to the "nomads of Gerrha and those who plough their fields by the Euphrates" (*The Poems and Poetical Fragments*, A.S.F. Gow and A.F. Scholfield, eds., [Cambridge: Cambridge University Press, 1952], 111).

[23] Megalommatis, 31.

[24] I refute this association, however, in *Nabonidus and the Queen of Sheba: Roots of a Legend* (Norwich: Piriŝtu Books, 2024).

# 11        FURNACE AND FIRE

Today, metallurgy is considered only as a craft, making it difficult to believe that Yahweh was formerly the god of metallurgy. In addition, our ignorance of this reality results from the exclusion of almost all direct evidence linking Yahweh to metallurgy in the biblical writings. However, … something about the 'metallurgic roots' of Yahwism was certainly known at least by the authors of the book of Genesis, Exodus, Numbers, Kings, Isaiah, Jeremiah, Ezekiel, Amos, Obadiah, Habakkuk, Zechariah and Job. For this reason, the hiatus existing in the Bible concerning the former identity of Yahweh should be considered as intentional. Understanding the source of this attitude may certainly help to elucidate many obscure points in the emergence of monotheism in Israel.[1]

## QENITES

One of the most intriguing theories about how the Israelites came to worship the deity Yahweh is the Qenite hypothesis, which basically suggests that the worship of Yahweh was inherited from the Qenites,

---

[1] Nissim Amzallag, "Yahweh, the Canaanite God of Metallurgy?" *JSOT* 33 (2009): 387-404, here 404.

the nomadic Midianites known for their metallurgical prowess and heritage. Though first broached by 19th Century biblical scholars, it is now experiencing a bit of a revival, especially among archaeologists.[2] In the singular, *qayn* "meant originally 'metal-worker, smith' as in Aramaic and Arabic; the meaning is clearly preserved in the appellation of the third son of Lamech in Gen 4:22, 'Tubal the smith, craftsman … worker in copper and iron'."[3]

Ancient lore from all over the world links metallurgy with magic and ritual. From Phoenician texts, for instance, we learn that a smelter is to be sought out if one wants to obtain a curse against an enemy; "the text … seems to compare—as a magic act—the smelting of lead to that of the enemies of the author of the text."[4] This should sound familiar, as the linking of smelters and enemies is found in the HB (e.g., 1 Kgs 8:51; Ezek 22:20).[5] According to Philon of Byblos, the ancient Phoenicians called the (iron) smith *chorosh* i.e., "magician," due to "his knowledge of the secret manipulations and necessary rites to purify the 'new, unclean metal'."[6] "There are ... indications that the Qenites enjoyed a certain status as ritual specialists or as the beneficiaries of a special relationship with Yahweh."[7] The smith is "generally an honoured and rich man, who inherits his craft. He is a potent magician, his fire is holy, his social position is high in proportion. … Apart from the guilds or clans of smiths we find many itinerant smiths … who are very specially considered to be powerful magicians."[8] This sounds like Aaron.

From the mining of raw materials from deep inside mother earth, where the chthonic masculine and feminine forces are deemed to be

---

[2] For instance: Nissim Amzallag, "Yahweh, the Canaanite God of Metallurgy?" *JSOT* 33 (2009) 387-404; "From Metallurgy to Bronze Age Civilizations: The Synthetic Theory," *A.JA* 113 (2009): 497-519; Joseph Blenkinsopp, "The Midianite-Kenite Hypothesis Revisited and the Origin of Judah," *JSOT* 33 (2008):131-53; J. M. Tebes, "The Archaeology of Cult of Ancient Israel's Southern Neighbors and the Midianite-Kenite Hypothesis," in *The Desert Origins of God: Yahweh's Emergence and Early History in the Southern Levant and Northern Arabia,* J. M. Tebes & Ch. Frevel, eds., Special Volume of *ER* 12/2 (2021).

[3] W. F. Albright, "Jethro, Hobab, and Reuel in Early Hebrew Tradition," *CBQ* 25.1 (1963): 1-11, here 9.

[4] José Ángel Zamora López, "Bronze and Metallurgy in Phoenician Sources," in *Phoenician Bronzes in the Mediterranean,* Javier Jiménez Ávila, ed., (Madrid: Real Academia de la Historia, 2015), 29-45, here 36.

[5] Also, as refiners of the soul, e.g., Prov 17:3; Mal 3:3.

[6] R. J. Forbes, *Metallurgy in Antiquity: A Notebook for Archaeologists and Technologists* (Brill, Leiden, 1950), 82.

[7] Forbes, 153.

[8] Forbes, 64.

manipulated and controlled, to the oven/kiln/furnace, which is "considered a sacred object, an object of adoration, a magical uterus,"[9] the metallurgists work with secret knowledge and divine resources. They conduct their work on auspicious days, set by "tradition, premonitions, or by astrologists"; they make sacrifices to their furnaces with accompanying "liturgical and even cosmological ceremonies"; and their attention to purification rituals is meticulous.[10] Purification often involves rites centred around water but also blood,[11] and includes abstinence from sexual relations.

The role of a smith/metallurgist is a professional one but also a social one, and is hereditary;[12] the role is conferred upon the next generation "through a program that resemble[s] a mystical initiation."[13]

> During the work the smelters live in temporary shelters in a state of strict taboos. They may not enter their own home, nor shall their wives wash, anoint themselves or put on ornaments .... The men moulding the kiln for smelting the ores are not allowed to drink any water!

> ... Practically every operation such as the lighting of a kiln, the starting of a new piece of smithing, etc., are carefully regulated and they should be accompanied by certain offerings or ceremonies. This even covers the digging of the ores. Especially sexual taboos are prescribed all over the world. The smith has to avoid the company of women; no woman, more particularly a pregnant woman shall enter the smithy; the workers often work naked. The fire shall be kept pure, for does not the god who gives the smith power reside in it? ... The fire shall always be kept burning and shall be purified by regular offerings.[14]

---

[9] Mihai Rotea, et al, "Bronze Age Metallurgy in Transylvania: Craft, Art and Ritual Magic," *AMN* 45-46/I, 2008-2009 (2011): 5-36, here 9-10.

[10] Rotea, 11.

[11] Rotea, 10.

[12] López, 38.

[13] Rotea, 11. Millennia of oral and written tradition notwithstanding, there are those who reject this perspective, arguing that the due to the paucity of definitive *archaeological* remains, the smith, "commonly envisioned as a highly specialised male person who controlled the secret and magical knowledge of metalworking–and his supposed itinerancy–remains largely a theoretical construct" (Maikel Kuijpers, "The Sound of Fire, Taste of Copper, Feel of Bronze, and Colours of the Cast: Sensory Aspects of Metalworking Technology," in *Embodied Knowledge: Historical Perspectives on Technology and Belief* [Barnsley, UK: Oxbow, 2013], 137-150, here 141). For a pro-elite perspective, see Amzallag, "A Metallurgical Perspective on the Birth of Ancient Israel," *ER* 12.2 (2021): 11-18.

[14] Forbes, 81. There are several quotations from this work only because there is so little material on the subject; Forbes himself says he knows of only one or two others. He writes: "most writers have shunned this labyrinth and skipped over this subject with a few

Already we can begin to see some familiar concepts and themes, e.g., the purity concerns, the formality of offerings and liturgical rites, the rule of abstinence, and even the idea that they work "naked" (which might explain the insistence of adding the underclothes to the attire of those who learn how to attend to the altar [Exod 28:42-3], i.e., it is for the protection [against the heat and/or sparks] of their delicate parts, perhaps not being quite as hardy as the Qenite smiths).

Hymns "are sung during the work, and the connection between the smith and music is one of the most interesting themes of the many legends and myths.[15] "The ... typical tinker ... carries his smithy, anvil, fire hearth and tools along .... At the same time he is the fortune-teller and the musician, a combination that is a regular feature of itinerant smiths in other regions.[16]

This, too, might relate to Aaron, whose wife, Miriam, is a songstress; perhaps he sometimes accompanies her when she sings and plays the timbrel.

Some other notable references about the ancient smithy/tinker:

⋆ The smithy was a temple of the spirits ... and the fire; the smith a priest who by certain rites could accelerate or cause the birth of the metals, the furnace an altar on which the rite was enacted.[17]

The sacredness of the "altar" in the tabernacle, the rituals developed for the proper tending of the fire and the altar itself, and the addition of the protective garment for those who approach the altar may suggest what sits within the tabernacle is a ceremonial furnace, or the means for creating one, i.e., to emulate the sacred furnaces on Mount Sinai (see below). This could help to explain scenes such as Num 11:1-3, where there seems to be some sort of accident with the "fire of the Lord" that resulted in the area being scorched (and perhaps the tabernacle destroyed?).

⋆ Portable charcoal fires are depicted on ancient Egyptian reliefs. The use of olive wood and charcoal made from it is mentioned in late Hellenistic Gnostic papyri. These charcoal fires easily attain a temperature of 9000 C, and the temperature can be raised by the application of blast air, it was therefore eminently suitable for the production of small quantities of metal and it served the skilled

---

paragraphs of generalities" (122). I thank him for his diligence!

[15] Forbes, 81.

[16] Forbes, 77.

[17] Forbes, 85.

Egyptian goldsmiths well![18]

Is the ark of the covenant some sort of mobile sacred furnace? If not for carrying a raging fire, perhaps for carrying the smouldering embers of the perpetual fire/coals. This is something nomads have always done, i.e., moving fire from place to place (it is itself an art form).

★ This air is provided via bellows or a blowpipe. "The blowpipe was far better suited for the work of the smith. It gave a stronger air-blast which could be directed on the exact point of the fire where it was wanted. It raised the temperature of the glowing charcoal far better and it was eminently suited for the work of the goldsmith and the jeweller, for which purpose (granulation work, etc.) it must have been used very early, for the oldest Egyptian pictures of blowpipes often occur in scenes depicting the work of goldsmiths. ... The Egyptians probably used metal pipes with clay tips, possibly also reeds like the Sumerians and Babylonians."[19]

Consider "Aaron's rod," which is the one used when the first sign is performed with the snakes (Exodus 7); might this have been his blowpipe? It is said to be one of the special items kept alongside/inside the ark, i.e., rather than Moses' staff.

★ ... the heating chamber (which may be a simple crucible) is movable. Such a process is used in Antiquity for refining gold .... In most furnaces there is a certain zone in which the essential reactions take place or where the temperature is such that corrosive compounds are formed .... Such conditions determine the life of the furnace and many of the most primitive furnaces served only once.[20]

This would explain the effect the ark has on the Philistines, if they are attempting to use it for similar purposes, or are just tinkering with it to see how it works. They become sick (the depiction of illness in the HB is rather limited, and is usually a dose of "leprosy" or boils) because of the noxious fumes (building up inside) they have not been trained to deal with. The wooden form of the ark need not be affected by the fire, if the crucible within is made of stone, perhaps.[21]

---

[18] Forbes, 107.
[19] Forbes, 113-14.
[20] Forbes, 125.
[21] In discussing the "copper altar" of Leviticus 9, Amzallag suggests a similar, pragmatic explanation: "... wood cannot resist the temperatures reached during the

⋆ The earliest form of casting was open mould casting using stone, loam, or clay moulds. The moulds were either temporary or permanent. The use of moulds of more parts, valved and closed moulds comes later. Permanent open and closed moulds made of stone (steatite, etc.) were generally used for small mass products such as votive and ornamental objects and coins. Temporary moulds were often formed over stone models.[22]

This demonstrates that stone was used in some capacity. Aaron, in making the golden calf, uses a mould (Exod 32:4), which means he may be carrying one with him. As an itinerant craftsman, this might be expected. However, the "open cast" mould can be "created either in a sand tray or chiselled into the floor of the workshop,"[23] which would mean Aaron, a skilled artisan, can make basic votive objects in compacted sand, anywhere.

⋆ Gold is easy to work with "even without the application of heat and, since only small quantities were worked at a time there was no need for large and intricate apparatus."[24]

A portable box with basic tools of the trade suffices. Forbes describes hoards of smiths' implements, ingots, moulds, tools, and products that reminded him of a "commercial travellers" who carried about with them samples of their craft to earn work on their journeys.[25]

The HB refers to many metallurgical themes and employs metallurgical terms:[26]

⋆ Tools: *pa'am*, the anvil (Isa 41:7); *makkabah*, the hammer for carpenters (Isa 44:12); *pattish*, the stone-hammer (Isa 41:7); *mal kachim*, the pincers; *ma alappu'ach*, the bellows (Jer 6:29); *matzreph*,

---

combustion of burnt offerings. But a stone altar coated with copper was set in the courtyard of the Jerusalem temple (1 Kgs 8:64; 2 Kgs 16:14–15; Ezek 9:2; 2 Chr 1:5–6), and its temple counterpart likely inspired the copper altar of the Tabernacle." Nissim Amzallag, "A Metallurgical Perspective on the Birth of Ancient Israel," *ER* 12.2 (2021): 29-30

[22] Forbes, 133-4.

[23] Lucas Braddock Chen, "Sumerian Arsenic Copper and Tin Bronze Metallurgy (5300-1500 BC): The Archaeological and Cuneiform Textual Evidence," *AD* 9.3 (2021): 185-197, here 192.

[24] Forbes, 143.

[25] Forbes, 6.

[26] The list is a summary of the description in "Metal," *McClintock and Strong Biblical Cyclopedia*, www.biblicalcyclopedia.com.

the crucible (Prov 17:3); *kur*, the melting-furnace (Ezek 22:18).

⋆ Preparation of metals: smelting (Isa 1:25; Ezek 22:18-20); mixing of material in the smelting, such as alkaline salts, bor (Isa 1:25), and lead (Jer 6:29).

⋆ Casting of images: always of gold, silver, or copper (Exod 25:12; 26:37; Isa 40:19).

⋆ Hammering of metal: making it into broad sheets (Num 16:38; Isa 44:12; Jer 10).

⋆ Soldering and welding (Isa 41:7).

⋆ Smoothing and polishing (1 Kgs 7:45).

⋆ Overlaying: plates of gold, and silver, and copper (Exod 25:11-24; 1 Kgs 6:20; 2 Chr 3:5; cf. Isa 40:19).

⋆ Trade names: blacksmith, the "worker in iron" (Isa 44:12); the brass-founder (1 Kgs 7:14); and the gold and silver smith (Judg 17:4; Mal 3:2).

# VOLCANOES

Linked to this interest in the Qenites is the idea that volcanoes might offer some insight into the worship of Yahweh, e.g., as a mountain deity who descends with fire and smoke, making the earth tremble, for instance:

⋆ Exod 19:18: Mount Sinai was wrapped in smoke, because the Lord had descended upon it in fire; the smoke went up like the smoke of a kiln, while the whole mountain shook violently

⋆ Exod 24:17: the glory of the Lord was like a devouring fire on the top of the mountain

⋆ Deut 33.2: The Lord came from Sinai and dawned from Seir upon us; he shone forth from Mount Paran. With him were myriads of holy ones at his right, a host of his own

⋆ Ps 104:32: who looks on the earth and it trembles, who touches the mountains and they smoke

⋆ Judg 5:5: The mountains quaked before the Lord

Certainly, these descriptions might offer some substantiation for an ancient practice of volcano-worship but there is very simple reason why this cannot be the context of a *conventional* interpretation of Moses in Exodus, i.e., there are no volcanoes on the Sinai Peninsula. The majority of recorded ancient eruptions are in the Mediterranean area, for which there are records of aftereffects being experienced in Egypt, but this has more to do with particles in the air blocking out the sun and ruining crops, or lowering the depth of the Nile.[27]

There are, however, geologically young basaltic volcanic fields in Northwestern Arabia running parallel to the Red Sea, i.e., the Harraat; a line of peaks runs right through the territory we are interested in, i.e., the land surrounding Tayma. In fact, there are two volcanoes very close by: 1) Harrat ar Rahah is the northernmost, sitting just south of the town of Tabuk. It last erupted about 10,000 years ago; 2) Harrat 'Uwayrid is located about 120 km east of the Red Sea and the only known eruption was in 640 CE, when it spewed "fire and stones, killing (Bedouin) herdsmen and their cattle and sheep."[28] According to Victor Camp, et al., there have been twenty-one *recorded* eruptions on the Arabian peninsula in the last 1500 years,[29] so it is possible such a sight was witnessed during the mid-6th Century BCE. There seems to be no real doubt that volcanism lies somewhere at the root of the pre-Israelite Yahweh but does this suit the specific descriptions we find in the HB, especially in Exodus?

One would think, for example, that the resulting fallout killing both people and animals (as in the 604 CE incident) would be the expected outcome of being physically close to an erupting volcano, yet Moses is said to bring the people up to the "foot of the mountain" to "meet God" (Exod 19:17). Why, and how, would he do this if it was truly a volcano going through an effusive eruption? Why is there no mention of damage to the encampment? Rather, we see Moses merrily shepherding the sheep right below the "mountain of God," leaving them without concern, to ascend (in fact, it is made explicit that no damage is done, in Exod 3:2-4).

When considering the smoke and the fire elements, we need to see that there are two kinds of smoke/fire in the exodus narratives. One represents the phenomena that physically travel with the group, seemingly of their own volition, usually in front of them, as in Exod 14:19-20, etc., and one where they remain either on Sinai or with the ark.

The first instance is fully explained by Trumbull as a well-attested

---

[27] E.g., Will Sullivan, "Volcanic Eruptions May Have Contributed to Unrest in Ancient Egypt," InsideScience.org, January 21, 2022.

[28] Information thanks to www.volcanodiscovery.com.

[29] Victor Camp, et al., "The Madinah Eruption, Saudi Arabia: Magma Mixing and Simultaneous Extrusion of Three Basaltic Chemical Types," *BV* 49 (1987): 489-508, here, 490.

method of guiding caravans and armies in the East, as employed by Alexander the Great on his campaigns, who adopted the technique from indigenous desert armies. The use of fire by night and smoke by day is similarly mentioned in the Anastasi Papyri, where a commander of an army himself is deemed the "flame in the darkness"[30] (which may correspond to the "angel" God sends to lead the people, i.e., possibly "Joshua"/ Belshazzar).

I suggest there must be another explanation for the fire and smoke references with regard to Sinai and the ark, i.e., the metallurgical rites and rituals themselves.

# FIRE

## *Burning Bush*

The wood the smiths used would have been the locally abundant thorn-bushes[31] and was probably sacred in its own right. Doughty, on his travels through Arabia, mentions the Bedouins who light fires, *even in the rain*, using the thorn-bush, for it has a natural resin that will catch fire readily.[32]

Pliny says something rather intriguing:

> In the Territory of Mutina, there riseth up Fire also, upon Days devoted to Vulcan. It is found written, that if a Coal of Fire fall upon the arable Fields under Aricia, the Soil presently is on Fire. In the Sabines Territory, as also in that of the Sidicines, **Stones anointed will be set on Fire**. In a Town of the Salentines, called Egnatia, if Wood be laid upon a certain hallowed Stone there, it will immediately flame out. ... Besides, there be Fires that suddenly arise, both in Waters and even about the Bodies of Men.[33]

Anointing stones and setting them on fire to worship Vulcan? (Cf. Ezek 28:14-16 and the "stones of fire" on the "mountain of God.")

Strabo (16.1.15) mentions the use of *naphtha*, a liquid form of asphalt (found naturally in Babylonia and Persia) that spontaneously combusts when brought near a source of heat and is very difficult to extinguish; Alexander the Great apparently experimented with this product by smearing it on a boy

---

[30] Trumbull, *Kadesh-Barnea*, 397 and n. 1.
[31] Forbes, 107.
[32] Doughty, 1.618.
[33] Pliny, *Natural History in Thirty-seven Books*, II, 45. https://archive.org.

sitting in a bath and his body remained on fire until he was rescued (!). This might correspond to the "fire of the Lord" in 1 Kgs 18:38 that "fell and consumed the burnt offering, the wood, the stones, and the dust, and even licked up the water that was in the trench." 18:36 clearly states that there had just been a "burnt offering" (18:38), so maybe Elijah (slyly) "offers" molten asphalt by pouring it on the still smouldering fire and everything ignites and cannot be quenched.

My thought is that the skilful Qenites make a metal imitation of a thorn-bush (just some straight branches soldered together); they could then put something flammable on it to set it on fire, making it an everlasting sacred representation of the fire used in the liturgy of the smiths. When the resin burns away, the flames recede, but the iron thorn-bush remains, unconsumed.

Remembering the mythological foundation of Tyre and the eagle, serpent, and tree, it should be noted that Nonnus says: "From the flaming tree fire self-made spits out wonderful sparks, and the glow devours the olive tree all round *but consumes it not* (emphasis mine)."[34] The notion of an non-consuming fire thus has precedence.

Also, in his discussion of ancient Egyptian curses, in relation to the Sun-god mythology, Budge describes the ritual of burning wax effigies of serpents to illustrate the priests' symbolic battle against Apep, in order to help Re through his underworld journey through the Night. The magical ceremony included throwing the figure into a fire that was "made of a special kind of plant," linking fire to plant again.[35]

It would seem, then, that in the context of the period and the religious beliefs, a burning bush might not be such a miraculous, or even novel, thing after all.

## Sparks

The context of metallurgy, of smithing rather than smelting, perhaps, offers further insight into one of the most intriguing concepts concerning the HB's depiction of Yahweh, i.e., the nature of the heavenly "hosts." Simply put, I suggest these originally pertained to the flying sparks from the fire and/or the metal-on-metal hammering.

As when a man hammers metal on a smith's anvil, and rings the fiery

---

[34] Nonnus, § 40.448.

[35] E. A. Wallace Budge, *Osiris and the Egyptian Resurrection, Vol. 2* (London: Warner, 1911), 178.

clinks with unwearied sledge beating the mass below, the sparks leap
out in showers, spurting when the iron is struck, and heat the air;
under blow after blow first one goes up then another, one leaps after
another and catches it leaping in its fiery course ....

Nonnus, § 22.316

The Lord came from Sinai, And dawned from Seir upon us; He shone
forth from Mount Paran. With him were myriads of holy ones; At his
right, a host of his own.

Deut 33:2

The line "With him were myriads of holy ones" employs two nouns,
i.e., *riboboth*, from *rebabah* meaning "multitude, myriad, ten thousand,"
and *qodesh*, "apartness, sacredness." This seems to suggest a countless
multitude of sacred things. The fire of the smiths' furnaces, the enthusiastic,
ritualistic hammering of metal, creates thousands of sparks. On a dark night
these might be seen travelling great distances on the air, dancing around,
being created and then disappearing into the ether. This might be enough to
inspire awe, initially perhaps, but I wonder if the novelty would abate with
time. Like all religions that have a liturgy, or a following that requires signs
and wonders, I think something a little more intense and dynamic might have
been introduced to wow the crowd. It's just what we do.

I think something like the addition of saltpetre to the furnace, on some
predetermined cue, would have done the trick. Saltpetre, or potassium
nitrate, is easily available, even to nomadic groups, for all that is required is
organic matter that is left to decay, e.g., manure, dead animals or plants, etc.
It is best farmed in arid areas,[36] as rain washes it into the ground; the Arabian
desert is the ideal place for this crop and it is from Arabia that saltpetre
(rather than soda) arose as a notably different chemical substance.[37] They
called it "Chinese snow"; to the Persians it was "Chinese salt"; the Arabs were
the first to purify saltpetre to "weapons-grade"[38] but the Chinese, of course,
turned it into spectacular fireworks. Though not combustible itself, it accelerates
combustion and in the process creates intense fire, sparks, and smoke.

There is no way of knowing if, perhaps, in some dark and distant
corner of the Arabian Desert, someone, many generations earlier, realised
the volatile and impressive qualities of saltpetre in the context of
visual/religious ritual. "Saltpetre-including preparations act on the vascular

---

[36] Although saltpetre naturally occurs on the banks of the Nile after a flood and was
gathered by hand. Paul Forchheimer, "The Etymology of Saltpeter," *MLN* 67.2 (1952):
103-6, here 103-4.

[37] Prov 25:20 and Jer 2:26 preserve the early rendition of "nitre" which was a more
basic "soda" used in washing, etc.

[38] "Gunpowder compositions" Alchemy (Islam), www.chemeurope .com.

199

system and alter pulse frequency"[39]; this might accentuate the physiological and psychological processes already influenced by an intensely ritualistic ceremony (see discussion on Mount Sinai, below). It was already being used as a "flux in metallurgical operations,"[40] so any community with even a single blacksmith would have used it. Throw some into the fire at the right moment and, just like we do today when we watch fireworks, the crowd will "ooh" and "ahh" in amazement. If the uninitiated are kept ignorant of the ways of the smithy, of the rites and secret practices, i.e., they were kept at the foot of the mesa, they would, indeed, find the effect "indistinguishable from magic" (Arthur C. Clarke).

In the ancient tale of "Joseph and Asenath" which I have claimed is a later rendition of the Nabonidus-Nitocris relationship as found in the Song of Solomon,[41] the divine being who appears to Asenath is described thus:

> His face was like lightning, and his eyes like the light of the sun, and the hair on his head was like a burning flame, and his hands and his feet were like iron from the fire and sparks shot forth from his hands and feet (14.9).[42]

To me, this suggests an intended allusion to the metallurgical-fire foundation of Nabonidus' new, mystical deity. Similarly, in this same tale:

> [The spirits of the stars] were standing like fiery sparks around the chariots of the Omnipresent One. What did Metatron do? At once he clapped his hands and chased them all from their places. Immediately they flew up on wings of flame and fled ....[43]

Even in the 17th Century writings of the Rosicrucians we find a religious fascination with fire and its sparks; this excerpt discusses the "fire-theosophy of the Persians":

> See that spark from the blacksmith's anvil—struck, as an insect, out

---

[39] Raman Ramya, et al., "On the Villainous Saltpetre in Pre-Independent India," *Current Science* 110.5 (2016): 923–27, here 925.

[40] "Gunpowder compositions." See also Siran Liu, et al. "Copper Processing in the Oases of Northwest Arabia: Technology, Alloys and Provenance," *JAS* 53 (2015): 492-503, here 500.

[41] Tyson, 250-4.

[42] Ross Shepard Kraemer, *When Asenath Met Joseph: A Late Antique Tale of the Biblical Patriarch and his Egyptian Wife, Reconsidered* (New York: Oxford University Press, 1998), 121.

[43] Kraemer, 189, n. 166.

of a sky containing a whole cloud of such. Rare locusts, of which Pharaoh and the Cities of the Plain read of old the secret! One, two, three sparks; dozens come: faster and faster the fiery squadrons follow, until, in a short while, a whole possible army of that hungry thing for battle, for food for it—Fire—glances up; but is soon warned in again—lest acres should glow in the growing advance. Think that this thing is bound as in matter-chains. Think that he is outside of all things, and deep in the inside of all things; and that thou and thy world are only the thing between; and that outside and inside are both identical, couldst thou understand the supernatural truths! Reverence Fire (for its meaning), and tremble at it …. Avert the face from it, as the Magi turned, dreading, and (as the Symbol) before it bowed askance. So much for this great thing—Fire![44]

> *Glory be to thee ... Supreme Power*
> *Eternal One who burns his enemies, Flaming One*
> *Flame which shoots a tongue of fire*
> *Thou art the forms of the Eternal One*
> Great Litany of Ra, 71[45]

# STRANGE FIRE

An interesting episode occurs in Num 11:1-3, where the people are said to be complaining so much that "the fire of the Lord burned against them"; the site where this occurs is named "Taberah," i.e., "burning," from the verb *baar*, "to burn, consume." Another verb *baar* means "to be stupid, brutish" (Jer 10:8), and "inhuman, cruel, barbarous" (Ezek 21:36). Another *baar* denotes a "purging" or "purifying" (Ezek 20:38). When I first read these verses, it sounded like a simple fire-related accident; it occurs on the outskirts of the camp, which makes it seem not too significant, but now I think there is far more to be gleaned from the pericope.

Considering the magical, mystical nature of the metallurgical procedures, it is probable that some of Nabonidus' group have to be trained and initiated into this nomadic tribal cult of smiths, e.g., Abihu, for a start. Being unfamiliar with so many of the rites and rituals, the learning curve is steep and mistakes are made. What happens in Numbers 11 is potentially an alternative version of the "strange fire" incident of Lev 10:1-3.

---

[44] Hargrave Jennings, *The Rosicrucians: Their Rites and Mysteries*, 4th ed., (1907, 1870), 80, https://sacred-texts.com.

[45] Luigi Tripani, *The God Ra: Iconography (With all the Forms and Names from the 'Litany of Ra')* (Amentet Neferet: 201), 113.

The term "strange" (*zara*) is translated from the verb *zuwr*, "to be a stranger." *Strong's* suggests "profane; specifically … 'to commit adultery' — (come from) another (man, place)." Abihu, being Moses' "son" (as opposed to Aaron's) becomes, in effect, an allusion to Exod 2:22 and Moses' own identification as an alien in Midian; his son is "Gershom," meaning "stranger, exile," from the verb *garash*, "to drive out, cast out." As Nabonidus, of course, this fits the imposed exile of his seven-year stay in Tayma but also this current exile, after the Persian conquest. As a stranger Abihu is also etymologically linked to the idea of Nabonidus' reputation of being brutish, foolish, etc., as seen elsewhere. So, Moses' "Abihu" and Aaron's "Nadab" (the latter of which, I think, is for symbolic balance, i.e., one from each camp) are eliminated because of something they do *physically* that makes their incense offering "profane," "loathsome": Nadab, a Qenite, is possibly instructing Abihu but Abihu makes a mistake.

Laughlin makes a valid point, in that Lev 16:12 gives specific instructions for the fire that burns incense, i.e., the coals "are to be taken from the altar of Yahweh on which … the perpetual fire burned."[46] It would seem then, that Abihu takes the coals from elsewhere and Nadab, perhaps, doesn't notice. Laughlin goes on to suggest that this would be considered a "cultic sin" and the inevitable result would be death by God's wrath (i.e., he would have to be purified by fire).

However, to me, seeing this in a historical context, the incident in Leviticus 10 demonstrates that these were real people, who made huge adjustments to the new life they found themselves in. Abihu tries but fails (just like his "father" Nabonidus, in the Song) but in the end, the incident is to be blamed on ignorance and carelessness, e.g., coals taken from elsewhere may not have the same composition as those used for the altar fire, so when the incense (which must have contained volatile ingredients to create so much "smoke" it could obscure the ark from view) is added, there is combustion, perhaps even an explosion. As the tabernacle is said (twice) to be set up outside the camp (Exod 33:7), it isn't too much of a leap to suggest the similar indication made in Num 11:1-3, where "burning" also happens in a wrathful context, is an expression of the same event.

God supposedly had warned the priests that anyone who comes "near" to him must respect his holiness (Lev 10:3), i.e., in Qenite/metallurgical terms, must respect the dangers inherent in working with fire and combustibles. Abihu clearly had not respected the dangers and Moses, seemingly indignant, simply says "I knew this would happen!"

This applies also to the death of Uzzah, who happens to be in the

---

[46] John C. H. Laughlin. "The 'Strange Fire' of Nadab and Abihu," *JBL* 95.4 (1976): 559-65, here 561.

wrong place at the wrong time and attempts to stop the ark from crashing to the ground, only to be thanked by a bolt of divine wrath (2 Sam 6:7; 1 Chr 13:5-14). The ark, as discussed, possibly serves as the vehicle for several of the sacred ritualistic objects, ingredients, etc., and if the lid fell off and something caustic fell out *onto* Uzzah, he might well have died from his chemical burns, though not immediately (if there is a perpetual flame, the coals for this would be carried, smouldering, in the sanctified safety of the ark, and these might have ignited something unexpectedly).[47]

# SHESHBAZZAR

In Ezra's account of the exiles leaving Babylon after Cyrus' declaration of amnesty, he spends little time, perhaps surprisingly, on the very first convoy to leave for Jerusalem (Ezra 1:8-11). It should have been a cause for celebration, a momentous event but the only thing he describes is the hoard of gold and silver Sheshbazzar is provided. This instantly reminds us of Abraham and his many "goods," the focus on "wealth" in his narrative, and the emphasis on gold/silver (in particular) in Moses' tale. But the objects are not just jewellery, or objects that can be melted down, etc., they are the Israelites' temple vessels, supposedly taken by Nebuchadnezzar (1:7) when he conquered Jerusalem (in 587 BCE).

The most striking element of Sheshbazzar, to me, is the etymology of his name, which means, "fire worshipper." Some translate it as "O sun-god [or moon-god], protect the lord [or the son]."[48]

Ezra, as I mention throughout *She Brought*, has no time for anything Babylonian, least of all the women, and of them, least of all the temple servants who come from Solomon's (i.e., Nabonidus') temples.[49] His rejection of anything foreign, his insistence on the separation of mixed-race families, etc., stem from his experience under the rule of Nabonidus, whose laxity, fetishes, open revelry, etc., are deemed abominations. Like every dutiful scribe, however, he is compelled, or commissioned, to write an account of his own exodus from Babylonia to Canaan, and in doing so, he is

---

[47] For alternative suggestions see Gershon Hepner, "The Naked Truth Concerning the Deaths of Nadab and Abihu," *RB* 121.1 (2014): 108-11, who considers the two offered incense whilst naked; Gnana Robinson, "The Prohibition of Strange Fire in Ancient Israel: A New Look at the Case of Gathering Wood and Kindling Fire on the Sabbath," *VT* 28.3 (1978): 301-17, argues that their illicit worshipping practices signified "idolatry" (includes comments about other possible explanations [308-9]).

[48] "Sheshbazzar," *Hastings Dictionary of the Bible*, www.studylight.org.

[49] E.g., Tyson, 214-16.

beholden to include the true story of how this came about. "Sheshbazzar" is thus a resentful inclusion of the first wave of emigrants under the man Ezra detests, Nabonidus (who receives this pseudonym/commission name in keeping with the apparent agreement never to mention his name).

This perception may seem contrary to the epithet given in Ezra 1:8, i.e., "the," not "a," "prince of Judah," until you realise that the term *nasiy'* means "one lifted up, chief, prince, leader." This means the term might reflect royalty, but it might just as easily reflect a position as group *leader*. For the name "Judah," there is Yehudah which often means those from the tribe of Judah, but in Arabic it means, collectively, "the Jews." Ezra simply depicts Sheshbazzar as the ("Arabian"?) leader of the first Jews who leave Babylonia.

Historically, I find it highly unlikely that a conqueror would readily hand over such riches as gold and silver sacred vessels, to a 'mixed' contingent of emigrants, even if these objects still existed in their original form and were not distributed as booty or melted down for their own religious vessels, etc. Remember, this would have been before Nabonidus' time as King, so although he might have a more 'archaeological' or religious interest in such things, I think they would have been long gone by the time he came to the throne. There is evidence that Cyrus retained for his palace at Susa one of Nabonidus' votive bowls from the temple of Sîn in Harran, but this was made of stone.[50] I think, perhaps, the focus on the vessels here in Ezra links directly back to Dan 5:23 where Nabonidus is in possession of these same objects and is treating them profanely (if the decadent party before the fall of Babylon is true, the king's distasteful profaning of the vessels would have been widely known).

Sheshbazzar is tasked with placing these vessels "in the temple in Jerusalem" (Ezra 5:15) and *then* to lay the foundations, which seems back to front, unless you take this to mean some of these vessels were to be placed *under* the foundations (if there had been a ramshackle temple there already, such riches could not be safely stored there). Nabonidus is famous for focussing intently on the foundations of the temples he renovates, i.e., always searching for the original, marking its discovery, placing a memorial object of some sort under it, along with his predecessors', and then building anew from this base (e.g., Nab 2 ii 10-15; Nab 10 ii 8-10; Nab 15 i 36 - ii 6, etc.).

Sheshbazzar *is* Nabonidus, the man identified by abundant wealth and his previous association with the Jews of Babylonia. He is remembered for his worship of Fire (Exodus), for his solar-lunar dichotomy (Song of Solomon) and attempted synthesis (Exodus). He is the fire-loving "Eshcol" (Genesis). Mentioned once more in Ezra 5:14-16, Sheshbazzar is named as Cyrus' "governor" to Jerusalem, providing a satisfying inclusio with my initial suggestion.

---

[50] W&N, 21.

# 12                                              SINAI

*God is coming from Teman, the Holy One from Mount Paran.*
Hab 3:3

*YHWH, when You came forth from Seir, advanced*
*from the country of Edom, ....*
Judg 5:4

In order to find Sinai, we must assess the land surrounding it, i.e., the places Moses visits on the lead up to arriving at the mountain of God. This will provide us with enough information to pinpoint exactly where Mount Sinai is.

## HOREB

The name "Horeb" is used three times in Exodus (3:1 ; 17:6 ; 33:6) and is translated to mean "waste, arid, dryness," and stems from the verb *hareb* ("to dry up or lay waste"). It is usually defined as a pseudonym for Mount Sinai but, I suggest, like Paran, Horeb is an *area* that also has a eponymous mountain. Mount Paran *is* Mount Sinai, and it sits in the Wilderness of Paran (and also in the Arabian Wilderness of Shur, as Sinai is the other Rock, or *tsur*, recall, i.e., a play on words, linking a wall with a wall-like rock/cliff); this is also "the *horeb*." Rephidim is "in" the *horeb* (17:6, see below) and Mount Sinai is also called the Mount of Horeb (3:1; 33:6); the entire desert region, all the "Wildernesses" (Shur, Sîn, Paran) together make up (*the*) *horeb*; all mountains in the desert landscape might have their own name but all can be reckoned Mounts of Horeb.

In Exod 17:6, God says "I will be standing there in front of you on the rock (*tsur*) at Horeb" but the Hebrew word translated as "at" in the NRSV is translated as "in" by the King James Version and the Hebrew Interlinear text. In the "Hebrew *bə-ḥō-rêḇ*, the "bə" element is defined as: "Prep-b | N-proper-fs" and "Pre-b" is defined as "b  9996/be ('in')."[1] Exod 17:6 should therefore read: "the rock in (the) *horeb* (wilderness/desert, i.e., Split Rock)."

In 2 Kgs 23:13, we are told that in Jerusalem, Solomon raises high places for his wives on the "Mount of Corruption"; the noun here, *mashchith*, means "ruin, destruction." As *horeb* means "waste, or lay waste," this is potential substantiation for a Nabonidus-Solomon-Moses connection, all pointing to the inevitable downfall of the Babylonian king. We have to bear in mind that the story in Exodus, though superficially the tale of Moses the great leader is, just like the Song of Solomon, a two-tiered narrative, with a dark underbelly. It does not lavish praise on Moses (Nabonidus), it tells the true story of why he was eventually ousted by those who followed him through the deserts of Arabia. The others, who had followed him in the context of Abraham's story, had no such resentment/animosity; they got what they wanted. While hints of the Babylonian ex-king's old behaviour are detectable in Abraham, the overall feeling of Genesis' version of the exodus is positive; Exodus' is not.

# DEUTERONOMY NAMES

It will become evident that the author of Deuteronomy uses toponyms that represent, basically, the territory of Nabonidus in Arabia as we understand it today; he does not say this speech takes place at Sinai, but somewhere in the wilderness, between Canaan and the far side of Edom. We must always bear in mind that different authors were privy to different tales of Nabonidus and that many details could well originate in the first trip he made as "Abraham," during which, of course, he *did* enter Canaan.

Knowing that most people would not have visited, nor would be likely ever to visit the sites mentioned on the itinerary of Moses, what would be the point of providing a Hebrew-speaking audience with Arabic names for

---

[1] https://biblehub.com/hebrewparse.htm#.

every village or mountain? One desert village is much like another, one rock in the desert can be overlooked, one mountain blends in with the one next to it. The author of Deuteronomy preserves the location of the most dramatic, life-changing events in (his known) history by using a clever scribal skill. He creates commission names for every place where something significant happened, according to *his* received narrative. Each name mirrors in its etymology and nuances the story being told within that particular context. The following names solidify the action in the narrative, i.e., to give each event its own place in the great scheme of things, when maps were not available. This way, the events of the exodus become truly unique moments, preserved for posterity with both action and general location intact.

## *Suph*

The first instinct is to think this is just a shortened version of *Yam Suph*, "sea of reeds," but this is not the full story. The noun *sup* does denote "reeds" but it stems from the verb *sapap*, "to mark or cross a border," so the author of Deuteronomy is possibly making a distinction, highlighting the "border" allusion. Such a reed-border suggests a transitional landscape, from one that is watery on one side to one that is dry on the other. The verb *sup*, and the nouns *sop* and *supa* relate to something that comes to or makes "an end."

The group led by Nabonidus (as Abraham) travels in boats from Ur to Harran. The initial trip of Nabonidus into Egypt, to introduce Ennigaldi to Ahmose, is also carried out using boats through the Egyptian marshlands. On leaving Egypt after his second visit, as Moses, Nabonidus once again employs boats for a speedy getaway. The metaphorical notion of "Suph" is the transition from a watery journey to a desert one. Geographically, Moses' speech is, indeed, delivered "on the plain opposite Suph" (Deut 1:1), where Suph, in Deuteronomy at least, is the Red Sea. The author understood there were two bodies of water, not one, along the exodus route, i.e., the "Sea of Reeds" (*Yam Suph*, the Egyptian marshes), which does not really concern him, and the Red Sea (Suph), which forms the western boundary of Moses' territory ("opposite" the "plain" of Arabia).

### A Note on the Red Sea

The Red Sea was known to the Greeks/Romans as part of the "Erythraean Sea," their name for the Indian Ocean but *including* the Red Sea *and* the Persian Gulf. "Erythra" means "red." Although there was supposedly a Persian myth about a certain King Erythras, who rescued his beloved horses from a flood and built a settlement where he found them, the translator of this ancient text wrote:

> Here is manifestly a kernel of truth, referring, however, to a much
> earlier time than the Empire of the Medes and their capital
> Pasargadae. It suggests the theory of a Cushite-Elamite migration
> around Arabia ... the story of a people from Elam, who settled in the
> Bahrein Islands and then spread along South Arabia, leaving their
> epithet of "Red" or "ruddy" in many places, including the sea that
> washed their shores and floated their vessels: "Sea of the Red People,"
> or, according to Agatharchides, "of the Red King."[2]

Another explanation for the name of the Red Sea (as we know the body of water today) is that it simply represents a cardinal direction (South), because other colours have been used, historically, to designate directions. However, as R. Dixon pointed out in the 19th Century, a simple comparison of the uses of such a practice reveals too widespread a variation in the application of symbolic representation to warrant any claim to a more or less universal legend/key.[3] Dixon points out that unless one understands the local religious significance of colour symbolism, one cannot even claim to know why directions are given colours in the first place. So this theory is not convincing.[4]

Today, the discussion concerning the name "Red Sea" centres on two main theories, i.e., 1) it refers to seasonal blooms of the red-coloured algae *Trichodesmium erythraeum* near the surface (much as the Nile is Green, Red, or White, according to the mineralogical conditions at certain periods in its flow) and 2) it stems from a mistranslation by the authors of the Septuagint (in the 3rd Century BCE) of the Hebrew term *Yam Suph* used in the Book of Exodus, which is literally translated as "Sea of Reeds."

As mentioned earlier, Pharaoh Necho II began work on a canal to link the Nile with the (current) Red Sea (*Hist.* 2.158) but the task was allegedly abandoned when he received an ominous omen. Darius I took up the challenge and stelae preserve an account of his achievement, which he claimed was intended to show that he had conquered Egypt and had constant access to it from Persia.[5] Thus, although there is no direct waterway to the Red Sea from the Nile Delta during Nabonidus' reign, it is only a matter of a few years before access becomes practicable by connecting the intermittent bodies of water together, and this may or may not have been extant during Nabonidus' second visit to Egypt.

***

---

[2] Schoff, 50-1.

[3] Roland B. Dixon, "The Color-Symbolism of the Cardinal Points," *JAF* 12.44 (1899): 10-16.

[4] Dixon, 16.

[5] Henry Colburn, "King Darius' Red Sea Canal," *Fezana* 4.35 (2021): 27-30.

# Paran

"Paran" is possibly derived from the verb *paar*, meaning "to glorify"; the noun *peer* denotes a turban, i.e., the headdress of a priest (Exod 39:28; 44:18). The noun *tipara* suggests beauty or glory and often relates to descriptions of God (Ps 71:8, 1 Chr 29:11; Isa 63:14, Ps 96:6).

The Wilderness of Paran is commonly located in the Sinai Peninsula but it is first mentioned in Gen 21:21, where Hagar and Ishmael are sent after the split from Abraham and Sarah. Ishmael, as discussed earlier, represents the Arabian tribes (Gen 25:16), even if not one of their biological forefathers (often discounted today but potentially supported by a Nabonidus-interpretation). Mount Paran is mentioned in Deut 33:2, from which Yahweh is said to "dawn," using the verb *zarach* meaning "to rise, come forth, shine." This is most often used in reference to the Sun. God is also said to "shine forth" from Seir, using the verb *yapha*, "to shine out or forth, to send out beams, cause to shine." This verb is used in Job 35:15 to refer to lightning as a sign of God's wondrous power, i.e., too bright to look at.

Paran is a pseudonym for Sinai. It is the area from which "the glory" of Yahweh shines out, where the deity's essence/power is manifested in light and heat (or in both, e.g., Exod 19:16). It is the place where the new priesthood is envisioned (Exod 19:6; 28:1). The Wilderness of Paran is the desert immediately surrounding the Mount.

# Tophal

The verb *tapal* is used only in 2 Sam 22:27, where it means "to be cunning," or as *Strong's* puts it, "(morally) tortuous, to show one's self unsavoury." The adjective *taphel* means "tasteless or unseasoned" and has the connotation of "foolish, unsavoury, untempered."

If you have read *She Brought*, you will know where this is; it is Tayma. Everything about this name speaks to the unsavoury antics the amoral king at his height of madness, i.e., the entire issue with the blood rite (the Elixir Rubeus), the allusions to his loss of decency and honour, the folly of his ways, etc. Within the exodus narratives, however, the link to salt is paramount. As seen earlier, this too relates to Tayma via the "manna" and the covenant of salt (Exod 16:13-36).

# Laban

The verb *laben* means "to be or become white." It can be used figuratively or literally. The adjective *laban*, meaning "white," can be both positive (e.g., representing purity) and negative (the alleged skin disease after divine judgement, e.g., Lev 13:3; Num 12:10). The noun *lebanah* means "moon," which has immediate resonance with Nabonidus' worship of Sîn.

It might also suggest salt, e.g., of a sabkha.

There is, however, a more significant understanding, i.e., Laban is Leuke Kome (White Village), i.e., al-Wajh.

## Hazeroth

Often translated as "villages, or enclosures," the name has other connotations, i.e., it suggests a foundation, a starting point for something new, i.e., transition or transformation.

That Deuteronomy emphasises the beating of the rock scene, rather than the earlier instance of Moses on the shore of the Red Sea, suggests the group has moved beyond that point of transition ("Suph") and into new territory, i.e., the scattered settlements of Northwestern Arabia (where wall-enclosed villages are common).

<u>A Link to Numbers …</u>

The group leaves Paran (Num 10:12; 12:16), travels in three stages to Hazeroth (Num 11:35), and then journeys *back* to Paran (Num 12:16).[6] Although Moses apparently declares they are setting out for Canaan (10:29), they don't actually do this straight away; the "spies" are sent out in Num 13:17 *after* the group returns to Paran from Hazeroth. This could suggest Hazeroth is not north of Paran but south (i.e., the spies are sent out via Sela,

---

[6] Num 10: 29-34 is very strange (many commentaries deal with this issue). The ark suddenly seems to travel under its own power; it leaves the Israelites to fend for themselves for "three days." If we are to understand that it is God who takes the ark on this trip, why does he need humans to construct it from base materials like wood, gold, etc., and to carry it the rest of the time (Num 2:17)? Something is amiss here. Also, Hobab has only just been invited to be the scout for the group (10:31), so why does the ark go instead? The repetition of "three days" could be a transcriber's error, according to the Cambridge Bible for Schools and Colleges' commentary (https://biblehub.com); most seem to think the phrase "three days" is a common generalisation and is not to be taken literally. The Hebrew term for "day" is *yom*, which *Strong's* defines as "age, always, continually, daily, each, today," allowing for a less specific interpretation. I suggest something like "three times," or "three stages/journeys," with the ark being carried ahead (in front) each time.

to the north). The "manna" and "quail" scene, and Miriam's punishment, all seem to occur (in Numbers) on this excursion from Paran; in Exodus these seem to take place near Tayma. Hazeroth, therefore, must also be near Tayma. This is evidence, perhaps, of the extended residence in Tayma, with several visits to Sinai; something one doesn't really get from the encapsulated Exodus narrative.

On their journey, the group rests at two locations:

Taberah (Num 11:1-3)
One verb *ba'ar* means "to kindle, burn or consume"; a potential negative application might suggest anger or intense emotion. Another *ba'ar* means "to be stupid, brutish, beastly."; yet another suggests a the elimination of evil.

This is an allusion to the battle with Amalek, which had taken place at Rephidim, south of Tayma. God vehemently (angrily) vows that the scourge of (the evil) Amalek will be obliterated from the earth. Everything they represent, including their connection with Nabonidus, is considered "brutish, or beastly."

Kibroth-hattaavah (Num 11:35)
Commonly translated as "Graves of Desire" the name is derived from the verbs *qabar*, "to bury," and *'wh*, "to desire." The nouns *qeber* and *qebura* mean "grave." The verb *'wh* has the connotation of "coveting" rather than merely "wanting" (e.g., the greed alluded to in the manna scene of Num 11:34). Alternatively, the verb *'wh* can mean "to sign or make a sign, to mark, etc." Its obvious derivation is the noun *'ot*, meaning "sign or mark." This word is used for Cain's mark in Gen 4:15, while another verb pertaining to "marks," *naqab*, also means "to curse." Here, the "curse" element linked to Amalek is reiterated, confirming the location on the southern outskirts of Tayma. Similarly, this area (i.e., Kadesh) is where Miriam dies and where, I have suggested, the scene of Zipporah "cursing" Moses with the blood of Ishmael (Genesis 4) would be better placed.

There is, however, something else here that proves quite amazing:

> Archaeologists from the University of Western Australia (UWA) have determined that the people who lived in ancient north-west Arabia built long-distance 'funerary avenues' – major pathways flanked by thousands of burial monuments that linked oases and pastures – suggesting a high degree of social and economic connection between the region's populations in the 3rd millennium BCE. ... Whether on basalt plains or mountain passes, the densest concentrations of funerary structures on these avenues are located

near permanent water sources. The direction of the avenues suggests that many were used to travel between major oases, including those of Khaybar, al-Ula and Tayma.[7]

*Figure 14: Keyhole (pendant) graves near Khaybar (Image: Google Earth, 2024)*

The oases of al-Ula and Khaybar are both in the al-Hijr (Mada'in Salih) region, just south of Tayma; al-Ula is the modern name for Dadanu (or Dadan; in the HB, Dedan), one of the Arabian regions Nabonidus conquers whilst on his "wanderings" in Arabia (H2 A&B, 1.24).

These keyhole/pendant graves are simply part of the landscape for nomads, known for generations, their heritage obscured over the ages. Doughty mentions seeing them: "There are graves, set out in many places, in the Arabian

---

[7] "Mysterious ancient tombs reveal 4,500-year-old highway network in north-west Arabia," Royal Commission for AlUla, www.rcu.gov.sa/. For a detailed account of these graves see Matthew Dalton, Jane McMahon, Hugh Thomas, "The Middle Holocene 'Funerary Avenues' of North-west Arabia," *The Holocene* 32.3 (13 Dec 2021).

wilderness, more than twenty feet in length"[8] Here, in Numbers, they are used as an omen, a sign of "this fate will become you if you covet" (i.e., the "plague" punishment mentioned in Num 11:33). Having already looked at the covenant of salt, however, and knowing that the "manna" is likely to be salt from the brine-shrimp infested sabkha, this "plague" is possibly food poisoning (from eating salt left too long exposed to the decaying "worms"/shrimp, or from eating too much, which they had been warned against).

If Moses *is* Nabonidus, why would he *not* return to the places he already knows? Who would be foolish enough to enter the desert without knowing the routes and the watering holes?

## Di-zahab

A strange name, this means "having much gold," stemming from the noun *zahab*, "gold," and the adjective *day*, "sufficient."

Some suggest this may be Ophir, where the famed "King Solomon's Mines" were claimed to have been found in 1977, i.e., between Medina and Mecca.[9] Heck, however, places the richest gold resources in the Tabuk region, i.e., where Tayma is located.[10] I opt for the latter, being adjacent to all the other locations. Using the ever-elucidating etymology, we find that in the genealogies of Gen 36:9-19, Esau's firstborn is Eliphaz whose name means "God is gold," from *el* (Elohim/God) and the verb *pazaz*, meaning "to be agile or supple," and *Strong's* adds, "to solidify (as if by refining)," suggesting metallurgy; the other verb *pazaz* means, more plainly, "to refine, make the best," suggesting goldsmithing. Eliphaz's firstborn is Teman, i.e., Tayma (cf. Ezek 25:13). Reuel is Eliphaz's brother, i.e., Jethro. The family base is in the territory of Seir. i.e., the Harraat region.

So, we can see that all of these names pertain to Northwestern Arabia, not to the Sinai Peninsula. They all fall within the known extent of

---

[8] Doughty, 1.434.

[9] Lois Berkowitz, "Has the U.S. Geological Survey Found King Solomon's Gold Mines?" *BAR* (September, 1977), https://library.biblicalarchaeology.org/. That the Mosaic locations of Deuteronomy 1 includes not just one but two Solomon-linked sites does seem to suggest the author was privy to alternative sources for the story of the exodus, and that he was also under the impression the characters of Moses and Solomon were somehow connected. One would not need "ships of Tarshish" to get gold from somewhere inland; Ophir is somewhere else entirely (see my paper "Nabonidus, Tarshish, and Ophir" [2024], www.academia.edu).

[10] Gene W. Heck, "Gold Mining in Arabia and the Rise of the Islamic State," *JESHO* 42.3 (1999): 364-95, here 367-8.

Nabonidus' conquests and authority (as King of Babylon). They even have the potential of alluding to his other avatars in the HB.

# LOCATING SINAI

It seems scholars have been skirting around the idea of Sinai *not* being in the Sinai Peninsula for many years; Julien Cooper describes the situation thus:

> … the tradition of locating the Mount Sinai of the Hebrew Bible with Gebel Musa, the modern "Mount Sinai," only goes back to Christian times c. 4th Century CE. This has worried many scholars, who saw such an equation as an anachronistic invention of Christian monks and pilgrims, with no earlier material or proof for a local "pre-Christian" tradition at Gebel Musa …. As a result, alternative proposals have proliferated and gained in popularity, with some locating 'Mount Sinai' in the northern parts of the Sinai Peninsula, the Wadi Arabah, Jordan, or even Saudi Arabia.
>
> … Another implication of this equation is the etymology of "Sinai." One of the most commonly espoused origins for the name is a link to the Hebrew word *snh* "bush", an idea that finds its origin in the biblical narrative itself regarding the famed burning bush from which god spoke to Moses; although many other etymologies have been proposed, such as a link to the Wilderness of Sîn. The "bush" etymology is perfectly supported by this transcription of *Ṯnh(t)*, although it can only be guessed how a series of sound and dialect changes may have later reproduced a name like Hebrew *Sînay*.[11]

Because I am focussing on links to Nabonidus, I concentrated my search for "Sinai" on the area of Tayma. Tayma was renowned for being a rich, bustling trading oasis in the Arabian Desert, halfway between Egypt and Babylonia, at the crossroads of the great Frankincense Trail, which gave it access to the riches of the world. In terms of vegetation, acacia trees and a thorny shrub called *Astragalus spinosus*, prove to be dominant in the region.[12] This would tally with the "thorn bush" imagery/etymology, but I wasn't convinced, so I broadened my search parameters.

Modern archaeological analysis of the area, apart from discovering

---

[11] Julien Cooper, "The Earliest Mention of the Placename Sinai: The Journeys of Khety," The Ancient Near East Today (2023): 1-6, here 5-6, www.asor.org.

[12] Harald Kürschner and Reinder Neef, "A First Synthesis of the Flora and Vegetation of the Tayma Oasis and Surroundings (Saudi Arabia)," *PDE* 129.1 (2011): 27-58, here 28-42.

textual evidence for Nabonidus' stay in Tayma, unearthed a collection of painted pottery at a site just south-east of the city itself; the archaeologists call this pottery "Ṣināʿiyyah Pottery," as it was located within the small district known as Ṣināʿiyyah, or Sanaʾiye. This site, together with another called Talʾa, is predominantly a cemetery, with remains dating to the mid-first millennium BCE, i.e., Nabonidus' time.[13]

The name Ṣināʿiyyah/Sanaʾiye jumped out at me. The Arabic word *sinaeiun* means "industrial," i.e., utilitarian, so the archaeologists nicknamed the area of the graves the "Industrial Site." A modern scholar wouldn't formally name an ancient burial ground an "industrial site," so I wondered if the name might have a much older provenance. I contacted a few scholars working in the field, or who have written about this pottery, and asked if the word/name is ancient or modern (I knew the name for the *pottery type* is modern). No one could confirm one way or the other.

Then I found this: Gen 10:17 in the Latin *Biblia Sacra* uses the *exact* same word "Sinaeiun," which is translated into English as "Sinites."[14] As seen above, this term is also somewhat troublesome to etymologists but is generally understood to mean "Thorn Bush," or "Storage Facility," both of which suit the Tayma excavation site. Although a cemetery, there is also a circular building above, "not used for burial," which might very well have been a storage facility in its heyday.[15] So, the term is ancient, not invented solely for the use of the archaeologists.

Doughty, whilst visiting Tayma, noted meeting a *ṣâny*, a smith: "The smith's house was the last … going out of the town …. The former year he and his brother had made it with their own hands upon a waste plot next the wilderness …."[16] This is just where the graves are located at the southern end of the Tayma archaeological site, and probably why the area was referred to as the "Industrial Site" in later days.

Doughty goes on to say the *ṣunnʿa* (plural of *ṣâny*) are "braziers, tinkers, blacksmiths, farriers, and workers in wood and stone in the tribes and oases: thus they are villagers and nomads. … Artificers, they are men of

---

[13] *Roads of Arabia: Archaeology and History of the Kingdom of Saudi Arabia*, Ali Ibrahim Al-Ghabban, et al., eds. Catalogue of the exhibition, Musée du Louvre, Paris 14 July-27 September, 2010, 231.

[14] *Biblia Sacra: Vulgatae Editionis Sixti V Pontificis Maximi jussu Recognita et Clementis VIII; Auctorate Edita*, https://archive.org. (Searching the text from the Clementine Vulgate Project, which has been heavily edited from various sources, the word is not found, https://vulsearch.sourceforge.net/index.html.)

[15] Tayma Governorate, Tabuk Region, World Encyclopedia, https://www.qpedia.org.

[16] Doughty, 1.581.

understanding more than their ingenuous neighbours."[17] Recall that earlier I proposed that the fourth month of the journey from Egypt, i.e., the month of Tammuz, the month of the arrival at Sinai using the Hebrew calendar, had the zodiacal sign *nangar(u)*, an apt Assyrian word meaning "workman."

At this point, it looked like Mount Sinai might be linked to Tayma, but I wasn't sure how, as many aspects of the exodus narrative are centred *around* Tayma, but they also indicate a journeying away from this site to reach the mountain of God.

Still, I had a word that sounds a bit like "Sinai." The site of Moses' elevated encounter with God is referred to as "Sinai," I posit, to signify the importance of the metallurgical activity in this new-fangled religion of Nabonidus'.[18] The exiles are aliens in this strange land, recall, mostly the well-to-do who can afford to invest in this expedition (i.e., Nabonidus' own friends and family, mostly, perhaps signifying those he picks up on the way, in Harran, plus a few Jews as part of the deal with Cyrus); probably none has ever seen such things as furnaces, smithies, or rituals pertaining to fire. They hear the local word for these men/practices and refer to the site as something like, "place of the metalworkers." As metalworking is relatively ubiquitous in this region (from the Sinai Peninsula down to the Tayma region), "Sinai" might pertain to any industrialised (metalworking) location,[19] but there are specific details, i.e., criteria, that must comply with the HB version of events for the site to be acceptable as the "Mountain of God."

The most widespread theory concerning a possible Mount Sinai *within* Saudi Arabia is that concerning Jebel al-Lawz. There are many websites devoted to proving and/or disproving this as a contender, so I won't spend time rehashing the debate. Simply put: Jebel al-Lawz is *not* Mount

---

[17] Doughty, 1.669.

[18] As a point of interest, Nissim Amzallag and Shamir Yona ("The Metallurgical Meaning of מִקְנֶה in Biblical Hebrew," *HS* 59 (2018): 7-24, here 25) suggest that the term "*ʿśy* (*qal*) usually denotes making, manufacturing, or creating. In rare instances, it evokes the act of 'making wealth'…. This meaning is explicitly invoked in reference to Abraham's (Gen 12:5) and Solomon's (Eccl 2:8) servants, probably because 'possessing' servants was a sign of wealth. … מִקְנֶה denotes metal as a raw material used for the production of implements …." As I claim both Abraham and Solomon are based on Nabonidus, and that Moses is yet another avatar of this itinerant, trading, wealthy ex-king, the scene in Exodus 11-12 of the "plundering" of the Egyptians seems even more like a night-time raid to acquire the raw materials for creating the implements, etc., when they get to Sinai (the golden calf is possibly made from stolen Egyptian gold).

[19] Modern archaeological discoveries have shown that what we now call the "Sinai Peninsula," called Mafkat or "country of turquoise" by the ancient Egyptians, was actually a profoundly important site not only for mining turquoise but for high-quality copper mining/smelting also. So the *ṣâny* (metalworkers) connotation fits this area too, but that's not enough to make *it* the location of the "Mountain of God."

Sinai. Nothing about it, other than its location in Northwestern Arabia fits well enough to be taken seriously. Hopefully, this discussion will put paid to that idea and support a rather less dramatic but potentially perfect candidate, i.e., Qurayyah, the alleged capital of the Midianites.[20]

# MOUNTAIN OF GOD

Situated approximately 115 km from the Red Sea, northwest of Tayma, Qurayyah first became of interest to archaeologists in the 1960s, but extensive excavations began in 2014. The most obvious and outstanding element of the site is the 800 meters long, 300 meters wide, 50 meters high mesa.[21] This mesa, I argue, is the original Mount Sinai. It may not look like much but this site ticks all the boxes:

> ✶ *It is the "Rock" toward which Moses leads his group, after leaving the Nile Delta.* Archaeologists today describe Qurayyah as having "[f]lat topped jebels with a uniform appearance ris[ing] to a series of steep rock faces and flat terraces"; they remark on "the steepness of its flanks" (befitting *tsur*: "rock/cliff"), and calling the mesa itself the "Rock Plateau."[22] In the Numbers' Oracle of Balaam there is a reference to the Qenites (Num 24:21), which reads: "Enduring is your dwelling place, and your nest is in the rock," making a potential allusion to the Midianites (i.e., Jethro's clan) at Qurayyah. In Deut 32:4, the Song of Moses praises God: "The Rock, his work is perfect, and all his ways are just" (also, 32:30-2). Isa 30:29 makes it certain: "go to the mountain of the Lord, to the Rock of Israel." The Rock is equated with Sinai, and equated with God. (For pragmatic reasons the group returning from Egypt head to Tayma first, to regroup, then approach Sinai from the south-west, but the mount is the intended destination, as will be shown, below.)

---

[20] Marta Luciani, "Qurayyah in Northwestern Arabia," Archaeological Research Between Levant and Hejaz, International Congress on the Archaeology of the Ancient Near East, June 9-13, 2014, University of Basel, Switzerland. Others dispute this, e.g., Laura Hüneburg, et al. "Living at the Wadi: Integrating Geomorphology and Archaeology at the Oasis of Qurayyah (NW Arabia)," *JM*, 15:2 (2019): 215-26, here 216.
[21] Luciani and Aslaud, 167.
[22] Marta Luciani, "Mobility, Contacts and the Definition of Culture(s) in New Archaeological Research in Northwest Arabia," *The Archaeology of North Arabia Oases and Landscapes*, Proceedings of the International Congress held at the University of Vienna, 5-8 December, 2013; 21-56, here 30; 32.

⋆ *An accessible summit which can be reached from various angles, especially if a ramp or steps were created for regular ascents*: Nabonidus is an old man; he cannot be expected to hike up and down an actual mountain, let alone carrying heavy stone tablets. Josephus claims that Mount Sinai "is the highest of all the mountains that are in that country," that it was "very difficult to be ascended" because of its height and dangerous terrain, and that no one could look at it because of the rumour "that God dwelt there" (*A.J.* 3.5.1). This is in keeping with the Greek perception of Olympus perhaps, but not the rabbis' perception of the site. A Midrashic tale tells why Sinai was chosen to be the seat of Yahweh, i.e., Mounts Tabor, Hermon, and Carmel all jostled with pride to be the glorious mountain of God but Yahweh chose Sinai *because* of its humility, *because* it was "low" and "nondescript."[23] Once later generations latched on to the idea of a glorious mountain, the quiet little tale of a lowly mesa slipped into obscurity and into the children's section of the library.

⋆ *Low enough to still be able to hear the people below, when they raise a ruckus* (Exod 32:17-18). Unless the two parties are separated by a ravine that echoes, sound would soon be dissipated by the intervening landscape of a true mountain, especially a high mountain, with Moses supposedly at the top and the people kept at a distance below. At about 50 meters high, the voices of the crowd at the base of the mesa would be audible.

⋆ *A large area of associated fields e.g., for "grazing sheep" and rearing other livestock*: In Exod 3:1, Moses is tending Jethro's sheep;[24] he comes from "the wilderness" to the mount, Sinai. At Qurayyah, the fields, covering 750 acres, back onto the wilderness.[25] These fields, about 3 km square, are located some 5 km southeast of the mesa,[26]

---

[23] See Rabbi Berel Wein, "A Mountain of Inspiration," Parshas Behar, May 18, 2022 (5782), https://torah.org; and Rabbi Dina Rosenberg, "Humility and the Power of Language," www.sefaria.org.

[24] This is, on one level, a euphemism. In the Song, "pasturing his flocks" is understood as "servicing his ladies" (e.g., Song 2:16, and see Tyson, 77-8); it has a long-standing precedence in the poems of Tammuz and Ishtar, upon which much of the Song is formatted. The allusion here in Exod 3:1, therefore, suggests this is a reference to Nabonidus taking Jehudijah from her father's home to be a woman of his court, i.e., his harem. Of course, as King, he would not be herding animals for anyone (the common Mesopotamian epithet for the king as the people's "shepherd" may be what is alluded to here); the imagery is for "Moses" the character, but it is still required to fit the parameters of the physical setting, if this is an actual geological/historical site.

[25] Marta Luciani, "Archaeology in the Land of Midian: Excavating the Qurayyah Oasis," *BAR* (Winter 2023): 32-9, here, 35.

[26] Marta Luciani and Abdullah S. Alsaud, "The New Archaeological Joint Project

thus allowing for Moses to be at a distance. Nomadic shepherds do travel far and wide to find forage if grazing is scarce. In Exod 34:3, herds of livestock are apparently allowed quite close to the mesa.

⋆ *A residential site just below, large enough for locals and visiting (small) caravans*: Nabonidus would not have hundreds and thousands of people following him; this idea is simply outlandish. My guess is that the group who continue the journey to Tayma with Nabonidus number no more than a hundred or so. This is a relatively large oasis with all the amenities it seems.[27] Just as Exod 19:2 suggests, there is room for a "camp" to be placed "in front of the mountain."

⋆ *A plentiful supply of water*: "There is a complex system of cracks and fissures within the rocks. ... flowstones ... developed on the rock surface ... providing clear evidence of at least minor former spring activity in the area ... these springs may have been closely related to fractures channelizing the groundwater flow."[28] For the exodus narratives this means water is available for the scene in Exod 32:20 and Deut 9:21, where the golden calf is destroyed and its remains cast into the "stream that runs down the mountain." There are references to thunder and lightning (Exod 19:16), and Ps 68:7-8 speaks of heavy rains at Sinai.

⋆ *There are caves*: Luciani states that the two caves at the base of mesa (northeast) received little attention by archaeologists in the past, even though human and animal bones were found in them at the turn of the nineteenth century; this suggests a "non-residential" use.[29] According to 1 Kgs 19:9, Elijah found a cave at "Horeb" in which he sheltered from the storm; in 2 Macc 2:4-8 we are told that Jeremiah hides the ark in a cave at the mountain of God, declaring that the site will remain "unknown until God gathers his people together again and shows his mercy."

⋆ *The mesa is surrounded by rockfall*: As can be seen in *Fig. 15*, rocks have fallen to the base of the mesa in several places (this is a common attribute of mesas but not necessarily of "mountains," which would accumulate rocks in ravines, etc., unless there had been a landslide). Rockfall is greatest *just* where the caves are to be found, correlating

---

on the Site of Qurayyah, North-West Arabia: Results of the First Two Excavation Seasons," *PSAS* 48 (2018): 165-83, here 167, n. 4.

[27] It is described as "one of the largest and most significant oases of Northwestern Arabia" (Laura Hüneburg, "Living at the Wadi: Integrating Geomorphology and Archaeology at the Oasis of Qurayyah (NW Arabia)," *JM* 15.2 [2019]: 215-256, here 215).

[28] Hüneburg, 217.

[29] Marta Luciani, "Mobility," 35.

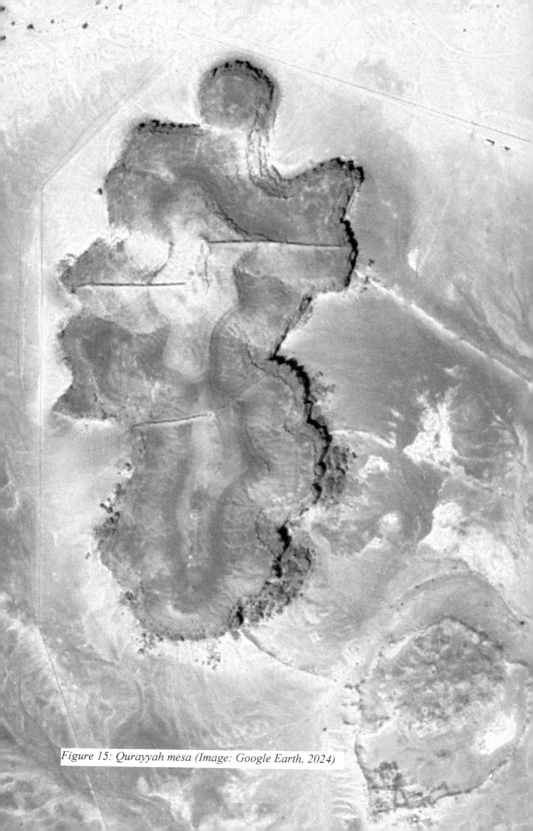

*Figure 15: Qurayyah mesa (Image: Google Earth, 2024)*

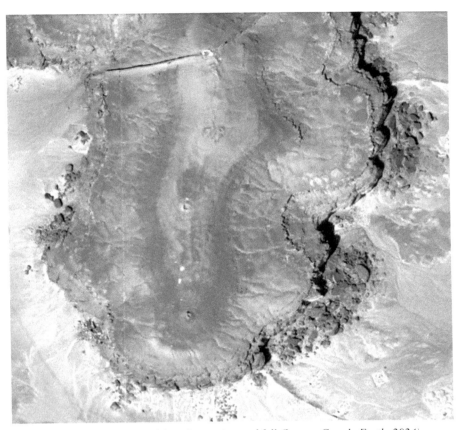

*Figure 16: Caves area (to right) and extensive rockfall (Image: Google Earth, 2024)*

✶ *"Metallurgical activities on top of the local rock plateau characterize the first settlement on the site."*[30] When I began this investigation, I always envisioned Sinai as an *accessible* site, with the fire and smoke on top, visible from below and afar; now the Qenite/metallurgy theory has been introduced, it makes such sense for the mesa at Qurayyah to be the site of multiple furnaces, crucibles, ceremonies, etc., that could not practically be used/performed on a steep slope. In the thick darkness of the desert night, the fires, with their heavenly hosts would be seen for miles, just as would the smoke, during the day. It would be a landmark, a guiding beacon.

---

[30] Marta Luciani and Abdullah S. Alsaud, "The New Archaeological Joint Project on the Site of Qurayyah, North-West Arabia: Results of the First Two Excavation Seasons," *PSAS* 48 (2018): 165-83, here "Summary."

✕ *It has superior acoustic properties*: This makes "it an ideal place for the celebration of highly relevant communal ceremonial and/or burial activities."[31] In Exod 19:16-19, the sound of the thunder and the trumpet is central to the overwhelming sensation of awe and fear felt by the crowd below. The area of archaeoaccoustics is relatively new and is a much anticipated field of study, as there is a glaring lacuna in the archaeological record. Recent studies have shown that sound, resonance, vibration, etc., can induce "ideas and thoughts similar to what happens during meditation, (and/or) images. .... Ancient populations were able to obtain different states of consciousness without the use of drugs or other chemical substances."[32]

As Nabonidus is probably still addicted to his favourite substance, but perhaps cannot source it (and Exodus seems to be telling of a testing of the man and his ability to put such things behind him), this new stimulus might be just what he is looking for (i.e., to replace the effects of the Elixir). The top of the mesa at Qurayyah reveals three walls that are yet to be explained fully; what if they were used as reverberation enhancers, a different resonance in each section? This might help to explain the reciprocity of speech (between Moses and God) insinuated by Exod 19:19 (as the trumpet is blown first and the "thunder" responds).[33]

## Getting High Up-High?

Analysis of samples from Qurayyah reveal arsenic-copper as the metal being treated here, "stemming not from the expected mines in the Jordan Valley but more likely from the Arabian Shield or possibly Oman."[34] "The high arsenic content ... combined with the fact that no tin bronze has so far been identified at the site may suggest that arsenical copper was *intentionally* (emphasis mine) produced at Qurayyah."[35] This use of arsenic, rather than

---

[31] Marta Luciani, "Qurayyah in Northwestern Arabia," *Archaeological Research Between Levant and Hejaz*, International Congress on the Archaeology of the Ancient Near East, June 9-13, 2014, University of Basel, Switzerland, Poster 9th ICAANE www.academia.edu; "Archaeology in the Land of Midian," 36.

[32] Linda Eneix, "Ancient Man Used 'Super-Acoustics' to Alter Consciousness (... and speak with the dead?)," June 16, 2014, https://sciencex.com.

[33] For a fascinating discussion on how we have perceived the echo through history, see Leendert van der Miesen, "Studying the Echo in the Early Modern Period: Between the Academy and the Natural World," *SS*, 6:2 (2020): 196-214.

[34] Luciani and Aslaud, 177.

[35] Siran Liu, et al. "Copper processing in the oases of northwest Arabia:

tin for alloying copper, Amzallag suggests, indicates a level of uniqueness that requires explanation, arguing that Qurayyah remained "largely uninfluenced by the technical developments observed in the ancient Near East at this time," and experienced a rather "autonomous development. If this premise is founded, we should expect to find in the Israelite theology some traces of a desert-shaped form of Yahwism reflecting the Northwestern Arabian reality."[36]

This is what I am attempting to reveal, i.e., not just some dim and distant connection to a metallurgy-based, nomadic society, but a hard and fast link to the "desert-shaped" exodus narrative that explains why Israel's Yahwism is so different. It all comes down to Nabonidus' strange ideas and powerful influence on those who would go on to tell the first stories of how Israel became Israel. It also rests on the uniqueness of Qurayyah's metallurgical practices, e.g., perhaps they "intentionally" work with arsenic-copper because a) they exploit its long-term physiological and psychological effects, in tandem with those of saltpetre, and the auditory stimulation of the trumpets, etc., in order to achieve an altered state of consciousness, and/or b) they prefer the silver-coloured copper that arsenic creates, rather than the reddish hue we now associate with copper;[37] this may further support a lunar-worship association.

## A Note on the Physiological Effects of Arsenic-Copper

Many mythological metallurgists, such as "the Greek Hephaistos, Roman Vulcan, Teutonic Wieland, Scandinavian Volunder, and the Finnish Ilmarinen are all lame. Such a widespread association of a particular symptom with a single occupation has led to the suggestion that this could have resulted from arsenical neuropathy."[38] As this aspect becomes part of the heroes' depiction, it must be seen as a divine attribute (the actual cause unrecognised) and therefore potentially emulated, or at least admired, much as physical deformities, e.g., dwarfism, etc., were often seen as special interventions/blessings from the gods.

Acute arsenic poisoning causes fairly rapid death, of course, but

---

technology, alloys and provenance," *JAS* 53 (2015): 492-503, here 501.

[36] Nissim Amzallag, "A Metallurgical Perspective on the Birth of Ancient Israel," *ER* 12.2 (2021): 65.

[37] Lucas Braddock Chen, "Sumerian Arsenic Copper and Tin Bronze Metallurgy (5300-1500 BC): The Archaeological and Cuneiform Textual Evidence," *AD* 9.3 (2021): 185-197, here 186.

[38] M. Harper, "Possible Toxic Metal Exposure of Prehistoric Bronze Workers," *BJIM* 44.10 (1987): 652-6, here 656.

chronic absorption often affects the skin, resulting in forms of skin cancer, boils, tumours, etc., which might reflect the incidents described in 1 Samuel 5-6, where the Philistines are affected by whatever was stored in the Israelites' golden box. As with previous accidents, resulting in the deaths of those who simply do not handle the volatile materials correctly, the sicknesses noted by the Philistines might well have to do with how they handled the ores they experimented with, exposing themselves to too many noxious fumes and/or the neat arsenic residues.[39]

Imagine how impressive Qurayyah must have been to a stranger. Moses has been there before, i.e., when he "tended Jethro's sheep" and married his daughter. To Nabonidus, it must have seemed, on his first encounter, like a natural ziggurat. When Woolley discovered the ziggurat *Ekišnugal* in Ur (the temple of Sîn), which Nabonidus completed, he found that the "total height of the 'Mountain of God' on which stood Nanna's Holy of Holies was just over 160 feet."[40] This equates to approximately 48.8 meters; the mesa is approximately 50 meters high. Nabonidus would have found this propitious.

With the sheer starkness, the imposing, isolated mesa in a desert sea, smiths working endlessly on its plateau, the noise probably deafening, the heat unbearable, the smoke interminable, Nabonidus has another of his great ideas. His previous, unfathomable idol of Sîn seems to have been inspired by a lunar eclipse;[41] its obscure symbolism was unappreciated. It was a chimera, a hybrid; taking form in Nabonidus' unique mind, its profundity and beauty so vivid in his imagination was lost in its translation to the public sphere. Now Nabonidus has a second chance and this time, he must be thinking, things will be different. They won't.

---

[39] Harper (654) adds: "The general toxicity of arsenical materials would have been recognised by early miners. ...a sublimate of arsenical oxides formed (as an extremely toxic white fume) during the process of breaking rocks with underground fires was said to attack wounds and ulcers as well as feet, hands, lungs, and eyes."

[40] Leonard Woolley, *Ur of the Chaldees* (London: Book Club Associates, 1982, rev. ed. 1929), 236.

[41] Tyson, 154-7.

# 13    JOSEPH'S BONES

There is something highly theatrical about Moses' encounter with God. There are elements of the old smoke and mirrors routine magicians used to use to impress an audience. Some of this flamboyance and drama could be attributed to the author, but I am of the opinion that the very *nature* of this encounter is strongly reflective of Nabonidus' own character as evidenced in the Song of Solomon and various historical inscriptions.

Consider how he appears in the Song, i.e., he is desperate for hidden wisdom; he is fascinated by Nitocris' Egyptian rites and rituals; he is overzealous; he challenges the priests and sages; he is a mediocre (spiritual) student who needs guidance; he is not overtly interested in kingship; and he has a predisposition for substance abuse. In Daniel 4-5 we learn that he has highly symbolic dreams that need interpreting; he sees the mysterious writing on the wall when no one else does, i.e., he has visions, perhaps hallucinations; the VA references his apparent "madness"[1] and strange behaviour, including the making of a bizarre idol of Sîn that dismays the people (1.7-8). He is also very interested in the occult, in priestly secrets, in esoteric practices; recall that as "Solomon," he is said to be "educated in all the wisdom of the Egyptians" (Acts 7:22). This is the man we need to see in "Moses" if we are to comprehend what is going on at Sinai.

In the Song, Nitocris attempts to teach Nabonidus the ways of *dod*,

---

[1] Tyson, 223-4.

that is, the all-encompassing, selfless, divinely-inspired form of "love" that lies at the root of her own religion and way of life. She teaches him, rather foolishly, about the Elixir Rubeus, one of the most secret and potent blood-rituals reserved, normally, for the Pharaoh and his priests. The question is, what else did she teach him? She acts the Scheherazade to Nabonidus' Sultan, keeping him (physically) at bay while she fills his head with secrets and stories.² That he feels he learns enough to be able to go back to Babylon and state he has discovered more "wisdom" than all the old sages, suggests he is inculcated quite deeply (for an outsider) into the Egyptian belief system:

> I have become greatest of the great, I have come into being among the beings who clear the vision of his sole Eye, I have opened and built up the injured Eye, for I am one of them. I know the ennead of On, into which The greatest of the seers was not initiated ....
>
> Coffin Texts, Spell 154³

In this verse, the spell is to invoke the powers of "On," or Heliopolis, the centre of Sun-god worship and the culture into which "Joseph" is indoctrinated/married, via the high priest's daughter.

Compare this to the Verse Account:

> It was he who once stood up in the assembly to praise himself, saying: "I am wise, I know, I have seen what is hidden. ... I have seen secret things. The god Ilteri has made me see a vision; he has shown me everything. I am aware of a wisdom which greatly surpasses even that of the series of insights which Adapa has composed!"
>
> VA 5.3

And to Ecclesiastes, which is thought to be the reminiscences of Solomon (i.e., I attest to this being someone else's philosophical musings on the Song of Solomon and the life of Nabonidus, who attempts to exonerate the biblical "Solomon" from his erroneous ways):

> I said to myself, "I have acquired great wisdom, surpassing all who were over Jerusalem before me; and my mind has had great

---

² Personally, I think this tale was also inspired by the Song of Solomon; another example of ancient interpreters beating me to it!

³ Coffin Texts (CT), Spells 154 (R. O. Faulkner *The Ancient Egyptian Coffin Texts, Vol. 1, Spells 1-354* [Warminster, UK: Aris & Phillips, 1973], 132). For other "I know (the souls of, or the "secrets" of the gods)" examples see, for instance, Spells 154-160.

226

experience of wisdom and knowledge." And I applied my mind to know wisdom and to know madness and folly.

Eccl 1:1-17

It would be likely that Nitocris divulges much to the king during their marriage; she very probably presented him with a copy of the Book of the Dead and explained the basics. He would certainly seek out further instruction on his trip(s) to Egypt, or from Egyptian priests, etc. He claims, openly, that his quest for hidden wisdom in Tayma did not stop at soothsayers and sages (Nab 47 3-4). So, what would he learn that could possibly find its way into the story of Moses on a stark mesa in the middle of the Arabian Desert?

Nabonidus, famous for his loyalty to the lunar deity Sîn, has lived with the high-priestess of Amun. His Egyptian father-in-law, Ahmose III, is, effectively, the son of Amun, a human avatar of Horus. He is the Sun-god incarnate. The battle between lunar and solar religions permeates the Song of Solomon and serves to underscore the great chasm between Nitocris and Nabonidus. Now, however, after learning so much, after seeing his kingdom fall (or perhaps, after *giving* it up), and after being drawn into Jehudijah's Yahweh-worship, in the context of metallurgical ritual and dynamism, he gets the idea to conflate everything he has learned into another chimeric form, i.e., a cosmological, Osirian blend of Sun, Moon, and Stars, with a smattering of Tyrian symbolism, and the dramatic liturgy of the Qenites.

Symbolically, Moses is the lunar representative; Miriam represents the Stars; and Aaron, whose role as a metallurgist (working with heat, fire, light, etc.) seems to be the obvious choice to represent the Sun in this new order. That is, *initially*; when Ahmose III dies, Nabonidus is inspired to steal his "bones" and thereby imbue his new portable deity with the very *essence* of the Sun-god. He creates the first recognisable reliquary (with a twist). A shocking idea, on face value, but I think there is enough evidence in the various legends and texts to substantiate the claim. In order to comprehend how this might have happened, in a historical sense, we must first take a look at the character of Joseph and the legend of Moses retrieving his bones from Egypt (Exod 13:19).

Both Jacob (Gen 50:1-14) and Joseph (Gen 50:26) are embalmed and placed in an Egyptian *aron*, or coffin. Jacob is repatriated to Canaan under great pomp and ceremony, involving not only his own people but a vast Egyptian contingent. Joseph asks Pharaoh for permission to do this on the promise that he will return (Gen 50:4-6), which he does. The body of Jacob is carried off to the same "Cave of Machpelah" where Sarah is supposedly buried. When the time comes for Joseph's death, however, a similar repatriation is hinted at (50:25) but is left unfulfilled; the last line of Genesis

227

is "he was embalmed and placed in a coffin in Egypt" (50:26).

In just this short summary we can see several of the elements of the subsequent Mosaic narrative, i.e., the need to go beyond Egypt to fulfil a duty; the necessary permission of Pharaoh; an excursion toward Tayma; the people on this (Genesis) trip include many Egyptian charioteers with their chariots (50:9), probably as an escort to ensure Joseph's return. One big difference is that no community, livestock, or children are taken (50:8); this is how I see Nabonidus' little exodus (camels for transport are not livestock for food).

Genesis 50 has several parallels to the funerary stele of Adad-guppi, Nabonidus' mother (Nab 2001), who died in 547 BCE, at the age of 104.[4] Joseph also supposedly dies a centenarian. She is said to have witnessed her descendants to the "fourth generation,"; Joseph does likewise (Ephraim, plus three generations). Joseph mourns his father for seven days, as Nabonidus and his kingdom mourn Adad-guppi for seven days. People from all over the kingdom make the journey to her funeral and a great show is made of their return to their own lands. Perhaps the stele, which influenced the Song of Solomon (i.e., allusion to its contents serve as a dating mechanism within the text),[5] influenced this narrative in Genesis also.

In Josh 24:32, Joseph is buried at Shechem, i.e., in Josephite, or rather, Ephraimite, territory. This suggests the book of Joshua was written after the Tayma-reign of Nabonidus-Solomon, and after Belshazzar's (Joshua's) lifetime. The north-south divide is accentuated, with Joseph's precious bones being symbolically taken home to Shechem, in Israel, rather than left in Judea. Shechem, recall, is the very first place Abraham sets up an altar at the tree of Moreh (Gen 12:6-8); to the later Jewish mind, of course, this is hostile territory, i.e., Samaria. I think this is a final nail in the coffin for the memory of Nabonidus' involvement with the early Jews, i.e., the authors of the book of Joshua reject Joseph's bones and *symbolically* send them to the heathen high places of the north, befitting their opinion of the much maligned Egyptian element in early Judaism.

There is potential for an Osirian link here, for a few scholars have debated the presence of a "Joseph"/Osiris centre of worship being at Shechem; both figures being associated with sacred trees.[6] This might suggest either the place was already an Osirian shrine when Nabonidus arrived there, or the Osirian connection sprang *from* Joseph/Ahmose/Osiris

---

[4] From "the twentieth regnal year of the Assyrian king Ashurbanipal (649) to the ninth regnal year (547)," according to W&N, 223.

[5] Tyson, 89-90.

[6] H. Abdul Al-Dahir, "Shechem Sacred to Osiris" (17 May, 2018) http://arabianprophets.com. Also, Wright, G. R. H. "An Egyptian God at Shechem." Zeitschrift Des Deutschen Palästina-Vereins (1953-) 99 (1983): 95-109.

influences peculiar to the exodus mission.

I suggest the latter is more probable, i.e., that Nabonidus brought his own beliefs to Shechem and after the Sinai years, the story of Joseph's bones took root there. Evidence for the connection between Joseph and Osiris appears in the ancient texts of Melito (a 2nd Century CE philosopher), who claimed that various ancient societies worshipped people (male and female) as gods, including the Hebrews, who revered Joseph as Serapis (Osiris-Apis);[7] and also Julius Firmicus Maternus (an early 4th Century CE Roman astrologer/theologian),[8] who described a statue of Joseph, as Serapis, in Egyptian temples, protected by guards; interestingly he claims Joseph was only called this *after* his death. Only the deceased can be called "an Osiris."

# THE "DOUBLE"

The character of Joseph is a difficult one to unpick. It is said that the first pharaoh in the Moses story does not know (of) him (Exod 1:8); how can this be, if he was supposedly of such renown and status? There would be records of previous viziers, funerary inscriptions, *something*, surely … if he had actually been who/what Genesis suggests he was.

On one hand, he reflects Ahmose III, i.e., both are outsiders, non-royals who rises to great heights in the Egyptian court; both are praised for being just and wise authority figures. The most intriguing parallel, however, is the depiction of Joseph in Gen 47:13-26, wherein he resolves to deal with the famine situation by gradually reducing the Egyptians' autonomy and ownership, until they are forced to become serfs to Pharaoh; they give up their money, their livestock, and their land, in exchange for food to subsist. Once their resources are forfeited, they are basically rented-back their lands at a cost of one-fifth of their profits. Seen in light of what we know of medieval serfdoms, this sounds mercenary and unfair perhaps, but in Genesis, the Egyptian people are grateful and readily offer themselves as "slaves" to Pharaoh. According to Herodotus (*Hist*. 2.177) and Diodorus (1.95) Ahmose legislates an annual income-tax for each male citizen, who has to prove that he can afford to *keep* his family (i.e., especially in times of famine, etc.); false or missing returns might cost him his life. Both characters succumb to harsh tactics to ensure a steady-state society, it seems.

Even the giving of land (Goshen) to the Israelites reflects Ahmose's

---

[7] Melito, "Discourse with Anoninus Caesar," Ante-Nicene Fathers, Vol. 8, www.tertullian.org.

[8] Firmicus Maternus, *The Error of the Pagan Religions*, Clarence A. Forbes, trans., (New York: Newman Press, 1970), 71.

supposed generosity toward the Greeks (as per Herodotus, *Hist.* 2.78-9), whom he subsidised in the Nile Delta, i.e., at Naukratis. Though modern archaeological assessments do suggest the Greeks were already ensconced in these areas during Psamtik I's reign, Ahmose is traditionally given credit for enhancing their presence and standards of living.[9] In Herodotus' time, however, which is not that long after Nabonidus' and Ahmose's time, this was not necessarily understood; such accounts from the early historians would be relatively unquestioned. This would be the perception of Ahmose the authors of the HB would have had (via Nabonidus), which is why they depict him as the magnanimous "Joseph." He was an 'honourary' Israelite.

On the other hand, Joseph seems to echo the same basic qualities/traits/actions of Nabonidus that his other avatars in the HB do, i.e., Abraham, Moses, Solomon, Samson, etc. (this is the primary material the scribes have to work with, cleverly devising ways to use the same details in a variety of characters). For instance, Joseph reflects the Babylonian king in that he is an alien in a foreign land (as Abraham, Nabonidus enters Canaan as a foreigner, and Moses is a stranger in Egypt); he is made the governor of the storehouses (Nabonidus *may* be sent as temporary governor of Jerusalem to set things up there); Joseph is welcomed into the Egyptian royal court (as Nabonidus is, to begin with); he is given a wife who is the daughter of a priest of On, i.e., a priest of the Sun-god (Nabonidus marries Nitocris, daughter of Ahmose, priest of Amun, the Sun-god); he is given a commission name (see below); Nabonidus is provided many pseudonyms in the HB. In this instance, however, the two characters appear together and thus cannot be identical, historically. There is something quite profound going on here.

In my work on the Song of Solomon, I discuss Solomon's commission name, "Jedidiah," which I contend potentially

> breaks down into three elements: *Jed*: Hand (sexual), *did/dod*: Beloved (cultic) … and *–iah*, the Egyptian lunar deity. The name *could* mean: Beloved hand of the moon god. This could be a deliberate signpost to the Egyptian women who serve as God's Hand. In that capacity, it would be intended as an *insulting* sexually-charged inference that the king (Nabonidus), himself, is "the hand" to Ahmose III (as a personification of Iah/Yah), a slur on the Babylonian king's strength as a man and ruler, e.g., that he is capitulating and/or emasculated even.[10]

---

[9] Carl Roebuck, "The Organization of Naukratis," *CP* 46.4 (1951): 212-20, here 213-15. Eliezer D. Oren, "Migdol: A New Fortress on the Edge of the Eastern Nile Delta," *BASOR* 256 (1984): 7-44, here 37.

[10] Tyson, 24.

This submissive, almost sycophantic depiction of Nabonidus comes through in the Song of Solomon but also in Exodus and Numbers (Genesis and Deuteronomy are predominantly pro-Nabonidus texts). Nabonidus becomes "pharaoh" in all but title, in that he is seen to be ingratiating himself into the sphere of Ahmose and is considered a collaborator with Egypt.[11] In this last regard, the name "Joseph" is translated to mean "one who increases, repeats, or doubles," from the verb *yasap*, "to add, increase, or repeat"; this seems fitting, i.e., Nabonidus is effectively added-to Ahmose, he attempts to emulate him, become his "double," etc. He has aspirations and perhaps covets the pharaoh's wealth, wisdom, status, etc., but now he envisions a way of exploiting the situation, helped by a little insider knowledge, in order to bring life to his new, chimeric deity.

In a Supplemental Note to *She Brought*, I discuss the various subsequent legends that seem to be telling the same story of Nabonidus and Nitocris; one of these is the Islamic tale of Asiya bint Muzahim, purportedly the wife of Pharaoh who discovered Moses in the river.[12] Many details of the legend, however, strongly suggest Nitocris is Asiya; some scholars have actually suggested the character is to be equated with Asenath (another Nitocris-based fable).[13] So, once again, the "daughter of Pharaoh" can be either Moses' mother *or* wife; the former would make Moses truly Egyptian, a member of the royal lineage (i.e., a pharaoh in waiting); the latter makes him Nabonidus, husband to Nitocris. Either way, the link to the pharaonic line is strong in this legend and provides grounds for suspecting there is more to the perception of Nabonidus attempting to emulate, or somehow exploit his affinity with Pharaoh.

Tayma is portrayed as "Jerusalem" in the Song of Solomon, and "Egypt" replaces Babylonia as the tyrannical, slave-driving entity that holds the Israelites in captivity.[14] Just as Nabonidus, Nitocris, and even Cambyses are intentionally struck from the official HB record, so too is Ahmose III (these blatant, similarly-dated omissions suggest both a postexilic context for much of the HB, and a definite agendum). Ahmose III, I claim, is fundamental to the entire exodus narrative, posthumously, and is therefore provided an avatar in the "bones of Joseph."

---

[11] See also the comments on "Hadad," Tyson, 236-7.

[12] John Walker, "Asiya, the Wife of Pharaoh," *MW* 18 (1928): 45-8.

[13] Tyson 255-6.

[14] It is a scribal safety-net for those writing of politically sensitive matters in a time of upheaval and the threat of repercussions. If anyone should ask, they simply say, "It's not about you … this is a story of our distant past!" This may also be why Nabonidus mirrors the pharaoh in some legends; he is just as responsible for not 'letting the people go' until it suits him, i.e., he probably retains the Tayma Jews to work on his temple/palace projects (as they would be experienced, via corvée).

Looking back at the burial of Jacob in Gen 50:13, we learn that his body is interred in the cave Abraham had bought for Sarah, i.e., the Cave of Machpelah, the "Cave of the Double," facing Tayma. This burial scenario provides the precedent for the transference of Joseph's bones, i.e., for Ahmose III's remains. The narrative in Genesis 50 sets the context for the inevitable rescue of the pharaoh's corpse, with the very obvious hint that the Cave of Machpelah will be the destination for Moses and the *aron*.

Now we know that Joseph is the "double" of Nabonidus (and vice versa), this special cave becomes the official burial site of Pharaoh, perhaps even the final resting place of Nabonidus. Though I am arguing that the bones become an intrinsic part of the ark (see below), like any religious relic, one small bone might suffice (and would be lighter to carry), whilst the rest are properly interred.

## Zaphenath-paneah

Joseph's Egyptian commission name is "Zaphenath-paneah." While most commentators consider this name difficult to translate on the basis that it is not Hebrew, arriving at a general consensus that it means something like "the god speaks and he lives," I think this name is wholly invented by the authors of Genesis who *know* Nabonidus. The *Jewish Encyclopedia* states:

> Targum Onḳelos gives the meaning of the name as "the man to whom mysteries are revealed"; pseudo-Jonathan, "one who reveals mysteries"; Josephus (*Ant*. ii. 6, § 1), "a finder of mysteries."[15]

This is profoundly significant once you realise who Joseph represents in a 6th Century BCE context, and where the story of Nabonidus and the exodus leads us.

The etymology may be derived from several potential root verbs such as *nuah* and/or *nahet,* both of which refer to "rest, settling down, being still/quiet," etc.; *naha,* which means "to lead, guide"; and perhaps most germane, *yaphah,* "to shine" or "to be beautiful, bright" and *sapan,* "to hide or store."

In a pharaonic context, this description alludes to Pharaoh as a solar-deity avatar, i.e., Horus, son of the Sun (Amun), and to deification. His "glory" or theophany, is symbolised by his golden statues, the gold in the temples, etc. He is "beautiful" as the deity is beautiful (this does not mean personally, or physically attractive, this is a symbolic, theologically

---

[15] Emil G. Hirsch, W. Max Muller, "Zaphenath-paneah," *JE,* https://www.jewishencyclopedia.com.

significant beauty that expresses divinity). He shines as the Sun, is brightness itself, etc.[16] The verb *sapan* I shall come back to momentarily.

More intriguingly, perhaps, *Strong's* suggests Zaphenath-paneah is from an unused root meaning "to extrude; a viper (as thrusting out the tongue, i.e. hissing): adder, cockatrice." The BDB translation is: 1) poisonous serpent, 1a) a viper snake or adder," citing usage in Prov 23:32; Isa 11:8, 14:29, 59:5; Jer 8:17.

So, the Egyptian name granted to Joseph when he rises from a nobody to having command over the entire nation (Gen 45:8) is equated with 1) a peaceful leader, perhaps after a tumultuous one;[17] 2) the symbolism of a Sun-god; and 3) serpents.[18] Not only does this commission name symbolise the recognition of Joseph as, effectively, Pharaoh, with the *uraeus* conferred upon him by his predecessor, it links him inextricably with what will come later, in Exodus, via his association with serpents.

# A WOMAN'S SECRET

Joseph, in the HB, becomes a major player in the Egyptian royal court, a vizier over all Egypt, second only to the Pharaoh. He is embalmed, i.e., mummified, and placed in a coffin, an *aron*. One rabbinical legend tells of his body being secured in a metal casket and sunk in the Nile (Sotah 13a:14). This proves very significant, for *why* would someone add this strange detail to the account in Genesis?

In Exodus, Moses falls out of favour with Egyptian officials, so we must question why he would he be given access to such a sacred, carefully-preserved royal tomb. The legends in the Talmud and Midrash provide many explanations for how Moses could possibly acquire the bones in the first place. The most striking is simply that a woman *tells* him where the body is hidden. This may sound rather dull but not when you know who it is that tells him: In one form of the story it is his "mother" Jochebed (*Legends of the Jews*, 3:1.3; more on this below) but in another, more prevalent, it is a woman named

---

[16] In my paper, "Nabonidus, Tarshish, and Ophir" ([2024], www.academia.edu), I discuss a link to this Egyptian name with regard to the building of Solomon's temple.

[17] And recall that Osiris, too, is said to bring peace and harmony to a previously brutish society.

[18] In the examples of usage listed, a "cockatrice" is mentioned, which is a (medieval) mythological cross between a bird and a snake, i.e., a flying, fiery serpent. The uraeus attacks enemies "with a flame called *nesery*, and Wadjet is hence sometimes called Neseret, 'the Fiery One' or 'Fiery Serpent'" (Edward P. Butler, "Wadjet," Henadology: Philosophy and Theology, https://henadology.wordpress.com).

"Serah" the "daughter of Asher."[19] This name is a play both phonetically and etymologically on "Sarah," who, we now know, is Nitocris. Like our Nitocris-Sarah, Serah is renowned for her beauty, her wisdom, her prowess as a seer, and as a commanding woman of authority.[20] She is also linked to music, singing, and playing an instrument (Sefer HaYashar, Vayigash 9).

"Asher" can be derived from the verb *asher*, which means "happy," and is always associated with Leah's second son of that name (Gen 30:12-13). The tribe of Asher is known for its prosperity (a fundamental basis for happiness for some), having been given prime territories near the Phoenician trading routes; they specialised in olive oil and became self-sufficient enough to eventually break away from the central conglomerate of Israel.[21]

This idea of prosperity lying at the root of happiness has a link to the tale of Sarah; Gen 12:16 states, "And for her sake he dealt well with Abram," i.e., Nabonidus (Abraham) *grows rich* on his trading caravan through Canaan (Mishlei 31:5) largely thanks to Sarah (i.e., pimping her out). Thus "Asher" becomes a pun, another pseudonym, playing on the increasing prosperity of Nabonidus, thanks to Nitocris (which is expressed also in the Song of Songs via references to the riches brought from Egypt and the selling of the Elixir).[22]

It would seem that Nabonidus receives the secret knowledge of the pharaoh's resting place from Serah/Nitocris, perhaps in one of their Elixir-induced moments when inhibitions were at an ebb. Perhaps it was a family secret, a long-held contingency plan for troubled times the king knew were just around the corner. Midrash also tells of a "secret of redemption" that was passed down the generations, purportedly concerning Moses as the redeemer of Israel, to which Serah was privy (Pirkei Derabbi Elazar 48b), but perhaps this originally pertained to the secret of the hidden burial (i.e., the redemption of Pharaoh's bones, rather than of the Israelites). Bechayei to Genesis 50:26 suggests Joseph's body was hidden so that the Jews *would not find it and take it away*, explaining that the Egyptians figured they would not leave Egypt without their patriarch. This proves really interesting.

A second pun (the first applying to Nabonidus and Nitocris) is in the use of "Asher" as a play on Osher, the Egyptian name for Osiris; the tribe of

---

[19] "Daughter" can refer to a number of relationships involving a female, and as Abraham lies about his connection to Sarah, we can legitimately read "daughter" as female companion, or even "sister" (as Sarah is depicted); "sister" can also suggest wife (especially in the Nitocris-based Song of Solomon).

[20] Mendy Kaminker, "Serach, the Daughter of Asher," www.chabad.org. Also, Pirkei Derabbi Elazar 48b; Rashi to II Samuel 20:18, quoting Genesis Rabbah 94:9.

[21] Morris Jastrow, Jr., J. Frederic McCurdy, "Asher: Tribe and Territory," *JE*, www.jewishencyclopedia.com.

[22] E.g., Song 3:6 (Tyson, 83-4); Song 5:15 (Tyson, 140), etc.

Asher becomes associated with Osher/Osiris via its territory, which sits on the border of the mythical land of Osiris' resting place, Byblos, on the Phoenician coastline.[23] Figuratively, if Nitocris is the daughter of Asher, she is also the daughter of Osiris. The dead Pharaoh, Ahmose III, becomes "the Osiris" in the afterlife (though Nabonidus' exploitation of this, later, confuses the issue a bit because *he* takes on the symbolism of Osiris); therefore, "Serah" *is* the daughter of Ahmose III, i.e., Nitocris (and in reality, Nitocris II was a staunch Osirian).[24]

Other legends relate to the effects of carrying this coffin/ossuary on the exodus itself. For instance, the ritual impurity of being in close proximity with the dead is discussed; the rationale involves a careful delineation of the wording so that it implies the *aron* is simply "in the same area" where Moses dwells and not necessarily close enough to be of concern (Pesachim 67a:10). Of course, such laws have yet to come into being in the context of the exodus narratives, but it does remind me of the comparison I made in *She Brought*, of the construction of the *millo* by Solomon (i.e., the *majal*, or cemetery of the *entus* Nabonidus restores),[25] which is vaguely alluded to in the HB discussion of the "daughter of Pharaoh" (Nitocris) having dwelt where the tabernacle once stood (2 Chr 8:11).[26]

Joseph's *aron* travels with the group for the full forty years of the exodus, and some of the people on the trip complain (familiar?) that an *aron* for the dead is getting the same treatment as the *aron* for the "living" "glory of God." Its proximity to the ark is said to be allowed because "The dead man enshrined in the one fulfilled the commandments enshrined in the other" (*Legends* 2:1.496-7).

The *aron* performs miracles and is attributed the power behind the parting of the Red Sea: "Shimon of Kitron says: In the merit of the bones of Joseph I will split the sea for them, viz. (Gen 39:12)" (Mekhilta DeRabbi Yishmael 14:15:2). It also provided "nourishment" for the sojourners in the desert, as Joseph had promised: "I will nourish you and take care of you" (*Legends* 2:1, 496).

One other aspect that is often referred to is that Moses allegedly goes

---

[23] David Prashker, "Osher (Osiris)" (2020), https://thebiblenet.blogspot.com.

[24] As evidenced in the funerary inscriptions on her sarcophagus (Mariam Ayad, "Some Remarks on the Pyramid Texts Inscribed in the Chapel of Amenirdis I at Medinet Habu," in *Egypt and Beyond: Essays Presented to Leonard H. Lesko* Stephen E. Thompson and Peter der Manuelian, eds. [Providence: Department of Egyptology and Ancient Western Asian Studies, 2008], 1-13, here, 8).

[25] In the original translation of Nab 34 by Clay is the transliterated word *majal*: "... the wall of the *majal* (resting place) of the ancient votaries, as it was of old, I constructed around it anew." Albert T. Clay, *Miscellaneous Inscriptions in the Yale Babylonian Collection* (New Haven: Yale University Press, 1915), 2.15.

[26] Tyson, 25-7.

in search of the bones of Joseph while everyone else is busy "plundering" the Egyptians for gold and silver (Mekhilta DeRabbi Yishmael 14:15:2; *Legends*, 2:1, 495). In other words, he creates a distraction, knowing this is going to be a dangerous and difficult theft. Notice that this forms yet another mirrored event in the narrative; Nabonidus (as Abraham) had stolen Jehudijah from Ur, and now, as "Moses," he steals Ahmose's bones.

The first trip to Egypt saw Nabonidus (potentially) attempting to return Ennigaldi to her grandfather, Ahmose. In fear of his life for angering the pharaoh, and humiliated by the revelation that the girl was never Nitocris' biological daughter, Nabonidus returns to Tayma, and to his Midian family. As Abraham, he had taken only "his wife" Sarah and Lot, according to Gen 13:1, which may support a clandestine entry into Egypt befitting the secret meeting to hand over Ennigaldi.[27] On the second trip, however, this time as Moses in Exodus 5, after Ahmose's death, Nabonidus has others with him, i.e., men willing to plunder and make a diversion for him.

In the Coffin Texts, a spell is recited on the occasion of the new moon: "The speaker demands access (to the Osirian tomb) on account of being one who *hbs ht*. Taken literally, this is 'one who covers things' and it can mean one who keeps a secret, as well as *one who gathers and embalms the members of Osiris* (emphasis mine)."[28] Covering his actions with a cloak of darkness and mischief, Nabonidus goes in search of Ahmose's corpse, and his intentions are *certainly* Osirian-based.

So, the next question must be: *Where* are the bones of Joseph hidden?

# SANCTUARY

Herodotus suggests (*Hist.* 3.16) that Ahmose's mummy was desecrated by the "angry" Cambyses soon after the conquest of Egypt in 525 BCE.[29]

I am one who argues for discretion when including Herodotus in any argument. His account of the marriage of Nitetis (*Hist.* 3.1) was key to my argument about Nabonidus marrying Nitocris II (in *She Brought*) but I questioned each element of his claim and concluded that he had got the wrong end of the stick, with regard to the identity of the groom in that

---

[27] Cf. Deut 26:5: "A wandering Aramean was my father; and he went down into Egypt and sojourned there, *few in number* …" (emphasis mine).

[28] Joergensen, 25.

[29] Also, John Dillery, "Cambyses and the Egyptian Chaosbeschreibung Tradition," *Cl.Q* 55.2 (2005): 387-406, here 393.

marriage. A major source of his material was from Egyptian priests, who clearly had their own agenda (as he himself admits), and many of his stories have proven to contain erroneous historical details. From my investigation into Nabonidus from the biblical evidence, I have become increasingly aware that several of Herodotus' accounts attributed to Cambyses (and at least one to Polycrates) fit more accurately the character and life of Nabonidus. Herodotus seems not to be very familiar with the Babylonian king, mentioning him as "Lybentius" only twice, so if he acquires tantalising information that he did not have a direct source for, he simply attributes it to Cambyses, of whom people would apparently believe the worst (even today) because that is what Herodotus wants them to think (e.g., "senseless madman as he was" [*Hist.* 3.25]).

Cambyses, for instance, is accused of vandalising Ahmose's remains. Such a desecration would imply (to Egyptians) that the pharaoh's soul could not be reborn in the afterlife, i.e., he would die the dreaded "second death." Although Ahmose's tomb has never been located, there is archaeological evidence proving that the tombs of other immediate family members *were* vandalised.[30] His wife Nekhtbastetru and son Iahmes, discovered at Giza, both had their sarcophagi defaced. While not quite as macabre and destructive as Cambyses' alleged attack, the very carefully chosen obliteration of key hieroglyphs was clearly intended to have the same result, i.e., to eliminate the occupiers of the tomb from the afterlife. Bolshakov, studying these mutilated inscriptions, suggests the act had to have been performed by a literate Egyptian who knew the text and knew which hieroglyphs to deface, as every name of a deity was left untouched.[31]

Herodotus claims that the Egyptians themselves suggest Ahmose knew something like this would happen, so he arranged for someone to hide his corpse, replacing it with a stand-in body (*Hist.* 3.17). There is no way of knowing, to date, if his wife and son died before or after Ahmose did; he might have been aware of the vandalism, especially if he had intended to be buried in the same tomb, as Herodotus suggests, and had visited it to make plans (which would indicate an earlier date for the damage). Maybe this is what gives him the idea to make alternative arrangements. Regardless, this provides a connection between the *hiding* of "Joseph's" bones and the *hiding* of Ahmose's corpse.

Joseph's Egyptian name, "Zaphenath-paneah," is also linked, etymologically, with "Baal-zephon," via the verb *sapan* and its derivatives (especially, *sapon*, "north, hidden, dark"; *sapin*, "treasure"). The clue is the

---

[30] See Andrey Bolshakov, "Persians and Egyptians: Cooperation in Vandalism?" in *Offerings to the Discerning Eye* (Leiden: Brill, 2010), 45-54.

[31] Bolshakov, 51.

statue of, or reference to, "Baal-zephon" in Exod 14:2. As previously mentioned, the Israelites go to Pi-hahiroth "where two rectangular rocks form an opening, within which the great sanctuary of Baal-zephon [is] situated"; there, Joseph is said to hide something of great worth but the Israelites run off with it (*Legends* 3:1, 11-12; Bechayei to Genesis 50:26). Somewhere deep within this piecemeal legend is a memory, a snippet of history that once pertained to the hiding of Ahmose's bones. This "sanctuary" of Baal-zephon is probably at Tahpanhes. The Baal-zephon statue, I posited earlier, possibly depicted a bird, i.e., an eagle (or mythical bird); in the Ugaritic poem mentioned in earlier, the phoenix is linked to the deity; the phoenix is the iconic symbol of immortality, the afterlife, resurrection, etc.[32]

One might say that the clue in Exod 14:2, i.e., "Baal-zephon," is pivotal, in that it not only provides the precise location where the first group is to gather in the Ur Temenos, but it also contains within it the entire purpose and goal of the journey into Egypt and the consequent escape—the acquisition of the bones of Pharaoh Ahmose III (i.e., the comparatively quiet leader who brings peace and prosperity, who is the shining embodiment of the beautiful Horus, who is represented by the serpent on his crown), to serve as the solar aspect of Nabonidus' newly revamped tripartite deity. Ahmose replaces Aaron as the physical representation of the "Sun" in the triad.

The son of the Sun-god's symbolic bone (probably singular) will be kept in a reliquary, i.e., the *aron*. The small ossuary can easily be taken out of the ark when the glory is induced, but because it represents the Sun on earth, it must remain within the black box (see below) of the tabernacle, unseen.

That the ark itself is relatively compact and not long enough to accommodate a full-length mummy (which would be very awkward to carry stealthily, and which would be at risk of damage by water, especially, as it would be transported through the marshes) suggests Nabonidus must dismember the corpse if he is to be successful in stealing it away. He must, necessarily, mutilate it, removing all the bandages (keeping the gold and silver), and breaking the body into manageable pieces. Though this may shock some readers, just remember what we, a so-called enlightened civilization, did when we first discovered the mummies of Egypt: We ground them up, made dye and face-cream, and even ate them!

Nabonidus' predecessors, the Assyrians, known for their violence and torture in battle, left a legacy of their bloody tactics in a plethora of stone reliefs. Ashurbanipal (669-31 BCE) provides a comprehensive list of what seem to be his favourite tactics, including the ravaging of kings' tombs and the desecration of their remains:

---

[32] Albright, "Baal-Zephon," 4, n. 2.

(vi 58) I had the sanctuaries of the land Elam utterly destroyed (and) I counted its gods (and) its goddesses as ghosts.

(vi 65) (As for) their secret groves, … my battle troops entered inside them, saw their secrets, (and) burned (them) with fire.

(vi 70) I destroyed (and) demolished the tombs of their earlier and later kings, … I exposed (them) to the sun (lit. "the god Shamash"). I took their bones to Assyria. I prevented their ghosts from sleeping (and) deprived them of funerary libations.[33]

It has already been ascertained that although Nabonidus seems to admire his Assyrian predecessors, and he is certainly depicted in some of his early inscriptions as being a warrior king, it is possible that he is the kind of man who simply lets his spin-doctors say for the record what they feel is necessary (propaganda), especially when he begins to exhibit signs of his alleged "madness." This perception of him is exploited by the authors of Exodus, especially, but they often turn military violence into a very personal violence that more truly depicts Nabonidus the man (as made clear in the Song).

Nabonidus has a conflicting and complex nature and it is more likely he would echo the sentiment of the Chaldean king Merodach-Baladan,

who actually dug the bones of his ancestors out of their graves in the Sea-land and took them with him into exile on the other side of the Persian Gulf. Presumably he feared the kind of treatment from Sennacherib which Assurbanipal later meted out to the remains of the Elamite kings ….[34]

Therefore, I think it is possible Herodotus' story of Cambyses dismembering and, note, "burning" Ahmose's corpse *may* be an erroneously attributed accusation based on a scrambled rumour about Nabonidus' daring raid and the apparent desecration of the king's corpse (in association with the fiery connotations of Sinai). In fact, Nabonidus is not removing the bones like Ashurbanipal (and Herodotus' Cambyses) did in order to negate Ahmose's chances of immortality, but to insure *against* such a fate. Like the Chaldean king, he gathers the bones and takes them with him, in order (he believes) to assure his father-in-law and once friend the fate he deserves (but don't think this is all altruistic and honourable; Nabonidus still has his own agendum).

---

[33] Inscriptions of Ashurbanipal 011, http://oracc.museum.upenn.edu.
[34] D. K. M. Bayliss, "Ancestry and Descent in Mesopotamia from the Old Babylonian to the Neo-Assyrian Period," 198 n. 68, https://eprints.soas.ac.uk/29750/1/10752722.pdf.

# OSIRIAN ASPECTS

I always say that anything that is repeated relatively quickly within a biblical text is crying out to be investigated; it is an intentional clue, or sign. Noegel points out, for instance, that in Gen 50:9-10 "threshing floor" is mentioned twice: "In Egypt, the threshing floor was most widely associated with Osiris and his cult. … the threshing of grain was interpreted as the dismemberment of Osiris"; he then suggests this, together with the *aron*, evokes "an Egyptian, if not Osirian subtext."[35] Indeed it does. Nabonidus is both Abraham and Moses, so the Egyptian influence is consistent; the entire book of Exodus is an arcane account of his fascination with and attempted imposition of his (probably insufficient) knowledge of the Osirian liturgies, etc., as is befitting his now familiar hubris.

There are several pertinent aspects of the Osiris myth that can shed further light on Nabonidus' quest:[36]

⋆ Osiris is tricked into laying down in an ornate *aron*, which had been secretly constructed to his precise measurements; his conniving brother, Set, had offered the casket as a prize for anyone who would fit into it. Set sealed it with molten lead and threw it in the Nile. As mentioned above, one of the later legends of Joseph's bones is that they were put in a metal casket and sunk in the Nile.[37]

⋆ The *aron* of Osiris is set in the Nile in the Delta region, near Tahpanhes, and is said to drift up the coastline, to Byblos. The sanctuary of Baal-zephon is probably in Tahpanhes; instead of travelling north, to Byblos, the new *aron* will travel south, to Sinai (hence the emphasis on deviating from the expected route).

⋆ The *aron* is enveloped by a sacred tree (echoing the mythology of Tyre, with its sacred tree), concealing it from view; the King of

---

[35] S. B. Noegel, "The Egyptian Origin of the Ark of the Covenant," in *Israel's Exodus in Transdisciplinary Perspective: Text, Archaeology, Culture, and Geoscience,* T. E. Levy et al., eds. (Germany: Springer, 2015), 223-242, here 232-3.

[36] These Osirian references (unless otherwise stated) from "The Myth of Osiris and Isis," https://ancientegyptonline.co.uk; Plutarch, *Plutarch's Morals: Theosophical Essays*: "On Isis and Osiris," Charles William King, trans. (1908), https://sacred-texts.com.

[37] Interestingly Plutarch's account of the myth includes an "Ethiopian queen" who helps in the demise of Osiris by secretly gaining access to his body-measurements (Plutarch, 11). Who but a wife would get so close? Could this possibly be an anachronistic memory of the allegedly conniving "Cushite" Nitocris, who used her magic to make the king vulnerable and thereby instigate his fall?

Byblos cuts the tree down and places it as a pillar in his own palace. If Nabonidus has the (some of the) bones of the pharaoh in an *aron*, he keeps them concealed, first on the mesa (away from the people), then in the tabernacle; they become an integral aspect of the site of worship and perhaps one or two become incorporated into the pillars of "Solomon's" temple (again, linked to Tyre, as discussed earlier).

⋆ Although Joseph has been embalmed, i.e., mummified, it is still apt to refer to his remains as "the bones": In many of the Pyramid and Coffin Texts, the dismembered corpse of Osiris is referred to as his "bones" even though he is always depicted as being a "mummy" (e.g., Utterance 637 § 1800-02; Spell 80 II, 38, 41-42).[38] Recall that Moses is at the Nile in time for the ritualistic raising and reconstitution of Osiris' bones.

⋆ As mentioned above, the ritual/mythological *mutilation* of Osiris might be seen to be the root of Herodotus' account of the alleged *mutilation* of Ahmose's corpse by Cambyses. Herodotus, knowing very little about Nabonidus, knows there is a legend concerning the body of the Pharaoh but assumes it must relate to Cambyses.

⋆ Isis hides the child Horus on "Pe," a floating island amidst the marshes, Herodotus calls Chemmis (*Hist.* 2.156), said to be near Buto, where he also claims to have witnessed "flying serpents (*Hist.* 2.75)" (the city, located on the opposite side of the Nile Delta from Tahpanhes, was known as a centre of Wadjet worship, i.e., the cobra goddess, depicted in hieroglyphs as a winged serpent). As just discussed, Joseph is associated with serpents; if he is equated to Pharaoh, he is also equated to Horus.

⋆ "Thus they place the power of Osiris within the Moon, and say that Isis, being the cause of his birth is also his consort."[39] In the Moses mythology, recall, his adoptive mother's attributes parallel those of Nitocris, Nabonidus' wife.

⋆ The rituals surrounding the celebration of the resurrection of Osiris include his body being placed on a barque/boat (i.e., which is *carried*) in a casket made of sycamore and acacia woods, both of which are "life-giving"; in the parallel opening of the mouth ceremony for the deceased, a serpent-shaped "wand" is used, called "the great

---

[38] Dnboswell, "This is My Body, Which is Broken: The Lunar Osiris Easter Special, Part 1" (April 21, 2019), https://mythodoxy.wordpress.com.
[39] Plutarch, 37.

magician.”[40] Clearly this echoes what we see in Moses' use of acacia wood for the ark, the serpent staff, and the narrative's focus on performing wonders.

✳ The soul of Osiris "sometimes took the form of a flame of fire."[41]

✳ Also a major aspect of the revivication of Osiris is the use of libations, incense, and a specific copper tool. The libations (i.e., water for the most part) represent the fluids lost after death/mummification; the incense serves as a medium for restoring the odours of life to the dead, and for communication (via the smoke); and the copper "chisel" is used to "open the mouth," i.e., to make communication possible.[42] Moses uses water, but more profoundly his own preference, i.e., blood, to anoint the altar, etc.; Re "was not regarded as a dead king, but as a living king, who, having become old, is rejuvenated by the blood of his people."[43] Incense is obviously a major factor in the exodus narratives, as it would have been in Babylonian temples but in Moses' case, there may be other inhaled substances to consider (to be explained); and the use of a "copper" tool for ceremonial rituals reminds us of the Qenites, who make their own copper tools and implements.

✳ Osiris "encircle(s) the underworld like a snake. He is also said (in the Pyramid Texts) to be with outstretched arms, sleeping upon his side upon the sand, lord of the soil."[44] Like the *mehen* serpent guarding Re as he journeys through the night (see below), Osiris guards the underworld as an ouroboros. Moses may consider himself such a protective figure.

✳ The Osirian temple at Abydos is subterranean, emulating the "cavern" in which Osiris' body dwells. At Qurayyah there are two caves; might these have been used as initiation caverns (see below)?

✳ The pharaoh's *ka*, or "double," departs his body upon death, adopting its new identity with the succeeding pharaoh, while the deceased king

---

[40] W. J. Perry, *The Origin of Magic and Religion* (London: Methuen, 1923), 51-5), 53. Perry describes the "opening of the mouth" ceremony that is performed to reanimate a corpse within the tomb. "The word for 'to fashion a statue' (*ms*) is … identical with *ms*, 'to give birth' (i.e. the idea of 'Giver of Life' in another form), and the term for the sculptor was *sa'nkh*, 'he who causes to live'." One can easily imagine Nabonidus seeing himself in this role.
[41] E. A. Wallace Budge, *Osiris and the Egyptian Resurrection*, Vol. 2 (London: Warner, 1911), 177.
[42] Perry, *Origin of Magic*, 54.
[43] Perry, *Origin of Magic*, 39.
[44] W. J. Perry, *Children of the Sun* (London: Methuen, 1923), 256.

becomes assimilated with Osiris. In Nabonidus' world, this is the moment when Ahmose's bones, i.e., adopting the role of the "Sun," are ritually united with the Moon and the Stars.

✶ Meanwhile, Pharaoh's *ba*, his soul, hovers above the corpse in the form of a mystical bird, a hawk. The sacred-bird synchronicity with "Baal-zephon" (i.e., the phoenix of) might stand out to Nabonidus, whose mind is drawn to such patterns.

✶ The symbolic union of Osiris and Re and the notions of Osiris as the avatar of the deceased pharaoh are ideologies forged over many generations via a theological battle of Sun and Moon. Perry writes:

> … the Solar theologians were forced ultimately to bow to popular superstition, and to raise Osiris to the sky, there to become inextricably confused with Re as the ruler of that realm. Further, in the Twelfth Dynasty, the ideas concerning Osiris had become very powerful. The Heliopolitan priests apparently were forced constantly to modify their doctrines, to add yet one element after another to their compilation; and in the end they were defeated by sheer weight of popular prejudice.[45]

The Song of Solomon alludes to a clash between solar and lunar beliefs, i.e., a chasm that may well have inspired the king to seek out new avenues of expression and resolution. With his interests spanning the Egyptian, Tyrian, perhaps the Hittite religions, and now the Qenites and the Hebrews, it can be no wonder he manages to create something unique. However, Nabonidus soon finds that the chimeric deity of his own desire is not quite what everyone else has in mind. The "I AM" that provides a general one-size-fits-all nomenclature doesn't seem to correspond with the man's complicated and specific deity. This is why ructions are soon apparent, and challenges to his authority are made. He simply hasn't learned that others do not see what he sees.[46]

---

[45] Perry, *Children*, 464.

[46] This is a reference to Daniel 5 and the "writing on the wall," which I claim was a hallucination brought on by Nabonidus' substance abuse and was, therefore, not experienced by anyone else, but was exploited by Daniel as a harbinger of the king's fall (Tyson, 223-4).

# Cosmological Context

*There is one glory of the sun, and another glory of the moon,*
*and another glory of the stars ...*
1 Cor 16:41

It is important to remember that many have seen a synthesis of astronomical elements in the narrative of Exodus.

The *Jewish Encyclopedia* states:

> The two names of Sinai and Horeb, meaning respectively "moon" and "sun," are of a cosmological nature. ... The object of E is to show that before the Exodus the Israelites were heathen until Yhwh revealed Himself from His mountain to Moses (Ex. iii. 9-14). In E, Jethro is not the priest of Midian, but is connected with the worship of Yhwh of Horeb. On the other hand, J makes Jethro the prince of Midian, and omits all the expressions used by E tending to connect the cult of Yhwh with the older cult.[47]

Josephus, too, writes a fascinating and somewhat surprising account of the cosmological symbolism of Moses' new priestly order:

> As to the tabernacle itself, Moses placed it in the middle of that court, with its front to the east, that, when the sun arose, it might send its first rays upon it.
>
> *A.J.* 3.6.3

> ... if any one do without prejudice, and with judgment, look upon these things, he will find they were every one made in way of imitation and representation of the universe. When Moses distinguished the tabernacle into three parts, and allowed two of them to the priests, as a place accessible and common, he denoted the land and the sea, these being of general access to all; but he set apart the third division for God, because heaven is inaccessible to men. And when he ordered twelve loaves to be set on the table, he denoted the year, as distinguished into so many months. By branching out the candlestick into seventy parts, he secretly intimated the Decani, or seventy divisions of the planets; and as to the seven lamps upon the candlesticks, they referred to the course of the planets, of which that is the number. The veils, too, which were composed of four things,

---

[47] Joseph Jacobs, M. Seligsohn, Wilhelm Bacher, "Sinai, Mount," *JE,* www.jewishencyclopedia.com.

they declared the four elements; for the fine linen was proper to signify the earth, because the flax grows out of the earth; the purple signified the sea, because that colour is dyed by the blood of a sea shell-fish; the blue is fit to signify the air; and the scarlet will naturally be an indication of fire. Now the vestment of the high priest being made of linen, signified the earth; the blue denoted the sky, being like lightning in its pomegranates, and in the noise of the bells resembling thunder. And for the ephod, it showed that God had made the universe of four elements; and as for the gold interwoven, I suppose it related to the splendour by which all things are enlightened. He also appointed the breastplate to be placed in the middle of the ephod, to resemble the earth, for that has the very middle place of the world. And the girdle which encompassed the high priest round, signified the ocean, for that goes round about and includes the universe. Each of the sardonyxes declares to us the sun and the moon; those, I mean, that were in the nature of buttons on the high priest's shoulders. And for the twelve stones, whether we understand by them the months, or whether we understand the like number of the signs of that circle which the Greeks call the Zodiac, we shall not be mistaken in their meaning. And for the mitre, which was of a blue colour, it seems to me to mean heaven; for how otherwise could the name of God be inscribed upon it? That it was also illustrated with a crown, and that of gold also, is because of that splendour with which God is pleased.

*A.J.* 3.7.7

Some of these ideas are, no doubt, later additions to the original Mosaic understanding, having had time to develop under the influences of more metaphysical ideologies, Hellenic myth, etc. They do reveal, however, a need to comprehend the legacy of a richly cosmological religion in a new age. What Nabonidus creates is, I think, peculiar to *his* mind-set; he is driven to this ideal of a unified theory of divinity, with all his favourite gods, Sîn, Shamash, and Ishtar melded into one, profoundly original god that can exhibit properties many can relate to (while leaving him as the sole intermediary, of course). There are, however, almost immediately, those who rail against this audacious project, seeing that the ex-king is really just doing whatever *he* wants. I think, perhaps, the ark itself, with its strong links to Egyptian royalty/divinity is conveniently lost when the naysayers outnumber the supporters; Judaism goes forward without this last tangible connection to Nabonidus but his strange ideas leave a lasting impression. For those who investigate, question, decipher, the clues to this relatively bizarre period in the Israelites' history remain in the received texts and demand explanation.

We can never get into the mind of Nabonidus as he stands atop the mesa at night, hundreds of furnaces blazing and spitting around him, arsenic-laden fumes rising in his nostrils, the noise of the trumpets reverberating against the mesa walls, incense and saltpetre in the air, but somehow, understanding the man as we do now, it seems inevitable he is going to see something different.

# JOCHEBED AND THE DIVINE BIRTH

Recall that one of the myths pertaining to Moses finding the bones of Joseph suggests the woman who provides Moses with the location of the relics is his mother, Jochebed. The name "Jochebed" means "Yah is impressive," from *yah*, "God," and the verb *kabed*, "to be impressive." What is quite surprising is that *kabed* is also used to denote the "glory" of God, in the context of it representing ... his phallus![48] Abarim provides a fuller account of this but briefly, the relationship between Yahweh and his creation is seen, metaphorically, as a marriage, i.e., a bonding of male and female energies, to make the whole. This is enhanced in the Zohar's highly sexualised rendition of the cherubim:

> Whenever Israel came up to the Festival, the curtain would be removed for them and the Cherubim were shown to them, whose bodies were intertwisted/arousing with one another, and they would be thus addressed: Look! You are beloved before God as the love between man and woman.
>
> Yoma 54a

In the Song of Solomon, there are several allusions to the *hieros gamos*, or sacred marriage, i.e., the ancient (Mesopotamian and Egyptian) ritual of emulating the divine nuptials, usually acted out by the king and the high priestess, in the seclusion of a temple chamber.[49] This was Nitocris' role in Egypt (if she did attain the position of God's Wife or God's Hand, as I posit) and also at Ur, where she served as regent-*entu* for the very young Ennigaldi. It is one of the celebrations Nabonidus is notably absent from in Babylon[50] but which appears frequently in the Song, i.e., when he is in Tayma. I therefore think it *was* important to him but, again, within his own

---

[48] When the Philistines steal the ark, it is mourned as the loss of the "*kabud* of Israel" (1 Sam 4:21-2). "Ichabod" is named to mark this event, for his name basically means "no glory," i.e., "no divine phallus."

[49] E.g., Song 2:4-7 (Tyson, 68-70); 3:9-10 (87-8), etc.

[50] "Babylon's most important festival, the New Year's Festival, had to be cancelled while the god Marduk's earthly representative, the king, was residing on the Arabian Peninsula"(W&N, 5).

frame of reference.

The couple's relationship proves highly sexual, though not in the way traditional interpretations of the Song suggest; Nabonidus learns about the Elixir Rubeus from his Egyptian priestess-wife, i.e., the symbolic "cup of abominations" (menstrual blood and semen).[51] The rite is said to make the imbiber at one with the gods. He learns about the Osirian myths of rebirth and resurrection, the loss of the god's phallus, etc.; he probably sees for himself, on his trip(s) to Egypt, the iconography (statuary, hieroglyphic, and funerary) of erect phalluses. Sexualised rebirth imagery is abundant in his own culture, too. It seems a logical component of a resurrecting-god's symbolism.

The solar deity Amun (Re) acquires "ithyphallic tendencies through syncretism with both Min and Atum" and Osiris sports an erect phallus when in the underworld, a sign of his imminent resurrection; "The erect penis is a sign not only of life, but specifically of new life."[52] Perhaps the metal-craftsmen fashion a golden phallus for the ossuary, if one is not already with the bones.

As this interpretation has steered toward themes of resurrection, rebirth, and Egyptian solar-deities, Jochebed's alternative etymology fits neatly; it also leads seamlessly into the next associated insight. The entire scenario of Moses being "drawn from the water of the Nile (Exod 2:1-10) is analogous to the birth myth of Re. The Exodus myth is symbolically set within the context of what we already know from the Song of Solomon, i.e., that Nitocris had a miscarriage early on in her marriage to Nabonidus.

We need to refer back to the Song constantly because this is where the tale of Moses really begins. Nabonidus, recall, was very keen for Nitocris to conceive his special child, who was destined to be the first *entu* at Ur for hundreds of years. In a bid to retain her cultic purity and status Nitocris, when she discovered her prophylactic methods had not worked, returned to her "mother" in Egypt to learn of greater magic that would end the pregnancy; she consumed a cocktail of plants and minerals that ensured she miscarried. I have suggested she loses the foetus in the first trimester.[53] We have already seen that a reference to this aborted foetus appears in Num 12:12, immediately after Jehudijah and Aaron mention the "Cushite woman," i.e., Nitocris.

Now look at the scene in Exodus:

---

[51] Tyson, 12-44.

[52] Stephanie Lynn Budin, "Phallic Fertility in the Ancient Near East and Egypt," in *Reproduction: Antiquity to the Present Day*, Nick Hopwood, Rebecca Flemming, Lauren Kassell, eds. (Cambridge University Press, 2018), 25-38, here 27-8.

[53] For the whole story, see Tyson, 93-119.

* Exod 1:15 introduces two "midwives," Shiphrah and Puah.

* "Shiphrah" means "fairness, beauty," from the verb *shaphar*, "to be fair, or comely." Note that Shiphrah of Exod 1:15 (as midwife) is called "Sepphora" in the LXX, just as Zipporah is, making them (etymologically) connected. Zipporah is Jehudijah, so Shiphrah is also Jehudijah.

* "Puah" means "radiant," from the verb *yapa*, "to radiate," and is therefore related to Joseph's Egyptian name, "Zaphenath-paneah." Joseph is Ahmose III. Therefore, Puah is identified as Nitocris. The focus on radiant beauty, rather than mere comeliness also alludes to the beautiful princess who is described in the Song as having no faults, blemishes, i.e., she is perfect. She reflects the 'radiance' of her father, Ahmose/Joseph.

* The two women, Nitocris and Jehudijah, side by side, are thus assimilated into the Moses birth-narrative.

* Moses' mother ("Jochebed" is not named here but the rabbinic literature makes the connection) "hides" the child for "three months" and then casts him out on the waters of the Nile.

* In Near Eastern birthing nomenclature, "waters" is used to depict either menstruation or the outflow of blood and water after a miscarriage/birth.[54]

* In Song 7:1, Nitocris' foetus is subtly alluded to by the visiting emissaries who are fully cognisant of what she has done, i.e., they refer to it as a "sandal," a type of abortion that results in a flattened, fish-like foetus.[55] This happens, commonly, *before* the second trimester, according to a pregnancy-prayer in the Talmud (Berakoth 60a), i.e., the foetus is hidden in the womb for no more than "three months."

Interestingly, Job 3:16 refers to the *burial* of a "stillborn child" (a miscarriage), the same verb, *taman* ("to hide, conceal, bury") being used for Moses' concealment of the murdered Egyptian (Exod 2:12). "It hints at some

---

[54] Joann Scurlock, "Medicine and Healing Magic," in *Women in the Ancient Near East: A Sourcebook*, Mark Chavalas ed. (United Kingdom: Taylor & Francis, 2013), 101-43, here 110. In ancient Egypt, menstrual blood was symbolised by "water," i.e., both being Life-giving fluids (Kenneth Grant, *Cults of the Shadow* [London: Frederick Muller, 1975], 56).

[55] Stol, *Birth in Babylonia*, 18, n. 95. See also Niddah 31a.

kind of secret, hurried, and perhaps impious action."[56] I have already suggested that the "Egyptian" Nabonidus "kills" is probably Nitocris (i.e., he is, at least, held responsible for her death), and that in Ishmael's circumcision scene, Jehudijah marks Moses as a murderer (of Miriam). It seems a fitting foil, therefore, to have the ex-king's new Egyptian-influenced "priestly kingdom" symbolically drawn from the waters of the miscarriage that was fated to make the king both mad and kingdomless.[57] I see Jehudijah's hand at work here, if only by proxy (posthumously). The Sun-god aspect of the new deity rises from the ashes of destruction, like the phoenix, but as with most scenes in the exodus narratives, there is an underlying anti-Nabonidus theme that cannot be ignored.

Jehudijah, Nitocris' counterpart throughout all these narratives, is the living witness, the one who picks up the pieces, so to speak, by allowing her child to be taken/adopted by the Queen (at Tayma). It is Jehudijah who is being promoted in this scene, i.e., as the mother figure (and recall that 1 Kgs 3:16-28 is a reference to the two women's battle over motherhood[58]) who secretly saves, or rescues, the distraught Nabonidus by her seemingly generous (though probably coerced) action.[59] It is she who plucks Life from the "waters" where certain death had been expected.

Leviticus Rabbah 1.3 *identifies* "Jochebed" with Jehudijah (for different reasons, but this is still amazing).

This baby in the Nile scenario, then, is an allegory of rebirth, resurrection, and solar-divinity. The two Exodus "midwives" (aka Nitocris and Jehudijah) become synonymous with Isis and Nephthys, the midwives who bring Re into the world from the waters ("amnion") of Nut.

> *The majesty of this god goes forth from her hind part.*
> *He proceeds to the earth, risen and born (...)*
> *He opens the thighs of his mother Nut.*
> *He withdraws to the sky (...) He opens his amnion.*
> The Book of Nut[60]

---

[56] Marianne Grohmann, "Metaphors of Miscarriage in the Psalms," *VT* 69.2 (2019): 219-31, here 227.

[57] The BDB associates the verb *mashah*, "to draw," with an Arabic term that means "to cleanse the uterus." https://biblehub.com.

[58] Tyson, 220.

[59] In this respect, Jehudijah effectively outshines Nitocris at last, seemingly providing a greater "*dod*" than the queen, in Song 7:11-12 (see Tyson, 183-5).

[60] Susanne Töpfer, "The Physical Activity of Parturition in Ancient Egypt: Textual and Epigraphical Sources," *Dynamis* 34.2 (2014): 317-36, here 325.

> *Isis and Nephthys lift you up when you come forth*
> *from the thighs of your mother Nut.*
> Hymn to Re[61]

In the inscriptions at the Cenotaph of Seti I, Abydos, the two mythical Egyptian sisters are again midwives, this time to the birth of Horus; Isis serves as *both* mother and midwife.[62] I think this is what we are seeing in Exodus, i.e., the "mother" is also one of the midwives, ergo, "Jochebed" must be either Nitocris or Jehudijah. From the above discussion, we see she must be Jehudijah. It is she who symbolically draws the infant from the waters.

This is further confirmed when we note the etymology of "Nephthys":

> To the Ancient Egyptians she was Nebthwt (Nebhhwt or Nebthet) meaning "the Mistress of the House". The word *"hwt"* ("house") may refer to the sky (as in *Hwt-hor*, the "House of Horus" – the name of Hathor), but it also refers to either the royal family or Egypt as a whole.[63]

Jehudijah's secret code in the Song, the ultimate meaning of the sevenfold mentioning of "Solomon" that serves as her own signature, plays on two words, i.e., "wean" and "house."[64] It also becomes evident that although Nitocris is depicted in Hathoric terms during her supposed pregnancy (in the Song), it is Jehudijah who bears the child and is the true mother, the *real* "Hathor" of the Song (and thus of the "House of Hathor" allusion to the temple at Ur).

"Isis," on the other hand, is notoriously difficult to break down etymologically, but suggestions centre around "queen" with overtures to "knowledge."[65] Nitocris is Queen of Tayma and Babylon and is the keeper of arcane knowledge. Later, Isis becomes associated with Astarte (Ishtar), who is the primary avatar of Nitocris in the Song. The goddess is also associated with magic and dream interpretation (just like Nitocris). Only the motherhood aspect is not a true fit, but given that motherhood is effectively imposed upon Nitocris at Tayma (in Genesis 18) and she is heralded as a mother/fertility goddess in Song 6-7, this *can* be said to apply, too, albeit erroneously, thanks to her deception.

Isis, who can be both mother and wife of Osiris, also takes the form of the snake goddess Renenutet and this, as discussed earlier, relates to the

---

[61] Töpfer, 323.
[62] Töpfer, 323.
[63] "Nephthys," https://ancientegyptonline.co.uk.
[64] Tyson, 216-17.
[65] "Isis," https://ancientegyptonline.co.uk.

Egyptian myths of Moses and his serpent-mother (... or wife).[66]

There is even an associated myth that Isis and Nephthys compete to become the mother of Anubis; Nephthys, fed up with being overshadowed by the illustrious Isis (just as Jehudijah feels she lived in Nitocris' "shadow"),[67] tricks Osiris into impregnating her; Isis then adopts the child.[68] How close do things have to get before we acknowledge some level of cultural absorption?

So, the rabbinic legend of Jochebed as the one who tells Moses the whereabouts of Joseph's bones is really far more complicated and revealing than expected. It brings together multiple concepts, e.g., the two sisters; the mother-wife issue; the connection to Egyptian legends concerning Moses' mythical mother; snakes; solar birthing imagery; and the memory of when it all began, i.e., from the moment Nitocris' bloody waters ended her potential for motherhood and Jehudijah filled the breach.

# BLACK BOX

The passage of the Sun-god Re through the darkness of the night is one of the most significant of ancient Egyptian myths/beliefs. It appears in the Pyramid Texts and funerary poems and images, and lies at the foundation of the concept of regeneration and immortality. Re rides in his celestial barque (boat) through the heavens but the twelve night hours force him to travel in the darkness, through Rosetau, the realm of Sokar (a funerary form of Osiris), i.e., a desert land of giant serpents ruled by the Moon. Re's barque is led by the same two "midwives" that brought him into existence, i.e., Isis and Nephthys, this time as protective serpents. One account of this nocturnal passage is called *Amduat: Book of What is in the Duat*, discovered in the tomb of Pharaoh Tuthmosis III (ca. 1479-1426 BCE):

> Total darkness and silence ... and knowledge of the words of power ... accommodate the process of healing initiated. Renewal and rebirths are preluded by thick darkness and isolation.
> ... Re has the Wadjet-serpent or Uraeus on his brow. His knowledge of the Duat and its mysterious, secret process (represented

---

[66] " ... in ancient society the imperial power descended through the female line. In that case the heir to a throne is the daughter of a king. To retain a throne a son of a king must marry his sister, or failing a sister, his own mother. In the Sumerian myths we have both circumstances represented" (Perry, *Children*, 242).

[67] E.g., Tyson, 218-19.

[68] "Nephthys," https://ancientegyptonline.co.uk.

by serpents) is complete and protected.

... In Ancient Egypt, the role of serpents can be beneficial or afflictive. As serpents love darkness to hide from the Sun, the Duat is associated with them. Magic is needed to deal with them ... and this implies knowledge empowering one's entry into their world. Assimilating the power of that which one needs to control is the way of the shaman.[69]

The serpents in this myth are vital to Re's regeneration; one helps initiate his transformation by illuminating the darkness, another tends to the body of Re and returns him to his place of renewal, and a third protects him in his vulnerable stage just after his rebirth. The serpent-sceptre and the Uraeus link to the pharaoh's identification with Re; after death, the king makes this same nocturnal journey, becoming one with the Sun-god, and thereby ensuring his immortality (later, this is the anticipated journey for all the dead, not just Pharaoh). The actual process of Re's renewal is hidden, secret, in a "cavern of fire" tended by Isis:

This generates the first spark, which is completed (actualised) in the 6th Hour. So this hour anticipates the actual *Ars obscura* of the 6th and offers **the protective device, a secret "black box," a mysterious cavern or cave necessary to contain the initiation of the fusion, as well as to maintain the continuous circulations of energy** (within creation and between creation and precreation) to allowing total transformation.[70]

> *Invisible and imperceptible is this secret image*
> *of the land which bears the flesh of this god.*
> *Amduat*, 5th Hour, 384-6

Re regenerates only after he has passed through the darkest regions of the Duat, the "thick darkness" of the land, or the cavern of Sokar; he must meld with and supress Osiris in order to renew his former solar energy. He and the Moon-god become one within the darkness. At dawn, Re completes his journey through the twelve hours of night and is reborn on the other side to start the process again. In his role as the embodiment of Horus, therefore, the divine king (the pharaoh) temporarily represents both Sun *and* Moon, both Re *and* Osiris, merged as one deity.

The "cavern" becomes, in a sense, a crucible in which Re is transformed;

---

[69] Much of this account of the passage of Re is thanks to Wim van den Dungen, "The Book of: The Hidden Chamber, ca. 1426 BCE, or: The Twelve Hours of the Night and the Midnight Mystery," www.sofiatopia.org.

[70] Dungen, www.sofiatopia.org.

the walls of the cavern become a huge, all-encompassing, protective serpent. During the fourth hour of this journey through the night, Re enters a desert teaming with poisonous snakes. His sacred staff is transformed into a serpent, serving as protection against the evil serpents who dwell in the darkness. His barque also transforms into a fire-breathing snake, guarded by Thoth and Sokar, as he makes his slow progress through the desert.[71]

*Figure 17: Amun-Re on his barque with serpent-staff, surrounded by the mehen serpent (Image: Budge, From Fetish to God, 166)*

In the Fifth Hour of the *Amduat*, Re must pass over the subterranean lair of Sokar, his "cave"; it is the place of chaos and danger, where his foe, Apep is held captive.

In Exod 33:12-23, Moses is depicted as debating with God (again); in fact, it is almost emotional blackmail, as Moses insinuates that if God doesn't continue to reveal his "glory," he will lose face for having failed to emancipate the Israelites. God gives in (in a very Mesopotamian-deity sort of way) and shows his "glory" to a keen and eager Moses. This is the scene where Moses has to hide in a crevice of the rock so God can pass over him safely; Moses is only allowed to see the deity's back.

# "BACK" OF THE SUN

Rachel Adelman argues that Exod 33:21-3 serves as "a paradigm for God's seeming absence in our own post-Holocaust reality.... the image of God's "back" (becomes) an act of withdrawal that leaves room for human agency by invoking the possibility of forgiveness."[72] Diana Lipton, also sees the pericope as pertaining to the disappearance of the divine in a world of sin but with a glimmer of hope for the future (i.e., where God's "back" is a metaphor for the future).[73]

---

[71] "Sokar," Ancient Egypt Online. https://ancientegyptonline.co.uk.

[72] Rachel Adelman, "From the Cleft of the Rock: The Eclipse of God in the Bible, Midrash, and Post-Holocaust Theology," in *Ehyeh Asher Ehyeh* (New York: New Paradigm Matrix, 2019), 170.

[73] Diana Lipton, "God's Back! What did Moses see on Sinai?" in *The Significance of Sinai: Traditions About Sinai and Divine Revelation in Judaism and Christianity*, George John Brooke, Hindy Najman & Loren T. Stuckenbruck, eds. (Leiden: Brill, 2008), 287-311. Interestingly, in an ancient Egyptian text referred to as the "Speech of the Creator," is this line: "As for 'yesterday', that is Osiris. As for 'tomorrow,' that is Re" (ANET, 4). Similarly,

The Talmud understands that this crevice or "cleft" is a cave, in fact, the same (physical) cave Elijah is said to have stood in at Sinai (1 Kgs 19:9-18).

> Rabbi Yoḥanan says: If there had been an opening as large as the eye of a needle in the cave in which Moses and Elijah had stood, they could not have withstood its light, at it says: "For no one shall not see Me and live."
>
> B. Megillah 19b, on Exod 33:20

This is a start. The text of Exodus 33 does not say that Moses is *on/up* Mount Sinai when this encounter with God takes place; rather, we have just been given an explanation of how he sets up the tabernacle on the outskirts of the village (Exod 33:7-11). This must be to indicate his location for the upcoming scenario, i.e., he is in the tabernacle, having one of his secret conversations with the deity. God says, in Exod 33:21 "there is a place *by me* where you shall stand on the rock"; if God lives on top of the mesa, one of its two caves would qualify as being "near" him. Both are strewn with rocks (*tsur*), so if Moses stands at the entrance of a cave, this, too, would qualify.[74] But I am not convinced this is all there is to it. I suggest there is some sort of initiation going on here that is partly to do with the Qenite-metallurgical influence, and partly the Osiris-Re mythology.

In the first context, what if Nabonidus is instructed to undergo a dramatic test of his commitment to the Qenite belief system, i.e., to be brought into the fold as a priest? Perhaps this takes the form of an orchestrated, bright/dangerous explosion (e.g., the metalworkers would surely know how to create such special effects) from which he has to find his own way of protecting himself. He chooses to hide in the cave and this is then represented, retrospectively, as God's will. Perhaps it is a memory of an accidental explosion that is then turned around to be of divine origin and therefore significant (but otherwise left unexplained). He cannot, i.e., *does* not, witness the blast itself (e.g., perhaps it is a fireball) from his location, but sees the aftereffects when he exists the cave. By suggesting God will "save whom I wish and kill whom I wish," the indiscriminate nature of a fatal blast is potentially alluded to. Note that Moses is warned (Exod 34:3) not to let anyone else on the entire mesa, and even to keep the livestock away from its base, suggesting the moment of "passing" will be dangerous.

---

in the *Amduat*'s illustration of the 11th Hour, Re becomes the god/master of Time, effectively preparing the duration/passage of (solar) time for the next day.

[74] "Rock" can mean either "a rock" (generic) or "*the* rock"; in this latter case, it must imply the mesa, i.e., the "rock plateau" at Qurayyah, as the scene is set at Sinai, not in Rephidim by Split Rock. That "mountain" is not used does suggest it is not the mesa Moses stands upon, but a rock *from* the mesa (e.g., one of those scattered by the caves?).

The Osirian aspect of this scene, however, is far more profound. There is a reference in CT 237 to Osiris "turning his back" in his "moments of inertia"; in other words, he become oblivious to everything while he is *dead*.[75] The rebirth of Re must occur in absolute darkness, in secret, beyond the sight of any mortal; it does make sense that at some point in the narrative's quasi-Osirian theme the moment of this awakening has to be dealt with. Moses is instructed to come to the top of the mesa "in the morning" (Exod 34:2), an allusion to sunrise, "Dawn" etc., the new solar day (i.e., after Re's nocturnal rebirth).

Also, the verb *abar* ("to pass over, through, or by") here echoes its use in Exod 12:23, where God passes through on the night of the last "plague." The repetition forces an allusion to *imminent death* in Moses' "crevice/cave" scene, whether physical, or metaphysical. In both instances God passes over but here he protects those he wishes to protect by shielding them, in this case with his "hand" (i.e., replacing the blood of the Genesis scene). In the latter scenario, however, in the more sophisticated, Nabonidus-as-initiated-high-priest depiction, it is the Sun-god himself who must die, so that his natural heir (in the myth, Horus) can live on (at Sinai, Nabonidus' chimeric "I AM").

There is another little detail that supports this idea. Lipton offers a more precise translation of "you will see my back" i.e., "lit. my behind, *behind me*" (emphasis mine).[76] This is not, as some online bloggers like to suggest, God mooning at Moses. I think it has to do, again, with the nocturnal journey of Re. In the 6th Hour of the night, the Sun-god regenerates in the "deepest layers of the Duat, the thick darkness of the sinister Land of Sokar":

> The Ba-soul of Re assumes the death posture, and 'becomes' Osiris as the corpse of Re. After igniting the alchemical fire in the 5th Hour (in the Cavern of Sokar erected on the Lake of Fire), the soul of Re moves to the First Time (spiritualizes by becoming Akh) and returns rekindled.[77]

This Lake of Fire is referred to in CT Spell 247[78] as being the fire "behind" the deity. In Osirian terms, Moses witnesses only the Lake of Fire (that everyone in the Duat can see) "behind" Re, but not the Sun-god himself (he is too bright for human eyes).

---

[75] Faulkner, 185-6.
[76] Lipton, 290.
[77] Dungen, 1.5-1.6, www.sofiatopia.org/maat/hidden_chamber03.htm.
[78] Faulkner, 193.

*This image is like this in the thick darkness.*
*The (cavern) is illuminated*
*by the two eyes of the heads of the great god (the serpent).*
*His two feet shine in the coils of the great god, while he protects his image.*
*A noise is heard ... like the thundering ground of the sky in a storm.*
Amduat, 5th Hour, 443-5

*Glory be to Thee, oh Ra, Supreme Power,*
*Darkened One in His Cavern, He Who decrees that there be darkness*
*in the Cavern which hides Him Who is in it.*
Great Litany of Ra (9)[79]
*The Lord has said that he would*
*dwell in thick darkness.*
*I have built an exalted house,*
*a place for you to dwell in forever.*
1 Kgs 8:12-13[80]

Recalling Nabonidus' relatively recent relationship with Nitocris, the First Prophet of Amun, and her certain influence on him, there is an ancient hymn to the Sun-god (ca. 1413-1377 BCE) that says of Amun: "When thou crossest the sky, all faces behold thee, (but) when thou departest, thou art hidden from their faces."[81]

There is also an amazing correlation with a scene in the Song of Solomon, i.e., Song 2:14. Here, Nabonidus is newly enamoured with Nitocris, dazzled by her beauty, of course, but keen to learn what she can teach him. He begs her to let him see her face and hear her voice, key (but ominous) themes in the Song that have deep meaning regarding the king's desire for wisdom.[82] These words are spoken in the contexts of a "cleft" in the rock and anticipated birth. This should be considered a direct intertextual allusion, with Exodus reiterating Nabonidus' quest for intimacy with the divine, with universal knowledge, and with the mysteries of rebirth.

In the 6th Hour, Re passes over the tomb of Osiris and "calls out," just as Nabonidus' deity passes over and calls out his name (Exod 34:5-6):

This god calls out above these mysterious tombs (of Osiris), and it is (his) voice which this god hears. Then he passes on, after he has called out.
Amduat - 6th Hour, 485-8

---

[79] Luigi Tripani, *The God Ra: Iconography (With all the Forms and Names from the 'Litany of Ra')*, (Amentet Neferet: 2015), 99.

[80] This reveals the arrogance and hubris of Solomon (Nabonidus) so perfectly, for even though the deity *wishes* to dwell "in darkness" the king pursues his dream of an exalted temple to beat all others.

[81] ANET, "A Universalist Hymn to the Sun," 368.

[82] Tyson, 73-4.

At the hour of the night when the Sun becomes melded with the corpse of Osiris, it disappears; figuratively, it would be like the god momentarily placing his hand over the eyes of the human, so he *cannot* see the divine light that is about to be rekindled.

In the 12th Hour, Re is regenerated. Leaving the cavern and the corpse of Osiris behind, he boards his day barque and sails off into (or to become) the sunrise. From a human perspective, only his "back" is visible as he drifts farther away; the illustrations of the *Amduat* actually *show* this transformation, for once Re's regeneration is consolidated, his momentum toward Dawn assured, the entourage guiding his barque suddenly (9th Hour onward) all face the same direction, i.e., right, or East, when before, they were split between those facing back (left) and those facing forward (right).

It's all in the wonderful imagination of the early Egyptians who felt compelled to understand how the universe works.

Notice how in Exod 33:20 a similar pattern exists as in 10:28-9, i.e., basically, 'if you see my face you will die.' The *pharaoh* is the medium through which the "glory" of Re is transmitted to humans; we are invited to make the connection between the 'seeing-the-face' idea from the Sun-and-Moon-in-opposition context of Exodus 10, and the "glory" that passes over Moses in the latter scenario, i.e., the two scenes both involve Pharaoh as the solar aspect.

Recall this reference, in the discussion of "Sparks," earlier, where I suggested the "host" might be represented by the brilliant, flying spark from the furnaces:

> The Lord came from Sinai, And dawned from Seir upon us; He shone forth from Mount Paran. With him were myriads of holy ones; At his right, a host of his own.
>
> Deut 33:2

In a similar vein, i.e., in a symbolic rather than literal context of a furnace, we see Re here, in the furnace of the Duat, about to be reignited, about to regenerate and become volatile and release his energy. He is accompanied throughout his journey by a myriad of attendants. Perhaps this is the inspiration for the "heavenly host" idea.

# SINAI'S 12, 40, AND 73

## *12*

I have often wondered *why* there are twelve Israelite tribes; it is just taken for granted. But in both Solomon and Moses' case (both are Nabonidus, recall), "twelve" is significant for potentially non-tribal reasons.

In 1 Kgs 4:7, we are told that "Solomon had twelve officials over all Israel, who provided food for the king and his household; each one had to make provision for one month in the year." Walsh points out that the boundaries of these districts don't seem to tally with traditional tribal allotments.[83] This may simply be Nabonidus (as Solomon) carrying on the regular tithing inherited from his Babylonian administration, but it does support a non-tribal rationale for the "twelve."

The number twelve is central to the *Amduat*, however; the barque is towed through the twelve Gates of the Duat[84] by one extra figure per hour of the night, until the twelfth hour is reached (Dawn). Twelve guardians journey with Re during all hours of both night and day. Twelve goddesses (wearing fire-spitting serpents) and twelve gods witness his rebirth.

I suggest that the idea of twelve representative leaders (of tribes/clans, etc.) stems from Nabonidus' desire to emulate the entourage of Re. In Exod 24:4 he sets up twelve pillars[85] but note the context in which he does this: He is about to enter his "forty days and nights" stint on the mesa plateau, i.e., his initiation isolation (see "Sloughing at Sinai" below). What I think might be going on here is that Nabonidus is intent on carrying out his own version of the *Amduat* ritual for Ahmose, who had supposedly been denied eternal peace by the ravages of war.[86] As his "bones" now constitute the solar aspect of the

---

[83] Jerome T. Walsh, "The Characterization of Solomon in First Kings 1-5," *CBQ* 57.3 (1995): 471-93, here 489.

[84] *The Amduat* and the *Book of Gates* are distinct texts but similar enough to combine for our purposes. The twelve sections in the *Book of Gates* each have an "enormous gate shaped like a New Kingdom temple pylon" (Bojana Mojsov, "The Ancient Egyptian Underworld in the Tomb of Seti I: Sacred Books of Eternal Life," *MR* 42.4 (2001): 489-506, here 498).

[85] Recall that as "Solomon" Nabonidus is influenced by Hiram of Tyre, whose religion is that of Melqart, and this is represented by simple pillars. The aniconic nature of the Qenites is supposedly evidenced in Timna, where archaeologists discovered a Midianite shrine composed of a tent with pillars inside (defaced and looted from the old Egyptian Hathor temple) and no other form of iconography. Moses adopts the pillars as a form of representation to mirror the "image with no image" idea of the "I AM" (still to be discussed). This is a clear example of his tendency to be influenced by whomever he is following at the time (i.e., as "Solomon," first Hiram, then Nitocris; as "Moses," the Qenites). For the archaeological evidence at Timna see Nissim Amzallag, "Who was the Deity Worshipped at the Tent-Sanctuary of Timna?" in *Mining for Ancient Copper,* Erez Ben Yosef, ed. (Tel Aviv: Tel Aviv University, 2018), 127-136.

[86] "Egyptian beliefs preach that the soul of the dead visits the grave multiple times. The soul returns firstly on the third day and then consecutively seven, fifteen and forty days after death" ("The Visiting Soul," Egypt, https://myend.com /country/egypt-modern-

ark, the Osirian resurrection rite of the Sun-god would seem apropos.

In Hebrew gematria: 12 is represented by 10 + 2. 10 is the Hebrew letter *yod*, meaning "Jew"; 2 is the letter *bet* or "house."[87] Thus each pillar represents, retrospectively, a "house" (tribe/clan) of the Jews.

## 40

In Gen 50:3 the embalming of Joseph takes forty days; this is a clue that something different is going on here, for this timeframe is "at variance with Herodotus' statement that it required 70, the period which the Bible assigns to the Egyptians' mourning for Jacob."[88] Thus, "40" is a direct allusion to what will occur on Mount Sinai, i.e., a re-enactment of the mummification of Osiris (which is what the process of embalming is supposed to represent), possibly involving various purification rituals, magical spells, etc., to allow the pharaoh his dignity and his immortality.[89] This is, after all, the ultimate reason for the ark, and it is the symbolic source of the mystical "glory."

In terms of gematria, the number 40 (*mem*) "represents a metamorphosis, a transformation. After forty days, the embryo of a child begins to assume a recognizable form."[90]

Moses' forty-day stint as an initiate parallels Ahmose's underworld forty-day rebirth. Again doubles, both men metamorphose and share in a unified spiritual regeneration.

## 73

In the myth of Osiris' death, there are seventy-three conspirators;[91] in Exod 24:1-2; 9, Moses attends the mesa with seventy-three others. Though not necessarily a full-on conspiracy on the mesa, it is whilst Moses is otherwise engaged on the mesa that the seeds of ill-will, resentment, and ultimate rejection (death) are sown (e.g., in Exodus' golden calf scenario, and Numbers' "Peor" and "Korah" incidents). It is immediately after this gathering that we see Aaron

---

death-practices/).

[87] Raskin, "Yod"; "Bet," Letters of Light, www.chabad.org.

[88] "Embalming" www.jewishvirtuallibrary.org.

[89] Perhaps a re-binding of the bones (except the token relic) in preparation for eventual interment is involved.

[90] Raskin, "Mem," Letters of Light, www.chabad.org.

[91] James George Frazer, *The Golden Bough: A Study in Magic and Religion* (London: Oxford University Press, 1994 [1890]), 367.

has been replaced by Joshua as Moses' right-hand-man.

Gematria: 70 + 3; where 70 (*ayin*) suggests "leadership, responsibility" and 3 (*gimmel*) signifies "the ability to combine two contrasting forces—to bring about integration." [92] This is what is being attempted on the mesa, with all the leaders present, i.e., a meeting is held (immediately after the ten commandments have been agreed upon and inscribed) to unify the variant notions of "I AM," liturgy, hierarchy, etc. The board meeting ends with a feast.

# SAPPHIRE

Emphasising this potential link to Ahmose's bones and the profundity of what is about to occur, the description of the deity is limited to the base upon which it stands. There is no description of the god, as should be expected. The "pavement" (i.e., *libnah/lebenah*, pertaining to "bricks") is said to be made of "sapphire." Most exegetes concur that this probably means lapis-lazuli, as true sapphire was discovered during the Roman Period (they were considered forms of jacinth), "and prior to that time *sapphiros* referred to blue gems in general."[93]

Lapis is sacred to both the Egyptians and the Mesopotamians. It is the chosen stone to represent royalty. In the Sumerian myth "Enki and the World Order" the creator places lapis "beards" on the gods, including Utu, the Sun-god (ETCSL 1.1.3, 368-80). Enki's temple itself is made from silver and lapis-lazuli (ETCSL 1.1.4, 1-8), which are said to symbolise "shining daylight."

To the ancient Egyptians, lapis emulates the "supernatural" forces of the firmament, the dark blue evokes the darkening sky, and the crystals within represent the stars; the ceilings of their temples are painted to represent this lapis-sky.[94] "A hymn to Nisaba" (ETCSL 4.16.1, 27-35) states: "… he has opened up Nisaba's house of learning, and has placed the lapis-lazuli tablet on her knees, for her to consult the holy tablet of the heavenly stars."

With that understanding, representing an imageless sky-deity, be it the Moon or the Sun must be difficult, but for those of the period, whether they stem from Babylonia or Egypt, the mere mention of lapis-lazuli inspires

---

[92] Raskin, "Ayin"; "Gimmel," Letters of Light, www.chabad.org.

[93] ChemEurope.com, "Sapphire," www.chemeurope.com.

[94] Ahmed Mansour, "The Minerals as Divine Epithets: Notes on the Use of Lapis Lazuli in Divine Epithets," in *Environment and Religion in Ancient Coptic Egypt: Sensing the Cosmos through the Eyes of the Divine*, Archaeopress Egyptology 30, Alicia Maravelia and Nadine Guilhou, eds. (Oxford: 2020), 195-204, here, 195.

awe, reverence, submission to royalty, and the sky. Nabonidus is anticipating the voyage of Re through the firmament and all that will entail; he is preparing for Ahmose's symbolic resurrection as the new Sun-god in the Sinai triad. What better than lapis-lazuli to represent this?

# IMAGE

The notion of an "image" is very strong in the *Amduat*, i.e., seeing and comprehending the "image" (of the dead Osiris, of Sokar in the cavern, etc.) is the key to following the passage to Re, and thus the attainment of eternity with Re. The closing text of the *Amduat* is:

> The beginning is light, the end thick darkness. ... the secret writing of the Duat, which is not known by any person, save a few. This image is done like this, in the secrecy of the Duat, unseen and unperceived. Whoever knows this mysterious image will be a well-provided Akh-spirit. Always will he leave and enter again the Duat, and speak to the living.[95]

The "image" is thus a secret; only the pharaoh (or his representative the high priest) is permitted to see the deity face-to-face within the Holy of Holies:

> What is revealed should never be said. It is a secret, or "*bs.*" ... The "secret of secrets" was the secret image of the deity or "*bsw*" ("*besu*").
> ...
> "I am a priest knowledgeable of the mystery,
> Who's chest never lets go what he has seen!"[96]

This is just the sort of elitist, enigmatic, profound mystery that would capture Nabonidus' interest, and it helps substantiate my argument that he is not deifying himself at Sinai; this is a gross misunderstanding, even by those in his own time, for his self-deification occurred at Tayma, many years earlier.[97]

The tabernacle is thus a portable cavern, or "black box," made dark by all the layers of curtains, including the thickest, black goat-hair curtains, like those of the Qedar tents in Song 1:5 (Exod 36:8-19). It houses the bone(s) of Pharaoh (Sun) symbolically melded with the Moon and the Stars;

---

[95] Dungen. www.sofiatopia.org/maat/hidden_chamber03.htm.
[96] Dungen.www.sofiatopia.org/maat/peret_em_heru.htm.
[97] Tyson, 103-6.

only the initiated are permitted entry.

The tale of Nadab and Abihu being killed by the "strange fire" is reminiscent of the *Amduat*'s telling of the Lake of Fire:

> This Lake of Fire is a place of fiery punishment for the damned, but the blessed dead drink cool water from it. This "fire-water" is a powerful alchemical symbol, related to Philosophical Mercury (Aqua Mercurii). Dependent on one's attitude and condition, this water changes function. Constructive (blue) to some, it is destructive (red) to others. Burning Water implies to gain access to the inner planes of consciousness and imagination.[98]

It would seem, perhaps, that these two have dared to peek inside the "black box"; they have not been sanctioned to approach as they are not initiated, therefore they are impure. Their fate is certain death. On a more pragmatic level, one might suggest Nabonidus himself puts these two to death for daring to question his authority, or for attempting to "perceive" what is profoundly secret (and "his").

The idea of an "image" that is not an image will have intriguing significance to modern archaeological finds within Nabonidus' Arabian sphere, and will be discussed in due course.

# DARKNESS WITHIN

Moses ascends to the "lower sky", i.e., the symbolic plateau at Qurayyah, to commune with the deity in secret, hidden from view by the smoke of the fires, the furnaces of the smiths performing their sacred rites on the mesa. He symbolically enters the serpentine realm of the Duat, in a bid to assimilate their power and thus aid the transition of Ahmose's spirit so he can be reborn as the Sun aspect of "I AM." This is the way of the shaman, the path difficult and dangerous.

Nabonidus' own proclivity for the more esoteric practices, even when he was King in Babylon (e.g., his fascination with dream interpretation and with the *entu* priesthood, whose training seems to have included how to trigger trances and visions), even before he discovered the wonders of Egyptian religion or the mysteries of Arabian cultures, suggests Nabonidus might well imbibe something, or inhale something to aid his spiritual experience.[99] The smoke rising from the ceremonial furnaces may be laced

---

[98] Dungen, www.sofiatopia.org/maat/hidden_chamber03.htm.

[99] For instance, in the Sumerian text "Lugalbanda in the mountain cave," the king follows suit, i.e., he "… [lies] down not to sleep, he [lies] down to dream" (ETCSL 1.8.2.1,

with hallucinogenic substances as part of the shamanistic quest. One can imagine him feeling quite at home with this cult at Qurayyah, with this community who do not judge him as crazy for seeking an alternative reality and insight into the divine. They do not mock him for seeing shadows; they participate, they assist, they encourage.

In Nabonidus' not so normal reality, extreme visions and sensory experiences are what drive him, from the complex dreams he had early in his reign, to the Elixir-induced trips in Tayma. He seems to live for the next thrill, the next morsel of "hidden wisdom" that he can acquire, as if building his own esoteric library. His devotion to Sîn is not diminished but augmented by an increasing appreciation for the balance between lunar and solar energies. Through his understanding of the Osirian philosophy, via Nitocris, and his own investigations into the supremacy of the solar deity Re, Nabonidus believes he can create the perfect god that will satisfy his own need for spiritual superiority, and satisfy the dynamic that awaits him at the foot of Mount Sinai. This is classic Nabonidus hubris, so evident in the Song of Solomon, and in the propagandistic references to him in both cuneiform inscriptions (e.g., the VA especially) and the HB (e.g., Daniel 4-5).

This experience on the mesa, steeped in allusions to the regeneration and rebirth of Re and Osiris, has one thing in common with the old Sumerian/Akkadian rituals of the dreamers/seers, such as the *entus*, i.e., this overpowering "darkness." As we see in the Song, Nitocris, an active remote-viewer herself, twice goes into a deep reverie in order to "see" beyond reality. Both times, she does this in the dark of the night.[100] She was to instruct little Ennigaldi in the art, which had long been forgotten in Babylonia; in ancient days, the *entu* would spend the night in the darkness of the chamber at the top of the ziggurat, probably having taken something to aid her concentration, in order to enter the spirit realm and return with insights.

Darkness affects the human brain on a biochemical level; serotonin is produced in reaction to light, allowing us to perceive things in the waking reality, while melatonin is produced in darkness, converting to pinoline, thereby aiding dreaming and altered states of consciousness. Dungen suggests that those who enter the "Hidden Chamber" and witness the "dark light" within, are necessarily transformed, but it is a fine line between enlightenment and madness:

> The Osirian priests of Ancient Egypt, prophets of Judaism, the mystics of Christ and the prophet of Islam have all experienced the

---

§326-50). The two states are distinguishable and the process is ceremonial: Lugalbanda imbibes an alcoholic drink, prepares a "couch" of special herbs, and dons a sacred garment in preparation for his "dream."

[100] Song 3:1-2 and 5:2-3 (Tyson 79-80; 125).

hidden, dark light "seen" in total darkness. Christian mystics like John of the Cross speak of the "dark night of the soul," in which the depth of one's existential misery is faced and overwon. If not, *insania amoris* or primal rage ensue. In the dark, the need to cling to a sense of ego, Self or personhood is lost.[101]

In the Song, Nitocris becomes frustrated with the king because she truly desires him to learn but he proves an impatient, inattentive student, making mistakes and crossing the line once too often. He desires wisdom so he can boast about it, like his fancy chariots and beautiful horses; he hasn't the patience to be taught well. Because of his nature, the secrets he is privy to become like a drug to him, and he loses his sense of reason, his grasp on reality. This is why the legend of Ashmedai was created (Gittin 68), i.e., to give a context, or rationale, for the king's seemingly unnatural behaviour (concerning the blood-rite and his insatiable appetite for menstruating women).[102] This is what Daniel 4 and the "beast" is all about. Here, then, at Sinai, and indeed throughout the narrative, we see Moses walking a fine line between invoking the sacred and *dictating* the sacred, between experiencing the illuminating darkness and *becoming* that darkness.

Jehudijah sees the darkness in Nabonidus; she alludes to it in the Song many times. His "sense of ego" is accentuated not negated within the darkness, and his previously tentative hold on reality is easily triggered, revealing itself once again, e.g., he argues with God on Mount Sinai (Exod 32:7-14). He simply hasn't the cognitive prowess or experience to handle the fire (pun intended) he is playing with.

> Osiris is Atum, the one who accomplished the cycle, whose other face is Re, one being the nocturnal part, the vital strengths, the other the diurnal part, the luminous strengths, according to the famous formula of the tomb of Nefertari.[103]

# RA-MESES

For want of a more appropriate place to recount my own interpretation of "Rameses," I include it here, now the concept of the Re/Osiris amalgamation has been discussed.

The reason why "Rameses," rather than the historically correct Pi-

---

[101] Dungen, www.sofiatopia.org/maat/hidden_chamber03.htm.

[102] Tyson, 27-9, et al.

[103] Nadine Guilhou, "Les deux morts d'Osiris, d'après les textes des Pyramides," *EAO* 10 (1998): 19-26, here 25.

Ramesses is mentioned in Exod 1:11 is because the authors are suggesting a symbolic connection between the apparent solar focus of Nabonidus' new religion/deity and his alleged self-deification. They are playing with the name.

It has often been suggested that "Moses" is a shortened version of a longer Egyptian theophoric name, such as Thutmose or Ramesses,[104] yet modern commentators steer away from inferring a solar meaning for the Exodus character. The name "Rameses" or *Ra*-moses, however, is translated as "Son of Ra" i.e., "Son of the Sun" (from Egyptian *mes*, or *mesu*, meaning "child or son"). The name "Samson" means "Sun Man" and is also a pseudonym for Nabonidus, I claim;[105] the fact that the tale of Moses also contains a term that directly associates with "Samson" supports the notion that both are potentially founded on the same person. In the Song of Solomon, also, Nabonidus is identified by subtle reference to a place name, i.e., Baal-hamon (Song 8:11), which itself is a pun pointing us to the ancient Akkadian epic "Atrahasis" and the centre of the world, Babylon.[106]

Bearing in mind the double nature of the relationship between Ahmose III and Nabonidus that is hinted at in the HB, the names "Samson" and "Rameses" both point toward a solar symbolism for Nabonidus, which might seem odd, in that he is known for his lunar worship (of Sîn). When you realise, however, that "Ahmose" means "Son of the Moon" (or "The Moon is Born"), yet as Pharaoh he represents Amun/Horus, the Sun, the doubling technique is maintained and a synthesis of solar and lunar symbolism is effected between the Egyptian and Babylonian kings.[107]

I suggests this is also why in LXX Exod 1:11 a third "city" is included, i.e., On, or Heliopolis ("City of the Sun"). Heliopolis is the ultimate solar cultic centre, devoted for millennia to the worship of Atum, Re, and Amun-Re, and it sits just up-river from Heroopolis (Pithom), on the same Pelusiac branch of the Nile. In the Egyptian Creation myth, Heliopolis is where Atum began his creation of the world/universe; the LXX authors include Heliopolis because they *know* of the solar aspect of Moses' (Nabonidus') mission and they wish to accentuate this for those who fail to see the connection with "Pithom" or "Rameses."

Uphill provides support for this idea that Rameses in Exodus 1 is meant to be interpreted as a person, not a place, by describing a small collection of statues in the Pi-Ramesses area that seem to indicate the

---

[104] For an in-depth analysis of the name see Michael P. Carroll, "A Structuralist Exercise: The Problem of Moses' Name," *AE* 12.4 (1985): 775-8.

[105] Tyson, 18-20.

[106] Tyson, 205-7.

[107] Ahmose III's namesake, Ahmose I (Dynasty 18), had a son called Ramose, which might be the inspiration for this clever symbolic allusion, linking Nabonidus to Pharaoh by hinting as his close but subservient relationship to Ahmose.

possible self-deification of Ramesses II. He is depicted sitting with "divine-symbolism … almost without parallel in Egyptian art and iconography when applied to the reigning king," i.e., he sits with the solar deities, wearing a solar disk on his head.[108] There is also an inscribed obelisk at Heliopolis, calling Rameses "Son of the Sun."[109] Uphill states:

> A special cult of the reigning king is known to have been established for soldiers serving in the eastern Delta …. These show that four colossal statues of the king were the object of the cult …. One is called "Ramesses the God" ….

Again, this is information that would be on public view, known to the locals, not hidden away in a tomb; the Exodus authors may be drawing on what they learn of Ramesses II from the territory they pass through (and they are sure to know of Nabonidus' self-deification years ago in Tayma) to hint at a similar self-perception in the character of "Moses."

There may also be a subtle play on words, here, for the Akkadian "RA" means "to hit, beat upon" (Moses violently "strikes" several things, including "an Egyptian," the Nile, and the rock/Miriam); it also suggests "to drive" (Moses drives his caravan through the land); and also "to impress" as in a seal (in the Song, Nabonidus is warned to keep Nitocris' words as a seal upon his arm, to remember the warnings, etc. [Song 8:6]).[110]

While *ra* in Egyptian clearly pertains to the deity Ra, in Hebrew, the noun *ra* means "evil" (e.g., Isa 5:20). Perhaps "Rameses" is a fabricated name to reflect the early experiences under the influence of Nabonidus in his Egyptian phase? A Hebrew Studies website suggests that Hebrew words are supposed to have a minimum of three letters, so to make *ra* a legitimate Hebrew word, you have to repeat the last letter, so *resh ayin* (*ra*), becomes, *resh ayin ayin* (*raa*).[111] This is how Rameses is spelled in Exod 1:11, i.e., "Raameses," indicating that the name is not meant to be understood as an Egyptian one, but as an intentionally constructed Hebrew one that has its own, specific significance. Remember, Exodus is basically an anti-Nabonidus text.

---

[108] E. P. Uphill, "Pithom and Raamses: Their Location and Significance," *JNES* 28.1 (1969): 15-39, here 31.

[109] Uphill, 35.

[110] Tyson, 195-6.

[111] Hebrew Word Study: "Evil" (RA, Resh Ayin), www.chaimbentorah.com.

# 14    CHERUBIM

## "… THERE I WILL MEET WITH YOU"

T hat the ark has Egyptian nuances and is linguistically linked to Joseph's coffin (via the word *aron*), is not news. I apply these notions in a different way, to illustrate the ark's profound significance to Nabonidus' perception of the new deity at Qurayyah; it is integral to the entire context of the "glory" being made *mobile* and not being merely a localised phenomenon at Sinai. The secrecy element, the darkness element, the purity element, all need to be dealt with and an enclosed box serves all three.

The ark's cherubim, I suggest, are not "sphinxes," as Noegel describes,[1] but winged serpents, emulating Wadjet as she protects both Pharaoh and deity (Re) on their sojourn through the desert. I would even dare to suggest that the original description *was* "seraphim" not "cherubim" but as soon as Nabonidus' influence was deemed a thing of the past, this was downplayed and changed, the serpent iconography rejected. Isa 6:2, however, might just retain evidence of this: "I saw the Lord sitting on a

---

[1] Scott B. Noegel, "The Egyptian Origin of the Ark of the Covenant," in *Israel's Exodus in Transdisciplinary: Perspective Text, Archaeology, Culture, and Geoscience*, T. E. Levy, et al., eds. (Switzerland: Springer, 2015) 223-42, here 224.

throne ... Seraphs were in attendance above him."

> An adoration of Re in BD spell 15A2 says of Re, "Thou risest, thou growest remote in the sky, while the twin Wadjets abide on thy head," while a hymn to Osiris in BD spell 185K says, "Hail to thee ... lord of gladness ... on whose brow have been fixed the twin Wadjets." The twin Wadjets are the double crown, representing sovereignty over the idealized Egypt, the universal kingdom.[2]

In terms of the practicalities of the ark as a potential container for the eternal flame of "I AM," i.e., the coals/embers, and the (toxic) raw ingredients for a mobile "glory machine" (cf. Exod 33:14, "My presence will go with you"), the ark cherubim might have functioned as chimneys,[3] the resulting smoke itself considered sacred. Just as the Oracle of Delphi inhaled noxious fumes in order to receive her divine messages, so Moses is told: "...from above the mercy seat, from *between the two cherubim* (emphasis mine) ... I will deliver to you all my commands for the Israelites" (Exod 25:22). In other words, "place your head between the chimneys and breathe in the essence of God." The instruction of Exod 25:20 to make the cherubim so that they face downward, toward the ark itself, is odd, yet hardly anyone discusses a rationale for this.

In Egyptian motifs a winged serpent (Wadjet, uraeus) is always pictured with its head high (i.e., in the attack pose). I think the instruction to have them with bowed heads is vital to understanding what is going on here: The fumes from whatever concoction is being kept inside (when activated) are strong and dangerous; if they exit the box via the chimneys straight into the nostrils of those close by, the effect may be detrimental or even fatal. However, if the fumes are first directed downward, the touching wings form a sort of basin in which the chemicals can intermingle, react, or dissipate, leaving the desired smoke relatively safe to inhale. Basically, the inhaler gets high, has visions, speaks to God, etc. It is this procedure that is highly secretive, magical, and restricted.

It is possible that the design for the ark comes to Nabonidus in one of these visions, whether fume-induced or in a dream. There is at least one precedent for this (but possibly several others). Nabonidus creates a special dagger to augment his idol/statue of Sîn, claiming the god told him to make it:

---

[2] Edward P. Butler, "Wadjet," *Henadology: Philosophy and Theology*, https://henadology.wordpress.com.

[3] "Classical authors often refer to the necessity for chimneys as an adjunct to ore mineral roasting in order to disperse the noxious vapours of sulphur and arsenic" (M. Harper, "Possible Toxic Metal Exposure of Prehistoric Bronze Workers," *BJIM* (1987) 44.10: 652-6, here 654. Also, Forbes, 123-4.

(This is) the dagger, a request of the god Sîn, lord of the god(s), that he requested from Nabonidus, king of Babylon, in a dream.

Nab 53

This is so suited to the Nabonidus we have come to know; it is simply another exploitation of someone else's beliefs and practices to suit his own insatiable desire to know the will of the gods (cf. 33:18, "Show me your glory, I pray," even though he has supposedly witnessed God many times by now, i.e., he wants *more*). It's also a replacement for the Elixir, which is no longer readily available; perhaps this aspect of the Qenites' rituals drew him to Sinai in the first place.

*Figure 18: The ark as an olfactory stimulus for divination*
*(Image: Author's construct)*

This is my rendition of what I think Nabonidus might have created for the ark. The winged serpents guard the deity within, just as in Egyptian hieroglyphics. The description of the ark's construction in Exod 37:2-3 suggests a "moulding of gold" was made around it. The Hebrew term for the "moulding" is *zer*, defined by *Strong's* as a "circlet, border," suggesting it is like a "crown" but the BDB suggests "originally, that which presses, binds," adding, "bracelet, wreath, crown, ring" With the allusions to Re in the Sinai scenario, it is fair to suggest the bodies of the snakes encircle the *entire* ark (*Fig. 17* shows the tails ending, but this is *my* limitation; they would probably continue down the sides of the box), just as the *mehen* serpent does the solar deity as he travels through the night. As the "cavern" in the solar myth becomes an all-encircling snake, so too the ark. A skilled craftsman could easily apply the motif of the snakes' bodies to the surface of the box, dividing the bodies at the junction between the top/lid and the container itself. An inscribed representation underneath would suffice to make the symbolism complete. The "glory" within the ark is thus spiritually protected by a continuous serpentine "ring, bracelet, etc.," as it is carried through the inhospitable desert.

The presence of winged serpents, while a direct Egyptian influence, would still be somewhat familiar to a Mesopotamian, for winged creatures, both deities and demons, are commonplace in the cultural iconography. Herodotus' remark on the "winged serpents" that travel from Arabia to Egypt and are thwarted by hungry ibis (*Hist.* 2.75-6) has been interpreted by some as a sighting of snake-like (i.e., salamander) fossils in a specific area of the Negev desert, 85 km south of (the conventional) Beersheba.[4] Herodotus' description of piles of bare bones *might* suggest fossils, and the hostile landscape reveals a predominance of ammonites, etc.[5] The illustrations used to support the argument for winged-snake fossils, however, are somewhat unconvincing and would have to be witnessed *very* closely, i.e., not easily noted by passers-by.[6] For there to be piles of these all visible on the surface and considered by travellers to be recently devoured prey doesn't seem to tally. I think Herodotus is, once again, inventing connections between snippets of information he deems too good to ignore but for which he has no concrete explanation.

Herodotus' Arabian flying serpents come straight from the legends of Moses. If the ark, as I suggest, has winged serpents on the top, and it is carried in procession everywhere the Israelites go, many people would see it. With the later Philistine debacle, its notoriety as a powerful object would be enhanced. Herodotus might have heard stories about the winged serpents that came from Arabia (i.e., on the ark, from Sinai/Qurayyah), in the context of a dangerous and sometimes lethal phenomenon that had something to do with Egypt, i.e., knowing that the winged serpent is familiar in Egyptian iconography. He also links the serpents with the ibis, suggesting this is why the Egyptians consider the birds sacred, i.e., they eat the snakes before they reach Egypt (*Hist.* 2.76).[7]

Ibis seldom, if ever, eat snakes, according to ornithologists; they feed on small crustaceans, worms, insects, etc., and sometimes other birds' or reptiles' eggs. A fourteen-year scientific study of the Sacred Ibis states

---

[4] Karen Radner, "The Winged Snakes of Arabia and the Fossil Site of Makhtesh Ramon in the Negev," *WZKM* 97 (2007): 353-65, here 365.

[5] Fossilised ammonites "were thought to be petrified coiled snakes, and were called snakestones. They were thought to have magical powers in Medieval times" (https://en.wikipedia.org/List_of_mythological_objects) but a coiled snake does not suggest a winged snake.

[6] Radner, 365, *Figs. 4a* and *4b*.

[7] In *Hist.* 3.107, Herodotus suggests that Arabian frankincense is protected by these creatures, further linking the serpents to Nabonidus' world of incense, trade, etc.

"regurgitations in nests underestimate some rare cases of killed but non-swallowed vertebrates, possibly by a few specialized individuals,"[8] thereby confirming that a union of snake and ibis is very rare indeed (and may only occur when a snake attempts to attack eggs in a nest?).

In the early 19th Century, French archaeologists opened several mummified ibis and did find snakes in the abdominal cavities. However, "Jules-César Savigny, who investigated the habits of the ibis, … noted that the embalmers had apparently been serving 'truths deeper than mere facts of natural history'," i.e., the embalmers were alluding to a symbolic connection by *placing* snakes in the birds *post-mortem*.[9]

Josephus (*A.J.* 2.10.2) tells the story of Moses' early years in Egypt and how he was sent to Ethiopia to stop an incursion into Egypt. Coming to a certain impasse filled with flying serpents, Moses unleashes baskets of ibis that hastily set to work devouring the creatures. He and his army are free to pass and arrive at their opponents' territory early enough to surprise and thereby conquer them. Earlier, I told of Moses being worshipped as Thoth-Hermes, and as being held responsible for the sanctity of the ibis; Thoth's zoomorphic form is the ibis. There seems to be a kernel of truth in both Herodotus' and Josephus' renderings of Moses' snake-eating birds, but if they weren't ibis, what were they?[10]

# SOLOMON'S CHERUBIM

> He put the cherubim in the innermost part of the house; the wings of the cherubim were spread out so that a wing of one was touching the one wall, and a wing of the other cherub was touching the other wall; their other wings toward the centre of the house were touching wing to wing. He also overlaid the cherubim with gold.
>
> 1 Kgs 6:27-8

There are many ways of imagining these statues; most illustrations show two winged *humanoid* figures. The word "cherubim" is, in the HB, *kerub*, with an unknown etymology. They are first mentioned in Gen 3:24, in a way that suggests either that something is missing (e.g., a previous explanation for

---

[8] Loïc Marion, "Is the Sacred Ibis a Real Threat to Biodiversity? Long-term Study of its Diet in Non-native Areas Compared to Native Areas," *CRB* 336.4 (April 2013): 207-220, here (online version) §4.2.2, "In the native area," www.science direct.com.

[9] "Savigny and the Sacred Ibis," Napoleon and the Scientific Expedition to Egypt, https://napoleon.lindahall.org/sacred_ibis.shtml.

[10] See my paper, "Nabonidus, Tarshish, and Ophir" ([2024], www.academia.edu), for a discussion on "peacocks."

what these creatures were), or "cherubim" were *already known* to the authors of Genesis and to its intended audience. I think it is the latter.

My first instinct was to imagine a larger replica of the paired, winged serpents on the ark, positioned with their wings arranged like Wadjet's (i.e., with one wing raised in protection, the other lowered in deference), which might find corroboration in Isa 6:2's "seraphs"; the "throne" of the deity *is* the ark (the seat of power), and the serpents are above it.

The serpentine connection is not fundamental to the Solomon narratives as it is to those of Moses, however, so the cherubim attributed to the temple's design and purpose, I propose, are quite different, and more in tune with Nabonidus' Assyrian/Babylonian cultural heritage.

Emulating Esarhaddon and Ashurbanipal, Nabonidus installs statues of "wild bulls" (*rīmū*) to guard temple gateways,[11] but he also places one *within* the Holy of Holies of Sîn's temple in Harran:

> I stationed a wild bull of shiny *zaḫalû*-metal, which aggressively gores my foes (to death), in his (Sîn's) inner sanctum. I firmly planted two long-haired heroes of *ešmarû*-metal, who overwhelm my enem(ies), in the Gate of the Rising Sun, (on) the right and left.[12]
>
> Nab 28 ii 14-17

Though tempting, these *rīmū* bulls are not to be mistaken for the winged *lamassu/shedu* bulls of Nineveh and Babylon, which are considered deities in their own right. They too guard entrances to temples, or gates in walls, etc., and usually come in pairs; they are chimeric beasts, which would please Nabonidus, but they are relatively passive entities.

Nabonidus' freestanding bulls are described as being made of shiny metal, and it is assumed that they were plated wood, not solid metal,[13] just as we see in 1 Kgs 6:28.

Rather, these *rīmū* bulls are probably representations of the mighty aurochs, the original wild bovine found in prehistoric cave art and Minoan frescoes. Known for their ferocity, their most noticeable feature was their horns; wide, sitting low, they resembled the crescent Moon, hence their connection to lunar worship, and potentially the honour of guarding Sîn's Holy of Holies.

Solomon's cherubim are not described as having wings, nor are their heads bowed, i.e., two striking deviations from the ark cherubim that need to be explained. Aurochs horns could reach over 1 meter in length

---

[11] W&N, 9, n. 69.

[12] Cf. the two pillars, "left and right," in Solomon's temple.

[13] W&N, 9; 11 n. 88; 178 n. i 5.

(prehistoric specimens, 2 meters).[14] If the Holy of Holies in Solomon's temple is about 4.5 meters long and 4.5 meters wide (ten by ten cubits), two such statues side by side would fill the space, horns touching each other and the outer walls. Domineering and threatening, they would have been a powerful symbol of protection.

The serpentine iconography is peculiar to the ark but the protection of the Holy of Holies from "foes" must fall to the king's mighty, reliable bulls. This provides for a wonderful symmetry, or fusion, of both solar (serpentine) and lunar (bovine) iconography within the Holy of Holies.

Anyone having joined Nabonidus' little exodus from Harran (during "Abraham's" stopover) would have known of these "wild bulls" of the temples, or from the public stele description. As it has already been mentioned that he replicates the Babylonian precedents for his temple/palace at Tayma, it seems likely Nabonidus copies these bulls, too, as he is obviously very proud of them.

*Figure 19: Lamassu (Image: By 0x010C, https://commons.wikimedia.org)*

As for "cherubim" etymology, there are several Assyrian/Babylonian terms that offer potential insight: *kurību* (an ethereal spirit, a spirit being, a cherub, a figure of a cherub); *karūbu* (an epithet of deities meaning "reverently greeted"); *kāribu* (a supplicant deity or genie); *karbu* (blessed); and several other related terms pertaining to priestly blessings,

*Figure 20: A modern aurochs (Image: www.sheppardsoftware.com).*

offerings, prayers, etc.[15] The term *kuribi* appears in an Esarhaddon inscription pertaining to the rebuilding of the temple of Assur: "*Lahme* [plural] and *Kuribi* [also plural] of brilliant, ruddy electrum, I placed on either side [of the entrances to the temple] (KAH, I, 75, obv. 24)."[16]

---

[14] "Wisent and Aurochs," www.northseafossils.com.

[15] www.assyrianlanguages.org/akkadian/list.php.

[16] Daniel David Luckenbill, "The Egyptian Earth-god in Cuneiform," *AJSL* 40.4 (July 1924): 288-92, here 290.

There is nothing in "cherubim" that suggests their form; 2 Sam 22:11 (Ps 18:10) describes God as "thundering" from the heavens on the back of a cherub, so it must be a formidable beast (e.g., a winged bull), but in the Zohar (13th Century esoterica), the "cherubim" in the Holy of Holies of the temple in Jerusalem are male and female beings intertwined, as lovers, i.e., "the mystery of masculine and feminine together."[17] This is the basis for the humanoid cherubim, probably.

So perhaps *any* physical form might be used; it is the sacredness of the creature and perhaps the innate protective quality that are paramount, which is why both snakes and bulls might serve as divine guards. If "seraphim" *was* originally intended as the description of the ark's cherubim, and Nabonidus' famous *rīmū* bulls for the temple of Solomon, both would have to be expunged from the record by those who wish to negate Nabonidus' influence. Isaiah's allusion slipped through the net! "Cherubim," I posit, is a Hebrew version of the *kuribi*, a benevolent, supplicant entity that bears no resemblance to anything deemed offensive by the early Jews. Nabonidus would not have recognised them.

Of course, there is no sign of the ark once construction gets underway on the temple in Jerusalem; it was never there. It is taken from Sinai to Tayma and probably stays there until Nabonidus dies, is taken on a few campaigns to show strength, political allegiances, etc., and then dismantled for the gold once the legend surrounding its original meaning is lost to the desert winds.

---

[17] Moshe Weinfeld, "Feminine Features in the Imagery of God in Israel: The Sacred Marriage and the Sacred Tree," *VT* 46.4 (1996): 515-29, here 518-20.

# 15                                  SERPENT KING

In his monograph *Ophiolatreia*, Hargrave Jennings describes how the Egyptian deity Thoth (the Egyptian god whom Moses is said to have been worshipped as) is renowned for introducing serpent-worship to Egypt. He first created a *hybrid*, supreme deity he called Cneph, "whose symbol was a serpent. ... He is generally represented leaning upon a knotted stick which has around it a serpent."[1]

At Sinai, Nabonidus-Moses is introduced to practical ophiolatry, the worship of snakes. He must already have a fascination, as the Egyptian solar religion is heavily imbued with serpent iconography and myth. That the Qenites also have a close relationship with serpents must seem divine providence to Nabonidus.

Meeks provides a brief appraisal of the phenomenon as it relates to Yahweh and the HB:

> ... the serpent cult was so closely knit with the Yahweh cult and continued right down to the time of Hezekiah ... and was only eradicated under the influence of the vigorous polemic of the prophets against idolatry (2 Kgs 18:4). The presence of "serpent" as an element in Hebrew proper names is another indication of the influence of the serpent cult on the Hebrew religion, as are likewise the name of the

---

[1] Hargrave Jennings, *Ophiolatreia* (London: 1889), 98-9.

altar erected by Moses, *Yahweh-nissi*, "Yahweh is my rod" (Exod 17:15; cf. the "rod" of Exod 4:2 ff.), and the ascription to Yahweh of the art of healing (Exod 15:26; 23:25). The "serpent" ... of Num 21:8 appears again in the "seraphim" ... of Isa 6:2, 6 (cf. also Isa 14:29; 30:6; Deut 8:15); and still another evidence of the serpent cult may be found in the "serpent's stone" of 1 Kgs 1:9, 38, and in the "dragon's spring" of Neh 2:13.1.[2]

Many scholars have rejected the possibility that serpent worship played any active role in the development of Yahwism, for instance:

Nowhere in ancient Israel do we find any possibility of developing a positive attitude towards serpents, as was the case in Egypt, Greece and Italy. There was certainly never any serpent cult, as in Mesopotamia and Egypt. This—more than inclusion of serpents in Ugaritic mythology—accounts for the fact that serpents were considered cultically unclean.[3]

Amzallag offers a fascinating argument, suggesting that the serpent, in the form of the *saraph*, or "flying snake" has a very early and important representation in Canaan as a symbol of divine protection, i.e., the protection of Yahweh's copper resources (mining regions).[4] Clearly, this echoes the idea of Moses' bronze serpent, the Nehushtan, being raised to protect the people from poisonous snakes in the desert (Num 21:6-9, discussed below).

Serpent worship has also been shown to be endemic in areas such as Dan, northern Galilee (the hill country), and in Beth-shan, a name some consider to mean "House of the Snake" and where multiple serpent-related objects were discovered, including a "serpent house" (ca. 12th Century BCE) that resembles a box for carrying an idol.[5] Admittedly, no serpent iconography has been found in Jerusalem itself, which most attribute to the reforms of Hezekiah (though there are remnants of names, e.g., the "Dragons Well" and the "Serpents' Pool"). With the rise in population, constant upheaval due to war, and limitations on excavations, however, this lack of evidence may be due to extenuating circumstances, rather than an absolute absence of artefacts. It may, on the other hand, be due to the anti-Nabonidus sentiment prevalent in early Judaism.

---

[2] T. J. Meeks, Some Religious Origins of the Hebrews," *AJSL* 37.2 (1921): 101-31, here 117-18.

[3] H. J. Fabry, "nḥs," *TDOT* 356-69, here 539.

[4] Nissim Amzallag, "The Origin and Evolution of the *saraph* Symbol," in *Antiguo Oriente: Cuadernos del Centro de Estudios de Historia del Antiguo Oriente* 13 (2015): 99-126, here 114-16.

[5] J. H. Charlesworth, *The Good and Evil Serpent* (New Haven: Yale University, 2010), 75-9.

# MOTHER SERPENT

Recall that Moses' adoptive mother is mythologically linked to the Egyptian goddess Renenutet. The traditional iconography of this goddess is that of a woman with the head of a cobra. She is also the mother of a rather more significant deity called Nehebkau, who is a fully-fledged serpent god. In more ancient stories he was an evil entity, untrusted and a threat to Re (cf. Apep) but, the legend goes, Atum touched the snake's spine with his fingernail and it became gentle, benevolent, and a protector/assistant to Re (and eventually succeeding him in the hierarchy of the afterlife). Poacher turned gamekeeper. One of the most striking legends pertaining to Nehebkau is that *he devoured seven uraei* which made him invulnerable to fire, water, and magic.[6] He is depicted as a multi-coiled snake and his likeness was used as an amulet against evil, ill omens, etc. This, of course, has ramifications for the Nehushtan discussion, but it also suggests a symbolic link between Moses and Nehebkau, who are both sons of Renenutet.

In the HB we have Moses and Aaron depicted as "brothers" in a religious context; serpent symbolism is employed in their initial portrayal, and the serpent is strongly linked to solar-worship. With this in mind, another sideways glance at the name "Moses/Moshe" may reveal an intriguing potential play on words, for in Akkadian, the word for "snake" is *muš* (*mush*).[7] As the mother of the serpent deity, Renenutet symbolically plucks Moses from the water as the new serpentine demi-god, like a water snake from the marshes.[8] He and his brother Nehebkau (Aaron) then become the protective assistants to the deity, i.e., a chimera of astronomical deities comprised of Sun, Moon, and Stars.

Nehebkau, or the "*n 'w* serpent," is identified in the Coffin Texts as the one who bestows and takes away powers; "I am he who assumes the powers of the gods."[9]

Renenutet's consort is the crocodile–headed Sobek, who rises in the

---

[6] Coffin Texts (CT), Spells 85; 88 (R. O. Faulkner *The Ancient Egyptian Coffin Texts, Vol. 1, Spells 1-354* [Warminster, UK: Aris & Phillips, 1973], 89-91).

[7] Composite words include: *muškû* ("snake eater" or bird of prey); *mušlaḫḫu* (snake-charmer); and *mušlaḫḫūtu* (the art of snake-charming); from Akkadian Dictionary, www.assyrianlanguages.org.

[8] In the Egyptian myth of Re traversing the underworld, his greatest enemy there is Apep (or Apophis), the giant snake who dwells in the marshes; this might be another hidden jibe at Nabonidus' intended amalgamation with Egyptian solar symbolism, from an author who, just as in the Nile scene, wants to discredit Nabonidus and present his mission as being doomed from the start. If he is equated with Apep, he is both the villain of the story and, ultimately, a failure.

[9] CT 86 and n. 5 (Faulkner, 90).

pantheon to become an avatar of Re, but what interests me is the fact that in the Pyramid Texts he is called "Neith's son."[10] Pharaoh Ahmose III (Nitocris' father) is called "son of Neith." However, if Renenutet is an avatar of Nitocris, which she seems to be, Sobek must reflect Nabonidus, but he was never a pharaoh. The convoluted point is this: The Sobek allusion pertains to the one who is associated with the goddess Renenutet (Thermuthis), i.e., one would think, Nabonidus (as Moses), but the epithet "Neith's son" is adopted by both Cambyses II and Darius I when *they* become Pharaoh (as conquerors).[11] Cambyses is really the only other contender, besides Nabonidus, to be linked with "Pharaoh's daughter" because he (or his father, Cyrus, who is at this point deceased) is presumed to be the intended husband for "Nitetis" (Nitocris) in Herodotus' confusing tale(s) of the Persian invasion of Egypt in 525 BCE.[12]

Sobek is the god of the Nile. Like Nehebkau, he has apotropaic qualities, in that he can be invoked for protection against evil influences and danger, especially danger from the Nile itself. Etymology for "Sobek" suggests "to impregnate" (*sbk*) and this is substantiated by a reference to him in the Pyramid Texts: "...lord of semen, who takes women from their husbands ... according to his heart's fancy."[13] To me, this sounds much more like Nabonidus, given his history (in the Song) but we must remember the close association between Pharaoh and Nabonidus, i.e., as "doubles," sharing traits and connections.

As I argue for an exilic/postexilic HB, I am of the opinion that many references to an ancient Egypt, a mysterious "Pharaoh," etc., are part of a broad scribal technique to protect the authors from possible repercussions, i.e., because the real focus of their ire is still living and has their lives still firmly in his grasp ... Cambyses.

# PETRA-GLYPHS

Wenning describes a snake-themed relief in the vicinity of Petra (one of several; this one is at Wadi al-Qantara, 2007):

The steeply uprising snake is depicted in three slight coils. The tail is

---

[10] James P. Allen and Peter Der Manuelian, eds., *The Ancient Pyramid Texts*, (Society of Biblical Literature: 2005), 60.
[11] Elias J. Bickerman, "The Edict of Cyrus in Ezra 1," *JBL* 65.3 (1946): 249-75, here 266.
[12] Tyson, 7-10.
[13] Allen and Der Manuelian, 60.

not resting on the ground. ... It is not easy to define where the mouth ends, and the head does not seem to widen greatly. ... The snake does not threaten, but rather seems to have a protective character. It does not belong to the types of the snakes representing the *genius loci* or the *agathos daimon*. The best parallel is that of the harmless snake of Aesculapius.

... The object hangs like a garland. It is not clear if the snake is attacking or devouring an animal. It is also possible that the snake is touching an object. The mouth and uprising coiling of the snake give a wrong impression of being a seahorse instead of a snake.[14]

*Figure 21: Snake in a boat from rock with Nabonidus inscription near Tayma (Image: Author's rendition after Hayajneh, 85).*

This description reminded me of the illustration that appears next to the Nabonidus-related "Inscription 1" from Ramm, south-west of Tayma (*Fig. 20*).[15]

There are two strikingly obvious things to note about this image: 1) something is *in a boat* in the middle of the desert; 2) the thing in the boat does not look human, i.e., compare almost any other ancient petroglyph of humans and you can instantly recognise the human form, with two legs and two arms, at the very least.

1). The boat motif may suggest a river boat, as it has no obvious mast. The object on the bow is a figurehead, probably a bull's head; the bow is pronounced and the bottom is flat. This suggests a wooden vessel, rather than a reed one.[16] I put it that this glyph is contemporaneous with the inscription that mentions Nabonidus arriving in the area, in the context of an "emigration": I put it that the boat illustrates how they arrived (as I have claimed, by small boats).

2). The figure in the boat is not a human but a rearing snake. It does have the likeness of a "seahorse" as Wenning claims for the glyph at Petra

[14] Robert Wenning, "Snakes in Petra," *From Ugarit to Nabataea: Studies in Honor of John F. Healey*, George Kiraz and Zeyad Al-Salameen, eds. (Piscataway: Gorgias Press, 2012), 235-54, 279-82 (Plates), here 246, with n. 59. For images see 281.

[15] Hani Hayajneh, "First Evidence of Nabonidus in the Ancient North Arabian Inscriptions from the Region of Tayma," *Proceedings of the Seminar for Arabian Studies, Vol. 31*, Papers from the thirty-fourth meeting of the Seminar for Arabian Studies held in London, 20-22 July 2000 (2001), 81-95, here 85.

[16] Robert S. Neyland, "The Seagoing Vessels on Dilmun Seals," in *Underwater Archaeology Proceedings from the Society for Historical Archaeology Conference*, Donald H. Keith and Toni L. Carrel, eds., (Kingston, Jamaica: Society for Historical Archaeology, 1992), 68-74, here, 69. Illustrations on pp. 69-70 show various forms of people in boats, standing in different positions; all show obvious arms and legs.

(though this one is much cruder). From early Mesopotamian cylinder seals we know that Shamash, the Sun god was seen to travel through the sky in a boat, and cultic statues were often placed in boats for ritual processions.[17] Of course, Re also rides through the sky in a boat, or "barque."

So, we may be seeing, very close to Tayma, a Nabonidus inscription that speaks of a journeying group, next to a glyph of a serpentine deity in a boat. Amazingly, Wenning's account of the Petra monuments upon which the snake glyphs are carved ends with this comment (emphasis mine):

> These monuments can be grouped together with votive niches with baetyls and figural deities (e.g., Isis, Dushara-bust, and eagle), and it is significant that from among these a specific type developed around the snake. *Two of the monuments seem to depict a scene from a narrative .... As no Nabataean mythological texts are known,* we are unlikely to be able to explain these contexts or even to tell which deity the snakes represent. However, this new group of monuments does support the idea of a snake cult or snake-deity in Petra.[18]

What if that mysterious "narrative" tells of the strange amalgamation of the Sun, Moon, and Stars into one deity, or is the same tale that would later become the basis of the HB's book of Exodus? Although the serpent was revered in the region long before the Babylonian ex-king first rode through Petra as conqueror, it is just possible that his interest in the solar aspects of ophiolatry inspired later generations of Nabonidus supporters to create more visible depictions of the deified snake.

# SLOUGHING AT SINAI

A riddle from the Tur Abdin region (Mount Masius)[19] reads: "I know something that takes off its [shirt] once a year and fasts forty days until it has come off—the snake."[20] The Sumerians and Akkadians were fond of a

---

[17] "Maritime Archaeology," www.brown.edu/Departments/Joukowsky Institute /courses/maritimearchaeology11/files/18404468.pdf, 11.

[18] Wenning, "Snakes," 250. Wenning previously proposes the serpentine imagery may pertain to the solar deity Dushara (239).

[19] Tur Abdin is a plateau region in the Anti-Taurus Mountains of south-eastern Turkey, on the western side of the Tigris River. It has strong Assyrian connections dating back to the 10th Century BCE.

[20] W. F. Albright, "The Goddess of Life and Wisdom," *AJSL* 36.4 (1920): 258-294, here 279.

parable, of symbolic debates between surprising opponents, e.g., grain and sheep (ETCSL 5.3.2); heron and turtle (ETCSL 5.9.2). I can imagine such a riddle as this would have been popular in Nabonidus' (Solomon's) court. Perhaps this notion of the "forty-day" sloughing of the snake's skin was a common one and found a place in the account of Moses ascending Mount Sinai, entering "the cloud," and remaining there for "forty days and nights" (Exod 24:18) without food. In a quasi-magical/mythical sense, Nabonidus is sloughing off his old skin (as King of Babylon) and reinventing himself as the high priest of "I AM."

He is going through a formal ordination/initiation ritual atop the mesa. Just as Song 5:1 tells of the king's initiation into the sacred rites of the Elixir Rubeus, etc.,[21] so Exodus allows for a seven-day pre-ordination period (for purification, Exod 24:16). He is then inculcated into rituals and rules of the Qenite religion, becoming one with the fire and the "glory."

Nabonidus' deity is not the Yahweh of the Qenites, the metallurgical, volcanic god of the nomads; he imbues his chimera with as much originality, arcane symbolism, and personal preferences as he did his "image" (idol) of Sîn. The serpent that once burned bright from the copper furnace at Qurayyah, takes on new meaning in Nabonidus' mind; it becomes the new *mehen*, the all-encircling, protective snake of the barque of Re who, so Nabonidus seems to think, is still ensconced in the bones of Joseph, i.e., the bones of Pharaoh Ahmose III, son of the Sun-god.

## HOBAB THE SNAKE

In Num 10:29, Hobab is named as Reuel's son, with Reuel ("friend of God") being another name for Jethro ("excellence, leader"), the (high) priest of Midian. In Judg 4:11, Hobab is again mentioned, this time as the "father-in-law" of Moses. Albright argues that "Hobab, *son-in-law* of Moses, was a Midianite belonging to the clan of Reuel and a smith by profession. Jethro, priest of Midian and father-in-law of Moses, was a member of the same clan (Reuel)."[22] Indeed, Hobab *is* Moses' son-in-law, *not* his "father-in-law"; Hobab is Aaron, married to Moses' daughter, Miriam; Jethro *is* Moses' father-in-law because Jehudijah is Jethro's daughter. However, I don't see the need to make "Reuel" a clan name, for why would it not be mentioned as such (e.g., cf. Judg 4:17, "the clan of Heber")? Once you can accept commission names, pseudonyms for new contexts, there is no discrepancy.

---

[21] Tyson, 120-4.
[22] W. F. Albright, "Jethro, Hobab and Reuel in Early Hebrew Tradition," *CBQ* 25.1 (1963): 1-11, here 9.

The "friend of God" translation of "Reuel" is also (exclusively) applied to both Abraham (2 Chr 20:7) and Moses (Exod 33:11), i.e., both representing Nabonidus, the person introduced to Jethro's deity. Introductions are made by friends, normally. "Reuel" is the first commission name for Jethro because this is where he is the instigator of Moses' experience with the "I AM." It is a role, an office (a commission).

The word used for the relationship between Hobab and Moses is the same term used for that between Zipporah and Moses in Exodus 2's "bloody husband" scene, i.e., *chatan. Strong's* defines this as "A primitive root; to give (a daughter) away in marriage; hence (generally) to contract affinity by marriage - join in affinity, father in law, make marriages, mother in law, son in law." "Father in law" is one option and is, I think, assumed; once the alternative context of that scene is understood, the definition must shift. In 1 Kgs 3:1, the conciliatory "treaty" between Solomon and his Egyptian bride (Nitocris) is also defined by *chatan*.

To reiterate: Hobab is Aaron, Moses' Qenite son-in-law.

The name "Hobab" means "Serpent." Meeks provides additional insight, with respect to the Levitical connection:

> A further connection between Levi and the serpent cult is to be found in the probable connection between Levi and Leviathan, both being derived from Arabic *lawa*, "to twist, coil." Finally, the presence of serpent names among the Levites would point in the same direction, although these, it must be confessed, are few in number, due doubtless to the fact that serpent names, like animal names in general, came to be suppressed as out of accord with later religious ideas. ... P preserves the name of Aaron's brother-in-law as Nahshon (Exod 6:23), and with the Chronicler we have Naas as the name of a Levite (1 Chr 26:4 LXXB), and Shuppim, "serpents" (1 Chr 26:16).[23]

"Nahshon" means "enchanter" (*Strong's*) or "serpent, bronze, oracle" (Abarim) from the noun *nahash*, i.e., he is a snake charmer. No name in the Bible is gratuitous; there has to be a reason why "Nahshon" is mentioned other than the fact that he is someone's brother, otherwise it is a waste of words. I posit he is there to illustrate the cultic community, guild, or trade both of Jethro's sons (in the broader sense) are involved with. An associated etymology is passed down the line, to "Phinehas," Aaron's grandson (Num 25:10. *Strong's* suggests "from *peh* and a variation of *nachash*; "mouth of a serpent"), a character who will prove very important in a scene involving

---

[23] Meeks, T. J., "Some Religious Origins of the Hebrews," *AJSL* 37.2 (1921): 101-31, here 109-10.

Jehudijah, later. Serpent symbolism is therefore strongly linked to the Qenites, i.e., to Jethro and especially to Aaron.

Abarim's alternative rendering of "Hobab" is "beloved, embrace," from the Hebrew verb *habab*, "to love, embrace" (used only in Deut 33:3) nearly threw me off course, as it suggested a strong connection with the Song of Solomon, i.e., where Nabonidus is called the "beloved" and the ritual "embrace" becomes a matter of serious contention. This made me wonder if the "serpent" etymology was pointing to Hobab being Moses, but this would have been illogical. The verb *habab* appears surreptitiously, however, within the context of hidden love in Song 2:1. Jehudijah's Song is filled with double meanings; she writes of Nitocris but imbues the text with her own passion. In the "rose" of Sharon (*chabatstseleth*: a conflation of *habab/chabab*, "to love" and *basal*, "flower bud") she hides this attestation of a love she was compelled to keep to herself.[24]

Jehudijah's secret love preserved in the Song may have a correlation in the tale of the exodus; she no longer loves Nabonidus (Moses) but we know that she has had intimate dealings with Aaron, who is already known to Jethro via their mutual metallurgy-related worship. Indeed, later, we will see Jehudijah being admonished for a sexually-related incident, so don't rush to dismiss this idea.

In Num 10:29-34, Moses seems to invite Hobab to come with the group into Canaan, with the added incentive of "whatever we get you will have a share in." Hobab firmly states that he does not wish to go with Moses, and has plans to return to his "own land and kindred," i.e., to his nomadic life with the Qenites. This scene postdates the killing of Miriam, so it suggests Aaron does not wish to remain with the man who killed his wife; perhaps Moses convinces Aaron to remain longer but when Aaron's tale ends, we find him well and truly home.

The rationale for providing Aaron with the pseudonym "Hobab" is to make a distinction between the priest who works wonders and the ordinary man, the prophet right-hand-man of Moses, and the man who effectively cuckolds the ex-king. One might even suggest a play on words by the authors, i.e., on the etymology of "Hobab" as "serpent," in that they are insinuating a lasciviousness that is unbecoming, an echo of the serpent in Eden, etc.

## Levite

Aaron/Hobab is thus a nomadic Qenite, an itinerant metal-worker/artisan, whose home is farther afield, away from the community who dwell near Sinai.

---

[24] Tyson, 64; 219.

Jethro would have known him first through Jehudijah's relationship. He is introduced as "the Levite" in Exod 4:14, and while most see this as being an attribute of the later Levitical priests, there is an alternative understanding. Meeks, for instance, argues that "the Levites were originally a tribe" rather than a "priestly caste or profession," and that the attribution of Aaron as "the Levite" is probably a much later insertion.[25] In the analysis provided here, however, the two are *not* mutually exclusive, for Jethro and his priestly tribe might well be considered "levites" simply by virtue of their tightly-knit (joined) community, and the fact that they twist metal as part of their religious expression. By naming Aaron, directly, as a levite, he (as opposed to Moses) is defined as a member of Jethro's original religious family.

I suggest, therefore, that the term "levite" originally pertains to a member of the religious community at Sinai (in Arabia); it is later adopted by the Israelite priests, retaining its undeniable association with the nomadic priestly individuals (recall the Jewish Levites are given no lands in Gen 49:5-7) who attend to the ritualistic aspects of their religion (e.g., as those who light the fires, stoke the flames, prepare the tools).[26]

# NEHUSHTAN

As mentioned earlier, during the fourth hour of Re's nocturnal journey through the night/underworld, his staff is turns into a serpent. Just as Aaron's serpent-staff devours the Egyptian priests' serpent-staffs, so Moses' Nehushtan (Num 21:6-9) becomes a "fiery serpent" to emulate Re's powerful magic; it wards off the "fiery serpents" (*seraphim*) that threaten safe passage through the desert. This is, perhaps, one of the most striking examples of a biblical author *realising* the significance of Nabonidus' fascination with the Egyptian solar mythology, and *intentionally* including it in the narrative.

Discussing the *aron*, previously, I mentioned the lore pertaining to the carrying of Joseph's bones and the associated complaining by the Israelites, who deemed it unfair that the *aron* for the dead was getting the same respect and protection as the *aron* for the "glory." I see this as the only potential rationale for the Nehushtan in terms of it being a *historical entity* and not a fictional device for the narrative, i.e., the people complain (incessantly) that they are not given the same protection from their leader, so Moses orders the Nehushtan

---

[25] Meeks, 113.

[26] Interestingly, Meeks suggests the opposite, i.e., the Jewish Levites seem to have influenced the Arabian concept of priesthood (116).

fashioned[27] to represent the same power of the cherubim, the winged (fiery) serpents on the ark (thereby confirming that Nabonidus has no qualms about figurative representations). Raised up high, its symbolic venom covers a wider area, and its wings cast a greater protective shadow; everyone can see it. It can't genuinely revive people who have been bitten by real snakes; it is more sympathetic magic, fighting fire with fire to appease the people.

*Figure 22: Wadjet (Image: Public Domain)*

The Nehushtan is made of bronze because that is the material most commonly worked with in the region. Late Bronze Age (bronze) serpents have been discovered in Gezer, Timna, Hazor, and Tell Mevorakh,[28] suggesting the only novelty about the Nehushtan is that this one probably has wings (it is a *seraph*).[29] The Nehushtan is, I suggest, a replica of the cherubim but with her head held high, i.e., an image of Wadjet, doing what she does best, i.e., protecting the pharaoh, protecting Re and, by extension, protecting the people. As a goddess of Lower Egypt, this fits well with the Delta context of the exodus. As she is considered the "eye of the moon" in relation to Horus being the "eye of the sun,"[30] she also identifies with both solar and lunar worship, making her an ideal panacea for a frightened, "mixed" crowd.

---

[27] I.e., by a smith, a metalworker in bronze; *he* is not a smith, as many seem to have understood this. He is a ruler, an ex-king, a powerful man; he orders something done, it gets done and he claims the credit, just like the temples, palaces, stelea, etc. It is the way of royalty.

[28] Albert Leonard, Jr., "Archaeological Sources for the History of Palestine: The Late Bronze Age," *BA* 52.1 (March 1989): 4-39, here 22.

[29] I see no contradiction with the destruction of the Nehushtan by Hezekiah in 2 Kgs 18:14, as I am a proponent of an exilic/postexilic HB, i.e., *everything* is written from the vantage point of at least the 8th Century BCE but predominantly later. The Nehushtan is inserted into this history retrospectively, as it is a familiar object, exemplifying the notion of idolatry, reminding us of the golden calf that had also been broken into pieces. If it *were* an artefact, it *would* have been preserved and probably revered as a relic in later times. Nabonidus' "Nehushtan" seems a prime candidate for public eradication (even if only symbolically).

[30] Richard H. Wilkinson, *The Complete Gods and Goddesses of Ancient Egypt* (London: Thames & Hudson, 2003), 176.

# 16

## MOSES IN TAYMA

### DEIFICATION

*"... you shall serve as God for him (Aaron)"*
Exod 4:16

*"I have made you like a God to Pharaoh."*
Exod 7:1

Nebuchadnezzar, the ruler of the whole world, to whom even the wild animals paid obedience, his pet was a lion with a snake coiled about its neck, did not escape punishment for his sins. He was chastised as none before him. He whom fear of God had at first held back from a war against Jerusalem, and who had to be dragged forcibly, as he sat on his horse, to the Holy of Holies by the archangel Michael, he later became so arrogant that he thought himself a god, and cherished the plan of enveloping himself in a cloud, so that he might live apart from men. A heavenly voice resounded: "O thou wicked man, son of a wicked man, and descendant of Nimrod the wicked, who incited the world to rebel against God! Behold, the days of the years of a man are threescore years and ten, or perhaps by reason of strength fourscore years. It takes five hundred years to traverse the distance of the earth from the first heaven, and as long a time to penetrate from the bottom to the top of the first heaven, and not less are the distances from one of the seven heavens to the next. How, then, canst thou speak of ascending like unto the Most High 'above the heights of the clouds'?" For this transgression of deeming himself more than a man, he was punished by being made to live for some time as a beast among beasts, treated by them as though he were one of them. ... For forty days he led this life. As far down as his navel he had the appearance of an ox, and the lower part of his body resembled that of a lion. Like an ox he ate grass, and like a lion he attacked a curious crowd, but Daniel spent his time in prayer, entreating that the seven years of this brutish life allotted to Nebuchadnezzar might be reduced to seven months. His prayer was granted. At the end of forty days reason returned to the king, the next forty days he passed in weeping bitterly over his sins, and in the interval that remained to complete the seven months he again lived the life of a beast."[1]

The world of biblical interpretation is gradually approaching a consensus that Daniel's "Nebuchadnezzar," at least the one who is given this dreadful fate, *is* the last King of Babylon, Nabonidus.[2] After researching the Song of Solomon, there is no doubt for me.[3]

In Song 4:8, the king takes Nitocris, symbolically, to the heights of Lebanon, where he makes them *both* demi-gods; they look down upon their people, as though they are "Baal" and "Lady" of the mountain,[4] though the actual divine names are not provided. Nitocris, I argue, would only have gone along with this plan to placate the king because, at this juncture in the Song's narrative, she is in a desperate situation. The verse seems to point to Nabonidus' desire for apotheosis. It is also evident that Nabonidus, whilst

---

[1] Louis Ginzberg, *Legends of the Jews* (1909), www.sefaria.org, here, Book 10 (The Exile): "Nebuchadnezzar a Beast."

[2] E.g., see A. M. Davis Bledsoe, "The Identity of the 'Mad King' of Daniel 4 in Light of Ancient Near Eastern Sources," *CS* 33 (2012): 743-58; John Joseph Collins and Adela Yarbro Collins, *Daniel: A Commentary on the Book of Daniel* (United States: Fortress Press, 1993), 217. The argument on authorship of Daniel suggests Chapters 1 through 6 are far earlier than those of 7-12 and, according to Collins, have been deemed most likely applicable to the reign of Nabonidus since the discovery of the Prayer of Nabonidus (DSS) in 1854.

[3] Tyson, 50. I suggest in *She Brought* that the names of Nebuchadnezzar and Belshazzar are pseudonyms that both allow for the veracity of the exile experience *and* maintain the anonymity of Nabonidus. Belshazzar is not, historically, in Babylon when it falls. The passage in Daniel is far less confusing when you see this tactic behind its construction.

[4] Tyson, 103-7.

King, erects statues of himself in various temples and boasts that worshippers "kissed his feet," i.e., as they would a cultic statue of a deity.[5]

Look at the significant elements of this excerpt from the *Legends of the Jews* (above):

★ *The king's pet is a lion with a snake coiled around its neck*: Solomon has lions protecting his throne; Moses uses a coiled snake on a staff.

★ *Nebuchadnezzar was never "chastised"*; Nabonidus was, posthumously.

★ *Jerusalem is mentioned in a way that suggests he would have been expected to be at war with the city* ... but he wasn't. In Dan 5:3, Nabonidus makes a mockery of the Jews, so if he does offer himself as their escort back to Jerusalem, it might seem odd to some.

★ *He has to be dragged to the temple*: Nabonidus is considered negligent toward his routine temple duties.

★ *He becomes arrogant*: Nabonidus is accused of being proud and arrogant (in the VA and in the Song).

★ *A plan to envelop himself in a cloud*: In the Song, Nabonidus is deified atop a mountain; as Moses, he goes up a mountain shrouded in a cloud.

★ *Inciting the world to rebel against God*: Nabonidus' preference for Sîn is considered a rebellion, as the pseudonym "Mered" suggests.[6]

★ *Fourscore years (by reason of strength)*: why make this statement at all, unless his age and extraordinary fitness is significant? Nabonidus is in his sixties when he becomes King; as Moses, he is 80-plus; his mother dies a centenarian, so longevity is in the blood.[7]

★ *Deemed himself more than a man*: In the Song of Solomon, Nabonidus deifies himself and Nitocris, and he does begin to show signs of hubris and arrogance as Moses.

★ *He serves penance for seven years* (in reference to Daniel's curse). This is the length of time Nabonidus lives in Tayma with Nitocris; their marriage is stormy and destructive.

---

[5] Tyson, 143-4; Nab 3, v 1-7.

[6] Tyson, 22-3.

[7] "... Nabonidus was (by the standards of the time) quite old when he became king" (W&N, 3, n.19); however, I suggest a man in his fifties might be considered as 'getting on'.

✮ *His reason does return to him temporarily* (i.e., on his return to Babylon, perhaps) but then he loses it again (on the exodus?). This is reminiscent of the Ashmedai myth.[8]

✮ *He weeps over his sins.* This is an allusion to Solomon and Ecclesiastes, i.e., written long after the Song of Solomon.[9]

Then there is:

> How you have fallen from heaven, O Day Star, son of Dawn! How you are cut down to the ground, you who laid the nations low! You said in your heart, "I will ascend to heaven; I will raise my throne above the stars of God; I will sit on the mount of assembly, on the heights of Zaphon; I will ascend to the tops of the clouds; I will make myself like the Most High."
>
> Isa 14:12-14

Isaiah's "taunt against the king of Babylon" (14:4) is another direct allusion to the assumed deification of Nabonidus. The epithet of "Dawn" is given to the deceased pharaoh in PT utterance 306;[10] it relates to his solar aspect. With the consistent allusion to Nabonidus being the "double" of Pharaoh, and the added mention of "Zaphon," i.e., Tahpanhes, the sanctuary where Ahmose's "bones" might have been hidden, does seem to be a sarcastic reference to Nabonidus' apparent self-deification, in terms of him emulating Ahmose III.

So, although I think we can be fairly certain that Nabonidus, at some point, deifies himself, I have a suspicion the later accounts of this are a little jumbled and probably exaggerated, conflating what is supposedly seen to be happening at Sinai with what was a sex-drug-induced aberration during the difficult years at Tayma.[11] To me, seeing things from Nabonidus' perspective, rather than from a Jewish or Christian perspective, I can appreciate how he would have ancient precedents in mind (something that defines his very character, as anyone studying Nabonidus will concur), such as the flamboyant Shulgi, the second Sumerian king of the Ur III Dynasty (ca. 2112-2004 BCE), whose lengthy self-proclamations of divinity are

---

[8] Tyson, 28-9.

[9] Tyson, 29.

[10] Edward P. Butler, "Soped," Henadology: Philosophy and Theology, https: //henadology.wordpress.com.

[11] For a detailed analysis of early Mesopotamian royal deification, see Audrey Pitts, "The Cult of the Deified King in Ur III Mesopotamia" (PhD Diss., 2015, Harvard University, Graduate School of Arts & Sciences). Also, Tyson, 103-7.

something to behold (ETCSL 2.4.2.01). The fact that other than a brief allusion in the Song of Solomon, there is no inscription from the reign of Nabonidus (as yet discovered), that represents him as anything but a king and loyal worshipper of deities, does seem to support the theory that his momentary dabble in apotheosis was an aberration. He did not continue with that notion after he returned to Babylonia from Tayma.

I think the events at Sinai are not mis*interpreted*, as the Osirian themes are so consistently represented, but intentionally mis*represented*, e.g., especially given the two biblical quotations, above, which undoubtedly fuelled suspicions, even though in the original Hebrew, they seem less controversial ("God" is rendered *elohim* in both, i.e., "the gods"; Moses becomes "like the gods," which, ironically, is exactly how we wishes to be remembered, for to be "like the gods" one has to acquire wisdom).[12] Recall that I claim Exodus and Numbers are generally anti-Nabonidus texts; the theophany, the overly dramatic representation of Moses' interactions with the deity atop the mountain are surreptitiously geared toward proving he was pursuing his own deification once again. The authors *know* the man; they know of his past; they want to discredit him so that there is no hope of him being allowed into the Promised Land. All of this, of course, must be seen to be the will of God. The Egyptian element must be downplayed, though without it, Nabonidus would never have bothered to do any of this, I am certain.

I don't see self-deification in these scenes. I see a man who is genuinely determined to find answers to his deep-rooted questions about the universe. He seeks arcane wisdom from Nitocris; he converses with learned individuals on matters of philosophy and religion; he wants to know the great universal Truths. He is easily swayed by those with wisdom to offer and he throws himself headlong into each new mystery, like an overly keen student. He is a man at odds with himself; according to his publicity a violent tyrant, according to his depiction in the HB full of self-aggrandisement, but between the lines, and even in his own words, he is also a sophist.

If anything, I see more of a *priestly* identification for Moses, i.e., given the Osirian nature of much of what transpires in the account of his acquiring "Joseph's bones," the nature of the tabernacle, the ark, and his face-to-face audiences with the deity, it seems he is, rather, attempting to emulate Pharaoh as the ultimate High Priest who has almost exclusive access to the divine. In discussing the Osirian temple at Abydos, Dungen describes the priestly initiation as a form of "sacerdotal deification," or a consecration of the initiate's "own priestly state."[13]

---

[12] In the Epic of Gilgamesh, Enkidu learns about Life from a devotee of Ishtar, and she says to him: "You are wise, Enkidu, and now you have become like a god" (*The Epic of Gilgamesh*, N. K. Sanders, trans., revised ed. [London: Penguin, 1972], 65).

[13] Wim van den Dungen, "Egyptian Initiation," www.sofiatopia.org.

As Budge says:

> To possess the knowledge of the secret names of God, and those of the gods, and of things animate and inanimate, was the magician's chief object in life, and his desire to acquire it is easy to understand ; for, according to the belief of the period, it made him master of all the powers in this world.[14]

As Nabonidus' deity, "I AM" is non-sectarian, accommodating all possible options, and this is the name he relays to the group, it might appear that he is withholding information for his own advancement, i.e., exploiting this secret intimacy with the intention of discovering the true identity of the deity (as Isis did with Re). From my perspective as a 21st Century researcher, I see this as Nabonidus attempting to keep everyone placated; it is *his* name for *his* new god, so in reality, he already has the power of the magician (magi), hence his association with Thoth in later legend.

> *(...), but into the divine book,*
> *I have been initiated.*
> *Of Thoth, I have seen glory,*
> *and among mystery, I introduced myself.*
> Statue of Amenhotep, son of Hapu[15]

Nabonidus' apparent fascination with Pharaoh is seen as early on as the Song of Solomon; now he has risked life and limb to locate and steal his "bones"; he has created a suitably ostentatious and regal *aron* to convey them through the desert, and a tabernacle to emulate the Osirian cave. He conflates the deities but he usurps the position of Pharaoh in a cosmological context (not a political one). Thus, as the Moon, he finally unites with the Sun, (Ahmose) in the makeshift Duat, and in that sense, earns himself an everlasting "life," for here we are, thousands of years later, keeping his memory alive (when the early Jewish authors had hoped to avoid this; perhaps his own protective serpent worked, too, in the darkness of those millennia).

In the Coffin Texts (CT) there are spells for becoming deified, for becoming one-with-Re, for example: "*Ascending to the sky, going aboard the Barque of Re, and becoming a living god*: ... make a way for me in the darkness, the chaos, in the Abyss and in the gloom."[16]

Perhaps it is via this forty-day initiation and the re-enactment of the

[14] E. A. Wallace Budge, *Osiris and the Egyptian Resurrection, Vol. 2* (London: Warner, 1911), 88.

[15] Dungen, "Egyptian Initiation," www.sofiatopia.org.

[16] R. O. Faulkner, *The Ancient Egyptian Coffin Texts, Vol. 1, Spells 1-354* (Warminster, UK: Aris & Phillips, 1973), CT 76.

Duat journey of Re that Nabonidus believes he will find what he most desires, i.e., to *know* God, not to *be* God.

An essential element in this initiation was justification and the declaration that this had happened, so the adept was called a *"maa(t) kheru"* or "True of Voice," a title ordinarily only given to the deceased after a favourable judgement of the balance (in the "Hall of Maat").[17]

In the Song, whilst making her poppet of Nabonidus (Song 5:10-16), Nitocris alludes to this concept by calling the king's voice "sweet," suggesting he is *maa(t) kheru* She has *just* initiated him into her secret religion, the Elixir Rubeus, and probably the Osirian myths. It is, however, an ironic, or rather, an intentionally misleading attribution, for he turns out to be nothing of the sort.

There are two scenes in which one might suggest Moses is *acting* like a god, i.e., in Num 13:16, he takes it upon himself to confer a commission name, normally a divine prerogative. Joshua is originally "Hoshea," i.e., his name shifts from meaning "salvation" to "Yah saves"; this may be an attempted accusation of Nabonidus' apotheosis, or simply an example of his hubris in thinking he doesn't need to get God's permission. In Num 20:10 he brazenly suggests he and Aaron can "bring water" for the people (from the "stone"), thereby assuming divine powers rather than attributing the deed to God. Is this enough to suggest he thinks he *is* a god? No, I don't think so, especially when you can see what is happening, historically, in the scenes, i.e., on a very human level. He just has a bad habit of revealing his hubris.

Also, we must recall Joseph's Egyptian name, "Zaphenath-paneah" includes the notion of "shining, radiating light," i.e., a theophany. Moses, in the Osirian perspective, represents Osiris, the Moon, awaiting the union with the Sun, i.e., Ahmose III, whose avatar in the tale is Joseph (or his bones). Joseph's bones are thus a source of divine light.

When Moses descends from his communion with "I AM" (Exod 34:29-35), his face is visibly flushed (transformed) from the heat of the ceremonial furnaces/rituals, and the people pull away from him in fear. Over the millennia this has often been interpreted to mean Moses is reflecting God's shekinah, his "glory," etc., which is too much for the people to witness, so he covers his face when not in the tent of meeting. I think this is plausible, but only part of the actual meaning of this scene. In fact, this may be one of the most significant moments in the entire book of Exodus, as far as Nabonidus is concerned.

In the Assyrian texts, there is something called a/the *melammu*:

---

[17] Dungen, "Egyptian Initiation."

It denotes a characteristic attribute of the gods consisting in a dazzling aureole or nimbus which surrounds the divinity. This radiance is shared by everything endowed with divine power or sanctified by divine presence: the holy weapons and symbols of the gods as well as their chapels and temples have all such a *melammu*. It may be noted that this supernatural glamour could be granted by the principal divinities and withdrawn again ....

The king as representative and likeness ... of the gods, also has such an aura which constitutes the divine legitimation of his royalty. This *melammu* is bestowed upon him when he becomes king ....[18]

So, we may consider that Moses, i.e., Nabonidus, the already self-deified king, is depicted as descending from the mesa displaying his divinely granted *melammu* (much as tradition holds), but there are other aspects of the *melammu* that might have a bearing here. For instance, according to Oppenheim, the *melammu* is usually mentioned in connection with an article of clothing, or a type of headwear, i.e., just as we see with Moses wearing a veil. In the Near Eastern texts, this article of clothing is understood to be a "mask"; it is often used by demons, making them "unrecognizable," and thereby inspiring fear/terror in those who encounter them.[19] This is the familiar seed of doubt, the little niggling negativity in the subtext that must be addressed; it is there for a reason. This, I suggest, is the moment Nabonidus is most likely to be misinterpreted as attempting to become deified (by those who not know of his previous attempt). I think those with him at Sinai are beginning to sense his rather self-centred and controlling handling of the entire situation, i.e., this is *his* plan, *his* deity, *his* new little kingdom.

Interestingly, early Midrash expounded the possibility that Moses was, or was seen to be a *king*; he was granted two signs of kingship on Sinai, i.e., a crown and a special garment (with supernatural powers), i.e., with "glory and majesty."[20] "Midrashic literature interprets the radiance of Moses' face as evidence of his wearing a crown."[21] Does this not echo the notion of the *melammu* and the item of clothing/veil/mask? For such similarities to span the thousand-odd years between Nabonidus at Sinai and the Midrash authors suggests there might be something to this notion, i.e., is this the moment in Nabonidus' own journey when he makes himself, for all intents and purposes, "King of Israel"? As Solomon, he is said to reign "in Jerusalem" (at Tayma) for forty years (1 Kgs 11:42); as Moses, he "leads"

---

[18] A. L. Oppenheim, "Akkadian Pul(u)ḫ(t)u and Melammu," *JAOS* 63.1 (1943): 31-4, here, 31. The nimbus is first represented visually in the 7th Century BCE.

[19] Oppenheim, 32.

[20] Rimon Kasher, "The Mythological Figure of Moses in Light of Some Unpublished Midrashic Fragments," *JQR* 88.1/2 (1997): 19-42, here 28-31.

[21] Kasher, 30.

the Israelites for forty years.

Nabonidus acts the king, he still wants everything his own way, and now he is symbolically transformed into the demon-in-divine-clothing. Recall that this scenario of the veil is just before the cleft of the rock pericope, and the making of the second set of tablets. As Moses he has already demonstrated his shortness of temper and his violence; he not only smashes the original tablets in a fit of pique, but supposedly orders families to slaughter their own kin for worshipping the golden calf. He is becoming dangerous, not deified.

From Nabonidus' own Osirian perspective, however, he enters the tent of meeting as the (human, i.e., priestly) avatar of Osiris, to merge, symbolically, with the Sun-god, represented by Joseph's bones. A very small detail confirms this: Joshua (i.e., Belshazzar) remains in the tent whenever Moses leaves (Exod 33:11); Osiris *never* leaves his subterranean cavern in the darkness of the Duat, i.e., there must always be an avatar of Osiris within the tent of meeting, at least during this initial Duat-reconstruction phase. As the high priest is later ascribed a deputy to take his place if he is unable to minister in the Holy of Holies,[22] so Joshua (Belshazzar) is granted the role of proxy while Moses takes a break.

Nabonidus becomes one with Osiris, with Re, and thus acquires the status of Ahmose, Pharaoh and High Priest (in his own mind). In Eccl 8:1, "Solomon" (assumed) is pondering on the concept of "wisdom":

> …who knows the interpretation of a thing?
> Wisdom makes one's face shine,
> And …one's countenance is changed.

The entire process for Nabonidus has been for this very reason; he *seeks* wisdom, the more arcane and restricted the better. As Solomon (in 1 Kgs 3:8-9), Nabonidus prays for wisdom; in the Song of Solomon he finds his Egyptian wife is a source of profound cosmic secrets. This experiencing of the divine atop the mesa is the pinnacle for him. When his face shines, he is filled with God-given wisdom (hubris again), but this wisdom, being so deeply rooted in Osirian rituals, is meant to be kept secret. The veil may be a token of this concealment by Nabonidus, who keeps secret what is meant to be secret. This is then perceived by the people as something sinister.

Also worth mentioning is the fact that the "idea of radiance and sparkling is always implied when the *melammu* is mentioned" and that even in the case of demons, this is an astronomical reference, i.e., they are equated to twinkling (mischievous) stars.[23] In Moses' case, the idea that he somehow

---

[22] E.g., Mishneh Torah, Kelei haMikdash 4:7-10 on Leviticus 21.
[23] Oppenheim, 34, n. 8.

sprouts "horns," a confusion regarding the rays of light that supposedly shine from his face, is an ancient one, best exemplified by Michelangelo's statue of Moses holding the tablets.[24] In the Babylonian astronomical Series *Enuma Anu Enlil*, however, "the astronomer is advised: If the sun's horn (*si*) fades and the moon is dark, then (explanation:) in the evening watch, the moon is having an eclipse (and in this context,) *si* means 'horn', *si* means 'shine' ...."[25]

So, there is a known connection between the "shining" and the "horn" of the Sun; and there is also a Mesopotamian connection between the Moon and horns, for Sîn has long been identified as the celestial bull, his young crescent form being represented as bull's horns. Moses represents Sîn, the Moon of the triad, the Moon of Osiris, in the Sun-Moon conflation ritual (the moment of the "passing" of God in Exod 33:19-34:8) atop the mesa. Perhaps the "horns"/"shining" ambiguity is, indeed, intentional, for it is only via an eclipse (the melding of Sun and Moon) that the horn(s) of the Sun *can* be seen. Thus, Moses' shining face becomes a subtle astronomical allusion to this symbolic solar-lunar conjunction.

> *Glory be to Thee, oh Ra, Supreme Power,*
> *Shining Horn, Pillar of the West, He of the darkened looks when tired.*
> *Thou art the forms of Shining Horn.*
> Great Litany of Ra (53)[26]

If the Hebrew scribes know of Nabonidus' motivation, his fascination with the Egyptian mysteries, which they clearly seem to, it may be that the constant allusions to subtle concepts like this in their depiction of what ensues during the exodus, lost on the masses, are seen as evidence of his aspirations for apotheosis. I think they would have had enough knowledge of the basics as part of their sacerdotal training (just as they supposedly learn magic in order to judge against magicians).[27]

Modern archaeological finds can shed some light on this, though even today the jury is out concerning whether or not Nabonidus *depicts* himself as a deity or not. I will suggest he does not, at least not post-539 BCE. The quotations: "... you shall serve as God for him" (Exod 4:16) and "I have

---

[24] For this debate see William H. Propp, "The Skin of Moses' Face: Transfigured or Disfigured?" *CBQ* 49.3 (1987): 375-86.

[25] Seth L. Sanders, "Old Light on Moses' Shining Face," *VT* 52.3 (2002): 400-6, here 403.

[26] Luigi Tripani, The God Ra: Iconography (With all the Forms and Names from the 'Litany of Ra') (Amentet Neferet: 2015), here 109.

[27] There is a fascinating body of references to the "Sky Ladder (Stairway)" in the Coffin Texts (e.g., Spells 21; 62; 297 especially); it is a means of attaining deification by accessing the realm of the gods. In Gen 28:10-28, Jacob has a vision/dream of the ladder/stairway to heaven as a portal to the heavenly realm.

made you like a God to Pharaoh" (Exod 7:1) declare Nabonidus (Moses) to be acting *like* a god, serving in the place of a god (i.e., he is granted the authority of a god), not that he *is* one. Admittedly, Nabonidus' own appreciation for this delineation becomes questionable as the narrative continues, but I think his self-importance, his daring to challenge the deity, and his testing of his powers can all be put down to hubris, not apotheosis.

# TAYMA STONE

Discovered in the Tayma oasis by Charles M. Doughty in 1876, the Tayma Stone tells how the priest Salmshezib, son of Pet-Osiri (another Osirian link?) introduced a new deity, "Salm of Hagam," into the pantheon at Tayma. A hereditary priesthood was inaugurated.

The figure on the side of the stele employs the same iconography as Nabonidus, i.e., he is standing; wears a coned hat and a long robe; he holds a staff in one hand "surmounted by a prominent feature"[28]; the other hand is stretched out; a winged disk is above. This image is referred to as "Salm," i.e., "Image"; Salmshezib's name evokes the deity's, i.e., "Oh, [divine] Image, save me."[29]

J. Rohmer states: "The text is dated to the 22nd year of a king, whose name has unfortunately been erased. Although the iconography obviously bears a strong Neo-Babylonian imprint, a date under Nabonidus, who reigned only for 17 years (556-539 BCE), is impossible."[30] This inscription may pertain to Nabonidus as the ruler *of Tayma*; his reign as King of Babylon ended in 539 BCE, but if there *was* a deal with Cyrus, that included Nabonidus' return to Tayma, he would have made sure it was as the local King, not merely a resident or even governor (it would be this period in which he becomes the exceedingly wealthy "King Solomon"). Belshazzar was initially sent back to Tayma (having left Babylonia surreptitiously as "Lot") to keep things ticking over whilst Nabonidus made his journey through Canaan with the Jews (as "Abraham"), joining his father from time to time, such as when the two went after their stolen goods. If we take 538

---

[28] C. J. Gadd, "The Harran Inscriptions of Nabonidus," *AS* 8 (1958): 35-92, here 41.

[29] Gadd, "Harran," 41.

[30] J. Rohmer, "The Political History of North-west Arabia from the 6th to the 1st Century BCE: New Insights from Dadān, Ḥegrā and Taymā'," in *The Archaeology of the Arabian Peninsula 2: Connecting the Evidence*, Proceedings of the International Workshop held at the 10th International Congress on the Archaeology of the Ancient Near East in Vienna on April 25, 2016, OREA 19, Marta Luciani, ed. (Vienna: Austrian Academy of Sciences Press, 2021), 179-98, here 186.

to be the first year of Nabonidus,' reign as King of Tayma, 22 years later would be 516 BCE, some six years or so after the start of the Sinai saga that began in 522, when he returned to Egypt to seek out "Joseph's bones." I think there are too many 'coincidences' for this *not* to be Nabonidus' stela/baetyl.

## Salm

Scholars have translated and interpreted the Tayma Stone for many years, with some identifying the deity as lunar god, and others a solar god.[31] I think, in this instance, it is neither.

One of the leading authorities on the deity Salm is Stephanie Dalley. In her first paper on the Tayma Stone's inscription, she explains that the word *salmu* is an Akkadian word meaning "image, statue, representation"; the adjectival homonym means "black, dark."[32] The Akkadian deity Salmu is attested from the second millennium BCE, as a name for the Sun god Shamash, but this is deemed a rare title that faded from use after the fall of Nineveh in 612 BCE until, that is, something sparked an interest in the name in the region of Tayma/Dadan, where stone inscriptions bearing the name have been found. Dalley suggests this might be evidence of a Northwestern Arabian origin for the solar deity.[33]

Dalley also posits that the name "Salm" might be a shortened version of Salmu-sari, which means "Salmu of the king," i.e., a title used by a legal representative of the deity in the context of witnessing an oath. Moses is twice involved in an oath-taking situation, i.e., once in the covenant of salt, and once in the covenant at Sinai, but it is the "representative" aspect we need to note. For Nabonidus, a man who is used to and enjoys getting his own way, who is depicted throughout Exodus/Numbers as being somewhat of an authoritarian, such an inscription demanding loyalty and respect to him as this divine agent may suffice as an explanation for the Tayma Stone's unique content. This aspect of Dalley's argument I fully accept.

In a later paper, Dalley provides further evidence for the solar aspect of Salm, and for the winged-disk emblem, which she says is also strongly linked to the taking of oaths of loyalty (to either the ruler or the depicted

---

[31] Paul-Alain Beaulieu, *The Reign of Nabonidus, King of Babylon 556-339 B.C.* (New Haven: Yale University Press, 1989), 177.

[32] Stephanie Dalley, "Stelae from Teima and the God Ṣlm (Ṣalmu)," *PSAS* 15 (1985): 27-33, here, 28.

[33] Dalley, "Stellae from Taima," 28-9.

deity).[34] While I concur that the solar aspect of "I AM" is vital to our comprehension of that deity, I argue that it is but one aspect of it, not its entire nature.

Gadd's original interpretation that Nabonidus is presenting himself as the deity Salm is deemed "eliminated" by Dalley[35] but he wasn't the only one to suggest the Babylonian king *had* deified himself; Beaulieu also claimed it might be Nabonidus.[36] But the notion seems hard for people to accept, as the general opinion is that Babylonian kings simply *weren't* deified:

> It is difficult to accept the suggestion of Beaulieu that the worshipping of Salm is the same as that of the divine king, Nabonidus .... The deity Salmu was known before the time of Nabonidus.[37]

Assyrian and Babylonian religious beliefs had been averse to deification of living rulers for the millennium preceding the reign of Nabonidus.[38] Neo-Babylonian religious protocol was, we know, opposed to the supremacy of Sîn over Marduk, to the introduction of hybrid idols, and to a king who did not perform the rites and rituals expected of him, yet Nabonidus ripped up the rule book and did all this anyway. Why would he stop there, especially if given the relative freedom to do as he wished once out of Babylonia and away from those who would thwart him? The Song of Solomon depicts Nabonidus performing *some* sort of deification ritual with Nitocris, during his stay in Tayma, and this perception is carried through to the Persian propaganda and the post-biblical legends.

Both Esarhaddon (680-669 BCE) and Ashurbanipal (669-630 BCE) were referred to as "the very image (*salmu*) of Shamash" and "Bel" respectively; they were considered the essence of the deity,[39] a representative on earth. Similarly, solar affiliations are not unheard of, i.e., "Ashurnaṣirpal II boasted that 'his protection was spread like the sun's rays over his land' and Adad-nirari II, Tukulti-Ninurta II, Ashurnaṣirpal II,

---

[34] Stephanie Dalley, "The God Salmu and the Winged Disk," *Iraq* 48 (1986): 85-101, here 99.

[35] Dalley, "The God Salmu," 86.

[36] Beaulieu, *Reign of Nabonidus*, 176-8.

[37] Mohammed Maraqten, "The Aramaic Pantheon of Tayma'," *AAE* 7 (1996): 17-31, here 19.

[38] Beaulieu, *Reign of Nabonidus*, 176.

[39] E. Frahm, "Rising suns and falling stars: Assyrian kings and the cosmos," in J.A. Hill et al., eds., *Experiencing Power, Generating Authority: Cosmos, Politics and the Ideology of Kingship in Ancient Egypt and Mesopotamia* (Philadelphia: University of Pennsylvania Press, 2013): 97-120, here 102.

Shalmaneser III, and Esarhaddon all claimed to be 'the sun of all the people'."[40] The Sun god "was occasionally called *(d)salmu* in the ancient Near East; in a passage from the lexical list ḪAR-gud, this very name is associated with Saturn, the planetary avatar of the sun," i.e., the "black star."[41] In the solar context of Moses' communion with "I AM," the element of darkness is highly significant, as it emphasises the nocturnal journey of the Sun and its rebirth.

The "association of Saturn with the Sun is explained folk etymologically by a pun based on the homophony of *salmu* 'black' and *salmu* 'statue', the latter term also being an acknowledged epithet of the Sun or even of the symbol of the winged disk."[42] It is just this sort of wordplay that we see the early authors of the HB, and even Nabonidus himself employing to create new meaning (e.g., on the cylinder depicting the dedication of his daughter Ennigaldi to Sîn, he plays with the concept of the "eclipse"[43]).[44]

In Ugaritic and Akkadian personal names, however, the term *salmu* "has nothing to do with the god Salmu"; "The only Aramaic references for *slm* are from North Arabia, namely from Tayma'…."; interestingly, the Neo-Assyrian version of Salm is heavily rooted in Harran.[45]

That adjectival *salmu* means "dark, black" is even more intriguing, as the *Concise Akkadian Dictionary* includes in its translation "black-haired [*salmat qaqqadi*]."[46] The Sumerians/Babylonians call themselves the "black-headed" people, due to their pure black hair (e.g., ETCSL 1.7.4, 10-14: "After An, Enlil, Enki and Ninhursag had fashioned the black-headed people").[47]

This is an excerpt from an incantation performed during the

---

[40] Frahm, 100.

[41] Frahm, 114-15.

[42] Marinus Anthony van der Sluijs-Seongnam and Peter James, "Saturn as the 'Sun of Night' in Ancient Near Eastern Tradition," *AOr* 31/2 (2013): 279-321, here 280; 294, www.ub.edu/ipoa/wp-content/uploads/2021/08/20132AuOrVander Sluijs.pdf.

[43] Tyson, 154-7.

[44] Jeremy Black, Andrew George, Nicholas Postgate, eds., *A Concise Dictionary of Akkadian*, (Weisbaden: Harrassowitz Verlag, 2000), 295: "…these word-plays only worked because Saturn's black colour was presupposed; it did not derive from them – black hardly suggests a solar quality." Ironically, in modern astrophysics, the Sun is called the "blackest" object in the solar system because it reflects no light.

[45] Maraqten, 20.

[46] Black, 332-3.

[47] Also, Nab 1, ii 12-16: "the black-headed (people), all humankind." This suggests that humanity as a whole bore this epithet but the Sumerians/Babylonians saw themselves as the centre of life on earth, so it really is an expression of how they perceived themselves, as they must have encountered fairer-haired peoples.

ritualistic production of a divine image from the hide and tendons of a sacrificed bull:

> You, choice bull, are the creation/product of the great gods.
> You were created and are being brought forward for the work of the great gods.
> … In the heights of the heavens your *salmu* is treated as a supreme divine office (lit. rite of Anu-ship).
> … As for that *salmu*, its assigned fate is with the gods, his brothers.[48]

Lenzi goes on to explain that in "making this celestial connection and assertion of rank for the *salmu*, the incantation makes the *salmu* (bull and image) worthy of (or 'suitable for') divinity."[49] It does not imply, *ipso facto*, deification.

The stele's *salm*, then, might represent Nabonidus as the "image" (i.e., Dalley's "representative") of the universal "I AM" (the nebulous deity who takes no specific name or form),[50] just as later, the high priest would become the representative on earth of the divine entity that is hidden in the Holy of Holies. One would not say the High Priest *is* the deity, even when communing with it in the privacy of the sacred space. If we think more along the lines of Ahmose, or any other pharaoh, who is accepted as the proxy of Amun, who is given the authority and status of that deity *on earth*, even though everyone knows he is human, he cannot perform miracles, and does not return to the heavens intermittently, that is more along the lines of what Nabonidus is wanting to express, I think.

Therefore, I cannot agree that the reference to *salm* on the Tayma Stone suggests a connection to Nabonidus' *own* deification (which originally probably compared to a demi-godship, like Tammuz, or Gilgamesh). The two are distinct. *Salm* is the "image" of the earthly (human) representation of the deity, just as Esarhaddon and Ashurbanipal were the *salm* of Shamash and Baal. Nabonidus is "Salm" but "Salm" is not the god.

On the mesa, Nabonidus is the one who interacts with "I AM"; he is the one who later intercedes on behalf of the people. It makes sense that he

---

[48] Alan Lenzi, "Material, Constellation, Image, God: The Fate of the Chosen Bull According to kar 50 and Duplicates," in *The Scaffolding of Our Thoughts: Essays on Assyriology and the History of Science in Honor of Francesca Rochberg,* C. Jay Crisostomo, et al., eds., (Leiden: Brill, 2018), 58-96, here 68-9.

[49] Lenzi, 79 and n. 91.

[50] Exod 6:1-9 seems to me to be a later addendum to rationalise the shift in terminology for this deity; if Moses had truly been raised an Egyptian, he would probably not know of the legends of Abraham, Isaac, and Jacob. If Abraham is Nabonidus, there would be no time for such legends to have been formed (like mentioning the "Ishmaelites" during the supposed lifetime of Ishmael).

promote himself as this intermediary, as the one to whom others will say "Salm, protect/save me"; this does not necessitate Nabonidus identifying *as* the deity (and this might link back to the scene with Jethro and the judges in Exodus 18, i.e., Nabonidus originally takes it upon himself to be the *only* intermediary but others want that role, too, providing further rationale for the disgruntled attitude of Korah).

As the King of Babylon, Nabonidus' stelae, cylinders, and rock inscriptions are relatively prolific; as "Abraham" he sets up baetyls on his journey. It would be the natural thing to do at Tayma, too.

## Salmshezib the Priest

The other human to appear on the Tayma stele is the priest called "Salmshezib," i.e., "Salm save me,"[51] or "Salm has saved."[52] Clearly, there may be many people with "deity has saved me" names, but consider for a moment that if this object can be attributed to Nabonidus, this priest may, if not *should*, be someone close to him; someone he trusts. I think there is a person who would fit the bill, given the etymology in the narratives we are following, i.e., Phinehas.

Phinehas' iconic actions at "Peor" (Num 25:6-13; discussed in Chapter 18) earn him special commendation from God: "I hereby grant him my covenant of peace. It shall be for him and his descendants … a covenant of perpetual priesthood …." The etymology of "Phinehas" is based on the serpent/metallurgical themes of the priestly Qenites, but his role as saviour lies in the fact that he is said to thwart God's original plan to destroy ("consume") the Israelites. Phinehas, however, is only mentioned in Exodus in the genealogy list I claim is a later addendum (Exod 6:14-25), meaning someone thought it necessary to provide Phinehas (of Numbers) with a provenance. By the time the book of Joshua is written, Phinehas is "*the* priest."

Looking at Josh 24:19-28, we see that Joshua (whom I considered first, as his name *means* "Yah saves") is following in his father's footsteps by erecting a stone/stele as a "witness" to the covenant, i.e., to "all the words of the Lord"—in other words, it stands as a *salm* of/for Yahweh. It represents, embodies, symbolises the essence of Yahweh, without being a likeness of Yahweh.

I can envision a situation, therefore, where such a stele/stone is set up at Tayma, i.e., as a "witness" to the new priesthood, the new covenant with the temple/priests at Tayma, and Nabonidus' role as intermediary.

---

[51] C. J. Gadd, "The Harran Inscriptions of Nabonidus," *AS* 8 (1958): 35-92, here 41.

[52] Beaulieu, *Reign of Nabonidus*, 176.

"Phinehas" is thus, potentially, Salmshezib, the first serving priest of the new order (with Nabonidus as the high priest at first).

## Salm of Hagam

This leads us into a potential explanation for the name given to the new deity welcomed into the pantheon at Tayma: Salm of Hagam (*slm zy hgm*). If the king depicted on the stele *is* Nabonidus, Hagam would not be simply a town somewhere, as is generally supposed (especially in Yemen,[53] where he never went, as far as we know; it is possible, however, as there are many lacunae in the historical record, and toponyms that have yet to be identified, geographically) but a reference to Nabonidus himself. In Arabic, "*hagam*" means "bleed" and "*hagāma*" means "bleeding."[54] Put this together with Salm having the allusion to "dark-haired," and we might be looking at a translation *something* like, "This is the image of the black-headed one who worships bleeding/blood."

I am certain an open-minded Near-Eastern linguist could wrestle even more from these snippets but the fact that "blood" has *any* potential connection is yet further support for my theory that Nabonidus' reputation in Tayma is one based on an addiction to blood. Perhaps he gave the local priests no choice in the matter, i.e., they found him intimidating and just said "Yes" to his demand for formal recognition (but if the priest is Phinehas, supported by the army general Belshazzar, no permission would be needed).

# ROCK INSCRIPTIONS

Amazingly, two Nabonidus rock inscriptions have been discovered at al-Hait, Province of Ha'il, within a decade. The first, recorded by

---

[53] Maraqten, 20.

[54] Captain H. F. S. Amery, *English-Arabic Vocabulary for the Use of Officials in the Anglo-Egyptian Sudan* (Cairo: Intelligence Dept., of the Egyptian Army, 1905), 38. (It can also mean "accuse" [5]; "assail/assault" [22]; "attack" [23]; and "storm" [348]. Each of these could be applied to Nabonidus in a metaphorical sense, as a violent man who attacks, one who is accused and/or accuses, and one who has a symbolic connection with the thunder and lightning on Sinai). Also, "*hagam* (i): to attack," in Walter Lehn and Peter Abboud, *Beginning Cairo Arabic: Preliminary Edition* (Austin: University of Texas, 1965); and "*hagama* - "draw blood (with a cup)" in Wolf Leslau, "Analysis of the Ge'ez Vocabulary: Ge'ez and Cushitic," *RSE* 32 (1988): 59-109, here 105 (listed as a "loanword from Arabic"). It seems to be a word no longer in use.

archaeologists in 2012 shows the king in his usual, iconic stance, i.e., one arm raised, the other holding a long staff (*Fig. 22*).

The crescent Moon (Sîn), the winged disk (Shamash), and the Star (Ishtar), his regular triad, are duly represented, but there is another emblem (above), half destroyed, which is captivating. What could it represent? Hausleiter suggests that "the loop-shaped symbol cannot yet be found among the symbols of Arabia."[55] He also says: "Contrary to all other known representations of King Nabonidus abroad, this text and image seem to include local deities, expressing respect towards them – a rare exception to Babylonian self-understanding."[56] The scene with Abraham and Melchizedek (Gen 14:18-20), where Nabonidus reaches Jerusalem and pays tithes to the local king/priest,[57] demonstrates that living in Arabia has taught the old king how to be a gracious visitor, how to be an alien in a strange land without losing his head. The covenant of salt at Tayma proved this point.

The figure of Nabonidus in these inscriptions, if you did not already know this to be the King of Babylon, might be mistaken for Moses himself, with his signature raised arm and long staff. I warrant this is where the biblical imagery comes from, i.e., the landscape inscriptions from the king's earlier campaigns witnessed first-hand by those on the exodus. Nabonidus himself writes that Marduk gave him a staff that "subdues enemies" (Nab 44, Obv. 7–19),[58] providing a basis for the staff being employed to subdue Pharaoh, but also to beat the rebellious Miriam. He is not given this staff by God; he already has it (Exod 4:2), from when he was King.

*Figure 23: Author's rendition of Nabonidus as he appears in relief (Image: after the drawing by H. Kosak, in Hausleiter, "Rock Relief," 235).*

---

[55] A. Hausleiter and H. Schaudig, "Rock Relief and Cuneiform Inscription of King Nabonidus at al-Ḥā'iṭ (Province of Ḥā'il, Saudi Arabia), Ancient Padakku," *ZOA* 9 (2016): 224-240, here 235, n. 28.

[56] Arnulf Hausleiter, "A New Rock Relief with Cuneiform Inscription of King Nabonidus from al-Ḥā'iṭ (Hausleiter and Schaudig, forthcoming, in collaboration with S. Baier, A. al-Dayel, Kh. al-Ha'iti, M. al-Ha'iti, N. al-Rashidi, and S. al-Rowaisan, ATLAL) ATLAL - *JSAA* 4, www.academia.edu.

[57] This is a standard Babylonian custom, even for royalty (Dougherty, *Nabonidus and Belshazzar*, 87). I think Melchizedek is Jethro (recall that "Jerusalem" is Tayma in the Song of Solomon; the King of Sodom is also present, making the scene undeniably in the Tayma/Khaybar region). This is possibly the 'moment' Nabonidus *introduces* his new deity to the resident priests at Tayma.

[58] Also in Neriglissar 1, i 26-36 (W&N, 37). This seems to be a standard perception of the royal staff.

The more recent inscription (*Fig. 23*, discovered 2021) is yet to be assessed fully but the iconography is better preserved: Now we can see the U-shaped icon is a snake! In fact, it may be that the original inscriptions only had the triad and that after the Sinai years the snake was added. The first inscription does look like the snake is an afterthought, added above for lack of room; the second has the snake sitting slightly higher than the others, so might also be a later addition. Nabonidus would not make new inscriptions after losing his title as King, and with his new god "I AM" that is effectively an amalgamation of all his favourite deities, the serpent serves as its glyph, its icon).

Hausleiter surmises that Nabonidus …

> had to pay homage to the numen loci in the first place. At least, the positioning of the visible rest of the Arabian symbols above the Babylonian ones gives the impression of an 'equating correspondence'. … Contrary to all other known representations of King Nabonidus abroad, this text and image seem to include local deities, expressing respect towards them—a rare exception to Babylonian self-understanding."[59]

Unique indeed but, I suggest, for different reasons.

"Furthermore," Hausleiter continues, "we can read the name of the god Nusku, hinting at more divine names which are however badly eroded (e.g. Ishtar in line 19 ….)."[60] Nusku is the Babylonian god of Fire, son of Sîn. Recall that as "Sheshbazzar," Nabonidus is called the "fire worshipper."

In his analysis of the Harran stele, Gadd describes the staff in Nabonidus' hand (*Fig. 24*) as "bearing many coils, or rings, probably of some shining, reflective metal that emphasizes the worship of Nusku, whose emblem is a lamp, and his epithets include 'light', 'god light', and 'bearer of the shining

*Figure 24: Author's rendition of a press-release photo showing Nabonidus and a serpent motif (Image: Saudi Press Agency; see n. 60).*

sceptre'."[61] Nusku is a messenger to the gods; he is invoked when sacrifices are made and serves as the intermediary between the gods and the people offering the sacrifice. He is also classified as a solar deity, due to his

---

[59] Hausleiter, "A New Rock Relief," 3-4.

[60] Hausleiter, "Rock Relief," 234.

[61] C. J. Gadd, "The Harran Inscriptions of Nabonidus," *AS* 8 (1958): 35-92, here 40-1. Some suggest he is the god of the stylus, also.

association with Fire, and he shares a responsibility with Ea as the protector of humanity.[62]

The rings around Nabonidus' staff (*Fig. 24*) may represent a snake's coils, wrapped around a tree-trunk, as in the Tyre myth; in fact, Gadd does suggest the staff is reminiscent of Assyrian sculptures of the "sacred tree" and the "bands" around its trunk (though he stops short of suggesting serpent iconography).[63] He claims there is no other depiction of a king's stave to compare it to, which means, once again, Nabonidus is doing his own thing. Could this staff be an initial concept, an evolving idea that culminates in the Nehushtan, i.e., the bronze, 'fiery' serpent (i.e., the solar Wadjet), wrapped around the staff, symbolically protecting the people?

Beaulieu states that the Harran stele dates to the period *after* the return of Nabonidus from Tayma,[64] so it is possible the influence of his early encounters with Jehudijah's father, Jethro (i.e., according to the Song of Solomon Jehudijah had been taken into the king's harem during his early days at Tayma, before Nitocris was even introduced

*Figure 25: Ringed staff of Nabonidus (Image: Harran Stele detail, BM 90837).*

in 549 BCE), left a lasting impression on Nabonidus, enough to inspire him to

---

[62] Morris Jastrow, *The Religion of Babylonia and Assyria* (Boston: Athaneum Press, 1898), 279.

[63] Gadd, "Harran," 40. Sidney Smith was one of the first to notice a correlation between Osirian and Ashur/Marduk mythology, stating: "It is very tempting to see in them the same metal bands that are round the tree with which Ashur is connected. Perhaps it was this very feature that the Osiris myth attempted to explain by the story of a tree growing round the chest which held the body of Osiris. Should this comparison be accepted, it seems impossible to the present writer not to believe that Ashur and Osiris, whose cult objects are similar, as well as their myths, have a common origin" (in "The Relation of Marduk, Ashur, and Osiris," *JEA* 8.1/2 (1922): 41-4). This might be used to support the "Asher" link to Osiris mentioned earlier. Smith adds: "According to a translation of an Arabic text recently published ... the early Arabs were in the habit of placing rings made of precious metal on logs or trunks of trees which in some way had become sacred. In the instance quoted the log of wood had a mysterious origin and performed miracles, and Solomon determined to preserve it" (44).

[64] Paul-Alain Beaulieu, "Nabonidus the Mad King: A Reconsideration of His Stelas from Harran and Babylon," in *Representations of Political Power: Case Histories from Times of Change and Dissolving Order in the Ancient Near East*, M. Heinz and M. Feldman, eds. (Winona Lake: Eisenbrauns, 2007), 137-66, here 143.

devise a new deity to encompass everything he had learned (from Egyptian, Tyrian, and Qenite religions). During the four to five years from his return to Babylon and his departure for Canaan, he would be drawing up plans, making provisions, securing his allies, etc. The ringed staff may be the just first expression of an envisioned serpentine iconography, not to represent "I AM" per se, but to mark Nabonidus' priestly status.

The serpentine theme remains (potentially), in the ark's decoration (i.e., the cherubim), where it does not represent the deity but still has specific meaning (the protection of the "glory"). A simple snake icon is easy to inscribe and many worshippers would have preferred/expected *some* sort of visual representation;[65] I therefore think that the snake glyphs on the two inscriptions mentioned above (*Figs. 22 and 23*) were added by Nabonidus' devotees later, to encapsulate what *they* deemed the most dynamic and vital aspect of the "Sinai" phenomenon.

> Remarkably, archaeologists found at Qurayyah "a stone relief with a depiction of the ancient Semitic god Salm .... Also visible on the relief are a wavy line (perhaps representing water or a snake) and a stylized human figure with upraised arms ...."[66]

That a Salm inscription is found at both Tayma *and* Qurayyah, and the latter with a potential snake glyph, must be pause for thought.

# JEWISH TAYMA

Schaudig makes interesting comment:

> There is also a group of graffiti found in the vicinity of Tayma, written in a North-Arabian script .... Several of these graffiti give the names and professions of individuals who took part in the campaign of Nabonidus in Arabia. The names are commonly regarded as Arabic, and some may even be Greek, .... None, however, are Judean, as one might have expected in view of the later Judean traditions about Nabonidus and Tayma.[67]

---

[65] Nabonidus' indefinable "image" probably failed to inspire a great rush of converts (as his strange idol of Sîn made many uneasy), but I can see how this might have initiated the aniconism of Islam.

[66] Marta Luciani, "Archaeology in the Land of Midian: Excavating the Qurayyah Oasis," *BAR* (Winter 2023): 32-9, here 37.

[67] Hanspeter Schaudig, "Edom in the Nabonidus Chronicle: A Land Conquered or a Vassal Defended? A Reappraisal of the Annexation of North Arabia by the Late

From the tale of Abraham, Nabonidus receives a positive depiction for posterity, i.e., from those who had left Babylonia with him in the hopes of finding their fortunes, or their roots, in Canaan. These, who are responsible for the Genesis narrative of Nabonidus, isolate themselves (just as they did in Babylonia, probably) by rigidly defining the parameters of Abraham's sojourn, i.e., he does *not* enter Arabia. He is the version of the leader *they* wish to preserve.

The tale of Moses, on the other hand, is written by less than admiring scribes who tell of a more harrowing experience. These stories come from the "Jews" (and others) who follow him beyond Canaan and into the Arabian Desert, to Tayma. They stay there for many years; one can only imagine that some are too scared of the Desert to risk heading out alone and so they just settle down and become Nabonidus' yes-men in Tayma, perhaps enjoying the good life, or perhaps being retained as a workforce for the building of his temple there. The degree to which they "complain" suggests they like their home comforts and rather resent the situation.

I would suggest that the notion of a "Jewish Tayma" stems from the Sinai days, i.e., the post-539 BCE years, long after Nabonidus' original forays into Arabia as King. There would, therefore, be no references to Judean names in the discovered inscriptions because he hadn't brought them there yet.

## *Nabonidus' Local Names*

The Arabs held a tradition that Tayma was built by Solomon;[68] we can now see this has to be Nabonidus. This single legend should be enough to change our perception of the biblical narratives, yet it is seldom mentioned, let alone assessed in terms of its potential significance, simply because it challenges the status quo. When I first discovered this Arabic lore years ago, I got goose bumps. For me, it changed everything.

There was also a tribe of Bedouin who …

> occupied the towns of Teima and Kheibar. Of this now vanished tribe Al-Kalkashendy gives the following account: the Beni Suleim area powerful tribe of Keis; **the patrial noun from their name is Sulamy** ; they are of the posterity of Suleim, … **Suleim had a son Buhta (Buhtah), through whom his whole race is descended.**[69]

Babylonian Empire," in *About Edom and Idumea in the Persian Period: Recent Research and Approaches from Archaeology, Hebrew Bible Studies, and Ancient Near East Studies*, B. Hensel, E. Ben Zvi, and D. V. Edelman, eds., (Sheffield: Equinox, 2022), 251-64, here 260-1.

[68] Raymond P. Dougherty, "Nabonidus in Arabia," *JAOS* 42 (1922): 305-16, here 306, n. 6.
[69] Dr. George A. Wallin, *Notes Taken during a Journey through Part of Northern*

The Arabic name for Solomon is Sulaimān. "Solomon" *is* Nabonidus. Coincidence? Or did the Sulamy attribute their existence to Nabonidus' son, Belshazzar (Buhta), who returned to Tayma after the Persian invasion of Babylon (i.e., just as Jacob, rather than Abraham, becomes the Jews' symbolic forefather). The name "Buhta" in Arabic means "a false accusation; calumny; defamation," which may just suggest Belshazzar was, they thought, wrongly accused, or painted with the same brush his father had been, perhaps, and did not deserve it.

In the Song of Solomon, Nabonidus' relationship with Nitocris is set in Jerusalem as part of a campaign to diminish them; Jerusalem itself would have been derelict at the time the group passed through from Harran. Soon after publishing *She Brought*, I discovered an interesting comment about Huldah, the female scribe (wise-woman) to whom the newly discovered book of the law is brought in 1 Kings 22. Na'aman argues that the Mishneh quarter, where Huldah is supposedly dwelling, had been "deserted for hundreds of years" up to the 2nd Century BCE, arguing that the author should have "avoided locating the prophetess in a deserted quarter" and "placed her in the City of David."[70] This would have tied in nicely with my argument that the HB authors, especially Ezra-Nehemiah, demeaned and humiliated strong, sacerdotal women, often within the etymology of their names. Here, they ridicule Huldah's perceived importance by placing her, retrospectively, in such a derelict location, as if her word meant little, her position now defunct (and I did suggest the statement she provides about the book is probably not her own but propaganda).[71] Therefore, just as Huldah is set in the context of a dilapidated quarter of Jerusalem in order to reduce her significance, so Jehudijah might have thought this unimportant, broken, and challenged Jerusalem the perfect setting for her tale of the disastrous and doomed marriage of Nabonidus and Nitocris (the Song of Solomon).

The association stuck, however, and Nabonidus' original dropping off of a few Jews along the way (in Canaan) seems to have been exaggerated by those who needed to secure their position in the land (a tactic we see in the *huge* numbers of Israelites who served as soldiers, etc.; it is mere chest-puffing, similar to the exaggerated numbers of captives mentioned on Mesopotamian victory stelae, for instance). Nabonidus (as Solomon) subsequently becomes "King of Israel" by default; his palace and temple are 'in Jerusalem' only because the growing Jewish nation cannot possibly allow it to be in Arabia (and Jehudijah had set a precedent that could serve their purposes). They can denounce Nabonidus' unseemly ways, conceal his

---

*Arabia*, in 1848 (London: Clowes and Sons, 1850), 39.

[70] Nadav Na'aman, "The 'Discovered Book' and the Legitimation of Josiah's Reform," *JBL* 130.1 (2011): 47-62, here 57.

[71] Tyson, 35-6.

beliefs beneath layers of symbolism, and duplicate all the Arabian cities in the Promised Land (considering there would be no reason to think any Jew from Canaan would ever go down into Arabia to see for themselves), but they *cannot* remove him from their heritage.

Doughty, the intrepid 19th Century adventurer I relied on for much of the first-person Tayma-region geographical information, describes being shown the ruins of "old (Mosaic) Tayma":

> They showed me a hillock even with the wall-height, and thereupon a heap of building stones; this they call "*Kasr Bedr Ibn Johr*, Prince of Old Tayma of the Yahud."[72]

The word *qasr* means "fortress or palace" but what is interesting is the name of this "Prince," i.e., Bédr (or Béder). The name is Arabic, of course, and it means "Full Moon."[73] Ibn (son of) Jôher: This intrigues me. I am not a linguist, hands up, so someone else might come to a completely different conclusion but from what I can discern, "Johar" means "a jewel, pearl, gem," etc., and can also mean "knowledge, secret" or "essence, substance, gist, etc."[74] Nabonidus has declared himself the "image," i.e., the essence, of the deity ("I AM"); he is renowned for seeking arcane wisdom; and if he is the son of a "jewel," this might relate to the prestigious and memorialised visitation of his much-admired mother, Adad-guppi, for the occasion of the king's marriage to Nitocris.[75] Perhaps the Tayma locals deemed this very old and frail woman something of a marvel and liked her.

Whichever you prefer, each translation suggests Nabonidus, yet Doughty wrote these words in 1888, a year before archaeologists began excavating in Nippur, and a decade before anyone lifted a trowel in Babylon, so Doughty was unaware of Nabonidus the King of Babylon, making this a wholly independent attestation of a Tayma ruler who was strongly identified with the Moon, had an illustrious mother, and was somehow connected with the Jews.[76]

---

[72] Charles M. Doughty, *Travels In Arabia Deserta* (New York: Random House, reprint 1921 [1888]), 1.600.

[73] "Bidar" can also be a Persian name meaning "awake" (a bearing on his quest for wisdom?), https://quranicnames.com/badr/; "in the Persian version the 'i' is a long sound, as Beedar" (https://quranicnames.com/bidar/).

[74] "Johar," Muslimname.com.

[75] Tyson, 90.

[76] For a very short discussion on Nabonidus as the Quran's Abraham and a direct link to Tayma, see my paper, "Nabonidus, Abraham, and the Buraq" (www.academia.edu).

# 17         SCRIBAL CRAFT

## TABLETS

T he account of Moses ascending the mountain and receiving the "ten commandments" (in Exodus 19) is not so straightforward. Not only are there at least three different sets of laws, there are many inconsistencies that suggest multiple versions have been superimposed.[1] It is commonly known that a priestly influence has expanded upon a much simpler account, as with many other aspects of Exodus, but what interests me is the nature of the tablets themselves, and what they would mean to Nabonidus, ex-King and lover of wisdom.

### *Clay Tablets*

Exod 24:7 refers to Moses reading the "book of the covenant" to the people. Books, as we understand them today, were not extant in Mesopotamia; there

---

[1] "The Decalogue and Covenant Collection are written by Moses on a scroll (Exod 20-24:11); Moses inscribes the Cultic Decalogue on tablets (Exod 34); God gives Moses tablets containing an undefined "teaching and commandment" (Exod 24:12)" (from Rabbi David Frankel, "What Did God Write on the Tablets of Stone?" www.thetorah.com).

was nothing to make paper with, even if the process was known. There were no indigenous trees for the mass production of pulp; the beloved cedars of Lebanon were used for temples and palaces, not quick notations. Babylonia had an abundance of clay/mud so as well as building their ziggurats out of it, they fashioned the now familiar clay tablets for preserving their knowledge. Nabonidus might have learned from Nitocris how to write with ink (with everything that was going on during the Tayma years, I doubt he had time to become proficient).[2] He would have seen papyrus texts from Egypt, of course, but the technique of making the marshland plant into paper had not transferred to Mesopotamia, despite the extensive marshes there (which did contain papyrus in some places). Had this happened, however, we would not have the abundance of records for study that we do, for papyrus does not preserve well (as the very limited number of Egyptian texts proves).

> When alphabetic Aramaic reached Assyria and Babylonia from the west at the turn of the first millennium BCE, it was quickly adopted for an increasing range of everyday writings, almost always on perishable media like animal skins and papyrus. Whereas in early Mesopotamia cuneiform literacy had been primarily a tool for controlling the ownership and rights to assets and income (some 95 percent of extant tablets attest to this function), in the first millennium it increasingly became a prestige medium. With cuneiform, the scribes communicated with the gods, learned and created intellectual culture, and wrote certain sorts of legal documents.[3]

So "book" (here) really needs to be understood as a collation of inscribed (cuneiform) information, i.e., be it on clay tablets, or wax-coated wooden boards, using a stylus.[4]

Most of the clay tablets we know of now come from a few major caches, including one from Elba, Syria (ca. 2300-2550 BCE); the first ever organised library of Tiglath-Pileser (1115-1077 BCE) in Assur, Assyria; and the most famous from the library of Ashurbanipal (668-627 BCE) in

---

[2] "Ink had long been used by cuneiform scribes for various purposes. Scribes working in the royal city of Nineveh in the 7th century sometimes wrote the colophons to library tablets in ink. It was much more commonly used for writing Aramaic" (Jonathan Taylor, "Writing Cuneiform on Other Media," *Nimrud: Materialities of Assyrian Knowledge Production* [2019], The Nimrud Project at Oracc.org).

[3] Robson, 3.

[4] This holds for the references in Daniel, too (Dan 7:10; 10:21; 12:1). For a short treatise on tablet books see Eleanor Robson, "The Clay Tablet Book in Sumer, Assyria, and Babylonia," https://discovery.ucl.ac.uk/id/eprint/1476493/2/Robson_c05-2015-07-27.pdf.

Nineveh, Assyria.[5] The Elba hoard was a fluke find, as the tablets (mostly containing accounting records) were preserved intact due to the building they were housed in being set on fire by invaders; they were kiln-baked to perfection. Ashurbanipal, on the other hand, created a true library for his own personal edification, consisting of thousands of clay tablets, hundreds of which turned out to be scribal texts such as the Epic of Gilgamesh and the Epic of Creation.

Ashurbanipal boasted that he had "achieved the highest level in the scribal art," and that "among the kings … none had learned such an art."[6] He was very protective of his tablets; only designated officials could access them and even then under direct supervision. Curses were inscribed on some, condemning anyone who took, defaced, or damaged a tablet to be "cast down," his "name, his seed" stricken from the land forever![7] Even later libraries that allowed lending (to priests and scribes) were very strict; anyone making the writing illegible was warned that the gods would be very angry with the perpetrator.[8]

The Assyrian king organised his library by using two key tools of the trade: Tablet boxes, and colophons. A box would be constructed to house a collection of tablets/texts and a colophon (i.e., a note providing the name of the scribe, the owner of the tablet, the date, etc.) was attached to the lid to identify what lay inside. One of these colophons reads:

> Palace of Ashurbanipal, King of the World, King of Assyria … whom Nabu and Tashmetu gave wide open ears and who was given profound insight …. The wisdom of Nabu, the signs of writing, as many as have been devised, I wrote on tablets, I arranged [the tablets] in series, I collated [them], and for my royal contemplation and recital I placed them in my palace.[9]

The preservation of information on tablets has proven so successful that today, the Memory of Mankind Project is recreating a similar cache of human wisdom to last the ages. Certain that some future catastrophe will wipe out all of our digital databases, the Project aims to produce records of knowledge, history, even personal writings, and store these deep underground in an old salt mine, for posterity. The point is, these new records, including my books, are going to be preserved on *tablets*!

---

[5] For a concise account of tablets in the ancient Near East, see Lionel Casson, *Libraries in the Ancient World* (New Haven: Yale University Press, 2001), 1-16.

[6] Casson, 9.

[7] Casson, 12.

[8] Casson, 13-14.

[9] Casson, 10.

Admittedly, the clay is now high-spec ceramic and the stylus a laser but the irony is worth a mention.[10]

## *Stone Tablets*

> The use of stone, the most commonly attested class of inscribed materials apart from clay, would have entailed learning to chisel signs into a hard surface rather than impressing them into a soft one. This, in turn, involved a substantially different set of motor skills and familiarity with material properties and tools.[11]

The art of inscribing stone was, originally, the job of the smith, the artisan who knew how to bring raw materials into the divine sphere, how to manipulate their nature so as to make a product imbued with heavenly meaning. They were knowledgeable in shaping and decorating metal, so it must have seemed an obvious transition to work with stone (for the most talented).

> *Beliš-tikal, chief smith, man of my choosing, who can write tablets,*
> *I will give you orders, let my orders be carried out!*
> ETCSL 2.1.4 B, 25-34

However, when we look at Exod 20:25, it is made very clear that using a "chisel" on the rocks of the *altar* would profane it. Although a common focus here is on the "chisel" (i.e., *chereb*, "sword," i.e., a metal tool i.e., weapons are made with metal, so *chereb* is unsuitable for an altar), I see a connection to the aniconism of the Qenites, for to carve something, however crudely, is to apply your own, human perception of what that rock should look like—you *make* it an "image." Unhewn stones are God's handiwork, which is deemed perfection. Solomon (Nabonidus) knew of this directive but circumvented it by locating the mystical *shamir* to do the hewing for him (Gittin 68a-b); this is Nabonidus' hubris and his underlying rebellious nature coming to the fore again.[12]

Whether stone tablets held more authority than clay ones is a question scholars are debating; for instance, "how far were certain documents set up for civic, democratic purposes, how far for accountability before the

---

[10] See www.memory-of-mankind.com/.

[11] Susan Pollock, "From Clay to Stone: Material Practices and Writing in Third Millennium Mesopotamia," in *Materiality of Writing in Early Mesopotamia*, Thomas E. Balke and Christina Tsouparopoulou, eds. (Berlin: De Gruyter, 2016) 277-92, here 283.

[12] Tyson, 28.

gods"?[13] Clay tablets can be stored for personal use but stone is almost always used for public display, which seems to make sense, yet time has proven that under the right conditions clay tablets can last indefinitely, while exposed stone eventually succumbs to erosion (many a discovered inscription cannot be translated due to weather damage).

Large stone stelae, such as the Code of Hammurabi, inscribed (ca. 1755-1750 BCE) on a black basalt rock that stands over two meters tall was copied onto palm-sized clay tablets for distribution to schools and courts.[14] The choice of clay verses rock really depends, therefore, on the context and the intended purpose. It has been generally assumed that Moses comes down the mount with nothing but stone tables; in a real-world scenario, perhaps this isn't so black and white (see below).

## Fate Tablets

> The Tablet of Destinies in his hands, Anzu gazed,
> And fixed his purpose, to usurp the Enlil-power.
> Anzu often gazed at Duranki's god, father of the gods,
> And fixed his purpose to usurp the Enlil-power.
> 'I shall take the gods' Tablet of Destinies for myself,
> And control the orders for all the gods,
> And shall possess the throne and be master of the rites![15]

In the Babylonian myth of Enlil and Anzu, there is but one "Tablet" that bears the fates, or destinies, of all living things. The Anzu bird, in Sumerian literature quite harmless, is transformed into a malevolent character in later Babylonian lore,[16] where even the place of his birth provides a sense of chthonic trepidation, for he is born "in mountain-rocks," i.e., in a cave (like a bat).[17] Enlil's Tablet of Destinies, however, proves irresistible to Anzu (like a shiny object to a magpie) and he steals it. Ninurta the hero warrior-god slays Anzu and retrieves the Tablet, returning it to Enlil (but only after

---

[13] Rosalind Thomas and Nikolaos Papazarkadas, "The Dynamics of Publication on Stone in Democracies and Oligarchies" (Project Outline), www.humanities.ox.ac.uk.

[14] Osama Shukir Muhammed Amin, "Law Code Tablet of King Hammurabi from Nippur," World History Encyclopedia, www.worldhistory.org.

[15] Stephanie Dalley, *Myths from Mesopotamia: Creation, the Flood, Gilgamesh, and Others* (Oxford: Oxford University Press, 1991), 207 (I iii).

[16] Dalley, *Myths from Mesopotamia*, 203.

[17] Dalley, *Myths from Mesopotamia*, 206 (I ii). For the cave/bat link see William W. Hallo and William L. Moran, "The First Tablet of the SB Recension of the Anzu-Myth," *JCS* 31.2 (1979): 65-115, here 70 and n. 18.

a little temptation of his own to keep hold of it, much like the ring in Tolkien's *Lord of the Rings*).

Later, in the *Epic of Creation* (*Enuma Elish*), it is said that Tiamat, the feminine deity who represents the primordial sea, has in her possession the fabled Tablets of Destiny (now plural).[18] When she sends her son, Qingu, into battle she places the tablets on his chest as symbols of power. Marduk, a latter-day Ninurta, is created for the sole purpose of destroying Tiamat and when he succeeds, he takes the Tablets of Destiny and fixes them to his robe as a sign of victory and kingship.

Sonik argues that the Tablets' "rightful keeper" is determined by their "innate qualities, power, and position in the pantheon, and varies according to chronological and geographical context"; she adds that the Tablets serve "as a familiar and prominent device in several Mesopotamian texts that explore the nature of legitimate and illegitimate divine power and rulership ...."[19] Wisnom suggests that when Marduk is proven victorious, he is elevated above all things in the universe, including the constellations; "since

*Figure 26: Marduk with multiple tablets adorning his robe (Image: Public Domain)*

the movements of the stars communicate the fates that have been fixed by the gods," control over the firmament is a "display of the ultimate control over destinies."[20] So, the Tablets of Destiny are worn not so much as a sign of magical prowess but as trophies, i.e., he has not simply slain the enemy, he has proven himself the king of the gods by seizing the fate of the universe. While Enlil possessed just one Tablet, Marduk acquires *multiple*, implying that in the period of this later Babylonian myth, there are multiple deities who dictate the destinies, and his conquest is over all of them:

May the Anuna determine the destinies in your midst (ETCSL 1.1.3, 192-209).

I (Enki) decree good destinies ... (ETCSL 1.1.3, 61-80).

---

[18] E. A. Wallis Budge, *The Babylonian Legends of Creation*, (1921), at www.sacred-texts.com.

[19] Karen Sonik, "The Tablet of Destinies and the Transmission of Power in Enūma eliš," in *Organization, Representation, and Symbols of Power in the Ancient Near East: Proceedings of the 54th Rencontre Assyriologique Internationale at Würzburg*, Gernot Wilhelm, ed. (Winona Lake: Eisenbrauns, 2012), 387.

[20] Selena Wisnom, "Blood on the Wind and the Tablet of Destinies: Intertextuality in Anzû, Enūma Eliš, and Erra and Išum," *JAOS* 139.2 (2019): 269-86, here 23-4.

... majestically you (Inanna) extend your arm in order to determine
destinies ... (ETCSL 4.13.05, 5-12).

You have won complete dominion, every single rite ... the shrines of
the gods of fates (are) granted to you.[21]

The tablets of the gods relate to the deeds and consequences, the fates,
of humans, both individuals and nations, and are sometimes referred to as
"the Tablet(s) of Life."[22] There exists a delineation between tablet entries
that are positive and those which are negative. Also, such records, though
divinely inscribed and supposedly unalterable, do seem to have an out clause
in some situations:

May his sin be shed today, may it be wiped off him, averted from him.
May the record of his misdeeds, his errors, his crimes, his oaths, (all)
that is sworn, be thrown into the water.[23]

## Women and Tablets

In the Sumerian texts, several females are put in charge of, or actually
inscribe, tablets:

Bring, bring, bring my sister! Bring my Geshtinana, bring my sister! Bring
my scribe proficient in tablets, bring my sister (ETCSL 1.4.3, 19-24).

Ninimma[24] ... you are the heavenly scribe. You ...... the tablet of life
(ETCSL  4.21.1, 1-18).

I keep an eye upon the black-headed people: they are under my
surveillance. I hold the tablet of life in my hand and I register the just
ones on it. The evildoers cannot escape my arm; I learn their deeds.
All countries look to me as to their divine mother (ETCSL 4.28.1, 75-
82).[25]

---

[21] Dalley, *Myths from Mesopotamia*, 219-20. This refers to Ninurta but is just as
applicable to Marduk.

[22] Shalom M. Paul "Heavenly Tablets and the Book of Life," *JANES* 5 (1973):
345-54, here 351-2.

[23] Paul, 346, n. 13.

[24] Ninimma (Lady of Clay Tablets) is sometimes depicted as the consort of Ninurta,
who is known for his connection to the Tablet of Destinies.

[25] This is from a hymn to Ningal, a goddess who is often identified with Inanna-
Ishtar. She claims to have the authority to dictate destinies from birth, and to judge the good

Nisaba[26] ... the book-keeper ......, the wise one, the holy woman
......, ...... the oracle, has placed his (?) name on the tablet of life
(ETCSL 2.5.8.1, 37-48).

And finally, a nod to one of my favourite women of all time,
Enheduanna, the first *entu* of Ur, the first *known* author:

The compiler of the tablets was En-ḫedu-ana. My king, something has
been created that no one has created before (ETCSL 4.80.1, 543-4).

# NABONIDUS AND TABLETS

## *Reading and Writing*

The most well-known and charismatic of the early Mesopotamian kings,
Shulgi, King of Ur in the Ur III period (ca. 2094-2046 BCE), who *also* deified
himself, and who boasts one of the longest and substantially preserved praise
poems in history, did not claim to be able to write. Rather, he makes it clear
that he dictated the words of the gods to a scribe, who then inscribed a lapis-
lazuli (i.e., stone) tablet, to last forever (ETCSL 2.4.2.05, 240-57). This seems
to be what we see happen (between the lines) on the mesa at Qurayyah.

When Leonard Woolley excavated the *giparu* at Ur in the 1920s,
where Jehudijah and Ennigaldi lived, he discovered a small collection of
artefacts with museum-like labels on them (Nabonidus was an archaeologist
at heart and perhaps shared his enthusiasm with his young daughter who
collected objects in emulation of her father). Next door to the "museum," he
found a vast collection of used clay tablets, upon which were written practice
sentences, several beginning with the same letter or syllable, as though
teaching the alphabet. On one tablet he found the inscription "Property of
the boys' class"; from this Woolley surmised Ennigaldi must have kept a
school.[27] Ennigaldi, however, was about six years old when Babylon fell, so
it was not, I submit, she who ran the school; more likely, it was Jehudijah.

This type of school is an *edubba*, or "tablet-house," where scribes
would learn their craft over many years, beginning quite young; it was also
called a "place of wisdom."[28] The training was incredibly complex, bilingual

---

and the evil.

[26] Nisaba is Enlil's mother-in-law; she is the goddess of wisdom, writing, and grain.

[27] Leonard Woolley, *Ur of the Chaldees* (London: Herbert Press, 1982), 251.

[28] Christopher J. Lucas, "The Scribal Tablet-House in Ancient Mesopotamia,"

(Sumerian and Akkadian), and covered a multitude of topics that would be considered specialisms today. For instance, a novice scribe

> is examined over different types of calligraphy and occult script. There are questions about the various classes of priests and other types of professions ... the preparation of official documents and seals. ... categories of songs and problems of choral direction. ... explicate technical details of the "tongues" ... of the several classes of priestly officials, of silversmiths, jewellers, shepherds, and master shippers. The master poses mathematical problems relating to the allocation of rations and the division of fields. Finally, there is a query about the use and techniques employed in playing musical instruments.[29]

In the *edubba*, "royal petitions were preserved in a fixed canonical form" and were studied by generations of scholars; hymns and literary texts were composed, or "having been handed down in an oral tradition, were first committed to written form" there.[30] The advanced levels of instruction were reserved for those entering the scribal profession, such as exorcists, lamentation priests, diviners, etc.

> *A scribe is told by his mentor: "They should recognise*
> *that you are a practitioner (?) of wisdom."*
> ETCSL 5.1.3, 62-72

It is possible that the original ten commandments are inspired by Nabonidus' own knowledge of the Decad, the ten compositions advanced students of the *edubba* were expected to study (these included such works as the Praise Poem of Shulgi [ETCSL 2.4.2.01], the Exaltation of Inanna [ETCSL 4.07.2], etc.).[31] While there is much to be found concerning the number of Decad tablets discovered, their size and form, where they were found, etc., the content of these texts and *why* they were chosen for the advanced students of the *edubba* doesn't seem to be much debated. Perhaps this is a topic for a future investigation, but I think it should be considered as a potential influence on a man who sets so much store in his own learning and writing skills.

> It hardly needs pointing out that an understanding of Mesopotamian educational systems is a key component of an understanding of the

---

*HEQ* 19.3 (1979): 305-32, here 309.
[29] Lucas, 314.
[30] Lucas, 310.
[31] Paul Delnero, "Sumerian Extract Tablets and Scribal Education," *JCS* 62 (2010): 53-69, here 59.

society, ideology, religion and politics of Mesopotamia—a key component, in other words, of an understanding of any aspect of the uses of literacy in a cultural complex which is in many ways defined by its use of the technology of writing.[32]

The ultimate ambition of the scribe, it seems, was to be skilled enough to be chosen to inscribe stone:

> "Now," directs the examiner, "write your name in lapidary form (i.e., as it would appear incised in stone)." The student prepares to comply. "If you can, you will write (for yourself)," cautions the master. His charge apparently succeeds, for the teacher pronounces the words, "You are a scribe," and he proceeds, as it appears, to warn the boy not to be overly impressed with his accomplishment.[33]

The *edubba,* however, was an Old Babylonian institution, replaced over time by private tutors.[34] This seems fitting, as Nabonidus is renowned for being retrospective and attempting to encourage a resurgence of old traditions. That Nabonidus locates this place of wisdom within the temple at Ur, in the care of his all-female *entu* priesthood, also confirms his strong (though skewed) belief in the innate power of women. He would have learned this from his mother, Adad-guppi, who was a strong role-model, but also from Nitocris, whose powers captivated him on all levels of interpretation. Lucas suggests that although women in Old Babylonian times were both literate and actively involved in business, etc., there are few known female scribes; this means there *were* some, and it means there is hope of finding more as tablets continue to be translated.[35] In Ezra 2:55, there is the female scribe "Hasophereth" (i.e., the name means "the [female] scribe"; in Neh 7:57 she is recorded as Sophereth).[36] There is also Huldah (2 Kgs 22:8-20), the wise woman/scribe to whom the newly discovered book of the law is brought for authentication.[37] In the exodus narratives we see the beginnings of an outright desecration of female wisdom and authority, i.e., beginning with the murder of Miriam, and culminating in the misogynistic apartheid of Ezra-Nehemiah.

---

[32] Steve Tinney, "On the Curricular Setting of Sumerian Literature," *Iraq* 61 (1999): 159-72, here 170.

[33] Lucas, 314

[34] Lucas, 310.

[35] Lucas, 312, and n. 25.

[36] Meir Bar-Ilan, *Some Jewish Women in Antiquity*, Brown Judaic Studies 317, ed., Shaye J. D. Cohen (Atlanta: Scholar's Press, 1998), 36.

[37] Tyson, 35-6.

The ex-Babylonian king has a cultural inheritance that cannot be ignored. He proudly asserts his admiration of his Assyrian predecessors but also admires the ancient Sumerians. To both societies, the skill of writing on tablets (cuneiform) was synonymous with wisdom. Ashurbanipal was thus given "profound insight," the "wisdom of Nabu," and "the signs of writing" (i.e., the skills of reading and writing cuneiform), yet nobody deemed *him* mad, as they apparently did Nabonidus. Novotny and Jeffers claim that Ashurbanipal, as a younger son of a king, was not the next in line for the throne, so he received a formal education as a scribe, about which he speaks in the "School Days Inscription":

> [The gods Šamaš (and) Adad] placed at my disposal the lore of the diviner, a craft that cannot be changed; [the god Mardu]k, the sage of the gods, granted me a broad mind (and) extensive knowledge as a gift; the god Nabû, the scribe of everything, bestowed on me the precepts of his craft as a present; the gods Ninurta (and) Nergal endowed my body with power, virility, (and) unrivalled strength. I learned [the c]raft of the sage Adapa, the secret (and) hidden lore of all of the scribal arts. I am able to recognise celestial and terrestrial [om]ens (and) can discuss (them) in an assembly of scholars. I am capable of arguing with expert diviners about (the series) "If the liver is a mirror image of the heavens." I can resolve complex (mathematical) divisions (and) multiplications that do not have a(n easy) solution. I have read cunningly written text(s) in obscure Sumerian (and) Akkadian that are difficult to interpret. I have carefully examined inscriptions on stone from before the Deluge that are sealed, stopped up, (and) confused.[38]

From my perspective, this might well have been written by Nabonidus. It parallels the later Verse Account's mocking of the Babylonian king, yet it possibly served as Nabonidus' inspiration and mantra.

The VA's damaged Tablet IV reveals only a few lines of discernible text, yet they prove the most intriguing, for in just a few cuneiform markings we learn that "the king is mad," "portents were observed," and there is mention of the writing stylus twice, i.e., one on its own, and one that reads: "Lord of the Stylus."[39] The acerbic rejection of something so specific as this

---

[38] Jamie Novotny and Joshua Jeffers, *The Royal Inscriptions of Ashurbanipal (668–631 BC), Aššur-etel-ilāni (630-627 BC) and Sîn-šarra-iškun (626-612 BC), Kings of Assyria, Part 1*, Royal Inscriptions of the Neo-Assyrian Period, Vol. 5. (Winona Lake: Eisenbrauns, 2018), 13.

[39] This translation from James B. Pritchard, ed., ANET, 314. For a more recent translation see Hanspeter Schaudig, *Die Inschriften Nabonids von Babylon und Kyros' des Grossen: samt den in ihrem Umfeld entstandenen Tendenzschriften. Textausgabe und Grammatik*. Alter Orient und Altes Testament 256 (Münster, 2001), 576.

title, linked to scribal ability, surely reveals its veracity; if Nabonidus had not promoted himself *as* a scribe, this would not make sense. He could not fake such an ability, especially as he conversed regularly with the astronomers/priests concerning the omen tablets, which they physically brought to him to inspect (RChr iii 1-5a); what would be the point if he could not read them? Again, as a work of propaganda (written after his defeat) to subtly discredit the king's comprehension of priestly matters, the Royal Chronicle adds, "he did not heed (what the tablets said and) he did not understand anything it (*Enuma Anu Enlil*) said" (iii 1-5a). Yet, they also claim that he *could* read and write: "He inspected the tablets (carefully) and became af[raid]" (iii 5b-12a)"; "[He] wrote down [...] and [...] the god Sîn, [..., an]swered him (ii 10-12)."

In Nab 34 (i 34-35), Nabonidus states that he had found some ancient cuneiform deposits in the foundations of the old Egipar (the *giparu*, or dwellings of the *entu* priestesses at Ur): "I carefully inspected the ancient tablets and writing boards and made (it) as (it had been) in ancient times." Due to his archaeological interests over the years, he would have acquired *some* knowledge of cuneiform simply by osmosis; although he obviously had scribes at hand to read inscriptions out to him, knowing how inquisitive and eager he was to learn, it seems almost impossible that he never picked up a working knowledge of the written language, even if he did make mistakes (cf. VA 5.3-4). Beaulieu states: "The alleged royal confession of not knowing the art of cuneiform writing on line 10 (VA) is in flagrant contradiction with the opposite statement of Nabonidus, that he received the scribal craft from the god Nabu[40] himself."[41] He further suggests that "...the claims laid by Nabonidus (i.e., concerning his ideas on religion/wisdom), far from embodying the fantasies of an eccentric, *stemmed from the mainstream tradition of cuneiform learning* (emphasis mine)." That is, from the scribal school curriculum.[42]

## Usurper of the Fates

In *She Brought*, I suggest Nabonidus is sent into Arabia as part of a

---

[40] Nabu's symbol was a stylus wedge. Nabonidus displays such a symbol on his staff on the Harran Stele. Paul-Alain Beaulieu, "Nabonidus the Mad King: A Reconstruction of His Steles from Harran and Babylon, in *Representations of Political Power: Case Histories from Times of Change and Dissolving Order in the Ancient Near East,* M. Heinz and M. Feldman, eds. (Winona Lake: Eisenbrauns, 2007), 137-66, here 148.
[41] Beaulieu, "Mad King," 162.
[42] Beaulieu, "Mad King," 142.

conspiracy to get him as far away as possible from Babylon, where his allegedly mad ideas were causing too much interference for the Marduk priests, etc.[43] One of the claims I made, which must have seemed strange at the time, was that on a symbolic level Nabonidus was being accused of attempting to "steal" the Tablet of Destinies, i.e., he was usurping the power of the gods.[44] During this current research, however, it has become evident he was not the first king to be linked to the Tablet(s); the neo-Assyrian kings Sennacherib (705-681 BCE), Esarhaddon, and Ashurbanipal are all depicted in terms of possessing Marduk's Tablets of Destiny.

In 2009, archaeologists uncovered a cache of tablets at Tell Tayinat, in Turkey, which included the "single most important epigraphic find, a new manuscript of the so-called Vassal Treaties of Esarhaddon, best known from eight tablets discovered at the Assyrian city of Nimrud."[45] A tablet known as T1801 (dated 672 BCE) proves to be intriguing because it is the Succession Treaty of Esarhaddon and includes the remains of three distinctive seals of the deity Ashur. As discussed above, the Tablets of Destiny legitimise their owner and this sample of an oath tablet, upon which vassals would reiterate their allegiance to the sovereign, is no different. The three seals on the document are thought to be likenesses of the deity, which implies they were "images" or icons in their own right.[46] In the aniconic Mosaic context, these are replaced by the sprinkling of blood to "seal" the treatise/testimony (Exod 24:6-8).

Tablet T1801, "like the Nimrud tablets, needs to be rotated along its vertical, and not its horizontal, axis in order for a reader to move from the obverse to the reverse."[47] This means that the writing, *on both sides* (just as is made explicit in Exod 32:15), is not just visible but legible to all who stand before it; the tablet itself is pierced for attaching it to a pole (i.e., the tablet could then be rotated).[48] This is in stark contrast to the writing on ordinary, handheld clay tablets, which are written in such a way that the reverse appears upside down. T1801 was discovered, face down, in a temple, having fallen from a podium when the temple was destroyed in antiquity; the archaeologist surmise this to be evidence of a public presentation of the tablet but are not

---

[43] Tyson, 1-7.

[44] For our purposes the singular and plural of "Tablet/Tablets" are interchangeable; it is the concept that matters.

[45] Jacob Lauinger, "Some Preliminary Thoughts on the Tablet Collection in Building XVI from Tell Tayinat," *JCSMS* 6 (2011): 5-14, here 5.

[46] Lauinger states that although the images themselves are no longer extant, the corresponding inscription begins, "'Seal of Aššur, king of the gods', part of a caption that the Nimrud tablets have fully preserved" (9).

[47] Lauinger, 9.

[48] Lauinger, 11.

convinced if this was purely for oath-taking, or if the tablet itself was being venerated. This serves as a precedent for Nabonidus creating similar public-display tablets, *possibly* intended for a temple setting. In the interim, they are housed in the ark, i.e., the necessary, portable "tablet-box."

> The seal's inscription explicitly reveals the function of the Seal of Destinies to have been the sealing by Aššur of both human and divine destinies, as irrevocably decreed by him in his position as king of the gods. There can be little doubt that the document ratified by Aššur's sealing is, on the mythological plane, the Tablet of Destinies.[49]

Intriguingly, other tablets in this cache from Turkey revealed tongues extending from their top edges which had been pierced through, in order to allow the objects to be suspended.[50] Compare this to the priestly "breastpiece of judgement" (Exod 28:15-30), the tablet of stones representing the tribes that is hung around the high priest's neck and rests on his chest, much in the manner of Marduk, when he retrieved the Tablets of Destiny from Qingu (*Enuma Elish*, IV 122: "He sealed it with a seal and fastened it on his breast"). Might this be the more practical, mobile version of the Tablet of Destinies, symbolising the fates of the Israelites? What was once a symbol of divine kingship is usurped by the new priesthood for their own agenda and authority.[51]

Nabonidus' connection to Nabu, the god of the scribal arts and "bearer of The Tablet of Destinies of the gods,"[52] in his own words (above), and in his name, suggests he identifies himself as one worthy of the Tablets, dictated and sealed according to the will of "I AM." It's as if he is aware of the accusation laid against him, i.e., of trying to steal the Tablet(s), and now he attempts to go about things in a different way, using ceremony, ritual, public oaths, and legally-binding testimonies, to prove his claim.

The Epic of Gilgamesh was supposedly written on a stele by Gilgamesh himself; the stele was then copied onto clay tablets which were then buried "under the walls of Uruk as a foundation deposit to be retrieved by future generations."[53] As with several other allusions to Gilgamesh,[54] Nabonidus

---

[49] A. R. George, "Sennacherib and the Tablet of Destinies," *Iraq* 48 (1986): 133-46, here 141.

[50] Lauinger, 10, Fig. 6.

[51] Cf. Tyson 37, concerning the usurpation of Ishtar's symbolic rosette by the high priest.

[52] George, 141.

[53] Beaulieu, "Mad King," 142.

[54] E.g., Paul-Alain Beaulieu, compares Nabonidus' quest for "hidden things" and "secret knowledge" as "a direct allusion" to Gilgamesh (1.7), i.e., in the poem, the same two words (*katimu* and *niṣurtu*) are used to "embody the knowledge that Gilgamesh seeks on his quest for antediluvian wisdom" ("Mad King," 162).

possibly intends to make these tablets not an element of veneration in their own right, but as future foundation deposits for his temple at Tayma (not Jerusalem). This is a phenomenon mentioned in many of the ex-king's accounts of the renovation of temples (e.g., RCh iii 5b-12a; Nab 13 ii 1-8; Nab 16 ii 20-27, etc.), so it would be in keeping with his character and his cultural experience.

Protected from the elements, hidden from human eyes until such a time that the temples need rebuilding and the stones once again see the light, foundation stones can last millennia. The "memorial tablets" of Tiglath-Pileser (745-727 BCE), are inscribed with instructions to the finder in future days: "Let him anoint my (stone) tablets and my clay prisms with oil," offer sacrifices, and then put them back. The finder is invited to add his name to the king's but if he erases the king's name and puts his there instead, he is cursed.[55]

## *Blessings/Curses*

As a researcher, there are moments when you think you are really going out on a limb with a suggestion but then you happen upon precisely the same notion in another paper/book. On the one hand you are disappointed someone beat you to it, but on the other, elated that you are at least on the right track. A case in point is this neo-Assyrian oath tablet T1808. I independently made the connection between Nabonidus and the Tablet of Destinies some years ago, but only recently recognised the positive/negative attributes of similar Assyrian tablets as potentially echoed in the blessings and curses on the mountains of Shechem in Deuteronomy 28. Then I came across a fascinating paper by Hans Steymans that explains this fully, so I won't go much further into this topic but will direct you to his brilliant analysis.[56]

## *The "Book"*

Similar to the dual nature of the "death of the firstborn" threat (where it is initially declared as the punishment for Egypt but is pre-empted by the other plagues), so it is with the description of the ten commandments. In Exod 24: 4-7, Moses is told to write the words, which he then reads out (again demonstrating Nabonidus can read and write), as the "book of the covenant";

---

[55] Daniel D. Luckenbill, *Ancient Records of Assyria and Babylonia, Vol 1* (Chicago: University of Chicago Press, 1926), 90.

[56] Hans U. Steymans, "Deuteronomy 28 and Tell Tayinat," *VEcc*, 34.2 (2013): 1-13.

the people all agree to honour the commands ... and that should have been the end of it, but the narrative then takes another great leap into extensive descriptions of the laws, i.e., addenda to the original text by those with a vested interest, i.e., the later priests.

In the British Museum (BM 91022) sits a large inscribed stone monument that is considered a forgery; written in "archaising writing," it alludes to the privileges supposedly granted to the priests of the Shamash temple in Sippar, ca. 2269-2255 BCE. It was made to provide legitimacy and an ancient precedent for what was happening centuries later, in the Neo-Babylonian period (i.e., 8th to 6th Century BCE).[57] So again, Nabonidus would be fully entrenched in this idea of writing things in stone to confirm and make absolute the will of the king/gods (providing, perhaps, the original basis for the common Jewish phrase, "it is written"). The priests, on the other hand, have a precedent for manipulating evidence to suit their own agenda.

The original ten commandments, if they were truly part of Nabonidus' agreement with the Israelites, would be the very simple statements of Exod 20:1-17. This list, impressed with a stylus by Nabonidus' own hand, would easily fit on a single clay tablet held in his palm.[58] However, I think that he makes notes for himself, written drafts of more lengthy prohibitions, descriptions of visions whilst inhaling the fumes on the mesa perhaps, ideas for the ark and the tabernacle that come to him while dreaming. Everything from 20:18 to 23:19 is probably *based* on those musings, clarified by subsequent priestly scribes (who, I suggest, are solely responsible for Exodus 34).

Another tablet in the British Museum (BM 38770) is a "crudely-fashioned ... 'pillow-shaped' tablet" that contains mistakes and flaws; intended to be a first draft of an inscription for a gift to Ishtar, it is thought to be "a scribal exercise made by a student or a copy prepared by an inexperienced scribe."[59] This is probably the degree of Nabonidus' scribal skills. The whole point of the order to bring *only* Aaron with him up to the summit of Sinai in Exod 19:24 is so that he (Aaron) can edit the text, being a man of such learning (e.g., recall that it is he who is instructed to be Moses' prophet before Pharaoh). As a skilled smith, he has the skill to inscribe the words.

I suggest, then, it is either a small collection of draft tablets, or a writing board (see below) that comprises the "book" of the covenant, i.e.,

---

[57] British Museum. www.britishmuseum.org.

[58] As mentioned earlier, it is possible that he can write with ink on some sort of perishable medium, such as an animal skin, etc., but there is no hint of this from the text and, as we saw from the quotation from Robin's work on clay books, it would seem unlikely, given the gravitas of the situation, that anything but formal cuneiform is used.

[59] W&N, "Commentary" (Nab 6), 81.

the first draft of the agreement for the new community. There is no mention of stone tablets yet; the process seems to be one of a ratification of the clauses, *then* a final creation of the stone tablets to make them law and preserve them for posterity, just as with any stone tablets commissioned by the kings of Mesopotamia. There are several first draft texts from Ashurbanipal's hoard of clay tablets that reveal themselves much refined in their final, stone-etched, versions.[60]

Writing boards are in evidence in Babylonian administrative records well before Nabonidus' reign. Consisting of two thick planks of wood, hinged together on one side, and covered in wax for receiving cuneiform text, they more aptly represent what we now think of as a book. In fact, Nabonidus himself makes reference to them in his account of preparing the Ur temple precinct for his daughter, the new *entu*, i.e., he discovered some writing boards left by a previous king; in Nab 34 (i 34-5) he states: "I carefully inspected the ancient tablets and writing boards and made (it) as (it had been) in ancient times."

It is quite possible for Nabonidus to employ a writing-board for his own notations concerning the upcoming covenant for, as MacGinnis explains, there were "distinct advantages in (waxed) writing boards over clay tablets: they were lighter, less fragile, they were easily updated, and could be re-used."[61] He adds that in the case of "contracts" (e.g., the "covenant"), writing boards would not be used:

> These were traditionally formatted as tablets sealed with cylinder seals and here the fact that clay could not be written on after drying was its great advantage, preventing alteration of the contract. Also, Mesopotamian sealing practice was perfectly adapted to use on clay tablets and clay tablets were particularly well suited to contracts: the sealed tablet could be inspected without destroying the information. Wooden writing boards could be sealed (with a bulla on string) but the information could not then be viewed without destroying the integrity of the sealed unit (breaking the seal or cutting the string).[62]

It does seem much more practical for Moses, the very old man, to use this lighter form of palimpsest to take up to the top of the mesa and formulate his new treaty (cf. Deut 31:24).[63] He reads from his probably messy notes on

---

[60] Novotny and Jeffers, 2; 24; 38.

[61] John MacGinnis, "The Use of Writing Boards in the Neo-Babylonian Temple Administration at Sippar," *Iraq* 64 (2002): 217-36, here, 223.

[62] MacGinnis, 223.

[63] As we are dealing with the Arabian Desert, here, I did check to see if beeswax would be available for the boards, and I was glad to see that it would have been in abundance (see A. S. Alqarni, et al., "The Indigenous Honey Bees of Saudi Arabia

the waxed writing boards, adjusting the phrasing before he finalises the text for the stone tablets, i.e., only then does he commission Aaron to write down "the words of the Lord" (Exod 24:4), just as Shulgi commissioned his scribes to do. In Exod 24:12, God declares he will give Moses the stone tablets on his next visit. In 31:18 and 34:1, the writing on stone is allegedly done by the "finger of God," that is, from the divine hand, not tainted by human industry (and this, in turn, echoes the idea of the unhewn stones).[64] Aaron is the one who performs the work (probably during the time spent on the mesa in Exod 24:9-11) but he is not given the credit.

This brings to mind the making of cultic statues in Babylonia, for which the craftsmen would ritually denounce having made them, in order to remove the stigma of their own profane and unworthy contributions:

> … the statue manifests the god by virtue of the fact that it is really made by the craft deity Ea and not by earthly craftsmen. On the very first day of the two-day ritual, along the river bank, the *mis pi* ritually distances … the god/statue from the human craftsmen (*mareummani*) who worked on it in the temple atelier (*bit mummi*). Their tools are sewn up in the body of a sheep and consigned to the river, the domain of Ea. On the second day, each craftsman's hands are bound with red yarn and ritually cut off with a wooden tamarisk sword while he swears, "I did not make you, rather the craft-god made you." The cult image is ritually established as *acheiropoietos*, "unmade by (human) hands."[65]

Aaron is deliberately left at the foot of Sinai (in part) *in order to disassociate him from the tablets* and it is Joshua who accompanies Moses, to ceremoniously retrieve the tablets and descend with them (Exod 24:13). In other words, Nabonidus desires his son, his once-coregent Belshazzar, to be with him. It is a moment of sombre, legal import.

All "ancient Near Eastern binding agreements, oral or written, involved divine participation. It seems that the collection of oaths and the conclusion of a treaty were accompanied by rituals."[66] This is also the time

---

(Hymenoptera, Apidae, Apis mellifera jemenitica Ruttner): Their Natural History and Role in Beekeeping," *Zookeys* 134 (2011): 83-98.

[64] Exod 34:1 God says *he* will write on them but in 34:27, he instructs Moses to do it. 34:27-8 seems like an addendum, reiterating the forty-day fasting and providing a name for the "ten commandments/words," where one was not required before. There are not two distinct forty-day fastings on the mesa.

[65] Michael B. Dick, "The Mesopotamian Cult Statue: A Sacramental Encounter with Divinity," in *Cult Image and Divine Representation in the Ancient Near East*, Neal H. Walls, ed., American Schools of Oriental Research Books Series 10 (Boston: 2005), 43-67, here 60.

[66] Daniel Beckman, "The Use of Treaties in the Achaemenid Empire," (PhD diss.,

of Nabonidus' forty-day initiation into the Qenite cult, the transformative, ritualistic "sloughing-off" of his previous life and the new, highly symbolic amalgamation with the Sun-god. Thus, the treaty or "testament" of the new kingdom *is* accompanied by many rituals.

## *Tantrum*

The first set of stone slabs, thought by some to have been made from lapis-lazuli because of the mention of this stone in Exod 24:10, is probably taken from the rockfall at the base of the mesa, split and shaped to uniform rectangles by Aaron before he ascends with Moses (Exod 19:24). Though supposedly written by God, Moses hurls them at the ground during another of his temper tantrums (32:19). Interrupted by the noise rising up from below the mesa, his spiritual initiation brought to an unseemly, perhaps premature end, he casts these sacred, valuable, crafted objects to the ground as if they mean nothing. Recalling the curses on the tablets in Ashurbanipal's library, this act in itself would have been deemed unforgivable, for it demonstrates a lack of respect for the words of the gods and a lack of appreciation for the scribal craft and the wisdom it represents.

Nabonidus is accused, in RChr 3.5-10, of "unwittingly" or "ignorantly" manhandling sacred tablets, i.e., of being "impious" and a bit rough around the edges.[67] I wonder if this perception of the ex-king, which we also see in Exod 15:25 and his chucking of the wood into the water at al-Wajh had an influence on the scene here with the tablets. What deity would simply shrug off such disrespect and violence toward their divine covenant/decrees?

To be honest, I don't think there *are* two sets of tablets at all. I don't even think there were *two* original tablets (see the upcoming discussion concerning the golden calf). I suggest there is only one, which the angry Nabonidus breaks. Someone (Aaron?) retrieves the pieces and places them in the ark. Nabonidus has proven to be an impatient man who likes to get his own way; I cannot see him going through the entire process a second time. That the tablets are never mentioned in terms of being on display, or being in the ark when it is stolen by the Philistines, etc., surely suggests they were not as fundamental to his long-term plan as we like to think they were. The jar of "manna" is mentioned as being placed in the ark in Exod 16:33-4, and

---

University of California, Los Angeles, 2017) 27-8, https://escholarship.org /content/qt0bh180f4/qt0bh180f4.pdf.

[67] Paul-Alain Beaulieu, *The Reign of Nabonidus King of Babylon 556–539 B.C.* (New Haven: Yale University Press, 1989), 129-31.

"Aaron's rod" in Num 17:10, but these are, in my opinion, afterthoughts, retrospectively inserted because of their unique qualities in the narrative. Think of them as relics, or as talismans; they can be easily forged and perhaps even allowed to be touched, invoking awe and reverence. In 1 Kgs 8:9 and 2 Chr 5:10, however, Solomon is said to place the ark in his new temple (in Tayma); there is a most adamant statement that "there was *nothing* in the ark except the two tablets of stone that Moses had placed there at Horeb" (1 Kgs 8:9). I think this statement is probably contemporaneous with the additions to Exodus/Numbers about the manna and the rod, i.e., later priestly authors add these items as substitutions for what *really* lay inside the ark, i.e., the "bones of Joseph"/Pharaoh. Somebody wished to repress that memory and all its associations, but as it was known to many that the ark contained something magical, the manna and the rod had to suffice.[68]

The archaeologist in Nabonidus might later consider repairing the original stonework; he had probably repaired objects himself and certainly had replicas made for his museum.[69] The repair of stone (and clay) objects is evident in the archaeological record dating to about 9500 BCE and includes quite sophisticated techniques (later including the use of metal staples) that allow for artefacts to be reused rather than discarded.[70] Aaron himself, a skilled smith, a man trained also in stonework, might consider this a future project, to preserve something unique and irreplaceable. Craftsmen who worked solely on repairing objects were probably itinerant workers, like Aaron, and their existence is known only from the specialist repairs themselves.[71] It remains a possibility.

As the tablets of the testimony/covenant seem to disappear from the narrative fairy quickly, however, it may be that they are buried deep under Tayma's temple once Nabonidus completes his mission with the Jews. Or perhaps the broken stone pieces become simple mementoes, placed in one of Nabonidus' curiosity museums, reminding him of his days on the mesa, and how difficult it was working with people who simply didn't grasp what he was trying to do.

---

[68] That Aaron's rod is included after it miraculously sprouts (Numbers 17), showing divine preference for the house of Levi, should be seen as somewhat suspicious, in that it legitimises the subsequent priestly clan.

[69] Leonard Woolley, *Ur of the Chaldees* (Book Club Associates: 1982, 1929), 251-5.

[70] Julia Hsieh, "The Practice of Repairing Vessels in Ancient Egypt: Methods of Repair and Anthropological Implications," *NEA* 79.4 (2016): 280-3, here 280.

[71] Hsieh, 283.

# 18

IDOLS

T here are two main interests here: What does the golden calf represent and why is Nabonidus (Moses) so angered by its creation?; and, How is it constructed and why does Aaron suggest he didn't make it?

## "I AM"

Aaron is left at the foot of the mesa while Moses goes up to retrieve the tablets; this, I have claimed, is to disassociate him from the tablets themselves, much in the way Babylonian craftsmen ceremoniously disassociated themselves from the cultic statues they fashioned. The allusion, however, reiterates Aaron's skills as a craftsman; he goes from making the tablets, to making the calf statue. That's his profession. This is probably why he comes across as blasé about the incident when questioned by Moses (see below); he is simply doing the work he has been asked to do.

The people ask Aaron to make *elohim* for them, "gods" that can be placed before them, to bring comfort and assurance, to guide, protect, etc. Moses had set himself up to supply all these things but he is not there; he is up on the mesa conversing with "I AM." This is immediately contrasted against the statement (in Exod 34:1) concerning Moses, "the *man*"; it is another subtle snipe at Nabonidus. The mixed-heritage people desire their familiar deities to fill the void left by Nabonidus, yet he is off on his own, allegedly *becoming* a god (erroneously); the 'bringing up from Egypt' phrase is mentioned three times, first with respect to Moses (32:1), then the gods (32:4), then Moses again (32:7). One might suggest this repetition is to highlight the perception that Moses sees himself as one of these gods[1] but, as usual, I think it is far more nuanced than that. His divine authority is essentially negated here; he is declared just a "man."

So how does one statue suddenly become multiple deities? The answer is to be found, primarily, in the nature of Nabonidus' chimeric god, "I AM."

Beaulieu suggests that earlier in his career, Nabonidus "tried to conflate" two views into one theology, i.e., the tradition of "the god Anu as demiurge" and that of Nabu as "divine hero," both manifestations of "Sîn as new moon."[2] This is, therefore, a precedent for Nabonidus creating a hybrid deity and is not, as I am sure you might be wondering, *my* unfounded and eccentric notion. It seems as though the first attempt had its failings, with too many people in opposition; here, in the desert of Arabia, far from the Marduk priests, far from politicians, he can try again. The ambiguity of "I AM," the new amalgamation of Sun, Moon, and Stars that includes the familiar Mesopotamian themes (e.g., the obvious echoes of Gilgamesh), a strong Egyptian element, the Arabic Qenite influences, etc., must seem to Nabonidus the perfect balance that will appeal to the largest demographic.

The calf in Exodus 34 is a bull-calf (*egel*). There are many adult-bull representations of deities from both Egypt and Mesopotamia (e.g., representing Ptah, Osiris,[3] Horus, Sîn, Adad, etc.) but the *calf* iconography is special. I have discovered only three examples: 1) Baal, the storm god, when depicted as the warrior-deity, is a bull-calf;[4] 2) Marduk is called in Sumerian, "Bull-Calf of the Sun."[5] His father is the Sun-god, Shamash; and

---

[1] For more on this idea see Jack M. Sasson, "Bovine Symbolism in the Exodus Narrative," *VT* 18.3 (1968): 380-7.

[2] Paul-Alain Beaulieu, "Nabonidus the Mad King: A Reconstruction of His Steles from Harran and Babylon, in *Representations of Political Power: Case Histories from Times of Change and Dissolving Order in the Ancient Near East,* M. Heinz and M. Feldman, eds. (Winona Lake: Eisenbrauns, 2007), 137-66, here 154.

[3] Plutarch says: "… the Apis, the 'Image of the soul of Osiris'," ; "… the Ox that is kept at Heliopolis, which they call Mnevis (sacred to Osiris, and which some believe to be the sire of the Apis) …. they consider the ox as the animated image of Osiris." (17; 28; 33).

[4] Hundley, 560-1 n. 3.

[5] Michael B. Hundley, "What Is the Golden Calf?" *CBQ* 79.4 (2017): 559-79, here 571.

3) Ra is depicted as a white bull-calf.[6] The latter two, clearly, are solar deities. Gold is associated with solar symbolism and is synonymous with the flesh of the gods. Together, the bull-calf and the gold most likely represent the Sun-gods. By linking the idol with the actual departure from Egypt, once you see the solar and Marduk/Tiamat themes inherent in that narrative, it makes perfect sense that the small statue represents Re to some, but Marduk to others.

Linking the "I AM" with bovine iconography (though not specifically with a bull-calf) is a fascinating little detail in an illustration from the tomb of Seti I depicting the "Heavenly Cow." Inscribed on a hind inner-thigh of the beast (i.e., an avatar of Hathor) are the words "*iw.i im.i,*" translated as "I am who I am" (the same as in the Hebrew, *'ehyeh 'ăšer 'ehyeh*), while the ceremonial inscription refers to "the Infinite Ones who are."[7] If this isn't a precedent for the all-encompassing "I AM" and the notion of a singular bovine representing multiple deities, I don't know what is.[8]

In the pro-Moses book of Deuteronomy, "I AM" is called "God of gods and Lord of Lords, the Great God" (10:17), thus implying that there was never meant to be a complete banishment of other deities, just a new hierarchy. The worship of multiple deities by those exposed to both the Yahweh tradition and the Egyptian pantheon is recorded in a fascinating papyrus entitled "The Aramaic Text in Demotic Script." The "liturgy of the New Year's festival of an Aramaic-speaking community in Upper Egypt ... seems to have been dictated by a priest of the community, possibly at the beginning of the 3rd Century BCE, to an Egyptian scribe trained in the 4th Century BCE"; the authors of the text appear to have been residents of Bethel, "joining the foreign colonists settled there by earlier Assyrian kings," before going to Egypt.[9] What proves fascinating for me is that this mixed community worships, in unison, both Horus *and* Adonai:[10]

> May Horus answer us in our troubles; may Adonai answer us in our troubles.

---

[6] See images in Luigi Tripani, *The God Ra: Iconography (With all the Forms and Names from the 'Litany of Ra')* (Amentet Neferet: 2015), 70-2.

[7] Edward F. Wente, *The Literature of Ancient Egypt An Anthology of Stories, Instructions, Stelae, Autobiographies, and Poetry*, William Kelley Simpson, ed., R. K. Ritner, V. A. Tobin, E. Wente, Jr., trans. (Yale University Press, 2003), 293-4.

[8] Cf. Judg 5:5 : "... the One at Sinai."

[9] Steiner, Richard C. "The Aramaic Text in Demotic Script," in *The Context of Scripture. Vol. 1: Canonical Compositions from the Biblical World*, William W. Hallo and K. L. Younger, eds. (Leiden: Brill, 2003), 309-27, here 310.

[10] "Adonai" is a title meaning "Lord" (like "Baal") from the noun *adon* ("lord, mister, sir"); often equated with Yahweh.

O crescent (lit., bow) / bowman in heaven,
Sahar[11] / shine forth;
… from Zephon may Horus help us/
May Horus grant us what is in our hearts; …
All <our> plans may Horus fulfil …
may Adonai not fall short in satisfying — every request
of our hearts.

A Psalm from Bethel (xi 11-19)[12]

They continue by claiming "Mar is our god" but then they add, amazingly, "Horus-Yaho, our bull, is with us," i.e., a reference to the *bovine union of the solar deity Horus and the lunar deity Yahweh*:

With reference to the discussion on the symbolic meaning of Baal-zephon, in the context of the escape from Ur, this papyrus seems to substantiate such a perception (i.e., that it was a sign of assistance from the north; I did not know of this poem at that point in the research) only now, we can appreciate the connection to the solar deity Horus also (and thus underscore the link between the "bones of Joseph" and Pharaoh Ahmose III):

Who is like you, Horus, among gods?
Come from Shur,[13]
take vengeance
for those who call upon you,
… make us strong again, beneath you, Horus, beneath you,
Adonai, Resident of Heaven; like the phoenix, Horus,
Resident of Heaven.
Call out to us your words …and make us strong again,
Baal from Zephon.
Arise, Horus, to our aid / help us.
May Adonai give heed to my prayer.
… Horus, may you grant protection ….

A prayer to Adonai (xii 11-17)[14]

So, with all this in mind, why should Nabonidus react so violently when he discovers what the people have done? He comes from a world intensely focussed on multiple deities and the worship of idols. Have the Qenites truly influenced him so much that he now rejects everything he has believed in and practiced his entire life? No, of course not. I don't think for

---

[11] God of the dawn.
[12] Steiner, 318.
[13] In this context, the Way to Tyre, on the Phoenician coast, but see how this parallels the idea of Yahweh coming from Paran, etc. (in the Wilderness of Shur).
[14] Steiner, 318.

a moment this has anything to do with the representation of the gods; it has to do with Nabonidus' nature and the dogma of the early priests.

Remember that throughout the anti-Nabonidus exodus narratives (e.g., Exodus and Numbers), the old man is being tested (by the new generation); he is constantly forced to prove himself able and willing to change, in order to earn a place in this highly anticipated and divinely-sanctioned new kingdom of Israel. This is wholly the Jewish authors' invention. Nabonidus could not be more indifferent to the notion; that was *never* his plan. If the golden-calf incident actually occurred, and is not a contrivance of later scribes, I think what might have happened is that whilst up on the mesa undergoing his sombre initiation (this is more what he is interested in), he first becomes agitated due to the noise emanating from the revelry below. Descending to find that the crowd have not done as *he* commanded, have disregarded the solemn oaths they have only just made with *him*, their king (in all but name), he simply loses control. His old nature kicks in again, i.e., the nature we saw glimpses of in the Song of Solomon, when Nitocris broke the rules or got on his nerves. This same nature surfaced when Miriam crossed him, and when Jehudijah was found out. He responds with anger and violence. Hundley proposes that Moses' anger is exhibited in the phrase "great sin" which appears three times (Exod 32:21, 30, 31); in other HB texts this refers to the breaking of a contract, in the context of being unfaithful through idolatry, etc.,[15] so this also suits the context here but for a slightly different reason. It is not that the people are being unfaithful, but that they have humiliated Nabonidus by making a mockery of his carefully thought-out covenant/treaty.

Nabonidus has a deity in his mind. This is *his* project, *his* time to make an impact on history by resolving the worship of Sun, Moon, and Stars, into one, simple, non-denominational god. This is supposed to be *his* hour, when the Akhenaten side of him overwhelms the Henry VIII side, where wisdom is supposed to outweigh the base passions, but the masses have become too bothersome and have ruined the moment. Just like Enlil in the Babylonian *Atrahasis* epic,[16] Nabonidus reacts with the destruction of not only the tablets but also the golden calf and then the worshippers! The words of Exod 32:7-10 I see as a paraphrase of what Nabonidus *might* have said, especially as it implies the Israelites are to be vanquished for their behaviour, but the

---

[15] Michael B. Hundley, "What Is the Golden Calf?" *CBQ* 79.4 (2017): 559-79, here 576.

[16] For how this relates to Nabonidus in the Song, see Tyson, 205-7. Just for balance, there is a similar tale from the Egyptian culture, in the *Book of the Heavenly Cow* (the same text mentioned above, with the "I AM" inscription), which tells of Re threatening to destroy the rebellious humans by sending Hathor, as the lioness Sekhmet, to kill them all. Again, humanity is eventually spared.

deity still sees Moses as worthy of founding a "great nation" (it just has that haughtiness about it that suits Nabonidus' character). But 32:11-14 I consider an addendum by subsequent scribes to explain why the nation was not actually "consumed," in light of what had already been "written" in Genesis.

*Atrahasis* tells of how Enlil, Lord of the Gods, disturbed by the ruckus humanity is making, vows to destroy them; the tale of the Flood ensues, where the hero Atrahasis is told he will be the only one to survive, along with "two of everything" (i.e., animals), he is to place in the ark. To the average Babylonian-reared exile, this scene with Moses being singled out as the only one to benefit from this encounter with God at Sinai, when all the rest are punished (Exod 32:10), the parallels must seem clear, right down to the obligatory "two" tablets being placed in the ark. Not only does this suggest Nabonidus is *not* playing the role of the deity (i.e., in an assumed apotheosis, for he is seen as Atrahasis/Noah, from whom the resulting civilization will arise) but also, it foreshadows the issues that soon threaten the status quo, i.e., insurgencies and challenges to Moses' authority.

A Note on 1 Chr 3:20-3

Just as in the Song of Solomon, where Jehudijah leaves us her signature by hinting at her specific role in the royal court via the distribution of the name "Solomon,"[17] so here, in 1 Chronicles, we are provided a potential confirmation that "Solomon" is/was "Moses." In the genealogies of the "descendants of Solomon," we find a curious numbering: In 3:20 we have the number "five," in 3:22 is "six," in 3:23 is "three," and in 3:24 is "seven." This entire genealogical list is full of mystery, which I am still working on, but these numbers are unique in such a context. They total 21. In terms of gematria, this equates to the word *'ehyeh* (in *'ehyeh 'ăšer 'ehyeh*: I am who I am); it equates to "I AM." Thus the "descendants of Solomon" ultimately equate to those who experienced, or followed, "I AM," the deity of Sinai, of Moses/Nabonidus.

# "… OUT CAME THIS CALF!"

When Aaron is left at the foot of the mesa while Moses takes Joshua with him to retrieve the tablet(s), his skill as a metallurgist is called upon to create the *elohim* for the crowd.

---

[17] Janet Tyson, *She Brought the Art of Women: A Song of Solomon, Nabonidus, and the Goddess* (Norwich: Pirištu Books, 2023), 216-17.

In Exod 32:4, Aaron receives the gold from the people; he then fashions it with *cheret*, "an engraving tool," i.e., a stylus used for writing, inscribing, etc. This ties together both Aaron's employment as the carver of the inscriptions on the tablets and his profession as a (gold)smith.

There is much debate on whether the idol is constructed as a solid gold statue or a gold-plated wooden form. Jeremiah's famous condemnation of idols (Jer 10:3-15) supports the traditional Babylonian method of crafting such statues from wood, overlaid with precious metal (silver/gold). Similarly, Isa 40:18-20 mentions a statue first prepared by the artisan (i.e., carpenter), then by the goldsmith. Isa 44:13 actually mentions the stylus: "The carpenter stretches a line, he marks it out with a stylus; he makes it with planes, and marks it with a compass; he shapes it into the figure ...." It would appear that Aaron uses the stylus to inscribe, perhaps, the animal's features, or symbols pertaining to various gods, etc., into the surface of the mould he is about to use. The Hebrew term used to describe the idol is *maccekah*, i.e., "a libation, molten metal or image"; he makes a moulded calf.

As I like to discover the pragmatic, historical veracity of scenes like this, I did a few calculations and came up with how large a statue could be made, given an entourage of about a hundred people (the "seventy" of Exod 1:5, is symbolic but I have argued that very few people went on this trip; even 100 is generous, I feel), who each give two earrings to the cause. Each earring might weigh about five grams (a modern jeweller suggests anything over five grams per earring is considered "heavy" and not for everyday wear;[18] the Israelites would wear their earrings all the time). Aaron can thus work with approximately 1kg of gold. While that sounds like a lot of precious gold, it would result in a statue no larger than about 10 x 5 cm (consider that King Tutankhamun's gold mask weighs 11 kg and stands 54 x 40 cm). That's quite small but add a wooden plinth and place it high, it might suffice.

Aaron is a metalworker; Qurayyah is filled with metalworkers, furnaces, moulds, etc., i.e., everything that would be needed to melt gold at 1000° C and make a molten image. It is not until Exod 32:24 that we learn Aaron *puts the gold into a fire*; only a furnace can reach those temperatures. Although Aaron seems to back-peddle, claiming he collected the gold, put it in the fire, and out popped a cultic statue, this is our modern perception of his words, for isn't that exactly what putting molten gold into a mould does? It turns earrings into calves, as if by magic! He keeps the process a trade secret, as expected.

That Exod 32:24 mentions the act of putting the object into a fire as one sort of thing, and it coming out as another, speaks to its authenticity, for

---

[18] Desiderate, https://desiderate.com.au.

why would someone invent this for the narrative?; the calf has already been described (in 32:4), so it would be superfluous if not actually witnessed. It was a mysterious episode that was noted but not understood. If the calf had been made of wood, throwing it into the fire would simply destroy it, as we see in 32:20; besides, he says he put the *gold* into the fire, not the finished statue itself, and the description does not remotely suggest the gold miraculously changed into wood.[19] Rather, the scene reinforces the metallurgical skills of Aaron, the craftsman.

In Exod 32:20, Moses is said to burn the idol and pulverise (*tachan*, "to grind") the remains. This is not so easily done with a solid gold object; it would take a long time and some serious steel files, or it would simply melt.[20] Only a wooden statue would burn so readily in a fire, to produce the "powder" (from the verb *daqaq*, "to crush, pulverize, thresh") he then puts in water and forces the crowd to consume. Because it has been demonstrated that the idol cannot be made of wood if it is to resist Aaron's fire, and due to the impracticality of grinding up 1kg of solid gold (I should think the heated moment would pass in the meantime),[21] I cannot see this part of the iconic tale as *history*. Besides, it seems to be the basis of Num 5:11-22; why didn't the author of Numbers (also leaning towards an anti-Moses sentiment) simply relay the same tale, instead of making the enforced drinking of sacred dust (this time from the floor of the tabernacle, rather than from a cultic statue) yet

---

[19] I did explore the possibility that Aaron uses a burnishing/gilding technique, which would involve a fire, but the text we have does seem to suggest the transition from gold to calf was speedy, while gilding takes time and several other processes It also requires the use of liquid mercury (which they might have had access to as this comes from cinnabar, present in volcanic rocks, but there is no evidence I could find to suggest they used this in 6th Century BCE Arabia); plus, there is no mention of wood *at all* in the HB text which, if historically true, would have been included to balance with the object's alleged method of destruction (this suggests the latter episode is a later addendum, and the scribe is not permitted to change what is already written).

[20] Mortar and pestles were used to grind *ore* (i.e., rock) and extract the desired metals (Lucas Braddock Chen, "Sumerian Arsenic Copper and Tin Bronze Metallurgy (5300-1500 BC): The Archaeological and Cuneiform Textual Evidence," *AD* 9.3 (2021): 185-197, here 190). Making a powder from a metal object is possible only with either modern grinding machines or chemicals ("Making Metal Powder," § Metal Powders: Types, Characteristics, and Applications, The Metal Powder Industries Federation, www.mpif.org).

[21] Samuel E. Loewenstamm (in "The Making and Destruction of the Golden Calf," *Biblica* 48.4 (1967): 481-90, here 483-5) provides Ugaritic precedents for this form of destruction, in terms of the symbolic killing of Mot, the god of Death. His body is burned, crushed, and scattered in water. The version in Deut 9:21 is succinct and does not involve the enforced drinking; this is a pro-Moses text, so the tendency to skirt around the difficult bits is obvious here.

another 'let's use a woman's menses against her if she strays from what we require of her' curse? The ritual in Numbers pertains to adultery, the punishment for the woman being a direct attack on her uterus, i.e., infertility.[22]

I can see how the adultery theme might be superimposed onto the Moses story but not in the manner traditional interpretations might explain it. That is, the calf *itself* is not something Nabonidus would have been angry about; it supposedly represents the very gods that the entire scenario at the Nile was all about, i.e., those who represent the Sun and the "son of the Sun," Re and Horus, but also Marduk. Remember his nonchalant attitude to Eldad and Medad and their secret liaison in the tent (Num 11:26-30); it didn't rattle him because this was behaviour he was familiar with.

Nabonidus is angered by the people's impatience and willingness to put Aaron in charge of their cultic depiction, rather than wait for the final ratification of the covenant, i.e., the sealed tablet(s). He has no qualms with the iconography of the Sun, Moon, and Stars; he has designed the ark with cherubim (as Solomon, he creates even larger cherubim for the temple, adorns his throne with lions, etc.). He just wants "I AM" to be *his* idea, and I think it is from this episode, not just the influence of the Qenites, that he realises an aniconic deity would be best, to ensure the broadest acceptance. It is not the deity who is "jealous"; it is *Nabonidus*. He would see this as the opportunity for a new beginning, but the people are still content with the past; his response is a visceral reaction to what he sees as a personal snub. In a real-life scenario, I can see him ranting and raving and threatening to ram the idol down their throats, yes, but this is then over-egged in the narrative and taken up by the author of Numbers, who tries to make sense of it by making it about Moses' main source of frustration, i.e., women! It is another scenario that is predominantly symbolism, not history.

As mentioned in the description of the river ordeal allusions in Exod 7:20-25, the idea of a trial by water is deeply engrained in the Babylonian mind. The Exodus 7 example, recall, also revealed an anti-menses theme. There must be a connection.

Tensions between Moses and Aaron are increasing. The first sign of a problem is in Numbers 12, which describes the scene of Aaron and Miriam discussing Nitocris, the "Cushite" wife. As discussed earlier, it is Miriam who is punished for her 'rebelliousness' immediately by being expelled from camp for seven days, *as if* she is menstruating,, while Aaron is left pleading her cause, only to make things worse by (bizarrely) mentioning Nitocris' miscarriage. Nabonidus remains unnervingly silent, as if waiting for the right time to make his anger felt. The blood theme seems to be the uniting element.

---

[22] This is the passage from which we derive the awful pseudonym for menses, i.e., "the curse."

In the Babylonian tradition of an ordeal by drinking (magical, spiked, etc.) water, it is said that those who "successfully completed the ordeal were sometimes sent to the king … for further questioning, perhaps due to the principle of *"din napištim ana šarrim,"* according to which litigation over life belonged to the king: the king personally had to decide all of the cases that would result in loss of life."[23] The resulting massacres in both Exodus 32 and Numbers 5 suggests Nabonidus is still very much *acting* the king.

Thus, the imposition of the ordeal by water, using the calf itself as the sacred dust that must be consumed to demonstrate innocence or guilt, stems from the same mindset as the River Ordeal of Exodus 7, in that it demonstrates Nabonidus' folly. The scene at the Nile alludes to the inevitable profaneness of his plan (from the Jewish perspective), and the scene with the calf basically proves the point, fulfils the omen of the Nile, i.e., that Nabonidus would (metaphorically) destroy his own gods. The blame for the golden calf incident is set squarely on Aaron's shoulders (Exod 32:25, 35) but his punishment is yet to be devised.[24]

Even in the early stages of their relationship, one can discern a looming conflict between Moses and Aaron. Initially Moses' "prophet," Aaron was to use his skills to impress the pharaoh, to bolster Moses' impact, but very quickly it is Moses who takes the lead, demanding more of the credit. Joseph's bones replace Aaron as the solar representative of the chimeric deity, marking the irreversible shift in the depiction of Aaron from Moses' once brother and member of the original triad (the Sun), to someone of relatively little import. The multi-skilled goldsmith is soon replaced in the narrative by the bright young artisan Bezalel (Exod 35:31-3), who is commissioned with the construction of the tabernacle.[25] God, it is said,

> … filled him with divine spirit, intelligence, and knowledge in every kind of craft, to devise artistic designs, to work in gold, silver, and bronze, in cutting stones for setting, and in carving wood, in every kind of craft.

Bit by bit, Aaron is nudged into a less influential position until, once his task of preparing the tablet(s) is completed, he is relegated to this supervisory role at the foot of the mesa. The scene in Exod 32:25-6

---

[23] Joanna Töyräänvuori, "Trial by Water through the Ages," *SAA* 27.2 (2021): 301-30, here 312.

[24] See Midrash Tanchuma, Ki Tisa 19:2-5 which claims the murder of Hur by the crowd forces a subservient Aaron to do as he is told; Rabbeinu Bahya, Devarim 9:20:1 suggests Aaron's punishment is the death of his children.

[25] This is a harbinger of Solomon's appointment of Hiram-abi, the multi-talented smith from Tyre (1 Kgs 6:13-14), about which I intend to write a paper at a later date.

encapsulates the mood: Are the people on Moses' side, or Aaron's?

The emphasis on Aaron as the high priest in the exodus narratives is the invention of later priestly scribes.[26] Nabonidus sees *himself* in this role but, because this is not made explicit, it *is* possible to channel the high-priestly role to Aaron, thereby avoiding the acknowledgement of Nabonidus as such, and complying with the rule that the original story remain intact.

# DANIEL'S STATUES

While I don't want to get into the dating, structure, etc., of the book of Daniel, it is worth noting that the general consensus does indicate chapters 1-6 date from a much earlier time than the subsequent chapters (i.e., ca. 6th Century BCE), and may have served as a sort of catalyst for the increasingly apocalyptic visions that follow.[27]

Our own cultural perceptions and biases, in terms of literary criticism, etc., affect how we understand ancient symbolism and metaphor. As historians, we constantly need to remind ourselves that the interpretation of texts must, first and foremost, involve removing ourselves from our modern take on things and experience the imagery and the context within the framework of what is known from the *past*, not what is allegedly prophesied of the future; when you are working with biblical texts that can be tricky.

As I argue that the early words of Daniel relate to Nabonidus, and not Nebuchadnezzar (i.e., as a means of subverting the *name* of "Nabonidus," as explained in *She Brought*),[28] I must interpret Daniel's statues in terms of what I think this particular author would have *known*, historically. I have previously argued that Daniel (i.e., the biblical character known by that name) knew Nabonidus and Belshazzar intimately and even stayed with the Babylonian king whilst the latter was residing in Tayma.[29] I therefore suggest Daniel 1-6 is a commentary on what transpired leading up to the fall of Babylon, but with the *hindsight* of what ensued after, i.e., with "Moses"

---

[26] Moses Aberbach and Leivy Smolar ("Aaron, Jeroboam, and the Golden Calves," *JBL* 86.2 (1967): 129-40, here 130) suggests Aaron "function(s) in a sacerdotal capacity … in connection with the preparation for the calf worship" but adds: "The consecration of the Levites and of the priests had not yet taken place. There is no reason to assume that Aaron had any priestly status" (130, n. 7).

[27] For the apocalyptic perspective, see Michael Segal, "The Four Kingdoms and Other Chronological Conceptions in the Book of Daniel," in *Four Kingdom Motifs before and beyond the Book of Daniel*, Andrew B. Perrin, et al., eds., (Leiden: Brill, 2021), 13-38.

[28] Tyson, 50-1. See also 4-6; 50; 140; 223-4.

[29] Tyson, 125 (see also 6, 36 on 4Q242 "Prayer of Nabonidus").

and the exodus (or at least the rumours that drifted back to Babylonia/Persia). As with most, if not all biblical texts, a certain amount of editing has gone on to meld these earlier sections with the later, and this has led to some misinterpretations.

With this parameter set, let's take a closer look at the two statues that appear in Daniel 2 and 3.

## *Four Metals and Clay*

Previously, I suggested the statue-dream in Dan 2:31-45 was part of Daniel's subtle campaign to encourage Nabonidus to step down, i.e., to abdicate in favour of his son, Belshazzar.[30] The feet of iron and clay, I posited, represented the mixed marriage between Nabonidus and Nitocris that would eventually cause the entire kingdom to fall (which it did) and which could not be condoned by Daniel. Now I have continued into this new field of investigation, it seems clear to me that although that interpretation sufficed for the Song of Solomon's analysis, there is more to be gleaned from the two statues described in Daniel, in terms of how they reflect the subsequent Nabonidus years, i.e., the Abraham/Moses years.

The statue in Dan 2:36-49 is an retrospective omen. Consisting of all the major metals used by civilization at that time, i.e., gold, silver, bronze, and iron, plus an added ingredient, "clay," the omen-statue represents Nabonidus' precarious position *in hindsight*. It is but one of three steps in Daniel that lead to the downfall of the great kingdom of Babylon, i.e., 1) the composite statue, 2) the gold statue, and 3) the writing on the wall.

In the "second year" of the king's reign, i.e., the same year Nabonidus witnesses the first of the portentous 13 Ululu lunar eclipses, which marks his departure from Babylon (in 553 BCE),[31] "Nebuchadnezzar" dreams that this huge statue, seemingly robust, is brought low by a simple stone (reminiscent of David and Goliath). Daniel interprets this dream by first making sure the king knows that the *King of Babylon* is represented by the shining gold "head": "—you are the head of gold" (Dan 2:38). The following description, I posit, is where the apocalyptic editors show their hand. I do not support, as said several times already, any notion of absolute prophecy; what is written must be already *known*. As this section of Daniel is unmistakably and generally agreed to be ca. 6th Century BCE, there is no way anyone can claim to know what or how many "kingdoms" will follow Nabonidus' reign. If the statue is

---

[30] Tyson, 137.
[31] Tyson, 154-7.

authentically a part of the original tale, it must have meaning within a 6th Century BCE context, no later.

We have seen how Nabonidus attempts, at Sinai, to make a chimeric deity from the Sun, Moon, and Stars, amalgamated with the symbolic union of Osiris and Re in the darkness of the Duat. When we look at the metallic statue in Daniel, we find the "gold" is Nabonidus, i.e., the Crown, the pinnacle, in one sense, but also the Sun, for he has been depicted in both the Song of Solomon and Exodus as being the double of Pharaoh (and as "Samson" he is the Sun Man). Of course, this is erroneous, as Nabonidus retains his loyalty to Sîn, the Moon, but the information, as we see in the early historians, like Herodotus, reaches these authors as incomplete or misunderstood reports from distant lands. This is the kind of thing that fuelled the fairly widespread idea that the Babylonian king had become deified during the Sinai years.

The statue's metals, I suggest, symbolise the hybrid nature of Nabonidus' supposedly 'future' deity. The gold represents the Sun; silver, the Moon; bronze the Stars; and iron, the Underworld.

* Gold, of course, needs little explanation. It is synonymous with solar worship, the flesh of Re, etc. It is strongly depicted in Egyptian iconography.

* Silver is the metal of the Moon in many civilizations due to its colour; "the Egyptians associated silver with the moon, ritual purity, and the bones of the gods."[32]

* Bronze is a little more complicated but can be summed up using two concepts, i.e., copper metallurgy and the symbolic representation of the cosmos, and serpent worship.

To many civilizations, the celestial sphere, or dome, that held the stars was made of metal, e.g., the Sumerians thought it to be made of tin, while the Greeks' preferred metal was either bronze or iron.[33]

The alchemical symbol for copper is also the planetary symbol for Venus., i.e., the circle with a cross beneath ♀. Venus, of course, is the planet associated with Ishtar, the "star" in Nabonidus' triad. Though a later identification, alchemical symbols are often derived from ancient ideas.

As we are in a copper-based community at Sinai, it makes sense to see the firmament (stars) in terms of burning copper:

---

[32] Deborah Schorsch, "Silver in Ancient Egypt," *Heilbrunn Timeline of Art History* (New York: The Metropolitan Museum of Art, 2000–), September 2018, www.metmuseum.org.

[33] N. F. Gier, *God, Reason, and the Evangelicals: The Case Against Evangelical Rationalism* (Lanham: University Press of America, 1987), 285.

The book of Ezekiel points to a link between the divine presence in the temple of Jerusalem (Ezekiel 10) and in the celestial universe (Ezekiel 1), both milieus being described in almost the same terms. Interestingly, the first Ezekiel vision (Ezekiel 1) describes the celestial throne of YHWH as a universe of fierce fire (vv. 4, 13, 27), radiance (vv. 13, 27-8), glowing coals (v, 13), and blowing wind (vv. 20-1), all associated with a circular structure (v. 27). This representation of the celestial universe is similar to that encountered in the vision of the celestial universe in Daniel. There, the prophet envisions this divine domain as a fiery environment from which a scorching molten matter flows (Dan 7:9-10). Both descriptions fit the representation of the celestial universe as a furnace at work.[34]

This is then associated with the idea of the serpent, i.e., the copper/bronze serpent Moses raises in Num 21:9. Interestingly, in Daniel, the term for "bronze" is uniquely *nechash*, while elsewhere it is *nechosheth*; *nechash* is a play on *nachash*, which means "serpent." This is why the belly and thighs of the statue are made of bronze, for snakes travel on their bellies. The HB connection between the copper/bronze and the serpent is Mosaic: Num 21:9 and 2 Kgs 18:4 both refer to Moses' snake-on-a-stick as "Nehushtan": Amzallag suggests that "wordplay between serpent (*nāḥāš*) and copper (*nāḥāš /něḥōšet*) invites us to look for a metallurgical context of interpretation."[35]

Thus, the statue's bronze belly signifies both the firmament in the triad (the stars) and the serpentine cultic influence in Nabonidus' chimeric idol/deity (in the dream of Daniel 2), which itself becomes a symbol of the Sinai/Qurayyah/copper influence on Nabonidus' new religion.

✶ Iron then, the heaviest of metals, the darkest, the one used to make tools and weapons, the one that requires sophisticated smithing techniques and is most associated with the legends of Vulcan, etc., becomes synonymous with the deep earth, the underground, or, in Nabonidus' case, the underworld. This is the dark realm of the dead Re, the "black box," the "cavern" where Osiris and Re are fused together by fiery, subterranean forces.

---

[34] Nissim Amzallag, "A Metallurgical Perspective on the Birth of Ancient Israel," *ER* 12.2 (2021): 65 §27, doi: 10.46586/er.12.2021.8742§27. And recall that I have discussed the "sparks" in terms of the "heavenly host"/stars.

[35] Amzallag, "Metallurgical Perspective," §14.

> *The sky over your head shall be bronze, and the earth under you iron.*
> Deut 28:23[36]

The only thing left is the clay. My first thought was to see this as the earth with which God supposedly creates Adam, and I saw this as a possible denigration by the human element, i.e., Nabonidus himself is the human element, so it is his weaknesses that make the kingdom unstable and vulnerable. Due to his creation of Adam from the earth, God is often referred to as the divine "potter," so this was the first image that came to mind. As I always say, however, the etymology is key.

The word for "clay" in Daniel 2 is *chasaph* ("clay, or potsherd"), not *aphar* ("dry earth, dust") or *adamah* ("ground, land"), as in Gen 2:7. *Chasaph* has the same Aramaic root as the verb *chaspas*, meaning "scaled off," therefore, scale-like;[37] *chasaph* is sometimes translated as "potsherd" (which can have the shape of a fish-scale). This is why Dan 2:42 suggests the feet are "partly brittle" (pottery is brittle, even though the clay is malleable). So, seeing some sort of wordplay here, I searched for another example of *chaspas*. The *only* other instance of this verb in the HB is in Exod 16:14, that is, in the description of the "manna" as a "fine flaky substance." This event takes place at the Tayma sabkha.

So, my initial instinct seems to have been on the right track. The "clay" in the feet of the statue in Daniel 2 represents Nabonidus' Tayma, i.e., one half the "divided kingdom" (which would then translate into Solomon's divided kingdom, as Solomon is based on Nabonidus, too). Considering Herodotus' impression that it was Nitocris who ruled Babylon (*Hist.* 1.185-7), it isn't a far leap to imagine Daniel (as I say in *She Brought*)[38] using the weakness of the clay to symbolise Nabonidus, and the "iron" in the feet of the statue the strong Nitocris. The kingdom was supposedly doomed the instant he married her, as the Talmud implies, i.e., God plans the future destruction of the temple at the moment the royal couple consummate their marriage (Avodah Zarah, 1:2, 39c).

From a scientific perspective, however, Tayma clay is proven to produce more brittle pottery than Qurayyah clay: "Tayma crucibles were made with normal clay but lack the rich quartz temper found in the Qurayyah crucible."[39] This could explain why more successful pottery production is

---

[36] Cf. Lev 26:19, which speaks of the punishment for idol worship: "I will break your proud glory, and I will make your sky like iron and your earth like copper." It reverses what would be considered normal.

[37] BDB, https://biblehub.com.

[38] Tyson, 140.

[39] Siran Liu, et al., "Copper Processing in the Oases of Northwest Arabia:

found at Qurayyah, but it also suggests a distinction between the geology of Tayma and everywhere else. Also, studies into the high-rate of damage to structures in modern Tayma reveal that "The shale is a fine grained weak rock composed of sedimentary deposits mainly clay or silt, oriented and laminated, *flaky in nature* (emphasis mine), often referred to as silty shale or clayey shale."[40] Shale breaks into sherds, or scale-like fragments. Still just a coincidence?

The metal figure[41] is destroyed by the unhewn rock that comes from the "mountain" seemingly under divine volition (2:34, 45). It strikes at the foundation of the statue, its feet, shattering the brittle clay sherds, toppling the entire structure, the resulting "chaff" being blown away by the winds, as if it had never been. The stone, however, becomes "a great mountain" (2:35) and is deemed invincible. While the common understanding is that this is a metaphor for the kingdom of God (which it is), the allusion in a historical context is to the rise of the kingdom of Israel (as the representative of that god; the little stone that slay the giant). Hence, we see in Gen 49:24 the "Rock of Israel," and in Dan 2:34 "the stone," using the same Hebrew word, *eben* ("stone").

With the hindsight of knowing what eventually transpires in the Arabian Desert, the author(s) of Daniel 2 illustrate Nabonidus' hubris and audacity, for the king in the narrative pays no heed to the dream interpretation but goes on to create another statue, this time one of pure gold.

## Golden Statue

This statue, in Daniel 3, is not an omen. Nor is it a representation of a deity. It is a parody of the golden calf scenario at Sinai (suggesting "Daniel" knew what had occurred there).

Parallel elements in the depiction include:

★ *The sound of musical instruments (the first mentioned is the "horn") used as a signal to the people to worship the golden statue*

---

Technology, Alloys and Provenance," *JAS* 53 (2015): 492-503, here 501, §6.1.2. "Tayma."

[40] Muawia Dafalla and Mosleh A. Al-Shamrani, "Swelling Characteristics of Saudi Tayma Shale and Consequential Impact on Light Structures," *JCEA* 8.5 (2014): 613-623, here 614.

[41] Tim Meadowcroft (in "Metaphor, Narrative, Interpretation, and Reader in Daniel 2-5," *Narrative* 8.3 (2000): 257-78, here 265) raises the question of whether we should be seeing this statue as a representation of one person (the king) or of "empire" itself (rather than the sequential kingdoms idea).

*(Dan 3:5)*. The Israelites hold a festival in honour of the golden calf where much noise is made, i.e., in Exod 32:18 it is the "sound of revellers" and in the Numbers 25 "Peor" incident, we learn that musicians and songstresses are there. It is also the trumpet that represents Moses' conversation with his deity in Exod 19:19, and it becomes the symbolic duty of the priests to replicate this horn-blowing[42] both as a call to arms and as a command to assemble: Num 10:10 makes it clear that trumpets are to be blown at all festivals to remind them of "I AM."

✳ *Those refusing to worship the statue are threatened with "furnace" and "fire" (Dan 3:6)*. At Qurayyah, furnaces and fires abound and much of the Sinai imagery/symbolism is linked to fire, which may substantiate this subtle allusion. In Exod 32:27-9, those who *do* worship the golden calf are put to death. In both scenarios the people are informed upon by others, revealing a profound schism in religious beliefs and a precarious social structure. The threat of death if due reverence is not shown is central to both situations and Nabonidus' ire is raised by the fact that the people do not behave the way *he* wants them to (respecting *his* new vision). The Babylonian audience, by the time they hear the tale, believe the mad old king is simply up to his old tricks of imposing his own beliefs onto the people; the result is a parody of the now famous temper tantrum, i.e., a reversal of the original details of the golden-calf scenario, where those who *do* worship the idol are slain (a technique used often in the Bible to indicate alternative meaning).[43]

✳ *Three men defy the king's orders to worship the statue and are executed by fire (Dan 3:12)*. I suggest Daniel's three religious abstainers represent the three significant people killed by Nabonidus as a direct result of the golden-calf incident, i.e., Hur, Jehudijah, and Aaron, in that order (the latter two will be dealt with in the following chapter).

"Hur" seems to come from the root *harar* ("to be hot, burned or charred") or *hara* ("to burn or ignite"), which links him, thematically, with Uri (Hur's father in Exod 31:1), whose name means "Ya is light, fiery, a flame," from the verb *or* ("to be or give light; to shine") and *Yah* (God). This, in turn links to his

---

[42] I wonder if the symbolism of the horn has anything to do with the magical blowpipe of the artisan, e.g., as Aaron possessed. When it is blown, the "glory" appears (in the agitated fire/sparks).

[43] E.g., in the Song, the reversal of the expected format for making an idol/statue is indicative of Nitocris' allegedly sinister motives (Tyson, 135; 143).

grandfather, Aaron, whose etymology speaks of "light" or "brightness." The family business of metalworking (with furnaces/fire/light) is consistently represented in the names. "Hur" is also linked to the name "Nahor" via *harar*; Genesis' Nahor is Exodus' Aaron.

In rabbinical texts, Hur is said to be *the son of Miriam*,[44] by Caleb (Rashi Exodus 17:10), but Caleb is also said to be Mered of 1 Chr 4:17 (Daf Shevui to Megillah 13a, 5), whom I claim is Nabonidus. The point is, even the early rabbis knew the basic "they were brothers and sisters" set-up of Exodus and its main characters didn't really work historically, so they attempted to find more logical relationships. In the end, we both agree that Miriam must be Hur's mother, but I claim Aaron is his father.

In Rashi on Exodus 32:6, the death of Hur is explained as angry retaliation by the crowd when he stands against them and criticises their worship of the calf; but Hur is actually killed as part of the Midian war. In Num 31:8; Zur is also one of those killed; this is Jethro/Reuel, with the pseudonym that means "Rock," identifying him as the priest of Yahweh (the "Rock") who dwells on the rock at Qurayyah. Thus, Nabonidus is seen to wipe out his own Midian relations.

✲ *The king mocks the absenters, saying "who is the god who will deliver you out of my hands?" (Dan 3:15).* The most famous line from the golden calf scene is "These are your gods, O Israel, who brought you up out of the land of Egypt!" (Exod 32:4). Daniel's king is being sarcastic, malevolent, as if referring directly back to this precedent. Nabonidus is again likened to the pharaoh with the hardened heart (Cambyses) who would not release his grasp on the Israelites and allow them to worship in their own way, in their own temple.

✲ *There are ten statements that "Nebuchadnezzar" made/raised a statue (Dan 3:1, 2, 3 (twice), 5, 7, 12, 14, 15, 18).* There are ten commandments associated with the golden calf scenario. In both Daniel and Exodus, the ramifications of the people's unease with being forced to comply with Nabonidus' blinkered perception of religion include disharmony and violence.

In the process of this dream interpretation, Daniel begins the threefold denunciation of Nabonidus; just as the bloody Nile scenario, which showed the ex-king's plans to be futile from inception, and thereby his new religion proven a vain and useless demonstration of his arrogance, etc., so Daniel's

---

[44] Josephus argues that Miriam is married to Hur (*A.J.* 3.54).

three major scenes (two statues and the writing on the wall)[45] ridicule and denounce the king who has no conscience but a surfeit of hubris.


## A Note on "666"

Using the ancient system of gematria is fun and often enlightening but there are many ways of dealing with the numbers (e.g., adding the values of letters or entire words, adding the digits of a large number together, etc.), and many different sources of potential meanings or correlations, so care must be taken. Early scribes used gematria whilst *composing* their narratives, sometimes encoding information that was not considered for everyone, such as political biases, or subversive claims about people who might still be a threat, etc. The *context* of what it is you are deciphering must always be paramount so, for instance, if you are analysing a word or phrase that sits within a clearly negative context, it is of no use to you if the gematria you work out has positive connotations. Clearly something is wrong somewhere. My mantra has always been, "if I have to force it, *I'm* probably wrong." I include it in my work as and when it proves irresistible. The golden statue is a case in point, for we are given precise numbers to work with: The statue measures 60 cubits high by 6 cubits wide.

Immediately it becomes clear that these are not the dimensions of a human. 60 cubits is approximately 100 feet (30 meters), so the breadth is just ten percent of this, i.e., this is more a monolith than a figure. In fact, the HB text does not imply the statue is of a person at all, which is itself a clue. Early exegetes attempted to rationalise this discrepancy by suggesting the statue was in the style of a seated pharaoh (i.e., as witnessed by Nebuchadnezzar when he invaded the country; they claimed he made it of gold to surpass the stone colossi in Egypt), but then the 6-cubit width was still a problem, so it was explained as being not shoulder to shoulder but chest to back (which is not the way one would measure a statue or a person, normally).[46]

The intended gematria might be 60 x 6, which would give us 360. The gematria of the phrases "to glow," and "to burn"[47] (echoing the glowing of the solar deity, the burning of the furnaces, the gold in the statue, etc.), is 360. This

---

[45] For the writing on the wall scene see Tyson, 223-4.

[46] Charles Taylor, *Calmet's Dictionary of the Holy Bible* (London: Holdsworth and Ball, 1832), 535-6. It should be noted that Herodotus (*Hist.* 1.183) describes the sacking of the Esagila temple in Babylon in 482/1 BCE; a huge golden statue of a "man" was taken (many presume this to be the statue of Marduk but there is no evidence of this), so the allegory in Daniel might have been based on an actual statue, but given a twist.

[47] Bill Heidrick, "360," Hebrew Gematria, www.billheidrick.com.

is not really enough to warrant including precise measurements, I feel. If we *add* the numbers, however, 60+6, we get 66, and this proves more interesting, for the gematria of "spoil or booty, riches or wealth" is 66.[48] This is sounding more germane to both the Abraham and Moses tales … but also, and perhaps even more so, to that of Solomon.

Solomon's fortune is described in 1 Kgs 10:14-29. The very first element of his hoard of personal wealth is the vast amount of gold per year, i.e., 666 talents; ten percent of this number is 66. As impressive as his accumulation of treasures might be they are, throughout Jewish lore, considered one of the two main faults/sins, of Solomon:

> Apart from having married a Gentile … the king transgressed two other biblical laws. He kept many horses, which a Jewish king ought not to do, and, what the law holds in equal abhorrence, he amassed much silver and gold.[49]

"Solomon's" wealth exists because Nabonidus spends many years trading in the land of "milk and honey"; he is friends with two of the wealthiest men in the land, Hiram of Tyre and a retired Croesus. He takes booty wherever he goes, including Egypt, and sends everything back to Tayma, where his immense, ostentatious fortune grows and is on display. Resentment also grows when a king sets himself up in such a way and forces his subjects not only to do the hard graft (e.g., as corvée labour) but also to honour him and be forced to pay for the pleasure, e.g., in 1 Kgs 10:24-5, it is made clear that those seeking an audience with Solomon bring gifts of great value, perhaps a requisite. At the end of the Song of Solomon, the king's love of money is equalled by his love for the Elixir, which he sells for profit in the temple in Babylon.[50]

This consistently negative depiction reflects an antipathy toward Nabonidus that permeates almost every allusion to him. He has a *really* bad reputation.

Deut 17:14-20, written after the demise of Nabonidus, has this precise situation in mind, for the *nature* of any future "king" is given very specific prerequisites: He must not be a foreigner (17:15), as Nabonidus was. He must not acquire horses (17:16), which is one of Solomon's favourite acquisitions. He must not send the people back to Egypt under the auspices of acquiring "more horses" (17:16); Moses takes some of the Jews with him into Egypt to acquire the "bones of Joseph." The new king must not "acquire many wives for himself, or else his heart will turn away (17:17); this is said

---

[48] Heidrick, "66."
[49] "The Marriage of Solomon," *Legends of the Jews*, 4.5 (22).
[50] Tyson, 207-10.

of Solomon in 1 Kgs 11:1-3. "Silver and gold he must not acquire in great quantity for himself" (17:17); as Abraham, Moses, and Solomon, Nabonidus' reputation is heavily influenced by his desire for riches. And, finally, it is made clear that this new king will be subject to the law that is put into his hand on the day he is enthroned ... *by the priests* (17:18-19); as Moses, Nabonidus attempts to impose the laws of his own making upon the people, which leads to strife and revolt. It is clear, therefore, that even by the time of Deuteronomy, and even though the narrative itself presents a positive perception of Moses, the underlying trepidation that another Nabonidus might come along is palpable. Everything he represented is nullified and made anathema by this new law dictated by a Nabonidus-weary priesthood.

Might this "666" be the "beast" of Rev 13:15-18?:

> And that no man might buy or sell, save he that had the mark, or the name of the beast, or the number of his name. Here is wisdom. Let him that hath understanding count the number of the beast: for it is the number of a man; and his number is six hundred and sixty-six.

This warning is presented in terms of buying and selling; the number refers to "a man"; anyone who does as this man does (i.e., creating excessive wealth) is effectively tarred with the same brush. Money may be the root of all evil but might Nabonidus' reputation with the Jews be so deplorable that even hundreds of years later he is remembered (though still not named) by his association with "666"?

The following words/phrases also have a gematria of 666: "height"; "excellence; gain, emolument"; and "hidden" (Heidrick, "666"). The first suits the statue context, the second the wealth accrued by Abraham/ Moses/Solomon, and the third just screams Nabonidus and his search for arcane wisdom. The ten-percent allusion might be to Abraham, who is explicitly depicted providing a ten-percent tithe to Melchizedek (Gen 14:20),[51] thereby reiterating the link to Nabonidus and wealth.

***

So, getting back to the golden statue in Daniel 3, with its gematria of 66, taking the above perception of Nabonidus into consideration, we can deduce the following: 1) The statue is purposefully represented as an ingot of solid gold,[52] representing "wealth"; 2) This wealth is "worshipped" by the

---

[51] Saite pharaohs were known to offer ten-percent tithes to temples (Astrid Möller, *Naukratis: Trade in Archaic Greece* [Oxford: Oxford University Press, 2000]), 207-8.

[52] For an illustration of a long and narrow ingot (on a smaller scale) see

king and this worship is expected from others; it is considered idolatrous by the Jews; 3) The riches are acquired by means that are probably considered illicit (stolen, borrowed, sourced from foreigners, etc.); 4) The golden statue alludes to Nabonidus as "King Solomon."

The gematria of the phrase "the son of David" is, you guessed it, 66.[53]

# NABONIDUS' STATUES

In the historical record (to date), there are several references to Nabonidus' penchant for statues; if there were an inherited responsibility, or a cultural norm for the King of Babylon to be *so enamoured* with these objects, there would be no need for such references in texts that are on public display, that require much work to produce, and where space for wording is at a premium. Although, in a way, he is not doing anything his predecessors have not done, i.e., by creating likenesses of himself, or placing statues about the city, etc., I think Nabonidus' personal interest in statues is profound and unique, which is why they are employed to mock him in certain sources.

☆ In the Song of Solomon, the king himself is depicted as a cultic statue/idol, constructed by the goddess-like Nitocris (Ishtar), piece by piece (Song 5:10-16).[54] This is to parody his own apparent self-deification (and to emphasise the magical, therefore sinister, qualities of the Egyptian, Nitocris). There is also a subtle scene wherein the king is being taught to make an idol of his own, but he fails to complete the task, being distracted by more base desires (Song 4:1-7).[55] In a third statue-related scene, Song 7:1-7 is a parody of Nitocris' statue/idol of the king, with the woman as the subject, i.e., a fertility goddess.[56]

From formal inscriptions come the following examples of Nabonidus-related statues:

☆ Two fragments of a pedestal for a statue were discovered at Tayma. Part of the inscription (Nab 57) reads: "Statue of Nabonidus, kin[g of]

---

"Ystradowen finger ingot" (Matthew Knight, National Museums Scotland, www.nms .ac.uk).

[53] Bible Gematria, §"Tubal Cain is the Name," www.biblegematria .com.

[54] Tyson 135-42.

[55] Tyson, 101-2.

[56] Tyson, 171.

Babylon, mighty king, son of [Nabû-balāssu-iqbi, ...].''[57]

✷ In RCh iii 29 - iv 5, Nabonidus discovered the statue of Sargon whilst renovating Shamash's temple Ebabbar; he employed craftsmen to refashion its broken head. He then put it on public display and "firmly established *taklīmu offering(s)* for it" (i.e., homage was paid to it).

✷ Nab 46 is a stele inscription that actually opens with the proud declaration that the king had repaired several statues and rehomed them, according to the gods "commands" (i 1-8).

✷ Following Esarhaddon's and Ashurbanipal's example, Nabonidus "installed copper(-plated) statues of *mušḫuššu*-dragons as gateway guardians ... as well as statues of goat-fishes (*suḫurmāšū*);[58] (and) long-haired heroes (*laḫmū*) ...."[59]

✷ In the VA (i 6-8), the strange, chimeric idol/statue of Sîn is denounced and ridiculed as an abomination thought up by a mad man.

✷ Also in the VA (i 6-7). Nabonidus is said to have erected statues of the Anzu bird, i.e., the "Storm Dragon" and the "Wild Bull."

✷ He openly declares: "I securely placed an inscription of mine and an image of my royal majesty in the presence of the god Shamash and the goddess Aya ..." (Nab 26 i 33-ii 1; Nab 24 ii 7-10), thereby conferring sanctity upon a royal image.

---

[57] W&N, 20.
[58] W&N, 8-9.
[59] W&N, 11, n. 88.

# 19

## END DAYS

## REVELRY AND MASSACRE

D eut 4:3-24 tells of Moses warning the people that they must *not* make idols; they must *not* worship sun, moon, or stars, etc. (4:19). It is strenuously emphasised that they did *not—categorically—*they *did not* see any form or idol at Horeb! The author doth protest too much, perhaps, placing his own dogma in the mouth of *his* heroic "Moses."

This Moses apparently claims he was punished by God because of what the *people* did but what did they do? They are told to remember what happened to those who "followed" Baal-Peor (or Baal of Peor, Deut 4:3), i.e., they were slaughtered. Once again, this vengeful, violent, blood-thirsty deity is condoning the slaying of "thousands" of Israelites.

Who was Baal-peor? The name means "Lord of the wide opening" from the verb *ba'al*, "to be lord," and the verb *pa'ar*, "to open wide." In Numbers 25 the Israelites behave badly with the women of Moab, in a place called "Shittim." This name is the plural of the feminine noun *shitta*, "acacia tree"; in Exod 25:5 and Deut 10:3, for instance, it relates to the making of the ark of the covenant. Acacia, whatever the species, is renowned for its thorns, hence Moses' "burning bush" (*seneh*, Exod 3:2) is described as a "thorny bush." However, "the word *shitim* in Hebrew means *shtus*, 'folly'," and this suggests a "spirit of folly" that enters into a person and causes him/her to "sin."[1] The verb *sata* means "to turn away," e.g., with regard to being unfaithful (to a person or one's faith).

In Num 23:28, Balak and Balaam go "up" Peor, which suggests it is a mountain; it overlooks Jeshimon. Jeshimon means "wilderness, desolate," etc., i.e., the same as *horeb*.

What we are seeing is an *alternative rendition* of the golden-calf scenario at Sinai:[2]

★ There is a desert/wilderness

★ The wood (thorny acacia) for the ark is available

★ There is a mount

★ The group below the mount "revel" (32:6-29, esp. v.18)

★ A mass slaughter ensues

★ Those who perform the slaughter are made priests

★ Both refer to a "plague" (Exod 32:35; Num 26:1)

The misbehaviour of the men with the women of the area is described in terms that are overtly sexual, using the verb *zanah*, "to cause to commit fornication, continually, great, be [or] play the harlot" (*Strong's*). The name Peor, however, easily (and often) overlooked, suggests much the same thing, i.e., from *paar*, meaning "to open wide" (i.e., euphemistically, the legs or mouth). From the Song, we know that Nabonidus' penchant is for cunnilingus, especially with menstruating women; we know he is confronted with his past behaviour in the metaphorical battle with Amalek. A similar verb *paar* means "to glorify one's self," or "to boast," which may be another jibe at Nabonidus, whose self-interests, including his intimate relationship with the deity on Sinai, seem to lead to several rebellious incidents (and of course, he is later considered arrogant by those who accuse him of self-deification).

Just as in the Song of Solomon, Nabonidus is provided a "Baal-" pseudonym;[3] this is *his* mountain. *He* is Baal of Peor (of Sinai), "Lord of the wide opening," basically, the Lord of Sex. This is his reputation in the Song,

---

[1] Raskin, "Kuf," Letters of Light, www.chabad.org.

[2] Num 25:1 calls the area "Moab" but then in subsequent verses it becomes "Midian"; recall that we do not know the precise boundaries of Moab, Edom, etc., but this does mean we are looking at the same region as Qurayyah and the Qenites, i.e., Sinai and the Wilderness of Paran.

[3] Tyson, 205-6.

in rabbinical literature, in Herodotus, and in the HB, if you look carefully.

The task for the HB authors who redact, edit, and finalise Torah is to tell the truth but hide all the unsavoury bits (just as in the Song), for they believe God will know if they lie. Thus, we see Nabonidus/Moses being the one who damns the people for acting the way *he* used to (and clearly still does); we see *him* bringing the "plagues" to Egypt—but this is all manipulation, poetic justice, placing the ex-king at the core of the events (the *history*), whilst using him as his own foil in the narrative. He is hoisted by his own petard, so to speak, i.e., the damnation is upon him in each instance, ironically coming from his own lips. It seems to be standard scribal practice throughout the Bible.[4]

The incident at Peor leads to a battle with the Midianites, i.e., the very people Moses is said to be related to through marriage, i.e., to Zipporah, daughter of Jethro (Reuel). The battle with Amalek in Exodus 17 is a test to prove Nabonidus has removed himself from the influence of the "blood-lickers" he revelled with at court, consuming the blood extracted from women forced to comply.[5] Nabonidus, as recorded between the lines of the Song, created a lucrative business from the Elixir Nitocris had introduced him to; the reputation of this practice even reached Herodotus, and it was probably one of the reasons Nabonidus became such a villain in the eyes of the Babylonian exiles (e.g., to the point of never mentioning his name).

The question, then, is: Why be so exact in naming the first two who are killed at Peor (Num 25:14-17), when so many die; what is the significance of the two characters, Cozbi and Zimri, who are speared through, together?

☆ First, Moses responds to the event by ordering that the group slaughter everyone involved, i.e., "the chiefs of the people, i.e., their own people, and *impale them in the sun* before the Lord" (Num 25:4-5)

☆ The words used for "in the sun" are *neged*, "in front of, in sight of, opposite to" and *shemesh*, the Sun (Shamash, the Akkadian Sun god). Thus, those killed are to be set up on stakes in front of Moses' new (*apparently* solar) deity as an offering, rather than burying them (see below)

---

[4] Deuteronomy is a pro-Moses text yet the warning about "Baal of Peor" is placed on Moses' lips, much as Genesis and Exodus place the destruction of the "gods" in Moses' own hands. The effect is reversed, however, in that Moses is seen to be openly *denouncing* everything that he once condoned (sex, revelry, etc.), i.e., something he failed to do in Exodus.

[5] Tyson, 30-38; 120-33; 205-9.

✴ The woman is Cozbi ("false, lying," from the noun *kazab*, "a lie, falsehood, or deception"; the adjective *akzab* means "deceptive or disappointing");[6] she is twice referred to as the *daughter of a leader of Midian*, i.e., the daughter of Zur (Jethro)

✴ Jethro/Reuel/Zur is a (high) priest of Midian

✴ The slain man is Zimri (see below)

✴ The two are killed, together (as lovers), by Phinehas "in sight of Moses" and in sight of the congregation; why mention Moses separately?

✴ Phinehas means "the bronze-coloured one," "bronze snake," "mouth of brass" (e.g., prophet). Aaron is called a "prophet" in Exod 7:1; he is the metallurgist, the craftsman

✴ Phinehas is "son of Eleazar, son of Aaron" (Num 25:11); young and zealous (Num 25:11)

The name "Zimri" (the man who is speared) is potentially translated as "my musician," or "song of Yah." It comes from the verb *zamar*, which means "to sing or praise" (e.g., Judg 5:3, Ps 18:49), or "to play musical instruments" (Pss 33:2, 71:22). Its derivatives are: *zimra* (f. noun), meaning "song or music"; *zamir* (m. noun), "song"; and *mizmor* (m. noun), denoting a "song of praise."

Cozbi (Numbers 25) is the same woman as Zipporah (Exodus 2 and 18), i.e., she is Jehudijah. Recalling the discussion on the etymology of "Zipporah," the verb *sapar* was said to be linked to her use of a sharp object to circumcise her son (i.e., she pierces his skin). I think, perhaps, her first name serves as a foreshadowing of this current scenario, where she, herself, is pierced by a sharp instrument.

When I discovered this etymology, I nearly cried, for this means that the first couple put to death under Nabonidus' own legislation is none other than Jehudijah and "her musician." The name "Jehudijah" means "Praise Yah/Iah" and is etymologically linked to *huyyedot*, "songs of praise"; in *She Brought* I suggested that this helps to substantiate my theory that she had written the Song of Solomon.[7] As a professional poet, she would certainly

---

[6] The name "Cozbi" (from *kazab*) can also mean "to disappoint or fail" (Hab 2:3, Isa 58:11), i.e., figuratively, a flow of water that dries up (BDB, cf. Isa 58:11); in the context of Nabonidus' desire for a constant blood supply, and the symbolic relationship between wells/water and female blood, this should, perhaps, be taken as another sign that Zipporah has outlived her usefulness to Moses (Nabonidus).

[7] Tyson, 215-16.

have someone to accompany the recital of her songs.[8] Clearly he was also her lover.

This, perhaps is why "Cozbi" is rendered as "lie/falsehood," for Jehudijah had made it so clear in the Song of Solomon that she had (once) loved the king more than anyone; it would seem the unobservant Nabonidus simply never comprehends (or indeed knows of) the venom in her song about him and just thinks of her as a lying harlot. Not only has Moses learned that Ennigaldi (Miriam) was *not* Nitocris' child (and therefore did not have Egyptian royal blood in her veins), he has also (probably) discovered that Jehudijah has had other sons with Aaron. Now she is cavorting with another man, in public (recall that she has been the second-wife of a king, mother to some of his children, and the *entu*'s guardian, responsibilities that require her to be impeccable, despite the Babylonian leniency toward sexual exhibitionism). She has repeatedly defied him, publicly cursed him; he has had enough. He *orders* her death and doesn't seem to flinch at her demise.[9] Phinehas, ambitious and keen to make an impression volunteers to start the culling.

Josephus, a Moses apologist, has a strange account of Phinehas's killing of the couple, in that he

> … characterizes Phinehas' act as a "heroic" military operation in reaction to the sedition and lawlessness in the camp and with which Phinehas can be described as "victorious" over his foe. Phinehas, in Josephus' conception, was acting in a tactical capacity—not with spontaneous zeal for God.[10]

This brewing mutiny, it seems Josephus puts down to Zimri's daring and brutal verbal attack on Moses. Josephus has Zimri declare:

> … thou shalt not have me one of thy followers in thy tyrannical commands: for thou dost nothing else hitherto, but, under pretence of laws, and of God, wickedly impose on us slavery, and gain dominion to thy self: while thou deprivest us of the sweetness of life; which consists in acting according to our own wills: and is the right of free men, and of those that have no Lord over them. Nay indeed, this man

---

[8] Tyson, 213-22.

[9] This woman, Jehudijah, is close to my heart, even more so than Nitocris, who fascinates me. She broke through all the conventions and taboos, against the odds, and shone through for me as one of the strongest, cleverest women of ancient times. She belongs in the same league as Enheduanna and Hypatia. To see her come to this demeaning and unwarranted demise is greatly saddening. She was a real person, not just an obscure name in the Bible; I hope anyone reading this will remember her.

[10] Yonatan Miller, "Sedition at Moab: Josephus' Reading of the Phinehas Story," § "Phinehas' Killing: A Military Matter," www.thetorah.com.

is harder upon the Hebrews then were the Egyptians themselves: as pretending to punish according to his laws every ones acting what is most agreeable to himself. But thou thy self better deservest to suffer punishment, who presumest to abolish what every one acknowledges to be what is good for him: and aimest to make thy single opinion to have more force than that of all the rest, and what I now do, and think to be right, I shall not hereafter deny to be according to my own sentiments. I have married, as thou sayst rightly, a strange woman: and thou hearest what I do from my self, as from one that is free: for truly I did not intend to conceal my self. I also own that I sacrifice to those gods to whom you do not think it fit to sacrifice: and I think it right to come at truth by enquiring of many people: and not like one that lives under tyranny, to suffer the whole hope of my life to depend upon one man. Nor shall any one find cause to rejoice who declares himself to have more authority over my actions, than myself.

*A.J.* 4.6.11

This is precisely the atmosphere I see developing in Nabonidus' camp, with squabbles, retaliations, accusations, resentments, etc. It is not a happy place to be and cannot persist under such conditions. How interesting, though, for Josephus to invent this diatribe against Moses, in order to separate church from state (i.e., the priestly heritage from the violent aspects). This surprising criticism, placed on Zimri's lips must be, to some degree, how Josephus saw Moses' unilateral dominance but he placing it on the lips of one who is damned anyway makes it unattributable to him.

There is an issue with the etymology I wish to address here: Phinehas is listed as "son of Eleazar, son of Aaron the priest" (Num 25:11) but Eleazar's etymology is not a match for Phinehas'. That is, Phinehas' name alludes to serpents, bronze, etc. (strongly Aaronite) and his actions demonstrate the definition of "Nadab," i.e., "willing, volunteer," from the verb *nadab*, meaning "to willingly give, incite, or impel." I think Phinehas is of the priestly line of "sons" (sacerdotal not filial) running from Aaron to his *successor* Eleazar, which is why "Aaron the priest" is emphasised (and this also suggests a later composition, i.e., after the exodus and once the 'priestly nation' is formalised). Because of his zeal at Peor, Phinehas inherits the priesthood for *his* descendants, bypassing Aaron (Num 25:13).

In direct response to this debacle at the foot of the Sinai mesa, God orders Moses to "harass and defeat" the Midianites, suggesting the whole affair was due to their "deception." In other words, Moses has to sever all contact with his Midianite family and ventures; it is, perhaps, a post-exodus attempt to begin the process of removing Moses entirely from the Arabic sphere, so that his story can be transposed onto Israelite ground. It is devised, however, as another test for Nabonidus; will he comply?

In Num 31:13-18, we see that even after the slaying of his own wife in front of him, Moses orders *more* killing after the battle. Just as at Split Rock, he is told to do one thing but takes it upon himself to go even further. "Harassing and defeating" does not have to entail a total massacre but that is what ensues. All young males and all non-virgin women are to be slain but the virgins are kept for the troops, naturally. This sounds like the Nabonidus we have come to know.

There is historical precedence for Nabonidus' violence and the seemingly gratuitous gore we see in Numbers 25 and 31:

> In the month Ayyāru (II) of the third year (553), [... Bab]ylon, he took command of his troops. [He] mustered [...] and, on the thirteenth day, they arrived at [...]. **He cut off the [... (and)] heads the people living in the city** Ammanānu and [...] **in heaps. He hung [(their) king on a p]ole and divided the city** [...].
>
> RChr iv 27-41

So, "staking" people is something for which Nabonidus has form (at least in his propaganda). Assyrian kings, whom he admires, often worked with the premise that violence brings fear, and fear inhibits opposition. Rule can be ultimately peaceful if you beat all potential opposition out of your subjects, e.g., "I killed foes, slaughtered enemies, (and) suppressed all of the unsubmissive. I constantly established justice in the land (and) peacefully shepherded my widespread people."[11] Remember, too, the inscription detailing Ashurbanipal's destruction of the Elamite royal tombs, mentioned earlier; here, the king declares that he *"exposed [them] to the sun"* (emphasis mine).[12] Exposure to the sun like this is a defilement of the dead, a denouncement of any afterlife or belief in the afterlife. It negates everything by allowing the body to decay, be eaten, etc. This is what we see Nabonidus doing to those who are killed after the Peor incident ... including Jehudijah, who had cursed *his* name for eternity. In this case, the phrasing of "in the sun before the Lord" allows for the idea of a sin offering placed in front of the deity; the expiation of the sins of Israel *is* mentioned as the rationale for this barbarity (Num 25:4).

---

[11] Neriglissar 1, i 37 - ii 4. Ibid, 37.

[12] Daniel David Luckenbill, *Ancient Records of Assyria and Babylonia Vol 2: Historical Records of Assyria* (Chicago: University of Chicago Press, 1927), 310, #810.

# AARON'S DEMISE

Aaron seems to disappear without ceremony in the book of Exodus; one minute he is with everyone, eating and drinking with God, the next, we see another priest taking on his supervisory role, i.e., his "son," Ithamar (biologically *and* cultically here in Exod 38:21). Numbers 20 provides the explanatory narrative for this event.

In Num 20:22, the group is travelling in the region of Kadesh, i.e., south of Tayma. They have avoided going through Edom (Num 18:20-1), to the north of Tayma, because this is where the Midianites/Qenites live. It hasn't been long since Miriam was killed, and perhaps Nabonidus fears retaliation from Jethro.

Quite abruptly, it seems, Aaron is "gathered to his people" on Mount Hor. Back in Exodus 4 Aaron had been brought from somewhere to meet with Moses in the wilderness. I suggest he is symbolically, if not historically, returned to his home turf for his death scene.

Aaron has been to the top of Mount Sinai *with* Moses, also seeing God face-to-face (Exod 24:9-10). When the time comes for him to end his days, he is escorted up Mount Hor by Eleazar and Moses. Moses "strips" Aaron of his garments (Num 20:22-8) but the Hebrew verb employed here is *pashat*, which means "to plunder, to deploy in hostile array, to invade," etc., thus implying a stronger, more violent image than, perhaps, *sheylal* ("to strip naked") would have done (cf. 1 Sam 19:24, Job 19:9). Also, the word for "garments," *beged*, is defined as "treachery" (*Strong's*: from *bagad*, "to act or deal treacherously") and yet it is used as a word for any sort of apparel, or cover. Due to later priestly attributes for Aaron, these garments are considered "vestments" but in the core Exodus narrative he has not been made a priest. As a smith, he would most likely have worked naked, as mentioned earlier, so we can't even suggest they were garments pertaining to the rites of the smith. This leaves, more emphatically, the notion of "treachery." Does this pertain to Moses and Eleazar, or to Aaron?

What seems to be implied by the use of *pashat* in Numbers 20 is that Aaron is *forcibly* removed from his office; the 'special garments' are then handed over to Eleazar to signify a transfer of commission/office. The two men leave Aaron's body, unceremoniously, up the mountain. There is no suggestion that they bury him (cf. Deut 10:6).[13] One might think that dying

---

[13] Deut 34:6 states that Moses' place of burial is a secret, a mystery, which is tantalising, as it echoes both the secretion of Ahmose's corpse at Baal-zephon (e.g., Nabonidus is doing likewise by having his body hidden), and the fact that Nabonidus himself seems to have kept the location of his mother's interment a secret (Nab 2001 iii 5-16a).

up a mountain would be a good thing, a symbol of being close to God perhaps, but it is not. Deut 32:51 insinuates that the deaths of both men up mountains (symbolically) is due to fact that they "broke faith," so it is to be seen as a punishment, not an honour.

Nabonidus is systematically culling everyone who challenges him. Miriam, Jehudijah (Zipporah/Cozbi) and Aaron. This means, on the cosmological level, Nabonidus has removed both the (first) Sun (Aaron) and the Stars (Miriam) from the equation. As the Ordeal by Water and the golden calf scenarios foreshadowed, he is destroying his own gods.

The traditional "Mount Hor" location for Aaron's death is preserved in both Numbers and Deuteronomy; the latter calls the place both "Hor" (Deut 32:50) *and* "Moserah" (10:6), which proves enlightening.

"Moserah" is a veritable anagram of "Ramose/Rameses," ("Son of the Sun"), i.e., Moserah is "Ramoseh." Something that is reversed in the HB often signifies a negative intention, such as dark spells, evil intentions, etc. (by introducing chaos into order, on a symbolic level, e.g., the procedure for making the magical poppet in the Song of Solomon, for instance).[14] It may be that Moses sees Aaron as a pretender to the sacerdotal "throne"; by reversing the highly symbolic name "Rameses" the pro-Moses Deuteronomy author admonishes Aaron and marks him for eternity as a dissident who got what he deserved.

I do have a suspicion, however, that Aaron might be the man killed along with "Cozbi" (Jehudijah); as a "Simeon," Zimri is linked to the Ishmaelites via *shama'*, "to hear"; this means he is an Arabian (as opposed to an Israelite or Babylonian). Zimri's father is Salu, which means "raised up, exalted" from *salal*, "to cast up/heap up, exalt, extol, make plain, raise up." Jethro, Aaron's sacerdotal father is the esteemed leader of the Qenites at Sinai. There is a subtle connection between Iye-abarim (in Numbers 33; see Appendix 4) and the idea of "heaping up" that relates to the Harraat, Aaron's home. In the gematria of "Nahor" there is a potential allusion to "cutting through" being "felled" etc.[15] And as a smith, recall, he would also probably have been a musician. Being already intimately involved with Jehudijah from earlier years, and having been widowed relatively recently, knowing Nabonidus' jealous and rash nature, he might well suspect the two of cavorting, or planning something together behind his back. He kills two birds with one spear. The scene atop the mountain is added for symbolic reasons, and because Aaron is later used as the alternative to Nabonidus as the high priest figure; his death must be seen to be God's will, not the mad king's.

---

[14] Tyson, 135-42.

[15] See my paper "Nabonidus and the Arabian Genealogies (Genesis 10 and 11)" (2024), §4, www.academia.edu.

Aaron *has* proven somewhat disloyal, perhaps, and has humiliated Nabonidus more than once (i.e., by being Jehudijah's former lover, by gossiping with Miriam about Nitocris, and by siding with the calf-worshipers). This is reflected in the term *beged* ("treachery").

"Moserah" stems from *asar*, meaning "to bind" and though this can be used innocently in the context of tying up animals, for example, most instances pertain to the binding of *prisoners* (e.g., Gen 39:20; 42:24, Judg 15:10; Isa 49:9, etc.).

With respect to the Midianites, a similar word, *masar*, is used to describe Moses' "conscripted" soldiers, whom he sends to battle with the Midianites (Num 31:5). This word means "to commit, deliver," hence "conscript" in the HB. Just as Joshua was sent into a battle (with Amalek) that was meant for Moses, others are forced to do his dirty work here. Slaughter ensues.

Putting the two contexts together, it seems likely that Aaron is physically bound, forced away from the crowd (who like him), stripped of his official titles and accoutrements, and killed alongside his paramour.[16]

## Hor

"Mount Hor" literally means "Mount Mountain/Hill," from the noun *har*, "mountain, hill." On the other hand, once you know to look into the etymology of names a little deeper, you will notice that *har* is also a factor in the etymology of "Aaron," so the site on which Aaron dies is simply "Aaron's Mountain/Hill."

The noun *har* is also an element of "Harraat," i.e., the volcanic lava fields of Northwestern Arabia. The verb *harar* means "to scorch." You can see from the landscape in *Fig. 27* why this is apt. This is also an element in the name "Nahor" (Genesis' Aaron).

---

[16] In Num 33:39, Aaron is given the age of 123 at his death. In gematria terms, this is the numerical equivalent of e.g., "to smite hard" (in terms of divine judgment) but it can also mean "a plague" (physiological e.g., leprosy, boils, etc.). As $100 + 20 + 3$, it relates to: $100 = kuf$, "monkey" (unholy, base, negative); $20 = kaf$, "bend, crown"; $3 = gimmel$ "wean, nourish." Note the pattern here: the first two are the same as Moses and Sarah (Nabonidus and Nitocris), where the negativity of 100 is blatant, the "crown" of 20 is a reference to submitting to an authority, in this case, Nabonidus, and 3 relates to Jehudijah's signature of "weaning." Aaron is considered an adversary/reprobate; he is overcome by Nabonidus' authority, his wife, Miriam is stricken with a 'plague', and his relationship with Jehudijah is at the root of his demise (as Zimri).

# *Seir*

Esau, Jacob's brother, whose appearance is described as "red" and "hairy" (Gen 25:25, ) settles in Seir, which is in the land of Edom (Gen 32:3, 36:8). The name "Edom" has connotations of "redness" (Gen 25:30) and "Seir," of being "hairy."

The etymology of "Seir" is, at first glance, a little odd. It stems from the *s'r* root which can have a rather negative meaning, e.g., *sa'ar* (*sahar*) means "horror, terror." In cognate languages *sh'r* words often suggest a tearing apart, a violent breaking up or splitting in two, etc. On the other hand, *sear* means "hair," *sa'iyr* means "hairy," and *sa'ar* (*sawar*) means, "to sweep or whirl away" (as in windswept hair) but can also be used to imply fear or trepidation (e.g., Deut 32:17).

I propose that "Seir" is none other than the Harraat, the volcanic lava fields around which Nabonidus leads his caravan, from Ezion-geber, through Dadan, and up to Tayma.[17] Mount Hor (Aaron's Hill/Mountain) is one of the scorched volcano peaks (hence "Seir" is called "the Horite" in Gen 36:20, i.e., it simply means the Harraat; Nahor/Aaron is a Horite).

In Exod 19:2, the group travels from Rephidim to Sinai, suggesting nothing of significance stands in their way and it is a direct route (i.e., the author's concern is not to identify the route but to highlight the symbolic significance of their arrival). However, look at the pragmatic itinerary in Deut 2:1-3:

> After you had stayed in Kadesh as many days as you did, we journeyed back into the wilderness, in the direction of the Red Sea … and skirted Mount Seir for many days. … Then the Lord said … "Head north …." …So we (left) behind the route of the Arabah[18] … and Elath and Ezion-geber.

Thus, Nabonidus leads his group out along the same path they travelled *to* Tayma, i.e., the Wadi al-Jizl and Wadi al-Hamd caravan route, "skirting" around Seir, the Harraat, eventually getting onto the safe "passage" to the north, via the route mentioned earlier, i.e., the "Aarab

---

[17] Isa 21:11-14 says: "One is calling to me from Seir … O caravans of Dedanites … O inhabitants of the land of Tayma." Nevertheless, modern suggestions for Mount Seir place it along the Jordan border somewhere between the Dead Sea and the Gulf of Aqaba.

[18] "Arabah" is the feminine version of the Hebrew name for Arabia; in the HB it is applied to diverse regions e.g., east of the Jordan (Deut 1:1, 7; 3:17, 2; Sam 2:29), west of the Jordan (Deut 11:30; Josh 8:14), and near Mount Seir (Deut 2:8). The narrow parameters assigned to the Arabah today seems unjustified; like *horeb*, I think *arabah* is a vast, nebulous entity.

Agabah," which runs along the coast of the Red Sea and on up to Moab (Sela/Kadesh-barnea).[19]

From the accounts of explorers in the 19th Century, who were the first modern westerners to traverse the vast and desolate Arabian landscape, the two things that stand out from their descriptions of the Harraat are a), it is a place of horror, a frightening, dark, awful place to find oneself, and b), the lava flows in one place in particular, i.e., Jabal al Quidr (Qedar), in the Khaybar region, have the appearance of twisted, windswept hair!

Early explorers write of their passage through the Harraat:

*Horror, etc.:*

That black wilderness had become like a nightmare with its horrible boulders and little tortuous paths, which prevented the camels from doing more than about two miles an hour.[20]

We passed through a burial ground of black volcanic mould and salt-warp: the squalid grave-heaps are marked with headstones of wild basalt. That funeral earth is chapped and ghastly, bulging over her enwombed corses (*sic*), like a garden soil, in springtime, which is pushed by the new-aspiring plants. All is horror at Khaybar—nothing there which does not fill a stranger's eye with discomfort.[21]

*Split in Two:*

Regarding the "black hills" of the Harraat: "Some are two-headed— it is where a side of the crater is broken down."[22]

*Hair (Whirling):*

The volcanic field is a stony flood which has stiffened; long rolling heads, like horse-manes, of those slaggy waves ride and over-ride the rest …. (like) bunches of cords ….[23]

---

[19] You can find this route today, on Google Maps, still in use.

[20] Anne Blunt, *A Pilgrimage to Nejd: The Cradle of the Arab Race*, Vol. 1 (London: John Murray, 1881), 75.

[21] Doughty, 2.96-7.

[22] Doughty, 2.87.

[23] Doughty, 2.88.

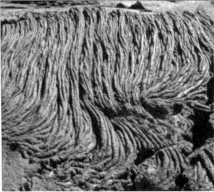

*Figure 27: Hair-like lava in the Harraat (Images: courtesy of Jean-Claude Latombe, Professor Emeritus, Stanford University, https://ai.stanford.edu /~latombe/mountain/photo /saudi-arabia-10/khaybar-10.htm).*

If this is how seasoned travellers two hundred years ago experienced the stark, lonely, and daunting landscape, imagine how the Babylonian emigrants felt. Most were probably wealthy, used to a relatively luxurious life in Babylon, and certainly more acclimatised to the Mesopotamian weather and flora, not searingly hot, glass-like mounds of black lava under foot, with not a soul in sight,[24] nor a palm, nor a river. No wonder Exodus has them "complaining" all the time!

Doughty further describes walking through this lava field with its "glassy" crests and dangerous footing, stating it had "a likeness to molten metal," adding: "That this soil was ever drowned with burning mineral, or of burning mountains, the Arab have no tradition."[25] Apart from the one eruption we know of in the 7th Century CE, which clearly didn't make that much of an impact on the inhabitants farther away from the craters, it would seem that no devastating or profoundly inspiring volcanic eruption occurred here that might substantiate a volcanic basis for the worship of Yahweh in Northwestern Arabia. The resulting lava fields, on the other hand, force themselves upon the unsuspecting wanderer, standing in their way, defying them to proceed at risk of death and injury. Mount Seir is thus several mounts, bonded together by this once oozing but now vitrified mass that leaves far greater an impression on the imagination than some long forgotten rumbling.[26]

However, evidence of a limited erruption might be found in the tale of Lot fleeing Sodom and Gomorrah; when angels tell him to flee "to the

---

[24] Like the biblical Esau, there were nomads who dwelt in the Harraat in Doughty's day (e.g., "the Bishr and Heteym," 2.87), as they probably still do.

[25] Doughty 2.88.

[26] It is to this huge expanse of volcanic hills that "Hor-haggidgad," mentioned in the discussion of the name "Nahor," seems to relate, i.e., as foothills.

hills," he fears the disaster will catch up with him, i.e., the "sulfur and fire" will rain on his head. He is doubting the safety of running toward the very hills (of the Harraat) that are errupting, fearing other seemingly dormant volcanoes will errupt also. He opts to go to a village instead but later, he takes his daughters up the very hills he was advised to in the first place, so he must realise they are safe, after all (and the erruption is over).

That Nabonidus himself found the terrain here challenging is recorded in the *Royal Chronicle*, which describes his approach to Dadan as having "difficult roads, [...], difficult [terr]ain [where access was bloc]ked (and) approach was not possible" (v 13-24).

*Figure 28: The stark reality of the Harraat (Image: NASA)*

## *Ithamar*

The name "Ithamar" has a strange etymology, i.e., "Palm Coast" from the noun *'i*, "coast land," from the verb *wh*, "desirous," and the noun *tamar*, "palm tree." We know of two places where trees are etymologically significant, i.e., al-Wajh and Tayma; the "desirous" element was noted in the etymology of Kibroth-hattaavah, which we found to refer to the graves between Tayma and Harrat Khaybar. As I argue that Aaron meets his death in this Harraat region, it is possible that this is also Aaron's original homeland, and thus his son's, "Ithamar's" (who perhaps represents those who lived nearer the coast).[27]

## *Heber and the Harraat*

From 1 Chr 4:18 we learn that "Heber" is Mered and Jehudijah's son. His name is said to mean "associate, companion," from the verb *habar,* "to join." We have come across a similar etymology, i.e., in "levite." Although the names stem from different verbs (levite is from *lawa*, "to join, twist, etc."), the end result is analogous: Heber is one of a group, a collective, e.g., a priestly clan (with a nod to both metallurgy, with the bending and twisting of metals, and to the worship of snakes, the coiled/twisted serpents).

Jehudijah is Jethro's daughter; Heber is *her* son, therefore Heber is Jethro's grandson. Although 1 Chronicles 4 lists this son as Mered's (Nabonidus'), the inference of the etymology suggests he is might be another of Aaron's sons.

Heber the Qenite moves away from the central hub of the Qenites (at/near Sinai) just before his wife Jael performs her murderous deed and kills Sisera (Judg 4:17-22).[28] He camps "as far away as Elon-bezaanannim, which is near Kadesh" (Judg 4:11). This is one of several names that link to "Elim" and "Eloth" via the notion of terebinths, or tall trees (i.e., "Elon" means "oak tree," from the noun *allon*, "oak," from the verb *alal*, "to protrude"; these related words often suggest foolishness, worthlessness, folly, etc., any of which can be an allusion to Nabonidus' reputation at Tayma, and therefore hint at a near-Tayma location). "Zaanannim" means "wanderings, journeys, etc.," from the verb *sa'an*, "to move about." Qenites are traditionally nomads.

As with other toponyms that correlate with characters (e.g., Temen,

---

[27] There is an "Itamara the Sabaean (of Saba)," who appears in an inscription of Sargon II (c. 709 BCE), who brings tribute to the king, along with the Arabian Queen Shemshi. This *may* suggest our name is alluding to a more southerly location but nonetheless, it confirms it is an Arabian name.

[28] For how this echoes Nitocris in the Song, see Tyson, 98; 111.

Terah, etc.), "Heber" is linked to "Hebron," which means "place of joining, place of an alliance," from the verb *habar*, "to join." Thus, "Hebron" is linked to metallurgists via the "joining" allusion, and is symbolically linked to the "City of Four," the place of the anti-Cyrus "alliance," and therefore to the Tayma region. The various definitions suggest a location somewhere between Eloth (al-Wajh) and Elim (Tayma). With Aaron's death, and another of his sons names ("Ithamar") being linked to Seir in the Harraat, we may conjecture that Heber returns to Aaron's dwelling place ("clan" in Judg 4:17) amidst the dormant volcanoes, near the Arabian Kadesh, just south of Tayma.

# DEATH OF MOSES

According to the Jewish tradition, Moses is said to end his days on a "mountain of the Abarim range" (Num 27:12-14) as a punishment for his behaviour in Kadesh (where the "waters of Meribah" refers back to Exodus 17). Hardly an honourable death for the saviour of the Israelites, but fully in keeping with the Jewish need to put Nabonidus, once and for all, in his place.

The Abarim range is contiguous with the Arabah, which stretches from the Sea of Galilee, to the Gulf of Aqaba. This means the Abarim 'range' could well be anywhere within this broad region.

The name "Abarim" stems from the root *abar*, meaning to "pass/cross over, through, etc.," in terms of *physical* transition and movement. One might suggest this is apt for the territory marking the borderline between Moses' old world and Joshua's new world (cf. Deut 34:4); between the Israelites as exiles and the Jews as returnees.

Islamic tradition, on the other hand, holds that Moses' tomb lies about thirteen kilometres south of modern Jericho, at a place called Ein Feshkha (quite close to Qumran). Without going into an analysis, here, it is intriguing that Moses (i.e., Nabonidus) is acknowledged by Arabic sources as having *been in Canaan*, despite the Jewish insistence that he was never permitted to cross the Jordan.

In addition, the legend that tells *why* the grave of Moses is where it supposedly is, has a remarkable similarity to something I have already presented in this book, i.e., the death of Osiris. The Islamic tale suggests that when Moses is told by an angel that he is to die, he wanders off into the desert for six years *away* from Jerusalem; when he is rediscovered, the angel tricks him into getting into his own grave/tomb by asking him to judge whether it is big enough. Recall that Osiris is likewise tricked by his brother Set. Osiris is cast into the Nile, while Moses' tomb is miraculously transported to the edge of the Dead Sea (so pilgrimages can be made from

Jerusalem to his tomb).

Personally, I don't think Nabonidus, the historical figure, dies at this stage; I think he returns to Tayma to live out his days in comfort. The story of Moses' death is only preserved in Deuteronomy, the pro-Moses exodus narrative (32:49-50; 34:1-6), in a bid to prove he had been doing the will of God by helping the Israelites. In reality, Nabonidus really doesn't seem that bothered, as I suggested before; he exploits the people in his charge, he leaves them stranded in the desert with him, under his authoritarian control, and he apparently has no qualms about killing them off if they get out of hand. But Deuteronomy, as with Genesis, preserves its own relatively happy ending whilst maintaining the undeniable truth that "Moses" (Nabonidus) did not re-enter Canaan after his Egyptian escapade.

As Abraham, Nabonidus had visited Jerusalem, had traversed the land building his own wealth and dropping off those who wished to settle there. For him it was a land to trade in, to invest in property, not a land to make home; that was never the intention. A parting gift from the author of Deuteronomy to his hero is his association between Moses' death and one of the names mentioned in Num 33:47, i.e., "Nebo"; both are based on the same inherited tales.

"Nebo" is commonly translated as "prophet, spokesman," from the Hebrew *nabi* ("spokesman or prophet") e.g., Aaron is Moses' *nabi* (Exod 7:1). From the Arabic *nabah*, it means "to be high or prominent." As suggested earlier, "Nebo" is a reference to Nabonidus himself.[29] Just as Aaron dies on "Aaron's Mountain" so Nabonidus dies on "Nabonidus' Mountain." The Nabo/Nabu element of his name pertains to Nabu, the Babylonian god of wisdom and writing. In cuneiform, Nabonidus' name is "Nabû-na'id" and means something like "Nabu is exalted" or "Nabu is praised."

Beaulieu states:

> The fact that Nabu conferred kingship in Babylon and possessed a lunar aspect explains why the god occupied an important place in the theological thinking of Nabonidus. After all, Nabonidus' own name ... could not be a better expression of his personal devotion.[30]

Thus, the author of Deuteronomy ends his favourable account of

---

[29] See p. 173.

[30] Paul-Alain Beaulieu, "Nabonidus the Mad King: A Reconstruction of His Steles from Harran and Babylon, in *Representations of Political Power: Case Histories from Times of Change and Dissolving Order in the Ancient Near East*, M. Heinz and M. Feldman, eds. (Winona Lake: Eisenbrauns, 2007), 137-66, here 159.

Moses with a bit of a twist. He seems to be fully aware of the general rule of anonymity for Nabonidus (whose name was cursed by Jehudijah at the beginning of the Song of Solomon), so he uses "Nebo" as a pseudonym, taken, no doubt, from the Sela inscription the Israelites would have had pointed out to them (i.e., "Nabû-na'id"). Nabonidus' lasting and most important quality is his never-ending search for wisdom, so his official 'last stand' is aptly named after the god of wisdom and writing.

Moses is said to die at the age of one hundred and twenty (Deut 34:7), which is the author's concession to the overwhelming evidence that Nabonidus was not a nice man and had issues, for this is the same number we looked at with respect to his relationships with Hiram of Tyre (1 Kgs 9:10-14) and the Queen of Sheba (1 Kgs 10:10), revealing the gematria to be wholly negative and concerning. To find this number linked to his death suggests Nabonidus (Moses) never changed.

Compare this to the number associated with both Joshua's (Josh 24:29) and Joseph's (Gen 50:22) ages at death, i.e., one hundred and ten years. If we look at 100 + 10, we find the now familiar allusion to the negative meaning of 100, i.e., the letter *kuf* with its derogatory meaning of "monkey," symbolising falsehood and impurity.[31] But there is the added 10, which has quite a different meaning, i.e., the letter *yod* means either "Jew" or the "Hand of God"; it pertains to divinity and Raskin calls it a "corridor to a heightened level of connection and understanding."[32] Basically, a small positive (ten percent) is added to the foundation of a negative.

Joshua, i.e., Belshazzar, Nabonidus' son, earns his honorary age by challenging his father's brutal and salacious ways, recognising the need for change in a new land. He serves as the strong and inspiring leader Moses really wasn't (the fact that an Arabian tribe near Tayma revered Belshazzar, not Nabonidus, as their founding father attests to this favourable perception of him).[33]

Joseph, on the other hand, is an Egyptian, not a Jew, but because of his magnanimous, peaceful reputation as Pharaoh Ahmose III, and his ultimate (intimate) association with the origins of Judaism, he is granted an honorary place in the annals as a "Hebrew" (a Jew), like so many others in the HB.

In the Egyptian context of Osirian burial rituals, there is a CT spell

---

[31] Raskin, "Kuf," Letters of Light, www.chabad.org.

[32] Raskin, "Yod" Letters of Light, www.chabad.org. The "Hand of God" connection is explained by Raskin as relating specifically to the escape from Egypt by God's hand.

[33] See pp. 306-8; see also my paper "Shishak and Rehoboam in a Nabonidus-based Paradigm" (www.academia.edu) that sheds new light on the later Jewish perception of Belshazzar, which isn't so positive.

that says:

> As for any man who knows this spell
> He will complete 110 years in [life]
> … The ritual [craft] consists of what
> a man does, being ignorant or being
> knowledgeable.
> If he proceeds to the realm of the dead,
> he will eat bread beside Osiris.[34]

The one hundred and ten year lifespan is, to an Egyptian, synonymous with breaking bread with Osiris. Despite all his efforts, Nabonidus does not qualify; his alleged "one hundred and twenty years," as discussed, leaves him with an unenviable reputation.

The death of Nabonidus is not a concern for the Israelites who write the HB. The death of "Moses" though, is a necessity. There has to be a cutting off point, a way of passing on the mantle to the younger generation, of ridding themselves of the Babylonian yoke once and for all. Theologically, the unsavoury aspects of the Sinai episode, i.e., the attempted synthesis of cosmological deities, the internecine violence, the rebellions, etc., have to be expunged for the Jews to find their own path, to cross over.

Beaulieu sums up Nabonidus thus:

> Nabonidus, while appealing to deeply entrenched Babylonian traditions in presenting himself as religious leader and teacher of wisdom, nevertheless failed in his endeavour to create a new theology that would reflect the complex political reality of the Babylonian Empire at the transcendental level. In this respect, he exemplifies the failure of an old monarchy to maintain its legitimacy in times of dissolving order and the incapacity of an ancient but waning civilization to reinvent itself in a world dramatically transformed.[35]

Now we can potentially see how this "transcendental" undertaking panned out, I almost pity the old king … *almost*.

---

[34] R. O. Faulkner *The Ancient Egyptian Coffin Texts, Vol. 1, Spells 1-354* (Warminster, UK: Aris & Phillips, 1973), 181-2.

[35] Paul-Alain Beaulieu, "Nabonidus the Mad King: A Reconstruction of His Steles from Harran and Babylon, in *Representations of Political Power: Case Histories from Times of Change and Dissolving Order in the Ancient Near East,* M. Heinz and M. Feldman, eds. (Winona Lake: Eisenbrauns, 2007), 137-66, here 163.

# Appendices

## 1. The Song and its 'Mad' King

It is 549 BCE. King Nabonidus has just settled in Tayma, Arabia, having spent a few years "wandering" around the Arabian Desert, conquering cities. In this year, he joins a coalition with three other kingdoms against the growing threat of Cyrus; the most significant ally is Ahmose III, Pharaoh of Egypt. As part of the treaty with Babylon, Ahmose grants Nabonidus his most illustrious daughter, Nitocris II, who is First Prophet of Amun, a high-priest (she retains the male title).

Nitocris is sent to Tayma where she is expected to get pregnant quickly, for Nabonidus has a dream, i.e., to re-establish an ancient and rather controversial female-only priesthood in the ancient temple at Ur, Babylonia (the high priestess was called the *entu*). The only thing is, Nitocris really doesn't want to get pregnant; her sacerdotal devotions would have to be forfeited and she is not willing to allow this to happen. Needless to say, this causes much anxiety in the royal court, and Nabonidus reveals himself an impatient and volatile man. More than once he throws his weight around, humiliates Nitocris, and demands to have his own way. Though besotted with this exotic, beautiful woman, his behaviour is less than romantic and he forces himself on the young woman, who then conceives. To celebrate, Nabonidus deifies both Nitocris and himself, in a mystical ceremony atop a mountain.

Unbeknownst to Nabonidus, Nitocris has acquired certain plants and potions that induce a miscarriage in the first trimester. She endeavours to gain control of her situation, attempting to keep the king at bay, sexually, by telling him of the wonders of her religion. Ever the inquisitive student, Nabonidus has a fascination for arcane wisdom and this Egyptian priestess has much to teach him. He is a man, however, with a short span of attention; he loses interest at times, preferring sex to learning, and sometimes her aloofness brings on dangerous moods in him. Eventually, her control over the king increases; she employs sympathetic magic to ensure he is snared and under her spell (so the author of the Song suggests). When this begins to weaken, she resorts to introducing Nabonidus to the one thing she is trying so hard to protect, i.e., the Elixir Rubeus rite, which involves drinking male and female efflux in a mind-bending, hallucinogenic ritual meant only for the Pharaoh and his priests. Nabonidus becomes addicted to the effects of this and so triggers his eventual downfall. He loses his senses, so rabbis would later explain, because he was possessed (or had been replaced) by a demon.

As with any situation where one person controls another, the worm finally turns and Nabonidus breaks free from this mesmerisation and is not a happy man. Nitocris, fearing for her life, and/or her position, makes a rash decision to *pretend* she has conceived again, to placate her husband. He falls for it. She is hailed the "mother" of the first *entu* in centuries and things settle down. Nitocris is in a quandary, however, for she must find a baby to serve as hers when the time comes. She does this by going to the place where the harem ladies who are pregnant go to isolate themselves and give birth. There, she finds Jehudijah, one of the ladies at court who had been in love with the king from afar and was just another of his conquests, impregnated, forgotten.

A deal is made to bring up this child as Nitocris'; this is Ennigaldi-Nanna, Nabonidus' daughter who becomes the *entu* dedicated to Sîn at Ur. The child's birth-mother is kept on as a wet-nurse (just as in the Moses story). When priestly emissaries from Egypt come to see how their princess is getting on with Nabonidus, Nitocris is put in a very awkward and dangerous position because they seem to know everything she has done to hide the truth from her husband. They put her on the spot, threatening to reveal the scam of the fake pregnancy if she does not either return with them or grant them continued access to the Elixir. Nitocris is the supreme source for this potion, being the high priestess.

Nitocris manages to get the king and her small family away from Tayma before much damage is done, and the Song ends with a scene of the women ensconced in the temple at Ur declaring they will never let such a thing happen to the little girl. We also learn, in the final verses, that the Song is written soon after the fall of Babylon, that Nabonidus had introduced the sacred rite of the Elixir to the masses, for money, in Babylon, and that the biological mother of Ennigaldi, whom I identify as Jehudijah, is the author of the Song, exposing her rage and her desire for revenge on the man who, she felt, did not deserve her love. She includes in the Song a curse on both Nitocris and Nabonidus, to make them forever her enemies, and forever damned.

The tale ended there, or so I thought, until I discovered the same story in various ancient legends, right up to the Medieval Period; all telling the same fundamental tale, some with extraordinary parallels and repeated details.

# 2. PRIMARY COMMISSION NAMES

**Aaron:** Nabonidus' son-in-law / m. Miriam / (original Sun in triad, Exodus) Nahor / Hobab / Mamre / Zimri

**Abraham:** Nabonidus / m. Sarah / (Moon in triad, Genesis)

**Amram:** Exodus' version of "Terah" / symbolic (lunar) "father"

**Belshazzar:** Isaac / Lot / Hoshea / Joshua / Eliezer / Aner

**Cozbi:** Jehudijah

**Eleazar:** Aaron's sacerdotal 'son'

**Eliezer:** Abraham's servant / Moses' son / son of Dodavahu of Mareshah / Joshua-Lot / Nabonidus son, Belshazzar

**Elisheba:** Aaron's once concubine / Jehudijah

**Ephron:** Croesus, King of Lydia

**Ges(h)em:** Nabonidus in Arabia

**Hagar:** Jehudijah

**Heber:** Nabonidus-Jehudijah's son (in 1 Chr 4) / Aaron's via etymology

**Hobab:** Aaron / Nabonidus' son-in-law

**Hur:** Miriam-Aaron's son

**Isaac:** Belshazzar, Nabonidus' firstborn son

**Iscah:** Nitocris

**Ishmael:** Representative of Nabonidus supporters in Arabia

**Jehudijah:** Nabonidus' second-wife / Jethro's daughter / Hagar / Zipporah / Elisheba (Aaron's concubine) / Reumah / Cozbi / Miriam's mother / Author of Song of Solomon

**Jethro:** Jehudijah's father / Moses' father-in-law / Aaron's sacerdotal father Miriam's grandfather / Amram / Reuel / Amminadab / Zur / (possibly Melchizedek)

**Joseph:** Pharaoh Ahmose III (replacement Sun in triad, Exodus) / "double" of Nabonidus

**Joshua:** Isaac / Aner / Hoshea / Lot / Eliezer / Belshazzar

**Keturah:** Moses' wife (to be explained in a forthcoming book)

**Lot:** Joshua / Eliezer / Belshazzar

**Milcah:** Miriam / Ennigaldi-Nanna

**Miriam:** Ennigaldi-Nanna / m. Aaron / Nabonidus-Jehudijah's daughter / (Stars in triad, Exodus)

**Moses:** Nabonidus (Moon in triad, Exodus) / Abraham

**Nabonidus:** Abraham / Moses / Solomon / Samson / Baal-hamon / Eshcol / Baal-peor / Jethro's son-in-law / Dodavahu of Mareshah / Sheshbazzar

**Nahor:** Aaron (original Sun in triad, Genesis)

**Nitocris II:** Sarah / Iscah / Puah / Asenath / Nabonidus-Solomon's Egyptian wife / Ahmose III's daughter (and First Prophet of Amun) / Serah

**Pharaoh:** 1st - Ahmose III ("double" of Nabonidus) / 2nd - Cambyses

**Phinehas:** Aaronite sacerdotal 'son' / Salmshezib

**Sarah:** Nitocris, posthumously (Stars in triad, Genesis)

**Solomon:** Nabonidus

**Sheshbazzar:** Nabonidus

**Terah:** Symbolic Sîn, lunar deity / Nabonidus' 'father'

**Zimri:** Jehudijah's musician lover / possibly Aaron

**Zipporah:** Jehudijah / daughter of Jethro / Nabonidus' second-wife

# 3. ABRAHAM, ISAAC, AND SOLOMON

Isaac, like Lot, was difficult to understand within the parameters of Nabonidus being the inspiration for the three main characters of Abraham, Moses, and Solomon. I still think "Isaac" is an invention of sorts, i.e., to serve as a means of humiliating Nitocris posthumously but, as usual, there is more to it. I have decided to put this short assessment in the Appendices section because it is a work still in progress. I feel I am on to something but it requires far more attention than I can afford it for this current book.

What draws my attention is that Solomon is the one who is overtly associated with "Molech" in 1 Kgs 11:5-7, and yet it is Abraham who physically prepares and is fully intent on dispatching his own child to placate a deity.[1] I'm not concerned with which spelling of "Molech" is authentic, or whether the word is used to depict a cultic site, a rite of sacrifice, or a deity's name.[2] In the end, it simply comes down to the generally accepted fact that child sacrifice did happen during the early days of Israel, i.e., whether by Israelites, or by foreigners.

Molech is certainly perceived as a deity in Lev 18:21; 20:2-5, and I have a theory that much of the so-called "priestly" addenda to the original exodus narratives are indicative of a backlash against everything Nabonidus had introduced or had practiced. For instance, in the closing statements of Numbers 36, there is a sudden and almost surprising focus on murder; there is talk of refuge cities, blood-guilt, capital punishment, and the inheritance of daughters. Knowing now what seems to have been the case with Nabonidus, i.e., he murdered, or had killed, several people beyond the scope of War; as "Moses" he fled from punishment for killing and was denounced by his own wife as a murderer; and the issues surrounding Ennigaldi's rightful place in the scheme of things *might* have triggered heated discussions on where her inheritance was to go after her death (she was very prestigious in her own right, a princess, etc.), especially considering she crossed over into the local

---

[1] Jephthah (in Judg 11:39), behaving much like the impetuous Nabonidus, makes a rash promise to God that if he wins the battle against the Ammonites, he will sacrifice the first person he sees after the fight. The person who greets him as he returns from the battlefield, much in the manner of Miriam with her timbrel and dancing is, of course, Jephthah's virgin daughter. Not only does he carry through on his promise, God *allows* it, despite grave castigations of the practice elsewhere in the HB.

[2] For various arguments see Francesca Stavrakopoulou, "The Jerusalem Tophet Ideological Dispute and Religious Transformation," *SEL* 29-30, 2012-2013: 137-58; Moshe Weinfeld, "The Worship of 'Molech' and of the Queen of Heaven and its Background," *UF* 4 (1972): 133-54.

Qenite tribes after her marriage to Aaron.

So, too, I think, the emphasis on child sacrifice to Molech is a direct consequence of what Nabonidus was up to during his post-539 BCE life at Tayma, i.e., as "Solomon." He dabbled in other religions, cherry-picking what pleased him, what suited is worldview. He seems to have been a man easily led, fickle, and impulsive. He possibly met someone who worshipped this deity "Molech" and got drawn in, just as he did with Nitocris and her Amun-Re/Osiris-based religion. His curiosity overwhelmed his caution, perhaps.

Given this premise, I think "Isaac" is meant to be a young Belshazzar but I don't think the "sacrifice" scene is in any way historical. I suggest Gen 22:1-15 is the author(s)' depiction of the "Solomon" he/they had witnessed in Tayma. It is a tale of unquestioning, blind faith in the extreme, i.e., almost a fanaticism, which suits the Nabonidus we have come to know. It surreptitiously links Abraham with Solomon in the strange context of child sacrifice, which must have *some* sort of connection to reality, or any intended allusions would not make sense. I posit, therefore, that the "sacrifice of Isaac" scenario is intended as a foreshadowing (and a retrospective confirmation) of the shared identity of Abraham (who is willing to sacrifice his child), Moses (who threatens death of the firstborn), and Solomon (who worships Molech). It is a stark motif that is meant to be noticed.

Recall that in Num 13:16, Moses is said to change "Hoshea" to "Joshua" (son of Nun), i.e., from meaning "salvation" to "Yah saves." This seems to be a last-minute insertion to indicate the connection between the young Isaac who represents Abraham's salvation (as the sacrifice to appease the deity) and the post-ritual son whom the god has saved.

Nabonidus had already sacrificed one child to a deity, i.e., Ennigaldi-Nanna was ceremoniously dedicated to Sîn, at the age of three years old. Though she was not killed and presented as a "burnt offering," she was put into the service of the deity for her lifetime in a manner that was highly publicised and obviously of great import to the king. In the end, as we have seen, she, Nabonidus' "firstborn" daughter, dies by her father's own hand. I think the death of Miriam (Ennigaldi) haunted the early Jews, which is why they created the myth of "Miriam's Well" and why they remembered her at Kadesh-barnea. This is another of those myths, preserving the unswerving determination of a man on a mission … until something *else* catches his attention.

Cue the ram in the thicket.[3]

The blinkered, resolute Abraham, lying to both his companions and

---

[3] Cf. the image of a golden ram in a thicket statue (one of a matching pair) found at Ur by Leonard Woolley (*Ur of the Chaldees* [London: Book Club Associates, 1982; rev. ed. 1929], 99).

his son, keeping the burnt offering a secret until it is about to happen (like Moses keeps much a secret from his companions; one cannot prevent or question something that is hidden), is stopped in his tracks by the sight of the ram caught by its horns in the bushes/thicket.

The ram here, I suggest, is the symbol for what will ensue in the subsequent tale of Moses; it is the spark of inspiration, the moment of clarity Nabonidus experiences when Ahmose III dies. He is on a quest to create his own deity, a blend of everything he thinks is needed to unite all religions, perhaps. Just before the deed is done, the ram, symbolizing Amun-Re, shines from within the thicket and gives Moses the sign he seeks. When I say "shines," this isn't obvious in the HB text, of course, but the fact that "horns" are mentioned can be seen as an allusion to the "horns" of the Sun and the Moon, as mentioned previously.

The ram is central to the depiction of Amun-Re, i.e., the Sun god. When Rameses II dedicated the temple of Abu Simbel in the 13th Century BCE …

"the sun when it penetrated into the shrine of the temple was in conjunction with the first stars of the constellation (we call) Aries, and this fact doubtless led the King to honour Aries in connection with the god Amun. The Egyptians called Aries 'the Lord of the Head'."[4]

The avenue of sphinxes approaching the temple of Abu Simbel is the route taken by a special procession "when Aries specially dominated the ecliptic"; the cultic statue of Amun was carried "to the Necropolis, from which place the constellation Aries was fully visible."[5] The arrangements for this festival began "before the full moon next to the spring equinox, and on the fourteenth day of that moon all Egypt" celebrated "the dominion of the Ram"; the "Persians, who called Aries 'Bara', had a similar festival."[6]

This might be the moment Nabonidus envisions what he is going to do; Ahmose is Horus, son of Re; he is Amun-Re's representative on earth. He is "the Osiris." Like the ram tangled in the bushes, the pharaoh's corpse is "hidden," held somewhere, but Nabonidus has the key to unlocking its whereabouts.

In Gen 22:2, Abraham takes the sacrificial Isaac to the "land of Moriah" ; this is the same "Moriah" where Solomon supposedly builds his temple (2 Chr 3:1).

Belshazzar, i.e., as "Hoshea," is given another name that implies

---

[4] William Tyler Olcott, *Star Lore Myths, Legends, and Facts*, (Mineola, NY: Dover, 2012), 56.

[5] Olcott, 56.

[6] Olcott, 56.

being saved from something by God ("Joshua"); I suggest this is to remind us that he is the character "Isaac," rescued (figuratively) at the last minute by one of Nabonidus' surreal moments of divine inspiration.

If such a tale was invented to expose the nature of the man, Nabonidus, perhaps it *was* based on an observed rift between father and son, which seems possible, given the references to his son (in inscriptions) mentioned previously, and the potential alliance against the king with Daniel, etc. This may provide fuel for the theory that Belshazzar then goes on to denounce his father's legacy as soon as he crosses over into Canaan (see Appendix 6). We must consider, however, that this entire perception of Belshazzar by the early Jews might be propaganda, i.e., a 'holding on to' their brave general as some sort of deeply psychological anchor in a scary new world.

Just as the Arabian Sulamy tribe attribute their heritage to the "son" of Nabonidus, Belshazzar (suggesting he was not merely a temporary resident), so the Israelites (Jews) come to attribute their heritage to Isaac, i.e., the 'saviour' Belshazzar they also know as "Joshua." The Jericho rejection scenario is a necessity, to draw the final line between the exiles and their perceived oppressor, between Babylon and Canaan, between good and evil. Like Abraham in Genesis, the tale of Joshua ends with contentment and praise, allowing the hero to die peacefully in his own land at the symbolically charmed age of 110.

Historically, however, Belshazzar probably assists the Israelites to seize certain territories in Canaan before returning once more to Tayma, to build a trading empire with his father, who will assert his role as "King Solomon," and whose fleet at Ezion-geber will make him one of the wealthiest and most famous men in the world (if he wasn't already).

# 4. 400 OR 430 YEARS IN CAPTIVITY?

With regard to the character "Abraham," recall that he purchases a plot of land from the Hittite (Croesus) in order to secure a burial ground, ostensibly for "Sarah" (who is an avatar of the already deceased Nitocris, suggesting this is a ruse). We also know that the Cave of Machpelah, the site of this tomb, is the "Cave of the Double." Nabonidus is seen by the HB authors as Ahmose III's "double," not in the way that makes the former a great leader and honoured king like the latter, but because Nabonidus consistently reveals his desire to emulate the pharaoh. But Moses is also Abraham's "double" (both are avatars of Nabonidus); the name "Machpelah" has the gematria of 175,[1] the same as Abraham's lifespan (Gen 25:7). Thus, Abraham, the Cave of Machpelah, and Moses are united, symbolically.

The cave is bought for four hundred shekels (Gen 23:16). The number 400 is represented by the Hebrew letter *tav*, the last letter of the alphabet, with a meaning of "truth, sign, life or death."[2] 400 is also the number of years the Israelites are said to have lived oppressed, in Egypt, according to Gen 15:13; yet Exodus 12:40 suggests the period was 430 years. If we take the 400 of Gen 15:13 as an indication that within this narrative there is a particular "truth" or "sign" that has something to do with "life and death," we can suggest this might point to Nabonidus' (true) quest to procure the corpse of Ahmose III. This really is a matter of life and death, both in terms of the danger of the mission, and in terms of the Life/Death symbolism attributed to the bones at Sinai.

The captivity is lengthened in Exodus by adding 30 to the 400; 30 is represented by the letter *lamed*, which means "teach, learn."[3] This is often related to the learning/teaching of Torah, i.e., to the complexities of the writings, to the hidden truths, wisdom, etc., that take time to see and understand. This is precisely what I am trying to articulate, i.e., the narratives contain far more than we can see, at first, with hidden layers that we must learn how to reveal. So, for me, the 430 of Exodus is a sign to the reader to relate back to the beginning, to Genesis' 400 (this is another one of those too-obvious anomalies that serve as signposts to deeper realms within the text), in order to make the connection between Abraham, Machpelah, Joseph (Ahmose III), and Moses, and the hidden tale of the acquisition of the Son of the Sun in Ipip, 522 BCE.

---

[1] Heidrick, "175," www.billheidrick.com.
[2] Raskin, "Tav," Letters of Light, www.chabad.org.
[3] Raskin, "Lamed," Letters of Light, www.chabad.org.

# 5. NUMBERS 33 AND THE 40 CAMPS

1. Rameses to **Succoth**

2. **Etham:** Edge of the wilderness of *Yam Suph*

3. **Pi-hahiroth:** They passed through the sea into the wilderness (of Shur), three days on the marshes, then a camp by the shore before they row/sail across the Red Sea

4. **Marah:** Red Sea

5. **Elim:** Tayma

6. **Red Sea**

7. **Wilderness of Sin:** Surrounding Tayma

8. **Dophkah:** "To beat violently, knock"; used in Song 5:2 when Nabonidus forces his way into Nitocris' chamber; also translated as "Palm," so again, Tayma (with echoes of Kadesh).

9. **Alush:** "Wilderness, wild place" (Wilderness of Sin, in this region)

10. **Rephidim:** South of Tayma

11. **Sinai:** Qurayyah

12. **Kibroth-hattaavah:** "Graves of desire"; keyhole graves between Tayma and Khaybar

13. **Hazeroth:** "Villages," from *haser*, "settlement, village"; Song 7:11 uses *kaphar* for "villages" but it is an important concept, for this is where Jehudijah is residing when she gives birth (Nitocris and the king go there to retrieve the child); outskirts of Tayma

14. **Rithmah**: From *ratham* "to bind, attach" BDB suggests, "compare Arabic thread bound to finger as reminder"; Song 8:6, "set me as a seal"

15. **Rimmon-perez:** From *rimmon* ("pomegranate"), from *rum*, "to be high"( Abarim Publications explains: "Ripe and ready-for-harvest of fruits") and *paras*, "to break through." In Song 4:3, Nitocris' cheeks are compared to the two halves of a pomegranate, and in 8:3, she promises to let Nabonidus drink her pomegranate juice (i.e., the Elixir); it is this delicacy the king is after when he 'breaks into' her apartments.

16. **Libnah:** "White"; al-Wajh ("White Village")

17. **Rissah:** from *racac*, "a ruin ("as dripping to pieces" – Abarim); from *rasas,* "to moisten"; *raciyc*, "to moisten (with drops)"; to temper. Two

allusions to drops: Nabonidus as being wet with dew (Song 5:2) and the manna in the Tayma sabkha being seen after the dew (Exod 16:13)

18. **Kehelathah:** "Assembly, place of assembly," from *qahal*, "to assemble"; Tayma (place of coalition; City of Four)

19. **Mount Shepher:** "Beauty, harmony," from *shaphar*, "to be pleasing to the eye"; Abarim states: "It appears to be related to an Arabic verb that denotes the removal of the veil [normally of a woman], which also may mean to shine"; used in Song 4:8 in the context of mountain-top apotheosis (while living at Tayma); shining is the solar aspect at Sinai; Moses removes his veil on Sinai. Also, Exod 1:15 introduces the "midwife," Shiphrah, i.e., Jehudijah, who hails from this region. Sinai/Qurayyah mesa

20. **Haradah:** "Tremble, fear," from *harad*, "to shake, to tremble with fear," or to be "anxiously careful" (BDB); Rephidim is where Moses shakes/trembles when he avoids facing Amalek; the verb *nua* in "Kadesh-barnea" also means "to shake, stagger, quiver, tremble, wander, be unstable"

21. **Makheloth:** "Assembly, place of assembly," from *qahal*, "to assemble." Tayma (place of coalition; City of Four). Note the identical etymology in Kehelathah (18); this is a recurring pattern used in the Genesis genealogies[4] that highlights Nabonidus' naming of Split Rock ("Massah/Meribah")

22. **Tahath:** "Beneath, support," from *tahat*, "under, below"; it can also mean "substitute"; At Rephidim, Joshua is Moses' substitute in the battle against Amalek

23. **Terah:** "The Moon, wanderer"; Tayma; Nabonidus

24. **Mithkah:** "Sweetness" Manna

25. **Hashmonah:** "Envoy, ambassador"; feminine of *chashman*, envoy, ambassador"; also translated as "fatness/fertile" (BDB). In Song 7, Egyptian envoys come to Tayma (the only place *chashman* is used directly is in Ps 68:31, in the context of Egyptian envoys arriving!). The scene in the Song is when Nitocris is feigning her pregnancy and is awaiting the chosen child to be weaned; "fatness" relates to pregnancy[5]

26. **Moseroth:** "Bond, bonds"; from *asar*, "to bind (e.g., a prisoner)"; "Moserah" is used by Deut 10:6 as the name of Aaron's burial site (as claimed here, in the Harraat, in the context of him being a prisoner, then killed); the Song's "set me as a seal" (8:6) might also be germane

---

[4] See *Nabonidus and the Queen of Sheba: Roots of a Legend* (Norwich: Pirištu Books, 2024), 12-13; 42; Appendix, 119.

[5] Tyson, 111.

27: **Bene-jaakan:** "Sons Of Jaakan"; from the plural of *ben*, "son," and Jaakan, from *aqam*, "to twist"; Qenites/Qurayyah, the metallurgists/smiths; Deut 10:6 includes "Beeroth" or "the wells" of Bene-jaakan, hinting at Jethro's "well of seven"

28: **Hor-haggidgad:** "?Impassioned cutting," from *harar*, "to be hot, burned, charred," and *gadad*, "to cut or invade"; *harar* used to denote the volcanic Harraat (Aaron's burial place), but I think more the figurative heat of anger and zealotry in the killing of Zimri and Cozbi at Peor/Sinai (Num 25:6-18); both are impaled/stabbed/cut

29. **Jotbathah:** "Pleasantness, goodness," from *yatab*, "to be or do good"; Deut 10:7 describes it as "a land flowing with streams"; Tayma is watered by eighty-plus springs; cf. Gen 13:10, where Lot moves into the northern Hijaz region that is "well-watered" and like a garden (he returns to Tayma)

30. **Abronah:** "passage, pass" from *abar*, "to pass over, through"; the passage leading along the shore of the Red Sea to Moab

31. **Ezion-geber:** Solomon's (Nabonidus') port on the Red Sea; located at al-Wajh

32. **Wilderness of Zin (Kadesh):** The wilderness across the Jordan Valley, adjacent to Sela (i.e., a mirroring of the Wilderness of Sîn near Tayma, but using the later, Jewish preference for not mentioning the lunar-deity post-Exodus)

33. **Mount Hor:** Aaron's symbolic burial site in the Harraat, where he is from (i.e., "Seir")

34. **Zalmonah:** "Place of the image/idol" (from *selem*, "image"); Tayma; place of *slm*, the "Image"

35. **Punon:** "Man with a dark mind" (Abarim) from *pun*, "to be distracted, confused, hopeless"; Tayma is where Nabonidus loses his mind under the influence of Nitocris

36. **Oboth:** Abarim suggests "Lunacy / seductive teacher" (from *ob*, a "seductive tutor", [Abarim] in the context of a pupil falling for their instructor); *Strong's* has "necromancer / water-skin"; Nabonidus, the Moon King is driven to madness by his seductive teacher, Nitocris (in Tayma); it might be said that at Sinai, Nabonidus invokes the spirit of the dead Ahmose

37. **Iye-abarim:** Although the most common translation seems to be "Ruins of crossing over" (from *iy*, "ruin," *avah*, "heap," and *abar*, "to cross over"), there is the alternative "Heaps/mounds of the Abarim" which I think may be more fruitful. In Num 21:11 the site is said to be "in the wilderness bordering

Moab toward the sunrise" (i.e., the term *shemesh* is used, meaning "sun" and can mean either "sunrise" or "sunset"; towards Arabia, "the East" suggests sunrise); Num 33:44 simply says it lies on the border of Moab. This, I think, refers to the eastern banks of the Jordan Valley where Sela is located, but more specifically, where Moses parts company with the Israelites

38. **Dibon-gad:** "Angry exposure or cutting" (from *dub*, "pining", with connotations of anger, shame, loneliness, sorrow; and *gadad*, "to cut, expose") Zipporah is Jehudijah. She once pined for Nabonidus; her anger/sorrow fills the Song of Solomon and is evident in Exodus. She curses Nabonidus in the Song and openly curses Moses in Exodus, i.e., cutting him down, exposing him; she also 'cuts' Ishmael, i.e., circumcision; suggests Qurayyah region (Midian); possibly an allusion to the Zimri/Cozbi killings

39. **Almon-diblathaim:** "Hidden cakes," from *alam*, "to be hidden," and *dobela*, "fig cakes"; from *dabal*, "to collect, press together," "lump or mouthful"; Tayma's sabkha provides "manna" (salt) that is seen as bread from heaven; Num 11:8 compares it to "cakes"; it is hidden from them until the conditions are perfect for it to form

40. **Nebo:** From *nabi* ("spokesman or prophet") e.g., Aaron is Moses' *nabi* (Exod 7:1); from the Arabic *nabah*, it means "to be high or prominent"; However, this name pertains to Nabonidus as King of Babylon, i.e., Nabû-na'id, where Nabû is not only a family name, it reflects his desire for Wisdom. Elsewhere I have suggested this site is synonymous with Sela, the last post on the eastern side of the Jordan Valley, where "Moses" had a panoramic view of Canaan, but beyond which he did not venture (again). Sela is also the location of one of the largest Nabonidus inscriptions, both "high" up and "prominent," figuratively stamping his name on the site

This is a wonderfully constructed illustration of three things: 1) The "forty years" of wandering around with Nabonidus, i.e., there are forty *symbolic* camping stations to depict itinerancy; 2) every single one of them pertains to either a place, a person, or an event in the narratives; 3) the group do not stray from the Hijaz during those years, i.e., they meander about 'in circles', toing and froing between the Harraat, Tayma, Qurayyah, and the Red Sea (which is precisely what Deut 2:1-3 insinuates, i.e., they skirt around the same area for a long time). They are commission names that are intended to preserve specific memories; thus, we see several pseudonyms for Tayma, several for Sinai, etc., using events that have been recorded either in the Song or the exodus narratives.

# 6. JERICHO AND BELSHAZZAR

Jericho was allegedly uncovered in 1868 by Charles Warren:

> Although there is a significant deviation in views over the exact date of the destruction and abandonment, archaeological analyses of Jericho generally agree on the manner in which the city met its end, including a widespread fire, collapsed mudbrick walls, burning of the stored grain, and abandonment.[1]

For all intents and purposes this does sound a rather general description of what would have been a ubiquitous destruction of a city in ancient times. Fire would have been the best, if not only practical weapon for the greatest damage; mudbrick walls were everywhere, from Mesopotamia to the Nile; one would expect them to collapse if breached; stored grain burnt during the conflagration was just a casualty of war (why would they take the time to rescue it?); and a destroyed city was often abandoned. What makes this undeniably the "Jericho" of Joshua? Kennedy seems convinced;[2] countless others have accepted its location at the top of the Dead Sea without question but I cannot.

As most of what we have discussed here occurs at Tayma, Qurayyah and its environs, and Sela, why would the crossing into Canaan include a very long trek from there to the far tip of the Dead Sea? Or are we still accepting that "God willed the Israelites to wander aimlessly"? At Kadesh-barnea the Israelites, having left Sinai, are readying for battle, for their incursion into Canaan; military context cannot be ignored, despite the laboured symbolism of a Moses-like, ritualistic 'water crossing' closer to Jerusalem.[3] They would choose the most strategic route, which would be via the wadi near Sela. Nabonidus would have had contacts and probably stored provisions on this side of the Arabah, from his earlier travels as "Abraham."

Nabonidus left an inscription at Sela during his original wanderings through Arabia, so we can be certain he knows this area first-hand. The

---

[1] Titus Kennedy, "The Bronze Age Destruction of Jericho, Archaeology, and the Book of Joshua," *Religions* 14.6 (2023): 796, Abstract, https://doi.org/10.3390/rel14060796.

[2] He states: "… archaeological excavations and analysis at Jericho appear to place the destruction of the final Bronze Age city ca. 1400 BC in a manner consistent with the account in the book of Joshua" (Kennedy, Conclusion).

[3] This is a fabricated crossing to mirror Moses', as many agree, but with the understanding of the rejection of the Arabian connection, the necessity for such a blatant 'new beginning', replacing Moses' tarnished version, replacing Arabian locations with Canaanite ones, it is a scenario that simply *had* to be invented.

inscription, high on an overhanging rock, facing all who enter the narrowing, oppressive passage, boldly declares, "I am Nabû-na'id, King of Babylon," and subsequent (legible) text includes a reference to "troops," making this a military landmark.[4] The idea for this entire military pericope might have been *inspired* by this inscription, but it is also plausible that Nabonidus already knows the landscape, its tactical advantages, and so makes this the intended location for the final push (knowing he does not intend to go beyond this point again).

Interestingly, a recent tour of the site by Assyriologists raised the issue of whether or not the inscription could be seen by passers-by, as it is awkwardly situated very high up and seen well enough to read (when the text was still legible) only by those immediately below it, in the dried up wadi; the idea was posited that the inscription was meant for divine rather than human eyes.[5] Two things come to mind: 1. Nabonidus did not hide his light under a bushel. Even when there was a foundation deposit, there was also an inscription to tell of it. The dominance of the Sela inscription, hovering over the viewer, would have made it all the more impressive (unlike seeing it as a billboard from a distance). 2. If the entry into Canaan was to be stealthy, and the men wished to remain 'under the radar', they would be in the perfect position to see the inscription; there would be no reason for them to be far away, on the opposite bank.

One other possibly insightful note these Assyriologists made was that the inscription had been altered at a later date, with an extra column of text and, uncannily, the *solar* icon (of Shamash) made more elaborate. Might this also be evidence of a post-Sinai modification of Nabonidus' inscriptions to attest to the fact that the events at Qurayyah were profoundly solar in nature? If only we could read the text! It might also have mentioned the subsequent passage of Nabonidus' son via the same route.

Jericho would need to be relatively close to the troops' emergence from the protection of the wadi. That they would encounter no opposition until they travelled all the way to the other end of Canaan is simply unbelievable. So, I suggest the first city to be razed by Joshua was somewhere in the Arabah, opposite Sela. There is no way of determining its name; it didn't matter then, so it doesn't matter now, i.e., "Jericho" is a commission name (toponym).

That "Jericho" is the *first* formal mission for Joshua may prove significant for one variant of the name's etymology suggests a translation of "City of the Moon" (from *yareah*, "moon," from *arah*, "to wander or travel"),

---

[4] Bradley L. Crowell, "Nabonidus, as-Sila'', and the Beginning of the End of Edom," *BASOR* 348 (2007): 75-88, here 88.

[5] "A visit to Nabonidus at Sela, Jordan," (4, September, 2022) https://tuppublog. wordpress.com/.

i.e., the City of Sîn, ergo, the City of Nabonidus. Alternatively, "place of fragrance," from *reah* ("scent or fragrance"). In the absence of Moses, Joshua the warrior, the Marduk-like hero, charges into this city with such vehemence and intent, it suggests this is not just any border town that needs to be subdued to get the Israelites into Canaan; it is treated as a special place. The ritualistic encircling, seven times, the sounding of trumpets, the curse against anyone rebuilding it (Joshua 6) on pain of death for not just the firstborn but the "youngest" also, hints at something much more profound and final.

If this attack on Jericho is truly historical and not wholly symbolic, I think Joshua, i.e., Belshazzar, like his father before him, is being tested for his fidelity to the Israelites by defying his father, who is fundamentally synonymous with the lunar deity, Sîn. Thus "Jericho" becomes a symbol of Nabonidus and all he stands for, ritualistically defeated by the young Marduk-like saviour; the walls come tumbling down and everything Nabonidus had created is razed. This would be utterly symbolic, of course, written into the story to rationalise the retention of Belshazzar as their leader in Canaan, even though the group had rid themselves of Nabonidus. It is a cleansing of sorts.

Even in the alternative name for Jericho, i.e., "Ir-hatamarim" (Deut 34:3; 2 Chr 28:15; Judg 1:16, 3:13) there is a fascinating correlation. This name stems from *ir* ("city") and *tamar* ("palm tree"), so "City of Palm Trees," or suchlike. This may sound vague enough, until you recollect that in *She Brought* I explain that *tamar* (in the Song of Solomon) relates to both Nabonidus and Nitocris as the avatars of Tammuz and Ishtar in the context of the sacred marriage (thereby underscoring their self-deification at Tayma).[6] Of course, Tayma itself is renowned for its palms and, as Solomon, Nabonidus decorates his temple with imagery of palms (1 Kgs 6:29-35). Once again, then, the focus of the Israelites' (Joshua's) attack on "Jericho" is Nabonidus and everything he stood for.[7] (There was no need to 'conquer' Jerusalem, as Nabonidus had already been there, with the Jews, as "Abraham.")

It seems this final act of defiance against Nabonidus and Nitocris begins a new chapter in the lives of the "Israelites." From this point on there is a concerted shift from the Arabian landscape to the Canaanite. The toponyms now refer to conquered lands, not the left-behind world of the Hijaz. Appropriated names bear witness to what happened, historically, but the new context is purely Jewish and firmly rooted in the Levant.

---

[6] E.g., Tyson, 83; 178-9.

[7] Even the alternative rendering of the translation, as "fragrance" ties in with the discussion on "Keturah" I present in *Nabonidus and the Queen of Sheba: Roots of a Legend* (Norwich: Pirištu Books, 2024), Chapter 3. For a discussion on the rejection of Nitocris in a similar vein, see my paper, "The Three Namaahs" (2024), 7-8, www.academia.edu.

# BIBLIOGRAPHY

## PRIMARY SOURCES

*The Ancient Egyptian Coffin Texts, Vol. 1, Spells 1-354.* Faulkner, R. O. Warminster, UK: Aris & Phillips, 1973.

*Ancient Near Eastern Texts Relating to the Old Testament.* Edited by James, B. Pritchard. Princeton: Princeton University Press, 1994.

*The Ancient Pyramid Texts.* Edited by James P. Allen and Peter Der Manuelian. Leiden: Brill, 2005.

*The Aramaic Inscriptions of Sefire*, 2nd ed. Translated by Fitzmyer, J. A. Rome: Pontifical Biblical Institute, 1995.

Ashurbanipal (Inscriptions). http://oracc.museum.upenn.edu.

*Biblia Sacra: vulgatae editionis Sixti V Pontificis Maximi jussu recognita et Clementis VIII; auctorate edita.* https://archive.org.

*The Book of the Dead.* Papyrus of Mes-em-neter. "Coming Forth by Day." https://en.wikisource.org.

Diodorus Siculus. *The Library of History.* https://penelope.uchicago.edu.

"Dynastic Prophecy." Livius.org.

Electronic Text Corpus of Sumerian Literature. https://etcsl.orinst.ox.ac.uk/.

*Enuma Elish: The Babylonian Epic of Creation.* www.worldhistory.org.

Eusebius. "Chronicle." www.attalus.org.

*Ezekiel's Exagoge.* Translated by Howard Jacobson. https://bingweb. binghamton.edu.

Firmicus Maternus. *The Error of the Pagan Religions.* Translated by Clarence A. Forbes. New York: Newman Press, 1970.

Herodotus, *Histories*. Edited by Tom Griffith. Hertfordshire: Wordsworth, 1996.

Homer. *Odyssey*. Translated by Samuel Butler. 1900. www.perseus .tufts.edu.

Josephus. *The Complete Works of Josephus*. Translated by William Whiston. London: Ward, Lock & Co., 1873 (1737).

Melito. "Discourse with Anoninus Caesar." *Ante-Nicene Fathers Vol. 8*, www.tertullian.org.

*Miscellaneous Inscriptions in the Yale Babylonian Collection*. Traslated by Albert T. Clay. New Haven: Yale University Press, 1915.

Möller, Astrid. *Naukratis: Trade in Archaic Greece*. Oxford: Oxford University Press, 2000.

Nicander of Colophon. *The Poems and Poetical Fragments*. Edited by A. Gow and A. Scholfield. Cambridge: Cambridge University Press, 1952.

Nonnus. *Dionysiaca*. Cambridge, MA: Harvard University Press, 1940. https://topostext.org.

Pausanias. *Description of Greece*. Translated by W. H. S. Jones. www .theoi.com.

*The Periplus of the Erythraean Sea: Travel and Trade in the Indian Ocean by a Merchant of the First Century*. Translated by Wilfred Harvey Schoff. New York: Longmans, 1912.

*The Pyramid Texts*. Translated by Samuel A. B. Mercer. 1952. https://sacred-texts.com.

Philostratus. *The Life of Apollonius of Tyana, the Epistles of Apollonius, and the Treatise of Eusebius*. Translated by F. C. Conybeare. London: Heinemann, 1912.

Pliny, *Natural History in Thirty-seven Books*. https://archive.org.

Plutarch. "On Isis and Osiris." Translated by Charles William King. 1908. https://sacred-texts.com.

*Proclus: The Commentaries of Proclus on the Timaeus of Plato, in Five Books*. Translated by Thomas Taylor. London: A.J. Valpy, 1820.

*The Royal Inscriptions of Amēl-Marduk (561–560 BC), Neriglissar (559–556 BC), and Nabonidus (555–539 BC), Kings of Babylon*. Edited by Frauke Weiershäuser and J. Novotny. The Royal Inscriptions of the Neo-Babylonian Empire, Vol. 2. University Park: Eisenbrauns, 2020.

*The Royal Inscriptions of Ashurbanipal (668–631 BC), Aššur-etel-ilāni (630–627 BC) and Sîn-šarra-iškun (626–612 BC), Kings of Assyria, Part 1*. Edited by Jamie Novotny and Joshua Jeffers, Royal Inscriptions of the Neo-Assyrian Period, Vol. 5. Winona Lake: Eisenbrauns, 2018.

Strabo. *Geography*. Edited by H. C. Hamilton and W. Falconer. https://www .perseus.tufts.edu.

"Translation of 1Q Genesis Apocryphon II-XXII." Translated by John C. Reeves. https://pages.charlotte.edu.

"Translations of Hellenistic Inscriptions: 258," c. 264 BCE (Pithom Stele), Cairo CG 22183 [TM 58344]. Translated by Eduard Naville. https://www .attalus.org.

Verse Account of Nabonidus. www.livius.org.

Xenophon. *Cyropaedia*. Translated by H. G. Dakyns. London: Dent & Sons, 1992 (1914).

# SECONDARY SOURCES

Aberbach, Moses and Leivy Smolar. "Aaron, Jeroboam, and the Golden Calves." *JBL* 86.2 (1967): 129-40.

Abudanah, Fawzi, Saad Twaissi, et al. "The Legend of the King's Highway: The Archaeological Evidence." *ZOA*, Band 8 (2015): 156-87.

Adelman, Rachel. "From the Cleft of the Rock: The Eclipse of God in the Bible, Midrash, and Post-Holocaust Theology." Pages 169-92 in *Ehyeh Asher Ehyeh*. New York: New Paradigm Matrix, 2019.

Akcil, Ata. "Mining History in Anatolia - Part 1." *CIM Magazine* 1.1 (2006): 90-92. www.researchgate.net.

*Akkadian Dictionary*. www.assyrianlanguages.org.

Al-Amoudi, Abeer. "Haddaj: An Enduring Well in an Ancient Oasis." 23 June 2020. www.wafyapp.com.

Albright, W. F. "Baal-Zephon." Pages 1-14 in *Festschrift, Alfred Bertholet zum* 80. Geburtstag: J. C. B. Mohr Tübingen, 1950.

_____. "The Goddess of Life and Wisdom." *AJSL*, 36.4 (1920): 258-94.

_____. "Jethro, Hobab and Reuel in Early Hebrew Tradition." *CBQ* 25.1 (1963): 1-11.

Al-Dahir, H. Abdul. "Shechem Sacred to Osiris." 17 May, 2018. http://arabian prophets.com.

Al-Fassi, Hatoon Ajwad. "The Taymanite Tombs of Madāʾin Ṣāliḥ (Ḥegra)." *PSAS* 27 (1997): 49-57.

Al-Ghabban, Ali Ibrahim, eds. *Roads of Arabia: Archaeology and History of the Kingdom of Saudi Arabia*. Catalogue of the exhibition, Musée du Louvre, Paris 14 July - 27 September, 2010.

Alibaigi, S. "The Gawri Wall: A possible Partho-Sasanian structure in the western foothills of the Zagros Mountains." *Antiquity*, 93.370 (August, 2019): e22. doi:10.15184/aqy.2019.97

Allen, Spencer L. *The Splintered Divine: A Study of Ishtar, Baal, and Yahweh Divine Names and Divine Multiplicity in the Ancient Near East*. Berlin: de Gruyter, 2015.

Alqarni, A. S., et al., "The Indigenous Honey Bees of Saudi Arabia (Hymenoptera, Apidae, Apis mellifera jemenitica Ruttner): Their Natural History and Role in Beekeeping." *Zookeys* 134 (2011): 83-98.

Amery, Captain H.F.S. *English-Arabic Vocabulary for the Use of Officials in the Anglo-Egyptian Sudan*. Cairo: Intelligence Department of the Egyptian Army, 1905.

Amin, Osama Shukir Muhammed. "Law Code Tablet of King Hammurabi from Nippur." World History Encyclopedia. www .worldhistory.org.

Amzallag, Nissim "A Metallurgical Perspective on the Birth of Ancient Israel." *Entangled Religions* 12.2 (2021).

_____. "From Metallurgy to Bronze Age Civilizations: The Synthetic Theory." *AJA* 113 (2009): 497-519.

_____. "The Origin and Evolution of the *saraph* Symbol." *AO* 13 (2015): 99-126.

_____. "Who was the Deity Worshipped at the Tent-Sanctuary of Timna?" Pages 127-36 in *Mining for Ancient Copper*. Edited by Erez Ben Yosef. Tel Aviv: Tel Aviv University, 2018.

_____. "Yahweh, the Canaanite God of Metallurgy?" *JSOT* 33 (2009) 387-404.

Amzallag, Nissim and Shamir Yona. "The Metallurgical Meaning of מִקְנֶה in Biblical Hebrew." *HS* 59 (2018): 7-24.

"Anatolia from the end of the Hittite Empire to the Achaemenian Period." www.britannica.com

"Ancient Ports in the Red Sea." www.ancientportsantiques.com.

"The Antiquary's Note-Book (Ancient Egypt: Remarkable Discovery)" in *The Antiquary: A Magazine Devoted to the Study of the Past*, Vol 14. London: Eliot Stock, 1886.

"Archaeological research at the oasis of Tayma, Saudi Arabia." General Commission for Tourism and Antiquities, Riyadh, and the German Archaeological Institute, Berlin. https://studylib.net/doc/7406744.

Archer, George. "A Short History of a 'Perfect Woman': The Translations of the 'Wife of Pharaoh' Before, Through, and Beyond the Qur'ānic Milieu." https://pubs.lib.uiowa.edu/mathal/article/2738/galley/111540/view/.

Astour, Michael C. "The Origin of the Terms 'Canaan,' 'Phoenician,' and 'Purple'." *JNES* 24. 4 (1965): 346-50.

Ataç, Mehmet-Ali. "The 'Underworld Vision' of the Ninevite Intellectual Milieu." *Iraq* 66 (2004): 67-76.

Aubet, María Eugenia. "Tyre before Tyre: The Early Bronze Age Foundation." Pages 14-30 in *Nomads of the Mediterranean: Trade and Contact in the Bronze and Iron Ages, Studies in Honor of Michal Artzy*. Edited by Ayelet Gilboa and Assaf Yasur-Landau. Leiden: Brill, 2020.

Ayad, Mariam. "Some Remarks on the Pyramid Texts Inscribed in the Chapel of Amenirdis I at Medinet Habu." Pages 1-13 in *Egypt and Beyond: Essays Presented to Leonard H. Lesko*. Edited by Stephen E. Thompson and Peter der Manuelian. Providence: Department of Egyptology and Ancient Western Asian Studies, 2008.

Azzoni, Annalisa. "Women and Property in Persian Egypt and Mesopotamia" (paper presented at the Women and Property Conference, Centre for Hellenic Studies, Harvard University, n.d.), 1-28. https://classics-at.chs.harvard.edu.

Baker, Luke "Ancient Tablets Reveal Life of Jews in Nebuchadnezzar's Babylon." Feb 23 2015. www.reuters.com.

Bagg, A. M. "The Unconquerable Country: The Babylonian Marshes in the Neo-Assyrian Sources." *Water History* 12 (2020): 57-73.

Bar-Ilan, Meir. *Some Jewish Women in Antiquity*, Brown Judaic Studies 317. Edited by Shaye J. D. Cohen. Atlanta: Scholar's Press, 1998.

Beaulieu, Paul-Alain. "Nabonidus the Mad King: A Reconsideration of His Stelas from Harran and Babylon." Pages 137-66 in *Representations of Political Power: Case Histories from Times of Change and Dissolving Order in the Ancient Near East*. Edited by M. Heinz and M. Feldman. Winona Lake: Eisenbrauns, 2007.

____. *The Reign of Nabonidus King of Babylon* 556-539 B.C. New Haven: Yale University Press, 1989.

Beckman, Daniel. "The Use of Treaties in the Achaemenid Empire." PhD diss., University of California, Los Angeles, 2017.

Beitzel, Barry J. "Was There a Joint Nautical Venture on the Mediterranean Sea by Tyrian Phoenicians and Early Israelites?" *BASOR* 360 (2010): 37-66.

Bennett, Ellie. "The 'Queens of the Arabs' During the Neo-Assyrian Period." PhD diss., Helsinki 2021.

Berkowitz, Lois. "Has the U.S. Geological Survey Found King Solomon's Gold Mines?" *BAR* (September, 1977). https://library.biblicalarchaeology.org/.

Bible Gematria. www.biblegematria.com.

Bickerman, Elias J. "The Edict of Cyrus in Ezra 1." *JBL* 65.3 (1946): 249-75.

Bijovsky, Gabriela Ingrid. "The Ambrosial Rocks and the Sacred Precinct of Melqart in Tyre." Pages 829-34 in *XIII Congreso Internacional de Numismatica, Madrid – 2003. Actas – Proceedings.* Actes I. Madrid. 2005.

Black, Jeremy, Andrew George, Nicholas Postgate, eds., *A Concise Dictionary of Akkadian*. Weisbaden: Harrassowitz Verlag, 2000.

Bledsoe, A. M. Davis. "The Identity of the 'Mad King' of Daniel 4 in Light of Ancient Near Eastern Sources." *CS* 33 (2012): 743-58.

Blenkinsopp, Joseph. "The Midianite-Kenite Hypothesis Revisited and the Origin of Judah." *JSOT* 33 (2008):131-53.

Blunt, Anne. *A Pilgrimage to Nejd: The Cradle of the Arab Race, Vol. 1.* London: John Murray, 1881.

Bolshakov, Andrey. "Persians and Egyptians: Cooperation in Vandalism?" Pages 45-54 in *Offerings to the Discerning Eye*. Leiden: Brill, 2010.

Brettler, Marc Zvi. "Some Biblical Perspectives on the Haggadah" (The Ten Plagues). www.thetorah.com.

Brooks, W. E. and Matos, G. R., "Flow Studies for Recycling Metal Commodities in the United States." Pages 1-21 in *Mercury recycling in the United States in 2000*, Sibley, S.F., comp. U.S. Geological Survey Circular 1196–U (2005).

Brown, Lawrence Parmly. "The Cosmic Eyes." *The Open Court* (n.d.): 685-701. https://opensiuc.lib.siu.edu.

Brownsmith, Esther. "To Serve Woman: Jezebel, Anat, and the Metaphor of Women as Food." Pages 29-52 in *Researching Metaphor in the Ancient Near East: An Introduction*. Edited by Ludovico Portuese and Marta Pallavidini. Wiesbaden: Harrassowitz Verlag, 2020.

Budge, E. A. Wallace. *The Babylonian Legends of Creation*. 1921. https://sacred-texts.com.

____. *From Fetish to God in Ancient Egypt.* New York: Benjamin Blom, 1972.

_____. *Osiris and the Egyptian Resurrection.* Vol. 1. London: Warner, 1911.

_____. *Osiris and the Egyptian Resurrection.* Vol. 2. London: Warner, 1911.

Budin, Stephanie Lynn. "Phallic Fertility in the Ancient Near East and Egypt." Pages 25-38 in *Reproduction: Antiquity to the Present Day.* Edited by Nick Hopwood, Rebecca Flemming, Lauren Kassell. Cambridge University Press, 2018.

Butler, Edward P. Henadology: Philosophy and Theology. https://henadology.wordpress.com.

Camp, Victor. et al. "The Madinah Eruption, Saudi Arabia: Magma Mixing and Simultaneous Extrusion of Three Basaltic Chemical Types." *BV* 49 (1987): 489-508.

Campbell, Joseph. *Myths of Light: Eastern Metaphors of the Eternal.* Novato: New World Library, 2003.

Carlson, Stephen C. "For Sinai is a Mountain in Arabia: A Note on the Text of Galatians 4:25," *ZNW* 105.1 (2014):80-101.

Casson, Lionel. *Libraries in the Ancient World.* New Haven: Yale University Press, 2001.

Chabad.org. "12-Facts -Every-Jew-Should-Know-About-Eliezer."

Charlesworth, J. H. *The Good and Evil Serpent.* New Haven: Yale University, 2010.

ChemEurope.com. "Sapphire." www.chemeurope.com.

_____. "Lapis Lazuli." www.chemeurope.com.

Chen, Lucas Braddock. "Sumerian Arsenic Copper and Tin Bronze Metallurgy (5300-1500 BC): The Archaeological and Cuneiform Textual Evidence." *AD* 9.3 (2021): 185-97.

Christian, Mark A. "Phoenician Maritime Religion: Sailors, Goddess Worship, and the Grotta Regina." *DWO* 43.2 (2013): 179-205.

Cobbe, H. M. T. "Alyattes' Median War." *Hermathena* 105 (1967): 21-33.

Colburn, Henry. "King Darius' Red Sea Canal." *Fezana* 4.35 (2021): 27-30.

Collins, John Joseph and Adela Yarbro Collins. *Daniel: A Commentary on the Book of Daniel.* United States: Fortress Press, 1993.

Cooper, Julien. "The Earliest Mention of the Placename Sinai: The Journeys of Khety." The Ancient Near East Today (2023): 1-6. www.asor.org.

Cowie, Ashley. "Did Ritual Use of Cinnabar Cause Mercury Poisoning in Ancient Iberia?" Updated 18 November, 2021. www.ancient-origins.net.

Crowell, Bradley L. "Nabonidus, as-Sila‘, and the Beginning of the End of Edom." *BASOR*, 348 (2007): 75-88.

Dafalla, Muawia and Mosleh A. Al-Shamrani, "Swelling Characteristics of Saudi Tayma Shale and Consequential Impact on Light Structures." *JCEA* 8.5 (2014): 613-23.

Dalley, Stephanie. "The God Ṣalmu and the Winged Disk." *Iraq* 48 (1986): 85-101.

_____. *Myths from Mesopotamia: Creation, the Flood, Gilgamesh, and Others.* Oxford: Oxford University Press, 1991.

_____. "Stelae from Teima and the God Ṣlm (Ṣalmu)." *PSAS* 15 (1985): 27-33.

Dalton, Matthew, Jane McMahon, and Hugh Thomas, "The Middle Holocene 'Funerary Avenues' of North-west Arabia." *The Holocene* 32.3 (13 Dec 2021).

Deffke, Uta. "The Story of a Dried-up Lake in the North Arabian Desert." 24 March, 2022. www.gfz-potsdam.de.

Delnero, Paul. "Sumerian Extract Tablets and Scribal Education." *JCS* 62 (2010): 53-69.

Derricourt, Robbin. *Antiquity Imagined: The Remarkable Legacy of Egypt and the Ancient Near East.* London: I. B. Taurus, 2015.

Dever, William G. *What Did the Biblical Writers Know, and When Did They Know It?: What Archaeology can Tell Us about the Reality of Ancient Israel.* Grand Rapids: Eerdmans, 2002.

Diakonoff, I. M. "The Naval Power and Trade of Tyre." *IEJ* 42.3/4 (1992): 168-93.

Dick, Michael B. "The Mesopotamian Cult Statue: A Sacramental Encounter with Divinity." Pages 43-67 in *Cult Image and Divine Representation in the Ancient Near East*. Edited by Neal H. Walls. American Schools of Oriental Research Books Series 10. Boston: 2005.

Dillery, John. "Cambyses and the Egyptian Chaosbeschreibung Tradition." *ClQ* 55.2 (2005): 387-406.

Dixon, Roland B. "The Color-Symbolism of the Cardinal Points." *JAF* 12.44 (1899): 10-16.

Dnboswell. "This is My Body, Which is Broken: The Lunar Osiris Easter Special, Part 1." April 21, 2019. https://mythodoxy.wordpress.com.

Dougherty, Raymond P. "A Babylonian City in Arabia." *AJA* 34.3 (1930): 296-312.

____. *Nabonidus and Belshazzar: A Study of the Closing Events of the Neo-Babylonian Empire.* 1929 repr. Eugene: Wipf & Stock, 2008.

____. "Nabonidus in Arabia." *JAOS* 42 (1922): 305-16.

____. *The Sealand of Ancient Arabia.* Yale Oriental Series 29. New Haven: Yale University Press, 1932.

Doughty, Charles M. *Travels In Arabia Deserta* [1888]. New York: Random House, 1921.

Drews, Carl and Weiqing Han. "Dynamics of Wind Setdown at Suez and the Eastern Nile." PLoS ONE 5(8): e12481. doi:10.1371/journal.pone.0012481.

Dumbrell, William J. "The Tell El-Maskhuta Bowls and the 'Kingdom' of Qedar in the Persian Period." *BASOR* 203 (1971): 33-44.

Dungen, Wim van den. "The Book of: The Hidden Chamber, ca. 1426 BCE, or: The Twelve Hours of the Night and the Midnight Mystery." www .sofiatopia.org.

Eames, Christopher. "Camels: Proof That the Bible Is False?" Armstrong Institute of Biblical Archaeology. March 28, 2019. https://armstronginstitute.org.

Encyclopedia of the Bible, www.biblegateway.com.

Encyclopedia Iranica. www.iranicaonline.org.

Eneix, Linda. "Ancient Man Used 'Super-Acoustics' to Alter Consciousness (... and speak with the dead?)," June 16, 2014. https://sciencex.com.

Englander, Henry. "Problems of Chronology in the Persian Period of Jewish History." *JJLP* 1.1 (1919): 83-103.

Fabry, H. J. "nḥs." Pages 356-69 in *Theological Dictionary of the Old Testament* Vol. 9. Edited by G. J. Botterweck, H. Ringgren, H. L. Fabry. D. Green, trans. Grand Rapids: Eerdmans, 1974.

Feld, Lisa Batya. "Miriam's Well." www.sefaria.org.

Fiema, Zbigniew T., et al. "The al-ʿUlā–al-Wajh Survey Project: 2013 Reconnaissance Season." ATLAL 28 Part Two, 109-31. https://hal.science/hal-03064753/document.

Fleming, Wallace B. *The History of Tyre.* New York: Columbia University Press, 1915.

Flusser, David and Shua Amorai-Stark. "The Goddess Thermuthis, Moses, and Artapanus." *JSQ* 1.3 (1993): 218-19.

Forbes, R. J. *Metallurgy in Antiquity: A Notebook for Archaeologists and Technologists* Leiden: Brill, 1950.

Forchheimer, Paul. "The Etymology of Saltpeter." *Modern Language Notes* 67.2 (1952): 103-6.

Fragkaki, Mary. "Spartan Identity and Orestes' 'Repatriation'." Pages 287-298 in Ancient History: Interdisciplinary Approaches. Carmen Soares, José Luís Brandão. 2018. doi:10.14195/978-989-26-1564-6.

Frahm, E. "Rising Suns and Falling Stars: Assyrian Kings and the Cosmos." Pages 97-120 in *Experiencing Power, Generating Authority: Cosmos, Politics and the Ideology of Kingship in Ancient Egypt and Mesopotamia.* Edited by J.A. Hill, et al. Philadelphia: University of Pennsylvania Press, 2013.

Frandsen, Paul John. "The Menstrual 'Taboo' in Ancient Egypt." *JNES* 66.2 (2007): 81-106.

Frankel, Rabbi David. "The Death of Pharaoh's Firstborn: A One Plague Exodus." www.thetorah.com.

_____. "What Did God Write on the Tablets of Stone?" www.thetorah.com.

Frazer, James George. *The Golden Bough: A Study in Magic and Religion.* London: Oxford University Press, 1994 [1890].

Freedman David Noel, Allen C. Myers. *Eerdmans Dictionary of the Bible* Amsterdam: Amsterdam University Press, 2000.

Freedy, K. S. and D. B. Redford. "The Dates in Ezekiel in Relation to Biblical, Babylonian and Egyptian Sources." *JAOS* 90.3 (1970): 462-85.

Gadd, C. J. "The Harran Inscriptions of Nabonidus." *AS* 8 (1958): 35-92.

_____. *History and Monuments Of Ur.* London: Chatto & Windus, 1929.

Galpin, Francis W. *The Music of the Sumerians and their Immediate Successors, the Babylonians and Assyrians.* Librairie Heitz: Strasbourg University Press, 1955.

Gardiner, A. H. "House of Hathor." *Recueil D'études Égyptologiques Dédiées à la Mémoire de Jean-François Champollion.* Paris: 1922. https://archive.org.

Gautschy, Rita. "The Star Sirius in Ancient Egypt and Babylonia." www.gautschy.ch /~rita/archast/sirius/siriuseng.htm.

George, A. R. "Sennacherib and the Tablet of Destinies." *Iraq* 48 (1986): 133-46.

Gier, N. F. *God, Reason, and the Evangelicals: The Case Against Evangelical*

*Rationalism*. Lanham: University Press of America, 1987.

Ginzberg, Louis. *The Legends of the Jews*. 1909. www.sefaria.org.

Giroux, Chandra. "The Power of Bones: An Intertextual and Intermaterial Reading of the Retrieval of Theseus' Bones in Plutarch's *Life of Cimon*." Pages 539-50 in *The Dynamics of Intertextuality in Plutarch*. Leiden: Brill, 2020.

Goedicke, Hans. "Papyrus Anastasi VI 51-61." *SAK* 14 (1987): 83-98.

Good, Edwin M. "Capital Punishment and Its Alternatives in Ancient Near Eastern Law." *SLR* 19.5 (1967): 947-77.

Graham, Lloyd D. "King's Daughter, God's Wife: The Princess as High Priestess in Mesopotamia (Ur, ca. 2300-1100 BCE) and Egypt (Thebes, ca. 1550-525 BCE)." www.academia.edu/34248896.

Grant, Kenneth. *Cults of the Shadow*. London: Frederick Muller, 1975.

Green, Tamara M. *The City of the Moon God: Religious Traditions of Harran*. Leiden: Brill, 1992.

Griffith, R. Drew. "Honeymoon Salad: Cambyses' Uxoricide According to the Egyptians (Hdt. 3.32.3-4)." *Historia* 58.2 (2009): 131-40.

Grohmann, Marianne. "Metaphors of Miscarriage in the Psalms." *VT* 69.2 (2019): 219-31.

Guilhou, Nadine. "Les deux morts d'Osiris, d'après les textes des Pyramides." *EAO* 10 (1998): 19-26.

"Gunpowder Compositions." Alchemy (Islam). www.chemeurope .com.

"The Hagarites/Gerrhaeans." Nabataea.net. https://nabataea.net/explore/history/hagar/.

Hallo, William W. and William L. Moran. "The First Tablet of the SB Recension of the Anzu-Myth." *JCS* 31.2 (1979): 65-115.

Hammer, Rabbi Jill. "Priestesses, Bibliomancy, and the Anointing of Miriam" (2013). https://rabbijillhammer.com/2013/11/25/priestesses-bibliomancy-and-the-anointing-of-miriam.

Harper, M. "Possible Toxic Metal Exposure of Prehistoric Bronze Workers." *BJIM* 44.10 (1987): 652-6.

Hausleiter, Arnulf. "A New Rock Relief with Cuneiform Inscription of King Nabonidus from al-Ḥāʾiṭ." Hausleiter and Schaudig, forthcoming, in collaboration with S. Baier, A. al-Dayel, Kh. al-Ha'iti, M. al-Ha'iti, N. al-Rashidi, and S. al-Rowaisan. ATLAL 4. www.academia.edu/24575559.

_____. et al. "Al-Ula, Saudi-Arabia: Archaeology and Environment from the Early Bronze Age (3rd mill. BCE) Onwards. Season 2019." From e-Forschungsberichte des Deutschen Archäologischen Instituts, 2021-1, § 1-22. doi: https://doi.org/10.34780/b5t2-t686.

_____. and H. Schaudig. "Rock Relief and Cuneiform Inscription of King Nabonidus at al-Ḥāʾiṭ (Province of Ḥāʾil, Saudi Arabia), Ancient Padakku." *ZOA* 9 (2016): 224-40.

Hayajneh, Hani. "First Evidence of Nabonidus in the Ancient North Arabian Inscriptions from the Region of Taymāʾ." Pages 81-95 in *PSAS 31: Papers from the thirty-fourth meeting of the Seminar for Arabian Studies held in*

*London, 20-22 July 2000.* Archaeopress, 2001.

Hebrew Word Study. www.chaimbentorah.com.

Heck, Gene W. "Gold Mining in Arabia and the Rise of the Islamic State." *JESHO* 42.3 (1999): 364-95.

Heidrick, Bill. Hebrew Gematria. www.billheidrick.com.

Helfgot, Nathaniel. "'And Moses Struck the Rock': Numbers 20 and the Leadership of Moses." *Tradition* 27.3 (1993): 51-8.

Hepner, Gershon. "The Naked Truth Concerning the Deaths of Nadab and Abihu." *RB* 121.1 (2014): 108-11.

Hirsch, Emil G. and James K. Hoffmeier, *Ancient Israel in Sinai: The Evidence for the Authenticity of the Wilderness Tradition.* Oxford: Oxford University Press, 2005.

____. and M. Seligsohn. "Pi-hahiroth." www.jewishencyclopedia. com.

____. and W. Max Muller. "Gershon." www.jewishencyclopedia.com.

Hoffmeier, James K. *Ancient Israel in Sinai: The Evidence for the Authenticity of the Wilderness Tradition.* Oxford: Oxford University Press, 2005.

____. Thomas W. Davis, and Rexine Hummel. "New Archaeological Evidence for Ancient Bedouin (Shasu) on Egypt's Eastern Frontier at Tell el-Borg." *ÄL* 26 (2016): 285-311.

Hogarth, Peter J. and Barbarah J. Tigar. "Ecology of Sabkha Arthropods." Pages 267-82 in *Sabkha Ecosystems Vol. 1: The Arabian Peninsula and Adjacent Countries.* Edited by H. J. Barth and Benno Böer. Netherlands: Kluwer Academic, 2001.

Hsieh, Julia. "The Practice of Repairing Vessels in Ancient Egypt: Methods of Repair and Anthropological Implications." *NEA* 79.4 (2016): 280-3.

Hundley, Michael B. "What Is the Golden Calf?" *CBQ* 79.4 (2017): 559-79.

Hüneburg, Laura, et al. "Living at the Wadi – Integrating Geomorphology and Archaeology at the Oasis of Qurayyah (NW Arabia)." *JM*, 15:2 (2019): 215-26.

Jacobs, Joseph et al. "Moses." §"In Hellenistic Literature." *JE* www.jewish encyclopedia.com.

Jacobs, Martin. "'A Day's Journey': Spatial Perceptions and Geographic Imagination in Benjamin of Tudela's Book of Travels." *JQR* 109.2 (2019): 203-32.

Jacobsen, Thorkild. "The Waters of Ur." *Iraq* 22 (1960): 174-85.

Jalbout, Ziad. "Sacred Water." §3.7. https://phoenicia.org/Decoding-Canaanite-Phoenician-Temple.html#sdfootnote149anc.

Janzen, J. Gerald. "The Character of the Calf and Its Cult in Exodus 32." *CBQ* 52.4 (1990): 597-607.

Jastrow, Morris. *The Religion of Babylonia and Assyria.* Boston: Athaneum Press, 1898.

Jawad, Laith, et al. "The Southern Marshes of Iraq." Ornithological Society of the Middle East the Caucasus and Central Asia, 7th August, 2021, https://osme.org/2021/08/the-southern-marshes-of-iraq/.

Jeenah, Na'eem. "Bilqis - A Qur'ānic Model for Leadership." *JSS* 13.1 (2004): 47-58.

Jennings, Hargrave. *Ophiolatreia.* London: 1889.

_____. *The Rosicrucians: Their Rites and Mysteries.* 4th ed. 1907 [1870]. https://sacred-texts.com.

Jewish Virtual Library. www.jewishvirtuallibrary.org.

Joergensen, Jens. "Secrets, Knowledge and Experience in Ancient Egyptian Religion: The Spells of Knowing the Powers of the Sacred Sites." MA-thesis University of Copenhagen (2006). www.academia.edu /39358296.

Johnson, Daniel. "Meet Spica, the Ear of Grain." Sky & Telescope. May 6, 2019. https://skyandtelescope.org.

Kaminker, Mendy. "Serach, the Daughter of Asher." www.chabad.org.

Kasher, Rimon. "The Mythological Figure of Moses in Light of Some Unpublished Midrashic Fragments." *JQR* 88.1/2 (1997): 19-42.

Katzenstein, H. Jacob. "Tyre in the Early Persian Period (539-486 BCE)." *BA* 42.1 (1979): 23-34.

Kennedy, Titus. "The Bronze Age Destruction of Jericho, Archaeology, and the Book of Joshua." *Religions* 14.6 (2023): 796. https://doi.org/10.3390 /rel14060796.

Kiel, Yishai. "Dynamics of Sexual Desire: Babylonian Rabbinic Culture at the Crossroads of Christian and Zoroastrian Ethics." *JSJ* 47.3 (2016): 364-410.

_____. "Why the Midrash has Abraham Thrown into Nimrod's Furnace: The Historical Association of Abraham and Nimrod with Zoroaster, the Founder of Zoroastrianism." www.thetorah.com.

Kleber, Kristin and C. van der Brugge. "The Empire of Trade and the Empires of Force: Tyre in the Neo-Assyrian and Neo-Babylonian Periods." Pages 187-222 in *Dynamics of Production in the Ancient Near East 1300-500 BC.* Edited by J. C. Moreno García. Oxford: Oxbow Books, 2016.

Klein, Isaac. *A Guide to Jewish Religious Practice.* New York: Jewish Theological Seminary of America, 1979, 1992.

Klein, Rabbi Reuven Chaim. "Haircut Time." April 2022. The Anatomy of a Mitzvah. https://ohr.edu/this_week/the_anatomy_of_a_mitzvah/9811.

Knauf, Ernst Axel and Robin M. Brown. "Edom." 2018. Oxford Bibliographies. doi: 10.1093/OBO/9780195393361-0258.

Knight, Matthew. "Ystradowen Finger Ingot." National Museums Scotland. www.nms.ac.uk.

Kraemer, Ross Shepard. *When Asenath Met Joseph: A Late Antique Tale of the Biblical Patriarch and his Egyptian Wife, Reconsidered.* New York: Oxford University Press, 1998.

Kuijpers, Maikel. "The Sound of Fire, Taste of Copper, Feel of Bronze, and Colours of the Cast: Sensory Aspects of Metalworking Technology." Pages 137-50 in *Embodied Knowledge: Historical Perspectives on Technology and Belief.* Barnsley, UK: Oxbow, 2013.

Kürschner, Harald and Reinder Neef. "A First Synthesis of the Flora and Vegetation of the Tayma Oasis and Surroundings (Saudi Arabia)." *PDE* 129.1, (January 2011): 27-58.

Laughlin, John C. H. "The 'Strange Fire' of Nadab and Abihu." *JBL* 95.4 (1976): 559-65.

Lauinger, Jacob. "Some Preliminary Thoughts on the Tablet Collection in Building XVI from Tell Tayinat." *JCSMS* 6 (2011): 5-14.

Leahy, Anthony. "The Adoption of Ankhnesneferibre at Karnak." *JEA* 82 (1996): 145-65.

Leeman, Diane. "The Nomes of Ancient Egypt." 2019. www .academia.edu/41245583.

Lehn, Walter and Peter Abboud. *Beginning Cairo Arabic: Preliminary Edition*. Austin: University of Texas, 1965.

Lemche, Niels Peter. "Is it Still Possible to Write a History of Ancient Israel?." Pages 391-414 in *Israel's Past in Present Research: Essays on Ancient Israelite Historiography* Vol. 7. Edited by V. Philips Long. USA: Eisenbrauns, 1999.

Lenzi, Allen. "Material, Constellation, Image, God: The Fate of the Chosen Bull According to kar 50 and Duplicates." Pages 58-96 in *The Scaffolding of Our Thoughts: Essays on Assyriology and the History of Science in Honor of Francesca Rochberg*. Edited by C. Jay Crisostomo, et al. Leiden: Brill, 2018.

Leonard Jr., Albert. "Archaeological Sources for the History of Palestine: The Late Bronze Age." *BA* 52.1 (March 1989): 4-39.

Leslau, Wolf. "Analysis of the Ge'ez Vocabulary: Ge'ez and Cushitic." *RSE* 32 (1988): 59-109.

Levy, Y. and J. R. Gat. "Isotope Hydrology of Inland Sabkhas in the Bardawil Area, Sinai." *LO* 23.5 (Sept 1978): 841-50.

Lewy, Julius. "The Late Assyro-Babylonian Cult of the Moon and its Culmination at the Time of Nabonidus." *HUCA* 19 (1945): 405-89.

Liddell, Henry George and Robert Scott, eds. *A Greek-English Lexicon*. Oxford: Clarendon Press, 1940.

Lipton, Diana. "God's Back! What did Moses see on Sinai?" Pages 287-311 in *The Significance of Sinai: Traditions About Sinai and Divine Revelation in Judaism and Christianity*. Edited by George John Brooke, Hindy Najman & Loren T. Stuckenbruck. Leiden: Brill, 2008.

"List of Provinces ('Nomes') of Ancient Egypt." Digital Egypt for Universities, University College London (2000). www.ucl.ac.uk.

Liu, Siran, et al. "Copper Processing in the Oases of Northwest Arabia: Technology, Alloys and Provenance." *JAS* 53 (2015): 492-503.

Loewenstamm Samuel E. "The Making and Destruction of the Golden Calf." *Biblica* 48.4 (1967): 481-90.

Lloyd, Alan B. *Herodotus, Book II Commentary 99-182*. 2nd ed. Leiden: Brill, 1993.

_____. "Necho and the Red Sea: Some Considerations." *JEA* 63 (1977): 142-55.

López, José Ángel Zamora. "Bronze and Metallurgy in Phoenician Sources." Pages 29-45 in *Phoenician Bronzes in the Mediterranean*. Edited by Javier Jiménez Ávila. Madrid: Real Academia de la Historia, 2015.

Lucas, Christopher J. "The Scribal Tablet-House in Ancient Mesopotamia." *HEQ* 19.3 (1979): 305-32.

Luciani, Marta. "Archaeology in the Land of Midian: Excavating the Qurayyah Oasis." *BAR* (Winter 2023): 32-9.

____. "Mobility, Contacts and the Definition of Culture(s) in New Archaeological Research in Northwest Arabia." Pages 21-56 in *The Archaeology of North Arabia Oases and Landscapes*, Proceedings of the International Congress held at the University of Vienna, 5-8 December, 2013.

____. and Abdullah S. Alsaud. "The New Archaeological Joint Project on the Site of Qurayyah, North-West Arabia: Results of the First Two Excavation Seasons." *PSAS* 48 (2018): 165-83.

____. "Qurayyah in Northwestern Arabia." *Archaeological Research Between Levant and Hejaz*. International Congress on the Archaeology of the Ancient Near East. June 9-13, 2014. University of Basel, Switzerland. file:///C:/Users/PC/Documents/Documents/New%20Writing/Exodus/sourc es/Luciani_M_2014_Qurayyah_in_Northwestern.pdf.

Luckenbill, Daniel David, *Ancient Records of Assyria and Babylonia Vol 2: Historical Records of Assyria.* Chicago: University of Chicago Press, 1927.

____. "The Egyptian Earth-god in Cuneiform," *AJSL* 40.4 (July 1924): 288-92.

Macalister, R. A. *The Excavation of Gezer*, Vol. 1. London: John Murray, 1911.

MacGinnis, John. "The Use of Writing Boards in the Neo-Babylonian Temple Administration at Sippar." *Iraq* 64 (2002): 217-36.

Machiela, Daniel. "Who is the Aramean in 'Deut' 26:5 and What is He Doing?: Evidence of a Minority View from Qumran Cave 1 ('1QapGen' 19.8)." *RQ* 23.3.91 (2008): 395-403.

"Making Metal Powder." § Metal Powders: Types, Characteristics, and Applications. The Metal Powder Industries Federation. www .mpif.org.

Mansour, Ahmed. "The Minerals as Divine Epithets: Notes on the Use of Lapis Lazuli in Divine Epithets." Pages 195-204 in *Environment and Religion in Ancient Coptic Egypt: Sensing the Cosmos through the Eyes of the Divine.* Archaeopress Egyptology 30. Edited by Alicia Maravelia and Nadine Guilhou. Oxford: 2020.

Maraqten, Mohammed. "The Aramaic Pantheon of Tayma'." *AAE* 7 (1996): 17-31.

Margalith, Othniel. "The Kelābīm of Ahab." *VT* 34.2 (1984): 228-32.

Marion, Loïc. "Is the Sacred Ibis a Real Threat to Biodiversity? Long-term Study of its Diet in Non-native Areas Compared to Native Area." *CRB* 336.4 (April 2013): 207-220. www.sciencedirect.com.

"Maritime Archaeology." www.brown.edu/Departments/JoukowskyInstitute /courses /maritimearchaeology11/files/18404468.pdf.

Maunder, E. W. "The Triad of Stars." *The Observatory* 31 (1908): 303-307. SAO/NASA Astrophysics Data System (ADS). https://articles.adsabs .harvard.edu.

*McClintock and Strong Biblical Cyclopedia.* https://www.biblical cyclopedia.com.

Meadowcroft, Tim. "Metaphor, Narrative, Interpretation, and Reader in Daniel 2-5." *Narrative* 8.3 (2000): 257-78.

Meeks, T. J. "Some Religious Origins of the Hebrews." *AJSL* 37.2 (1921): 101-31.

Megalommatis, Shamsaddin. *Meluhha, Gerrha, and the Emirates: Introduction to the Ancient History of the Emirates.* Germany: Dictus Publishing, 2012.

Meiliken, Jeffrey. "Sarah Lives Continued: There's Much More than Meets the Eye." Nov 25, 2008. https://kabbalah secrets.com.

Meyers, Carol. "Jachin and Boaz in Religious and Political Perspective." *CBQ* 45.2 (1983): 167-78.

Michalowski, Piotr. *The Correspondence of the Kings of Ur: An Epistolary History of an Ancient Mesopotamian Kingdom.* Penn State University Press, 2011.

Michaux-Colombot, Danièle. "Bronze Age Reed Boats of Magan and Magillum Boats of Meluḫḫa in Cuneiform Literature." Pages 119-53 in *Stories of Globalisation: The Red Sea and the Persian Gulf from Late Prehistory to Early Modernity.* Edited by A. Manzo, C., D. J. de Falco. Leiden: Brill, 2019.

Miesen, Leendert van der. "Studying the Echo in the Early Modern Period: Between the Academy and the Natural World." *Sound Studies*, 6:2 (2020): 196-214.

Millard, Alan R. "A Wandering Aramean." *JNES* 39.2 (1980): 153-55.

Miller, Yonatan. "Sedition at Moab: Josephus' Reading of the Phinehas Story." www.thetorah.com.

Mir, Mustansir. "The Queen of Sheba's Conversion in Q. 27:44: A Problem Examined." *JQS* 9.2 (2007): 43-56.

Mohammad, Yaser B. and Salih M. Awadh. "Salt Crystallization and Mineralogy of Sabkhas in Abu Ghraib, Western Baghdad, Abu Graib, Iraq." *IGJ* 56 (2023): 263-72.

Moro, Caterina. "Hero and Villain: An Outline of the Exodus' Pharaoh in Artapanus." Pages 365-76 in *Israel's Exodus in Transdisciplinary Perspective: Text, Archaeology, Culture, and Geoscience.* Edited by T. E. Levy, T. Schneider, W. H. C. Propp, BC. Sparks. Heidelberg: Springer, 2015.

Mojsov, Bojana. "The Ancient Egyptian Underworld in the Tomb of Sety I: Sacred Books of Eternal Life." *MR* 42.4 (2001): 489-506.

Muller, W. Max. "Ramases." *JE.* www.jewishencyclopedia.com.

Mumford, Gregory. "The Sinai Peninsula and its Environs: Our Changing Perceptions of a Pivotal Land Bridge Between Egypt, the Levant, and Arabia." *JAEI* 7.1 (2015): 1-24.

Munson, Rosaria V. "The Madness of Cambyses (Herodotus 3.16-38)." *Arethusa* 24.1 (1991): 43-65.

Muss-Arnolt, W. "The Names of the Assyro-Babylonian Months and Their Regents." Part 1. *JBL* 11.1 (1892): 72-94.

____. "The Names of the Assyro-Babylonian Months and Their Regents." Part 2. *JBL* 11.2 (1892): 160-76

"The Myth of Osiris and Isis." https://ancientegyptonline.co.uk.

Na'aman, Nadav. "The 'Discovered Book' and the Legitimation of Josiah's Reform." *JBL* 130.1 (2011): 47-62.

_____. "From Conscription of Forced Labor to a Symbol of Bondage: Mas in the Biblical Literature." Pages 746-58 in *"An Experienced Scribe who Neglects Nothing": Ancient Near Eastern Studies in Honor of Jacob Klein*. Bethesda: 2005.

_____. "Hiram of Tyre in the Book of Kings and in the Tyrian Records." *JNES* 78 (2019): 75-85.

Naville, Edouard. *The Store-City of Pithom and the Route of the Exodus*. London: Trübner, 1885.

Nehmé, Laïla. "Land (and Maritime?) Routes in and Between the Egyptian and Arabian Shores of the Northern Red Sea in the Roman Period." In *Networked Spaces: The Spatiality of Networks in the Red Sea and Western Indian Ocean*. Lyon: MOM Éditions, 2022. doi: https://doi.org/10.4000 /books.momeditions .16486.

Neusner, Jacob. *The Comparative Hermeneutics of Rabbinic Judaism: Seder Tohorot. Tohorot through Uqsin, Vol. 6*. United States: Academic Studies in the History of Judaism, 2000.

Neyland, Robert S. "The Seagoing Vessels on Dilmun Seals." Pages 68-74 in *Underwater Archaeology Proceedings from the Society for Historical Archaeology Conference*. Edited by Donald H. Keith and Toni L. Carrel. Kingston, Jamaica: Society for Historical Archaeology, 1992.

Nikaido, S. "Hagar and Ishmael as Literary Figures: An Intertextual Study." *VT* 51.2 (2001): 219-42.

Noegel, Scott B. "Dreams and Dream Interpreters in Mesopotamia and in the Hebrew Bible (Old Testament)." Pages 45-71 in *Dreams and Dreaming: A Reader in Religion, Anthropology, History, and Psychology*. Edited by Kelly Bulkeley. Hampshire: Palgrave-St. Martin's Press, 2001.

_____. "The Egyptian Origin of the Ark of the Covenant." Pages 223-42 in Israel's *Exodus in Transdisciplinary Perspective: Text, Archaeology, Culture, and Geoscience*. Edited by T. E. Levy et al. Germany: Springer, 2015.

Nourel-Din, Mustafa. "The Great Eastern Canal in Egypt." *ÄL* 32 (2022): 199-230.

"Numbers 1-40 and their meanings." Hebrew Linguistics and the Bible. www.gods-abcs.com.

Oestigaard, Terje. "Osiris and the Egyptian Civilisation of Inundation: The Pyramids, the Pharaohs and their Water World." Pages 72-99 in *A History of Water Vol 5: River and Society. From the Birth of Agriculture to Modern Times*. Edited by Terje Tvedt and Richard Coopey. London: I. B. Tauris, 2017.

Olcott, William Tyler. *Star Lore Myths, Legends, and Facts*. Mineola: Dover, 2012.

Olmstead, A. T. *History of the Persian Empire*. Chicago: University of Chicago Press, 1948.

Oppenheim, A. L. "Akkadian Pul(u)ḫ(t)u and Melammu." *JAOS* 63.1 (1943): 31-4.

Oren, Eliezer D. "Migdol: A New Fortress on the Edge of the Eastern Nile Delta." *BASOR*, 256 (1984): 7-44.

_____. Martha A. Morrison, and Itzhak Gilead. "Land of Gerar Expedition: Preliminary

Report for the Seasons of 1982 and 1983." BASORSup 24 (1986): 57-87.

Ouysook, Peerapat. "A Study of the Composition of Nebuchadnezzar II's Royal Inscriptions." PhD diss., Department of Archaeology University of Cambridge, 2021.

Papazian, Sjur Cappelen. "Hydra, Cancer and The Serpent" (July 15, 2018). *Cradle of Civilization: A Blog about the Birth of Our Civilisation and Development.* https://aratta.wordpress.com/2018/07/15/hydra-cancer -and-the-serpent/.

Paton, Lewis B. "The Civilization of Canaan in the Fifteenth Century BC," *BW* 20.1: 25-30.

Paul, Shalom M. "Heavenly Tablets and the Book of Life." JANES 5 (1973): 345-54.

PBS. "Desert Survival: Transportation." https://www.pbs.org/lawrenceofarabia /revolt/transport.html.

Perry, W. J. *Children of the Sun.* London: Methuen, 1923.

_____. *The Origin of Magic and Religion.* London: Methuen, 1923.

Petrie, W. M. Flanders. "The Nomes of Egypt." Pages 22-9 in *Historical Studies.* British School of Archaeology in Egypt: Studies Vol. 2. London: 1911.

Pinch, Geraldine. *Handbook of Egyptian Mythology.* Santa Barbara: ABC-CLIO, 2002.

Pitts, Audrey. "The Cult of the Deified King in Ur III Mesopotamia." PhD diss., 2015. Harvard University, Graduate School of Arts & Sciences.

Plunkett, Emmeline. *Calendars and Constellations of the Ancient World.* London: Senate, 1997, [1903].

Pollock, Susan. "From Clay to Stone: Material Practices and Writing in Third Millennium Mesopotamia." Pages 277-92 in *Materiality of Writing in Early Mesopotamia.* Edited by Thomas E. Balke and Christina Tsouparopoulou. Berlin: De Gruyter, 2016.

Potts, Daniel. "On Salt and Salt Gathering in Ancient Mesopotamia." *JESHO* 27.3 (1984): 225-71.

Priskin, Gyula. "The Depictions of the Entire Lunar Cycle in Graeco-Roman Temples." *JEA* 102 (2016): 111-44.

Propp, William H. "The Skin of Moses' Face: Transfigured or Disfigured?" *CBQ* 49.3 (1987): 375-86.

_____. "That Bloody Bridegroom (Exodus IV 24-6)." *VT* 43.4 (1993): 495-518.

Radner, Karen. "The Winged Snakes of Arabia and the Fossil Site of Makhtesh Ramon in the Negev." *WZKM* 97 (2007): 353-65.

Ramya, Raman. et al. "On the Villainous Saltpetre in Pre-Independent India." *Current Science* 110.5 (2016): 923-7.

Raskin, Rabbi Aaron L. "Letters of Light: The Meaning of the Hebrew Alphabet." www.chabad.org.

Reid, John Nicholas. "Slavery in Early Mesopotamia from Late Uruk until the Fall of Babylon in the *Longue Durée.*" PhD diss., University College, 2014.

Retsö, Jan. *The Arabs in Antiquity: Their History from the Assyrians to the Umayyads.* London: Routledge, 2003.

Ritner, Robert Kriech. *The Mechanics of Ancient Egyptian Magical Practice.* Chicago: Oriental Institute of University of Chicago, 1993.

Robinson, Gnana. "The Prohibition of Strange Fire in Ancient Israel: A New Look at the Case of Gathering Wood and Kindling Fire on the Sabbath." *VT* 28.3 (1978): 301-17.

Robson, Eleanor. "The Clay Tablet Book in Sumer, Assyria, and Babylonia." https://discovery.ucl.ac.uk/id/eprint/1476493/2/Robson_c05-2015-07-27.pdf.

Roebuck, Carl. "The Organization of Naukratis." *CP* 46.4 (1951): 212-20.

Rochberg, Francesca. *In the Path of the Moon: Babylonian Celestial Divination and Its Legacy.* Leiden: Brill, 2010.

Rogers, John H. "Origins of the Ancient Constellations: 1. The Mesopotamian Traditions." *JBAA* 108.1 (1998): 9-28.

Rohmer, J. "The Political History of North-west Arabia from the 6th to the 1st Century BCE: New Insights from Dadān, Ḥegrā and Taymāʾ." Pages 179-98 in *The Archaeology of the Arabian Peninsula 2: Connecting the Evidence*, Proceedings of the International Workshop held at the 10th International Congress on the Archaeology of the Ancient Near East in Vienna on April 25, 2016. Edited by M. Luciani. OREA, 19. Vienna: Austrian Academy of Sciences Press, 2021.

Rosenberg, Rabbi Dina. "Humility and the Power of Language." www.sefaria.org.

Rotea, Mihai, et al. "Bronze Age Metallurgy in Transylvania: Craft, Art and Ritual Magic." *AMN* 45-46/I, 2008–2009 (2011): 5-36.

Sala, Renato. "The Domestication of Camel in the Literary, Archaeological and Petroglyph Records." *JALS* 26.4 (2017): 205-11.

Sánchez, M. I., B. B. Georgiev, P. N. Nikolov, et al. "Red and Transparent Brine Shrimps (*Artemia parthenogenetica*): A Comparative Study of their Cestode Infections." Parasitol Res 100 (2006): 111-14.

Sanders, N. K. *The Epic of Gilgamesh.* Revised ed. London: Penguin, 1972.

"Sands of Time," www.pulpinternational.com.

Sasson, Jack M. "Bovine Symbolism in the Exodus Narrative." *VT* 18.3 (1968): 380-7.

"Savigny and the Sacred Ibis." Napoleon and the Scientific Expedition to Egypt, https://napoleon.lindahall.org/sacred_ibis.shtml.

Schaudig, Hanspeter. *Die Inschriften Nabonids von Babylon und Kyros' des Grossen: samt den in ihrem Umfeld entstandenen Tendenzschriften. Textausgabe und Grammatik.* Alter Orient und Altes Testament 256. Münster, 2001.

_____. "Edom in the Nabonidus Chronicle: A Land Conquered or a Vassal Defended? A Reappraisal of the Annexation of North Arabia by the Late Babylonian Empire." Pages 251-64 in *About Edom and Idumea in the Persian Period: Recent Research and Approaches from Archaeology, Hebrew Bible Studies, and Ancient Near East Studies.* Edited by B. Hensel, E. Ben Zvi, and D. V. Edelman. Sheffield: Equinox 2022.

Schneider, Stanley. "Moses in Cush: Development of the Legend." Researchgate 2019. www.researchgate.net.

Schorsch, Deborah. "Silver in Ancient Egypt." In *Heilbrunn Timeline of Art History*. New York: The Metropolitan Museum of Art, 2000. September 2018. www.metmuseum.org.

Scott, R. B. Y. "The Pillars Jachin and Boaz." *JBL* 58.2 (1939): 143-9.

Scurlock, Joann. "Medicine and Healing Magic." Pages 101-43 in *Women in the Ancient Near East: A Sourcebook*. Edited by Mark Chavalas. United Kingdom: Taylor & Francis, 2013.

Segal, Eliezer. "Sarah and Iscah: Method and Message in Midrashic Tradition." *JQR* 82.3/4 (1992): 417-29.

Segal, Michael. "The Four Kingdoms and Other Chronological Conceptions in the Book of Daniel." Pages 13–38 in *Four Kingdom Motifs before and beyond the Book of Daniel*. Edited by Andrew B. Perrin, et al. Leiden: Brill, 2021.

Shesh Kemet Egyptian Scribe. https://seshkemet.weebly.com.

Shirazi, Sayyid Abdul Husayn Dastghaib. § "What Does 'Becoming A'arab After Hijrat' Mean?" Greater Sins – Vol. 2. www.al-islam.org.

Shkop, Esther M. "And Sarah Laughed ...." *Tradition* 31.3 (1997): 42-51.

Shuaib, Marwan G. "The Arabs of North Arabia in later Pre-Islamic Times: Qedar, Nebaioth, and Others." PhD diss., University of Manchester, 2014.

Singer, Isidore, Ed., "Goshen" (1901) *JE*. www.studylight.org.

Sluijs-Seongnam, Marinus Anthony van der and Peter James. "Saturn as the 'Sun of Night' in Ancient Near Eastern Tradition." *AOr* 31.2 (2013): 279-321.

Smith, Sidney. *Isaiah XL-LX: Literary Criticism and History*. London: Oxford University Press, 1944.

_____. "The Relation of Marduk, Ashur, and Osiris." *JEA* 8.1/2 (1922): 41-4.

Smith, William Robertson. *Kinship and Marriage in Early Arabia*. Eugene: Wipf & Stock, 2023 [1903].

Soldt, Wilfred H. van. "Ordeal A. In Mesopotamia." Pages 124-9 in *Reallexikon der Assyriologie*. Edited by Erich Ebeling and Ernst F. Weidner. Berlin: 2019.

Sonik, Karen. "The Tablet of Destinies and the Transmission of Power in Enūma eliš" Pages 387-95 in *Organization, Representation, and Symbols of Power in the Ancient Near East: Proceedings of the 54th Rencontre Assyriologique Internationale at Würzburg*. Edited by Gernot Wilhelm. Winona Lake: Eisenbrauns 2012.

Spalinger, Anthony. "Some Remarks on the Epagomenal Days in Ancient Egypt." *JNES* 54.1 (1995): 33-47.

Spier, Jeffrey. "Meet the Mesopotamian Demons." May 11, 2021. www.getty.edu.

Staal, Julius D. W. *The New Patterns in the Sky: Myths and Legends of the Stars*. Blacksburg: McDonald and Woodward, 1988.

"Status of Mangroves in the Red Sea and Gulf of Aden." PERSGA Technical Series 11 (PERSGA, Jeddah: 2004). www.cbd.int.

Stavrakopoulou, Francesca. "The Jerusalem Tophet Ideological Dispute and Religious

Transformation." *SEL* 29-30, 2012-2013: 137-58

Steymans, Hans U. "Deuteronomy 28 and Tell Tayinat." *VEcc* 34.2 (2013): 1-13. www.scielo.org.za.

Steiner, Richard C. "The Aramaic Text in Demotic Script." Pages 309-27 in *The Context of Scripture. Vol. 1: Canonical Compositions from the Biblical World.* Edited by William W. Hallo and K. L. Younger. Leiden: Brill, 2003.

Steinert, Ulrike. "Fluids, Rivers, and Vessels: Metaphors and Body Concepts in Mesopotamian Gynaecological Texts." *JMC* 22 (2013): 1-23.

Stern, S. "The Babylonian Month and the New Moon: Sighting and Prediction." *JHA* 39.1.134 (2008): 19-42.

Stetkevych, Suzanne Pinckney. "Sarah and the Hyena: Laughter, Menstruation, and the Genesis of a Double Entendre." *HR* 36.1 (1996): 13-41.

Stol, Marten. *Birth in Babylonia and the Bible: Its Mediterranean Setting.* Cuneiform Monographs 14. Edited by T. Abusch, et. al. Groningen: Styx Publications, 2000.

_____. "The Moon as seen by the Babylonians." Pages 245-77 in *Natural Phenomena: Their Meaning, Depiction and Description in the Ancient Near East.* Edited by D. J. W. Meijer. Amsterdam: Royal Netherlands Academy of Arts and Sciences, 1992.

Stoneman, Richard, "Notes." *Xenophon: The Education of Cyrus.* Translated by H. G. Dakyns. London: Dent & Sons, 1992 [1914].

"The Strength of Sarah." www.chabad.org.

*Sudan English-Arabic Vocabulary*, Sudan Government, 1925.

Sullivan, Will. "Volcanic Eruptions May Have Contributed to Unrest in Ancient Egypt." January 21, 2022. www.inside science.org.

Taylor, Jonathan. "Writing Cuneiform on Other Media." *Nimrud: Materialities of Assyrian Knowledge Production* (2019), The Nimrud Project. http://oracc .museum.upenn.edu.

Tayma Governorate, Tabuk Region. World Encyclopedia. www.qpedia.org.

Tebes, J. M. "The Archaeology of Cult of Ancient Israel's Southern Neighbors and the Midianite-Kenite Hypothesis." In *The Desert Origins of God: Yahweh's Emergence and Early History in the Southern Levant and Northern Arabia.* Edited by J. M. Tebes and C. Frevel. Special Volume of *Entangled Religions* 12/2 (2021). doi: https://doi.org/10.46586/er.12.2021.8847.

Teeter, Emily and Janet H. Johnson, eds. *The Life Of Meresamun: A Temple Singer In Ancient Egypt.* The Oriental Institute Museum Publications 29. Chicago: University of Chicago, 2009.

"Tell el-Rub'a (Mendes)." March 3, 2009. Egyptian Monuments. https://egyptsites .wordpress.com.

Thomas, Rosalind and Nikolaos Papazarkadas. "The Dynamics of Publication on Stone in Democracies and Oligarchies." Project Outline. www .humanities.ox.ac.uk.

"Thonis-Heracleion: Finding a Legendary Port Under the Sea." https://the-past.com

Tinney, Steve. "On the Curricular Setting of Sumerian Literature." *Iraq* 61 (1999): 159-72.

Töpfer, Susanne. "The Physical Activity of Parturition in Ancient Egypt: Textual and Epigraphical Sources." *Dynamis* 34.2 (2014): 317-36.

Töyräänvuori, Joanna. "Trial by Water through the Ages." *SAA* 27.2 (2021): 301-30.

Tripani, Luigi. *The God Ra: Iconography (With all the Forms and Names from the 'Litany of Ra')*. Amentet Neferet: 2015.

Trumbull, Henry Clay. H. *The Blood Covenant: A Primitive Rite and its Bearings on Scripture*. Kirkwood, Mo.: Impact Books, 1975.

____. *The Covenant of Salt: As Based on the Significance and Symbolism of Salt in Primitive Thought*. New York: Scribners, 1899.

____. *Kadesh-Barnea*. Philadelphia: Wattles, 1895.

Tyson, Janet. *She Brought the Art of Women: A Song of Solomon, Nabonidus, and the Goddess*. Norwich: Pirištu Books, 2023.

Uphill, E. P. "Pithom and Raamses: Their Location and Significance." *JNES* 27.4 (1968): 291-316.

____. "Pithom and Raamses: Their Location and Significance." *JNES* 28.1 (1969): 15-39.

Valk, Jonathan. "The Eagle and the Snake, or anzû and bašmu?: Another Mythological Dimension in the Epic of Etana." *JAOS* 140.4 (2020): 889-900.

Van Seters, John. "The Geography of the Exodus." Pages 255-76 in *The Land that I Will Show You: Essays on the History and Archaeology of the Ancient Near East in Honour of J. Maxwell Miller*. Edited by J. Andrew Dearman and M. Patrick Graham. JSOTSup 343. Sheffield: Sheffield Academic Press, 2001.

Vincent, Peter. *Saudi Arabia: An Environmental Overview*. London: Taylor & Francis, 2008.

"Virgo Constellation." Arabian Nights. https://arabiannightsrum.com.

"The Visiting Soul." Egypt. https://myend.com.

Waerzeggers, Caroline. "Introduction: Debating Xerxes' Rule in Babylonia." Pages 1-18 in *Xerxes and Babylonia: The Cuneiform Evidence*. Edited by Caroline Waerzeggers and Maarja Seire. Leuven: Peeters, 2018.

Walker, John. "Asiya, the Wife of Pharaoh." *MW* 18 (1928): 45-8.

Wallin, Dr. George A. *Notes Taken during a Journey through Part of Northern Arabia, in 1848*. London: Clowes and Sons, 1850.

Walsh, Jerome T. "The Characterization of Solomon in First Kings 1-5." *CBQ* 57.3 (1995): 471-93.

Ward, William A. "Goshen." *The Anchor Bible Dictionary Vol. 2*. Edited by David Noel Freedman. New York: Doubleday, 1992.

Wein, Rabbi Berel. "A Mountain of Inspiration." Parshas Behar, May 18, 2022 (5782), https://torah.org.

Weinfeld, Moshe. "Feminine Features in the Imagery of God in Israel: The Sacred Marriage and the Sacred Tree." *VT* 46.4 (1996): 515-29.

____. "The Worship of 'Molech' and of the Queen of Heaven and its Background." *Ugarit-Forschumgen* 4 (1972): 133-54.

Weissman, Rabbi Moshe. *The Midrash Says: The Narrative of the Torah-portion in the Perspective of our Sages*. Brooklyn, NY: Benei Yakov Publications, 1980.

Wenning, Robert. "The Betyls of Petra." *BASOR* 324 (2001): 79-95.

_____. "Snakes in Petra." Pages 235-254, 279-282 (Plates), in *From Ugarit to Nabataea: Studies in Honor of John F. Healey*. Edited by George Kiraz and Zeyad Al-Salameen. Piscataway: Gorgias Press, 2012.

Wente, Edward F. *The Literature of Ancient Egypt An Anthology of Stories, Instructions, Stelae, Autobiographies, and Poetry*. Edited by William K. Simpson. Translated by R. K. Ritner, V. A. Tobin, E. F. Wente, Jr. Yale University Press, 2003.

West, Stephanie. "Croesus' Second Reprieve and Other Tales of the Persian Court." *ClQ* 53.2 (2003): 416-37.

Westermarck, Edward. *The Origin And Development Of The Moral Ideas* Vol I. London: Macmillan, 1924.

Whitcomb, Donald. "Aqaba." Pages 14-17 in *Oriental Institute 1994-1995 Annual Report*. Edited by William M. Sumner. Chicago: Oriental Institute, 1995.

White, Gavin. *Queen of the Night: The Role of the Stars in the Creation of the Child*. London: Solaria, 2014.

Wilkie, J. M. "Nabonidus and the Later Jewish Exiles." *JTS* 2.1 (1951): 36-44.

Wilkinson, Richard H. *The Complete Gods and Goddesses of Ancient Egypt*. London: Thames & Hudson, 2003.

Williams, P. J. "Shirya." Semantics of Ancient Hebrew Database, www.sahd.div.ed.ac.uk.

"Wisent and Aurochs." www.northseafossils.com.

Wisnom, Selena. "Blood on the Wind and the Tablet of Destinies: Intertextuality in Anzû, Enūma Eliš, and Erra and Išum." *JAOS* 139.2 (2019): 269-86.

Woolley, Leonard. "Excavations at Ur, 1929-30." *MJ* 21. 2 (June, 1930): 81-105. www.penn.museum.

_____. *Ur Excavations, Vol 9, The Neo-Babylonian and Persian Periods, Publications of the Joint Expedition of the British Museum and of the University Museum, University of Pennsylvania, to Mesopotamia*. London, 1962.

_____. *Ur of the Chaldees*. London: Book Club Associates, 1982; rev. ed. 1929.

Wong, Ka Leung. "'And Moses Raised His Hand' in Numbers 20:11." *Biblica* 89.3 (2008): 397-400.

Wright, G. R. H. "An Egyptian God at Shechem." *ZDP* 99 (1983): 95-109.

Yamauchi, Edwin M. and Marvin R. Wilson. *Dictionary of Daily Life in Biblical and Post-Biblical Antiquity*. Peabody, MA: Hendricksons, 2021.

Yasur-Landau, A. "The Baetyl and the Stele: Contact and Tradition in Levantine and Aegean Cult." Pages 415-22 in *Metaphysics Ritual, Myth, and Symbolism in the Aegean Bronze Age* Aegaeum 39. Leuven: Peeters, 2016.

# Index

Aaron
   age, 83, 24
   authority undercut,
      339
   base of mesa, 327
   calf, doing his job, 330
   called from
      somewhere else,
      26
   death of, 360
   dissident, 361
   gold calf, craftsman,
      194
   Hobab, 281
   inscribes tablets, 327
   magic, snake-rod, 101
   magician, 190
   metallurgy, music,
      192
   Moses' prophet, 25
   murdered, 362
   Nahor, 24
   proofreads, 325
   receives the gold, 336
   rod sprouting, 329
   stripped, 360
   the Levite, 25, 283
Aaron's rod
   blowpipe, 193
Abarim
   range, 368

Abib
   astronomical, Spica,
      112
   Ipip, Egyptian month,
      110
   new to exiles, 112
   Rosh Hashanah, 116
Abihu
   genealogy, 35
Abihu and Nadab, 201
Abimelech
   Sarah, 10
Abraham
   Abimelech, 27
   age 175, 382
   father Terah, 2
   Hebron, Tayma, 77
   in Gerar, 16
   introduction to, 6
   Moon in triad, 4
   Nabonidus as Jew, 69
   trader, wealth, 216
   two women, judge, 17
   Ur, Harran, 4
Abraham and Lot
   traders, 7
Abronah, 133
abzu (Apsu)
   Enki's marshland, 59
acacia, 214, 242, 353
Adad-guppi, 309, 319

Aramaean, 75
   dies, 38
   funeral stele, 228
   visits Tayma, 78
Adar
   Babylonian deity, 5,
      114
Ahmose III, 229, 230
   and Ladice, 157
   as Joseph, 227
   bones of Joseph, 231
   bones, corpse, 238
   coalition, 373
   corpse desecrated, 236
   corpse hidden, 237
   honorary Jew, 370
   income tax, 229
   Polycrates, 67
   Re, 281
   second pharaoh, 24
   son of Neith, 157, 278
Akki, the irrigator
   Sargon's adoptive
      father, 19
al-Hait
   rock inscription, 302
al-Naslaa Rock
   Formations, 161
al-Ula, 212
   al-Wajh route, 133
al-Wajh, 128, 134, 185,

210, 367
Ezion-geber, 133
Amalek
blood-lickers, 176
Joshua fights, 180
metaphor, 179
Nabonidus
inscription, 177
Sodom, Gomorrah,
187
Solomon's friends,
179
testing Nabonidus,
180
Ambrosial Rocks
Tyre foundation myth,
52
*Amduat*
journey of Re, 251
secret image, 261
Amminadab
Jethro, 33
Nadab, 35
Amram
lunar father, 24
Amun-Re
ram in thicket, 380
Anastasi Papyri
fire, smoke, 197
Great Wall, Egypt,
124
Shasu, Pi Tum, 95
Ankhnesneferibre, 31,
158, 177
Anzu
steals Tablet, 314
Apep
Apophis, 277
serpent, 253
underworld snake,
Ipip, 111
Apis, 105
Aqaba, 130
Nabonidus, 131
Araḥ Dumuzu
Babylonian month,
114
Aramaean
Nabonidus, 75
wandering, 74
archaeoaccoustics, 222
Aries

constellation, 112,
113, 380
ark
conveniently lost, 245
mobile fire, 193
tablet-box, 323
tablets within, 329
*aron*
coffin, 227
lore, 235
lore about, 235
Machpelah, 232
Nehushtan,
complaining, 284
Osiris, Nile, 240
Osiris, sacred tree, 240
ossuary, 238
Arsenic-Copper
effects of, 223
Artemia
brine-shrimp, 149
Ascent of Akrabbim,
172
Asher
play on Osher, Osiris,
234
pun on wealth, 234
tribe, 234
Ashmedai, 264
Ashur, 305
Ashurbanipal
library, reading, 312
read, write, wisdom,
320
Asiya bint Muzahim
Islamic legend, 231
astronomical elements
noticed by others, 244
Atrahasis, 8, 334
aurochs
Solomon's cherubim,
272
wild bulls, 272
Baal-hamon, 36
pseudonym for
Nabonidus, 8
Baal-zephon, 47
14th C. poem, 50
Egyptians allowed, 51
Hidden Things, 50, 51
in poem, as help from
North, 333

Joseph, 51
mockery, 289
pivotal clue, 238
sacred bird, 243
sanctuary, 238
statue, 49, 64, 66
Tahpanhes, 49
Zaphenath-paneah,
237
back
Sun-god, Dawn, 257
baetyl, 39, 301
Balshazzar
as Joshua, Jericho, 389
barque
*aron*, mock barque,
107
Baal-zephon, 50
Osiris, 107, 241
Re, 251, 253, 257,
258, 291
Re, *mehen*, 281
Shamash, 280
Beer-lahai-roi, 29
Beersheba
Elisheba, 33
Hagar, Zipporah, 29
seven, 27
Belshazzar, 37
Aner, 186
denounces father, 381
Eliezar, 138
honorary Jew, 370
in Tayma, 38
Isaac, 379
Lot, 39
Nabonidus concerned,
139
questions Nabonidus'
ways, 184
receives tablets, 327
revered by local tribe,
308
binding
of Aaron, 362
Bithiah
Moses' mother, 20
bitter
bitter waters, Meribah,
164
Marah, Miriam, 142
Bitter Sea (Ur)

*marratu*, 61
bitter water
  Mamre, 185
  Tiamat, 167
bitter waters
  Marah, saltwater, 128
  transitional, 129
black box, 252, 262
blood, 248
  curse, 168
  cursing with, 169
  libation, 242
  Salm of Hagam, 302
blood-avenger
  Jehudijah, 169
blood-guilt, 28
blowpipe, 14, 193, 346
  Aaron's rod, 193, 329
boats, 42
  dry ground, 65
  for escape, 207
  glyph, snake, 279
  Hiram, Euphrates, 66
  Osiris, 241
  Re, 251
  Red Sea, 128
  river, 65
  silent, 65
  wings, oars, 51
bones
  symbol of power, 80
book of the covenant
  drafts, 325
  tablets, boards, 310
bridegroom of blood, 28
bronze
  celestial, 342
  copper, Ishtar, 342
  serpent, 343
  Stars, 342
bull
  deities, 331
  Horus and Yahweh, 333
bull worship
  Horus and Yahweh, 333
bull-calf
  Baal, Marduk, Re, 331
burial site
  Sarah's, 75

burning
  plant, 198
burning asphalt
  *naphtha*, 197
burning stones, 197
burning tree
  not consumed, 198
Byblos
  body of Osiris, 241
  Osiris' body, 240
Cabul
  Hiram's land deal, 71
Cain
  mark of, 211
Caleb, 20
Cambyses
  50,000 men lost, 105
  death, eclipse, 113
  Herodotus, 104
  Herodotus, bones, 241
  Herodotus, corpse, 239
  in Egypt, 99
  King of Arabs, 96
  Pelusium, 99
  second pharaoh, 103
  son of Neith, 278
  still living, 278
  vandalising corpse, 237
camels
  Abraham, Nabonidus, 6
  at Tayma, 7
  Beasts of the Sea, 7
  considered anachronistic, 8
Canaan
  trade, 6
  traders' paradise, 79
canal
  Necho, Darius, 208
  Red Sea, 125
  Ur, 58
Carmania
  Nabonidus sent, 43
  no record, 46
casting
  metallurgy, 194
Castle of the Jew's Daughter, 69
cave

Elijah, 254
  Moses, 254
Cave of Machpelah, 76, 80, 227, 232, 382
cavern
  fire, Re, 252
Chemmis
  Pe, island, Horus, 241
cherubim
  as human lovers in Zohar, 246
  chimneys, 268
  etymology, 273
  facing down, 268
  Hebrew, passive, 274
  Solomon's temple, 271
  sphinxes, 267
chimera, 331, 342
chisel
  profane, 313
Choiak
  Egyptian month, 107, 115
circumcision, 28, 29
  Zipporah, 356
City of Four, 77, 368
  Kiriath-arba, 75
  Tayma, Kiriath-arba, 186
City of Osiris
  Pikehereth, 85
clay
  flakey, manna, 344
  potsherd, 344
  statue, weakness, 344
clay pavement
  Jer 43
    13, 122
cleft
  in Song 2
    14, 256
coalition (549 BCE)
  Tayma, 77
Code of Hammurabi
  stele, 314
commission name
  definition, 1
concubine
  Elisheba, 33
  Jehudijah, 29

Nitocris, 11
Reumah, 33
Conduit of the Infidel's
  Daughter, 69
conjunction
  astronomical, 107,
    111, 112, 295
corvée, 88
  priesthood, Ur, 90
  Solomon, 90
  two types, 89
cosmology, 244
covenant of salt
  Arabic, 152
  Nabonidus, 303
  Nabonidus, Gesem,
    95
  protection, treaty, 153
  Tophal, 209
  treaty, 186
Cozbi, 356
  Aaron, 361
  liar, 357
  Zipporah, ~Jehudijah,
    356
crevice
  Moses, 253
crocodile
  Pharaoh, Sobek, 101
Croesus
  consultant to Cyrus,
    79
  effectively Hittite, 78
  Ephron, coins, 79
  meets Nabonidus, 77
cultic statues
  gathered in time of
    war, 46
  humans profane, 327
cursing ritual
  with blood, 169
Cushite, 240
  miscarriage, 247
  Nubian, 155
  rabbis debate identity,
    15
Cyrene
  Libya, 158
Cyrus edict, 102
Cyrus the Great, 43
Damascus
  Eliezer, 139

Daniel
  book of, 340
  knows Nabonidus,
    340
  plot to remove
    Nabonidus, 341
Daphnae
  Tahpanhes, Ahmose
    III, 67
darkness, 107
  madness, 263
  mental state, 262
  Nabonidus, bones,
    236
  physical effects, 263
daughter of Pharaoh, 2,
    20, 21, 23, 156, 231
  purity concerns, 235
dawn
  Nabonidus leaves Ur,
    66
Dawn
  as epithet of pharaoh,
    289
Day Star, son of Dawn,
    289
death
  passover, crevice, 255
death of firstborn, 98,
    109
  caveat to Nabonidus,
    110
  only original
    punishment, 99
  Osiris, 109
Decad
  scribal school lessons,
    318
Decalogue, 310
deification, 265
  of Ramesses II, 266
  Osirian influences,
    121
  parodied in statue,
    Song, 351
Deuteronomy names
  Di-zahab, 213
  Hazeroth, 210
  Laban, 209
  Paran, 209
  Suph, 207
  Tophal, 209

Diodirus' Great Wall,
    126
Diqdiqah
  Euphrates ends, 60
  lagoon, 61
Di-zahab
  Deuteronomy names,
    213
Dodavahu of Mareshah,
    141
door, 317
Doughty
  Bedouin route (Red
    Sea), 134
  birds, sabkha, 152
  burning bushes, 197
  covenant of salt, 153
  graves, 212
  meets smith, Tayma,
    215
  rocks named, Tayma,
    162
  routes through Arabia,
    133
  ruins of Tayma, 309
  sabkha, Tayma, 151
  *ṣâny*, 215
  split rocks, 162
  Tayma Stone, 296
  the Harraat, 365
drag away
  Hagar and Jehudijah,
    16
drawn
  Moses, Re, 247
dream
  divine order, dagger,
    268
Dynasty 26, 68, 86, 157
eagle and snake
  Tyre foundation myth,
    52
eagles' wings
  metaphor, 51
  Tyre, 66
Ecclesiastes, 289
  wisdom, 226
eclipse
  Cambyses, 113
  Ennigaldi-Nanna, 299
  horns, 295
  idol of Sîn, 224

lunar, 13 Ululu, 553
BCE, 341
lunar, July 17, 522
BCE, 112
Nabonidus, 111
Eclipse Battle, 45, 77
Edom, 94
avoiding, 360
Esau, 363
Tayma, 136
*edubba*
Decad, 318
retrospective, revival, 319
tablet-house, 317
Egyptian
Hagar as, 17
Egyptian captivity
duration, 382
Ein Feshkha, 368
*Ekišnugal*
Temple of Sîn, Ur, 56, 224
*el Kasr el Bint el Yahudi*, 69
Eldad and Medad, 183, 338
Eleazar, 36
eleven days
Kadesh-barnea to horeb, 172
Eliezar
Belshazzar, 138
hero, 140
son of Dodavahu, 141
Eliezer
of Damascus, 138
Elijah
cave, 219, 254
rockfall, 220
uses asphalt, 198
Elim, 146
Tayma, 147
Eliphaz, 213
Elisheba, 33
Elixir, 11, 63, 120, 158, 165, 167, 168, 180, 209, 226, 247, 269, 281, 292, 349, 355, 375
Ennigaldi-Nanna, 70
making money from,

9
Nabonidus addicted, 374
Elon-bezaanannim, 367
Eloth, 136
embalming
Joseph, Osiris, 259
emigration
inscrition near Tayma, 177
empty
Nabonidus' name, 28
Enheduanna, 31, 317
Enki's temple
at Ur, 58
Ennigaldi-Nanna, 317
adopted by Nitocris, 374
dedicated to god, 379
eclipse, 299
*entu*, 56
exposed as not Nitocris' child, 67
little sister, 16, 75, 165
Miriam, 30, 33
Miriam, Kadesh, 165
rejected, 69
returned to Egypt, 64
ripe in Song, 34
*entu*, 247
builder of temple, 56
library at Ur, 319
Ephron
Croesus, 79
*Epic of Etana*, 51
equinox, 112
eruptions
Harraat, 196
Erythraean Sea, 207
Esau
red, hairy, 363
Eshcol
Sheshbazzar, 204
Eshcol and Aner
allies of Mamre, 186
Ethiopia
Moses, ibis, 271
Euphrates
boats taken overland, 131
boats to Ur, 48
Hiram's boats, 66

in marshlands, 60
Ordeal by Water, 119
reclaimed land, 49
rowing, sailing, 66
stops at Diqdiqah, 60
exodus
from Babylonia, 42, 43
exposure to the sun
sin offering, afterlife revoked, 359
Ezion-geber, 130
al-Wajh, 133
etymology, 132
wood, 135
feet
Moses', 29
fiery serpents
*seraphim*, desert, 284
finger of God
humans profane, 327
fire and smoke
guiding, desert, 196
precedent, 197
fire worshipper, 203, 304
First Prophet of Amun
Nitocris, 373
fish
Joshua, Enki, Marduk, 37
symbol, Enki, 59
flying serpents
Ethiopia, Moses, 271
Herodotus, Arabian, ark, 270
protect Horus, 241
flying snakes
copper mines, 276
*foetus compressus*
miscarriage, Nitocris, 160
forty days
Joseph, 259
snake, skin, 280
forty years
Solomon, Moses, 293
forty-days
initian, 328
fossils
Herodotus, snakes, 270

Frankincense Trail, 214
friend of God
    Abraham, 8
    Reuel, Abraham,
        Moses, 282
fugitive, 28
    Kadesh-barnea, 171
    wandering Aramaean,
        75
fumes
    from the ark, 268
furnace
    chemical reaction, 193
Gaza
    Judah boundary, 173
gematria
    '10', 370
    '100', 72, 370
    '12', 259
    '120', 71, 370
    '127', 76
    '137', 19, 26
    '175', 382
    '20', 71
    '205', 5
    '21', 335
    '3', 25
    '30', 382
    '318', 139
    '360', 348
    '40', 259
    '400', 382
    '60', 5
    '66', 349, 351
    '666', 348
    '73', 260
    Kabbalistic, 76
    using, 348
Genubath, 23, 66
Gerar, 184
    Arabian, 186
    etymology links
        Hagar and
        Jehudijah, 16
    Gerrha, 187
    King Abimelech, 10
Gerrha
    Gerar, 187
Gesem
    Arabic Goshen, 93
    Geshem the Arab, 93
    King of Qedari, 93

Nabonidus, 95
    Pithom, 93
*Ghirbal*
    timbrel, 32
Gilgamesh
    tablets, 323
*giparu*, 317
glory
    as phallus, 246
    mobile, 267
God's Hand, 230
gold
    amount of, idol, 336
    King, Pharaoh, Sun,
        342
    Sun-god, 332
golden calf, 330
    Aaron, stylus, 336
    bull-calf, 331
    burnishing technique,
        337
    construction, 336
    Daniel, parodied, 345
    death of worshippers,
        346
    in fire, 337
    in Numbers, drink,
        337
    Peor, 354
    pulverised, 337
    ten commandments,
        347
    these are your gods,
        347
    three killed, 346
golden phallus, 247
Goshen, 92
    *stratopeda*, 92
governor, 46, 47, 142,
    204, 230
graves
    al-Ula, 212
    in al-Ula, 211
Great Wall
    Wall of Shur, Egypt,
        124
Haddaj Well
    Tayma, 147
Hagar, 16
    flees, 18
    links to Well of Seven,
        27

haircut
    Zipporah, 29
hand
    Moses raises, Amalek,
        181
harbour
    Ur, 48
Harbour Palace
    at Ur, 56
Harraat, 94
    erruptions, 196
    lava fields, charred,
        186
    Seir, 363
    site of Hor, 362
    source of heat, 187
    volcanoes, 196
Harran
    centre of Sîn worship,
        4
    Salm, 299
    temple, statue, 272
    Terah dies, 5
Harran stele, 305
Harrat ar Rahah, 196
Harrat Khaybar, 367
Harrat 'Uwayrid, 196
Hasophereth
    female scribe, 319
Hazeroth
    Deuteronomy names,
        210
    in Numbers, 210
heavenly host
    attendants, Re, 257
    sparks, 257
Heber
    Hebron, 368
    Jehudijah, Mered, son,
        367
    metallurgy, snakes,
        priest, 367
Hebron
    Abraham, 77
    Heber, 368
    Tayma, 77
hedge
    in name Iscah, 14
Heliopolis, 226, 243
    Asenath, 157
    Great Wall, 125
    LXX, 265

On, Osiris, 117
  Ramesses II, 266
Herodotus
  misappropriation of
    legends, 236
Heroopolis
  Pithom, Pi Tum, 84
hidden
  body, 248
  foetus in womb, 248
*hieros gamos*
  sacred marriage, 246
high priest
  Aaron, Nabonidus,
    340
Hiram of Tyre
  aids Nabonidus, 70
  Aqaba, Suez, 132
  Hiram III, 54
  influence, 258
  Nabonidus, 52
  ships in Aqaba, 131
Hittite
  burial site, 75, 186
Hittites
  Nabonidus, 81
Hobab
  Aaron, 281
  as beloved, 283
  Moses' son-in-law,
    282
  snake, 281
  wants to leave, 283
Hobah
  hiding place, 140
Holy of Holies
  deputy priest, 294
  Jerusalem, 274
  priest, image, 261
  Sîn's temple, 272
  Solomon's temple,
    273
Hor, 362
  Horite, 363
  Moserah, 361
  Mount, Aaron's death,
    360
Horeb, 205
Horite
  Harraat, 363
horns, 295, 380
Horus

avatar of Pharaoh, 110
  Pe, floating island,
    241
Horus and Adonai
  worshipped together,
    332
Horus and Yahweh
  as bull, 333
Hoshea
  Isaac, 379
house
  Jehudijah, 250
House of Anger
  Pi-hahiroth, 63
House of Hathor
  Pi-hahiroth, 63
House of the Snake, 276
Huldah
  in derelict Jerusalem,
    308
Hur
  Aaron's son, 346
  death of, 347
  son of Miriam, 347
I AM, 243, 268, 304,
    330
  ambiguity, 331
  aniconic, 258
  bovine connection,
    332
  chimera, 331
  nonsectarian, 291
  not exclusive, 332
  not monotheistic, 332
  solar aspect, 298
I am who I am
  *'ehyeh 'ăšer 'ehyeh*,
    332, 335
Iah, 230
ibis
  African sacred, 59
  don't eat snakes, 271
  Herodotus, 270
  Moses, Ethiopia, 271
idol
  Terah as maker of, 3
Ilteri
  Tayma Moon god, 3
image
  Salm, deity, Tayma,
    296
  *salmu*, 298

secret, Re, 261
incest
  Abraham and Sarah,
    11
initiation
  Nabonidus, 281
  Sinai, 291
  test, 254
Ir-hatamarim
  Jericho, 389
iron
  Re's cavern, 343
  underworld, 342
Isaac
  Belshazzar, 379
  legitimacy, 13
  sacrifice, 378
Iscah, 14
  as Sarah, 14
Ishmael, 18
  archer, 18
  as part of curse, 169
  eponomous name, 94
  foreskin used to curse
    Moses, 168
  Shur, 124
Ishmaelites, 19
  Nabonidus supporters,
    19
Ishtar
  blood, Nile, 120
  followers revel, 184
  Jews hated, 121
  links Sarah and
    Nitocris, 13
  Stars in triad, 4, 5
Isis, 250
  mother, wife, 250
Isis and Nephthys
  midwives, 249
  serpents, 251
Ithamar
  Harraat, 367
ithyphallic
  Amun-Re, 247
Iye-abarim, 361
Jabal al Quidr
  hair lava, 364
Jachin and Boaz
  Solomon, pillars, 52,
    183
Jael

wife, Heber, 367
Jebel al-Lawz
    not Sinai, 216
Jedidiah, 230
Jehoshaphat
    ships damaged, 135
    Tarshish, Ezion-geber, 141
Jehudijah
    anger, 63
    as blood-avenger, 169
    as both mother and wife, 250
    as Nephthys, 250
    as Shiphrah, 248
    curses Moses with blood, 168
    escape, 65
    harbour palace, Ur, 57
    Hathor, 250
    haunted by Nitocris, 16
    introduction to, 2
    Jochebed, 249
    on the journey, 9
    overlooked, bitter, 68
    poetess, songstress, 31
    resentful, 17
    Reumah, 34
    saves the day, 249
    secret love, 283
    seized, 64
    songs of praise, 356
    unfaithful, 357
Jephthah
    child sacrifice, 378
Jericho
    Belshazzar, 387
    City of the Moon, 388
    location, 388
    symbolic, 389
Jerusalem
    expectations, 55
    governor, 46
    pseudonym, 46
    Tayma, 231
Jethro
    Amminadab, 33
    Salu, 361
Jewish Tayma, 306
Jochebed, 246
Jordan, 174, 368, 386

Joseph
    as Osiris, Coptic, 228
    Baal-zephon, 51
    body hidden, 234
    body in Nile, 233
    corpse mutilated, 238
    double, 231
    Egyptian name, 232
    Egyptian ruler, 229
    embalmed in Egypt, 227
    Genesis mirrors Exodus, 228
    Heliopolis, 226
    Nabonidus, 230
    Serapis, 229
Joseph and Asenath, 157, 200
    fiery sparks with deity, 200
Joshua, 36
    fights Amalek, 180
    Hoshea, Isaac, 379
    remains in tent, 294
    son of Nun, 37
    witness, stele, 301
judge
    Moses, 122
    two wives, 17
judgement
    Nabonidus at Nile, 118
Judith, 92, 93
Kadesh, 211
    Miriam's Well travels, 164
Kadesh-barnea, 170
*Ḳanâet Bint el-Ḳafir*, 69
Karnak
    priests, Nitocris, 65
*Kasr Bedr Ibn Johr*
    Prince of Tayma, 309
Keturah, 40
Khaybar, 152, 162, 186, 212, 364
Khenemibre
    Ahmose III, 23
Kibroth-hattaavah
    in Numbers, 211
king
    Deuteronomy rules

for, 349
King of Israel, 46, 293, 308
King of the Arabs, 96
    land, 81
    Nabonidus, 96
King Sargon of Akkad, 19
King Solomon's Mines, 213
Kiriath-arba
    City of Four, 75, 77
    City of Four, Tayma, 186
Korah
    disgruntled, 301
Laban
    Deuteronomy names, 209
Labynetus
    Nabonidus in Herodotus, 77
Ladice
    Ahmose III (Herodotus), 157
Lake of Fire
    underworld, 255, 262
Lake Tanis
    wind setdown, 127
*lamassu/shedu* bulls, 272
land purchase
    formal agreement, 80
landmarks
    mirrored, 42
lapis-lazuli, 260
    tablet, 317
laughing
    Sarah, 12
Layla and Majnun, 18
Leuke Kome
    White Village, 135
Levite
    Aaron, 25
Levites
    snakes, 282
    tribal metalworkers, 284
Libya
    Asenath, 157
    dark-skinned, 156
Lot, 39

disguise, 39
  kidnapping, 140
  Tayma region, 39
Lot's wife, 187
lunar names, 5
Lydia
  treaty, Media, 77
madness, 227
*majal*
  *entu* cemetery, 235
Mamre
  oaks, 185
  the man, 186
mangrove trees
  Eloth, 136
manna, 148
  colour, 150
  coriander, 150
  flaky, 149
  Mamre, 185
  melts, 150
  smell, 150
  taste, 151
  worms, 149
Marah, 128
  Moses, wood, magic, 142
  Red Sea, 128
Marduk
  Joshua, 37
  magic staff, 303
  tablets on robe, 315
Marduk and Tiamat, 99
marshes
  escape into (Ur), 65
  Iraq, Al-Hammar, 59
  Iraq, Al-Hawizeh, 60
  Iraq, Central, 60
marshlands
  of Nile Delta, inhabited, 71
Massah, Meribah, 172, 181, 182
*mehen*
  serpent, 281
*melammu*
  shining light, nimbus, 292
Melchizedek, 303
Melqart, 52
  pillars, 52
menstruation

anti-menses, 338
as waters, 248
Ennigaldi-Nanna, 70
Ishtar, Nile, 120
Mered and Bithiah, 22
  Miriam, 33
Meribah, 164
Meribath-kadesh, 170
Merris, 23
mesa
  Qurayyah, 217
metallurgy
  Aaron creates idol, 336
  biblical references, 194
  casting, 194
  in name "Nahor", 14
  magic, ritual, 191
  Massah, 182
  moulds, 194
  religious, music, 192
  ringing sound, 26
  rituals, secret, 191
  saltpetre, 200
  Sinai Peninsula, 216
  sparks, 198
  Yahwism, 189
Midian
  Moses' route, 86
Midian wife
  Zipporah, Jehudijah, 27
Midianites
  battle with, test, 358
  conscripts do killing, 362
  Ishmaelites, 19
  Qenites, 190
Migdol, 47, 57
  military fortress, 57
Milcah, 16
Miriam, 30, 159
  as Milcah, 16
  as Well, 164
  blood, 166, 167
  blood, well, 166
  daughter,wife, 32
  Ennigaldi-Nanna, 30, 33
  first rejection by Moses, 145

leprosy, 159
Miriam's Well, 164
  rock, 164
  sieve, 32
mirroring effect, 41
miscarriage
  Nitocris, 247, 374
  Nitocris, herbs, 247
Mishneh quarter, 308
Mizraim
  Hebrew for Egypt, 125
Molech
  child sacrifice, 378
moon
  disappearance of, 107
Moon god
  Arabian, 5
  in names of characters, 5
  in Song of Solomon, 5
Moreh
  Abraham, Shechem, 228
Moriah, 380
Moserah
  binding, 362
  Mount Hor, 361
Moses
  acting like god, 292
  as king, 293
  chastised by Zimri, 358
  death, 368
  face shining, 292
  horns, 294
  meaning, 20
  Thoth-Hermes, 21, 114
  veil, mask, 293
Moses/Moshe
  serpent, 277
mother
  consort, 241
moulding
  around ark, 269
Mount of Corruption
  Solomon, 206
Mount Paran, 209
mountain, 262
  death on, 361
murder

Moses, 248
murderer, 28
museum, 317
musical instrument
  Miriam, 30
myriads of holy ones
  sparks, 199
Nabonidus
  acting like king, 339
  addicted to Elixir,
    374
  against deification,
    298
  Ahmose III's body,
    227
  anonimity, 46, 86,
    340, 355, 370
  apotheosis, 290
  Aqaba, port, 131
  arbitrator, 45
  as Labynetus in
    Herodotus, 77
  as pharaoh, 231
  as protective hedge,
    15
  as protector, 6
  Assyrians, wisdom,
    320
  avatar of Osiris, 294
  bad reputation, Jews,
    355
  bones, precedents,
    239
  calf, jealous, 334
  camels, 7
  chimera, 281
  conflating deities, 331
  cuneiform, 321
  cut off from Israel,
    371
  deal with Cyrus, 64
  deification of sorts,
    291
  denounced, Daniel,
    347
  dismembers corpse,
    238
  Edom, Sela, 94
  Eshcol, 186
  esoteric interests, 262
  exploits Elixir for
    money, 9

favourite month,
  Tashritu, 115
first draft, 325
Gesem, 95
governor, 46
Hiram of Tyre, 52
history of being
  careless, tablets,
    328
hubris, 144, 183, 240,
  256, 263, 288, 292,
  294, 296, 313, 345,
  347
hybrid deity, 263
iconography, 296, 303
in local memory, 309
introduction to, 2
kills Midian family,
  347
kills opposition, 361
King of Babylon, 2
King of Israel, 308
leaves Ur, 62
leaves Ur at dawn, 66
Lord of Sex, 354
Lord of the Stylus,
  320
Nabu, 323
name cursed, 146,
  359, 370
nature, character, 225
no problem with idols,
  338
positive, Abraham,
  307
priest, 290
Qedarites, 94
rebellion, 259
receives *melammu*,
  293
rejected, 47
repair tablets, 329
ringed staff, 305
rock inscriptions, 302
scribal skills refuted,
  321
searches for bones,
  236
self-deification, 287
self-deification,
  erroneous, 330
sells Elixir in Babylon,

  374
serpentine imagery,
  279
seven years, penance,
  288
Sheshbazzar, 203
Sihon and Og, 173
statues in inscriptions,
  351
synthesis of gods, 227
temper, tablets, 328
treaty, Bedouins, 153
triad, 4, 5
two visits to Egypt,
  236
unites with Ahmose,
  294
Ur, writing boards,
  326
violence, 294, 359
wanderer, Moon
  (Terah), 3
wisdom, 11, 226
Nabu
  god of scribal arts, 323
  Nebo, 369
Nabû-balṭsu-iqbi
  Nabonidus' father, 3
Nadab and Abihu
  Lake of Fire, 262
Nahor, 14
  Aaron, 24
  Aaron's death, 361
  linked etymology,
    347, 362
Nahshon
  snake charmer, 282
naked
  metallurgy, fire, 191,
    192
name of God
  secret, powerful, 291
Nebo
  Nabonidus, 369
  Nabu, 369
  pseudonym, 370
Nebuchadnezzar, 92
  copies Egyptian
    statues, 348
  escaped exiles in
    legend, 73
  in Daniel, 340

mentioned, 104
Nabonidus, 45
pseudonym, 287
rain for pious, 144
ridiculing exiles, 88
seige of Tyre, 53
Necho
  lineage, Nitocris, 156
Negeb, 178
Nehebkau
  serpent god, brother to
    Moses, 101
  serpent, brother, 277
Nehushtan, 276
  copper, 343
  Re, 284
  Wadjet, 285
new moon, 107, 110,
  112, 236, 331
  third, at Sinai, 115
*niddah*
  Nile, 120
Nile
  beating (Miriam), 168
  Joseph's body, 233
  Ordeal by Water, 339
  Osiris, 240
  red, blood of Osiris,
    106
Ningal
  linked to Ordeal by
    Water, 120
Nisan
  equinox, 112
  Hebrew month, 110,
    113
  Jews prefer, 113
Nitocris
  as Asenath, 157
  as Puah, 248
  as Sarah, 9
  as wall, supressed, 75
  children, 12
  conciliatory wife, 373
  deified in Song, 287
  escape, 64
  feigned pregnancy,
    374
  First Prophet of
    Amun, 373
  God's Hand, *entu*, 246
  introduction to, 2

killed, 249
miscarriage, 247, 248
Queen of Babylon, 77
regent *entu*, 56
rejects pregnancy, 9
secret, bones, 234
seer, 263
teaches Nabonidus,
  225
visited by Egyptian
  emmisaries, 10
wisdom, 11
nomes, 85
  Moses passes through,
    86
Nonnus of Panopolis,
  52
Nubian
  Cushite, 155
number
  people on exodus, 42
Numbers 33
  forty camps, 383
Nusku
  Fire-god, 114
  in inscription, 304
  sacred number 10, 114
  solar, protector, 304
old boys' club
  Nabonidus, Croesus,
    Hiram, 79
ophiolatry
  snake worship, 275
Ophir, 213
Opis
  Battle, 45
  deal at, 46
  in Tashritu, 115
opposition
  astronomical, 107,
    109, 111, 257
Oracle at Delphi, 80
Ordeal by Water
  legal process, 119
  Ningal, Ishtar, 119
Orestes, 80
Osher
  Osiris, Asher, 234
Osiris, 233, 240
  110 years, 370
  and Re, 243
  as Moon, 241

Ashur, Marduk, 305
bones gathered, 236
bull as, 331
cavern, 242
City of, 85
death of firstborn, 109
Festival, 107, 115
first indications of, 84
Joseph, 228
judge of the dead,
  122
judgement of, 116
merges with Re, 252
Moses' tomb, 368
mumification, 259
mummy, bones, 241
new moon, 116
Nile, 105
Nile as blood, 106
nomes, 85
Osher, Ashur, 235
Pithom, 84
Re, astronomical, 111
resurrection ritual, 241
revived by incense,
  blood, 242
seat of power, 122
snake, 242
symbolism, 99
turns his back, 255
paper
  not common, 311
Paran
  Deuteronomy names,
    209
  Ishmael, 18
  Sela, 173
pasturing his flocks,
  218
Pelusiac
  branch of Nile, 88, 92,
    127
  topography, 92
Pelusium, 68, 86, 124,
  125
  Cambyses, 99
  route to Tahpanhes,
    126
Peor
  euphemism, 354
  warning, 353
*Periplus*

Red Sea ports, 134
Petra
  rock glyphs, 278
Phaophi
  Egyptian month, 115
Pharaoh
  makes labour difficult, 89
pharaoh with hardened heart, 102
Pharaoh's daughter
  as Nitocris, 2
  Moses' mother, 21
Pharmuthi
  Egyptian month, 113
Philistines
  affected by ark, 224
  effects of ark, 193
Phinehas
  as priest, 301
  etymology, 356, 358
  kills lovers, 356
  military hero, 357
  priest, Tayma, 301
  priesthood, 358
Phoenicians
  ritual, sailors, 49
phoenix, 238, 249, 333
  in poem, 50
  resurrection, 51
Pi Tum
  Pithom, 84
pierced
  Cozbi, Zipporah, 356
Pi-hahiroth, 62
  House of Anger, 63
  House of Hathor, 63
  site of Baal-zephon sanctuary, 51
Pikehereth
  City of Osiris, 85
  Moon, 86
pillars
  of Melqart, 52, 182
pimping out, 9, 74
Pi-Ramesses, 88
Pisgah, 173
Pithom, 83
  Moses,Midian, 86
  Pi Tum, 84
  Ptolemy II, Great Wall, 125

Serapeum, 85
storehouses, 88
Tahpanhes, 83
plagues, 98
  as omens in Mesopotamia, 108
  demeaning Nabonidus, 100
  number varies, 100
  omens, 108
  seasonal markers, 102
plunder
  gold, silver, 109
plundering, 216, 236
pomegranate, 34
portable
  cavern, tabernacle, 261
  tablet-box, 323
  tool box, 194
portable fire, 192
pregnancy
  ended, Nitocris, 247
  Nitocris feigns, 374
  Sarah, 9
  Sarah laughs, 12
priests
  law makers, 350
prophesying
  euphemism, 184
Puah, 33
  midwife, 248
Qedarites
  as archers, 19
  Cambyses, 96
  Gesem territory, 93
  Nabonidus, 94
  vast territory, 94
Qenites, 102, 189, 190, 195, 198, 217, 227, 242, 243, 258, 269, 275, 281, 283, 301, 313, 333, 338, 354, 367
  at Sela, 172
  magicians, 190
  metalworkers, 189
quail, 148
Queen of Sheba, 11
Quran
  princes of Egypt praise Sarah, 10

Qurayyah
  accoustics, 222
  arsenic-copper, 222
  caves, 219
  fit for caravans, 219
  furnaces, fire, 346
  grazing animals, 218
  hearing crowd, 218
  lower sky, 262
  metallurgy, 221
  Mountain of God, 217
  nondescript, legend, 218
  place for casting idols, 336
  rockfall, 219
  Salm, 306
  water supply, 219
Raameses
  'evil' Moses, 266
rain, 97
  manna, 148
  mist, dew, 149
  reward for piety, 144
  spell for, 142, 143
ram in the thicket, 379
Rameses, 264
  as person, 265
  Moserah, 361
  Son of the Sun, 265
  to hit, 266
Ramesses II
  store-cities, 88
Ramose, 265, 361
Re
  merges with Osiris, 252
  Osiris, astronomical, 111
  rebirth, darkness, secret, 255
  Sun god, 251
Red Sea, 207, 208
  algae, 208
  Marah, 128
reliquary, 227, 238
remote-viewing, 263
Renenutet, 20, 101
  as cobra, 21
  serpent goddess, 277
Rephidim, 133, 186, 211

Amalek, 37, 180
  *horeb*, 206
  meaning, 181
  Miriam's Well travels,
    164
  Moses weak, 171
resurrection
  Ahmose III, 261
  baby, symbolic, 249
  erect phallus, 247
  Marduk, 37
  moon, 116
  Osirian, Ahmose III,
    259
  Osiris, 116, 241
  phoenix, 51, 238
  Re, 111
Reuel
  clan, 281
  Jethro, Eliphaz's
    brother, 213
  priest, Midian, 356
  son, Hobab, 281
Reumah, 33
  Jehudijah, 34
rock
  stone hits statue, 345
Rock
  Qurayyah, Sinai, 217
  Sinai, 205
  Sinai/God, 130
  Tyre, 129
Rock of Israel, 217,
  345
rockfall
  used for tablets, 328
rocks
  in desert, named, 162
Rosh Hashanah, 116
Rosicrucians
  revere fire, 200
sabbath
  stems from Ishtar's
    menstruation, 120
sabkha, 148
  food poisoning, 213
  Khaybar, 187
  Nabonidus, treaty, 153
  white, 210
salm
  dark, black, 299
Salm, 297

deity, image, 296
Harran, 299
Qurayyah, 306
representative, 297,
  300, 301
suggested meaning,
  300
Salm of Hagam, 302
Salmshezib, 301
  priest of Tayma, 296
*salmu*
  Assyrian precedents,
    298
  black, statue, 299
  celestial, 300
Salmu
  deity, 297
salt-flats
  red, 150
saltpetre
  as flux, 200
  effects, 199
  for effect, 199
Salu
  Jethro, 361
Sambation
  symbolic river, 73
Samson
  Nabonidus, 265
sanctuary
  Baal-zephon, 238, 240
*ṣâny*
  smith, 215
sapphire, 260
Sara
  Ishtar, 13
Sarah, 9
  burial, 78
  burial site, 75
  burial, Tayma, 186
  Ennigaldi-Nanna, 70
  Gerar, 184
  Iscah, 14
Sarai, 13
sarcophagi
  defaced, 237
Saturn
  as Sun, 299
sea, 47
  in, on dry ground, 65
  Ur, 59
  waves, walls, 65

Sealand, 60, 61
  rapid flooding, 66
second-wife
  Elisheba, Jehudijah,
    33
secret, 226
seer
  Iscah, Nitocris, 15
Seir, 363
  hair, 364
  horror, 364
  horror, hairy, 363
  in Harraat, 363
  lava fields, 365
  shine forth, 209
  split, 364
Sela
  crossing, 387
  inscription, 387
  Kadesh-barnea, 171
Serah
  daughter, Ahmose III,
    235
  daughter, Asher, 234
Serapeum
  Pithom, 85
seraphim
  on ark, 267
seraphs, 272
Serapis
  Joseph, 229
serpent
  *Amduat*, cavern, 253
  as bronze, 343
  glyph near Tayma,
    279
  glyph, icon, 304
  glyphs, Petra, 278
  iconography, staff,
    cherubim, 306
  in Jerusalem, 276
  in Joseph's Egyptian
    name, 233
  *mehen*, 242, 269
  Nehebkau, 277
  staff, Re, 253
  Thoth, 275
  vital, Re, 252
  Wadjet, 241
  wand, 241
  Yahweh, 275
serpent goddess

Moses' mother, 22
serpents
    underworld, 251
Set
    birthday, 96
    Osiris, 116
seven years
    in Tayma, 157
    plague curse, 98
Shamash
    at Sela, 388
    Sun in triad, 4, 5
*shamir*, 313
Shasu, 95
    and Pi Tum, 95
Shechem
    Joseph, 228
Sheshbazzar, 43, 203, 304
shining face
    eclipse, 295
    Moses, 292
    wisdom, 294
Shiphrah
    midwife, 248
Shittim, 353
Shulgi, King of Ur, 317
sieve
    Well, timbrel, 32
Sihon and Og
    Nabonidus battles, 173
silver
    Moon, 342
silver and gold, 349
Simeon
    Zimri, 361
sin, 159
Sîn
    at Harran, Ur, 2
    Moon in triad, 4, 5
Sinaeiun
    means industrial, 215
Sinai, 205
    not in Peninsula, 214
Sinai Peninsula
    never enter, 136
    no volcanoes, 196
Ṣinā'iyyah
    industrial site, 215
Ṣinā'iyyah Pottery
    at Tayma, 215
Sinites, 215

Sirius
    heliacal rising,
        astronomical, 112
Sky Ladder, 295
slaves
    indigenous people, 90
    no evidence, 91
    prisoners, 89
smell
    manna, 150
Smerdis, 104
smith
    elitism, 191
    priest, 192
    *qayn*, 190
    *ṣâny*, 215
    snorting, blowpipe, 14
snake-rod
    eats priests', 101
snorting
    in name Nahor, 14
Sobek
    Nile, 278
    pharaoh at Nile, 106
    Pharaoh, crocodile,
        102
    Renenutet's consort,
        277
Sodom and Gomorrah,
    39, 185, 186, 187,
    365
Sokar, 255
    cave, Apep, 253
    cavern, 252
    form of Osiris, 251
Solomon
    Aqaba, 131
    cherubim, 271
    corvée, 90
    descendants, 335
    friends, Elixir, 180
    judging two women,
        17
    Mount of Corruption,
        206
    pillars, 52, 183
    wealth, 666, 349
    wisdom, 226
son of Neith
    Ahmose III, 157
songstress, 30
Sons of Moses

legend, 72
Sopdu
    Nome, 50
sparks
    heavenly host, Re, 257
Split Rock, 161, 181
    landmark, 182
    portent of doom, 183
staff
    metal coils, 304
    serpent, protection,
        Re, 253
    subdues enemies, 303
statue
    Baal-zephon, 66
    boat access, Ur, 58
    Daniel, golden, 345,
        348, 351
    Daniel, metals, clay,
        341
    divided kingdom, 344
    Nabonidus', 351
    Nebuchadnezzar
        copies Egyptian
        statues, 348
    Sîn, 49
    small stone, 345
    Song of Solomon, 351
    Ur harbour, 49
stillborn
    Aaron's defense of
        Miriam, 160
stolen, 5, 23, 63, 66,
    140, 145, 216, 236,
    351
store-cities, 87
strange fire, 201
    ritualistic error, 202
*stratopeda*
    as Goshen, 92
strike
    Moses condemned,
        163
    Moses, staff, 163
    murder, 163
stylus
    Aaron, golden calf,
        336
substance abuse, 168
Succoth, 85
Suez, 124, 126, 127,
    128, 132

Sulaimān
  Solomon, tribe, 308
Sun-god
  motion, astronomical, 111
Suph
  Deuteronomy name, 207
sympathetic magic
  rain spells, 142
Taberah
  fire of the Lord, 201
  in Numbers, 211
tabernacle
  furnace within, 192
  portable cavern, 261
Tablet of Destinies
  Anzu, 314
  Nabonidus, 115
  Nabonidus steals, 322
  Nabu keeps, 323
  oath tablet T1808, 324
  plural, Tiamat, 315
  seals, 323
  several leaders possess, 322
  trophies, 315
Tablet(s) of Life
  positive, negative, 316
tablets, 310
  amended by priests, 325
  blessings, curses, 324
  book of the covenant, 324
  both sides, public, 322
  buried, Tayma, 329
  caches, libraries, 311
  clay, 310
  clay, Gilgamesh, 323
  clay, Ur, 317
  curses for theft, damage, 312
  females, Ur, 319
  first owned by females, 316
  forgery, priests, 325
  in the ark, 329
  lapis-lazuli, 317
  libraries, 312
  Memory of Mankind

Project, 312
  Nabonidus careless, 328
  on chest, priest, 323
  repair, 329
  seals of deities, 322
  stone, 313
  stone for public display, 314
  stone inscribed by smiths, 313
  stone, inscribing, 319
  stone, rockfall, 328
  two or one?, 328
  two, *Atrahasis*, 335
Tahpanhes
  Abraham, Moses, Solomon, 67
  as remote, 67
  Baal-zephon, 49
  Baal-zephon sanctuary, 238
  bones, 289
  boundary, 99
  Daphnae, military camp, 92
  Hadad, 66
  in marshland, 126
  Osiris in Nile, 240
  Pelusium, Cambyses, 99
  Pithom, 83
  second visit, 51
Tammuz
  Hebrew month, 114
  Ishtar's consort, 114
  month of, 216
Tashentihet
  sarcophagus, 66
Tashritu
  Babylonian month, Nabonidus, 115
Tayma
  Amalek, 180
  as second capital, 2
  built by Solomon, 307
  Elim, 147
  Jericho, 389
  Jerusalem, 231
  landmark rocks, 161
  Sarah burial, 78
  wisdom, 147

Tayma Stone, 296
Teman
  Tayma, Eliphaz's son, 213
ten
  plagues, debateable, 100
  plagues, months, 114
ten commandments, 114, 310, 318, 324, 325, 327, 347
Terah, 2
Thermuthis, 20, 101, 250
  and Ps 107, 23
  Josephus on, 21
third day
  new moon (19 15), 116
Thonis-Heracleion, 71
thorn-bush, 197
  *sinaeiun*, Sinites, 215
Thoth, 291
  Egyptian month, 114
  serpent worship, 275
Thoth-Hermes
  Moses, 22, 271
thousand pieces of silver
  price for Sarah, 10
three days
  ark goes on its own, 210
  darkness, 107
three months
  Moses hidden, 248
  pregnancy term, 248
Tiamat
  Tablets of Destiny, plural, 315
Tiamat and Marduk, 167
timbrel, 30
Tishrei
  Hebrew month, 115
Tophal
  Deuteronomy names, 209
tower
  at Ur, 57
trade
  Abraham's goods, 7

camels, 6
Canaan, 6
treaty
 covenant of salt, 186
 Eshcol, Aner, 186
trees
 in name Elim, 146
triad, 4, 25, 109, 227,
 303, 343
 Sun, Moon, Stars, 4
tribes
 twelve, Solomon, 257
True of Voice, 117,
 121, 122, 292
Trumbull's Great Wall,
 126
Tubal
 as metalworker, 190
twelve
 *Amduat*, Re, 258
 pillars, 258
 tribes, 257
two wives/sisters
 motif, 16
Tyre
 burning tree, 198
 foundation myth, 52
 South Palace,
 Babylon, 54
 the Rock, 129
Ur, 317
 Abraham, 123
 Abraham's journey, 41
 adversaries in
 marshes, 61
 Baal-zephon, clue,
 238
 canal, 58
 centre of Sîn worship,
 4
 clay cones, 60
 *Ekišnugal* temple, 60
 Enki's temple, 58
 *entu* priesthood, 373
 harbour palace, 63
 layout, 47, 48
 leave at dawn, 66
 marshes, 60
 migdol, 57
 priests, Jehudijah, 65
 sea port, 60
 sea, marshes, 59

songstress, 31
timbrel, 32
tower, 57
women in temple,
 Ennigaldi, 374
writing boards,
 Nabonidus, 326
ziggurat, 56
Uzzah, 202
violence
 Nabonidus, 166
virgin bride
 Ennigaldi-Nanna, 70
Virgo
 constellation, 112
volcanoes, 195, 196
 Harraat, 196
Vulcan, 197
Wadi al-Hamd, 133,
 363
Wadi al-Jizl, 133, 363
Wadjet, 233, 272
 eye of the moon, 285
 flying serpent, 241
 Nehushtan, 285
wall
 meaning of *shur*, 124
 metaphor, 75
 pun, 129
 sea, waves, 65
Wall
 beyond is Shur, 127
 Diodorus, 126
 Trumbull, 126
wanderer
 Nabonidus as, 3
wandering
 Aramaean, 74
Warren, Charles
 Jericho, 387
water
 as feminine symbol,
 167
Way to Shur, 68, 96,
 129
wean, 31, 66, 250
 ripeness, 34
weapon
 Sarah, Nitocris, 9
well
 fertility/marriage, 27
Well of Miriam

 as vengeful spirit, 170
Well of Seven
 Beersheba, 27
white, 210
White Village, 210
wild bulls
 aurochs, 272
 Nabonidus' statues,
 272
Wilderness of Paran,
 209
Wilderness of Shur,
 123
 before Marah, 126
 beyond Great Wall,
 128
 byond the Wall, 125
 mirrored in Arabia,
 130
Wilderness of Sîn
 Elim, Sinai, 151
 surrounds Tayma, 151
wind setdown
 on Lake Tanis, 127
winged serpents
 ark, 269
 ark cherubim, 267
 Herodotus, 270
wings
 Abraham, protection,
 6
wisdom
 like the gods, 290
 Nabonidus, 226
 Nabonidus seeks, 290,
 294
 Sarah, Nitocris, 11
 Solomon, 11
 Tayma, 147
wise-woman
 Milcah as, 16
wood
 Ezion-geber, 135
 Moses throws, 142
wooden boards
 cuneiform, 311
worms
 manna, 149
worthless
 in name "Elim", 146
 in Song, Nabonidus,
 146

writing boards
  not for contracts, 326
  Ur, 326
  waxed, 326
Xenophon
  Nabonidus,
    Belshazzar, 140
*Yam Suph*, 126, 207,
  208
  as Nile Delta, 128
Zaphenath-paneah, 232

Baal-zephon, 237
  snakes, 233
  source of light, 292
Zedekiah
  daughters of, 69
ziggurat
  *entu*, chamber, 263
  seven levels, 56
  Ur, 56
Zimri, 356
  Aaron, 361

Josephus, castigation
  of Moses, 357
  musician, 356
Zipporah, 27
  as Cozbi, 356
  Jethro's daughter, 27
  not Nitocris, 156
  returned to Moses, 29
Zur
  father, Cozbi, 356
  Rock, 129

9 781739 315467